The Franco-Prussian War

The Franco-Prussian War

THE GERMAN INVASION
OF FRANCE, 1870–1871

MICHAEL HOWARD

DORSET PRESS

New York

FOR

Max Reese

AFTER TWENTY YEARS

This edition published by Dorset Press
a division of Marboro Books Corporation,
by arrangement with Routledge
1990 Dorset Press

ISBN 0-88029-432-9

Printed in the United States of America
M 9 8 7 6 5 4 3 2 1

Contents

Maps

Abbreviations Used in Footnotes

D.O.   *Enquête parlementaire sur les Actes du Gouvernement de la Défense Nationale: Dépêches télégraphiques officielles* (Versailles 1875).

D.T.   *Enquête parlementaire sur les Actes du Gouvernement de la Défense Nationale: Dépositions des témoins* (Versailles 1873).

G.G.S.   *The Franco-German War 1870–1871* (London 1874–84). Translated from: *Der deutsch-französische Krieg 1870–71. Redigirt von der kriegsgeschichtlichen Abteilung des Gross Generalstabes* (Berlin 1872–81).

Guerre   *La Guerre de 1870–71, publiée par la Revue d'Histoire, rédigée à la Section historique de l'Etat-Major de l'Armée* (Paris 1901–13).

M.M.K.   *Moltkes Militärische Korrespondenz. Aus den Dienstschriften des Krieges 1870–71* (Berlin 1897).

Reinach   *Dépêches, Circulaires, Décrets, Proclamations et Discours de Léon Gambetta. Publiés par M. Joseph Reinach* (Paris 1886–91).

Preface

I T is doubtful whether any war, the First World War not excepted, has been the object of more concentrated study in proportion to its length and extent than has the Franco-Prussian War of 1870–71. A bibliography compiled in 1898 could already list 7,000 titles, and the flood was to continue unabated for at least another decade. This is not surprising. In the first place, any event so dramatically catastrophic, occurring as it did in a century of such exceptional international amity as the nineteenth, was bound to attract the attention of a circle of writers, soldiers and historians far wider than those directly involved; and the forty-four years of peace which followed in Western Europe gave plenty of opportunity for detailed and leisurely research. Secondly, a substantial proportion of the literate population both of France and of Germany had, thanks to universal conscription, been directly involved. The educated soldier was no longer an exception in the ranks or in the officers' mess. On each side hundreds of temporary or professional soldiers kept diaries or were to recollect their tempestuous emotions in the tranquillity of their declining years; while leaders civil and military were to show no more restraint than those of our own day in publishing autobiographies making clear the influential or, alternatively, the innocuous role which they themselves had played. In France moreover the flood of invasion, the measures taken to meet it and the drama of the siege of Paris brought war in its most direct form into the lives of the most highly literate people in the world. Finally, in an age when technological change was transforming the nature of war in a manner as unpredictable as that of our own times, the events of 1870 for long provided the only examples which experts could study of the problems which principally perplexed them: the effect of modern weapons on tactics; the organisation and leadership of short-service conscripts; and the maintenance, movement, supply and medical services in the field of armies numbering hundreds of thousands.

The student of the subject therefore finds himself surfeited with material, ranging from analytical staff-studies of technical problems based on official archives to the diaries of French country *curés*, from the memoranda and table-talk of Bismarck to the cartoons of the Paris press. One man cannot master all this, much less digest it within the bounds of a single volume. Nevertheless a single volume, based on one individual's incomplete studies, may still be found useful, both by scholars and by the public at large; and it is in this hope that I have had the temerity to offer yet another book on what must appear at first sight to be a grotesquely over-studied subject. Only one single-volume study of any scholarly importance has appeared since 1914—that by Emil Daniels, published in 1929 as the sixth volume of Hans Delbrück's *Geschichte der Kriegskunst im Rahmen der politischen Geschichte*. Apart from the monumental work of General Palat, referred to below, this appears to be the only general history of the war to make use of the French documents whose publication by the Section Historique of the French General Staff between 1901 and 1913 rendered all previous studies out of date. The publication in full of the War Diary of the Emperor Frederick III in 1926 also gave new opportunities to the historian, of which so far only Dr Daniels has taken full advantage. And since 1929 yet further material has become available: in particular the definitive edition of Bismarck's works; Professor H. O. Meissner's edition of the diaries and letters of Grand Duke Frederick of Baden; and finally, most revealing of all, the secret war diaries of Colonel Bronsart von Schellendorf, which were published in Bonn in 1954. All this, together with the unfortunate fact that Dr Daniel's excellent work is almost unobtainable in this country, may make the present volume a little more acceptable to historians than the formidable catalogue of its august predecessors, from Lecomte's four volumes to Palat's fifteen, may at first suggest. But throughout this work I have been conscious how my path has been smoothed by these scholars of the past, and by General Palat chief among them. The lucidity, the scholarship, the eloquence and the passion of his volumes set a standard which no successor can hope to equal; and there is hardly a page which follows which does not owe an unacknowledged debt to his learning.

Not only the work of predecessors but the encouragement, co-operation or forbearance of contemporaries has made this book possible. Dr Werner Hahlweg of the University of Munster advised me on German sources. General de Cossé-Brissac, Head of the Service Historique de l'Etat-Major at Vincennes, M. Lemôine, Librarian of the École Supérieure de Guerre in Paris, Brigadier J. Stephenson O.B.E., Librarian of the Royal United Services Institution, Mr King, Librarian of the War Office, have all been consistently helpful, as have the officials of the Bibliothèque Nationale, the British Museum and the

London Library. The University of London provided a travel grant from its Central Research Fund. Mrs J. H. Naylor made invaluable transcriptions for me in the Archives at Vincennes. Captain B. H. Liddell Hart, Mr A. Marx, Mr C. H. D. Howard, Mr M. R. D. Foot, Mr Peter Paret and Mr J. H. Naylor read the work at various stages of its composition and saved me from an alarming number of solecisms and errors; though not, alas, from those which still remain. Mr Michael Clark of King's College, London, conducted me over the battlefields with patience and discernment; Miss P. McCallum compiled the Index; and but for the help of Mr Mark James it is doubtful whether the book could have appeared at all. To all these and to many others I am deeply indebted; and regret only that I have not produced a work of scholarship more worthy of their help.

King's College, London   MICHAEL HOWARD
March 1961

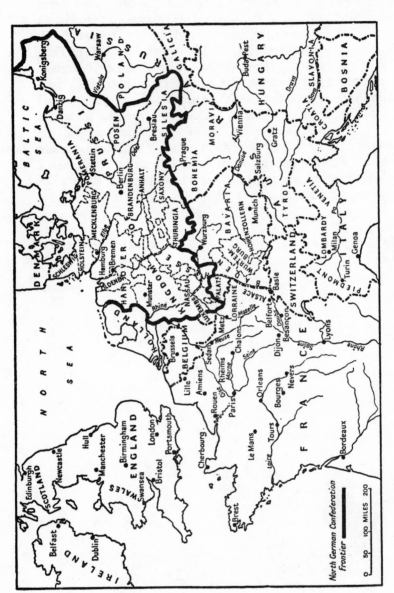

Map 1: Europe in 1870

CHAPTER I

The Antagonists

§1 The Technical Background

IN THE summer of 1870 the kingdom of Prussia and her German allies totally destroyed the military power of Imperial France. For nearly eighty years the defeated nation had given the law in military matters to Europe, whereas the victor, ten years earlier, had been the least of the continent's major military powers. Within a month Prussia established a military pre-eminence and a political hegemony which made the unification of Germany under her leadership a matter of course, and which only an alliance embracing nearly every major power in the world was to wrest from her half a century later.

There was little precedent in the history of Europe for so dramatic a reversal. To find one we must go back at least to the campaign of Breitenfeld in 1631 when within a few weeks Gustavus Adolphus broke the supremacy of the Catholic powers; and Gustavus had fought for years against the Danes, Poles, and Russians with an accumulating success which already marked him out as one of the great captains of history. In 1870 the Prussian army had to its credit the brilliant campaign of 1866 against Austria, but this was only one in the long series of defeats which the Hapsburgs had suffered at the hands of Prussia and France since the days of Eugene of Savoy. The completeness of the Prussian success in 1870 thus astounded the world. The incompetence of the French high command explained much: but the basic reasons for the catastrophe lay deeper, as the French themselves, in their humiliation, were to discern. The collapse at Sedan, like that of the Prussians at Jena sixty-four years earlier, was the result not simply of faulty command but of a faulty military system; and the military system of a nation is not an independent section of the social system but an aspect of it in its totality. The French had good reason to look on their disasters as a judgment. The social and economic developments of the past fifty years had brought about a military as well as an industrial revolution. The Prussians had kept abreast of it and France had not. Therein lay the basic cause of her defeat.

The military implications of the industrial changes and scientific discoveries which were transforming the world were little explored during the first half of the nineteenth century. Conservative War Ministries and parsimonious Treasuries allowed projects of every kind to collect dust in pigeon-holes or to be frittered away in endless experiment. This indolence was disturbed only by the change which occurred in the relations between the Great Powers in the 1850s. The Crimea showed that major war was still possible, and the growth of nationalist movements with the active encouragement of a new French Empire made it seem likely. Throughout Europe military writing began to multiply. The wars of the first Napoleon provided an inexhaustible field for study, and the principles which such authorities as Jomini, Willisen, Clausewitz and Rüstow derived from them provided the broad foundations for a theory of war equally valid for all ages. But two major technical questions were entirely open to speculation. How would the new means of communication—railways and the electric telegraph—affect strategy? And how would the development of breech-loading rifled firearms affect tactics?

The significance of railways for military operations had been discerned as soon as they were developed, in the 1830s. German writers were particularly alert to their possibilities, at a moment when a weak German Confederation once again seemed to lie at the mercy of a revived and ambitious France.[1] Some of them, notably Friedrich List, saw even deeper implications in the new form of transport. Hitherto, lying in the centre of Europe, Germany had been at the mercy of her more powerful and united neighbours. Railways would not only give her a new economic unity; they would transform her central position into an asset, enabling her to concentrate her forces rapidly at any point on her frontier to repel invasion.[2] It was in railways, therefore, that the real strength of national defence lay. "Every new development of railways", wrote Helmuth von Moltke, "is a military advantage; and for the national defence a few million on the completion of our railways is far more profitably employed than on our new fortresses."[3] Opinion in France and Austria was equally impressed by the military advantages

---

[1] Especially Friedrich Harkort, *Die Eisenbahnen von Minden nach Köln* (1833). See A. E. Pratt, *The Rise of Rail Power in War and Conquest* (London 1915) 2–3.

[2] Friedrich List, *Schriften, Reden, Briefe* (Berlin 1931–5) III i 155–270. See E. M. Earle, *Makers of Modern Strategy* (Princeton 1941) 148–52.

[3] "Welche Rücksichten kommen bei der Wahl der Richtung von Eisenbahnen in Betracht?" in *Deutsche Vierteljahresschrift*, 1843. Reprinted in *Vermischte Schriften des Grafen Helmuth von Moltke* (Berlin 1892) II 229.

of railway development and the military dangers offered by the advances of their neighbours. In 1842 alarmed French publicists urged the construction of a line from Paris to Strasbourg to counter the convergence of German lines on the Rhine; and even the British grew alarmed at the possibilities of a sudden French concentration on the Channel ports. In the campaign of 1859 the French and Hapsburg Empires, using railways, moved troops into Italy within a fortnight, which would have taken sixty days to march over the same distance. It was clear that the railway age would open a new chapter in the history of warfare.

Speed of concentration was only one of the advantages which railways provided. They carried troops rapidly to the theatre of war; and they enabled them to arrive in good physical condition, not wearied and decimated by weeks of marching. Armies needed no longer to consist of hardened regular troops; reservists from civil life could be embodied in the force as well, although the incidence of sickness and exhaustion in the combat area itself was consequently increased. Further, the problem of supplying large forces in the field was simplified. Military movements had hitherto been dictated by the necessity of living off the country, or from laboriously accumulated magazines: now, if the railway lines were intact, the trains smoothly organised, and supply from the railhead unhampered, armies could keep the field so long as there was blood and treasure in the nation to support them—and of this power of endurance the American Civil War provided the first great example. Supplies and reinforcements could come daily from home and the wounded could be quickly evacuated to base hospitals. With the burden of their supply-columns lightened, armies could be more mobile and their members more lightly equipped. Moreover, the distinction between army and nation was dissolved. No longer was the battle-area remote. Newspaper-correspondents could travel to and fro, sending back their reports by telegraph. Troops could come and go on leave. The wounded could be cared for and entertained at home. The nation at war thus became an armed camp—sometimes a besieged fortress—in which every individual felt himself involved in a mighty communal endeavour. In 1870 there dawned in Europe an age of "absolute war" in a sense which even Clausewitz had never conceived.

Finally, the development of railways gave an entirely new aspect to the fundamental principle of Napoleonic strategy—the concentration of overwhelming forces at the decisive point. This concentration could no longer be effected by movement of armies in the field: it was a matter of elaborate organisation which had to be undertaken long before the war began. The largest available number of men had to be called up, trained, and passed into an easily recallable army reserve. The peace-time armies of the European powers became largely training cadres; before they could take the field at all they had to recall their reservists, clothe and equip them from mobilisation-stores, and reform their units on a war-time basis. Efficient conscription, training, and mobilisation became a necessary preliminary to a successful concentration, and a successful concentration became more than ever the object of all strategy. The army which could first concentrate its masses not only secured an overwhelming advantage in the first, and possibly decisive, battle; it had also the chance of disorganising by invasion or deep raids the mobilisation of its adversary, reducing his plans to chaos, and leaving him defenceless. Prescient or predatory nations had the opportunity as never before to establish a military supremacy over their neighbours before hostilities even began.

The same advantage could be taken of those developments in weapon-technology which nineteenth-century advances in metallurgy, ballistics, and precision-engineering were simultaneously making possible. Between 1815 and 1870 the weapons both of infantry and of artillery were transformed. The muskets of the Napoleonic era were smooth-bores, barely accurate at fifty yards, and useless at more than two hundred. They were loaded at the muzzle and a skilled man might fire three shots in a minute if his flintlock mechanism did not misfire, as in wet weather it usually did. These weapons had remained virtually unchanged since the days of Marlborough, and so had the essence of infantry tactics. Infantry battalions deployed in line, two or three deep, to make the best use of their erratic fire; a formation of proved value in defence but of less use in the attack. For the attack the French army had developed a new technique: a line of skirmishers to wear down the defence with aimed harassing fire, columns of infantry to feed the firing line and where possible to charge, and, most important of all, mobile and powerful artillery to disorganise the defence before the infantry closed in. The guns, like the muskets, were smooth-bore muzzle-loaders, as virtually all guns had been since the fifteenth century; erratic and wildly inaccurate, with an effective range of a thousand yards or less.[1] Only in their greater mobility and rate of fire did they differ from the weapons

---

[1] The inaccuracy of these weapons was well expressed in the saying of Prussian artillerymen: "The first shot is for the Devil, the second for God, and only the third for the King." Prince Kraft von Hohenlohe-Ingelfingen, *Letters on Artillery* (London 1888) 56.

used by the armies of Montecucculi and Turenne. But by 1870 the principal armies of Europe were equipped with rifles scientifically accurate up to at least five hundred yards and with rifled guns which could be effectively employed at ranges of two to three thousand yards. The effect on the battlefield could only be revolutionary.

The revolution was made yet more violent by the simultaneous developments which made it possible to load firearms not at the muzzle but at the breech. This innovation had been regarded by military commanders with considerable suspicion. Only gradually was it discovered how the breech could be entirely sealed to prevent wastage of gas and consequent loss of range; and the advantage of greater speed in reloading seemed to be counter-balanced by the danger of wasting ammunition. The British, French, and Austrian armies therefore clung to muzzle-loading rifles, and with these fought their campaigns of 1854 and 1859. The Prussian army however had adopted a breech-loader, the Dreyse needle-gun, as early as 1843[1]; and although it had been used in minor campaigns in 1848 and in 1864, it was only in 1866, when it was for the first time matched against a first-class army equipped with muzzle-loaders, that its superiority became evident. The Prussian infantry, lying down to reload and firing six shots to the Austrian one, swept the Austrians from the field. Only then did the other Powers hasten to equip themselves with the breech-loaders whose patterns had lain neglected for years on the shelves of their Ministries.

In artillery pride of place still seemed, in 1866, to lie with the French. Theirs was the first army to be totally equipped with rifled cannon—the muzzle-loaders whose design and manufacture had been personally supervised by Napoleon III and which had proved so effective in Italy. The Prussian artillery in 1866 consisted partly of new breech-loading rifled ordnance and partly of old smooth-bores; but neither were used effectively, and their performance against the Austrian gunners compared unfavourably with the performance of the French seven years earlier. But in the four years which followed, the Prussian artillery was transformed. Thanks to the energy and foresight of the Inspector-General, General von Hindersin, the field batteries were entirely re-equipped with steel breech-loading field-pieces from the Krupp works.[2]

---

[1] F. W. Rüstow, *L'Art militaire au dix-neuvième siècle* (Paris 1869 tr. Savin de Larclause) II 40.

[2] Steel guns were unpopular with artillery specialists of the day, since the difficulty of cooling the barrel evenly during the casting process tended to produce flaws which shattered the weapon when it was fired. France and Austria

The tactical employment of these weapons was minutely studied and transformed and the introduction of a School of Gunnery set an entirely new standard for scientific precision of fire. The effectiveness of Prussian artillery was to be the greatest tactical surprise of the Franco-Prussian War.[1]

It was generally recognised that the introduction of these new arms would transform the conduct of armies in the field. An indication of the impending changes had been given by the improvement in the effectiveness of infantry fire when the percussion cap replaced the flint-lock earlier in the century, and in consequence an increasing importance was being attached to the initial skirmishing fire with which battles conventionally opened. It was already agreed that the skirmishing line must be strengthened at the expense of the columns held back for the final assault. Now the introduction of rifled weapons gave the defence, firing from prepared positions at known ranges, so evident an advantage that at first it seemed that the only answer was to close to attack with hand-to-hand fighting as quickly as possible. This could only be done, not by the traditional battalion-columns which could never survive on open ground swept by rifle-bullets and shellfire, but by flexible formations, making full use of cover, in which every man used his initiative.[2] The French showed the way in Italy in 1859. The whole emphasis of their infantry training, especially in their *chasseur* formations, lay in speed, agility, and individual intelligence. The *furia francese* was no myth; it was a quality which the Prussians recognised and envied.[3] The Austrians at Solferino were swept away by the charging French infantry before they could bring their rifle-fire fully into action; but when in 1866

---

therefore kept to the traditional bronze, while Britain preferred the wrought-iron guns, strengthened by exterior coils, developed by Sir Joseph Whitworth. See C. B. Brackenbury, *European Armaments in 1867* (London 1867) *passim*. For an account of the organisation and process by which Krupp overcame the difficulty of casting steel guns, see "L'Usine d'Essen et les Canons Krupp" in Louis Reybaud, *La Fer et la Houille* (Paris 1874).

[1] On the work of Hindersin, see Hohenlohe-Ingelfingen, op. cit. 165–90 and 247–67, and Kurt Jany, *Geschichte der Preussischen Armee* IV (Berlin 1933) 223–4.

[2] See Moltke's *Taktisch-strategische Aufsätze, 1857–1871* (Berlin 1900) 23–4. Also the tactical instructions issued by Marshal Lebœuf to the French army on 1st August 1870, reprinted in *La Guerre de 1870–71, publiée par la Revue d'Histoire, rédigée à la Section historique de l'Etat-Major de l'Armée* (Paris 1901–13) Hereafter referred to as *Guerre* IV, 67–75.

[3] Baron Stoffel, *Rapports militaires écrits de Berlin* (Paris 1871) 99. See also the famous pamphlet by Prince Frederick Charles, *Ueber die Kampfweise der Franzosen* (Frankfurt 1860).

the Austrians tried to copy the French tactics of close fighting, they found that against the needle-gun the result was disaster.[1]

The evidence of 1866 was overwhelming, that the new firearms gave to a well-sited defence a devastating advantage. In the French army the opinion spread that the essence of strategy must henceforth consist in finding and holding good positions.[2] The views of Helmuth von Moltke, Chief of the Prussian General Staff from 1857, differed only in that he aimed at combining this tactical defensive with a strategic offensive—that is, seizing and holding positions which the enemy would be compelled to attack. Enemy defensive positions, he agreed, should be by-passed wherever possible. If they had to be attacked, it should be only after heavy artillery preparation—which meant keeping the bulk of the artillery forward with the infantry divisions and not, in the Napoleonic tradition which had proved so useless in 1866, keeping them back in corps reserve until the battle had fully developed.[3] But such a defensive trend had everywhere to contend with a traditional and natural *penchant* for the attack. In the Prussian army the tendency shown in 1866 for the supporting columns to melt altogether into the skirmishing line was considered to be a grave error, and at subsequent manœuvres close formations were again restored.[4] In the French army the battalion column remained the rule until 1869. Field and general officers could not accept it as inevitable that in the age of rifled weapons the conduct of a battle devolved on the subaltern and non-commissioned officers. The twentieth century was to be well advanced before they did.

Finally the rôle of the cavalry arm had to be radically reconsidered. So long as infantry and artillery weapons were short in range and took long to load, cavalry used with skill and boldness could be a decisive arm on the battlefield, sweeping suddenly out of the mêlée to overrun shaken infantry and gunners. Cavalry regiments still commanded the highest social prestige, apart from royal household troops, in all the armies of Europe. On the Napoleonic battlefield they had been able to

---

[1] E. von Kählig, *Heere und Flotte der Gegenwart: Österreich-Ungarn* (Berlin 1898) 251–2.

[2] *Guerre* IV 19–22.

[3] *Taktisch-strategische Aufsätze* 9, 31, 56.

[4] Stoffel, op. cit. 331–2. The introduction into the French army of the *chassepot*, outranging the Dreyse rifle by 1000 yards, was used as an argument by the partisans of the attack. The King himself agreed "daß wir dem weit-tragenden Gewehr gegenüber dem Feinde dicht auf den Leib gehen müssen und das Gefecht auf Entfernung verlegen, wo unser Gewehr und unsere Schiess-fertigkeit ausgenützt werden können." Alfred Graf von Waldersee, *Denkwürdig-keiten*, ed. H. O. Meissner (Stuttgart 1922) I 84.

perform a useful as well as a spectacular rôle and so long as they remained the only mobile arm available to a commander their importance remained unquestionable. But it was becoming doubtful, in the 1850s and 1860s, exactly wherein that importance was to consist. Over the larger distances which the new firearms would make necessary, the difficulty of liaison and reconnaissance would certainly increase the need for cavalry to carry out these tasks, and numerous examples in the American Civil War showed what could be done by raids against enemy railway lines and supply-dumps. But such were not the traditions of European cavalry. For them shock-tactics still offered a fatal fascination; and whenever new rôles had been found for the cavalry—the light horse of the sixteenth century, the mounted infantry dragoons of the seventeenth—these had been gradually abandoned, and the regiments concerned grew into the likeness of the socially superior, sartorially more ornate heavy cavalry, trained only in meticulous formations for that consummation of the horseman's purpose in life—the charge *en masse*.[1] The French cavalry in Lombardy, the Prussian cavalry in Bohemia, had showed themselves equally incompetent at reconnaissance. But would there any longer be a place for the heavy cavalry at all? Doubts were growing. In France Marshal Niel, in Britain the Duke of Cambridge, in Prussia Moltke himself were sceptical.[2] But their scepticism had little impact on the minds of senior cavalry commanders. On both sides they entered the war of 1870 in the conviction that their regiments were to play the decisive rôle in great set-piece battles. Not even the experiences of that war were entirely to disillusion them.

§2 The Unreformed Armies

Military forces are shaped, not only by the weapons with which they are armed, but by the social background from which they emerge and the political function for which they are intended. During the forty years which followed the Napoleonic Wars, the powers of Europe raised and trained their forces at least as much for use at home as for fighting abroad. The main employment visualised for them was the

---

[1] E.g. General Du Barail, *Souvenirs* (Paris 1896) III 165.
[2] Baron D'Andlau, *Metz, Campagne et Négociations* (Paris 1871) 461–2. C. C. Chesney and H. Reeve, *Military Resources of Prussia and France* (London 1870) 46. Moltke, *Taktisch-strategische Aufsätze*, 22. But Moltke also realised the increasing scope for light cavalry actions on the battlefields of the future. The more dispersed the fighting, he pointed out, the greater the opportunity for "small-scale but brilliant coups," loc. cit. 33, 55.

suppression of revolutionary insurgents, domestic or alien. The first campaign of the Royal French Army had been fought to bring the Spaniards back to their Bourbon allegiance. The Austrian army survived as a police force to keep the Italian subjects of the Hapsburg Empire in due obedience, and it was diverted from that task only in 1848, to deal with risings in Budapest, Prague, and Vienna itself. The first major action fought by the armies of the Russian and Prussian monarchies after 1815 was against their insurgent Polish subjects in 1831; and the Prussians were next to go into action—apart from the brief and inglorious campaign against the Danes in 1848—against the rump of the Liberal Assembly of the German Confederation which had taken refuge in Baden. For such campaigns it was not necessary to maintain forces of the size and military efficiency which Napoleonic warfare had demanded. The essential quality of such troops was that they should be untroubled by liberal sympathies of their own, and remain loyal to the dynasty they served. Armies on the eighteenth-century model, small forces of long-serving regular troops with an exclusive, aristocratic officer-corps, were ideal for this purpose: they were politically reliable, and in the conduct of eighteenth-century wars they had been militarily serviceable. But the balance had now been upset. The French Revolution had introduced, and Napoleon had brought to maturity, a form of warfare which, with its unlimited demands on national resources, called for a different form of military organisation. Napoleonic warfare, *la Grande Guerre*, was a war of masses: masses raised by universal conscription, armed and equipped by large-scale state-intervention in industry, fed largely by requisition, making necessary new techniques of manœuvre and command. By his mastery of this new mechanism Napoleon had subjugated Europe and he had been defeated only when his adversaries began to turn his own weapons against him. The weapons were taken up with reluctance by the powers of Europe and quickly abandoned, but it was inconceivable that these techniques should be totally forgotten. If the fear of change which after 1814 dominated and paralysed the statesmen of Europe was ever to relax, and great issues were again to arise to engage the passions of their peoples, the conflicts which would develop could not be contained within the limits of the "Cabinet Wars" of the eighteenth century, or be resolved by eighteenth-century weapons.[1]

[1] E.g. F. W. Rüstow, *L'Art militaire au dix-neuvième siècle* II 9. "Ces campagnes avaient rendu à la guerre sa puissance primitive et montré ce qu'elle pouvait devenir."

The difficulty which was to face the Governments of Europe during the nineteenth century was, therefore, how to fashion armies which would be not only politically reliable but also militarily effective. The two categories seemed irreconcilable. The first called for a force of long-serving regulars: the second for the training of the whole nation in arms. An army composed of the manpower of a nation was politically a most unreliable weapon. It might contain revolutionary elements; it would certainly reflect internal dissensions and disagreements about policy, and its apparent military strength would be illusory if it brought political weakness in its train.[1] So long as internal dangers bulked larger than external, governments preferred their armies to be small and reliable, and in this attitude they found widespread support among their subjects. The aristocracy and land-owning classes could, save in such post-revolutionary states as France and Spain, preserve their monopoly of military commissions. The middle classes, unmilitary by instinct and growing in economic and political strength, approved of a system which made the lowest possible demands on the contents of their purses and the services of their sons. Everywhere armies languished in unpopular and impoverished isolation, and few thinkers in a Europe increasingly wealthy, materialist and optimistic saw in this any cause for regret. Even the restored and chastened French monarchy reconstructed its military system on a basis as alien to the Napoleonic as possible; and the state, curiously enough, which preserved most of the apparatus of Revolutionary military organisation was that paragon of all conservative régimes: the Hohenzollern monarchy of Prussia.

The Prussian army in the eighteenth century had been shaped by a succession of monarchs who were both military experts and political despots. It was officered by a serious and impoverished nobility compelled alike by tradition, law and economic necessity to serve the Crown in a civil or military capacity; and though based in theory on universal compulsion to military service, it was recruited from a combination of long-serving mercenaries and conscript peasants who were kept in order by ferocious discipline and drilled until the rapidity of their movement and the intensity of their fire made them unquestioned masters of the battlefields of Europe, capable of sustaining Prussia's equality among the larger, wealthier and more populous powers by which she was surrounded. Only when in 1806 this army collapsed

---

[1] See Albrecht von Roon's Memorandum of July 1858 in *Denkwürdigkeiten aus dem Leben des General-feldmarschalls Kriegsministers Grafen von Roon* (Breslau 1897) II 521.

before Napoleon did it become evident that the system was at fault: that the army, the personal instrument of the Crown, was divorced so completely from the rest of the community that its defeat was regarded with indifference by the nation at large. The Military Reorganisation Commission which was set up in July 1807 did not, therefore, attempt to reconstruct the old Frederican army; instead, under the leadership of Gerhard von Scharnhorst, it worked out the principles on which a new army could be built. Officer-schools were reformed and thrown open to the middle classes as well as to the nobility. The principle of universal service was reaffirmed; the savage code of discipline was swept away; and the confused administration of the army was centralised under a single Minister of War. It was Scharnhorst's avowed aim "to raise and inspire the spirit of the Army, to bring the Army and the Nation into a more intimate union".[1] In 1813 the Landwehr was created—a citizen militia separately armed and organised, which fought by the side of the regular forces in bringing about the downfall of Napoleon in the Wars of Liberation. It was in the white heat of that war, when conservative and liberal, Junker and bourgeois, forgot their differences in a new-found national unity, that the new Prussian army was forged.

Once the war was over the king was brought to regret his concessions, and the reformers were stripped of office; but not until they had enshrined their work in the Defence Law of 3 September 1814 and the Landwehr Law of 21 November 1815.[2] By the first, every native Prussian was "bound in duty to the defence of the Fatherland" from the age of twenty. The army was to be, in a phrase which summed up the full achievement of the reformers, "the chief training school of the whole nation for war". The Prussian conscript served for three years with the army, two with the reserve and then served until his fortieth year in a Landwehr which comprised not merely conscripts like himself, who had finished their five-year service with the regular army, but all able-bodied men who had not been called up with their annual contingent. The Landwehr had its own territorial organisation, and, like the English militia, its officers were drawn from local men of substance. This system of compulsory universal service, first with the colours, then with the reserve, finally with a territorial force, was by the twentieth century to be virtually universal among the Western Powers. Yet it

---

[1] Qu. G. Craig, *The Politics of the Prussian Army* (Princeton (O.U.P.) 1955) 41.

[2] Eugen von Frauenholz, *Entwicklungsgeschichte des Deutschen Heerwesens* (München 1941) V 180, 190.

grew out of two purely local considerations: the need to combine a standing army small enough to impose no great strain on a limited budget with a military potential large enough to enable Prussia to appear in Europe as a Great Power; and the desire of the reformers to perpetuate the spirit of Scharnhorst and blend together Army and Nation.

In this latter object they did not succeed. After 1819 the army reverted to the old Frederican pattern. The Officer Corps again closed its ranks against bourgeois candidates.[1] The distinction between the regular army and the Landwehr became sharpened. Budgetary parsimony combined with political caution to keep the annual intake low, and the strength of the standing army between 1815 and 1859 rarely rose above 200,000 men. In 1831, when the Polish revolt threatened Prussia's eastern frontiers and the Belgian and French revolutions her western, Prussia found herself militarily impotent. Only by calling out a largely untrained Landwehr could she mobilise enough men to make her a considerable military power. Such a situation was humiliating for the regular army, irritating for the settled civilians of whom the Landwehr was composed, and damaging to military efficiency. With its partly trained officers the Landwehr was doubtfully competent, and after the great civil disturbances of 1848 it was doubtfully reliable. When in June 1859 Prussia mobilised in support of Austria against France, a British observer wrote that the "regiments of the Landwehr were not in any fit state to take the field, being scarcely more mobile than our battalions of county militia".[2] Prussia indeed until 1859 had the worst of both worlds. Her armed forces were neither politically reliable nor did they give her an effective voice in the Concert of Europe; and in the nineteenth century, as in all other centuries, military effectiveness was the ultimate criterion of political power.

There was little question in 1859 who was the dominant military nation in Europe. Once again it was France. Her army had been toughened by thirty years of continuous fighting in Africa,[3] which had bred new regiments, *zouaves* and "*turcos*" (*tirailleurs indigènes*) in the in-

---

[1] Karl Demeter, *Das deutsche Offizierkorps* (Berlin 1930) 34–5.

[2] C. C. Chesney and H. Reeve, *Military Resources of Prussia and France* 4. French observers however were impressed by what they saw of the mobilisation, especially the use of railways and of blank orders drawn up in 1840, requiring only a date and a signature to make them valid. E. Guichen, *Les Grandes Questions Européennes* (Paris 1925–9) II 50.

[3] For the significance of these campaigns for the French Army see J. Regnault, "Les campagnes d'Algérie et leur influence de 1830 à 1870." *Revue historique de l'Armée*, December, 1953.

fantry, *spahis* and *chasseurs d'Afrique* in the cavalry, and made the reputation of a pleiad of brilliant commanders—Bugeaud, Canrobert, MacMahon, Bourbaki—who carried on the traditions of the Napoleonic marshals. These *beaux sabreurs* had as little in common with the elderly Junkers who commanded the Prussian forces as had the experienced veterans they commanded with the civilian reservists who made up the bulk of the Prussian army. They had carried off the honours of the Crimean campaign, and in Italy they had renewed the victories of an earlier Bonaparte at Magenta and Solferino. Napoleon III's supremacy in Europe may have been due ultimately to the dissensions and weakness of the three Vienna powers; but in the eyes of his admirers it rested, as had that of his uncle, on the victories of his troops.[1]

The military institutions of France had little in common with those of Prussia. There was no noble Officer Corps: between the army and the Faubourg St Germain there was, as Stendhal's heroes found, an almost impassable gulf. There was no short-term service, building up a small regular army and a mass of trained reservists. France had given birth to the ideal of the Nation in Arms, but in the nineteenth century she continually refused, for reasons political, military and economic, to base her military organisation on the pattern of her revolutionary armies. The rigours of the Napoleonic conscriptions, bearing off class after class of young Frenchmen to a service from which only too few returned, were cause enough for Louis XVIII to guarantee their abolition; and although a natural post-war absence of volunteers had compelled a return to the principle of compulsory service in 1818, this compulsion was no more than the recognition of a universal liability which the government enforced as narrowly as possible. Genuine universal short-term service would have produced an army far larger than the country needed or could afford to maintain. The idea was as repugnant to the soldiers, who like all professionals believed that only long practice could develop the necessary qualities of their trade, as it was to civilians who were concerned to save their sons the inconvenience of service and themselves the expense of supporting a large military establishment. The French practice between 1818 and 1870 was to select by ballot, out of the age-group liable, whatever number of men was necessary to make up the size of the army fixed by the Legislature. Far the larger part of the contingent—"the second portion"—was not called upon, remaining as an untrained reserve. The first portion served

[1] Turkey (1856) and Japan (1868) selected French officers and practices to guide them in remodelling their armies.

for a number of years which, after fluctuating between six and eight, was fixed in 1832 at seven, at which it remained until the reforms effected by Marshal Niel in 1868. This long service was intended to purge the conscript of all civilian dross and make a soldier of him. After seven years it was late to turn to another trade, and the conscript might reasonably be expected to re-enlist as a volunteer. Within the framework of universal liability for service, therefore, a small army of long-serving professionals grew up, which satisfied both the military preference for expert over amateur soldiers and the desire of the middle classes to remain undisturbed.

The only people who suffered under this system were the conscripts themselves, and to draw a *mauvais numéro* was a shattering piece of bad luck. But the State provided a loophole. The obligation of the individual was not necessarily to serve in person; it was to furnish military service. If he could provide somebody to take his place the military authorities raised no objection; indeed if he could find an experienced man to do his duty for him, so much the better. Thus there survived the institution of "substitutes" which was so notable a feature of the French military system. Agencies were established to provide substitutes, and con-scription became a risk against which one could insure as against fire, flood or hail.[1] It was an arrangement which enabled the upper and middle classes to escape the rigours of military service altogether, and the pure Republicans regarded it as iniquitous. "To desire that poverty should pay this blood tax" declared the Commission which examined the question during the drafting of the Constitution of the Second Republic, "and that wealth may avoid it by money, has seemed to your Commis-sion a monstrous iniquity". But the conservative majority in the Assembly successfully opposed their projected reform. "Burdens must be equal", agreed Adolphe Thiers, "but if you want to impose the same conditions and the same way of life on totally different individuals it is you who are offending against equality. . . . The society where everyone is a soldier is a barbarous society."[2] Substitution survived the Republic, and became an intrinsic and apparently irremovable part of the French military system.

Frenchmen, uneasily aware of the moral inferiority of such a system to the Prussian universal obligation without exemption to military

---

[1] Trochu, *L'Armée française en 1867* (Paris 1867) 49. See also J. Monteilhet, *Les Institutions militaires de la France 1841–1924* (Paris 1932) 25, and General Thoumas, *Les Transformations de l'Armée française* (Paris 1887) I 19.

[2] Monteilhet, op. cit. 29–30.

service,[1] argued that at least it was likely to provide a more compact and experienced force. It certainly provided an army consciously divorced from the rest of the nation, despising and despised by civilians.[2] Julien Sorel was not the only ambitious young man who discovered that in post-Napoleonic France "*le mérite militaire n'est plus à la mode*" and turned to a more peaceful and profitable profession. The aristocracy looked down on the army as a seed-bed of Napoleonic upstarts, the middle classes as a barbarous and unnecessary survival into an age of civilian prosperity and peace. This attitude was modified after 1848, when the possessing classes saw the army as the necessary guardian of social order against proletarian revolution; and the adventures of the army in Africa combined with the swelling flood of Bonapartist litera-ture to revive national pride in Gallic warrior traditions. In the glitter of the Second Empire the army, splendidly uniformed, its colours emblazoned with new battle-honours from the Crimea and Lombardy and the Far East, was once again held high in public esteem. But it remained apart from the rest of the nation, and Napoleon III deliberately kept it so, as a Praetorian Guard. "The ideal constitution", declared General Trochu, the most zealous of all military reformers, "is that which creates an army whose instincts, beliefs and habits make up a corporation distinct from the rest of the population."[3] In a régime so precarious as that of the Second Empire, bitterly opposed by an active and intelligent minority and resting on public apathy rather than popular consent, the army had police as well as protective duties to perform; and this intensified that spirit of clannishness which is perhaps inevitable, and not totally undesirable, in any regular peacetime Service. But in France it was given a bitter edge by the poverty in which army officers had to live, in the midst of a society which was feverishly and successfully obeying Guizot's instruction to "get rich". They did not

---

[1] The Prussian solution to the problem of reconciling the principle of univers-ality to the needs and interests of the upper and professional classes lay in the institution of the *Einjährige freiwillige*, established by Boyen's Law of September 1814. Young men with a sufficiently high standard of education could enlist, on passing a test, as "one-year volunteers". They provided their own uniform, lived out of barracks and wore plain clothes off duty, and were released to the reserve at the end of a year. The practice survived until the dissolution of the Imperial Army in 1918.

[2] For the changing relationship between the French army and civil society in the nineteenth century see Raoul Girardet, *La Société militaire dans la France contemporaine 1814–1939* (Paris 1953).

[3] G. Bapst, *Le Maréchal Canrobert* (Paris 1909) IV 52. See also P. Chalmin, *L'Officier français 1815–1870* (Paris 1958) 271.

have, like the equally impoverished Prussian Officer Corps, a social prestige to console them. Nor did they have, in the forty years which followed Waterloo, the prospect of an arduous campaign against a formidable European opponent to give them an interest and pride in their profession. There was little concern for military education: the standard of teaching at great military colleges, at St Cyr, Metz and Saumur was deplorable, and the intellectual calibre of the senior officers in no way corresponded to their panache. "When one wants anything done", complained Napoleon III, "only the officers of the specialist services are capable of doing it; but if one gives one of them an important command, all the other officers start complaining."[1]

Only a wealthy or well-educated minority of officers went through even these inadequate military schools, for entrance to them was by examination and fees were high.[2] By far the greater number were promoted from the ranks, and what they gained in experience they lacked in general education. The Marquis de Castellane complained that of ten new captains posted to his division at Perpignan in 1841 only two knew how to spell, and in 1870 the Germans were to be astounded at the illiteracy of the officers who fell into their hands.[3] These rankers on the whole did not attain high preferment.[4] They remained content as regimental officers, elderly but brave, experienced and respected by the men they led. But from their ranks was drawn at least one Marshal: François Achille Bazaine.

It may seem curious that such faults could survive and grow worse in an army which was from 1830 engaged almost continuously on active service. In fact, experience in Africa only intensified them. The campaigns there were conducted by small columns whose leaders required not so much technical *expertise* as courage, dash, and *coup d'œil*—the martial qualities which the French Army considered to be peculiarly its own. There was no call for the scientific study of military movements or for the skilful combination of the three arms in battle. There was no need for an elaborate supply-organisation: columns carried all they

---

[1] Bapst, *Canrobert* III 214.
[2] P. Chalmin, op. cit. 153 ff.
[3] See e.g. Ludwig Bamberger, *Bismarcks Grosses Spiel. Die geheimen Tagebücher Ludwig Bambergers*, ed. Ernst Feder (Frankfurt 1932) 188.
[4] Chalmin, op. cit., Annexe No. 2., points out that nearly two-thirds of the officers up to and including the rank of captain were drawn from the ranks. Thereafter the proportion dwindled to a quarter of the commandants and an eighth of the *généraux de division*. See also General Montaudun, *Souvenirs* (Paris 1900) II 27.

needed with them either on pack-horses or on their backs.[1] These habits they imported for European campaigns. The French soldiers were to go into action in 1870 carrying about 70 lb. weight of equipment and several days' supplies. These they naturally dumped before battle, and if the battle was lost they never saw them again.

The casual administrative habits which had distinguished the Napoleonic armies and whose evil effects had been counteracted only by the strategic genius of Napoleon himself[2] could thus be perpetuated in an army which none the less continued to be victorious. The ruling principle of the French forces continued to be *le système D: on se débrouillera toujours*—we'll muddle through somehow. They usually did, but at heavy cost. The full inadequacies of French military administration became evident when war broke out against a European enemy: Russia in 1854 and Austria in 1859. Headquarters, supply and administrative services all had to be created *ad hoc*. Troops were rushed out to the Black Sea in steamships and there remained in starving ineffectiveness until their supplies and guns arrived by sail.[3] In 1859, for a campaign politically foreseen for three years, the French army arrived in Lombardy in a state of astonishing confusion. The first units to cross the frontier had no blankets, tents, cooking equipment, fodder or even ammunition.[4] Shoes had to be borrowed from the Italians; shirts had to be torn up to bandage the wounded at Solferino while medical equipment lay piled up at the Genoese docks; and, in a theatre of war notorious for its waterways and fortresses, the army was provided with neither bridging equipment nor siege-train. Napoleon wired back from Genoa: "We have sent an army of 120,000 men into Italy before having stocked up any supplies there. This", he continued, with pathetic understatement, "is the opposite of what we should have done."[5]

Nevertheless the French had won both wars. Inadequate as their supply, administration and training may have been, that of the Russians, the British and the Austrians was demonstrably worse. It is hardly surprising that the French army was dominated, in the words of one who served in it, by "an all-powerful school, made up of soldiers as

[1] Thoumas, op. cit. II 632. Du Barail, *Souvenirs* III 151. His regiment landed from Africa in 1870 "avec leurs bagages de campagne au grand complet, traînant derrière elle une infinité de chevaux de bât et de mulets, comme si elles allaient manœuvrer dans le désert".

[2] See Jean Morvan, *Le Soldat impérial* (Paris 1904) *passim*.

[3] See St Arnaud's report to Napoleon III in C. Rousset, *Histoire de la Guerre de Crimée* (Paris 1877) I 115.

[4] Bapst, *Canrobert* III 192.

[5] Ibid. 193, 270.

fortunate as they were brave who loudly proclaimed their contempt for
the military art".[1] Some of the more perceptive commanders, led by
the Emperor himself, were seriously worried by the inadequacies
revealed in French military organisation by the campaign of 1859.
But for most of the army, and indeed for most of the nation, victory
provided all the justification necessary for preserving a system which,
with all its faults, had stood the test of time.

France vs Russia 1854
France vs Austria 1859

§3 The Reform of the Prussian Army

By 1860 the French army had beaten two of its chief European
adversaries. From the third, Prussia, there seemed even less to fear.
Indeed the French, at this period, hardly thought of the Prussian
forces as an army at all. In the French army it was widely considered to
be "a training school of the Landwehr".[2] Without general mobilisation
the Prussian army was too small to achieve anything, and general
mobilisation merely conjured up an ill-trained and undisciplined militia,
which the veterans of Africa and Italy felt, with some reason, that they
could afford to despise. Neither in administration nor in training did
the Prussian army seem to possess any advantage over the French.
So dismal a performance did it put up at the Royal manœuvres in 1861
that a French observer was heard to observe "*C'est compromettre le
métier*".[3]

By 1861 the evident weakness of their army had long been a cause of
concern to the Prussians themselves. Even the Liberals, opposed in
principle to the strengthening of a monarchical instrument which had
been wielded against them so effectively in 1848, were distressed at
Prussian inability to contest Austrian hegemony in Germany—a
hegemony, they realised, far more harmful to the cause of national
unity than that of monarchist Prussia. Such intelligent conservatives as
Albrecht von Roon, himself one of the most outspoken supporters of
Hohenzollern absolutism, saw the absurdity of a military system which
in time of crisis was dependent on the aid of precisely those civilian

---

[1] H. Bonnal, *Froeschwiller* (Paris 1899) 445.
[2] Trochu, *L'Armée Française en 1867* 6. Baron Stoffel, *Rapports militaires
écrits de Berlin* 53.
[3] W. Bigge, *Feldmarschall Graf Moltke* (München 1901) II 106.

elements which the Crown had most reason to distrust; and most concerned of all was Prince William of Prussia, who in 1858 became Regent of the Kingdom in place of his unbalanced brother Frederick William IV.

Prince William was the first professional soldier to come to the throne of Prussia since the death of Frederick the Great. He had served with the Prussian army in the campaign of 1814 against Napoleon; he had commanded the Prussian forces which had put down the Liberal revolt in Baden in 1848; and he loved the army with a passion for which one must go back to his ancestor Frederick William I to find a parallel. Military efficiency was for him, as it had been for Frederick William I, an end in itself. There is little evidence that he visualised in 1858 the use of his army to secure a Prussian hegemony in Germany, let alone in Europe. But reforms of the magnitude necessary if the Prussian army was to become once more a force capable of holding its own in European warfare could be achieved only by a political upheaval which subjected Prussia to a constitutional crisis as agonising as that which England endured between 1640 and 1660, and one whose outcome was quite as decisive for the future structure of the State.

The project of a general reform of Prussian military organisation was outlined in a memorandum which Albrecht von Roon drew up for the Regent in the summer of 1858.[1] In this he began by pointing out Prussia's need for an "inexpensive but at the same time impressively strong army" if she were to remain a Great Power, and he went on to argue that the existing reliance on the Landwehr did not answer that need. Disagreement about Government policy was inevitably reflected in the ranks of the Landwehr and made all "free political transactions" impossible. But such "freedom", he maintained, "was the first requirement for a strong independent government", and it could come only from the possession of a military force which did not argue but uncritically did what it was told. There must be a "more intimate blending" of the Landwehr and the Line. The separate civilian Landwehr organisation must be abolished. In its place "area commands" should be formed, staffed by officers of the Line who would train the Landwehr as an immediate reserve. Moreover men should pass into the Landwehr only after serving with the regular army—with the colours or in the regular reserve—for seven years; which would give the regular

[1] Reprinted in Roon, *Denkwürdigkeiten* II 521 ff. For other projects of reform see O. von der Osten-Sacken, *Preussens Heer von seinen Anfängen bis zur Gegenwart* (Berlin 1911–14) III 1–6.

army a strength of seven age-groups and make it less necessary to call upon the Landwehr at all. Thus the establishment of the regular army must be increased, and its cadres of regular officers and N.C.O.s must be augmented, by improved conditions of entry, training, and service.

With the essence of these proposals William wholeheartedly agreed. The confusion and inefficiency of the mobilisation of 1859 made the matter urgent,[1] and he set up a commission under Roon himself to examine and codify the proposals for legislation. The greatest political skill would be needed to steer through the Assembly proposals involving an increase in the military budget and the destruction of the independence of the Landwehr, and the Regent was prepared to make no concessions. Indeed he refused to support Roon's own suggestion that civilian opinion could be conciliated by reducing service with the colours to two years. "Discipline, blind obedience, are things which can be inculcated and given permanence only by long familiarity", he maintained, "and for these therefore a longer period of service was required."[2] The enlargement of the army must not lead to the weakening of its Hohenzollern traditions; and of those traditions long service was the only guarantee.

Thus modified, Roon's proposals could only awaken violent controversy. The Minister of War, General Edouard von Bonin, was so lukewarm in his advocacy of them that William replaced him in December 1859 by Roon himself. The dismissal of the liberal von Bonin and his replacement by a reactionary so avowed and notorious as Roon was in itself a challenge to battle, and opened a conflict between Crown and Assembly which was to rage for nearly eight years. With its course we are not here concerned, for Roon did not allow it to interfere with the methodical enactment of his reforms.[3] By September 1862 Parliamentary opposition had reached the point where the Assembly refused all further grants for the army, and William, on Roon's advice, summoned as Minister-President the ruthlessly unorthodox Otto von Bismarck. Bismarck's theory of "a gap" in the constitution, whereby in the event of a deadlock between Crown and Assembly the Crown

---

[1] Osten-Sacken, op. cit. III 13–17.

[2] Qu. G. Ritter, *Staatskunst und Kriegshandwerk* (München 1954) I 146. In practice this reduction had been made for the past thirty years.

[3] For full accounts see F. Löwenthal, *Der preussische Verfassungsstreit 1862–66* (Altenburg 1914) and K. Kaminski, *Verfassung und Verfassungskonflikt in Preussen, 1862–66* (Berlin 1938). Briefer summaries can be found in G. Ritter, *Staatskunst und Kriegshandwerk* I 159–206, and Gordon Craig, *The Politics of the Prussian Army* 138–79.

was entitled to take all measures necessary for the continued well-being of the State, enabled him to raise the taxes which the Assembly refused to vote. In September 1863 the Assembly was dissolved. Within six months Bismarck had involved Prussia in war with Denmark, and all the emotions which affect men once their nation is fighting foreigners strengthened the hand of the Government and weakened that of the Opposition. As the subsequent quarrel with Austria sharpened, the section of Liberal opinion which favoured unification of Germany under Prussian rule swung to Bismarck's support; and the constitutional crisis was virtually resolved on 3 July 1866, on the battlefield of Sadowa. Two months later the Assembly granted the Government a full indemnity for its unconstitutional expenditure over the last four years, and the following year the seal of parliamentary approval was set on the army reforms. On 20 October 1867 Roon could write jubilantly to the King that the struggle was over at last.[1] Not only had the Prussian army been remodelled according to his design, but the armed forces of the new North German Confederation, whose creation the victories of that army had made possible, were being brought into line.

Thus, by 1868, ten years after Prince William had succeeded his brother, the old army of Prussia had been transformed into the army of the North German Confederation[2]; and the military legislation of the Confederation was copied in essence from that of Prussia.[3] The King of Prussia was Commander-in-Chief of the Federal Army. Universal obligation to military service without substitution was again laid down, and the Army—with the addition of the Navy—was again described as "the training school of the entire nation for war". But there were significant differences. Service with the colours remained at three years, beginning at the age of twenty; but conscripts then served with the reserve for four years instead of two, before passing into the Landwehr; and in their first year of Landwehr service they could still be called up with the reserve. Thus the regular army when mobilised consisted, in addition to the cadres, of seven annual intakes—if necessary eight. Service with the Landwehr had been reduced from seven years to five—and that under a supervision of the regular army so direct that the force virtually constituted a second-line reserve. This

---

[1] Roon, *Denkwürdigkeiten* II 514.

[2] For an account of its detailed organisation, see G. Lehmann, *Die Mobilmachung von 1870–1* (Berlin 1905) 2, 177, Jany, *Geschichte der Preussischen Armee* IV 243–50, and Osten-Sacken, op. cit. III 117–77.

[3] Law of 9 November 1867. Frauenholz, op. cit. V 575.

supervision was exercised by the authorities of the army-corps areas into which Prussia had long been divided, and which were increased to cover the entire Confederation. Prussia itself was divided into eight areas, Schleswig-Holstein constituting a ninth, Hanover a tenth, electoral Hesse, Nassau and Frankfurt an eleventh, and the kingdom of Saxony a twelfth; with the Grand-Duchy of Hesse furnishing a single division.[1]

This corps organisation facilitated the extension of the Prussian military system to the remaining states of Germany. The authorities in each corps area were to a large degree self-sufficient. They drew their recruits locally, trained their own Landwehr and were responsible for their own mobilisation in time of war. Sovereign States could thus be embodied as new corps areas without too great offence being caused to local pride. But the Prussian military system could not be extended without friction, especially to those states such as Hanover and Saxony which had fought on Austria's side in 1866. Centralisation and uniformity had to be mitigated. There was no Federal War Minister; the armies of the States were linked to the Prussian Minister of War by separate military conventions, and Hesse, Saxony, Brunswick, and Mecklenburg retained a considerable degree of autonomy in their military administration. The States south of the Main, in uneasy equilibrium between Prussia, Austria, and France, followed yet more slowly. Baden, alarmed at French designs in the Rhineland, was Prussia's most enthusiastic disciple, adopting her system virtually *in toto*. Württemberg, while adopting Prussian regulations and equipment for her army, preserved her own uniform and Landwehr organisation; and Bavaria, although in January 1868 she also adopted conscription and many other features of Prussian military policy, stubbornly clung to her independence over questions of armament, uniform and tactical organisation. But even without the Southern States the army of the North German Confederation was formidably impressive. In 1870 its total strength, with reservists, was reckoned at 15,324 officers and 714,950 men, and the Landwehr provided a further 6,510 officers and 201,640 men.[2] When the test came Roon put into the field a grand total of 1,183,389 officers and men, 983,064 of them from the North German

---

[1] Each Corps contained two infantry divisions, and each division two brigades, brigades and divisions being numbered consecutively throughout the army. Thus IV Corps contained 7th and 8th Divisions, 8th Division containing 15th and 16th Brigades.

[2] *The Army of the North German Confederation. A brief description . . . by a Prussian General.* Translated by Col. E. Newdigate (London 1872) 65.

Confederation—a force unheard of, as a French historian ruefully remarked, since the legendary armies of Xerxes.[1]

Size and military effectiveness are not necessarily synonymous. The deployment and supply of such masses in the field presented enormous problems. The sword might be too heavy to wield. Napoleon had invaded Russia with an army little over half that size, and found himself quite unable to control it; whereas in 1797 and again in 1814 he was able with small forces to split up and defeat greatly superior foes. It was this argument that comforted the French as they watched Roon's reforms bearing their dragon-seed fruit beyond the Rhine.[2] But it was an argument which failed to take into account the changes which developments in science and industry were working in the conduct of war.

It would be wrong to conclude that the Prussian army as a whole was gifted with any special insight into the techniques of the new form of warfare. In railway organisation, in the mobilisation of reservists, in the training and conduct of the three arms, it committed plenty of mistakes —not only in 1864 and 1866 but in 1870. But its adversaries committed worse; and the Prussians at least studied their errors, and readjusted their training and organisation accordingly. They did so, not because the Prussian generals were more intelligent or harder-working than their opponents, but because the Prussians possessed, in their General Staff, a body whose object was to fulfil exactly this function: applying to the conduct of war a continuous intelligent study, analysing the past, appreciating the future, and providing the commanders in the field with an unceasing supply of information and advice.

In other armies the General Staff was no more than a collection of adjutants and clerks for the commander in the field. No more had been needed in days when armies seldom reached six figures in strength, and the frontage of battles was correspondingly restricted. But the dispersal of armies on the march made possible by the railway and the

---

[1] *Der deutsch-französische Krieg 1870–71. Redigirt von der kriegsgeschichtlichen Abteilung des Gross Generalstabes.* (Berlin 1872–81). English translation, *The Franco-German War 1870–1871* (London 1874–84) Hereafter referred to as G.G.S. I i 46. (Osten-Sacken, op. cit. III 179, gives 1,494,412 officers and men, citing no sources.) Pierre Lehautcourt (ps. B. E. Palat) *La Guerre de 1870* (Paris 1901–8) II 244.

[2] E.g. Émile Ollivier, *L'Empire libéral XV: Étions-nous prêts?* (Paris 1911) 247ff. Moltke himself admitted: "Sehr grosze Truppenansammlungen sind an sich ein Kalamität. Die auf einem Punkte konzentrirte Armee kan schwer ernährt, niemals untergebracht werden; sie vermag nicht existiren, sie vermag nur zu schlagen." ("Verordnungen für die höheren Truppenführer vom 24 juni 1869' in *Taktisch-strategische Aufsätze* 173.)

telegraph, and the dispersal in battle made necessary by rifled firearms, threw a far greater weight on subordinate commanders and created technical problems of supply and communication which had to be delegated to specialists and which only a trained expert could properly evaluate. Senior commanders needed not simply an adjutant but a professional adviser, who could appreciate what action was possible within the limits imposed by the technical difficulties of communication and supply.

On the great fields of manœuvre, moreover, there was little opportunity for direct control. An army headquarters might be several days' march from its forward troops when they engaged; and if the will of the commander was to make itself felt at all, it could only be through the reflexes which he had already inculcated in his subordinates through previous training; so that, even when deprived of his guidance, they should react to unexpected situations as he would wish. Such unanimity could not be expected from corps and army commanders who had undergone no such scientific training and who were often senior—and hostile—to the Chief of the General Staff. But their staff-officers could be trained; and although the staff-officer owed his commander an unquestioning loyalty and obedience, it was the loyalty of a mind already selected and shaped by the Chief of Staff himself. Thus the Prussian General Staff acted as a nervous system animating the lumbering body of the army, making possible that articulation and flexibility which alone rendered it an effective military force; and without which the French armies, huddled together in masses without the technical ability to disperse, found numbers a source not of strength but of fatal weakness.

That the Prussian General Staff was able to perform this function was due largely to the shape which Helmuth von Moltke had given to its organisation and training since his appointment as Chief in 1857. His work consisted not in innovation but in bringing to the selection and training of staff-officers the personal dedication and the mercilessly high standards of some great impresario or savant. Indeed Moltke's reflective temperament, the breadth of his interests and the fine-drawn austerity of his appearance all suggested a figure from the realms of the arts or letters rather than from that of the camp; and the affection and respect in which he was held by his officers was that of disciples and pupils rather than of subordinates. By temperament he was a liberal humanist, but by rigorous self-discipline he made himself the most exact and exacting of specialists and he trained the General Staff in his own image. He recruited it from the outstanding pupils who graduated annually from the *Kriegsakademie*: and as he selected only twelve from an annual class of about forty, itself selected by examination from a field of some hundred and twenty, he was able to skim the cream.[1] Even the successful candidates were on probation, working under Moltke's close personal control or accompanying him on the staff rides which he made a central part of their training, and if they did not give him the fullest satisfaction they were returned to regimental duty. Staff-officers had in any case to do a spell of regimental duty before each step in promotion—an intermingling of staff and line which not only kept the staff active and in touch with the troops, but which disseminated Moltke's ideas and standards throughout the whole army.[2] By 1870 the army had thus been largely formed to his ideas. Many brigade and divisional commanders had trained under him, and at the elbow of each corps and army commander stood a wary Chief of Staff; all impressed with the prime importance of keeping orders simple, of moving with their forces dispersed until the last moment, and of giving one another, virtually at any cost, the utmost mutual support.[3]

Training of his staff and, through it, of the army command as a whole was only one of Moltke's responsibilities. He had, in addition, the responsibility for drawing up war plans—a vital and complex task for a state with frontiers so vulnerable as those of Prussia. On the rapid assembly and correct deployment of forces the outcome of the entire war would depend, and skill in leadership or courage in battle shown by the armies in the field would avail nothing if those armies did not arrive in time, in adequate strength, and in exactly the right place. "A mistake in the original concentration of the army", wrote Moltke, "can hardly be made good in the entire course of the campaign."[4] He had therefore to ensure, first that the mobilisation of the Army ran smoothly; secondly that the necessary railway-lines were available and everything was prepared for their use; and finally that deployment-plans were drawn up to correspond to every conceivable political emergency.

The difficulties of the mobilisation of 1859 showed Moltke the size

[1] Stoffel, op. cit. 112 ff.
[2] See especially E. Kessel, *Moltke* (Stuttgart 1957) 230–2.
[3] See especially Moltke's "Verordnungen für die höheren Truppenführer, 24 juni 1869", in *Taktisch-strategische Aufsätze* 171 ff.
[4] Qu. D. von Cochenhausen, *Von Scharnhorst zu Schlieffen 1806–1906. Hundert Jahre preussisch-deutscher Generalstab* (Berlin 1933) 162.

of the problem with which he had to deal,[1] and thenceforward he worked tirelessly to solve it. One administrative arrangement made it easier: the decentralisation of mobilisation arrangements down to corps areas, whose commanders were closely in touch with the neighbourhood, and where the necessary lists and stores could be conveniently kept. In 1866 the mobilisation arrangements were sufficiently rapid to compensate for the time lost while King William, anxious to avoid all appearance of aggression against an Empire with which he felt such profound sympathy, hesitated to authorise them at all. By 1870 the machine was perfected. Every unit of the Army and the Landwehr, of the lines of communication and supply, had their orders which needed only a word and a date to bring them into operation.

The errors made in railway organisation in 1866 had also been carefully studied. In their campaign the Prussians had committed many of the errors of which the French were guilty in 1859.[2] Supplies had been sent forward with no consideration of the facilities for unloading at the further end, and unloaded wagons, urgently needed elsewhere, choked sidings and stations. Lines operated independently, and commanders in the field gave instructions to the local railway officials with no reference to Moltke or anyone else. All this was alleviated by the creation of a special Line of Communication Department of the General Staff, and a civil-military Central Commission to make all plans for the use of railways in time of war.[3] Detailed arrangements were again decentralised to corps, but an Inspector-General of Communications was appointed with general responsibility for supply, and one of Moltke's three principal assistants was made solely responsible for railway matters. Even in 1870 things were not to run entirely smoothly. Once again a glut of supply-waggons was to block the lines; and it has been suggested that only the capture of French stocks saved the invading armies from "a condition bordering on starvation".[4] But the frightful condition in which the French armies were to find themselves through incompetent railway administration provides evidence enough of the extent to which Moltke's attention to the *minutiae* of this department alone made possible

[1] E. Kessel, op. cit. 277. W. Bigge, *Moltke* II 42–67.

[2] E. A. Pratt, *The Rise of Rail Power in War and Conquest* 105–9. Lehmann, op. cit. 58.

[3] Details of the organisation and work of this Commission are given in the memorandum *The Railroad Concentration for the War of 1870–71*, reprinted in *The Military Historian and Economist* (Cambridge, Mass.) III No. 2 (1918). I am indebted to Mr Paul Guinn for this reference.

[4] Pratt, op. cit. 110–15. See also Albrecht von Stosch, *Denkwürdigkeiten* (Stuttgart 1904) 204.

even the relative success with which his armies in the field were kept supplied.

Finally there were the plans for deployment—the famous *Aufmarsch* which Prussia's central position in Europe made such an essential part of her strategy. Railways eased the problem of dealing with three potential enemies, but they could not solve it. There was still the question, against which adversary the main force should be deployed, and what minimum force should be left to defend the remaining frontiers. For this the most precise knowledge was needed about available communications, the forces of which France, Austria, and Russia could dispose, and the speed with which they could be mobilised and brought to the field. All the patient labours of the General Staff were crystallised in the deployment plans which Moltke drew up between 1858 and 1880; their intelligence about enemy and friendly resources, their work to improve and exploit the German railway network, their endeavours to ensure that German mobilisation should be the most rapid in Europe. Moreover these plans provide a barometer, recording the changing tensions of the political situation in Europe, the apparent threats to Prussia as they changed from year to year. Moltke's appreciation of these threats was inevitably influenced by his own political views. The conflict with Austria he considered a necessary but regrettable "cabinet war" in the old style, to settle the balance of power. With France he seems to have considered no permanent peace possible, either before or after 1870; and the danger from Russia seemed at times even greater. Hence the constant drafting and redrafting of plans for a war on two fronts, and a preoccupation with security which was to descend to his successors in a form which ultimately proved fatal to the peace of Europe.[1]

The post of Chief of the General Staff when Moltke assumed it was not one of great significance. Moltke was not consulted either during the drafting and passage of the Army Reforms nor at the beginning of the war against Denmark in 1864.[2] The commander of the Prussian forces at the outset of this campaign was the octogenarian Field-Marshal von Wrangel, who had commanded them in the unsuccessful campaign in 1848 and whose sanity was now a matter of some doubt; and he chose as his Chief of Staff the equally incompetent General Vogel von Falkenstein. Moltke's advice, that the Danes should be surrounded

---

[1] For a descriptive analysis of Moltke's political views as reflected in his *Aufmarsch* plans, see Rudolf Stadelmann, *Moltke und der Staat* (Krefeld 1950) 279–323.

[2] Kessel, op. cit. 339, 381.

and annihilated in their forward positions before they could withdraw to their unapproachable islands, was ignored. Only after three months of inconclusive fighting were Falkenstein and Wrangel succeeded by Moltke and the King's nephew, the flexible and soldierly Prince Frederick Charles, and then operations were conducted with a skill which established Moltke in the all-important royal favour for good. But Moltke still had far to go before he was universally accepted as the King's sole military adviser, and thus the virtual Commander-in-Chief of the Prussian forces in time of war. His plan of campaign against Austria had to be ratified by a sort of War Council, where it came under heavy criticism.[1] His distribution of forces was altered on Bismarck's insistence by the Ministry of War, to give protection to the Rhineland, and royal intervention was needed to uphold Moltke's original plans. Nor did his presence as the King's chief adviser inspire any great confidence in the public. "The King, in his seventieth year, at the head [of the armies]", said one officer, son of the great Boyen, "the decrepit Moltke at his side. What is the outcome likely to be?"[2] The army commanders were still wilful to the point of outright disobedience. Vogel von Falkenstein, commanding a detachment deployed against Hanover, defied Moltke's instructions and in consequence led his forces to humiliating, though short-lived, defeat. The Crown Prince, commanding the easternmost of the three armies with which Moltke planned to invade Bohemia, changed his position so as to give better protection to Silesia and thus nearly dislocated the whole plan of campaign. Frederick Charles, advancing in the centre, moved so slowly that it seemed at one moment as if Benedek, the Austrian Commander, would be able to fall on the isolated Crown Prince with overwhelming superiority and defeat the Prussian armies in detail. Moltke's decision to keep his armies separated and to unite them only on the battlefield came under the heavy criticism of most of his colleagues.[3] Finally, when at last the Austrians stood at bay before Frederick Charles, with the Crown Prince swinging in on their right flank and the army of the Elbe threatening their left rear, Frederick Charles, instead of fighting a holding action, launched his full forces in a premature attack which,

---

[1] *Prinz Friedrich Karl von Preussen: Denkwürdigkeiten aus seinem Leben*, ed. W. Foerster (Stuttgart 1910) Hereafter referred to as Frederick Charles, *Denkwürdigkeiten*, II 12.

[2] Kessel, op. cit. 444. Roon, *Denkwürdigkeiten* II 409.

[3] Kessel 472–3. See also the criticisms by Friedrich Engels in the *Manchester Guardian* of 3 July 1866, reprinted in W. O. Henderson and W. H. Chaloner, *Engels as Military Critic* (Manchester 1959) 133.

even had it succeeded, would only have driven the Austrians back to safety out of the closing jaws of Moltke's trap. Moltke's messenger checked the commander of his reserve division, General von Manstein, just in time; who then made the famous comment: "This seems to be all in order; but who *is* General von Moltke?" By nightfall the Austrian army was routed, losing twenty-four thousand men killed or wounded and thirteen thousand prisoners. The question was not asked again.

§4 The Reform of the French Army

A few French soldiers had studied Moltke's activities. "Be as rude as you like about this army of lawyers and oculists", warned General Bourbaki in 1866, who had visited Berlin two years earlier, "but it will get to Vienna just as soon as it likes."[1] But in general the French did not consider the Prussians as a force to reckon with on the same level as the Austrians who had resisted the French so stubbornly in Italy, and to them the news of Sadowa was a thunderclap. The obvious explanation of the Prussian victory, the one which was adopted with enthusiasm, was that the battle had been won by the Prussian needle-gun, and once the French army was also equipped with a breech-loading rifle its natural superiority would again be decisive.[2] But some of the wiser heads, the Emperor among them, saw that the roots of Prussia's victory lay deeper: in her success in training a short-service conscript army; in her power to mobilise it rapidly, and her ability to convey it, with its supplies, to the battlefield without the disorder which had attended the French army's entry into Italy. To cope with such an adversary France would have to attain new standards of efficiency in military administration, and she might even have to reconsider the fundamental principle of a small army of long-serving professionals, on which her military organisation had hitherto been based.

When in the autumn of 1866 the military authorities of France examined the situation, they estimated the military strength of Prussia to be about 1,200,000 trained men. That of France, according to one official estimate, was 288,000, out of which contingents had to be found

[1] Bapst, *Canrobert* IV 34.
[2] Du Barail, *Souvenirs* III 64. Stoffel, *Rapports* 3, L. M. Case, *French Opinion on War and Diplomacy during the Second Empire* (Philadelphia 1954) 234.

to meet commitments in Algeria, Mexico, and Rome.[1] A great increase in French manpower seemed imperative, and Napoleon set as a target a mobilised force of 1,000,000 men. When in November 1866 a conference of civil and military officials met at Compiègne to consider how this could be achieved there emerged two sharply contrasting points of view. One party, to which the Emperor himself inclined, advocated the adoption of universal short-term military service on the Prussian model. To this there were objections from both soldiers and civilians. The Minister of War, Marshal Randon, led the military opposition, and voiced its deep professional mistrust of reservists. "The basis for military organisation", he insisted, "is the army present with the colours"; and if the obvious solution, an increase in the size of the annual contingent, was impossible, then the length of service must be increased—if necessary to nine years.[2] At the same time the Emperor's proposal came under civilian attack. Universal service, maintained the lawyers, would be unconstitutional, as only the Corps Législatif could determine the size of the army. Ministers pointed out the damage that might be done to agriculture by a universal levy; and reports from the Prefects made it clear that any increase in military burdens would be violently unpopular with the electorate on which the self-liberalising régime of the Empire was coming increasingly to depend.[3]

Politically, indeed, the Emperor could hardly have chosen a worse moment for such a project. The liberal institutions with which he had been diluting his authoritarian empire were now too firmly established for him to be able to ignore public opinion; yet the memory of his oppression was too fresh for the opposition to accept any measure to strengthen the army with which he had carried out his *coup d'état* and which he had continued to use as an instrument of his rule. Moreover the Mexican fiasco was fresh in the minds of the public; what guarantee was there that the new forces would not be employed on more adventures of this sort? Round this nucleus of protest gathered all those interests, commercial, industrial, agrarian, and simply hedonist, which resented any increase in military expenditure, and which for five years had been forcing its reduction. For the prosperous and en-

---

[1] Figures presented by General de Castelnau to a meeting summoned by the Emperor on 11 September 1866. Bapst, *Canrobert* IV 53. See however Marshal Randon, *Mémoires* (2 vols Paris 1875–7) II 221–2, for a dissenting and more optimistic view.

[2] Randon, *Mémoires* II 196–9.

[3] See Gordon Wright, *Public Opinion and Conscription in France*, Journal of Modern History XIV (1942).

lightened bourgeoisie of mid-nineteenth century France, as optimistic and humanitarian as their Victorian counterparts across the Channel, war was becoming unthinkable. Denunciation of its evils and projects for its abolition proliferated. A *Ligue Internationale de la Paix*, whose members included some of the most respected and sincere men in France, held annual conferences, protesting against the burden of armaments and preaching the brotherhood of nations.[1] Napoleon had in fact to deal with all the elements of opposition which William of Prussia had encountered six years earlier, and which only the ruthlessness of Bismarck had enabled him to overcome. Ten years earlier Napoleon might have adopted a similar solution, but now it was too late. He was elderly and ill; the Duc de Morny, the only man who might have guided him on such a course, was dead; and he had gone too far along the path of constitutionalism to draw back. The lines of French military organisation had to be drawn within the narrow limits of what was politically possible for a people which grudged every penny spent on the army, distrusted its own rulers and was deeply divided in itself.

The Compiègne Conference therefore reached a deadlock; but a way out was indicated by one of its members, Marshal Niel, whose grasp of the problems involved, both political and military, and whose skill in argument and debate marked him as one of the few men capable of putting through a military reorganisation on the scale required.[2] The solution, suggested Niel, was to revive the *Garde Nationale* and make it serve the purpose which the Landwehr did in Prussia. The traditions of the *Garde Nationale* were not particularly auspicious. Founded as a bourgeois instrument for preserving order at the beginning of the French Revolution and thereafter merged into the revolutionary armies, it had been reconstituted in turn by Napoleon I, by Louis XVIII and by Louis-Philippe, always with the main rôle of protecting internal order and property against *le péril intérieur*. Membership had been confined to the propertied classes until 1848 when this restriction

---

[1] Founded in 1867. In general the 1860s saw a remarkable degree of international pacific activity. In 1864 Britain submitted to arbitration over the Alabama incident. In 1864 M. Durand had held the conference at Geneva, out of which had come the Geneva Convention establishing the neutrality of all medical services. In 1867 a further conference examined the gaps which the Austro-Prussian War had revealed in the Convention, and drew up further articles. But humanitarianism had not destroyed chauvinism: in the shrewd words of Pierre de la Gorce "la plus grande marque de chauvinisme était de croire qu'il suffisait que la France ne voulût point la guerre pour que la paix fût assurée" *Histoire du Second Empire* (Paris 1902-3) VI 144.

[2] Du Barail, *Souvenirs* III 84.

was abolished, and the units from the Faubourg St Antoine went down fighting savagely in the June Days against the government forces. For the dictatorship of Louis Napoleon the *Garde Nationale* would have been constant embarrassment, whether as the instrument of the middle classes or more genuinely as the nation in arms; and shortly after his *coup d'état* in 1851 he dissolved it altogether.

The *Garde Nationale* was thus not a body which could be properly compared to the Landwehr, but Niel none the less proposed making use of it in the same capacity. By his scheme the principle of calling up a small annual contingent would be maintained, and conscripts should serve for six years with the colours; but all other men of military age, both those who escaped the call-up and those who purchased exemption, should serve and receive intensive training with the *Garde Mobile*. So should conscripts on completion of their service. Napoleon himself took up the proposal and published it as a *ballon d'essai* in the *Moniteur* on 12 December 1866.[1] Such an organisation, he maintained, would create an army 824,000 strong on mobilisation, and a *Garde Mobile* of 400,000. His target of a million would therefore be reached. Randon would have none of it. "It will only give us recruits," he maintained. "What we need are soldiers."[2] Randon's objections could be easily dealt with: the Emperor dismissed him and in January 1867 Niel became Minister of War in his place. But the plan was also too extreme for the cautious bureaucrats of the *Conseil d'État*, and the Bill which was eventually laid before the Corps Législatif was a very diluted version of Napoleon's original proposals. The potential size of the army was to be increased by reducing the length of service with the colours to five years. An army reserve was created, on the pattern of the Prussian, partly of conscripts who would serve there for four years after their five years with the colours, and partly from the "second portion" of the contingent which was to receive only a minimum of military training; while the *Garde Mobile* was to consist of all men of military age who had purchased exemption from service, and of the "second portion" after their four years with the reserve.

The project was not well received by the Legislature. The traditionalists were discontented with the weakening of the principle of an all-professional army. "Instead of spending thirty millions a year on the *Garde Mobile*" suggested Thiers, "use the money instead for the regu-

[1] General Lebrun, *Souvenirs militaires, 1866–70* (Paris 1895) 9. De la Gorce, *Second Empire* V 329.
[2] Bapst, *Canrobert* IV 58.

lar army."[1] The supporters of the Government, who knew how unpopular the measure was likely to be in the country, were no more enthusiastic. Admittedly the principle of substitution was retained; but the proposal to make of the *Garde Mobile* an effective trained reserve introduced an element of compulsion against which neither the money of the bourgeois nor the *bon numéro* of the peasant would be of any avail. Police and prefectorial reports gave menacing accounts of the universal opposition to such an idea:[2] "We have got to vote this law as the Emperor wants it", grumbled one official deputy, "but we'll fix it so that it can't work."[3] As for the republican opposition, they demanded the destruction of the standing army altogether as wasteful and unproductive expenditure, and the entrusting of the defence of France to a militia on the Swiss model of all able-bodied men. The debates went on till the end of the year, and all the battles fought in the Prussian chamber over von Roon's proposals were rehearsed again.[4] Niel repulsed the project for universal two-year service on the same grounds as had William I of Prussia: that two years was not enough to imbue the conscript with *l'esprit militaire*. The liberals argued that a *dépaysé* army of professionals was an inferior form of defence compared to that of a People in Arms.[5] As for the proposals about the *Garde Mobile*, they saw in these simply a plan to militarise France. "Do you want to turn France into a barracks?" cried Jules Favre during a speech by the Minister of War. "As for you", replied the harassed Niel, "take care that you don't turn it into a cemetery!"[6]

The law finally passed the Legislature in January 1868 by 199 to 60 voices and on 1st February it came into force. With regard to the army Niel got most of what he wanted: a period of five years' service with the colours and four years with the reserve. The annual contingent was still divided into two parts, of which the second was to serve for five months only. Given an annual contingent of 172,000 and normal wastage, it was recognised that this would by 1875 give a total mobilised strength of 800,000 men.[7] The *Garde Mobile* would provide another 500,000 men, bringing the total well over the million which Napoleon had demanded. But of Niel's original proposals for the *Garde Mobile*, very little was

[1] De la Gorce, *Second Empire* V 339.   [2] L. M. Case, op. cit. 236–8.
[3] Bapst, *Canrobert* IV 69.
[4] Monteilhet, *Les Institutions militaires de la France* 48–51.
[5] R. D. Challener, *The French Theory of the Nation in Arms* (New York 1955) 21.
[6] Bapst, *Canrobert* IV 71.
[7] According to the calculations of Moltke. *G.G.S.* I i 11.

lcft. It was to consist, as planned, of men of military age who escaped the call-up, and service was for five years; but the annual training period was reduced from the three weeks demanded by Niel to two, and anyone who showed an adequate knowledge of drill and military education was exempt even from that.[1] Moreover, to avoid any possible militarisation of French youth, the fortnight's training had to take place a day at a time, for not more than twelve hours a day, and be held under conditions which enabled everyone to get home the same evening. Not for a single night might the civilian be subjected to the corrupting influence of the barracks. Not even the Legislature could really expect such conditions to be compatible with any sort of military efficiency; but, said their *rapporteur* hopefully, "whatever the speed of war today, a certain period will still be necessary to collect the reservists, incorporate them, concentrate the army and get it to the battlefield. That period seems to us more than enough to train the *Garde Nationale Mobile*."[2]

Niel decided to accept the measure as the best he could get. As it was, funds were not available to make more than a beginning in setting the *Garde Mobile* on foot, for any money spent on it had to be at the expense of the regular army. Few soldiers shared Niel's hopes for the institution, and General Lebœuf, who succeeded him after his premature death in 1869, regarded it with open distaste.[3] Political considerations also delayed the implementation of Niel's scheme. Imperial officials had doubted the wisdom of arming a people whom republican speakers and writers were daily inciting against the Government. The first "enrolment day" was made the occasion for menacing demonstrations.[4] The officers of the *Garde Mobile* were appointed by the Prefects, so their imperial sympathies could be guaranteed—though often at the expense of their military efficiency[5]—and the N.C.O.s were selected by the Army; yet the only regiments to be fully organised, those of the department of the Seine, showed so revolutionary and insubordinate a temper that the Government was reluctant to set on foot any more.[6] "To organise the *Garde Mobile*", maintained many senior officers, "will simply be to prepare an army for insurrection against the Government and society."[7]

[1] *Guerre: Mesures d'Organisation* 15–20.
[2] Monteilhet, op. cit. 94.
[3] *La Vie militaire du Général Ducrot* (Paris 1895) II 317.
[4] L. M. Case, op. cit. 239.
[5] See *Guerre: Mesures d'Organisation* 20–3, and the highly illuminating reports of Col. Berthaut reprinted in the Documents annexes 18 ff.
[6] Ibid. 19–20.
[7] General Jarras, *Souvenirs* (Paris 1892) 37.

Thus when war came in July 1870 the 500,000 men of the *Garde Mobile* on which Niel had counted to aid the regular army were still unorganised, unequipped and untrained.[1]

Improvements could be made in other directions. The introduction of the breech-loading rifle was, it is true, delayed by bureaucratic caution. The infantry would fire off their ammunition too quickly; the matter must not be rushed—further tests were still needed; the model under consideration might be surpassed within a few months by something even better; in any event it was not by improved weapons but by improved morale that the French army would win the next war. All these arguments were employed by Randon and his subordinates of the Ministry of War.[2] But the evidence of Sadowa was too strong. It was known that M. Chassepot, an employee in the artillery works at St Thomas d'Aquin, had been working on a breech-loading model, without official countenance, for ten years, and its adoption had been considered since 1863.[3] In 1866 Napoleon himself overruled Randon's objections and ordered the rifle to be put into immediate production. It was a magnificent weapon. The chief defect of the Prussian rifle was the lack of a really gas-tight breech. Chassepot solved this problem by introducing a rubber ring to seal the breech, which produced a rifle easier and safer to fire, while by giving the weapon a smaller calibre he increased the number of rounds which the infantryman could carry, and substantially increased the range. The Prussian needle-gun was effective only up to 600 yards: the *chassepot* was sighted up to 1,600. Niel hastened its production, and a million were available at the outbreak of war in 1870.[4] This was all that was needed to satisfy the army. Its morale, experience and traditions all were superior to the Prussians, and now its weapons were better as well. There seemed every reason to look forward to a conflict with complete confidence.

Artillery was another matter. The Prussian breech-loaders were known to be effective, but thanks to their faulty tactical employment they had played only a minor part in bringing about victory. It seemed rather that the Austrian gunners, whose disciplined and accurate fire had badly mauled Frederick Charles's divisions at the beginning of the Battle of Sadowa and had checked the Prussian pursuit at the end of it, had carried off the honours of the day. The French army, thanks to

[1] For an account of local problems in the organisation of the *Garde Mobile* see General Montaudun, *Souvenirs militaires* (Paris 1900) II 34–5.

[2] Du Barail, *Souvenirs* III 66, Lebrun, *Souvenirs* 20–1, Randon, *Mémoires* II 235–41.

[3] Bapst, *Canrobert* IV 48.   [4] Lehautcourt, *La Guerre de 1870* II 113.

Napoleon's expert interest, had been equipped in 1858 with the rifled muzzle-loading pieces which had done good work in Italy, and their conversion would be an expensive affair.[1] The government had spent 113 million francs on the *chassepot*. The 13 million it asked for the artillery was refused, and with the 2½ million voted it was in no position to effect any radical reforms.[2] Nor did the Army consider it necessary. When in 1867 French officers visited the Belgian army, watched tests of the Krupp breech-loader with which it was armed, and sent back disquieting reports of the superior range and accuracy of these weapons, no action was taken.[3] Next year Friedrich Krupp himself respectfully brought the excellence of his weapons to the attention of the French Government; but Lebœuf would not be convinced that any steel guns were reliable. Krupp's brochure and the reports on it were filed away with the comment "*Rien à faire*".[4] Even the Emperor, whose attention to military details and particular interest in artillery was unflagging, felt that nothing need immediately be done. He had the *chassepot*. He also had the *mitrailleuse*. With this he had been experimenting since 1860, and production had begun under conditions of great secrecy in 1866. In appearance it resembled the *fasces* of the Roman Lictors: a bundle of twenty-five barrels, each detonated in turn by turning a handle. It had a range of nearly 2,000 yards and a rate of fire of 150 rounds a minute.[5] Like the *chassepot* it was an excellent and ingenious weapon; but such secrecy surrounded its manufacture that training in its use was almost out of the question, and no useful discussion was possible about how it should be employed.[6] It was used at extreme range; sited in the open and in battery; and fired inaccurately and wastefully. The Germans were to treat it with respect, but its achievements on the battlefield were not remotely to fulfil Napoleon's expectations.

Reforms in the fields of recruiting and armament, however wisely conceived and expeditiously enacted, were bound to take some years to bear fruit. There were more immediate ways in which the army could be improved. Discipline, training, organisation, the use of railways,

---

[1] See Louis Napoléon Bonaparte and Capt. Favé, *Études sur l'Artillerie* (Paris 1846–71) V 223 ff.

[2] Albert Sorel, *Histoire diplomatique de la Guerre Franco-Allemande* (2 vols. Paris 1875) II 389.

[3] Lebrun, *Souvenirs* 33–43.

[4] *Les Papiers secrets du Second Empire*, No. *11* (Brussels 1871) 7–14.

[5] J. Godts, *Les Mitrailleuses* (Paris 1908) 18.

[6] In one division, on the eve of the battle of Froeschwiller, only one N.C.O. could be found who knew how it worked. *Guerre* II 27.

machinery for mobilisation and concentration, all were inadequate by Prussian standards. These points were made the subject for a new Commission, which was set up at the end of 1866 after the Compiègne conference had broken up. The report of this Commission submitted to the Emperor in February 1867 was a confidential document; but its contents were revealed in an anonymous publication by one of the Commissioners, General Trochu, entitled *L'Armée française en 1867*, which ran through sixteen editions in three weeks and created as much irritation in the army as it did interest in the public. Trochu was an able and ambitious Breton with a fine record of service in Africa, the Crimea and Italy; an officer whose outstanding intelligence set him apart from, and indeed made him suspect to, his more pedestrian colleagues. His book was doubly odious, both as a breach of confidence and as an attack on the legends and traditions on which the army prided itself: on the *grognards* of Napoleon, on the military superiority of the French to all other races, on the adequacy of *débrouillage* to overcome all defects of education, administration and training. He agreed with conservative opinion in believing that the path of army reform should lie not through any increase in size but through " the correction of certain errors and the perfection of military techniques "[1]; but this did not recommend it to his colleagues. "The man who destroys the legend destroys faith," proclaimed one of the most intelligent, "and whoever destroys faith destroys an immeasurable force in which every race, one after the other, has sought victory".[2] The fact that the work made Trochu popular with the Opposition only increased his isolation within the army; as an open Orleanist he could never achieve a position of influence at Court; and even potential sympathisers were repelled when they discovered on meeting him that the General was, even by the standards of those loquacious days, a long-winded bore.[3] His considerable abilities therefore were largely unused and when war broke out he was allotted a command which was almost an insult: an Army of Observation, to consist largely of *Mobiles*, on the Pyrenees.

Napoleon did not need the adjuration of Trochu to make him press on with the work of military reform as a matter of urgency.[4] He urged

[1] *L'Armée française en 1867* 270.
[2] Du Barail, *Souvenirs* III 83.
[3] Lebrun, *Souvenirs* 61. Palikao, *Un Ministère de la guerre de vingt-quatre jours* (Paris 1871) 21.
[4] After the war he published an account of his projects and efforts towards military reform. See Le Comte de la Chapelle, *Les forces militaires de la France en 1870* (Paris 1872).

the need for a General Staff on the Prussian model. Colonel Stoffel in Berlin spoke unequivocally of the all-important part which the Prussian General Staff had played in the recent victories,[1] and Napoleon himself was under no illusions. But what was clear to him and Stoffel was not yet general knowledge, and military conservatism clung to the *Corps d'État-Major* as it stood. Even a partial measure which attempted to break down the isolation of the staff by sending regimental officers on staff-courses created such ill-feeling that it had to be abandoned.[2] The efficiency of the Prussian mobilisation, Moltke's other great achievement, was also under-rated. Napoleon's warnings, that Prussia might pour 500,000 men into France within a week and that the only way to counter this threat was to establish a comparable peacetime organisation in France, passed unheeded.[3] By 1869 intelligence about Prussian capacities was too clear even for the overworked Niel to ignore;[4] but by then it was too late. Niel, like Napoleon himself, was suffering agonisingly from the stone, and in August he was dead.

Too much importance should not be attached to Niel's premature death. Napoleon found an active and competent successor in General Lebœuf, who, if he lacked Niel's political adroitness, was quite as energetic and possibly more popular with the Legislature. Certain projects of Niel's he allowed to fall into decay—not only the *Garde Mobile*, but, even more serious, the Central Commission on military movement by railway which Niel had set up in March 1869 and which before its sittings were suspended had done some useful preparatory work.[5] But he studied problems of mobilisation and frontier-defence as a matter of urgency, and for many of the inadequacies of his period of office the blame can be allotted elsewhere. The Legislature, between 1868 and 1870, chipped away ceaselessly at military expenditure, reducing appropriations for fortifications and armaments, and increasing the proportion of furloughs[6]; and the Liberal Ministry which came into power under Émile Ollivier in January 1870 was so optimistic about the possibility of a general disarmament in Europe that on 30th June it proposed the

[1] See especially his report of 23 April 1868, in *Rapports militaires* 112–31.

[2] D'Andlau, *Metz, Campagne et Négociations* 474.

[3] Lebrun, *Souvenirs* 47–54.

[4] Niel wanted at least to reduce the number of men on permanent leave in order to speed mobilisation, but this plan was also rejected by an Assembly intent on cutting costs. Sorel, *Histoire diplomatique de la Guerre Franco-Allemande* II 387.

[5] F. Jacqmin, *Les chemins de fer pendant la Guerre de 1870–1871* (Paris 1872) 18–19, 45. Jarras, op. cit. 17–19.

[6] De la Gorce, *Second Empire* VI 142–3.

reduction of the annual contingent by ten thousand men. The debates on these proposals once again followed familiar lines. The burden of arms was too crushing for the nation to endure. The French military establishment was a constant provocation to her peaceful neighbours. Armaments would not prevent but could only lead to war. Lebœuf combatted these arguments by ample reference to the menace beyond the Rhine, and Napoleon seconded him; writing personally to deputies, and preparing a pamphlet, *Une mauvaise Économie*, which compared the military strengths of France and Germany, and whose publication was forestalled by the outbreak of war.[1] Even Thiers, that old enemy of the régime, brought all his authority to bear. "To talk of disarmament in the present state of Europe one needs to be both foolish and ignorant," he declared. But it was a losing battle. Lebœuf was compelled to reduce his budget by thirteen million francs.[2]

Nevertheless by July 1870 Lebœuf had cause to be satisfied with the achievements of the past four years. The army available for active service, he reckoned, totalled 492,585, of which he hoped to have 300,000 mobilised within three weeks. The *Garde Mobile* was 417,366 strong on paper, of whom 120,000 might be immediately available for service. The supply situation was excellent: clothing, food, ammunition, remounts, *chassepots*, all existed in reasonable abundance, and a new mobilisation scheme was taking shape in the Ministry of War.[3] Lebœuf's gallant and disastrous assurances to the Ministry, that the French army was ready, had a solid foundation in fact. By the standards of its past campaigns the French army *was* ready; ready, as Trochu was later to write, "as it had been for the Crimean War, for the Italian War, for the Mexican adventure, for all the military enterprises of that era; that is to say, ready to fight successfully and sometimes with brilliance against armies constituted and trained like itself".[4] It was the tragedy of the French army, and of the French nation, that they did not realise in time that military organisation had entered into an entirely new age.

---

[1] It was discovered in the Tuileries and reprinted in *Le Soir*, and by Georges d'Heylli, *Journal du Siège de Paris* (Paris 1871) I 326.

[2] Émile Ollivier, *L'Empire libéral* XIII 602. *Enquête parlementaire sur les Actes du Gouvernement de la Défense Nationale: Dépositions des Témoins* (Versailles 1873) Hereafter referred to as *D.T.*

[3] *D.T.* I 41–5, 67.

[4] L. Trochu, *Œuvres posthumes I: Le Siège de Paris* (Tours 1896) 88.

CHAPTER II

The Outbreak

§1 The War Plans

THE SEARCH for the "responsibility" for the war of 1870 is one
which historians have long since abandoned. There can be no doubt
that France was the immediate aggressor, and none that the immediate
provocation to her aggression was contrived by Bismarck; but the
explanation that the conflict was planned by Bismarck as the necessary
climax to a long-matured scheme for the unification of Germany—an
explanation to which Bismarck's own boasting in old age was to give
wide currency—is one which does not today command general assent.
The truth is more complex. War between France and Prussia was
widely foreseen when, after Austria's defeat in 1866, the North German
Confederation was formed.[1] The resulting change in the European
balance of power could be made acceptable to France only if her own
position was guaranteed by those compensations on the left bank of the
Rhine and in Belgium which Napoleon instantly demanded and which
Bismarck point-blank refused. After 1866 the French were in that most
dangerous of all moods; that of a great power which sees itself declining
to the second rank. In all ranks of French society war with Prussia was
considered inevitable. It required little insight to see that a French
foreign policy based on prestige was incompatible with those swelling
forces of German nationalism to which Bismarck had so skilfully
harnessed the Hohenzollern monarchy; and the more concessions
Napoleon made to Liberal feeling in domestic policy the more bitter
was the clamour from the Imperialist element, headed so influentially
by the Empress, for a determined stand in compensation abroad. Bismarck could rely for certain on a succession of provocations, growing
with French military strength, which he could accept or not as he
chose.

In Germany war also was recognised as being sooner or later in-

---

[1] See L. M. Case, *French Public Opinion* 240.

evitable[1]; and a war with France was bound to be popular in a way that the *Brüderkrieg* with Austria was not. For the Prussian Conservatives the trauma of Jena and their consequent humiliation had never been healed: the Austrians and British had intervened in 1814-15 and prevented them taking their proper revenge. For the Liberals of the *Nationalverein* France, with her unsleeping hunger for the left bank of the Rhine, and her possession of that province of Alsace which Louis XIV had snatched from the old Empire, was the arch-enemy of German unity; while for the German people in general—as indeed for the British at the time— France with her record of past aggression and repeated revolution was the disturber *par excellence* of European peace. To render her impotent, and at the same time to reclaim the German lands of Alsace, would be to satisfy the demands both of practical policy and of the nationalist ideal.

No one held this view with greater conviction than did Moltke himself. For him France was the hereditary foe, and had been so since the Rhineland crisis of 1831. The safety of Prussia over which he watched could never, in his view, be guaranteed until France was deprived of all power to do harm. The war of 1859 he saw as plain notice of aggression. "France", he then wrote, "has until now fought for others: she will now fight and conquer for herself." In 1866 the fighting with Austria was hardly ended before he was urging on Bismarck the desirability— and feasibility—of attacking France at once while Prussian forces were still mobilised.[2] A year later during the negotiations over the future of Luxemburg, he again urged war. The Duchy of Luxemburg was a member of the old German Confederation, ruled by the King of the Netherlands as Grand Duke. Napoleon saw in this left-over rump of old Germany a very reasonable compensation for French prestige, and Bismarck, since the King of the Netherlands had professed his desire not to see the Duchy a part of the new North German Confederation, was prepared at least to negotiate on this basis. But the city of Luxemburg was a federal fortress garrisoned by Prussian troops; so Moltke had to be asked whether its abandonment was compatible with the military security of the North German Confederation. Moltke protested vigorously. The negotiations became publicly known and a furore arose in the Reichstag and the nationalist Press. This, said Moltke, was a

---

[1] Stoffel, *Rapports militaires* 302. Evidence of Thiers and Benedetti in *D.T.* I 7, 89.
[2] *Moltkes Militärische Korrespondenz aus den Dienstschriften des Krieges 1870-71* (Berlin 1896) Hereafter referred to as *M.M.K.* 66-70.

splendid opportunity. War with France was inevitable within five years and during that time German military superiority over France would daily diminish. "The present occasion is good", he argued, "it has a nationalist character and we should take advantage of it (*man benutze ihn also*)."[1] Bismarck took a more statesmanlike view, and the matter ended amicably with the Prussians evacuating the fortress and the neutralisation of the Grand Duchy under the protection of the Powers. Moltke could not deny the political sanity of Bismarck's solution, nor the primacy of political considerations over military; but, he lamented, "he will cost us many lives in his time".[2]

It was in the conviction that war with France was inevitable, that Moltke on assuming office in 1857 began to draw up his plans for the *Aufmarsch* to the west. For many years these were purely defensive. In 1858 the most likely eventuality seemed to be the invasion of Germany by an aggressive Napoleonic France, and to guard against this Moltke looked, as Prussian conservatives had looked since 1815, to a close alliance with Austria.[3] But unlike other Prussian conservatives, Moltke realised that the leadership of this alliance must be Prussian. Only Prussia, by concentrating a substantial part of her forces on the Main, would be in a position to bring immediate help to the invaded states of South Germany; and, he concluded with satisfaction, "the question, as important as it is difficult, of the Command-in-Chief, will resolve itself".[4] But the left bank of the Rhine would have to be abandoned. It would take thirty-three days for Prussia to mobilise a force capable of opposing any resistance to the French, and nearly seven weeks before there was an adequate balance of forces. The only hope therefore lay in remaining on the defensive behind the Rhine and the Main—a position which lay conveniently on the flank of a French offensive either into the Rhineland or into South Germany. But such a defence, both tactically and strategically, could not be decisive unless an offensive followed; and how should such an offensive be conducted?

By 1861, as Roon's reforms began to fill up the cadres, Moltke was able to start taking this aspect of a war against France into consideration in planning his concentrations behind the Rhine. A French attack would have to be checked in the Palatinate, and Prussia might then launch an outflanking offensive to north or south. The route through

[1] Qu. R. Stadelmann, *Moltke und der Staat* 190.
[2] Moltke, *Gesammelte Schriften* (Berlin 1892) V 298. E. Kessel, *Moltke* 533.
[3] "In dem Zusammenhalten der beiden Deutschen Grossmächte liegt die grösste Gewähr für den Frieden Europas" *M.M.K.* 11.
[4] *M.M.K.* 13.

Belgium had little to recommend it.[1] Its way lay through the fortress belt of northern France and there were no conquests to be reaped there, either as permanent acquisitions or as bargaining counters in negotiating for peace. An offensive to the south held out very much better hopes. "If the former German provinces of Alsace and Lorraine were conquered" he reflected, "it is conceivable that we might keep them";[2] and at very least they would provide very useful pawns at the peace conference. It is clear from the context that these invasion-schemes were no more than highly remote conjectures in a plan which was almost entirely concerned with the defence of German territory; but they offered some indication of the direction in which Moltke's mind was beginning to move as his forces and his confidence increased.

The events of 1866 transformed Moltke's plans. The proved effectiveness of Prussian forces and the increased numerical strength brought by the other contingents of the North German Confederation enabled him to abandon all thought of passively awaiting the French attack behind the Rhine. All now depended on the speed with which railways could be built so that the superior manpower of North Germany could be brought into play. With the construction of four more lines, he told Roon, the time needed to concentrate the thirteen corps of North Germany could be reduced from six weeks to four.[3] Meanwhile, he reckoned in the autumn of 1867, he could concentrate 250,000 men in twenty-five days, even if he had to leave 65,000 to watch the Austrian frontier; and the following spring he set to work in earnest on plans for the invasion of France.[4] Counting on the support of the South German states, he would have 360,000 men available in three weeks, 430,000 in four. With forces of this size, strategy would be simple: a massive movement of four armies across the frontier of the Palatinate, between the Rhine and the Moselle, aiming at Nancy and Pont-à-Mousson, sweeping up the French forces as they went. Even if Austria came to the help of the French she would take about eight weeks to mobilise and could be held in check by 110,000 men. 385,000 would still be available to deal with the French army which could not possibly, reckoned Moltke, total more than 343,000. Any French force taking the offensive into Belgium or South Germany would quickly have to fall back to deal with this invasion. Moreover, the disposition of the French

---

[1] *M.M.K.* 28–9. It is clear from the context that Moltke was relying on the French to be the first to infringe Belgian neutrality.
[2] Loc. cit.
[3] *M.M.K.* 71–4.
[4] Ibid. 87.

railway-system gave the French army, as a choice of bases, only Metz and Strasbourg; and a German offensive would separate the two. The French army would be defeated; the dynasty would fall; and "as we desire nothing from France", concluded Moltke, "perhaps a rapid peace could be signed with the new Government".[1] Evidently even at this stage Moltke had no settled designs on Alsace and Lorraine.

In the winter of 1868-9 the General Staff polished their plans down to what proved to be their final form.[2] Six railway-lines were now available to bring the forces of the North German Confederation to the Rhineland—a total, in three weeks, of 300,000 men. If Austria was quiescent and the South German states fulfilled their treaty obligations, the total would be 484,000. The maximum strength of the French army, it if embodied all its reservists, was still calculated at 343,000, but it was more likely to take the field with 250,000; and it was just conceivable that it would attempt a rapid attack to disorganise German mobilisation schemes with its peacetime strength of 150,000. If that happened, German forces would have to detrain on the right bank of the Rhine, where they would be able to meet the French with superior numbers. Otherwise, the German armies would concentrate in the Palatinate, the First Army round Wittlich, the Second round Homburg, the Third—including the South German contingents—round Landau, the Fourth in reserve.[3] Corps were allotted to armies and railway-lines to corps. Railway timetables were drawn up, so that every unit knew the exact day and hour that it would leave its barracks and reach its concentration area. Mobilisation and deployment would follow one another in a single smooth and exactly calculated operation.[4] By July 1870 Moltke knew that he had under his hand one of the greatest engines of war the world had ever known; and he was openly impatient to use it.

The French nation and army as a whole was slow to appreciate the full implications of the threat which Moltke's preparations held for them, but one or two voices were raised in warning. One of them was that of the Baron Stoffel, the French military attaché in Berlin, whose despatches were detailed, clear-sighted, and increasingly urgent.[5] Another belonged to the commander of the 6th Military Division,

---

[1] *M.M.K.* 108.
[2] Ibid. 114-30.
[3] In 1870 the Fourth Army was to be merged into the Second. See p. 60 below.
[4] Lehmann, *Die Mobilmachung von 1870-1,* 7, and *Anlage* 3 188.
[5] See especially his report of 12 August 1869, in *Rapports militaires* 289 ff.

General Ducrot, who from his headquarters at Strasbourg and on his frequent visits to South Germany could watch developments in Germany almost as closely as could Stoffel. Ducrot exaggerated the capacity and aggressive intentions of the Germans as much as Moltke did those of the French. In autumn 1866 he gave warning of an imminent invasion by armies 600,000 strong, and in August 1868, more precisely, he reckoned that Prussia could invade France with 160,000 men in forty-eight hours and 500,000 in eleven days.[1] To him, as to Moltke, the answer seemed to lie in striking first and for this purpose the sooner war came the better. A rapid offensive would take the Prussians by surprise, win over the wobbling loyalty of South Germany and make possible a junction with Austria. The French, he repeatedly urged, should cross the Rhine, seize Heidelberg, advance to meet the Austrians at Würzburg, and then, with a friendly South Germany at their back, march on Berlin; while simultaneously a sea-borne force pushed up the Weser to seize Hanover.[2] Of the sympathy of the Germans in the Rhineland and the south he had no doubt at all. The Grand Duke of Hesse assured him that "the slightest [French] success will determine all the states of South Germany to march with you". But it had to be done quickly. Within a few years the South would be irrevocably integrated with the Prussian military organisation, and then it would be too late.[3]

No plans comparable to Moltke's were made in France until the very eve of the war; and here again the fault was basically one of organisation. The Minister of War, like his opposite number in Berlin, had his hands full with the reorganisation and rearming of the army; and the Staff was a mere depot of information, which occupied itself zealously enough with collecting military information and producing maps of Germany. It had no further responsibilities.[4] The only major plan of campaign which seems to have been drafted between 1866 and 1870 was the voluntary work of General Frossard, Military Governor to the Prince Imperial, and this visualised a strategy of pure defence.[5] The Germans, he reckoned, would invade France over the Palatine frontier with 470,000 men, directed against the Moselle Valley and Alsace. Numerically inferior French forces would be able to hold them. An Army of the Rhine could defend the ridge of Froeschwiller in Alsace, which threatened the flank of any advance over the Lauter on

[1] *Vie militaire du Gén. Ducrot* II 146, 250.
[2] Ibid. II 183, 242.
[3] Ibid. 232, 287.
[4] Jarras, *Souvenirs* 1–13.
[5] Printed in *Guerre* I 79–115.

Strasbourg. An Army of the Moselle on the Cadenbronn plateau above Forbach would bar the way to Metz. A reserve army could be formed at the camp of Châlons and a second reserve, largely of *Gardes Mobiles*, in Paris. This memorandum provided the basis of the plan which Napoleon drafted in 1868 for the distribution of the French forces (which he optimistically assessed at 490,000 men) into three armies based on Metz, Strasbourg and Châlons; and until 1870 this was the assumption on which all plans and appointments were made.[1]

In the spring of 1870 there came a change. Hitherto French plans had visualised a duel with the North German Confederation; but France had a powerful potential ally in Austria–Hungary, whose Chancellor, the Saxon Count Beust, had since 1866 been intent on revenge against the vanquisher both of his native land and of his country of adoption. There were political reasons for the Austrians to be cautious. The influence of the Hungarians was strongly hostile to any more adventures in Germany, and the statesmen in Vienna hesitated to commit themselves to a war which would probably involve them, not merely with Prussia and her German allies but, thanks to Bismarck's diplomatic skill, with Russia as well. But relations between the Austrian and French staffs were cordial. Unofficial conversations had been in progress ever since the initiation of the large Austrian programme of military reform in 1868, and in February 1870 the Austrian Minister of War informed the French military attaché that his forces were now ready for action. His arsenals and magazines were full, his reservists were trained, and in six weeks he could put an army of 600,000 in the field.[2] A semi-official stamp was given to these conversations when, the same month, the Archduke Albert of Austria, son of the great Archduke Charles and the victor of Custozza, paid a visit to Paris. The Archduke was even more anxious than was Beust to reassert the honour of his army and his dynasty, and he proposed to Napoleon an allied strategy for Austria, Italy and France which held out good hope of victory. According to his plan,[3] each of the allies should send an army of 100,000 into South Germany to seize a base in the area Würzburg–Nuremberg. Behind this screen the main allied armies should concentrate, inviting the South German states to join them, until they were ready to strike north to Berlin. Between them he calculated that the allies could raise a force

[1] Lehautcourt, *Guerre de 1870* II 147.

[2] *Archives historiques de l'Armée*. Reconnaissances. Autriche Hongrie 1869–72, carton 1608. Reports of Col. Vassart for 19 Jan., 1 Feb., March 1869, 4 Jan., 15 Feb., 21 Feb. 1870.

[3] Lebrun, *Souvenirs* 69–173.

of nearly a million men, while that of the North German Confederation, even if joined by the South German states, he reckoned with absurd optimism, at less than 475,000. To conform with this scheme France would need to divide her forces into two armies: one based on Strasbourg to strike across the Rhine and join her allies in South Germany, and the other, based on Metz, to ward off any German invasion from the Palatinate, or to launch a diversionary attack towards Mainz.

The Archduke insisted, when he later developed his plans in Vienna to Napoleon's emissary General Lebrun, that the question was purely academic. But even as an academic exercise the plan still left much to be desired. The French Staff reckoned that they needed only sixteen days to mobilise and concentrate their army; but both Austria and Italy needed from six to eight weeks. The Archduke did not consider this difficulty insuperable. Prussia would take seven weeks, he estimated, to mount an invasion of France with eight corps, and by declaring a state of "armed neutrality" on the outbreak of war Austria and Italy would be able to pin down as large a Prussian force as if they were actually fighting. France need therefore, he assured the Emperor, have nothing to fear: with an army of 400,000 strong by her own calculations, she could easily sustain the fight alone for six weeks. But the French generals were not so sure. Lebrun suspected that the six weeks which Austria demanded were based on political rather than military calculation— that Francis Joseph could not run the risk of yet a third unsuccessful war.[1] At a conference on 19 May 1870 the whole plan was critically examined by Generals Lebœuf, Frossard, Lebrun, and Jarras, director of the *Dépôt de Guerre*. In their view the plan underestimated both the speed of the Prussian mobilisation and the reliability of the South German states, and they insisted that only if all three allies took the field simultaneously could it have any prospect of success.[2] When Lebrun visited Vienna the following month Francis Joseph himself made it clear that such simultaneity was politically and militarily impossible. But, he declared, if Napoleon appeared in South Germany "not as an enemy but as a liberator, I would on my part be compelled to make common cause with him".[3] Napoleon clung pathetically to the shreds of the Archduke's plan. It accorded with French political and military traditions of the offensive; it offered the possibility of gaining fresh allies in Germany; best of all, it provided at least a chance of a

[1] Lebrun, *Souvenirs* 79.   [2] Jarras, *Souvenirs* 42–7.
[3] Lebrun, *Souvenirs* 147.

brilliant military success which the Empire needed so badly, and which Frossard's cautious strategy did not. Torn between the projects of Frossard and the Archduke, Napoleon was to give his army the worst of both worlds.

§2 The Hohenzollern Candidature

Such was the state of military planning reached in France and Germany when in July 1870 the crisis of the Hohenzollern Candidature broke from a clear sky.

On 30th June Émile Ollivier, the President of the Council, declared to the Chamber that "at no period has the maintenance of peace seemed better assured". He was not alone in his optimism. On 5th July Lord Granville, taking up his duties as Foreign Secretary in Mr Gladstone's first Cabinet, was informed by the Permanent Under-Secretary that "he never had during his long experience known so great a lull in foreign affairs".[1] Yet the issue which shattered the peace was not a new one. The Spaniards had been seeking a monarch ever since their revolution against their unsatisfactory Queen Isabella in 1868, and the name of Leopold, Hereditary Prince of Hohenzollern-Sigmaringen, had figured very early in the list of possible candidates. He was a Catholic, married to a Portuguese princess and father of a family. His brother Charles had recently accepted the crown of Rumania. His relationship to the Prussian Hohenzollerns, would bring the goodwill of one great European power, and since there also ran in his veins the blood of Murats and Beauharnais it was to be hoped that Napoleon would be mollified as well.[2] In September 1869 his principal Spanish supporter Don Eusebio di Salazar visited Leopold and his father, Prince Charles Antony, to urge all these arguments upon him. But the Prince showed little desire to ascend the most unstable throne in Europe, and Salazar went empty away. In February 1870, however, after further canvassing by Bismarck's agents, Marshal Prim, President of the Spanish Council of Ministers, sent him back in an official attempt to renew the offer, and this time tried to enlist William I as an ally. This was a shrewd move. Both Charles Antony and Leopold were disciplined Hohenzollerns, quite

---

[1] Lord E. Fitzmaurice, *Life of Lord Granville* (London 1905) II 33.
[2] At one moment it looked as if this hope would not prove vain. See Randon, *Mémoires* II 306.

prepared to take their orders from Berlin. Neither had yet altered his views about the unattractiveness of the project, but Leopold wrote to William: "I consider it my duty as an Hohenzoller, soldier and subject to submit to the express will of his Majesty, our King, accepting it as the guiding line of my conduct if higher political considerations and the expansion of the power and lustre of our house so demand."[1]

William did not consider that it demanded anything of the sort. He had no wish to see his kinsmen scattered on unreliable thrones whose collapse could only involve him in humiliation. But Bismarck's reaction was different. He saw not only the advantages of a dynastic link with Spain, advantages both commercial and military, but the disadvantages which would arise if the throne were to fall into the hands of a party inimical to Prussia. On 28th May 1870 he wrote to Charles Antony a powerful letter pointing out the vital service he could render Germany by accepting the throne for his son. Charles Antony capitulated and his son Leopold reluctantly concurred. Salazar was sent for and on 19th June Leopold informed William I that he was resolved to accept the call to the Spanish Throne. William showed natural umbrage that negotiations on such a vital family matter should have continued without his knowledge or consent;[2] but he gave his approval to Leopold's decision, "though with a very heavy heart". By 21st June all was arranged and Salazar telegraphed the good news to Prim.[3]

William could claim, as he later did in the face of French attacks, that he had treated the matter as a private family concern throughout, and had used no influence to induce Leopold to accept the Crown. The same claim, when made before the Reichstag by Bismarck, was utterly false. The idea of the Hohenzollern Candidature may have originated in Spain,[4] but throughout the previous winter Bismarck had actively forwarded it. But for his intervention it would probably have been extinguished by the cold water poured on it by the Hohenzollern princes themselves. But that is no reason to see in his policy, as have so

[1] G. Bonnin, ed. *Bismarck and the Hohenzollern Candidature for the Spanish Throne* (London 1957) 67. See also, for a thorough and scholarly treatment of the whole subject, the chapter by M. R. D. Foot on *The Origins of the Franco-Prussian War and the Remaking of Germany*, in *The New Cambridge Modern History* Vol. XI. (Cambridge 1960).
[2] See the Memorandum of the Crown Prince of Prussia to Queen Victoria in *Letters of Queen Victoria 1862–78* (London 1926) II 22–4.
[3] For these negotiations see Bonnin op. cit. 158–96.
[4] Though it was certainly pressed from the beginning by the Prussian Minister in Madrid. R. H. Lord, *The Origins of the War of 1870* (Harvard 1924) 17–18.

many French historians, a "trap" deliberately laid for France. Bismarck knew quite well that a Hohenzollern on the throne of Spain would be highly unwelcome to France; but if all had gone as he had hoped, Leopold's election would have been over before Napoleon had a chance to intervene. "It is possible that we may see a passing fermentation in France", he wrote in June to one of his agents in Spain, "and without doubt it is necessary to avoid anything that may provoke or increase it . . . undoubtedly they will cry 'intrigue', they will be furious against me, but without finding any point of attack."[1] Once the election was complete France would have no grounds for intervention which did not gravely offend the sovereignty of the Spanish people, and Napoleon would be compelled, as in 1866, to acquiesce in a *fait accompli*.

As it was, things went wrong, and they did so in a manner which, if the French had kept their heads, might publicly and profoundly have humiliated Bismarck. While Salazar negotiated, Prim kept the Cortes in prolonged session in Madrid, until the news of Leopold's acceptance made it possible to proceed to formal election. On 21st June Salazar wired that all was well, and added that he would be back in Madrid by the 26th. By an error in deciphering this last date was read as the 9th; and rather than keep the Cortes sweltering for another idle fortnight in Madrid, Prim adjourned them until the autumn.[2] No election could be held until they were convoked again, and in the interval there was little hope of Leopold's acceptance remaining secret. As it was, it leaked out within a few days of Salazar's return; and on 2nd July Prim tried to repair the damage by officially informing the French Ambassador that Leopold had been offered and had accepted the Crown.

The news shocked Paris. It was clear that the German Chancellor had been engaged for at least six months in a discreditable and damaging intrigue, and the French Government with good reason was outraged. The Duc de Gramont, a career diplomat who had only recently taken over the Ministry of Foreign Affairs, told the British Ambassador that

[1] Lord, op. cit. 23–4. Lord however suggests that the fact that the document was written in French rather than German indicates that it was intended to be shown to the Spaniards to reassure them, and cannot be taken as a guide to Bismarck's real thoughts.

[2] The error was traced to a clerk in the Prussian Legation at Madrid. Bonnin, op. cit. 233–4. It has been pointed out also that the delay was almost certainly welcome to Prim, who was less sanguine than Bismarck about the probable French reaction and who hoped to use the interval to win over Napoleon III. See Leonardon, "Prim et la question Hohenzollern" in *Revue Historique* Nov.-Dec. 1900.

the affair was "nothing less than an insult to France". The bland and patently mendacious assertion by von Thile, Bismarck's Secretary of State, that "so far as the Prussian Government is concerned the affair does not exist"[1] heated tempers in Paris to a disastrous degree. The other powers of Europe were equally appalled at what *The Times* stigmatised as "a vulgar and impudent *coup d'état* in total contradiction to accepted diplomatic practice in handling such matters"[2]; and had Gramont kept his head and acted as the spokesman of the Concert of Europe, Bismarck might have found it difficult to justify his actions. But Gramont was no Talleyrand. Ollivier and his colleagues were inclined to conciliation, but the Empress, whose hand was to guide Napoleon's pen during the next ten days, was not. Lebœuf assured the Council that the army was ready to fight,[3] and on 6th July with imperial encouragement Gramont read a ministerial statement in the Corps Législatif, which filled the chauvinists with delight. While admitting the right of the Spanish people to chose whomever they wanted as king, he maintained that this right did not extend to disturbing the balance of Europe to the French disadvantage and "placing in peril the interests and the honour of France". "To prevent it", he went on, "we rely at once on the wisdom of the German and the friendship of the Spanish people. But if it proves otherwise", he continued, in a phrase inserted, curiously enough, by the pacific Ollivier,[4] "then, strong in your support and in that of the nation, we would know how to fulfil our duty without hesitation and without weakness." The right wing and its Press roared their approval;[5] and Bismarck, on reading the speech, commented "this certainly looks like war".[6]

On the purely diplomatic level the prospects of a settlement still seemed fair. William I, who disliked the Candidature and certainly

---

[1] *Documents sur les Origines diplomatiques de la Guerre de 1870* (29 vols. Paris 1910–32) Hereafter referred to as *Origines diplomatiques* XXVIII 31.

[2] 8 July 1870.   [3] Émile Ollivier, *L'Empire libéral* XIV 100.

[4] Henri Welschinger, *La Guerre de 1870: Causes et Responsabilités* (Paris 1910) I 52. A light is shed on the attitude of Ollivier and the *ralliés* Liberals at this time by a despatch from the Austrian Ambassador of 8th July, who asserts that Ollivier told him: "Nous en avons assez des humiliations que la Prusse veut nous imposer. Ce ne sont plus des Rouhers ou des La Valette qui ont à diriger la politique de la France. C'est moi, un Ministre du peuple, sortant du peuple, sentant avec le peuple, moi, un Ministre reponsable devant la Nation." *Origines diplomatiques* XXVIII 514.

[5] So did a large section of French public opinion. See L. M. Case, *French Public Opinion* 245–51, for a careful analysis of popular reaction to Gramont's policy.

[6] Keudell, *Fürst und Fürstin Bismarck* (Berlin 1901) 429.

did not want war, was at Ems accompanied by only one Foreign Office official, Abeken, and thus was only remotely susceptible to the influence of Bismarck, who was still on his estates at Varzin. Charles Antony and Prim were appalled at the furore which they had unwittingly unleashed, and it needed little persuasion to make them abandon the project. But although William was prepared, privately and as head of the family, to advise his cousins to withdraw, he maintained that this was an affair with which he as King of Prussia had nothing to do; and it was precisely this attitude which Gramont refused to accept. Count Benedetti, the French Ambassador to Berlin, was instructed, on 7th July, to demand a categorical statement that the King's Government did not approve of Leopold's acceptance and had ordered him to withdraw it. Having tried, and failed, to humiliate France, Prussia must now undergo a comparable humiliation herself. When Benedetti reported, on 9th July, that William would say only that he would acquiesce in Leopold's withdrawal in the same fashion as he had acquiesced in his acceptance, Gramont replied "if the King will not advise the Prince of Hohenzollern to withdraw, then it will be war at once, and in a few days we will be on the Rhine". He was himself being goaded by fear and by public opinion. If they delayed, he said, the Prussians would gain the lead in military preparations; and, he wired Benedetti a little pathetically on the 11th, "you cannot imagine how excited public opinion is. It is overtaking us on every side and we are counting the hours". He accused Benedetti of not being firm enough; and if no definite answer was forthcoming from the King by the 12th, it would be regarded as a refusal of satisfaction.[1]

In Gramont's eyes, and those of his supporters, the question of the Candidature itself had thus become secondary to the more vital point, of obtaining "satisfaction" from Prussia, of a kind which William, fortified by urgent advice from Bismarck, was determined not to give. Thus when on 12th July Charles Antony, besieged by envoys from Madrid, Paris and Ems and by letters from Queen Victoria and the King of the Belgians, renounced the throne on his son's behalf,[2] the news was received by Gramont and by the right wing deputies and Press with embarrassed irritation. Ollivier and the Emperor openly declared their delight at what they regarded as an honourable solution; but it was not a view which found much support in Paris.[3] To rest content

---

[1] *Origines diplomatiques* XXVIII 90, 155, 183, 190, 222. Of military preparations Stoffel, on 11th July, could see no sign (ibid. 223–4), but cf. p. 58 below.
[2] Bonnin, op. cit. 250–2. Lord, op. cit. 64–5.   [3] Ollivier XIV 232–5.

with such a settlement was generally considered to be shameful. The demand went up, inside and outside the Chamber, for "guarantees." The *Moniteur* suggested that Prussia should be compelled to evacuate the fortress of Mainz. Compared with such views, Gramont's demands were moderate, but they still insisted on the necessary humiliation of Prussia. He suggested to the Prussian Ambassador, Baron von Werther, that William should write Napoleon a personal letter of "explanation"; and he instructed Benedetti to obtain from William not only a declaration associating himself with Charles Antony's refusal, but an assurance that he would not permit the Candidature to be considered again.[1] It was from these instructions that the war was to arise. If such an assurance was not forthcoming France would consider that her just demands had not been met, and would continue with her military preparations.

There was nothing particularly dramatic about the famous interview at Ems on 13th July. Benedetti encountered the King in the public gardens during the early part of the morning, and William, with the courtesy which never failed him, came over to speak to the Ambassador himself, and congratulated him on the news of Leopold's withdrawal. Benedetti had to ignore this olive branch: as instructed he demanded a guarantee that the King would not consent to a renewal of the Candidature. The King refused to bind himself to any course of action in the indefinite future, and the two parted coolly. A little later William received Charles Antony's formal letter of renunciation and sent his aide-de-camp to inform Benedetti, and to tell him—a considerable concession—that he gave it "his entire and unreserved approval"; but when Benedetti requested another interview to raise once more the question of a guarantee he returned the answer that there was nothing further to discuss.[2]

Benedetti, it is clear from his reports to Gramont, was in no way conscious of being discourteously treated, but the temper of the King and of his entourage had risen higher than he realised. They had learned of the agitation in Paris for guarantees, and of Gramont's demand for a royal letter of explanation, and Werther was abruptly recalled for consultations. The report which Abeken wired to Bismarck of the day's events was thus considerably sharper than Benedetti's to Gramont.

His Majesty [he said], having told Count Benedetti that he was awaiting news from the Prince, has decided . . . not to receive Count

[1] *Origines diplomatiques* XXVIII 263.
[2] Count Benedetti, *Ma Mission en Prusse* (Paris 1871) 376, and his evidence in *D.T.* I 86–7. Lord op. cit. 92.

Benedetti again, but only to let him be informed through an aide-de-camp; ... His Majesty had now received from the Prince confirmation of the news which Benedetti had already received from Paris and had nothing further to say to the Ambassador. [He concluded] His Majesty leaves it to your Excellency whether Benedetti's fresh demand and its rejection should not at once be communicated both to our Ambassadors and to the press.[1]

From Abeken's telegram two conclusions emerge: first, that the King was considerably irritated by Benedetti's demand, and by the French refusal to consider the question closed; and secondly, that the King himself had the idea of making his rebuff to Benedetti public. Bismarck, in the version of the affair which he gave to the world, was to emphasize these considerations to the point of distortion: but he did not invent them.

Bismarck had viewed the worsening of relations with open satisfaction. A peaceful withdrawal of the Candidature would have meant an open defeat for his policy, and if war with France had to come, now was as good a time as any. The news of Charles Antony's renunciation, which greeted him on his arrival, flung him into the profoundest depression. It was a humiliation, he wrote later, "worse than Olmütz".[2] But no more than Gramont did he consider that the affair was ended. Suspecting what Gramont's next step might be, he telegraphed to Ems urging the King to give Benedetti no explanation of any sort. If anyone should explain themselves it was France; indeed, he informed the King, "the growing exasperation of public opinion over the presumptuous conduct of France" made it necessary "that we should address to France a summons to explain her intentions towards Germany"; and to make this possible he requested the King's immediate return to Berlin.[3]

Events had reached this stage when Bismarck, at supper with Moltke and Roon, received Abeken's telegram from Ems, and saw that with a very little editing Abeken's words, already sharp, could be made to seem so violent that war would inevitably follow. Moltke gave a final assurance that all was ready—indeed, he maintained, it would be better to fight now than in a few years' time, when the French military reforms would be taking effect. Bismarck therefore set about editing the telegram. There was no question of falsification; yet Benedetti's *démarche*

---

[1] Lord, op. cit. 221. H. Abeken, *Ein schlichtes Leben in bewegter Zeit* (Berlin 1898) 376.

[2] Bismarck, *Reflections and Reminiscences* (2 vols. London 1898) II 93.

[3] Bismarck, *Die gesammelten Werke* (15 vols. Berlin 1928–35) VI b. No. 1598 p. 358.

was made to appear positively insolent, and his dismissal final. "His Majesty the King", concluded Bismarck's version, "thereupon decided not to receive the French Ambassador again, and sent to tell him through the aide-de-camp on duty that his Majesty had nothing further to communicate to the Ambassador." This, he assured his friends, would have the effect of a red rag on the Gallic bull. Within a few hours a special edition of the *Norddeutsche Zeitung* carrying the telegram was selling on the Berlin streets. As a final touch the telegram was sent to all Prussian representatives abroad, with instructions that they were to communicate it to the Governments to which they were accredited. Nothing was left undone to goad the French into war.[1]

The effect was as Bismarck had anticipated. Both in Berlin and in Paris excited crowds gathered shouting "to the Rhine!" William I cried, on reading the telegram, "This is war!" So did Ollivier and Gramont. War could hardly have been long delayed if Bismarck had carried the King with him in his demands for "satisfaction" from France; but the sad irony is that on 14th July, when the news from Berlin reached Paris, the peace party in the French Government had precariously gained the upper hand. On the 13th the Ministers meeting in Council heard for the first time of the instructions which Gramont had sent Benedetti the previous evening; and though they somewhat reluctantly approved them, they added a rider that "the demand for guarantees was susceptible of mitigation and any honourable transaction would be welcome".[2] An urgent despatch from Lord Granville counselling the Imperial Government to rest content with Leopold's renunciation was read aloud and created considerable effect; and a proposal to decree mobilisation was voted down, to Lebœuf's chagrin, by eight votes to four.[3] Not till the following day did Benedetti's despatches and reports of Bismarck's "Ems Telegram" reach Paris; and then, by comparing the two, the Ministers were able to gauge the full extent of Bismarck's distortion and judge the bellicose purpose which lay behind it. Unanimously they consented to mobilisation and at 4.40 p.m. the orders went out. Then they had second thoughts, and for six hours they debated an

---

[1] Bismarck, *Reflections and Reminiscences* II 96. Moritz Busch, *Bismarck: Some Secret Pages of his History* (London 1898) I 405. Lord, op. cit. 103–4. Count Waldersee, reading the telegram in Paris, noted "Bismarcks Telegramm . . . war so grob, wie ich es kaum für möglich gehalten hatte." Waldersee, *Denkwürdigkeiten* I 79.

[2] De la Gorce, *Histoire du Second Empire* VI 273.

[3] Henri Welschinger, *La Guerre de 1870: Causes et Responsabilités* I 134, Ollivier, op. cit. XIV 355–86.

appeal to a Congress of Powers. A note to that effect was drafted and Napoleon prepared a message to Lebœuf to delay the recall of the reserves. "I doubt", grimly commented the Empress, who was attending the Council meeting, "whether that corresponds to the feeling in the Chambers and the country". The harassed Lebœuf threatened to resign. But as the evening wore on there came the news that Bismarck had officially communicated the Ems telegram to the Governments of Europe. In face of such provocation all thought of accommodation disappeared. By nightfall the French Government, like Bismarck himself, was resolved on war.[1]

When next day, 15th July, Gramont and Ollivier, addressing the Senate and the Corps Législatif respectively, demanded the necessary war credits, the voice of the opposition did make itself heard. The veteran Thiers, whose patriotism, political ability and military learning were above reproach and who had until the withdrawal of the Hohenzollern Candidature used all his influence to support the Government, followed Ollivier on the rostrum and, amid constant interruptions, denounced the war. "Do you want all Europe to say that although the substance of the quarrel was settled, you have decided to pour out torrents of blood over a mere matter of form?" The leaders of the Left supported him—Gambetta, Arago, Garnier-Pagès, Jules Favre; but on the solid majority of the Right and the Centre he could make no impression at all. The mastodon trumpetings of Guyot-Montpayroux— "Prussia has forgotten the France of Jena and we must remind her!"— fitted in better with their mood.[2] Ollivier, in replying to Thiers, accepted the heavy responsibility of the war "*d'un cœur léger*". He hastened to qualify the unfortunate phrase—"I mean with a heart not weighed down with remorse, a *confident* heart"—but for the rest of his long life he was never to be allowed to forget it.[3] A commission of the Chamber hurriedly examined him, Gramont and Lebœuf. Lebœuf stoutly assured them the army was ready. Better war now, he said, unconsciously echoing Moltke, than in a few years' time when the Prussians would have improved their rifles and copied the *mitrailleuse*—and, he added, before the Opposition in the Chamber had destroyed the army altogether.[4] Gramont, when asked whether France could rely on any allies, replied subtly: "If I kept the Commission waiting, it was because I had

[1] Duc de Gramont, *La France et la Prusse avant la Guerre* (Paris 1872) 212–23.
[2] P. Lehautcourt, *Les Origines de la Guerre de 1870: La Candidature Hohenzollern 1868–1870* (Paris 1912) 581.
[3] Ollivier, op. cit. XIV 422.
[4] Ibid. 451.

with me at the Foreign Ministry the Austrian Ambassador and the Italian Minister. I hope that the Commission will ask me no more."[1] The Chamber was satisfied by Lebœuf's soldierly bluntness and Gramont's diplomatic evasions, and by an overwhelming majority the votes of credit were passed. Outside in the streets the crowds greeted the news with roars of delight, and the demonstrations which the Republicans organised against the vote were drowned.[2]

Thus by a tragic combination of ill-luck, stupidity, and ignorance France blundered into war with the greatest military power that Europe had yet seen, in a bad cause, with her army unready and without allies. The representatives of Austria and Italy, like those of Russia, Britain, and the South German States, made it clear that they could not support France in such a struggle; and opinion in England, naturally gallophobe and sympathetic to the ally of Waterloo, was powerfully swayed when Bismarck released to *The Times* details of the proposals for the absorption of Belgium which Napoleon had so imprudently entertained in 1866.[3] But it was not due simply to the machinations of Bismarck that France had to go, alone and unpopular, to meet her fate.[4]

§3 The German Mobilisation

While the diplomats negotiated, the soldiers on both sides were taking their first precautionary measures. As early as 11th July the Prussian military attaché in Paris, the Count Waldersee, informed his King that the French had begun discreet preparations for war. Orders for forage were being placed in America; military commissions were being attached to railway companies; naval officers were being recalled from leave; transports were being prepared in Toulon to collect troops from Algiers and Rome, and the artillery depots were bustling with activity.[5] Properly alarmed, King William at once telegraphed orders to the

[1] Ibid. 454.
[2] See L. M. Case, *French Public Opinion* 264, for the improbability of the explanation that the pro-war demonstrations were officially inspired.
[3] D. N. Raymond, *British Policy and Opinion during the Franco-Prussian War* (Columbia 1921) Chapters 4 and 5, *passim*.
[4] The French declaration of war was not formally presented to the Prussian Government until 19th July, but the French Government's declaration of 15th July created a state of war, *Origines diplomatiques* XXIX 11 n. 1.
[5] Lehmann, *Mobilmachung* 23.

Ministry of War to arm the fortresses of Mainz and Saarlouis and to take measures for the defence of the Rhineland. Roon found these instructions embarrassing. No plans had been made for such partial mobilisation, and any improvisation would completely disorganise the total mobilisation and *Aufmarsch* which might have to follow. Yet total mobilisation, flowing automatically as it would into deployment and from deployment into invasion, meant war. The very perfection of Moltke's arrangements presented the Prussians with exactly the same dilemma that was to confront the General Staffs of Europe in July 1914. Moltke, who like Bismarck was on holiday on his estates, was sent for, and Roon, after consulting the Council of Ministers, explained to the King that "Military half-measures on our part would evoke similar measures on the enemy's side and we would be driven inevitably into war. If your Majesty believes that according to reliable reports of effective French measures war is inevitable, then only the mobilisation of the entire army at one stroke can be recommended."[1] The time for such action had clearly not yet come; but the Ministry of War was already checking over the mobilisation machinery, and on 12th July Podbielski was able to report that it was "completely in running order". All orders had been verified, and they would be sent out as soon as the French Chamber passed war credits or recalled their reserves, or Austria showed signs of military preparation.[2]

News of these precautionary measures reached France and there added to the excitement and alarm. The prefect at Macon reported on 12th July that Prussians in Lyons subject to Landwehr service were being summoned home. On 14th July the French consul in Frankfurt reported that reservists were being secretly recalled to the colours and broken in to the rigours of campaigning by forced marches. There were reports of Prussian agents buying horses in Belgium.[3] Thus military measures on both sides, protective though they were in intention, hastened the drift towards war, and when the French recalled their reservists on 14th July the matter was put beyond any doubt. On 15th July the King of Prussia returned from Ems to Berlin, and at Brandenburg his train was boarded by Bismarck, Roon, and Moltke, who together with the Crown Prince spent the rest of the journey back to Berlin urging him to order mobilisation. Even this formidable quartet found it difficult

[1] Lehmann, *Mobilmachung* 25. General J. von Verdy du Vernois, *With the Royal Headquarters* (London 1897) 5. Lord, *Origins of the War of 1870* 59.

[2] Lehmann, loc. cit.

[3] Lehautcourt, *Guerre de 1870* II 240. *D.T.* I 47. *Archives de Guerre* L⁰ 2 and 3. Dossier 12 Juillet.

to shake the cautious old King, who wanted at least to wait until the Council of Ministers met the following day. But on arrival at Potsdam they learned that war credits had already been voted in Paris. There seemed no alternative left open to the King; and the Crown Prince himself read the mobilisation order to the wildly cheering crowds.[1]

The Germans greeted the coming of war less with the excited enthusiasm displayed by the people of Paris than with a deep sense of earnestness and moral purpose. It seemed to them not merely a national but a profoundly just war, and they called with every confidence upon the God of Battles to defend their cause. Lutheran hymns mingled with patriotic songs in the celebrations; and British correspondents with the armies were to be reminded more than once of Cromwell's Ironsides. The letters of all participants in the war, from Roon and Moltke down to the junior officers and soldiers whose correspondence has survived, all breathe an impressive Lutheran piety; even if there is something repellently self-conscious in the contrast which many drew between their own earnestness and the attitude of the frivolous and atheistical foe.[2] Throughout North Germany swept a flame of impassioned patriotism fed by and reflected in the press.[3] In the South enthusiasm was, as one might expect, somewhat less. The Crown Prince wrote optimistically that "even in South Germany the population is so fired with a unanimous zeal for this war that Princes and Cabinets will find it impossible to stem the current, much as they might wish to"[4]; but from Schweinfurt there were reports of peasants cutting their corn green so that the enemy could not trample it, and by the enemy they meant the Prussians and not the French. In Mainz three-quarters of the judiciary were said to be waiting for the French as if for the Redeemer; in Hanover, it was said, "highly treasonable expressions" were to be heard; and even the official historian of the mobilisation was forced to admit that there were circles which "went their own way, grumbling and embittered, out of

[1] Lord, op. cit. 279. Lehmann op. cit. 28–9. *The War Diary of the Emperor Frederick III* (trs. A. R. Allinson, London 1927) Hereafter referred to as Frederick III, *War Diary*, 6.

[2] E.g. Ludwig Bamberger, *Bismarcks Grosses Spiel* 127, 143. Roon, *Denkwürdigkeiten* III 183–4.

[3] The French Minister in Hamburg wrote on 17th July: "La guerre prend, en effet, dans le Nord surtout, un caractère nationale irresistible; toutes les résistances autonomes sont entraînées ou brisées. M. de Bismarck a réussi par ses savantes manœuvres à exciter le sentiment de justice et de l'équité, si profond chez les Allemands, et il n'est personne de ce côté-ci du Rhin qui ne soit convaincu que la guerre était irrevocablement arrêtée dans notre esprit dès le début de l'incident espagnol." *Origines diplomatiques* XXIX 59.

[4] Frederick III, *War Diary* 8.

hatred for Prussia, and even sympathised openly or in secret with the enemy".[1] But there was a clear *casus foederis*; the southern States had no excuse for evading their treaty obligations, even if they wished to do anything of the sort. Bavaria and Baden began to mobilise on the 16th and Württemberg on the 17th July. Within eighteen days 1,183,000 men, regular and reservist, passed through the barracks in Germany and were embodied in the wartime army; and 462,000 were transported to the French frontier to open the campaign.[2]

Much of Moltke's work had been done long since, but one vital task remained: the appointments to the senior staff posts and army commands. Two of the army commanders were, inevitably, the King's son and nephew, the Crown Prince Frederick and Prince Frederick Charles, the joint victors at Sadowa. Political considerations dictated that the Crown Prince should take over the Third Army, in which served the contingents of the South German states. It was a delicate compliment to the susceptible Kings of Bavaria and Württemberg, on whom the Crown Prince at once paid courtesy calls, but the appointment filled him with alarm. The troops of South Germany he considered "ill disposed towards us and quite untrained in our school" and unlikely, he thought, to make much of a showing against so efficient and well prepared an adversary as the French.[3]

Frederick Charles was given command of the Second Army, which, embodying as it did the Fourth Army as originally planned by Moltke, contained the unwieldy total of six corps and two independent cavalry divisions—far too large a body, as Frederick Charles himself complained, for an effective command. But the Prince was a thoroughly reliable commander—almost too reliable. His nickname, "the Red Prince", acquired from the Hussar uniform he habitually wore, gave a misleading impression of dash and vigour. In fact he was a solid professional soldier, reflective, intelligent, but cautious to the point of timidity, as had been seen in 1866 and was to be proved again on the Loire.[4]

[1] Bamberger, op. cit. 135, 140. Lehmann, *Die Mobilmachung* 40.

[2] For an analysis of this railway concentration, see "The Railroad Concentration for the Franco-Prussian War" in *The Military Historian and Economist* (1918) III No. 2.

[3] Frederick III, *War Diary* 7–10. See also the Crown Princess to Queen Victoria, 22 July: "It is a dreadful position for him as the Bavarian and Swabian troops are so inefficient and undisciplined that they are of very little use—their leaders are more a hindrance than otherwise." *Letters of the Empress Frederick*, ed. Sir F. Ponsonby (London 1928) 79.

[4] F. Hönig, *Der Volkskreig an der Loire* (Berlin 1893–7) VI 287–92.

The charge of timidity, however, could not be levelled against the First Army Commander, General von Steinmetz, whose appointment was greeted among the *cognoscenti* with universal surprise. Certainly the septuagenarian general—he had been born in 1796—had emerged from the 1866 campaign with the greatest distinction of any general officer except Moltke himself. His corps at Nachod had held its own against attack by superior Austrian forces, driven them back, and next day pursued them in a series of victorious encounters which did much to make possible the *dénouement* at Sadowa; and for this Steinmetz's personal stubbornness and energy were rightly held to be largely responsible. Some hoped that he would be the Blücher of the new campaign. But he was wilful, obstinate, and impatient of control. Less than any other senior commander had he absorbed the lessons which Moltke had been patiently trying to hammer into their heads. "His judgment and activity had been affected," wrote one staff officer of him unkindly, "only his obstinacy remains."[1] One explanation of his appointment lay in Moltke's fear that the comparatively small First Army, which could deploy only two corps at the outset of the campaign, might have to take the full weight of a French offensive on the lower Moselle, and certainly Steinmetz would have been just the man to deal with such a critical situation.[2] As it turned out, he was a disaster. Moltke could do nothing with the old man. His insubordination was to wreck Moltke's plans, cause constant inconvenience, and at least once bring the whole German army within measurable distance of catastrophe.

There remain Royal Headquarters. The King himself, a well-informed and effective commander, was inhibited only by age—he was 73—from taking a yet more active part than he did. The position of Moltke as sole advisor to the King was now (except by Steinmetz) universally acknowledged. Lieut.-General von Podbielski served as Quartermaster-General and Lieut.-General von Stosch as the Intendant-General, a post for which his work during the past few years as head of the Militäroekonomie Department of the Ministry of War perfectly fitted him. Under Moltke's direct supervision worked the three heads of sections: Colonel Bronsart von Schellendorff in charge of movements, Colonel von Brandenstein of rail transport and supply, and Colonel Verdy du Vernois of intelligence. These three men were

[1] Bronsart von Schellendorff, *Geheimes Kriegstagebuch* 1870–1, ed. P. Rassow (Bonn 1954) 70.
[2] Waldersee, *Denkwürdigkeiten* I 87, G. Zernin, *Das Leben des Generals A. von Goeben* (Berlin 1895–7) II 44.

Moltke's principal instruments in the conduct of his strategy. Through Bronsart and Brandenstein went all orders for movement and supply, while Verdy, in addition to his intelligence duties, was to be used as a *Flügeladjutant* and given on his missions a degree of responsibility inconceivable except among the officers of the Prussian General Staff. They were known throughout the Army as Moltke's "Demigods" and not particularly liked. But thanks to Moltke's long training they did their work with a speed and economy which set a standard that staff officers have been aiming at, and not always achieving, ever since. The total establishment of the staff, apart from these heads of sections, was eleven officers, ten draughtsmen, seven clerks, and fifty-nine other ranks: not an over-large organisation for the control of armies which by the end of the war were to total some 850,000 men.[1]

This working military headquarters constituted only a small part of the retinue which was to accompany the King when he left Berlin to establish his headquarters in Mainz on the evening of 31st July. William was head of the State, as well as Commander-in-Chief, and with him had to travel the effective machinery of government—the Civil and Military Cabinets, Bismarck and the key Foreign Office officials, Roon and his assistants. There were experts civil and military, to deal with commissariat and communication problems. There were officials to take over the administration of occupied territory. And finally there was a host of privileged spectators, whose demands on billeting space and communication facilities were to exasperate the strained tempers of the staff officers who had under conditions inevitably uncomfortable to plan for and fight a complicated and large-scale war. The friendly and neutral war correspondents to whom Bismarck extended a wide and wise hospitality[2] were only to be expected. So were the military attachés of foreign powers. But there was little place for the crowd of princelings who, with their grooms and horses and valets and cooks, attached themselves to the armies as if they were attending a prolonged and highly fashionable meet. It is hard not to feel a nostalgic sympathy for these elegant *Schlachtenbummler* who, in days when war was being turned into a science as dreary and exact as economics, still insisted on regarding a campaign as their ancestors had the wars of Louis XIV: a royal and

---

[1] Verdy du Vernois, *With the Royal Headquarters* 24–6. Bronsart, *Kriegstagebuch* 36; also his *Duties of the General Staff* (London 1905) 259–62. The figure of 850,000 is that given for 1 March 1871 in Osten-Sacken, *Preussens Heer* III 268.

[2] See e.g. his letter to Roon of 26th July in *Gesamm. Werke* VIb No. 1712 p. 427.

seasonal sporting event. They were as anachronistic as a gilded figure-head on a modern battleship, but the anachronism only emphasised the functional efficiency of the rest of the war machine. And it was an efficiency with which on the French side there was nothing to compare.[1]

§4 The French Mobilisation

The plans which Lebœuf had made for mobilisation were based on Frossard's defensive project of 1868, for the creation of three armies at Metz, Strasbourg, and Châlons. The army of Alsace, three corps strong, was to be commanded by Marshal MacMahon, hero of the Crimean campaign and Governor-General of Algeria, and all the troops which could be spared from Algeria would form part. The army of Metz, also of three corps, would be commanded by Marshal Bazaine, leader of the ill-fated Mexican expedition; and that of Châlons, two corps strong, by Marshal Canrobert, whose reputation from the Crimea and Italy outshone even that of MacMahon. For five days all preparations were made on this basis; then on 11th July the Emperor ordered a complete reorganisation. There was now to be only one army, of eight corps, under his personal command, and the three marshals would be compensated with the command of exceptionally large corps, three divisions strong instead of two. It was the first of those vacillating, almost casual interferences by which Napoleon was to shake to pieces the army which he had done so much to build up. The change of plan was due partly to the insistence of the Empress, that Napoleon must command his army in person and leave the Government in Paris in the hands of a Council of Regency headed by herself: but Lebœuf attributed it to the suggestion of the Archduke Albert of Austria, that the suppression of intermediate headquarters would render the army more flexible and better able to play its part in the allied offensive strategy he had outlined. Certainly it created in the army, and especially in the mind of Lebœuf, the virtual certainty that the Austrians were going to intervene.[2]

The hopes of such intervention lingered into August. Beust, the

[1] Frederick III, *War Diary* 48, 55, 69. Bronsart, op. cit. 36, 196. Count von Blumenthal, *Journals, 1866 and 1870-1* (London 1903) 83. Verdy du Vernois, op. cit. 39.

[2] Bapst, *Canrobert* IV 140. Lebrun, *Souvenirs militaires* 181. Frossard, *Rapport sur les Opérations de 2ᵉ Corps de l'Armée du Rhin* (Paris 1871) 9. Baron d'Andlau, *Metz: Campagne et Négociations* 18-22.

Austrian Chancellor, had not concealed his surprise and displeasure at France's casual and premature declaration of a war for which Austrian opinion was totally unprepared, and at a moment when Russia, loyal to Bismarck as he had been to her during the Polish risings of 1863, threatened to match the Austrian mobilisation by one of her own.[1] But he could not entirely forswear the alliance which he had worked for three years to build. He accompanied Austria's declaration of neutrality on 20th July with profuse assurances of her devotion to the French cause, and the army began to make covert preparation.[2] Italy, without money, credit, or an army adequate for her internal needs, was equally in no condition to risk major war; and if there was an influential party in Florence which remembered what she had owed to France in 1859, there was another, no less strong, which remembered what she owed to Prussia in 1866. It was anyhow unthinkable for any Italian statesman to sign a treaty with France so long as French bayonets preserved the temporal power of the Papacy in Rome. But France, scraping up every man in her army to confront the Prussians, had already sent transports for her Roman garrison, and a military alliance might not be too high a price to pay for a guarantee that they would not return.[3] Throughout July, Austrian and Italian diplomats consulted on the maximum effort they were prepared to make on behalf of France, and on 3rd August the Italian military attaché in Paris brought to Napoleon's headquarters at Metz a draft treaty which embodied some of the proposals made by the Archduke Albert the previous spring. Austria and Italy were, as he suggested, to declare themselves in a state of armed neutrality, and press ahead with their war preparations until they were in a position either to offer armed mediation or to enter the campaign; and Austria was to use her influence to obtain the settlement of the Roman question.[4] But Napoleon found the draft unacceptable. Intervention, he insisted, must come at once; and on the Roman question he showed the stubbornness of despair. To yield Rome to the King of Italy would be finally to alienate his Catholic supporters, the more fanatical of whom were openly saying that they would have "rather the Prussians in Paris than the

[1] *Origines diplomatiques* XXVIII 212, XXIX 320, 407. Letters of Lieut.-Colonel Bouillé of 19th and 22nd July in *Archives Historiques de l'Armée*, Reconnaissances. Autriche Hongrie 1869–72. Carton 1608.

[2] *Origines diplomatiques* XXIX 32, 134, 361. Lieut.-Colonel Bouillé, loc. cit., 29th July. See also Francis Joseph's letter to Napoleon III in Oncken, *Die Rheinpolitik Kaiser Napoleons III* (Berlin 1926) III No. 920 p. 425.

[3] *Origines diplomatiques* XXIX 35, 53.

[4] *Origines diplomatiques* XXIX 440–97. Welschinger, *Causes et Responsabilités* I 204–46.

Italians in Rome." They were the last foothold of support on which he could depend as the Liberal and Republican tide rose all round him. It was the final tragic twist in a policy of shifts and compromises which seemed ever since his intervention in Italy in 1859 to have led him to disaster.

When he had first contemplated war, however, Napoleon still had some cause to expect that Austria might under certain circumstances come to his aid. Certainly only this assumption could justify the change of plans on 11th July and the increased work this imposed on an already overtaxed Ministry of War. The Minister himself, Lebœuf, had an immense burden to carry. In addition to his ministerial duties he became Major-General to the Emperor, a post equivalent to that held by Moltke in relation to William I; and it is doubtful whether even Moltke could have done the work of Roon as well as his own. As assistants—*Aides Major-Généraux*—he had Generals Jarras and Lebrun; officers who united later in denying that their position gave them any responsibility whatever for the conduct of operations.[1] At the Ministry of War, when he left for Imperial Headquarters at Metz, Lebœuf left as his deputy General Dejean, and the tasks which confronted that officer can be gathered from a memorandum which Napoleon sent Lebœuf on 23rd July. The eighteen items which the Emperor specified as needing ministerial attention included the military organisation of the railways, the complete organisation of lines of supply, the establishment of a requisition and a remount service, the provision of transport and supply for civilian specialists and observers with the army, and the provision of medical and veterinary services for the artillery and the engineers. There was hardly an item on the long list which did not require months if not years of preparation.[2] It is not surprising that to faults of planning and preparation in the French mobilisation and concentration there should have been added tragic inadequacies of execution.

A similar casualness prevailed in the appointment of senior commanders. Napoleon did not have, like the King of Prussia, a military cabinet to keep the record and reliability of his officers under constant review; nor like him did he have the expert knowledge and interest to keep track of them himself. Gallantry in the field and an agreeable personality were passports to court favour, and court favour was the passport to high command. Of the generals appointed to the command of corps in the army of the Rhine all save one were Imperial aides-de-camp. Bazaine, commander of 3rd Corps, had, it is true, been treated coldly

[1] Jarras, *Souvenirs* 61. Lebrun, *Souvenirs* 213.   [2] *Guerre* I 47

by the court ever since the revelations of his equivocal conduct of the disastrous Mexico campaign. But that very coldness together with his humble background had made him the hero of the Opposition, and to have passed him over would have been to provoke an outcry as great as that which eventually swept him into the command of the Army of the Rhine. MacMahon commanded 1st Corps with lion-hearted courage, but later tragically showed his incompetence as an army commander. He would have done better to emulate Canrobert, who felt he had reached his pinnacle with the command of 6th Corps and firmly refused to accept the command of the army of the Rhine when it was offered him. Of the other corps commanders, Frossard (2nd Corps) was a military engineer of distinction who had never commanded a unit in the field.[1] Failly (5th Corps), who had defended Rome against Garibaldi at Mentana, was to gain national execration by his incompetence. Ladmirault (4th Corps) and Félix Douay (7th Corps) were to show themselves fully up to their responsibilities, while Bourbaki, universally acclaimed for his exploits in the Crimea and Africa as a Bayard, if not a Galahad, was tragically misplaced in command of the Imperial Guard—a reserve force which in none of the great battles of the next six weeks was to be called upon to fight. As generals they were perhaps no worse than the average commanders of the Prussian corps, and if they had had, like the Prussians, the guidance of staff officers trained by a Moltke and had not been commanded by such successive incompetents as Napoleon and Bazaine they might have shown themselves incomparably better.

But it was neither the faults of French strategic planning nor the incompetence of French commanders, nor even the total numerical inferiority of the French army, which gave the Germans so overwhelming an advantage when the war began. It was the chaos of the French mobilisation. Lebœuf estimated, with some reason, that he could have a force 300,000 strong, with 924 guns, ready for action in three weeks.[2]

---

[1] Napoleon asked him whether he would not rather command the Engineers. Frossard replied that he was at the Emperor's service. No decision was taken for two days. Jarras, *Souvenirs* 53.

[2] *D.T.* I 41 ff. De la Chapelle, *Les Forces Militaires de la France en 1870* (Paris 1872) 78. The full strength of the army on mobilisation was 567,000 men, out of which garrisons had to be found for Algeria, Rome, and the French fortresses, as well as depôt and administrative troops. There were some 3,000 guns in the depôts, but a shortage of trained gunners and equipment made it impossible to use even a third of them. There were about 190 *mitrailleuses*. Lehmann, *Mobilmachung* 232, gives the total number of German guns available as 11,300; but 4,000 of these were smooth-bores.

Such a force, rapidly assembled and attacking at once, might have in-flicted fatal damage on the ponderous German armies. Alternatively, ensconced in the positions recommended by Frossard and putting *chassepots* and *mitrailleuses* to fullest use, it might impose on any invasion an indefinite delay, while reservists and *Gardes Mobiles* could be trained, troops could be brought up from Africa and Rome, and Austria and Italy, encouraged by the check to Prussian power, began actively to intervene. All depended on the speed with which the army could be assembled, and this Niel and Lebœuf knew very well. But speed was difficult to achieve. The regiments of the French army were neither garrisoned in their principal recruiting areas nor, in peacetime, organised in brigades and higher formations. They were scattered in garrisons throughout the country, changing post at frequent intervals and as a matter of deliberate policy. An army to take the field had to be made up *ad hoc* from units scattered all over France, which had seen neither one another nor their senior officers nor their supporting arms nor their services of supply—a process through which the Prussian army, organ-ised in peacetime as it would fight in war, did not have to pass. None the less the French army *had* to mobilise more quickly than the Prussian, if it were to have any hope of victory, and it was to solve this problem that Lebœuf decided that mobilisation and concentration should take place, not successively, but as a single operation. Regiments would not return to their depôts, to embody their reservists and war equipment and be grouped in fighting formations before entraining for the front. They went straight to corps areas on the frontier, and were embodied there. So far as possible regiments were allotted to the corps to whose areas access was easiest. 1st Corps at Strasbourg received the troops from Africa; 7th Corps at Belfort those from the Midi; 5th Corps at Bitche those from the neighbourhood of Lyons; 2nd and 3rd Corps, at Metz and St Avold, those from Paris and Châlons; and 4th Corps the troops from Lille and the North, where Ladmirault had already commanded them as governor of that military division. It was hoped by this means to have all reservists embodied by the fourteenth day of mobilisation. If this could be done there seemed every chance of launch-ing an assault across the Rhine before the German arrangements were complete.[1]

Lebœuf's sense of urgency was thus at least as great as Moltke's. On 9th July warning orders went out for the recall of troops from Al-geria, and on 11th July Lebœuf began checking the mobilisation

[1] *Guerre* I 34. *D.T.* I 69.

arrangements.[1] Two days later he was beseeching the Council of Ministers to order mobilisation—just as Moltke and Roon were to beseech their sovereign on the 15th—and, as we have seen, threatened resignation when they refused. On the evening of 14th July, a day ahead of the Germans, the order at last went out.[2]

The result was deplorable. The plans of the Ministry of War involved the movement of large bodies of men in every direction by railways imperfectly subjected to military control. Regiments had to go from their garrisons to their concentration areas, reservists from their homes to their regimental depôts and on to their regiments, and supplies had to be sent from central magazines to depôts and to regiments. One typical regiment whose depôt was at Lyons was stationed at Dunkirk; another, stationed at Lyons, had its depôt at St Malo. Reservists joining a regiment of Zouaves had to report to their depôt in Oran before they could join their regiment in Alsace. It is not surprising that a group of reservists who left Lille on 18th July for the 53rd Regiment's depôt at Gap never reached their regiment at all: it was destroyed at Sedan while they were still on the way, and they had to be embodied ultimately in the army of the Loire. Once the reservists reached their depôts, they were due to be sent up to their battalions in batches of a hundred; but there was some doubt as to whether they should be sent up with full equipment or not; and since faulty organisation at central stores and confusion on the railways often meant that delivery of equipment to the regimental depôt was delayed, the commanders of these depôts were torn between the clamours of their service battalions for more men and their natural desire to send them only when equipment was available and the railways were clear. The result was that by 6th August, the twenty-third day of mobilisation, only about half the reservists had reached their regiments, and many of these lacked the most essential items of uniform and equipment. The rest, if they had left their depôts at all, were marooned en route by railway delays and spent their days sleeping, drinking, begging, and plundering army stores.[3]

As for the *Garde Mobile*, its existence was largely confined to paper. In theory 250 battalions of infantry and 125 batteries of artillery had

---

[1] *Archives de Guerre*, Carton L° 2 and 3. File *Corr. Guerre* 11/17.

[2] *Archives de Guerre*, Carton L° 2 and 3. *Guerre* I 33. *D.T.* I 47, 138. Ollivier, *Empire libéral* XIV 292.

[3] The best general account of the French mobilisation is Lehautcourt, *Guerre de 1870* II 129 ff. See also *Guerre* II 90-1, 116, III 10. Lebrun, *Souvenirs* 204. Montaudun, *Souvenirs* II 63. A detailed analysis from the archives is given by A. Martinien, *La Mobilisation del'Armée* (Paris 1911).

been organised; in practice there were cadres and equipment for only a small proportion of these, and the orders which went out on 17th and 18th July for their embodiment and organisation into regiments, brigades, and divisions were simply the expression of a pious hope. The men who answered the summons found nothing prepared for them—neither accommodation, uniform, nor equipment. At best they could be fitted out with képi and blouse; but despairing telegrams poured into Paris from military authorities all over France asking whatever they were to do with the hordes of sullen or mutinous young men who had suddenly descended on them asking to be housed, clothed, and fed. Almost unanimously they suggested that their local *Mobiles* should be sent to some other part of the country where they might be kept under better discipline and be of more practical use. The *Intendance*, harassed enough by the demands of the army, maintained that equipment for the *Garde Mobile* was no business of theirs; and since there was no other source from which it could be supplied, the recruitment of the *Garde Mobile* was, on 4th August, suspended altogether. The regiments from Paris, which were already organised, were sent to the Camp of Châlons where Canrobert was assembling 6th Corps, and the Marshal, finding that not even his famous charm could dent their ferocious indiscipline, insistently demanded that they should be sent to fortresses to do garrison duty. But the fortress commanders as insistently refused to receive them, so they remained at Châlons, until Trochu took them back with him to Paris on 17th August.[1]

All this imposed an overwhelming strain on the railways; the more so as the recommendations made by Niel's commission were forgotten, and orders were given at random by officials qualified and unqualified, as the occasion seemed to demand. The movement of units was attended by lack of preparation, indiscipline and—especially with units departing from Paris—drunkenness and disorder which lasted throughout the journey and which regimental officers, interested only in leading their men into action, maintained that it was no business of theirs to quell.[2] The greatest source of delay was that which had caused such confusion for the Prussians in 1866 and was still to hamper them in 1870: the

---

[1] *Guerre. Mesures d'Organisation* 23–31. Bapst, *Canrobert* IV 154.
[2] Jacqmin, *Les chemins de fer pendant la Guerre* 113–24. Comte d' Hérisson, *Diary of a Staff Officer in Paris during the events of 1870 and 1871* (London 1885) 17. C. Sarazin, *Récits sur la dernière Guerre Franco-Allemande* (Paris 1887) 11, noted that in the case of troops coming from Africa "dans toutes les gares où les trains s'arrêtaient, des tonneaux de vin étaient mis à la disposition des soldats par les populations plus enthousiastes que réfléchies".

choking of the lines by loaded supply-trucks sent forward without consideration for the unloading facilities available at the end of their journey. Even where such facilities were available—as they were at Metz—trucks still remained unloaded because of uncertainty as to their ultimate destination. Eventually a tangle arose in which all the elements of an adequate organisation were present—enough rolling-stock, enough stores and adequate unloading space—yet the entire system was clogged with loaded trucks overflowing from the sidings on to the permanent way, containing supplies urgently needed elsewhere, while the trucks themselves were no less urgently needed for their next load. The Prussians had faced the problem without entirely solving it. The French only realised its existence too late.[1]

Thus a plan already faulty in principle was further marred by faults in execution; and as the army assembled around Metz and Strasbourg it found itself lacking not only men but the most elementary supplies. The trouble lay, not in the inadequacy of the stocks, but in the arrangements for their distribution. A survey by Lebœuf on 8th July had concluded, with some reason, "*Le personnel et le matériel suffisent pour une première campagne*".[2] The problem lay in the lack of transport and the lack of organisation in the *Intendance*. Horses and every sort of transport were short. Many vehicles, when they were brought out of store, were found to be unusable, and corps commanders had to obtain what they could by local purchase. Abundant medical stores lay centrally housed at the Hôtel des Invalides, yet it was not until long after the campaign began that proper ambulance facilities were organised for the fighting divisions.[3] Camping equipment, the little two-men *tents-abri* on which the French army relied entirely for cover, was insufficient, as were the cooking-pots on which the troops depended to make the rations issued to them in bulk fit to eat. There was no money to pay the troops. There were no maps available, except maps of Germany and a rough sketch-map entitled, optimistically, "Routes leading to the Rhine", and officers were driven to requisition maps from the local schools and estate offices.[4]

---

[1] The performance of the Compagnie de l'Est was none the less remarkable. By the evening of 27th July it had despatched 579 military trains at an average frequency of two per hour throughout 11 days. Jacqmin-Jarras, 28th July, in *Archives de Guerre*, Carton L^b.

[2] *Archives de Guerre*, Carton L⁰ 2 and 3. File *Corr. Guerre* 11/17.

[3] Bazaine-Lebœuf, 30th July in *Guerre* III 49. Also Failly, ibid. II 108. Lebrun, *Souvenirs* 205. Sarazin, *Récits* 12–13.

[4] *Trois mois à l'Armée de Metz*, par un officier de génie (Brussels 1871) 16, *Guerre* III 4, 42, 72. Ladmirault on 5th August acknowledged receipt of one

In short, the *Intendance*, understaffed and ill-organised, were over-whelmed by a task far above its strength.[1]

The gravest shortage of all was that of food. The pre-war accumulation of stores at Metz and Strasbourg, in spite of the confident reports rendered to the Ministry of War, was found to be inadequate. The Intendant-General wired from Metz on 20th July: "There is at Metz neither sugar nor coffee nor rice nor *eau de vie* nor salt, and not very much fats or biscuit."[2] Ducrot's messages from Strasbourg said the same. The stocks at Châlons could not be brought up because of the great jams of loaded rolling-stock piled up on the railway-lines; and when officials of the *Intendance* tried to buy supplies locally they found that the disorganisation of the railway system had cut the local contractors off from their sources of supply.[3] The troops were thrown on their own resources, and when they had exhausted the plentiful hospitality of the inhabitants of Alsace and Lorraine they turned inevitably to pillage. There was little enough discipline in the army as it was. The inhabitants of Froeschwiller, where MacMahon was concentrating his forces, saw with astonishment the slovenliness, the lack of self-respect and the open contempt for their officers which were displayed by regiments reputed among the finest in the army. "Everyone behaved as he wanted," observed the parish priest at Froeschwiller, "the soldier came and went as he liked, wandered off from his detachment, left camp and came back as he saw fit."[4] When such troops as these were left to fend for themselves they rapidly sank to the condition of the marauding bands which had terrorised Europe during the Thirty Years War. They might yet, with brilliant leadership, win victories; but they were in no condition to stand up to the shock of defeat.

Yet in outline the concentration of the army on the frontier between Luxemburg and Switzerland took place as it had been planned, with Bazaine in provisional command until Napoleon and Lebœuf could arrive from Paris. By 18th July, four days after the mobilisation had been

map of the Department of the Moselle, and asked whether he might have some more for his staff. *Guerre* VI 88.

[1] The Intendant of 3rd Corps wrote to complain, on 24th July as his corps left Metz to take up its positions, that he was so short of staff that in some divisions he had not even one official. The Intendant-in-Chief, Wolff, confirmed that "Pas un corps d'armée n'a le personnel le plus strictement nécessaire au service", *Archives de Guerre*, Carton LR9, dossier 7. 2°. *Instructions, Demandes, Ordres*.

[2] *Guerre* II 47.   [3] Ibid. 45–50.

[4] Pastor Klein, *La Chronique de Froeschwiller* (Paris 1911) 55–8.

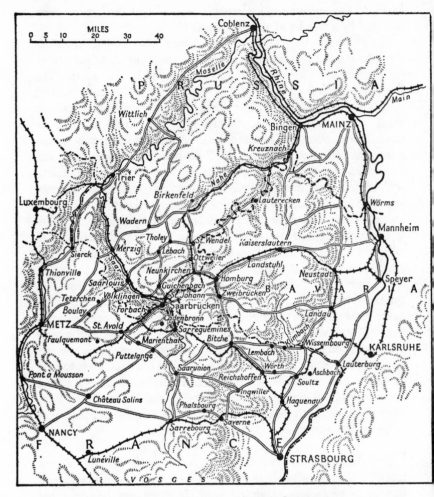

Map 2: Lorraine and the Palatinate

ordered, elements of four corps were in position before Metz. Ladmir-ault's 4th Corps was watching the Moselle at Thionville, with a division forward at Sierck; Frossard with 2nd Corps was on the frontier oppo-site Saarbrücken, based on St Avold, with Bazaine's 3rd Corps behind at Metz itself. At Strasbourg 1st Corps was being formed with Ducrot in provisional command until MacMahon arrived from Algiers, and between him and the left wing of the army Failly's 5th Corps uneasily straddled, based on Sarreguemines and Bitche. Bourbaki was forming the

Guard at Nancy; while Félix Douay's 7th Corps was gradually coming up to Belfort from the south to watch the upper Rhine. It was a simple cordon to cover the frontier while concentration was taking place, and on 20th July Bazaine passed on the word that no operations need be expected until the concentration was complete.[1] Cavalry patrols explored up to the frontier, attacked a few customs posts and occasionally exchanged shots with Uhlans,[2] but their activity was limited by Bazaine's directive, "Our reconnaissances should not be aggressive". They had neither maps nor medical supplies, and travellers from across the frontier all spoke of huge German concentrations on the very banks of the Lauter and Saar[3]; but the timidity of the French cavalry patrols contrasted unfavourably with the boldness of the Germans. German frontier detachments, finding no trace of the French on their side of the frontier, sent patrols over to seek them: not full squadrons such as the French used, compelled by their size to keep to the main roads, but small groups of one officer and two or three men, cutting telegraph lines, raiding railways and laying the foundations of that moral superiority which the German cavalry was never thereafter to lose. The adventure of the young Count Zeppelin, who took a small patrol over the Lauter as far as the village of Niederbronn, eight miles inside Alsace, where it was surprised gaily dining in a local inn, seemed exceptionally daring. It certainly astonished the French and set a pattern which they never attempted to emulate.[4]

On 23rd July Lebœuf, on the eve of his own departure for Metz, sent Bazaine orders for the first movement of the army according to a recognisable strategic plan. They provided for a concentration of forces on the axis of the Metz–Saarbrücken road—the main line of advance of the German forces which were evidently massing in the general area of Mainz. Such a concentration did not preclude the French themselves from taking the offensive; but it meant that if they did so it would have to be in a north-easterly direction into the Palatinate—not eastwards over the Rhine into Baden, as Ducrot in Strasbourg was urging in accordance with the Archduke Albert's plan. But if Austria was not to join her forces to those of France an offensive eastward across the Rhine would have little to recommend it. Militarily it was far wiser to seek out and disrupt the main German armies as they concentrated for battle

[1] *Guerre* I 59.
[2] Then, as in 1914, the term applied by the French to all German cavalry, whether Lancers or not.
[3] *Guerre* II 44, III 102, 106. [4] G.G.S I i 68. *Guerre* I 62.

before Mainz. On 24th July the movement took place, 4th and 5th Corps closing in towards Frossard's 2nd Corps, leaving flanking divisions at Sierck and Bitche, 3rd Corps moved up to Boulay, just behind Frossard at St Avold, and the Guard taking 3rd Corps' place at Metz. By evening the frontier cordon had turned into an arrow-head, pointing threateningly at Saarbrücken, and Lebœuf reached Metz to make the last arrangements before the Emperor himself arrived and the great offensive began.[1]

*   *   *

Before leaving Paris, however, Napoleon also had to give directions for the naval conduct of the war; for France had not only an army but a navy which had some claim to be the most efficient in the world. It had pioneered the new developments in naval warfare—shell-guns, steam, armour—and even the British for twelve years past had regarded it as a deadly threat to their traditional supremacy. At the outbreak of war it had in service forty-nine ironclads of which fourteen were frigates capable of fourteen knots and mounting twenty-four guns, and nine corvettes armed with 16-cm. and 19-cm. ordnance.[2] Against this force Prussia could show only a force of five ironclads—one of them, the *König Wilhelm*, more powerful than anything the French possessed —and about thirty other vessels fit for service; divided between two minor naval bases, Kiel and Wilhelmshaven, which were still in course of construction. Moreover, adjacent to the coast of North Germany lay Denmark—a power which, even more than Austria, was anxious to reverse the verdict of its earlier defeat. Exploratory talks held with Danish officials by the French Ministry of Marine had revealed that if the French could ship a force of some 30,000–40,000 men to Germany's North Sea coast Denmark would be prepared to add 30,000 on her own account. The joint force could then march on Kiel and possibly Hamburg; and it might even strike inland to Hanover and find allies there. It was a threat which the Prussians themselves took very seriously. Roon had worked hard, as war approached, to complete and arm the fortifications on which the Baltic and even the sandy North Sea coast would be dependent for their defence, and one regular and two Landwehr divisions were held in the areas of Hamburg, Bremen and Hanover— a force, together with depôt and garrison troops, of 90,000 men com-

[1] *Guerre* I 52–3.
[2] E. Chevalier, *La Marine française et la Marine allemande pendant la Guerre de 1870–1871* (Paris 1873) 15–25. H. W. Wilson, *Ironclads in Action* (London 1896) I 265–8.

manded by General Vogel von Falkenstein.[1] Apart from these unofficial Franco-Danish conversations, no preparations for a seaborne invasion had been made. When war broke out the French Minister of Marine had his hands full with the transport of the French army from Algeria and was preoccupied with the danger that a squadron of four Prussian iron-clads which had just set out from Plymouth on an Atlantic cruise might attempt a raid. In fact the Prussian squadron, with two damaged vessels, ran straight for Wilhelmshaven, where their commander, Prussia's only Admiral, Prince Adalbert, was at once sent to accompany the armies and his Vice-Admiral took command.[2] Once it was clear that French transports from North Africa would be undisturbed, a squadron was formed for service in the North Sea under Count Bouet-Willaumez, which sailed from Cherbourg on 24th July.

Meanwhile the idea of an amphibious attack had been revived from another quarter—by the Emperor's energetic and under-employed cousin, Prince Napoleon. At a conference on 19th July he suggested that he himself should lead such an expedition, with Admiral de la Roncière in naval and Trochu in military command. The Emperor was lukewarm; the combination of his liberal cousin and the Orleanist Trochu was unlikely to appeal to the Empress. Lebœuf firmly said the army could not provide a single battalion—it must be done, if at all, with the twelve thousand available marines; and Admiral Rigault, the Minister of Marine, equally firmly refused to give Prince Napoleon command of his ships. Nothing more was said. Rigault continued with the preparation of transports and a force of marines until the disasters of 6th August made him suspend all activity and instead devote his resources to the defence of Paris; while the French squadrons in the Baltic and the North Sea cruised uneasily off the German coast in an attempt to maintain a blockade, until the Government of National Defence summoned them back to France.[3]

Yet French seapower was not entirely wasted. Throughout the war French commerce continued to flourish, French overseas possessions were undisturbed and, as a result, French credit remained intact. The French Government was able to purchase armaments abroad and freely import them. Prussia could do nothing to stop the shiploads of war-materials which poured into Brest and Bordeaux and Marseilles through-out the second half of the year. It was a lesson not wasted on a later

[1] *D.T.* I 127. *G.G.S.* I i 80.
[2] *G.G.S.* I i 77.
[3] Trochu, *Œuvres posthumes* I 89–92. *D.T.* I 141–2.

generation of German sailors. But for a continental nation at grips with a neighbour, sea-power could never be more than an auxiliary weapon. It might create the conditions in which war could be won, but it could not by itself win them. The Franco-German conflict was to be settled by the methods of Clausewitz; not those of Mahan.

CHAPTER III

The First Disasters

§1 The Concentration of the Armies

IT WAS taken for granted by military opinion in Europe, informed and uninformed, that the war would begin with a French thrust into Germany, either northwards into the Palatinate or eastwards across the Rhine. The London *Standard*, which on 13th July gave a long analysis of the routes which Napoleon might take, did not even consider an invasion of France. "It seems impossible to our judgment", it explained, "that the Prussians will be ready in time to take the initiative"; and as Friedrich Engels pointed out in the *Pall Mall Gazette* of 29th July, if the French had not planned an offensive, their declaration of war did not make sense. The Germans themselves certainly expected invasion. The Crown Prince feared that it would cripple the mobilisation of the southern States; General von Blumenthal, his Chief of Staff, thought that such a thrust would be diversionary, and the main attack would be northwards towards Mainz. The King thought it unnecessary to have any maps of France immediately available at the beginning of the campaign.[1] Moltke himself believed that the movements of the French units towards the frontier even before their reservists had been absorbed made it likely that Napoleon was contemplating a spoiling attack with the 150,000 men he had immediately available under arms; but the prospect did not alarm him. This force would need at least six days' preparation before it could cross the frontier, and it would take another eight to deal with Prussian covering units in the Saar valley and reach the Rhine. By then he would have concentrated 170,000 men, and by 5th August he could meet the invaders with double their strength. Every day that passed without a French attack tilted the balance still further in the German favour; and by the beginning of August, as the trains from all over Germany poured uninterruptedly to the Rhine, Moltke could scarcely believe his fortune. Repeatedly he expressed his astonishment

[1] L. Schneider, *Aus dem Leben Kaiser Wilhelms 1849-1873* (Berlin 1888) II 139.

at a Government declaring war two weeks before they could be ready for it; and the Crown Prince wrote, as his army concentrated behind the Lauter undisturbed, "It may well happen that, for all the French sabre-rattling and all our age-long preparations against a sudden onslaught, *we* shall be the aggressors. Whoever could have thought it?"[1]

Lebœuf had no cause to believe, when he set out for Metz on 24th July, that such an offensive was impossible. The machinery for mobilisation had been set in motion; the problems which had inevitably arisen had, so far as possible, been rapidly resolved, and where this was not possible Lebœuf had no reason to suppose that his subordinates would not improvise with at least as much success as they had eleven years earlier in preparing the army for the invasion of Italy. But the situation which he discovered at Metz disillusioned him. Neither at the station nor at the magazine was there sufficient staff to handle the huge quantities of supplies, of ammunition, and of rations which were brought by every train. They were to remain stacked around the station, urgently needed but uninspected, uninventoried, and eventually forgotten; including millions of rounds of *chassepot* ammunition which the French were never to fire.[2] But if stores were piling up, men were not. By 28th July, the fourteenth day of mobilisation, Lebœuf had hoped to find the army of the Rhine complete with 385,000 men. The returns for that day showed 202,448. By 31st July, the total strength was still only 238,188; and since neither 6th Corps at Châlons (33,701) nor a substantial part of 7th Corps at Belfort (20,341) were immediately available for operations, the force at Lebœuf's disposal was less than 200,000 strong.[3] To take the offensive with such a force would be unwise, if not impossible; but a wisely planned defence might still have stood a chance of success.

Yet the Order of the Day which Napoleon issued when he arrived to take command of his armies on 28th July seemed to confirm the general expectation of an offensive, "Whatever may be the road we take beyond our frontiers", he wrote, "we shall come across the glorious tracks of our fathers. We shall prove worthy of them. All France follows you with its fervent prayers, and the eyes of the world are upon you. On our success hangs the fate of liberty and civilisation."

[1] *M.M.K.* 144–55. Frederick III, *War Diary* 7, 19. Blumenthal, *Journals 1866–70* 77. *Kriegsgeschichtliche Einzelschriften* XXXVI. *Moltke in der Vorbereitung und Durchführung der Operationen* (Berlin 1905) 116.

[2] Jacqmin, *Chemins de Fer* 122. Lebrun, *Souvenirs* 207–8.

[3] *Guerre* II 24, III 148. Lehautcourt, *Guerre de 1870* II 299.

Doubts about the practicability of an offensive, however, were beginning to grow. Intelligence about the German army was very incomplete, as was only to be expected in view of the total absence of any organisation for the collection of information.[1] The general impression was not inaccurate—the mass of the enemy armies in the area Mainz–Trier–Coblenz, with detachments moving forward towards the Saar and the Lauter; but there were also reports of large forces in the Black Forest, and, more curious, reports of a northern army under General Vogel von Falkenstein, menacing the French left flank.[2] On 26th July Frossard reported that 60,000 German troops were moving up from Cologne to the Saar. Lebœuf commented: "Without accepting this report as certain, I think it necessary to take the offensive as soon as possible." But at the same time he admitted that such an offensive was as yet out of the question: "Our intention is paralysed by lack of preparation, and we are losing precious time in insignificant operations." For though it had been generally agreed that an offensive was necessary, the senior officers of the French army had given very little thought to the tactical problems it would raise. "As for the offensive," Frossard wrote to Bazaine on 27th July, "we don't yet seem able to have any directive to guide us, so that we can plan ahead in any particular direction." There was no plan; there was a general disinclination, after the experiences of 1859, to advance without a plan; and nothing could be done until on 28th July Napoleon arrived in person at Metz, accompanied by his son, to take command.[3]

The arrival of the Emperor did nothing to clear the air. The French army, true to its traditions, awaited the impact of a dominant will; but such a will Napoleon was morally and physically incapable of providing. The campaign of 1859 had shown his total incapacity for generalship even when in good health; now he was suffering agonisingly from the stone, and in constant pain. To mount a horse was torture; at times coherent thought was impossible. The Empress was no longer at hand to guide his actions and none of his lieutenants could take her place. The only man with a positive suggestion to make was Frossard, whom Napoleon and Lebœuf visited at St Avold on 29th July. He for the past

---

[1] C. Fay, *Journal d'un Officier de l'Armée du Rhin* (Paris 1871) 36–7, significantly illustrates this. See also *Guerre* I 65, III 109.

[2] *Guerre* I 77, II 175–6, III 75, 100–2, 130, V 99. The German forces in the Black Forest totalled one regt. of infantry, one squadron of cavalry, and one battery of guns, based on Donaueschingen. Lehautcourt, *Guerre de 1870* II 323.

[3] *Guerre* I 57–61, 73. Bazaine, *Épisodes de la Guerre de 1870 et le Blocus de Metz* (Madrid 1883) 6. *Trois mois à l'Armée de Metz*, par un officier de génie 20.

week had been urging the occupation of Saarbrücken—not so much as the prelude to an offensive but to improve the position of the French forces by establishing them astride the lateral communications between the Moselle and the Bavarian Palatinate. He did not visualise any further move: his object was to fill in time. "Until the enemy's plans had become sufficiently clear, we have the opportunity of bringing the army nearer the frontier." Napoleon accepted the plan; and there can be no doubt that he did so for lack of anything better to do.[1]

Lebœuf's orders on 30th July provided only for a more intense and advanced forward concentration: 2nd and 3rd Corps one behind the other in the St Avold-Forbach valley, with 4th Corps on the left round Boulay and 5th Corps on the right at Sarreguemines; the army now constituting a tight lozenge round the Metz-Saarbrücken railway.[2] But the marches which began on 31st July were enough to show how incompetent was the French army to attempt anything more ambitious. Corps commanders overwhelmed Lebœuf with complaints about their shortages of essential equipment and supplies, and everywhere officers cursed the inefficiency of the organisation which held them paralysed.[3] But the *Intendance* could not be blamed for the confusion of the marches when the army began to move on 31st July—the first of a succession which were to increase in misery, inefficiency and pointlessness until they led the entire army into captivity in Germany three months later. There was no attempt to co-ordinate the movements of the different divisions; it was simply good fortune if their columns did not cross and delay one another for hours. The distances to be covered were not considerable—nowhere more than ten miles; but instead of bivouacking along the road, saving time and making the best use of local resources, the army had acquired in Africa the habit of closing up on the heads of their columns every night in divisional camps. Thus since the divisions seldom set out before 9 a.m., the rear battalions might not start until the afternoon, or reach their destination until long after dark. The officers were cheerful enough: "The general belief", wrote one of them, "is that we shall cross the Rhine and that the *grand choc* will occur somewhere around Frankfurt."[4] But the men, especially the reservists, sweating under their absurd shakoes, bent double by the

---

[1] *Guerre* II 16.

[2] *Guerre* III 166.

[3] Bazaine complained that he had no ambulances, Ladmirault that he had no draught horses, Bourbaki that his transport service was inadequate, Félix Douay that his commissariat arrangements had collapsed. *Guerre* III 64, 84, 194.

[4] Colonel d'Andigné, in *Guerre* III 150.

unaccustomed weight of their equipment, trudging glumly through the pelting summer rain, saw things differently.[1]

The attack on Saarbrücken on 2nd August achieved its very limited objective, as with six divisions concentrating against one infantry regiment and a handful of cavalry it could hardly fail to do.[2] Bazaine was in charge of the operation and his orders were meticulous; but they did not mention either the position of the enemy or the object to be achieved. There was no question of reconnaissance or of advance guard; the corps was to advance *en masse*, as if at a review, from the Forbach valley and the Spicheren heights towards the high ground a thousand yards ahead, the Winterberg and the Reppertsberg, which masked and dominated Saarbrücken.[3] The peacetime atmosphere was emphasised by a paragraph in the orders, suggesting that "officers and other ranks should take something to eat, as it is not known at what time they will return to camp in the evening."[4] To do Bazaine justice, he realised the inconsiderable nature of the operation[5]; but Napoleon thought that more might be involved. The reports of growing Prussian concentrations during the past few days had alarmed him; if Saarbrücken was to be seized at all he believed that it would be only in the nick of time, and there might be a considerable engagement. It was in this belief that he went up to 2nd Corps on the morning of 2nd August, taking the Prince Imperial with him, and subjected himself to the torture of sitting on horseback to watch his cheering troops go to action.[6]

The French advanced with an *élan* worthy of a better occasion. The three German companies and two troops of light field-guns posted on the heights south of Saarbrücken opened a brisk fire and then slipped away. By midday the French had won the heights at a cost of eighty-eight casualties—11 of them killed.[7] A few batteries opened fire on the railway station but the town was not occupied; it was too much overlooked. The bridges were not crossed; they might be mined. No attempt was even made to destroy the telegraph station beyond the river at the village of St Johann, and its employees were able to send back uninterrupted reports about French movements through the next four days.[8] Nobody who had taken part in the action could be under any illusions about its significance. But in even the best organised armies the importance of

[1] Lehautcourt, *Guerre de 1870* II 338–9.
[2] *G.G.S.* I i 93. *Guerre* III 8. [3] See Map on p. 86.
[4] *Guerre* IV 9.
[5] See, e.g., his letter to Ladmirault in *Guerre* IV 84.
[6] Lebrun, *Souvenirs* 219–24.
[7] *Guerre* IV 161. [8] *Guerre* IV 164–7, 237. *G.G.S.* I i 100.

actions become magnified as the distance from the front line increases; and the whole of France was waiting to hear of the beginning of that offensive which was so confidently expected. Both headquarters at Metz and the newspapers of Paris seized on this crumb of news with the greed of a starving man. "Our army", announced the *Journal Officiel* of 3rd August, "has taken the offensive, and crossed the frontier and invaded Prussian territory. In spite of the strength of the enemy positions a few of our battalions were enough to capture the heights which dominate Saarbrücken." It was enough to fire the Press, and it was widely reported that three Prussian divisions had been overwhelmed and Saarbrücken burnt to the ground. The expectations of the excited Paris public would be satisfied with nothing else.[1]

*　　*　　*

Meanwhile the German concentration had gone as planned. Moltke had divided his forces into two wings. The right consisted of the Second Army, six corps strong under Frederick Charles (III, IV, IX, X, XII, and the Guard: 134,000 men), which was advancing from the Rhine between Mainz and Bingen through the mountains round Kaiserslautern and St Wendel towards Saarbrücken; and the First Army, three corps under Steinmetz (I, VII, VIII: 50,000 men), converging from the lower Moselle at Trier and Wittlich to come into line beside the Second Army on the Saar below Saarlouis.[2] The Third Army under the Crown Prince (V, XI, two Bavarian Corps and one division each from Baden and Württemberg: 125,000 men) constituted the left wing. Separated from the right by fifty miles of mountain, this was concentrating in the Bavarian Palatinate, round Landau and Speyer, threatening Alsace and Strasbourg as the right wing threatened Lorraine and Metz. Military commentators noted the curious contrast between the German dispersal of forces over the hundred-odd miles between Karlsruhe and Coblenz and the French concentration between Saarbrücken and Metz[3]; but it was a dispersal as carefully thought out as that which Moltke had planned before Sadowa. It made supply easier in the approach march; and it enabled the advancing forces to encounter and outflank the enemy wherever he might appear.

Moltke did not originally visualise a simultaneous attack: he intended the Third Army to strike the first blow. It would take several days for

---

[1] See the press extracts printed in Émile Leclerc, *La Guerre de 1870: L'Esprit Parisien* (Paris 1871) 79.
[2] See Map on p. 72.
[3] E.g. Engels in the *Pall Mall Gazette*, 2nd August 1870.

Frederick Charles to get his six corps through the mountain defiles which lay between the Rhine and the Saar, whereas the Third Army round Landau was barely a day's march from the frontier of Alsace. If it advanced it could reach the Saar in time to fall on the flank of the main French forces just as the Second Army was engaging them front-ally, and the triumph of Sadowa would be repeated. On the evening of 30th July Moltke therefore sent to General von Blumenthal, the Third Army's Chief of Staff, the order to move.[1] It was not welcome. Blumen-thal was not nearly ready. Even his Prussian units had not yet received all their batteries and trains, while neither of the Bavarian corps had any trains at all. He had not visualised crossing the frontier until 7th August; certainly nothing could be done until 3rd August.[2] This blank refusal ruffled even Moltke's calm, and an angry telegram was drafted directly ordering the Third Army to attack. Fortunately for the internal peace of the armies, Moltke then had second thoughts. Verdy du Vernois visited Third Army H.Q. and satisfied himself that 4th August was in fact the earliest day that Blumenthal could be expected to attack. Blumenthal promised to cross the frontier on that day; but Moltke's hopes of immediate and overwhelming victory began to fade.[3]

Indeed it was becoming clear that Moltke's plans were more likely to be disrupted by his own subordinates than by the opposition of the French. He still assumed that the French would attack, and his main preoccupation during the first days of August lay in concentrating the Second Army in front of the Kaiserslautern forest before they did so. This was not easy: on 3rd August, for instance, Frederick Charles's forces sprawled over a depth of some fifty miles between his cavalry outposts in the Saar valley and his rear units moving down from the Rhine. Once concentrated, the Second Army would stand to receive the French attack north of the Saar; the Third Army would sweep up from Alsace to fall on the right flank of the French; and the First Army would strike down from the Moselle to close the trap. In preparation for this latter blow Moltke, on 3rd August, ordered Steinmetz to mass his forces round Tholey. But Steinmetz had different ideas. It was only with the greatest difficulty that he was brought to accept Moltke's authority at all: to understand Moltke's strategy was beyond him and he had no intention of implementing it. By 3rd August his army was ready,

---

[1] *M.M.K.* 181.

[2] *Kriegsgesch. Einzelschr. XXXVI: Moltke in der Vorbereitung und Durch-führung der Operationen* 119.

[3] Verdy, *With the Royal Headquarters* 46.

and he intended to attack. His cavalry reconnaissances had made it clear that he would be perfectly safe in doing so. He informed Moltke that he proposed next day to move south on Saarlouis and St Avold, and instead of holding back round Tholey he firmly pushed the units on his left wing forward to the St Wendel–Ottweiler road—straight across the Second Army's line of march.[1]

The formal courtesy of the correspondence which followed totally failed to cloak the deep personal animosity between the two generals. Moltke, once he realised that the French did not propose to advance beyond Saarbrücken, accepted Steinmetz's dispositions but forbade him to cross the Saar. Steinmetz in reply complained bitterly of having to abandon the chance of taking the offensive under such excellent conditions. "I do not understand", he added, "the strategic ideas which lead to the abandonment of the Saar which the situation does not make at all necessary."[2] Next day, 5th August, he appealed to the King over Moltke's head. If he had to stay round Tholey and Frederick Charles was moving forward on Neunkirchen and Zweibrücken, he pointed out, the Second Army would be taking up a position in front of the First; and, he concluded arrogantly, "as I have no orders about the offensive movement which would follow, I do not know whether I can play any useful part in it". The reply came back at once, not from the King, but from Moltke. The Second Army would not advance beyond Neunkirchen and Zweibrücken until the 8th. Steinmetz was to clear his troops off the St Wendel–Ottweiler road to let them pass; he might move up to the Saar on the 7th, and be ready to cross it on the 9th; but, concluded Moltke, "His Majesty has expressly reserved the giving of orders for the execution of this operation, since the manner of undertaking it, and the direction it is given, will depend upon the turn which events will have taken with the Third Army."[3]

Moltke was thus hoping to save something from the wreckage of his plans. Blumenthal's slowness and Napoleon's failure to attack had forced him to abandon his original intention of annihilating the French army in a battle of encirclement north of the Saar; but he might yet achieve his aim south of the river, if Frederick Charles attacked across it between Saarbrücken and Sarreguemines, and Steinmetz crossed downstream at Saarlouis and Völklingen, fell on the left flank of the

[1] G. Cardinal von Widdern, *Kritische Tage* (Berlin 1897) III ii: *Die Führung der I und II Armee und deren Vortruppen* 113 ff. Zernin, *Leben des Generals von Goeben* II 239.
[2] *M.M.K.* 195.   [3] *M.M.K.* 197.

French and pushed them away from Metz into the waiting arms of the Third Army. But Steinmetz was to ruin this last hope. On 5th August he ordered the evacuation of the St Wendel road; but, as he explained to Moltke next day, this involved "displacing troops, not only towards the west, but towards the south".[1] What he did, on the evening of 5th August, was to launch his two leading corps, VII and VIII, on the forbidden movement towards the Saar; and he moved them, not southwest towards Saarlouis, in the encircling movement intended by Moltke, but due south on Saarbrücken, where they would not only again cross the path of the Second Army, but find themselves involved with it in a blind frontal attack on the French; an attack which, however successful, would achieve nothing except to push the enemy back on its base. Moltke's plans were spoiled before his main forces were engaged at all.[2]

§ 2 Spicheren

With the advance on Saarbrücken on 2nd August the initiative of the main French forces had been exhausted. The inability of their army to take the offensive left the French commanders bankrupt of ideas, and reports of the German army's advancing through the Palatinate began to paralyse the initiative of the commanders at every level. The three days which followed the advance on Saarbrücken were spent by the French corps in Lorraine in a series of complex and ultimately purposeless marches which reflected the irresolution of their commanders. It is not easy to analyse the successive intentions of French headquarters in Metz between 3rd and 6th August, with such kaleidoscopic rapidity did plans succeed and merge into one another; but the result for the troops themselves was clear. They would be roused early from bivouacs which they had reached, probably in heavy rain, late the previous night, and shoulder their equipment for yet another march—often retracing their steps of the previous day. No one, from brigade commander down, knew where they were going or why. They had no maps, and the orders from Metz, so voluminous in their details about order of march, mode of encampment, security precautions, and even dress, gave no

---

[1] Ibid. 199–200.
[2] Cardinal von Widdern, *Kritische Tage* III ii 134. The German Official History [*G.G.S.* I i 104] gives the curious explanation of Steinmetz's movement that it was intended "merely as a measure of safety against the enemy".

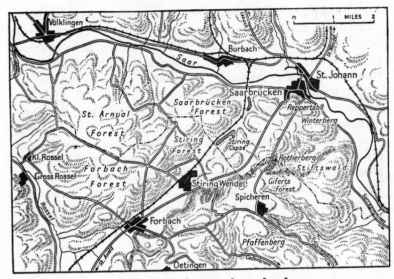

Map 3: Spicheren and Saarbrücken

information about the object of the movement or the disposition either of other French units or of the enemy.[1] For news of the latter the troops were dependent upon civilian information and latrine rumour. These blind marches seldom covered much ground, but, carried out in blazing sun or soaking rain and involving long delays as columns met, crossed, or accumulated on a single road, they effectively exhausted the men who had to carry them out; and each day would end like the last, long after dark in a rain-lashed field, with the men going to bed supperless, too weary to kindle a fire with their sodden wood. Such miseries may be swallowed up and forgotten in victory; but they are remembered, and heavily debited to the high command, when they lead only to defeat.

The first intention of Napoleon and Lebœuf after their easy triumph at Saarbrücken was to repeat it further downstream with an advance by 4th Corps on Saarlouis, to consolidate the French hold on the entire valley of the Saar.[2] But this last flicker of French initiative was stillborn, for what seemed feasible at Metz did not appear at all possible to Ladmirault. Placed on the left flank of the French army at Boulay, he was as alarmed by rumours of Germans massing opposite him as was Douay of 7th Corps at Strasbourg on the right. He knew by reports from Luxemburg that the German First Army, some 40,000 strong, was descending on him from Trier. What if this force were to penetrate unopposed up the valley of the Moselle, outflanking him by Thionville, and taking him in the rear?[1] On his own responsibility Ladmirault had sent a division to plug the Moselle valley at Sierck, twenty miles north of Boulay,[2] and with his corps thus extended concentration for an offensive was out of the question. The advance on Saarlouis was therefore abandoned. There were now clear indications, not simply from agents but from the English Press, whose most renowned correspondents were travelling with the German armies and sending back uncensored reports, of the German concentration north of Saarbrücken.[3] On 4th August therefore Napoleon and Lebœuf changed their instructions to 4th Corps and ordered it to concentrate behind Saarbrücken under command of Bazaine to meet the impending attack. But Ladmirault was stubborn. If he moved to the right, as Lebœuf demanded, he would uncover the Moselle valley. Sierck, he insisted, was "the key to the position and it is important to be master of it".[4] Lebrun, who had already been sent by Napoleon to examine the situation on the left flank, came down on Ladmirault's side; so Bazaine was ordered to take over, with 3rd Corps, some of 4th Corps's front, to enable Ladmirault to concentrate further to the north. Ladmirault thus compelled Napoleon to abandon his gains of 2nd August: for Bazaine could take over 4th Corps positions only by withdrawing the troops on 2nd Corps's left flank. Simultaneously Failly, on the right flank, was calling in the brigade of 5th Corps at Sarreguemines; and Frossard, considering himself dangerously isolated, fell back on 5th August from the Saarbrücken heights to the strong positions around Spicheren and Forbach from which he had set out with such *panache* three days before.[5] This withdrawal was, as we shall see, to have far-reaching results.

Napoleon abandoned his plans for a defensive concentration within a few hours of making them. While he hesitated on the Saar the Crown Prince had taken the initiative on the Lauter, and routed an isolated French division at the frontier post of Wissembourg; and at French headquarters when the news arrived on 4th August the reaction was one as much of anger as alarm. It was not only politically necessary that this setback should be compensated for as soon as possible; it was militarily essential that the Germans should be attacked at once, before their concentration was complete and the whole French army suffered the

[1] Ibid. 94–6, 247.   [2] Ibid. 326–7.
[3] *Guerre* V 296.   [4] Ibid. 332–8.
[5] Ibid. 301–5, VI 9–10.

fate of Abel Douay.[1] The army of the Rhine was now over 270,000 strong; the time had come to attack.[2]

With enthusiasm, the spell of indecision momentarily broken, Lebœuf and his advisers flung themselves into planning this new adventure, until the chief Intendant, Wolff, coldly pointed out to them that there was nothing for the French army to live on once it had crossed the Saar. Requisitions would be out of the question—the Palatinate would have been drained dry by the Germans already; and if they expected him to provide for them from magazines, he had at Metz, he said, only two days' supplies.[3] This scheme evaporated as quickly as it had arisen, and the staff devised yet another defensive deployment—this time one which presaged disaster. The French corps were now to be strung out in a cordon along the frontier, watching every avenue of approach, but too widely scattered to give mutual support. Ladmirault was to concentrate 4th Corps opposite Saarlouis; Frossard with 2nd Corps remained where he was, opposite Saarbrücken; Bazaine, while keeping 3rd Corps headquarters at St Avold, was to relieve Failly's troops at Sarreguemines, and Failly was to concentrate the whole of 5th Corps at Bitche. With 1st Corps watching the Vosges passes at Froeschwiller, and 7th Corps spread along the upper Rhine, the French were left with only two corps in reserve—the Imperial Guard, which was already moving up from Metz along the St Avold road, and Canrobert's untrained and ill-disciplined 6th Corps at the camp of Châlons, which on 5th August was ordered up to Nancy. Against forces so widely scattered it hardly required an ability so transcendent as Moltke's to gain an overwhelming victory. Yet the Germans, ironically enough, were to attack at the only point in the French defences where they seriously risked defeat.

To make the task of controlling his sprawling formations a little easier Lebœuf now divided them, for purposes of command, into two. The right wing—1st, 5th, and 7th Corps—came under the command of MacMahon; the left wing—2nd, 3rd, and 4th—under that of Bazaine. But much was left uncertain. The new commanders were still required to retain command of their own corps. They were allotted no additional staff, given no orders, and allowed no administrative control over their units. Imperial Headquarters at Metz remained intact, and the Emperor kept the Guard and 6th Corps under his own hand. It is not surprising that Bazaine regarded himself as a mere channel for conveying imperial

---

[1] See pp. 101–3 below. [2] *Guerre* V 300.
[3] Lebrun, *Souvenirs* 247–9.

orders to the units under his command, and continued to busy himself with the affairs of his own corps; nor that certain corps commanders, Failly in particular, were in doubt how far their new commander's orders should override those which they had previously received from Metz: two sources of confusion which were to be disastrous for the fortunes of the French army on and after 6th August.

On the German side also the chain of command left much to be desired. Steinmetz was growing increasingly impatient at what he considered the dilatoriness of Royal Headquarters, while his cavalry patrols were sending back reports of French movements which suggested a retreat. It had been bad enough that the enemy should have peacefully invaded the Palatinate; it was intolerable that he should now be allowed to slip away without a fight. On the evening of 5th August, in defiance of Moltke's restraining orders, he ordered, as we have seen, his leading corps forward towards Saarbrücken, through Guichenbach and Fischbach; a movement which separated the infantry of the Second Army, advancing down the Ottweiler–Neunkirchen road, from their cavalry divisions scouting ahead in the valley of the Saar. To Moltke he explained that his object was to facilitate the advance of the Second Army by drawing the French on himself and attacking them vigorously. Moltke merely annotated the despatch: "Would have exposed the First Army to defeat."[1]

Two overlapping German armies were thus advancing on Saarbrücken on the early morning of 6th August. Had Frossard still been in position on the hills above the town nothing might have happened that day. But soon after dawn the Second Army's cavalry patrols noticed that the watch-fires which had burned all night in the French positions were dummies: the heights had been abandoned. Curious, they crossed the river and advanced over the hill, till breasting the rise they saw the tents and the conspicuous blue and red French uniforms on the Spicheren heights a mile to the south. They reported back that the French were in retreat[2]; and in this mistaken belief the German commanders in both the First and the Second Armies were to throw overboard Moltke's careful plans, hoist a signal for general chase, and become involved in a battle as unexpected, as sudden, and as contrary to Moltke's intentions

---

[1] *M.M.K.* 199.
[2] *G.G.S.* I i 202. When this news reached Moltke, he commanded Steinmetz, in an order dated 6th August 1745 hrs, [*M.M.K.* 201] to cross the Saar downstream from Saarbrücken. In an attempt to cover up for Steinmetz the German Official History [*G.G.S.* I i 203] antedates the order by 24 hours. See Bonnal, *La Manœuvre de St Privat* (Paris 1904–12) I 226.

as the action at Froeschwiller which the Third Army was simultaneously unleashing forty miles to the south-east.

Frossard had no intention of retreating. Had he fallen back any further, Forbach would have been lost, and with it all the supplies accumulated for a French offensive.[1] He was established in one of those *positions magnifiques* of whose value he as an engineer was particularly conscious, and which he had delineated in his famous report three years earlier. The Spicheren heights projected into the valley of the Saar, forming a spectacular bluff which dwarfed the foothills between them and the river and commanded the country for twenty miles around. Their eastern slopes were covered by the forests of the Stiftswald and the Giferts Forest, and any assailant penetrating through these woods emerged at the crest of the ridge only to find a steep and narrow valley barring access to the village of Spicheren. Their western slopes fell into the Forbach-Stiring valley, a wooded defile through which ran the road and the railway from Saarbrücken to Metz; and the entry to this valley from the north was commanded by a feature jutting sharply out from the Spicheren heights; a spur called, from the red tinge of the soil laid bare where its three sides fall sheer to the valley, the Rotherberg. From the Rotherberg the French could overlook the whole valley between their positions and the heights above Saarbrücken which they had lately abandoned. If it fell, the assaulting force would still have to cross a narrow col dominated by the ridge of the Pfaffenberg rising to a height of 4,000 feet behind the village. On the other hand if the Rotherberg was lost, observation over the Forbach valley was lost as well; and here the heights descended too steeply to the valley to be easily defensible by fire. Moreover the entire position could be by-passed by an assailant crossing the Saar at Völklingen and striking south down the Rossel valley to come in on its rear at Forbach and Morsbach. Thus safety was not to be found by occupying the heights alone. It was necessary to have troops in the valley, and in making his dispositions Frossard bore this very much in mind. Of his three divisions, one, Vergé's, was placed in the valley, one, that of Laveaucoupet, was deployed on the heights, with two companies dug in on the Rotherberg; and the third, Bataille's, remained in reserve at Oetingen, whence it could deal with any attack on Forbach from Völklingen.[2] There were no outposts: no detachments remained to observe the river, and the cavalry was kept well behind the infantry positions. The first the French knew of the approach of the main

[1] Frossard, *Rapport sur les Opérations du 2ᵉ Corps* 35.
[2] *Guerre* VIII, Docs. annexes 24, 28.

German armies was the appearance, at about 6.30 a.m., of the Uhlan patrols on the line of hills above Saarbrücken which they had themselves recently occupied.

The first German infantry unit to learn of the French withdrawal was the leading division of the First Army, 14th Division of VII Corps, advancing on Saarbrücken by the Lebach road.[1] Its commander, General von Kameke, asked his corps commander for leave to attack: a purely formal request, since he continued to advance with the firm intention of doing so. He knew his superior officer. General von Zastrow was seventy years old and not standing up well to the rigours of the campaign. Zastrow replied authorising von Kameke to act as he thought fit.[1] This was a strange answer. Its vague passivity contrasted sharply with the masculine decisiveness usually characteristic of Prussian orders; and, what is worse, it betrayed a complete ignorance of Moltke's strategic intentions—an ignorance for which Moltke himself must certainly bear much of the blame. Zastrow's abdication of responsibility gave Kameke full rein; and without making any further arrangements for support, he launched his division into the attack.[2]

Now Kameke, in his bull-headed enthusiasm, was not only taking on an entire French corps. He had blundered into the only point on the frontier where the French had more than a single corps in a position to repel his attack. Behind Frossard, in an arc of some fifteen miles radius from Saarbrücken, lay the four scattered divisions of Bazaine's 3rd Corps: Decaen at St Avold, Metman at Marienthal, Castagny at Puttelange and Montaudun at Sarreguemines. Within fifteen miles of Spicheren lay 54,900 Frenchmen, and only 42,900 Prussians[3]; and had the French brought all their forces to bear at Spicheren the First Army might easily have received the drubbing which Moltke feared and which Steinmetz's blundering deserved. How did they succeed in escaping it?

It was certainly not because the German attack achieved strategic surprise. Earlier that morning, before the Uhlan patrols appeared, Lebœuf had wired to both Bazaine and Frossard, warning them to expect an engagement. Frossard querulously endorsed the message, "Then why not order Marshal Bazaine to concentrate his positions on mine and take over the combined command?"[4] But Bazaine, at

[1] *G.G.S.* I i 203.

[2] Cardinal von Widdern, *Kritische Tage* III iii: *Die Befehlsführung am Schlachttage von Spicheren* 112–22.

[3] *Kriegsgeschichtliche Einzelschriften*, IX (Berlin 1888) 403–414.

[4] *Guerre* VIII docs. 12.

St Avold, was not only Frossard's superior officer; he had also his own responsibilities as a corps commander, and he knew that Saarbrücken was not the only point at which the enemy might attack. Uhlan patrols had also been active on either side of the town, raiding the communications between Sarreguemines and Bitche and penetrating deeply into the St Arnual Forest. The main enemy attack might by-pass Frossard and come in on the left or the right flank of 3rd Corps itself. It is not surprising that Bazaine should have been cautious about committing his entire forces to Frossard's support until he was sure that the attack from Saarbrücken was serious; and not until nearly 6 p.m. did any message from Frossard suggest that it was.

Indeed for much of the day Frossard, repulsing the attack of a weaker enemy, had no need of support. His opening messages spoke simply of a reconnaissance in force, and indeed of a possible thrust on the left, through the St Arnual Forest.[1] Bazaine informed him, at 11.15 a.m., that a brigade of dragoons had been sent to watch the left, that Metman's and Castagny's divisions had been sent up to Bening and Thoding, four miles in rear, and suggested that Frossard should if necessary fall back in line with them on Cadenbronn.[2] Castagny indeed had shown an initiative rare in French commanders and had marched to the guns. But as he marched the gunfire seemed to die away; peasants told him that the battle was over; and he returned to Thoding to await further orders.[3] At 1.30 p.m. another message reached Bazaine from Frossard. The battle was developing. Could Montaudun be sent up from Sarreguemines on his right flank ? Dutifully Bazaine ordered Montaudun to march; but he sent off the order by messenger and not by wire. Montaudun received it at 3.30 p.m., and it was five o'clock before he had collected his outposts and set out on the seven-mile march to Spicheren.[4] The only other commander with whom Frossard communicated directly was Metman, whom he ordered up at 4 p.m. Unfortunately nobody had told Metman that he was at Frossard's disposal, and by the time he had checked with Bazaine and was ready to move it was almost 6.30 p.m.[5] Meanwhile the telegraph from Forbach to St Avold, which had been

[1] *Guerre* VIII Docs. annexes 14. *D.T.* IV 182.
[2] *Guerre* VIII 43.
[3] Castagny's evidence in *Procès Bazaine* 287.
[4] *Guerre* VIII 234, Docs. annexes 102. Montaudun *Mémoires* II 72–3.
[5] Lebrun declares [*Souvenirs* 276] that Frossard's unpopularity made his colleagues deliberately delay in helping him. One, having already started, stopped and "expressed his dislike of Frossard and his determination not to help him in terms of such crudity that I cannot repeat them here". On this question however Lebrun is not a particularly reliable source.

silent for most of the afternoon, had again sprung into life. At 5.30 p.m., in reply to an enquiry from Bazaine, Frossard reported that fighting seemed to be dying down; but ten minutes later he sent a frantic message: "My right on the heights has had to fall back. I am gravely compromised. Send me troops quickly and by every means."[1] To this appeal Bazaine reacted promptly. Montaudun and Metman, so far as he knew, were on their way. There was left only Castagny, whom he ordered up at once, and Decaen now his only reserve, to deal with any threat from the north; from whom he none the less detached a regiment and sent it up to Forbach by train. At 6.30 p.m., when a second message came from Frossard to "hurry on the movement of your troops as much as you can", he had nothing left to send; and the reinforcements already on their way arrived only to meet the débris of 2nd Corps streaming back from the Spicheren heights.[2]

All this is necessary to explain why it was that, whereas every German unit within earshot marched to the sound of the guns and built up a numerical superiority on the battlefield, Frossard fought until nightfall with no support at all. The very slowness with which the German forces arrived was fatal to him, for it prevented the French from realising their danger until too late. Moreover the Germans knew that they had only one battle to fight; that the noise of the cannon indicated the decisive point. The French could not be so sure. Of the divisions in 3rd Corps, Metman and Montaudun were understandably reluctant to leave the positions they guarded against possible German thrusts until they received a direct order.[3] The only man in a position to march straight to the guns was Castagny, and only ill luck prevented him from so doing. It was the fault neither of Bazaine nor of Frossard that virtually every unit in their corps was spread out in a thin defensive cordon, leaving them no effective reserve.[4]

The morning had passed uneventfully before Spicheren, except for an interchange of artillery fire which revealed at once the superior range and accuracy of the German guns.[5] It was not until nearly midday that

[1] *Guerre* VIII 17–18, 96.

[2] Bonnal, *Manœuvre de St Privat* I 333. P. A. Maistre, *Spicheren* (Paris 1908) 352 ff.

[3] See Montaudun's evidence in *Procès Bazaine* 287.

[4] Frossard himself considered that Bazaine gave all necessary orders to support him, and suggested only that he could have shown more energy in seeing that they were carried out. *Rapport sur les Opns. du 2ᵉ Corps* 54.

[5] *Guerre* VIII 44–5, and Docs. annexes 60.

Kameke's leading brigade was in a position to advance; two battalions being directed round each of the French flanks, in the Stiring valley and the Giferts Forest, while the remaining two assaulted the Rotherberg direct. This attack, launched with six battalions and four batteries on a front of some four thousand yards, was quite decisively repulsed. Thanks to the open formations of their company columns and the erratic fuses of the French shells, the Germans were able to cross the open ground before the Spicheren heights without suffering unduly. Their left wing made its way under cover of the trees to the southern edge of the Giferts Forest; but the violent fire of Laveaucoupet's men before Spicheren made it impossible for it to get further. The right wing, seeking cover among the woods and copses which flank the Forbach-Saarbrücken railway, wandered away from the direction of attack and was brought to an equally dead stop before Stiring Wendel by Vergé's division. As for the assault on the Rotherberg, we can only presume that Kameke had no idea what he was asking his men to do. To an observer from the heights of Saarbrücken the strength of the position is not a tall obvious. From here the Rotherberg is unimpressive. The plateau on its summit slopes invitingly, like a gang-plank giving access to the heights beyond, and its steep sides are veiled in trees and shadow. It was only as they approached the hill, and came in sight of its rocky and precipitous slopes, that the Germans could realise the difficulty of the assault. For a time they could only crouch in the shelter at its base; then, rallied by their officers, they charged and somehow gained a hold on the summit from which repeated French counter-attacks could not prise them loose.[1]

Frossard himself may have been slow to react to the German attack; his subordinate commanders were almost too prompt. Not only did Vergé and Laveaucoupet rapidly reinforce their forward troops but Bataille without waiting for orders roused his reserve division, divided it in two parts and sent them to the aid of the forward units; an action which, though a praiseworthy example of a French commander marching to the guns, left Frossard with no reserve and in consequence no chance to manœuvre—not that he showed any disposition to do so. The opportunity was excellent: by 3 p.m. Kameke's leading brigade was extended over a three-mile front, exhausted, and open to counter-attack. When Laveaucoupet brought forward troops to clear the Giferts Forest, the two German battalions established there, tired and unsupported, were flushed out after a very brief fight. But the French made

[1] *G.G.S.* I i 214. *Guerre* VIII 30–5, and docs. annexes 59.

no other move forward: they remained in their positions, awaiting the next German move; and that was not long delayed.[1]

When during the morning the optimistic and misleading reports of the cavalry patrols reached First and Second Army headquarters, both Steinmetz and Frederick Charles had given orders for a general advance through Saarbrücken. Steinmetz sanctimoniously declared that "in the interests of the Second Army" the French should be driven from the Spicheren heights and prevented from entraining at Forbach. Frederick Charles, furious at learning that the First Army was to cross his path, gave full powers to the commander of his leading division, General von Stuelpnagel, to clear them off the road.[2] Fortunately their subordinates did not translate these jealousies into action. The magnetic attraction of cannon-fire had already drawn the German divisions towards the battlefield long before they received formal orders to march. Kameke committed his remaining brigade to reinforce his right wing in the woods before Stiring; Zastrow ordered his remaining division, the 13th, to cross the river at Völklingen and carry out just that flanking movement on Forbach which Frossard so much feared. The leading division of VIII Corps, the 16th, came up and the corps commander, General von Goeben, took command of the action out of Kameke's hands. While these units of the First Army were converging on Saarbrücken from the north, those of the Second Army were approaching from the north-east, with the enterprising and able commander of III Corps, Constantin von Alvensleben, among the leading troops. Alvensleben was outranked by Goeben, and Zastrow, when he eventually came up, was senior to both. He was however vastly less competent, and made no difficulties about leaving the conduct of the operations in Alvensleben's hands on the excuse that he had no more troops to commit and Alvensleben had.[3]

From 3 p.m. onwards, therefore, German troops came pouring in to the aid of their hard-pressed comrades—and, even more useful than troops, German guns. If the French infantry held the Germans in check with their *chassepots*, the German gunners quickly swamped the French. They covered the French approaches to the Rotherberg and checked every attempt to reinforce or recapture it; they could support any attack by their right wing towards Stiring, and by forcing back the

---

[1] *Guerre* VIII 60.

[2] *G.G.S.* I i 205. *Kriegsgesch. Einzelschr.* XVIII. *Das Generalkommando des III Armeekorps bei Spicheren und Vionville* 486.

[3] *Kriegsgesch. Einzelschr.* XVIII. 509.

French guns and infantry from the edge of the heights, they made it
far easier for the German infantry to be brought forward to the assault.[1]
But the assaults were still unavailing. Alvensleben directed his leading
troops into the Giferts Forest, from which the first wave of the German
attack had now completely ebbed. French counter-attacks threw them
into confusion; further detachments came up to help them, both from
their own division and from VIII Corps, and by 7 p.m., as darkness
began to fall, the Giferts Forest contained a confused mass of some
thirty German companies, First and Second Army side by side, unable
to make any further headway since the southern edge of the wood was not
only separated from Spicheren by a considerable ravine but was swept
at a comfortable range by French rifle- and gunfire from the slopes
beyond.[2]

The attacks on the Rotherberg achieved equally little. Here also
units of III and VIII Corps came up to the help of the survivors of VII
Corps who still hung on to the edge. Covered by artillery fire, their
columns half-hidden in the smoke, these fresh troops stormed the spur
from every side; and finally drove the French back. The position was
taken; and as orthodox tactics demanded that cavalry should be put
in to pursue the beaten foe, a regiment of Hussars attempted to pick
its way up the narrow sunken lane which led to the summit. This was
disastrous: the French guns concentrated on the column, and created a
confusion which made it impossible to move in the lane at all. Next the
Germans tried to bring up artillery, and in this they succeeded. With the
help of the infantry eight guns were hauled up the slopes and came
into action at the top, sweeping the plateau and guarding against any
danger of counter-attack. By 5 p.m. the Germans were as securely
established on the Rotherberg as in the Giferts Forest—and as uselessly.
All they had captured was an outwork; the main French position still
lay before them on the broad slopes of the Spicheren and the Forbach
heights, and to reach these it was necessary to cross a narrow neck of
land swept by an artillery fire from the Pfaffenberg to which the German
guns were in no position to reply. A further advance was possible
only at the expense of casualties and exertions which the German

[1] The new Prussian tactics of deploying as many guns as quickly as possible
were here being put into effect with excellent results. The French still adhered to
the Napoleonic technique of keeping the mass of their artillery in reserve for
special concentrations. Many of Frossard's batteries did not come into action
at all. *Guerre* VIII 182.

[2] *G.G.S.* I i 226–7. *Guerre* VIII 80–1, docs. 61–9. Lehautcourt, *Guerre de
1870* III 421–3.

commanders were not prepared to ask of their weary and disorganised men.[1]

There was thus reason for the complacency which Frossard showed throughout the day about the position on his right wing; the real danger lay, he knew, on the left, where Kameke's and Vergé's divisions were waging a bloody and indeterminate fight among the goods-yards and factories of Stiring Wendel. Vergé was threatened not only in front but in flank, by the advance of the German 13th Division from Völklingen down the Rossel valley. His reserve brigade was at Forbach, watching this flank; but it was urgently needed at Stiring, where the threat was more immediate. Frossard decided to send it up, and wired to Metman to come and protect Forbach in its place. At the same time Bataille, commanding the reserve division, judged that the threat to the left wing was becoming dangerous and transferred a regiment from the heights to help Vergé deal with it. Thus strengthened, the French forces in the valley counter-attacked. The Germans crumbled in panic and all but a handful of men streamed back towards Saarbrücken. By 6 p.m. the whole German right wing seemed to be in a state of collapse[2].

To Alvensleben the position seemed critical. About the right wing he had little information—none of his men were engaged there; but on the left and in the centre his men were exhausted and unable to move; and if the French counter-attacked in strength they might pin him against the river. One last attempt had to be made to break the enemy hold on the Spicheren heights; and this could only be done, not by sending up more troops to those crowding the Rotherberg and the Giferts Forest, but by an attack straight up the slopes from the Stiring Valley, to come in on Laveaucoupet's flank. But even this attack, launched by six battalions, did not come up to his expectations. The first wave found themselves assailed by the point-blank fire of Laveau-coupet's left wing and disintegrated completely. The second wave, climbing up the tree-covered slopes of the Spicheren Forest, was checked by a flank-guard, which fell back so slowly up the wooded slopes that the Germans reached the crest long after darkness had fallen. Their arrival coincided with a last attempt by the French to drive the Germans from the Rotherberg and Giferts Forest by an ill-prepared and virtually spon-taneous counter-attack,[3] and the fire of the newcomers may have been

---

[1] *G.G.S.* I i 224–38. *Guerre* VIII 85. Lehautcourt, *Guerre de 1870* III 436–8.

[2] *G.G.S.* I i 216–35. *Guerre* VIII 63–86, docs. 24–41. Frossard, *Opérations de 2ᵉ Corps* 46. Lehautcourt, op. cit. III 433.

[3] See Bataille's report on this incident in *Guerre* VIII, docs. 45.

an effective contribution to the resistance which forced the French back to their own lines; but when, at about 7.30 p.m., Laveaucoupet decided to pull back his troops into a stronger and more concentrated position above Spicheren, it was not because he felt that his flank had been turned. The weariness of his troops, the need for tighter control as darkness set in, pressing problems of supply—these motives, and not any brilliant tactical stroke by Alvensleben, dictated the controlled retirement of the French right wing.[1]

Thus at nightfall the French front was still everywhere holding firm against superior numbers; and for this credit is due not only to the steadiness of the troops and the energy with which their officers rallied them to counter-attack, but to the skill with which Frossard and his divisional commanders had sited their positions. But this resistance had been made possible only by the commitment of almost every man under Frossard's command; and the reinforcement from 3rd Corps on which he had counted to bolster up his left wing had still not arrived. Instead, towards 7 p.m., the advance guard of General von Glume's 13th Division began to appear on the hills above Forbach. There were no troops to defend the town. A resourceful officer scraped together some reservists, but all his skill could not delay the enemy advance for more than an hour, and by 7.30 p.m. Frossard realised that he must abandon Forbach. Since this attack from the north made retreat west towards St Avold impossible he could now only fall back to the south, towards Sarreguemines and the hills round Cadenbronn. Vergé and Bataille had to withdraw their troops from the charnel woods and the blazing houses of Stiring—not an easy task with the Germans returning to the attack and pressing on their heels. The troops assembled on the dark slopes behind Spicheren; the wounded and their doctors were left in the village, and the reinforcements from 3rd Corps, coming belatedly up, found the hills covered with retreating columns of bitter and exhausted men.[2]

One French military historian has used the battle of Spicheren to illustrate the overriding importance of moral forces in war. "General Frossard, undefeated, thought he had been defeated, and so he was. General von Zastrow was half-defeated, but refused to be and so was not. This was the secret of the Prussian victory."[3] The Prussians had

[1] *G.G.S.* I i 235–42. *Kriegsgesch. Einzelschr.* XVIII 519–20. Bonnal, *Manœuvre de St Privat* I 286–9. *Guerre* VIII 108–14.

[2] *G.G.S.* I i 246–7. *Guerre* VIII 97–9, 117, 120–4, 170. Frossard, op. cit. 50.

[3] Bonnal, *Manœuvre de St Privat* I 338–9.

been punished severely, losing 4,500 casualties to the 2,000 French.[1] But the French also reported over 2,000 missing, of whom the bulk had been taken prisoner; Frossard's men retreating through the night certainly felt themselves to be vanquished, while the Germans, camped round their watch-fires on the battlefield, felt themselves to be victors. They were not to know that Frossard had been driven from the field, not by the frontal attack which had carpeted the slopes with Prussian dead, but by a barely developed threat in his rear. In retrospect the Prussian strategy seems masterly: drawing in the French reserves by frontal attack and then dislodging them by a threat to the flank; but no such idea had been in the minds of the German commanders, and with such disproportionate forces Frossard was almost bound to be forced back if a way round his flank could be found. Had German reconnaissance and consequent knowledge of the French positions been better, Frossard could have been forced from the Spicheren heights without the shedding of a drop of German blood. But the Prussian generals were true disciples of Clausewitz: for them battle was its own justification; and though Moltke's grand strategy was ruined by the premature and inconclusive engagement, a blow was also struck at the precarious equilibrium of the French High Command from which it was never to recover.

§ 3 Froeschwiller

Meanwhile Blumenthal had fulfilled his obligations, and the Third Army crossed the Alsatian frontier north of Wissembourg on the morning of 4th August.

Blumenthal knew that he was opposed by a force only two corps strong: 1st Corps, under MacMahon, based on Strasbourg, and 7th Corps, under Félix Douay, at Belfort—the latter indeed probably too distant to give effective help. MacMahon's units were moreover dangerously extended. He had decided not to defend the frontier but to establish himself in the position on the eastern slopes of the Vosges around Froeschwiller which Frossard had recommended in 1868. From there he could guard his communications with the rest of the army and threaten the flank of any force advancing south on Strasbourg.[2] The plan was wise but the details were poorly conceived.

---

[1] *Guerre* VIII 125. *Kriegs. Einzelschr.* IX 414.
[2] *Guerre* IV 54. This was also part of Frossard's original defensive plans. See *Guerre* VI 138.

MacMahon's four divisions were dispersed in a rough quadrilateral, twenty miles apart, just too far separated for effective mutual support. Corps headquarters, with Lartigue's division, lay at Hagenau; Raoult's division took over the strong defensive positions on the ridge at Froeschwiller where the whole Corps was eventually to concentrate; and Ducrot, given command both of his own division and that of Abel Douay—Félix Douay's brother—himself took up a position at Lembach, on the Bitche–Wissembourg road, and sent Douay forward to the frontier town of Wissembourg. Thus it happened that on 3rd August a single French division, about 8,600 men strong, twenty miles from the nearest supporting troops, took post within a few hundred yards of the frontier over which four German corps were to advance the following day.[1]

Two factors explain MacMahon's clumsy dispositions. One was the failure, which we have already discussed, of the *Intendance* to provide adequate supplies. The troops had to fend very largely for themselves, and both their own reserves and the resources of the hospitable but infertile countryside were quickly exhausted. The Corps thus had to disperse to live before it could concentrate to fight, and the resources of a town the size of Wissembourg, among these thinly populated and forest-covered hills, could not be lightly abandoned. The town lay at the foot of the Vosges, overlooked by the mountains to the north and by the slopes of the Bavarian Palatinate beyond the Lauter to the north-east, whence any attack would come. Its seventeenth-century fortifications and fieldworks—the famous "Wissembourg Lines", were now of purely antiquarian interest. The town was a tactical as well as a strategic death-trap, and tactical arguments would have dictated that Abel Douay should keep away from it and establish himself, as he might well have done, in a strong position among the mountains on the Klimbach road. But his overriding need was for food, and only the town could provide it. So one battalion occupied the town, the others lay encamped on the slopes immediately behind, and there they waited expectantly while officials of the *Intendance* explored the town's resources.[2]

The second factor was a disastrous failure on the part of Ducrot to appreciate the strength and intentions of the Germans. "The information I have received", he told Douay on 1st August, "makes me suppose that the enemy has no considerable forces very near his advance posts,

---

[1] *Guerre* V 55. *Vie militaire du Général Ducrot* II 348.
[2] *Guerre* II 35, V 230.

and has no desire to take the offensive."[1] Reports both from corps headquarters and from the civil authorities of Wissembourg that troops were massing beyond the frontier failed to shake his belief,[2] a belief, one can only suppose, firmly rooted in the picture he had formed over so many years in which it was to be the French who took the offensive and erupted over the Rhine. On 3rd August, from the famous viewpoint of the Col de Pigeonnier above Wissembourg, he inspected through a telescope the plain of the Palatinate and could not, he reported to MacMahon, "discover a single enemy post . . . it looks to me as if the menace of the Bavarians is simply bluff (*pure fanfaronnade*)".[3] His superior officers were less optimistic. Early on 4th August Lebœuf, disturbed by the German advance on the Saar, warned MacMahon to watch out for an attack. MacMahon telegraphed Abel Douay to be on his guard and, if attacked, to fall back along the Lembach road.[4] He prepared to go up to Wissembourg himself; but both the Marshal and his message were to arrive too late.

The Germans fell on Wissembourg in the morning of 4th August. The Bavarian troops who led the way felt anything but triumphant as they crossed the frontier. It had rained all night and they had slept miserably on the soaking ground; most of them were reservists suddenly recalled from their families to take part in a war at the behest of their late enemies in a cause for which their sympathies were doubtful; their boots hurt; and the wine and fruit so liberally supplied by the kindly population at the railway stations on their way to the front were beginning to have disagreeable results.[5] But the French were totally unsuspecting. Even when the first Bavarian shells began, at about 8.30 a.m., to fall in the town, Douay could not believe that they indicated more than a reconnaissance in force. He deployed his troops rapidly; one brigade around the Schloss Geissberg, an easily defensible group of buildings on the slopes a mile and a half south of the town, the remainder round Wissembourg station and within the town itself. Their fire halted the Bavarian infantry; the Bavarian gunners, moving clumsily among the vineyards, could bring no concentrated fire to bear in reply. The Bavarians therefore came to a halt and lay waiting for the Prussians who were coming up on their left to provide at least a diversion to enable them to move again.[6]

[1] *Guerre* IV 6.   [2] Ibid. 271–2.   [3] *Guerre* V 51.
[4] *Guerre* V 231–2. *Vie militaire du Général Ducrot* II 352.
[5] H. von Helvig, *Operations of the 1st Bavarian Corps* (London 1874) 16.
[6] *G.G.S.* I i 124. *Guerre* V 108–10, 195–7, 211–2. Frederick III, *War Diary* 23.

The two Prussian corps of which the Crown Prince disposed, V (General von Kirchbach) and XI (General von Bose), reached the Lauter below Wissembourg just as the roar of the Bavarian guns announced that battle had been joined. V Corps attacked the French position frontally, and XI outflanked the position to the south, to come in from the flank and rear. On the Prussian right wing a regiment was directed from Altenstadt against the southern gate of Wissembourg; an assault over a mile of dead-straight, poplar-lined road, flanked by water-meadows with very little cover. The Algerians round the station three times checked the advance by counter-attacks; but the Prussians moved stolidly on, the defending positions crumbled under a weight of shellfire to which the French gunners could make no adequate response, the *tirailleurs* were prised from their positions in buildings and ditches, behind railway-tracks and ditches, and soon after midday the station had fallen to the attack.[1]

Meanwhile Douay, attempting to organise his forces for a withdrawal, had been killed by a shellburst, and by the time his successor had taken over command XI Corps was threatening the French line of retreat. The increasing shellfire was shattering the French resistance. All who could do so escaped. The rest sought refuge in the enclosed courts and gardens of the Geissberg, which lay like a redoubt supporting the French position.[2]

The town of Wissembourg fell between 1 and 2 p.m.[3] The Geissberg held out for an hour or so longer against the Prussian assaults. The waves of infantry crowding up the slopes behind their colours, the generals and field-officers pressing up behind them on horseback to be in at the death, were held at bay by rifle-fire from walls and windows until six batteries were established on the slopes above and opened fire on the courtyards. The resistance was clearly hopeless. By 3 p.m. the battle was over. About a thousand Frenchmen were prisoner; a further thousand were dead or wounded; the rest were streaming miserably back along the road to Soultz.[4]

In an engagement where 50,000 men surprised 6,000 in a place totally unsuited to the defence, no other outcome was to be expected. The battle

---

[1] *G.G.S.* I i 123–9. *Guerre* V 114–16, 195–7.   [2] *Guerre* V 119–30, 217–20.

[3] The French commander tried to negotiate an honourable evacuation of his troops, but the Bavarian commander, with a regular soldier's command of military law, pointed out that this was permissible only for fortresses and *postes retranchés*, and that Wissembourg had been declassified as a fortress since 1867. *Guerre* V 143.

[4] *Guerre* V 131–5, 146–7, 220. *G.G.S.* I i 131–4.

was lost, not by the unfortunate Abel Douay, but by MacMahon and Ducrot whose joint responsibility it was that he had been placed in a position where the courage of his men could avail him nothing. One battalion had held up a Bavarian corps for five hours, and the two Prussian corps assaulting the position round the Geissberg bought their victory with nearly a thousand casualties. The timidity of the Bavarian and the rashness of the Prussian attack passed unnoticed in the completeness of the victory. So did the remarkable laxity of the German cavalry, which not only failed to pursue the retreating enemy—the most common of all military faults—but lost touch with him altogether. All these lessons had to be learnt later, and more expensively. Indeed the few hours' fighting round Wissembourg showed in miniature all the characteristics of the great battles which were during the course of the next few weeks to destroy Imperial France: the initial advantage of overwhelming numbers; the broad deployment which made tactics of envelopment almost automatic; the startling effectiveness of rifle-fire in checking mass assaults; and the ultimate reliance of the German infantry on their gunners to nullify the *chassepots* of the defence.[1]

MacMahon, with Ducrot, had witnessed the rout of Wissembourg from the heights of the Col de Pigeonnier. He could do nothing to help his luckless subordinate; indeed he could see, from the size of the black columns which were creeping by every road and track "like an oil-stain" over the frontier, that his own position was in serious danger.[2] But he remained impassive. By borrowing a division from 7th Corps he reckoned that he could still stand in the strong Froeschwiller position, as he had always intended, and if another corps were put at his disposal, he wired to Metz that night, he hoped to be able even to take the offensive. The Emperor replied by putting Failly's 5th Corps under his command; and on 5th August, while the divisions of 1st Corps concentrated round Froeschwiller and Félix Douay packed off Conseil Dumesnil's division from 7th Corps by train from Belfort, MacMahon summoned Failly to bring his corps south through the Vosges.

Failly was slow to react. His units were spread out along the frontier from Sarreguemines to Bitche, and he reckoned that no post could be evacuated until a relief had arrived. The troops at Bitche could not move till relieved by those at Rohrbach; nor those at Rohrbach till the

---

[1] For a detailed analysis of the performance of the German artillery see E. Hoffbauer, *Die deutsche Artillerie in den Schlachten und Treffen des deutsch-französischen Krieges 1870–71. Heft I: Das Treffen von Weissenburg.* (Berlin 1896).

[2] C. Sarazin, *Récits sur la dernière guerre* 24–5.

appearance of those from Sarreguemines; and Sarreguemines could not be abandoned until a relieving force from Bazaine's 3rd Corps had taken over.[1] All these snake-like evolutions would only produce, be it noted, one division. An impatient message from MacMahon on the evening of the 5th demanding the immediate advent of the whole corps only produced the bland reply, after some hours' delay, that there was only one division available and that would leave next morning. The remainder would follow "as soon as they could be concentrated and circumstances allowed."[2]

Later events in the campaign leave us in no doubt that Failly was a commander of remarkable sluggishness, but two points may be adduced

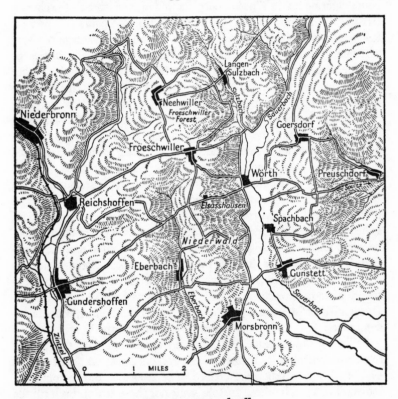

Map 4: Froeschwiller

[1] *Guerre* VI 18–29, 91–3.

[2] Montaudun's division of 3rd Corps took so long to reach Sarreguemines on 5th August that Failly's troops there, General Lapasset's brigade, never left at all, and joined up with Frossard in his retreat after Spicheren.

in his defence. His men had already carried out a long and tiring march on 5th August, and needed rest before they were fit to move, let alone fight, again; and secondly, his unwillingness to leave the frontier before him quite unguarded was natural enough. Admittedly it was not for him to entertain such fears, but to obey orders; but the chain of command in the French army was, as we have seen, uncertain; and blind obedience has never been an outstanding characteristic of the French.

Had Failly brought up his corps as ordered MacMahon would have had about 77,600 men at his disposal, with which he was confident of beating an equal number of Prussians. As it was, he found himself with some 48,000.[1] Even so he still had every hope of giving a good account of himself. The Froeschwiller ridge, like the Spicheren heights, was a *position magnifique*. To the traveller approaching the Vosges from the east by the Soultz road it seemed to rise in his path like a formidable wall. Closer inspection revealed it to be less of a wall than a pattern of alternating spurs and re-entrants, three to four miles in extent, comparable to a system of bastions and curtains; a natural fortress-system making possible a devastating cross-fire. Before it, moat-like, lay the flat valley of the Sauerbach: green water-meadows intersected by a stream which though passable on foot confined the passage of guns and transport to a few bridges well within range of the French guns. Thence the slopes rose gently and, except for vine-trellises, without cover, a perfect killing-ground a mile broad, to the crest crowned by the compact half-timbered village of Froeschwiller.

The configuration of these slopes can best be described as three prongs striking eastward from the central upright spine of the ridge, like a letter E. The northernmost prong lay just north of Froeschwiller, its northern slopes covered by the woods of the Froeschwiller Forest. Beyond it to the north a grassy alpine sward stretched down to the valley at Langensulzbach; and beyond that again the Vosges rose into high wooded peaks which effectively prevented any major movement of troops. The defence of this part of the front, the French left flank, was allotted to Ducrot's division. The centre of the French position, occupied by Raoult's division, lay across the next two prongs: that stretching from Froeschwiller down to the town of Wörth in the valley, and another, six hundred yards further south, on which lay the hamlet of

[1] 42,800 rifles, 5,750 sabres, 167 guns, against, on the German side, 89,000 rifles, 7,750 sabres and 342 guns. *Kriegsgeschichtliche Einzelschriften* IX 395. Bonnal's figures (*Froeschwiller* 176) of 43,000 against 150,000 are absurdly distorted.

Elsasshausen. To the south of Elsasshausen, beyond yet another re-entrant, lay the forest of the Niederwald: and here lay the weak point of the defence. The Niederwald was made the responsibility of Lartigue's division, the weakest in the corps. There were no clearly defined features to be occupied, no adequate field of fire. The wood was over a mile square, and its widely spaced pines offered no obstacle to the passage of infantry and cavalry; beyond it to the south towards the village of Morsbronn there stretched open slopes far too extensive for the French to defend. Lartigue had to sprawl his seven thousand men over a two-mile front, and could do little except scatter them round the edge of the wood, with a battalion forward in Morsbronn village.[1] Conseil Dumesnil's division, coming up piecemeal by the Hagenau–Reichshoffen railway, was fed in to strengthen Raoult's left wing at Elsasshausen; while the débris of Douay's division was held on the slopes behind Froeschwiller as a last reserve.

MacMahon's men arrived around Froeschwiller on 5th August, and in some disorder. Of Conseil's division only one brigade arrived that day; the rest came up next morning and the artillery never arrived at all. A number of reservists who were belatedly reaching their regiments on the eve of battle had never seen a *chassepot* and did not even know how to load it.[2] There was no explosive to destroy the bridges over the Sauerbach; there was no information about the enemy or about Mac-Mahon's own intentions—the content of the messages flowing in and out of the château at Froeschwiller where he had established his head-quarters was not communicated even to his divisional commanders; and above all, as might be expected after so sudden a concentration, there was no food. The resources of the local inhabitants, so unwisely generous to the troops during the opening days of the campaign, had been drained, and the *Intendance* had available six thousand rations for rather more than forty thousand men. By the 6th further rations had arrived and were distributed; but the evidence of the full cooking-pots which the Germans found after the battle showed that the troops were interrupted while preparing the first adequate meal which many of them had had for four days.[3]

---

[1] *Guerre* VII 86. The weakness of this flank had not escaped MacMahon's attention. His original plan had been for Lartigue to hold positions to cover it beyond the river, round Gunstett, with Conseil Dumesnil in the Niederwald in reserve. The late arrival of Conseil's division made this impossible. *Guerre* VI 162.

[2] A detail which Lebœuf's streamlined mobilisation had omitted. *Guerre* V 166, VII 30.

[3] C. Klein, *Chronique de Froeschwiller* 116.

This did not mean that the French were not confident. MacMahon trusted to his luck and to his splendid troops, and he doubted whether the Germans would really attack him at all; whether, under cover of a demonstration, they might not slip away to the west to join the rest of their forces on the Saar. Thus he merely replied to Failly's prevaricating messages, on the early morning of the 6th, with a telegram enquiring "on what day and by what route will you be joining me".[1] He considered an attack too improbable to make his troops dig trenches. As for his army, according to one member of it, "never were troops so sure of themselves and more confident of success".[2] They saw no reason to take any more precautions in fighting the Prussians than they had in fighting the Chinese. Douay's defeat was regarded as a mishap which might happen to anyone, and the sight of the grimy but cheerful survivors trudging back from Soultz to take up their positions to fight again roused in all who saw them a determination to fight at least as well as they had fought, and to succeed better. No sentries were posted; no defences were dug; the men wandered in to drink in the taverns of Wörth or to water their horses in the Sauerbach much as they pleased, and it was with some amazement that they saw, early in the afternoon of the 5th, little groups of German horsemen appear beyond the river.[3]

MacMahon's belief that the Crown Prince would not attack him was very nearly justified. Thanks to the sluggishness of its cavalry in failing to press pursuit beyond Wissembourg, the Third Army, on 5th August, had little idea of the French whereabouts. Blumenthal's orders— and in the light of Moltke's intentions for the Third Army they were surprising ones—were for a continuation of the march southwards towards Hagenau and Strasbourg.[4] While cavalry reconnoitred to the south and to the west, the army fanned out into a rough square, of which the base was formed by V Corps, at Preuschdorff, with XI Corps in the centre at Soultz and, on the left, the Württemberg and Baden divisions under General von Werder, coming up from Lauterburg to Aschbach. Five miles north of Werder lay I Bavarian Corps. Five miles north of V Corps II Bavarian Corps, which had toiled over the Col de Pigeonnier, watched the right flank at Lembach on the Bitche road.[5] It was a sensible formation, adaptable to almost any contingency.

[1] *Guerre* VII 4. *Vie militaire du Général Ducrot* II 376.
[2] H. Bonnal, *Froeschwiller* 205.
[3] *Guerre* VI 136. Sarazin, *Récits sur la dernière guerre* 30.
[4] Bonnal, *Froeschwiller* 148.
[5] *G.G.S.* I i 137.

Cavalry patrols found the French on the Sauerbach early in the afternoon, and the advance guard of V Corps moved into position opposite
them during the course of the evening; but the full significance of their
reports were evidently not appreciated at Army Headquarters. In the
orders issued for the next day Strasbourg was indicated as the objective,
and the presence of the French at Froeschwiller was recognised only
in the careful arrangements which were made for II Bavarian Corps
to come to the help of V Corps if it were attacked. Nothing in the orders
issued to the two corps on the left flank suggested that the army might
change direction towards the west; and nothing in any orders from army
headquarters indicated that the battle was either expected or desired.
The army was tired; the long, hot march over congested roads was
taking its toll of the reservists; the organisation of the supply-lines was
far from complete. Blumenthal looked forward to 6th August as a day
of rest and reorganisation.[1]

It was thus only by a series of mistakes and coincidences that the
German forces, both in Alsace and on the Saar, slipped simultaneously
into the first great battles of the war. We have seen how the leading
corps of the First and Second Armies were stampeded into the confused
action at Spicheren by the impetuosity of Steinmetz and Kameke.
At Froeschwiller the Third Army was pulled into battle like a workman
whose clothes have been caught in the cogs of a machine. The outposts
of the two armies, facing each other apprehensively across the Sauerbach,
had kept up a spattering exchange of shots throughout a night of pouring
rain, but the extent to which the Germans had established themselves
in the villages and houses beyond the stream had not, at first light on the
6th, been appreciated by the French. At 5 a.m. fatigue parties from
Lartigue's division going carelessly down to the Sauerbach to draw
water were astounded to find German bullets whizzing round their
heads. Further north, the outposts of V Corps opposite Wörth reported
noisy French activity in the town—activity consisting of the unofficial
arrival of large numbers of men coming to seek solace in the taverns of
the village after a wet night in the open. The Prussian brigadier ordered
his gunners to open fire; the Frenchmen scrambled hurriedly back to
their own lines; and the Prussian infantry regiment which advanced to
clear the town found it once more deserted. By 8.30 a.m. the Prussians

---

[1] See Bonnal's criticisms of the German dispositions, *Froeschwiller* 148, 172.
The success with which the Third Army adapted itself to the unexpected
conflict on 6th August, however, seems sufficient justification of Blumenthal's
plans.

had fallen back to their positions on the slopes to the east of the valley, and all seemed once again calm.[1]

This brief cannonade, like the first slight dislodgment of stones before an avalanche, had been enough to release forces of battle which were to grow in an accumulation of violence until every man and every gun available to the rival commanders was engaged in a struggle which could end only with the annihilation of one side or the exhaustion of both. Two miles to the north, near the village of Langensulzbach, the commander of II Bavarian Corps had heard the firing, glimpsed the French bivouacs on the slopes above him, and jumped to the conclusion that V Corps was being attacked. From the narrow, wooded Sulzbach valley he can only have had the vaguest idea of where the French positions lay, but he loyally launched his leading division up the hill, just as the outposts of V Corps were withdrawing from Wörth. It was difficult ground for an advance, thickly wooded slopes in which the Bavarians lost both direction and formation, and they emerged from the southerly edge of the Langensulzbach woods to find the open ground which lay before them swept by the *chassepot* fire of Ducrot's men. By 10.30 a.m. virtually the whole Bavarian 4th Division was extended in a single confused and unsupported skirmishing line, which Ducrot had no difficulty in holding in check.

Things were also warming up at the other end of the French line, where Lartigue opened fire with his artillery at about 8.30 a.m. XI Corps was moving into position on V Corps's left flank. Like the Bavarians, its advance-guards had been attracted by the sound of gunfire and the sight of the French lines round Froeschwiller and came hurrying up just as Lartigue's guns were deploying to fire. Four German batteries unlimbered on the slopes above Gunstett and replied with an accuracy, rapidity, and range which appalled the French. Fortunately the ground was soft with the recent rain and the percussion-fuses of many of the German shells did not explode; but within a very few minutes the French guns had been reduced to silence and the German dominated the battlefield. Thus at 8.30 a.m., although at Wörth itself all was peaceful, from both north and south there came the sound of brisk artillery fire; and the Chief of Staff of V Corps grew alarmed lest one of these engagements might presage a full-scale attack on his flank. He had no intention of launching an attack himself; but in order to pin down the French centre and deter MacMahon from attacking he ordered the entire artillery of V Corps to open fire. Fourteen batteries

[1] *G.G.S.* I i 151–2. *Guerre* VII 20. Bonnal, op. cit. 227.

deployed north and south of the main road, and they opened fire on the French positions at 9.30 a.m. Against them only two French batteries even attempted to reply, and that with a fire so inaccurate and ineffective that they were rapidly ordered to cease fire and save their ammunition for a better target.[1]

By now the commander of V Corps had come up to the gun line. General von Kirchbach was one of the most impetuous of the Prussian leaders. Two days earlier he had been wounded while directing, at absurdly short range, the attack on the Geissberg, and he was still unable to mount his horse. This did not impair his initiative. The exhilarating roar of his artillery, the evident trouble which it was causing the French, the encouraging sound of supporting gunfire on his flanks, all this was too much for him. He ordered his infantry to attack, and take not only Wörth but "the heights beyond". Simultaneously the leading infantry of XI Corps had been encouraged by the success of their gunners to attack over the stream opposite Gunstett. By 10 a.m. therefore, without any orders from Army Headquarters or any need to defend themselves against a French attack, three corps, more than half the strength of the Third Army, found themselves involved in un-expected battle.[2]

The French had taken up their battle positions during the preliminary engagements some three hours earlier. The divisional commanders deployed their men in the woods and vineyards, usually in two lines covered by a screen of skirmishers, with the reserves in close column behind. On the left flank Ducrot was well placed to hold off the Bavarians; Raoult dominated the slopes between Froeschwiller and Wörth; even Lartigue, his men thinly lining the eastern edge of the Nieder-wald, was able to repel the first attempts of XI Corps to get across the stream; while the cavalry divisions of General Bonnemains and the incomplete divisions of Douay and Conseil Dumesnil constituted a very respectable reserve. Thus the French troops were not only able to hold their ground; by repeated counter-attacks they swept the Germans back down the slopes and across the river, Bavarians and Prussians alike crumbling away before the bayonet-charges of MacMahon's Zouaves. At midday the French position still seemed intact.[3]

Indeed it was now the Germans who felt themselves threatened. The commander in Wörth sent back urgent demands to Kirchbach

---

[1] *G.G.S.* I i 153–6. *Guerre* VII 35–40, 46–8, 62. Lehautcourt, *Guerre de 1870* III 192–5.

[2] *G.G.S.* I i 157.   [3] *Guerre* VII 27 ff. 45, 55–7, 64–9.

for reinforcements, and Kirchbach still had a division in hand. True, he was forbidden to use it. The Crown Prince and Blumenthal at their headquarters in Soultz had heard with surprise and displeasure the noise of battle on V Corps's front which had been increasing ever since daybreak, and they sent a peremptory order to Kirchbach, that he was "not to continue the struggle, and to avoid everything which might induce a fresh one".[1] But such an order, by the time it arrived, no longer bore any relation to the situation. The Germans were too heavily involved to withdraw, and Kirchbach turned a Nelsonian blind eye to the signal of his superior officer. He told the Bavarians on his right that he was pressing his attack and asked them to do the same; from XI Corps on his left there came reassuring and reliable promises of complete support; so Kirchbach, sending back a firm if respectful message to his army commander, resolved to throw in his reserve division and hope for the best.

V Corps might have battered indefinitely against the French position above Wörth, but on XI Corps's front the situation was more promising. Lartigue had watched with alarm the columns converging on his thinly held position from the east, and warned MacMahon of the mounting danger. MacMahon was unhelpful: Lartigue was to stand firm and do his best, and if the worst came to the worst he had General Michel's cuirassier brigade to help him.[2] But by noon von Bose had assembled virtually his entire corps round Gunstett and the French saw "a black swarm of Prussians emerging at the run from the Gunstett bridge with every appearance of disorder. From this ant-heap, as if by magic, company columns shook themselves out and rapidly and without hesitation took up a perfectly regular formation".[3] The right wing gained the Niederwald where, sheltered from the French gunfire, they pushed the French infantry back up the hill; the left wing attacked Morsbronn, which the two French companies posted there prudently evacuated on their approach, and began to advance beyond.[4] But as they did so, Lartigue launched his cavalry to the attack.

Lartigue reckoned that his only hope of maintaining his position lay in re-establishing a line from east to west along the southern edge of the Niederwald. His object therefore in unleashing the cavalry was not to recapture Morsbronn but to hold off the Germans while his infantry scrambled back across the exposed slopes to their new positions. No

---

[1] *G.G.S.* I i 163. Frederick III, *War Diary* 32.
[2] *Guerre* VII 75, 79.
[3] Bonnal, *Froeschwiller* 315.   [4] *Guerre* VII: Docs. annexes 93–103.

French commander was under any illusion about the dangers involved to the protests of the cavalry generals Lartigue's Chief of Staff replied that there was no other way of saving the division, and they accepted this loyally. Michel launched his entire brigade down the slopes towards Morsbronn with an *élan* which it seemed that the scattered and winded Prussian infantry would be quite unable to withstand. But as they approached the village the horsemen found the smooth slopes before them cut up with hedges and vineyards, walls and trees, from behind which the Prussians directed on them a sustained and accurate fire. Shellfire from beyond the river tore great gaps in the charging ranks. The squadrons which reached the village found themselves trapped in a street barricaded at both ends, between houses from whose windows the Prussians fired at their leisure; a street which after the battle was piled so high with the carcasses of horses and the bodies of their riders that all attempts to get through it had to be abandoned. The rest of the squadrons swept round the sides of the village, to be picked off by riflemen, rounded up by Prussian cavalry, or find their way back, broken and useless, to their own lines. Nine squadrons were destroyed; it is doubtful whether a single Prussian infantryman lost his life.[1]

It was now about 2 p.m. An hour earlier the Crown Prince had arrived on the battlefield to discover for himself why the noise of battle, instead of dying away at his command, had been increasing; and finding that Kirchbach had committed V Corps without hope of retrieval he accepted the situation and attempted to impose some form on the battle. No more reserves were available in the centre: if Kirchbach's infantry collapsed he would have to rely on his gun line to break up a counter-attack. But all his remaining army corps lay within easy reach. General von der Tann was summoned to bring up I Bavarian Corps on Kirchbach's right flank; General Werder had already sent off the Württemberg division to help von Bose on the left, and the French would be squeezed between a pair of pincers of which each arm was forty thousand men strong. This was the plan worked out at Army Headquarters, and orders went out to corps commanders to this effect. But it did not work. Its achievement was to be totally distorted by the operation of the friction of war.[2]

In the first place it was not possible for Kirchbach to delay his

---

[1] *G.G.S.* I i 171. Lehautcourt gives a full account of the charge in *Guerre de 1870* III 231–6. See also the vivid account by Colonel d'Andigné, Lartigue's Chief of Staff, in *Guerre* VII, Docs. annexes 89.

[2] *G.G.S.* I i 167.

attack until more support could come up on his flanks.[1] His reserve division was already moving up through the villages of Wörth and Spachbach to be flung almost immediately against the French. A counterattack swept it back; but Kirchbach, undeterred, threw in his entire force. The men who had been in action since early morning, the fresh regiments which had just come up, all were assembled around Wörth and launched in a mass of company columns up the slopes. The German gunners beyond the river limbered up and came forward over the bridges which engineers had thrown over the stream, to deploy along the valley road, and to fire point-blank into the French ranks visible through the smoke barely five hundred yards away. Far from quietly waiting in the valley and letting the attack develop on the flanks, V Corps became locked on the slopes below Froeschwiller and Elsasshausen in a desperate and unsupported battle in which the French, in spite of the resilience and gallantry of their counter-attacks, were by sheer weight of men and gunfire gradually overborne.[2]

Nor did events on the right wing develop as the Crown Prince had intended. II Bavarian Corps was in no hurry to attack again, and I Bavarian Corps, struggling along steep and muddy lanes, seemed to the impatient army commander to be taking an absurdly long time to come up and to be curiously reluctant to attack when they did. The Bavarian military attaché passed an unpleasant five minutes with the Crown Prince, and was packed off to persuade his countrymen neither to abandon their allies nor to disgrace themselves.[3] In justice it must be pointed out that the task of the Bavarians was not easy. The country over which they had to approach and fight was far steeper and more thickly wooded than that on the left flank of the army. Control was more difficult and there was less space to deploy their guns. But the contrast between the military ability of the Bavarians and that of the Prussians, which had already been apparent at Wissembourg, was now made even more clear. Von der Tann's men lost their way, fired on one another, and fell back in a panic which Ducrot's Zouaves were quick to exploit.[4]

Eventually force of numbers began to tell. To defend the Froeschwiller Forest the French had only part of Ducrot's division and a regiment of Raoult's left wing, and during the afternoon the Bavarians,

[1] W. von Hahnke, *Die Operationen der III Armee* (Berlin 1873) 48–9.
[2] *Guerre* VII 103–8: Docs. annexes 61–9. Bonnal, *Froeschwiller* 350–2. G.G.S. I i 170–2.
[3] Frederick III, *War Diary* 36.   [4] *Guerre* VII 110. G.G.S. I i 188.

deploying against them the best part of two corps, were able gradually to make the French position untenable.[1] The wood was saturated with fire. Casualties multiplied; ammunition ran low; and messengers sent back for help were told by divisional and brigade commanders as desperate as themselves to hang on and do their best. Ducrot sent up his last reserves to hold the wood in which the dead were now so plentiful that "they seemed to make up a second line" a few yards behind the first; but nothing could be done about the wide outflanking movement which the Bavarians were making on Neehwiller, and nothing about the Prussians of V Corps advancing from Wörth through the vineyards to their right rear. By four o'clock the position of Ducrot's men was too hopeless even for retreat.[2]

Only on the left flank did the German attack go as had been expected; but since XI Corps had attacked on its own reponsibility the army commander could take little credit for it. It took XI Corps well over an hour to make its way through the Niederwald. The Prussian infantry could get little protection from their artillery and the zouaves were in their element sniping from behind trees. The French casualties were huge—in the 3rd Zouaves alone forty-five officers out of sixty-six, 1,775 men out of 2,200 were wounded or killed[3]; but Lartigue retained control of the survivors and withdrew them north-west beyond the Eberbach, avoiding the German left flank which was curving menacingly round his rear. At about 2.30 p.m. the men of XI Corps were beginning to debouch from the northern edge of the Niederwald, their supporting artillery following close behind, on to the right flank of the French forces struggling to hold Elsasshausen against V Corps attacks from the east.[4]

By 3 p.m. MacMahon's forces were compressed into a mile-square quadrilateral, every yard of which could be beaten by German guns. To the north and east Ducrot's and Raoult's men were still holding out against overwhelming forces, but to the south the few scratch units available could not stop the Prussians from storming into the blazing houses of Elsasshausen,[5] and to the west the French line of retreat was threatened, not only by the cavalry of XI Corps's right wing, but by the Württemberg Division which the Crown Prince had sent forward through XI Corps to come in from the south on the French rear. Fortunately for MacMahon the Württembergers, as they came up, were drawn into the battle round Elsasshausen: had they made straight for Reichshoffen,

[1] *Guerre* VII: Docs. annexes 31.   [2] Bonnal, *Froeschwiller* 401–5.
[3] Ibid. 341.   [4] *Guerre* VII 124–31.   [5] *Guerre* VII 136–7.

and had the Bavarians to the north hastened their own outflanking movement through Neehwiller, MacMahon might have been sur- rounded as completely as he was to be three weeks later at Sedan.[1] As it was, the chances of escape looked slim; and MacMahon turned, as Lartigue had done two hours earlier, to that resource of despair: the cavalry.

General Bonnemain's division of cuirassiers had remained un- employed on the battlefield all day, moving about the slopes behind Froeschwiller to avoid the increasing hail of enemy shells. At three o'clock MacMahon, without giving any precise objective, ordered the first brigade to charge the Germans advancing from the south. Like Lartigue he regarded the cavalry as a shock missile—a great mass whose impact would daze the enemy for long enough to enable the infantry to reorganise and get away. But over such country, broken up with vine- yards and walls, hop-plantations and fences, no such impact could be achieved. Nor did the Prussian infantry, scattered in small groups behind cover, offer any target. The cuirassiers charged repeatedly, only to be broken up by fire from invisible assailants. It does not appear that a single French horseman got within sabre-reach of any Prussian.[2] All that their courage had done was to prove that there was no place for cavalry on a battlefield dominated by breech-loading rifles; and that lesson was to be forgotten long before 1914.

MacMahon had still kept a reserve under his hand. He had eight batteries of guns, prudently husbanded until the German infantry was within range, and Abel Douay's division, which after its ordeal at Wissembourg could not be used again unless it was absolutely necessary. The guns he deployed before Froeschwiller, but too late. The Prussian infantry were already close enough to pick off the gunners with rifle-fire, and after firing a few rounds they had to fall back into shelter again.[3] That left only Douay's men to defend Froeschwiller and hold open the Reichshoffen road for the French retreat. At about 3.30 p.m. MacMahon brought one of their regiments over the crest. The fire which struck them drove them back in disorder; but they collected themselves again and charged pell-mell down the hill past Elsasshausen towards the Niederwald. As a manœuvre it was as gallant and as hopeless as the cavalry-charge. Three times they collapsed but were brought forward again by their officers; and when eventually they fell back they left their strength on the battlefield. The bodies of the fallen lay so thickly

[1] *G.G.S.* I i 185–6.   [2] *Guerre* VII 139–47.
[3] Ibid. 148. Lehautcourt, *Guerre de 1870* III 288.

together, in their light blue jackets, that they made the ground, according to one observer, look like a field of flax.[1]

By now twenty-five batteries of German guns were deployed in an arc to the south and east of Froeschwiller, their shells pulverising the shrunken area within which the French still fought. At about 4 p.m. resistance collapsed. From north, south, and east Bavarians and Prussians stormed cheering into the village, MacMahon and his staff remaining until the last moment. Few of the occupants of the Froeschwiller Forest escaped. Of one regiment, 2,300 strong, only three officers and 250 men got away, and long after Froeschwiller had fallen the Bavarians were mercilessly searching the wood for survivors.[2] By 4.30 p.m. it was all over; and the Crown Prince rode up through the shambles of the vineyards to receive, among the burning houses of Froeschwiller, the hoarse acclamations of his men. He had not intended this battle; he had not desired it to take the course it had; but the victory was complete, and the road through the Vosges to Lorraine lay open before him.[3]

The Germans had paid heavily for their victory, with over 10,500 killed or wounded—about six-sevenths of these being from the two Prussian corps. But MacMahon had lost half his strength. His killed and wounded totalled 11,000—about the same as the Prussian—but in addition 200 officers and 9,000 men fell unwounded to the enemy.[4] The number of bodies littering the slopes below Froeschwiller was appalling. It took three days for the combined efforts of the French and German doctors to bring into the dressing-stations all the wounded who lay where they had fallen in the woods and vineyards, and a further week before the inhabitants of Froeschwiller, helped by the inhabitants of more fortunate villages around, could bury all the dead.[5]

At Reichshoffen MacMahon found the long-awaited troops of 5th Corps, coming up in time only to deploy on either side of the narrow valley at Niederbronn and hold off the pursuing Württembergers while the débris of 1st Corps was hustled away. Failly had sent only one division, and that moved with no urgency.[6] He had no cause to suppose that the matter was urgent. The summonses which MacMahon had sent him, one the previous day and one early that morning, gave no indication that a German attack was expected; certainly their contents

---

[1] C. Sarazin, *Récits sur la dernière Guerre* 53.

[2] Lehautcourt, op. cit. III 301. *Guerre* VII 163. Bonnal, *Froeschwiller* 405.

[3] Frederick III, *War Diary* 37–8. Pastor Klein, *Chronique de Froeschwiller* 211–13.   [4] *Kriegsgesch. Einzelschr.* IX 395–6. Bonnal, *Froeschwiller* 442.

[5] Blumenthal, *Journals* 89. Pastor Klein, *Chronique de Froeschwiller*, passim.

[6] It took 8 hours to cover fifteen miles. *Guerre* VII: Docs. annexes 150–7, 162.

did not overcome Failly's obstinate obsession with the defence of the defiles of the Vosges against any possible threat.[1] The sound of the guns which rumbled through the mountains all day only made him sit the more fearfully expecting attack, and a message which reached him at 3.30 p.m. from Lebœuf, that Frossard at Saarbrücken was under heavy attack, paralysed him as completely as Buridan's legendary ass. Throughout the afternoon he remained at Bitche doing nothing, while the rumble of guns came from either side; till at 6.30 p.m. came a message from a railway official: "Enemy at Niederbronn. General collapse."[2] In panic he decided to abandon Bitche and fall back through the Vosges towards Phalsbourg. No attempt was made to call in the units on the flanks: one brigade was left at Sarreguemines to join up with Bazaine's forces, and Lespart's division at Niederbronn joined those of MacMahon. Baggage, stores, ambulances, even the corps funds were left behind at Bitche to lighten the march. Without having even seen the enemy Failly's corps fell into a retreat which would have been precipitate and disorderly after a lost battle.[3]

MacMahon, who throughout the day had never lost his composure, sent Napoleon a frank report. "I have lost a battle; we have suffered great losses in men and material. The retreat is at present in progress, partly on Bitche, partly on Saverne. I shall try to reach this point where I shall reorganise the army."[4] It was an independent decision which took no account whatever of the strategic requirements of the French army as a whole. Yet there was little else he could have done. To try to rejoin Bazaine through Bitche would put all his forces into a single defile where defence would be impossible; it was certainly safer to retire south-west through Ingwiller and Saverne towards the upper Moselle, and for this he gave the order. But his forces were too scattered for any immediate control; throughout the night every pass and mountain track in the Vosges was filled with straggling groups of men and horses, wagons and guns, 1st Corps and 5th Corps and 7th Corps intermixed, groping blindly westward; an army in unmistakable defeat.

The tragedy of Spicheren and of Froeschwiller lay in the very success with which the French had fought. Their defence had been stubborn,

---

[1] Reports from civil officials were full of them. The sub-prefect at Sarreguemines wired to Failly at 1000 hrs. that the Prussians were advancing in strength on Bitche via Rohrbach. Ibid. 169.

[2] *Guerre* VII 267.

[3] Failly, *Opérations et Marches du 5ᵉ Corps* (2nd edn. Paris 1871) 16.

[4] *Guerre* VII 176–7.

their counter-attacks persistent, and they retired only because, at Spicheren, they had been manœuvred out of position or, at Froeschwiller, overwhelmingly outnumbered. The quality of the French army was shown to be all that its admirers had claimed. The *chassepot* also had lived up to expectations. At Wissembourg the garrison in the town had held up a Bavarian corps for five hours, and the two Prussian corps which stormed the Geissberg bought their victory at a cost of a thousand casualties. At Spicheren the main French front remained intact throughout the day; and at Froeschwiller, when Ducrot's and Raoult's divisions eventually collapsed after nearly eight hours of fighting, they were broken not by German infantry but by German guns.

The German infantry did not, indeed, acquit themselves particularly well. The company columns in which they advanced into action disintegrated under fire into a ragged skirmishing line which quickly went to ground, and which officers and N.C.O.s urged forward in vain. In the woods and close country which lay before the French positions the temptation to 'get lost' was sometimes overwhelming.[1] Only close order could give the infantry confidence, and close order in face of breechloading rifles was suicidal. The answer to the problem, as the Germans discovered during the course of the campaign, was for the infantry, so long as its armament was inferior to that of the enemy, to hold back and leave matters to the guns; and German field artillery proved quite capable of settling matters itself. Its range and rate of fire gave it, at the beginning of both battles, such an ascendancy that the French gunners —including the dreaded *mitrailleuses*—were silenced in a matter of minutes. Even when they could keep firing, their effectiveness was limited by the time-fuses on their shells, which were set to explode only at 1,200 and 2,800 metres. The Germans, with percussion-fuses, suffered from no such drawback. Their shells exploded on impact, though in soft ground they sometimes buried themselves so deeply that they did little harm; and thanks to the meticulous training of General von Hindersin their gunners achieved an unprecedented degree of accuracy in their fire. Wars are rarely won by superior weapons alone; but the moral ascendancy which the Germans gained by their excellent artillery was of major, if not decisive, importance in bringing them victory in the field.

Finally, as the achievements of the German gunners on 6th August heralded the advent of a new age of applied technology in war, the

[1] See the much-quoted descriptions in K. W. Meckel, *Ein Sommernachtstraum* (Berlin 1888) 48 ff.

disasters to the French cavalry emphasised that an epoch in warfare was now ended. Michel's brigade at Morsbronn and Bonnemain's division at Froeschwiller had been sacrificed to no military purpose whatever. On this battlefield, as henceforth on all others in Western Europe, the only choice before horsed cavalry lay between idleness and suicide. But the lessons which now seem so evident in retrospect the armies of Europe were to take fifty years to learn.[1] Only the very clear sighted could have seen the triple significance of 6 August 1870: the collapse of the cavalry; the transformation of the infantry; and the triumph of the gun.

[1] See Edward L. Katzenbach jr., "The Horse Cavalry in the Twentieth Century—a Study on Policy Response" in *Public Policy, a Yearbook of the Graduate School of Public Admimstration, Harvard* 1958.

CHAPTER IV

The Army of the Rhine

§1 The Invasion

THE DEFEATS of 6th August were not in themselves catastrophic. One army corps had, it was true, been overwhelmed by superior numbers after a magnificent defence, but the other had merely withdrawn successfully from an untenable position after inflicting severe punishment on the enemy. But the implications were far-reaching. There was now no question of France invading Germany and repeating the triumphs of 1806; instead there loomed ahead, for the first time, a possibility of invasion and humiliation comparable to 1814 and 1815. The allies who might have rallied to her side if the campaign had opened with a resounding success began to mutter apologies and sidle away. Gramont had already abandoned hope of Austria. Even before the French defeats, the Czar's declared intention of matching any Austrian declaration of war with one of his own had enabled Moltke to summon the three army corps standing along the Austrian frontier to join the armies in the Palatinate. The news of Wissembourg created in Vienna an uneasiness which only victory could have dispelled; and by 10th August the Austrian army had abandoned all the military preparations which it had half-heartedly begun.[1] But Gramont still had hopes of Italy, and on 7th August he suggested that she should send an army corps of her own. "It could join us via Mont Cenis," he wrote, a little pathetically; "the same route that we took in 1859 to help Italy." But the Italians had no reason to be swept up in a French defeat. They began military measures which would provide within three weeks forces adequate to meet "both domestic and foreign eventualities"; but further than that they would not go.[2] Finally the Foreign Minister of Denmark, to whom Gramont had despatched the Duc de Cadore to negotiate an alliance, and who at first said encouragingly that the moment

[1] *Origines diplomatiques* XXIX 415. Lieut.-Colonel Bouillé, letter of 10 August 1870 in *Archives Historiques*, Reconnaissances, Carton 1608.
[2] *Origines diplomatiques* XXIX 422, 427, 438.

might come when "it would be possible for the Royal Government to abandon neutrality" now frankly regretted the "unexpected events which do not allow the Royal Government to adopt any other attitude."[1] France was on her own.

In Paris the shock of defeat was all the greater because the first news which came was of a splendid victory. When the truth was known, the feelings of Press and people found expression in an explosion of rage against the régime. The crisis which faced the Government was as much political as military. Should it yield to the cry rising on all sides for the summoning of the Assembly, the arming of the people, a *levée en masse* ? Should it attempt to preserve, or rather to reimpose, imperial despotism; or should it submit to the demand for a popular dictatorship in the revolutionary tradition ? The first course had its protagonists: the unrepentant Imperialists urged the arrest of the leading deputies of the Left, and to this Ollivier was not unsympathetic.[2] But such a course would have split the Ministry, and the Empress, to her credit, would not hear of it. There was no alternative but to accept the clamour for a meeting of the Legislature, with the almost certain consequence that the Ministry would be overthrown. Even before the Corps met, a deputation of the solid men of the centre and the right demanded Ollivier's resignation and the summoning of Trochu to the Ministry of War. But Trochu had already been approached by Ollivier, and would accept office only if he were allowed to expound from the tribune all the mistakes which the Government had made since 1866. Even Trochu's supporters agreed that this was no time for such an inquest. When Ollivier met the Corps Législatif on 9th August, he announced a programme of energetic military measures. Reserve forces totalling 450,000 men were being collected. A 12th Corps was to be formed under Trochu at Châlons and a 13th under General Vinoy in Paris. A state of siege was being proclaimed in the city and Marines and naval ordnance had been summoned to help in its defence.[3] This did not save Ollivier and he did not expect that it would; but the Corps declared itself ready "to support a Cabinet capable of providing for the defence of the country". When Ollivier announced that he had resigned, and that a Cabinet would be formed, not by Trochu, but by a figure of equal military renown, General Cousin de Montauban, Comte de Palikao, the hero of the Chinese expedition of 1860, who would act

[1] Ibid. 411, 437.
[2] Welschinger, *Causes et Responsabilités* I 262.
[3] *Guerre. L'Investissement de Paris* I 85. *Mesures d'Organisation* 58–9.

not only as President of the Council but as Minister of War, they agreed to give it a reasonable chance.[1]

The Left, both its journalists and its politicians, had been transformed by the course of the war. Before the cry of *"la patrie en danger"* all the pacifism and internationalism of the past twenty years vanished overnight, and the memory revived of the great revolutionary leaders, who had saved the nation in just such an hour of peril seventy-eight years before. The régime was now attacked, not for being bellicose, but for being incompetent. Some deputies of the Opposition demanded a *levée en masse* and the creation of a committee with dictatorial powers. Jules Favre urged the arming of the citizens of Paris with a vehemence he was later to regret. Léon Gambetta declared that "in presence of a nation in arms we too must raise up a nation in arms!"[2] The new administration at once took drastic measures. All fit bachelors and childless widowers between the ages of twenty-five and thirty-five were declared liable to service. The entire class of 1870 was called to the colours. The War Loan of five hundred million francs already voted was doubled; an issue of six hundred million francs of new paper was authorised, and the compulsory acceptance of bank-notes was decreed.[3] The French people and Government faced the invaders with a spirit of self-sacrifice and resolution not inferior to that of their grandfathers in 1792, and their children in 1914.

The same could not be said of Imperial Headquarters at Metz.

On the morning of 6th August, while the first German guns were firing on the Lauter and the Saar, Napoleon's staff had been drawing up yet another plan for the long proposed offensive. This time the army was to concentrate at Bitche whence its entire force could be brought into play. The telegrams which came in throughout the day from Bazaine at St Avold did not affect Napoleon's determination to attack. Frossard seemed to be holding his own; even when he fell back that night, it was, so he thought, on the yet stronger position of Cadenbronn. The only change needed in the army's disposition was for a concentration to take place at St Avold, to which the 4th Corps was now summoned and whither the Guard was already marching; and from there the French forces, four army corps strong, could fall on the advancing enemy with at least a local superiority.[4] To the excellence of this plan no less

---

[1] De la Gorce, *Histoire du Second Empire* VII 19–26.

[2] Lehautcourt, *Guerre de 1870* IV 67. J. P. T. Bury, *Gambetta and the National Defence* (London 1936) 40.

[3] *Guerre* IX 210.   [4] *Guerre* IX 2.

an expert than Moltke bore witness: in a letter to Blumenthal of 7th August he declared it to be quite the best thing the French could do. "But", he added shrewdly, "such a vigorous decision is hardly in keeping with the attitude they have shown up till now."[1] He judged his enemy rightly: it did not take long for this project to go the way of the others which had flashed through Napoleon's mind. Early on the 7th Napoleon and Lebœuf took train at Metz for St Avold to discuss their plan with Bazaine in the light of the news from MacMahon; but before they even left the station a message arrived that the Germans had taken Forbach, St Avold itself was in danger, and Frossard's where-abouts were unknown. This piece of news destroyed the last shreds of Napoleon's resolution. Without even leaving the train he ordered the entire army to fall back on Châlons, and returned to his headquarters in a state of moral and physical collapse.[2]

Frossard had at first fallen back on Sarreguemines. There he had heard the news of MacMahon's defeat at Froeschwiller; and on this he decided, without any reference either to Lebœuf or to Bazaine, that there was no chance whatever of making a stand. The only possible course for the entire army, he considered, was to fall back on Metz; so, picking up the brigade which Failly had left at Sarreguemines, he continued his march, not, as Bazaine had expected, to join forces with 3rd Corps at Cadenbronn, but towards Puttelange eight miles to the south-west, which he reached only on the afternoon of the 7th. His men were wet, hungry, and sleepless. They had left their tents and their cooking equipment on the battlefield, and since they were moving at a divergent angle to their line of supply through St Avold no replacements could be provided. No rations could be distributed until local purchases made this possible on the 8th, and without cooking equipment even these were almost uneatable. No wonder that Frossard's morale was low. "The concentra-tion on Metz, with its large entrenched camp", he wrote to Bazaine on the 8th, "is necessary and a sure raft (*planche*) of safety. The same could be said of Langres; the three corps of Alsace must concentrate there and nowhere else. There I hope we shall get out of this mess. Otherwise", he concluded with gloomy prescience, "the Empire is lost."[3]

By the decision he took in the railway carriage in Metz station on the

[1] *M.M.K.* 204.

[2] *D.T.* I 61. *Revue de Paris* 154 (Sept-Oct. 1929) 505–7. Napoleon III, *Œuvres Posthumes*, ed. le Comte de la Chapelle. (Paris 1873) 43.

[3] Frossard, *Rapport sur les Opérations du 2ᵉ Corps* 63. *Guerre* VIII Docs. annexes 16–21, IX 79.

morning of 7th August Napoleon acknowledged defeat. Thereafter he abandoned himself to his private agonies; and this abandonment was felt in the Army, not as a personal abdication of command to others more resolute and competent, but as a decision about the conduct of the campaign. It was the nemesis of a dictatorship. There was nobody at Metz to take up the reins which Napoleon had let fall; even Bazaine, when they were put into his hands, could not believe that he was entrusted with effective control; and this vacuum of command created in the French army a defeatism which military events had done very little to justify. The decision taken at French headquarters was the panic reaction of morally defeated men seeking safety in flight.

But such a decision only produced new problems. Where was the army to go? Already it had been divided into three parts by MacMahon's decision to fall back, not on Bitche, but on the upper Moselle, where he was separated both from Douay in Belfort and from Bazaine on the Saar. Strategic considerations alone would suggest that Bazaine should fall back to the south on Langres, whence the whole army could concentrate and threaten the flank of any German advance to the west—and perhaps even smash the Third Army with a superiority as crushing as the Crown Prince had enjoyed over MacMahon.[1] But when Bazaine suggested this plan Napoleon refused to listen. It was politically impossible: it would mean the abandonment of Paris; and the preservation of Paris had, since the days of Richelieu, been the very soul of French military thought. Napoleon, it appears, had forgotten that Paris had been equipped, at great expense, with fortifications, and did not depend for its protection on an army in the field. But if Bazaine was not to fall back on MacMahon, MacMahon must fall back on Bazaine. If he did so no concentration of forces could be effected east of Châlons; for to assemble the army at Metz would be to demand of MacMahon a dangerous flank-march across the front of the advancing enemy. If Bazaine were to halt at Metz and MacMahon to fall back to Châlons, this would only confirm the complete and dangerous division of the French army into two unequal parts unable to lend each other support. Yet for the whole army to fall back on Châlons, as Ollivier pointed out in a forceful telegram on 7th August, would have political consequences no less undesirable than the abandonment of Paris.[2] For a week the French were to hesitate between these unpalatable choices. For the moment however Napoleon allowed considerations of domestic politics to dictate

[1] *Guerre* IX 8–19. Lehautcourt, *Guerre de 1870* IV 19.
[2] *Guerre* IX: Docs. annexes 4.

his strategy. He accepted Ollivier's protest, and countermanded the order for retreat on Châlons. Instead he chose Metz as his objective. It would be difficult for MacMahon to reach it, and impossible for Félix Douay's corps at Belfort, so Douay was instructed to stay where he was. Canrobert would return to Paris, and there form the nucleus of a new army.[1]

This alteration of plan—which of course created havoc in supply arrangements[2]—was put into effect with the utmost clumsiness. Lebœuf only learned of it the following day, when all orders for the retirement on Châlons had already been drafted. Bazaine's place in the chain of command was ignored, with the result that Ladmirault received contradictory orders, from Bazaine to join him at St Avold, and from Napoleon to fall back straight to Metz. A little later Lebœuf himself forgot that the Guard was *not* under Bazaine's command but part of the Imperial reserve; for when Bazaine asked whether he should send the Guard back to Metz ahead of his own weary and slow-moving troops, Lebœuf sent the petulant reply: "You are the only person giving orders—do whatever you think best under the circumstances." Thus when on 9th August his command over 2nd, 3rd and 4th Corps was confirmed by Imperial decree and General Decaen assumed command of 3rd Corps, Bazaine had good reason to doubt how far his authority really reached.[3]

By 9th August Bazaine and Lebœuf had between them got the four army corps of the French left wing into position along the French Nied, ten miles east of Metz. Although the German cavalry pursuit consisted only of a handful of reconnaissance patrols, the retreat took place in conditions of confusion bordering on panic. Constant false alarms interrupted the cooking of the irregular meals and caused frequent and unnecessary standing to arms. No proper rear-guard was organised: the cavalry regiments, brought up in the tradition of African campaigning when it was unwise for small parties to wander far afield, remained closely under the protection of the infantry, impeding its movements and moving with maddening slowness. In spite of the urging of the corps commanders, the cavalry proved incapable of providing either information about the enemy or protection to their own troops; and thus movements could be watched by German reconnaissance

---

[1] Prince Bibesco, *Belfort, Reims, Sedan. Le 7ᵉ Corps de l'Armée du Rhin* (Paris 1872) 27. *Guerre* IX: Docs. annexes 75.

[2] Gen. Soleille's Diary, ibid. 127.

[3] Ibid. 1–5, 85, 94, 137.

patrols with an insolence which infuriated the French. Finally, to bewilderment, fatigue, hunger, and fear, a sudden spell of vile weather added a new intensity of physical misery. On the evening of 8th August, when one unit arrived in its billeting area, it was allotted a large field in which the regiment was to camp. "It was like a lake, with five centimetres of water everywhere. The men, overwhelmed with fatigue, put down their haversacks, sat on them, and many just went to sleep there, soaked to the skin . . . no guard was arranged, no sentries were placed; the regiments were piled up on top of one another."[1] This last complaint, of confusion of units in bivouacs and on the march, runs through all the documents. Divisional commanders, arriving after an exhausting march to find their bivouac areas already occupied by other units, raged in vain at the incompetence of the staff. Finally there were sinister indications of a collapse of discipline. One divisional commander reported "a slight tendency to indiscipline, marauding and even pillage of the local inhabitants which nothing, it seems to me, can stop. When they arrive in a village, weary and short of fresh food, they rush on it to get wood, straw, sleeping material." To such an extent can an army disintegrate, before it has fought at all.[2]

It was under these conditions that Bazaine's men fell back by good roads on Metz. MacMahon's and Failly's army corps struggling in disorder through the Vosges, demoralised, the one by defeat, the other by the incompetence and irresolution of its commander, reached even greater depths. At Saverne, thanks to the energy of Lebœuf and the Ministry of War, MacMahon found enough supplies to remedy the immediate needs of his men; but they were in no condition to confront the enemy, whose cavalry patrols were beginning to appear on their heels, and on the evening of 7th August 1st Corps and Conseil's division of 7th Corps moved on to Sarrebourg, where they were joined by Failly. MacMahon's main object, by his own confession, was to avoid any possibility of contact with the enemy; and since the patrols of the Crown Prince seemed to be probing due west towards the Moselle, he diverted his corps still further to the south, ignoring Lebœuf's attempts to make him fall back north-westwards to Metz.[3] 10th August found his force at Lunéville, where he entrained the most exhausted of his men for Châlons. The rest marched to Bayon and on across the Meuse; and as

[1] MSS. Reminiscences of Cmdt. Tarret, qu. Lehautcourt, *Guerre de 1870* IV 53 n.
[2] *Guerre* IX: Docs. 99, 258, 265, 281.
[3] Lebrun, *Souvenirs* 291.

the rain stopped, rations increased and the memories of Froeschwiller faded, their spirits began to revive.[1]

*   *   *

Had the German force required a breathing-space of two or three months after their victories, as had been usual enough in earlier wars, the French might yet have organised forces numerous and competent enough to make any further German advance sufficiently tedious and expensive to cause grave political trouble for Bismarck and give the neutral powers a chance to intervene. But the German armies needed no breathing-space. It took them only three days to recover from their two unexpected and costly battles. To neutral observers—and to members of the army themselves—the dusty roads from the Palatinate leading into Alsace and Lorraine, choked with troops and transport, seemed to be in a state of irremediable confusion. But Moltke's mind and intentions remained clear, and through the efficiency of his staff and the discipline of the troops he was able, in spite of the grumblings of Blumenthal, the mutinous insolence of Steinmetz, and the innumerable obstacles created by the friction of war, to keep his armies moving forward in an orderly and articulated mass, sufficiently dispersed for movement and requisition, yet concentrated enough for mutual support: a set of tentacles moving forward across the plains of France, any one of which could seize and hold its victim while the others closed round to destroy him.[2]

This advance was not achieved without difficulties and shortcomings which were to be analysed in their minutest details by a host of military critics during the next forty years. The most obvious point of criticism was the laxness of the German cavalry in losing contact with both MacMahon and Frossard. The Crown Prince was nervous about sending patrols through the passes of the Vosges, while the skilful withdrawal of Frossard had enabled 2nd Corps to break contact altogether. Thus the two most vulnerable corps of the French army were undisturbed in their retreat. It was only very gradually that the German commanders were prepared to use their cavalry with the boldness which the junior officers demanded and Moltke himself urged.[3] This sluggishness on the

---

[1] *Guerre* IX: Docs. annexes 7–8, 77, 202–4, 221–2.

[2] For the problems of keeping the supply-columns moving, see *Kriegsgesch. Einzelschr. XVII: Truppenfahrzeuge, Kolonnen und Trains bei den Bewegungen der I. und der II. Deutschen Armee bis zu den Schlachten westlich Metz, passim.* Each Corps train averaged 1,400 waggons and 5,000 draught-horses. Ibid. 463.

[3] G. von Pelet-Narbonne, *Cavalry on Service* (English edn. London 1906) 86.

part of his cavalry left Moltke in ignorance about the French movements. Had MacMahon withdrawn northward to Bitche or westward to Saverne? Was Bazaine moving south towards Langres or west to Metz? Not until 9th August did he feel sufficiently certain that the French were withdrawing westward to give out any further orders, and then these could only be for a general advance in a formation flexible enough to deal with the French wherever they were to be found.

These orders demanded that the Third Army was to move forward through Saarunion and Dieuze, the Second Army continue along the main St Avold road, while the First Army was to return to its original line of advance through Saarlouis on Boulay.[1] It was no simple matter to disentangle these last two armies and keep them separate on two roads which lay so inconveniently close together. Steinmetz did not make things easier. Since 6th August his relations with Moltke and with Frederick Charles had been sulphurous. He sent back the bare minimum of information about his movements and communicated with Moltke only to complain that the Second Army was poaching on his requisition-area and using his roads.[2] Altogether the Germans were more conscious of the administrative difficulties of the invasion than of its progress. The heavy rain made life perhaps even more miserable for them than for the French. They had a higher proportion of reservists unused to campaigning conditions; they had nothing comparable to the bivouac tents which made the rainswept fields barely tolerable to their enemies, and their sickness-rate during this first fortnight in August was correspondingly high. The problem of moving so dense a mass of men on such a narrow front was immense. The nine army corps marching on Metz had only two good roads for their fighting troops and for the echelons of supply, police, administrative, and medical services lumbering along behind. Then there were the *Etappen* troops—civil administration, telegraph, postal and courier services, railway specialists, and the rear medical echelons. There was Royal Headquarters, swollen, as we have seen, not only by the Royal Household but by the skeleton administration which Bismarck and Roon had brought with them to conduct the internal administration and international relations of Prussia. There were the German princes and their attendants, the foreign military attachés, and the representatives of the Press. It had been a comparatively simple matter to get this huge mass to the German frontier. Now the

---

[1] *M.M.K.* 207.
[2] Ibid. 207, 212, 214. Frederick Charles, *Denkwürdigkeiten* II 151. Stosch, *Denkw.* 191.

problem was to move it, over inadequate roads and in face of a hostile army, into France. The Official History confesses that "the sometimes endless mob of undisciplined park waggoners made the task appear almost hopeless"[1]; while Blumenthal, his always short temper rubbed raw by the strain of getting the Third Army through the passes of the Vosges, wrote querulously in his diary, "I cannot conceal from myself the notion that General von Moltke has manœuvred us into a pretty mess, and I think he has incorrect notions of what troops are capable of, and what they can be called upon to do and still retain their organisation. This crowded order of march fatigues the troops most unnecessarily."[2] The task of supplying and moving into action a mass army of the size made possible by railway transport was almost beyond the capacity even of the Prussian General Staff. It is not to be wondered at that, under a comparable strain, the French administration collapsed completely.

In view of these difficulties of movement and administration it was all the more vital that the advancing columns should be preceded by a thick cloud of enterprising cavalry to probe the enemy positions and give ample warning of attack. Yet on the right flank Steinmetz, so far from using his two cavalry divisions for reconnaissance ahead, kept one to guard his right flank, and the other he brought over the Saar *behind* his infantry, inflicting on them marches quite as tedious and frustrating as those which the French horsemen had to endure. On the Second Army's front the initiative of the cavalry was also restrained; but here the brake was imposed by the commander of the two cavalry divisions himself, General von Rheinbaben; a man whose sluggish nature unfitted him for his post and who had to be stirred into action by repeated messages from General von Voigts-Rhetz of X Corps, under whose command he had been placed. His outposts at Faulquemont, complained Rheinbaben on 10th August, were dangerously exposed. Voigts-Rhetz sent forward a staff officer who reported that they were nothing of the sort. "Having seen the French at large today", he reported, "I cannot take this view. The enemy is greatly depressed. I think, on the contrary, that the more we stick to the enemy's heels the more prisoners we shall make. . . . I think it would not be a difficult task to cut the railway from Nancy to Metz."[3]

The accuracy of this estimate was proved by the activities of a few audacious young patrol-leaders, operating far ahead of their main body.

[1] *G.G.S.* I i 289. [2] Blumenthal, *Journals* 91.
[3] Pelet-Narbonne, *Cavalry on Service* 153, 159.

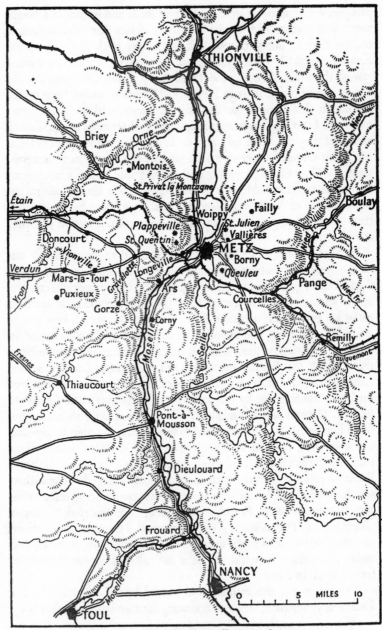

Map 5: The Moselle Valley round Metz

One, advancing on Nancy forty-five miles ahead of his infantry, cowed the astonished villages through which he passed by the simple expedient of ordering billets in each for large numbers of troops whose arrival he warned them to expect that evening. Another patrol, approaching the main French position before Metz, openly reconnoitred the enemy camp at a range of half a mile. A third rode up to the open gates of the fortress of Thionville, which were shut against them with only a few minutes to spare. On 12th August two patrols reached the Moselle, at Frouard and at Pont-à-Mousson, and crossed the river to begin demolitions on the vital railway-tracks which linked Metz with Nancy, Châlons, and Paris. French troops surprised them before much could be achieved, and at Pont-à-Mousson took the bulk of the patrol prisoner; but the moral effect of these cavalry patrols, like that of Guderian's armoured spearheads in France in 1940, was out of all proportion to their strength and their achievements. The activity of a dozen courageous and enterprising officers was enough to create that terrifying picture of "the Uhlans", ruthless, swift, and ubiquitous, which was to frighten the children of France and of Europe for forty years to come.[1]

The German armies thus soon found that there was nothing to check them except their own need of rest and replenishment. The Third Army, faced only by the retreating débris of 1st and 5th Corps, was able to advance without difficulty to the Moselle. Its cavalry occupied the acquiescent town of Nancy on 14th August, and two days later the infantry closed up to the river upstream as far as Bayon, while Army Headquarters followed comfortably to Lunéville. On the First and Second Army fronts resistance seemed more probable. A Prussian patrol discovered the main positions of Bazaine's army along the Nied on 10th August, and Frederick Charles wrote back to Moltke in some excitement. Here, he pointed out, was a chance for a second Sadowa. While Steinmetz attacked the French left flank, he could contain their centre with a weak screen and fall heavily on their right. "We must expect enormous losses", he prophesied cheerfully, "and perhaps a two-day battle."[2] But Moltke saw no need for such boldness. If the Germans delayed for two days they would have ten corps concentrated and ready for battle, and he therefore gave orders, on the evening of 11th August, for a purely defensive concentration on the German Nied between Boulay and Faulquemont. But these orders were out of date

[1] Pelet-Narbonne, op. cit. 185–225. *Guerre* IX: Docs. annexes 343–5. *Guerre: Batailles autour de Metz* I: Docs. annexes 66.
[2] Frederick Charles, *Denkwürdigkeiten* II 152–4.

before they were written: a message was already on its way to Royal Headquarters from the cavalry outposts that the French were abandoning their position on the Nied, and falling back on Metz.[1]

*   *   *

Lebœuf soon realised the disadvantages of the Nied position. Bazaine's army corps were tactically well sited, but they had no chance of holding their ground unless MacMahon and Failly could come and help, and those two commanders, deaf to Lebœuf's summons, were, as we have seen, marching their corps even further away. The Government was forwarding a stream of alarming messages about the strength and the intentions of the German army. Reports from Brussels declared that it was about to fall on the French with 450,000 men; those from Luxemburg said that the entire German army, including the Landwehr, was massed on the frontier, leaving the interior stripped bare; in Basel its strength was assessed at 550,000 men; another agent put it at 700,000. Finally, there were still disturbing reports of yet another army under General Vogel von Falkenstein, 150,000 strong, massing on the right flank to attack the French via Thionville; and it was this imaginary threat to their left flank that prompted the French on 11th August to fall back yet again to positions some miles west of the Nied, where they could be protected by the guns of the fortress itself.[2]

In Paris the Empress assessed the threat more coolly, but, in a message of 9th August, she warned Napoleon to expect an attack by 300,000 men, and advised him to summon all available troops from Châlons to meet it. So 6th Corps was directed, not on Paris as originally planned, but on Metz, by the highly vulnerable railway-line which, running first to Frouard and then down the Moselle valley, was throughout its last twenty-five miles unprotected against the activities of German cavalry patrols. In spite of constant alarms, breaches in the line and one minor battle among the trucks and station buildings of Pont-à-Mousson, most of Canrobert's infantry reached Metz safely; but before his cavalry, artillery, and ancillary service units could arrive the line had been finally cut.[3] Lebœuf had sent also for the Marines of the French navy,

[1] *M.M.K.* 215, 217.

[2] *Guerre* IX: Docs. annexes 188, 199, 297, 301. Many of the reports coming into Metz also bear evidence of a spy-mania comparable to that which affected France and the Low Countries in 1940. Englishmen and maids in the Metz hotels were particularly suspect, and suspicious signals were observed from the fortifications of Metz. Ibid. 302-3, and *Guerre: Batailles autour de Metz* I Docs. annexes 66 (Hereafter referred to as *Guerre: Metz*).

[3] *Guerre* IX: Docs. 337-40. *Procès Bazaine* 238.

but they also set out too late, and had to return to constitute part of the 12th Corps which was assembling at Châlons. Altogether by 13th August the French had assembled nearly 180,000 men at Metz and deployed most of them along a front about seven miles long.[1] The supply situation had improved: the Intendant-General reckoned that he had flour for three weeks, although the shortage of field bakeries made him dependent on Paris for bread or biscuit. Of other stocks he had a week or more in hand; and ammunition supplies were also satisfactory. In general what was lacking was not supplies but the machinery to distribute them to troops always on the march in the execution of plans which were continually changing.[2]

This uncertainty of French strategy was inevitable so long as Napoleon remained in even titular command. His immediate military advisers, Lebœuf, Lebrun, Bazaine, could tender professional advice on purely military questions; and, failing an immediate counter-attack, a concentration at Châlons or, as Bazaine suggested at one moment, on the flank of the German advance from Langres, were reasonable courses of action. But from Paris came a stream of advice based on purely political —indeed purely dynastic—considerations. It was well within the province of the Government to tender such advice; it was for Napoleon to balance military and political factors and reach a decision, as, later in the campaign, it was for William I to judge between the conflicting arguments of Bismarck and Moltke. Like William, Napoleon was at once the commander-in-chief of the army and the supreme repository of civil authority in the State. But he had devolved the exercise of the latter power on a Council of Regency under the presidency of the Empress, and it was becoming daily more evident that he was incapable of wielding the former. Officers who came into contact with him found him "much aged, much weakened, and possessing none of the bearing of the leader of an army".[3] A tactful intimate suggested to him that he was no longer physically competent to command in the Army. In Paris opinion was hardening against him, not only in the Press and the Chamber but within the Ministry itself. But could a Napoleon *not* command his armies? Could he return to Paris, alone and disgraced by two defeats, without precipitating the collapse of the régime? The Empress for one thought it impossible. "Have you considered all the consequences

[1] 178,629 men. *Guerre: Metz* I: Docs. annexes 30–2.
[2] *Guerre* IX: Docs. 239–40. *Guerre: Metz* I: Docs. annexes 8–10.
[3] Montaudun, *Souvenirs* II 85. *Papiers secrets du Second Empire* No. 12 (Brussels 1871) 34.

which would follow from your return to Paris under the shadow of two reverses?" she demanded, and he himself found this argument final.[1]

But at Metz he began to consider a compromise. He might go, not to Paris, but to Châlons and devote himself to the organisation of a new army there. Were he to do so, a commander-in-chief must be found for the Army of the Rhine. Lebœuf was a possible choice, but already Paris, remembering his unfortunate assertions about the readiness of the army, was howling for his blood.[2] The Corps Législatif demanded his resignation and on 9th August in spite of Napoleon's protests the Council of Regency voted his dismissal. It was a cruelly unjust decision—one too often passed on able and devoted soldiers who cannot, in the course of a few weeks, make up for a generation of incompetence and neglect. There was nobody of comparable ability to take his place, and from this decapitation the French army was not to recover. Lebœuf himself did not remain long unemployed; the mortal wound of General Decaen at Borny on 14th August created a vacancy in the command of 3rd Corps, which he was able to fill; but it was politically out of the question for him to be Napoleon's successor. Two other possible candidates were the two heroes of the Crimea and Italy, MacMahon and Canrobert: but MacMahon's reputation was in eclipse after Froeschwiller, and Canrobert, who had insisted in coming to Metz with his army corps in spite of the Empress's offer of the governorship of Paris, would not consider the command.[3] He was an officer who not only knew his limitations but had the strength of mind not to overstep them. He could serve his emperor as a commander of troops, in whom he inspired affection and confidence to an unparalleled degree; but into the spheres of higher strategy, and even politics, in which an army commander must inevitably move, he refused to venture. And that left, of the marshals immediately available, only François Achille Bazaine.

To judge Bazaine fairly we must forget the fate which was to overwhelm him and his army during the coming months, and the execrations heaped on his head by a generation of French historians, soldiers, and politicians, who saw in him not merely the instrument but the deliberate contriver of their national tragedy. One must also try to overlook, as did his contemporaries, his remarkably unprepossessing appearance; the tiny malevolent eyes set in a suety, undistinguished face, the heavy

[1] Lebrun, *Souvenirs* 280.
[2] *Papiers secrets du Second Empire* No. 12, 35.
[3] *D.T.* IV 273. C. Fay, *Journal d'un officier de l'armée du Rhin* (Paris 1871) 63.

bulldog jaw, the stout, flabby body sagging inelegantly on horseback in such marked contrast to the cavaliers with whom he was surrounded. The public knew him primarily as a ranker who had risen to one of the highest posts in the service by dint of good fortune and outstanding physical courage. It was partly this popularity, partly his appeal to the Left as a man of the people, and partly a purely irrational mania which made the Press and politicians of Paris, almost regardless of party, clamour during the second week of August for his appointment to the supreme command.[1] It was a clamour before which Napoleon was quite prepared to bow, and on 12th August the appointment was made. "Public opinion," he told Bazaine, "combined with that of the army, marked you out as my choice."[2] It was a choice which Bazaine was prepared to accept as an order.

But simultaneously with his appointment a check was imposed on Bazaine's powers as commander-in-chief. The first essential for any commander is a good chief of staff; but whereas Bazaine naturally wanted one whom he knew and could work with, Napoleon equally naturally wanted him to have an officer who was *au fait* with the general situation. Bazaine's own selections were brushed aside, and the appointment was given to Lebœuf's assistant, General Jarras—who was, again naturally, very unwilling under the circumstances to accept it.[3] Bazaine, like so many senior commanders since his namesake Achilles, was capable of temperamental sulks more in place in an opera house than on a battlefield. He ignored Jarras and continued to ignore him. He sent his orders direct to subordinates or at best instructed Jarras to work out the minor administrative details of plans of whose purport he knew nothing.[4] It is not surprising that the movement and supply arrangements of the forces tightly concentrated around Metz fell into confusion; and the confusion was increased by uncertainty whether Bazaine was really in command at all. He himself seems to have accepted his new appointment as a formality: Napoleon, so long as he was with the army, remained the real commander-in-chief. Headquarters at Metz did not volunteer any of the information about enemy movements, about reserves, about the general French military situation or about supplies, which would have been necessary for the formulation of any coherent plan, and it did not occur either to Bazaine or to Jarras to demand it.[5] So little attempt did Bazaine make to take over effective command

---

[1] *D.T.* IV 273. *Procès Bazaine* 221.   [2] Bazaine, *Épisodes* 49.
[3] Lebrun, *Souvenirs* 289. Jarras, *Souvenirs* 79.   [4] Jarras, op. cit. 81.
[5] *Procès Bazaine* 159, 215.

that he did not even move into Metz to be near Jarras and his staff. Thus while Bazaine remained with 3rd Corps in the front-line village of Borny, straightening bivouac-lines, siting gun-positions and sending well-intentioned but belated instructions to his corps commanders about the detailed conduct of operations,[1] Napoleon remained in Metz and played no smaller part than before in the formulation of plans. The only visible difference was that he no longer gave orders; he merely expressed desires but these, as Bazaine justifiably complained, were simply the "same idea in different words".[2] It is not easy to abdicate from a dictatorship after nearly twenty years.

On his appointment Napoleon wrote to Bazaine: "The more I think about the position of the army, the more critical I find it; for if a sector were driven in and we had to fall back in disorder, the forts would not prevent the most overwhelming confusion."[3] As an appreciation it was correct, if somewhat unhelpful, and it showed how Napoleon's mind was moving. The impossibility of concentrating 1st and 5th Corps with the others and the broad front on which the Germans were advancing made it ever more likely that if the army remained at Metz it would be outflanked and annihilated. The possibility of making a counter-stroke, the unwillingness to abandon a base into which men and stores had been piled in such profusion—and British readers who remember Tobruk in 1942 may well sympathise—sharply divided opinion at Headquarters and kept the French paralysed at Metz until it was too late to escape.[4] As early as 8th August Napoleon had ordered the construction of enough pontoon bridges to get the army rapidly over the Moselle and its tributary the Seille; but not until 13th August, when German cavalry was reported to be in Pont-à-Mousson and nearing Thionville, did Napoleon make up his mind to leave. Then he wrote to Bazaine urging him to withdraw at once; there was not a moment to lose.[5]

Inert and timorous as a commander Bazaine may have been, but he had been a general for long enough to realise that an army 180,000 strong crowded into a front of twelve miles, with its outposts already in contact with the enemy, cannot retreat at a moment's notice over a river provided with a very limited number of crossings. The situation was made worse by one of those pieces of ill-fortune which beset all armies

[1] *Guerre: Metz* I: Docs. annexes 3–5.
[2] Bazaine, *Épisodes* 67. D'Andlau, *Metz, Campagne et Négociations* 54.
[3] *Guerre* IX 309.   [4] Lebrun, *Souvenirs* 291–8.
[5] *Guerre: Metz* I: Docs. annexes 14.

and ruin inefficient ones. The heavy rains had caused a rise in the river the previous evening which had swept away or damaged every one of the bridges erected by the engineers during the last four days. None could be repaired before noon on the 14th and then only four would be available to supplement the three permanent crossings.[1] This would compress the army into a bottleneck at best three miles wide, and only the most exact staff-work could have got it through without confusion. From the bewildered and ill-informed Jarras such organisation was too much to expect; and Bazaine entrusted him only with the movement of 6th Corps, the army artillery, the engineers and the *Intendance*—services which for the most part were already over the river. To the rest of the army Bazaine gave orders direct[2]; and in the confusion one bridge— that at Longeville-les-Metz—was completely overlooked. The bottle-neck was thus reduced to a mile and a half and the number of bridges to six. Yet even these slender resources could not be fully exploited: the temporary bridges had to be approached through soaking water-meadows impassable to vehicles, so only infantry could safely make use of them. Horses and wagons had to go through the narrow winding streets of Metz to get at the two permanent bridges beyond the town. It was a problem which might well have baffled a better staff than the French.[3]

Bazaine was far from blind to these drawbacks. He dutifully gave warning orders for a withdrawal to take place either on the night of the 13th or the morning of the 14th, depending on when the bridges were ready; but in private he expressed violent opposition to the idea of such a retreat, and informed Napoleon that the Germans were watching them so closely that, rather than be caught while crossing the river, it might be better to stand his ground or even take the offensive.[4] In reply Napoleon forwarded a message from the Empress to the effect that not only was the Crown Prince by-passing Metz to the south, but Frederick Charles was outflanking to the north to link up with him at Verdun. There was no time to be lost; if an attack *had* to be launched, he insisted, it must not interfere with the retreat.[5]

[1] *Guerre: Metz* I 32–42.
[2] Jarras, *Souvenirs* 82.
[3] *Guerre: Metz* I: Docs. annexes 19–25.
[4] *Guerre: Metz* I: Docs. annexes 17. *Procès Bazaine* 255. Bazaine later asserted that he planned to drive the Germans back over the Nied and then take up a position on the plateau of l'Haye, west of Nancy, where he could concentrate the entire army with Toul as a base. *D.T.* IV 184. See also Lebrun, *Souvenirs* 291–8.
[5] *Guerre: Metz* I: Docs. annexes 18.

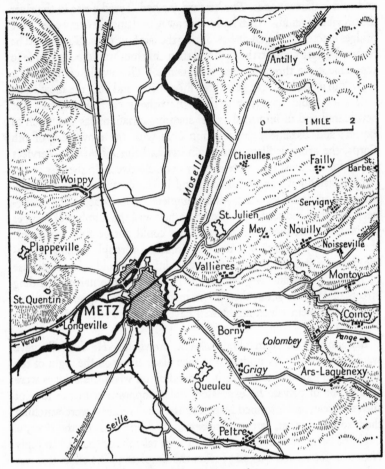

Map 6: The Fortress of Metz

On 14th August therefore Bazaine began to withdraw. A few hours
sufficed to show how badly the movement had been planned. The men
were ready to move at 4.30 a.m. Before the infantry could start the
baggage trains had to be got clear; but as these had all to pass through the
streets of Metz, a blockage was quickly built up in the town which made
further passage almost impossible. The two cavalry divisions which
should have led the way could not leave until the afternoon; and by the
time the infantry began to move in six vast converging columns, after
sweltering for hours in their full equipment under the blazing sun,

they found all approaches to the bridges jammed with horses and transport which should have been cleared hours before. Then at 4 p.m.,
when, nearly twelve hours after they had first stood to, the troops were at
last beginning to cross the river, there came from the positions they had
just abandoned the sudden roar of cannon. The Prussians had opened
fire.[1]

* * *

The news that the French had abandoned the Nied and fallen back
under the guns of Metz reached Moltke during the night of 11th–12th
August, and brought his hesitations to an end. Since the French were
evidently not planning an offensive he himself could pass to the attack.
On 12th August he issued orders, not for the battle of encirclement
urged by Frederick Charles, but for an advance on a wide front which
embraced the Third as well as the First and Second Armies. The
German forces were to fan out like a line of beaters and seize crossings
over the Moselle on a front more than fifty miles broad stretching from
the Crown Prince's left wing at Bayon to Steinmetz's right wing well
below Metz.[2] A more striking contrast with the French army, huddled
together in a tight group round the fortress, is difficult to imagine.
But once again Moltke's plans were modified in execution. Frederick
Charles, ordered to seize crossings over the Moselle at Pont-à-Mousson
and Dieulouard, did so on 13th August and pushed his ever bolder
cavalry patrols over the river as far as the gates of the fortress of Toul;
but the cavalry in the First Army, receiving no similar impetus from
their army headquarters, made no attempt to get across the river below
Metz.[3] After his reprimand at Spicheren, Steinmetz was conducting his
army with a defiant timidity. On 13th August, while the Second
Army flared out boldly towards the Moselle on either side of Pont-à-
Mousson, the First Army approached Metz with a circumspection very
different from its insouciant attack on the Spicheren Heights. In spite
of Moltke's orders[4] it made no attempt to by-pass the fortress with
cavalry to the north. Thus the threat to the French left flank, which had
so powerfully affected the minds of the French commanders, never
existed at all.

---

[1] *Guerre: Metz* I 82: Docs. annexes 130, 154, 252.
[2] *M.M.K.* 219.
[3] Pelet Narbonne 241–9, 265, 286. Frederick Charles, *Denkwürdigkeiten* II
158–9.
[4] *M.M.K.* 222.

The result for German strategy was far-reaching. The advancing armies, instead of moving forward in line, developed a formation comparable, on a large scale, to the famous Frederican "oblique order", with the left wing (Frederick Charles), boldly advanced, the right wing (Steinmetz), cautiously refused. This deployment has been hailed as an example of Moltke's strategic genius: wrongly. His genius lay in realising the advantages which circumstances had placed in his hands, and, instead of readjusting the line of his armies to fit in with a pre-arranged pattern, adjusting himself to the new situation and turning it to his advantage with a rapidity and smoothness comparable only to that shown by Bismarck in making use of circumstances and emergencies in the political sphere. In retrospect the imprisonment of Bazaine's army in Metz and the destruction of MacMahon's force at Sedan, both flowing so naturally from this "oblique order", seem to the strategist as much the result of careful planning as the unification of the German Empire seems to the politician. In fact Moltke, like Bismarck, achieved his ends by brilliant opportunism. Even the errors of a Steinmetz could be turned to effect.

The discovery on 13th August that the French were still on the right bank of the Moselle caused the Prussians some surprise. It did not occur to Moltke that the presence of the enemy could be explained by the indecision of his leaders and the inefficiency of his staff work; and Moltke began to wonder whether the French could be meditating an offensive after all. If they were, it would be foolish for Frederick Charles to go marching blithely across the Moselle while Steinmetz alone sustained the attack. On the evening of the 13th therefore Moltke modified his orders. The Second Army was now to pause in its advance, and send up its two northernmost corps III (Constantin von Alvensleben) and IX (von Manstein) to a position south of Metz from which they would be able if necessary to support Steinmetz by falling on the French flank.[1] Steinmetz was given no definite instructions, and in his new chastened mood he took this, and passed it on, as an order to his army to stay where it was.[2] On 14th August therefore the infantry of the First Army rested in their billets on the French Nied. But cavalry patrols went out as usual to inspect the French positions; and quickly their reports came back that the French camps had been raised, that columns were jamming the bridges across the Moselle and that the roads beyond the river were packed with transport, sending up huge clouds of dust. The French were getting away.

[1] *M.M.K.* 222.   [2] *G.G.S.* I i 306.

This was a situation which called for quick decision from the commanders on the spot. There were two corps of the First Army immediately concerned—I Corps under General von Manteuffel, which had joined the army too late to take part in the battle of Spicheren and was now leading the advance down the main Saarbrücken–Metz road; and VII Corps, under General von Zastrow, on the road which leads to Metz from Sarrebourg and the south-east. Manteuffel at once prepared for battle and asked Steinmetz's permission to advance. It was refused. Steinmetz would not risk royal wrath a second time for the same offence; so Manteuffel remained under arms and awaited events. But Zastrow seemed fated to be run away with by his subordinates. His leading brigade was commanded by the decisive and enterprising Major-General von der Goltz, an officer whose natural independence of mind had been increased by service with the General Staff, and for him the sight of the French slipping away without a shot being fired was altogether too much. Without consulting anybody he took the decision to attack; and Manteuffel, once he heard the guns opening up on his left, did not hesitate to join in. Once again the First Army had precipitated a battle, but this time in defiance of the wishes of its unfortunate commander.[1]

From their positions the Germans could command a magnificent view of the French. Beyond the Moselle to the west there rose a steep bluff, crowned by the outlying forts of Plappeville and St Quentin and stretching north and south in a line of tree-covered heights as far as the eye could reach. At its foot lay the city of Metz, a compact group of houses dwarfed by the elegant spire of its cathedral; a fortress battered through ten centuries by the invaders to whom it barred the path into the heart of France from the Palatinate and the Middle Rhine. The old fortifications had been replanned, and outlying forts were designed to keep a besieging army beyond bombardment range; but in 1870 these forts—Queuleu to the south, St Julien to the north, Plappeville and St Quentin to the west—were still incomplete. To the east the land rose from the Moselle in a huge saucer of gently undulating fields, overlooked for miles by the heights west of the river, and among these fields, some four miles east of the town, the French had taken up their positions. Their flanks had rested on the forts of Queuleu and St Julien, before which 2nd Corps and 4th Corps respectively were deployed; and 3rd Corps between them had its front covered by the

[1] Cardinal von Widdern, *Kritische Tage* I i: *Die I Armee bei Colombey-Nouilly* 57–9.

Vallières brook which flowed north for two miles from Ars-Laquenexy along a deep ravine before turning west and running through a wider valley into the Meuse just north of Metz. To the east of this ravine there branched out three small valleys, and along the two spurs which divided them ran the roads from Saarlouis and Saarbrücken along which Manteuffel was advancing. On the high ground to the south ran a smaller road from the French Nied at Pange, crossing the Vallières brook at the farm of Colombey; and it was on this road and the main Sarrebourg road through Ars-Laquenexy that there came the columns of VII Corps headed by von der Goltz.

At the moment when Goltz took his decision to attack, Frossard and Ladmirault had already withdrawn from their positions, and now 3rd Corps was beginning to thin out. But only the French outposts in the Vallières ravine gave ground before the German attack; after the first surprise the men of 3rd Corps stood firm. Their fire dominated the valley, and French artillery returned to the battlefield to make any further Prussian advance impossible. Within an hour Goltz's entire force was pinned down unable to move in the Vallières ravine; and I Corps, coming into action on the right, could do no better. Manteuffel was able to get both his divisions forward, the first through the Montoy valley and the second through Nouilly, but all further advance here also was checked by French rifle- and gunfire. By 5 p.m. the pattern of Spicheren had repeated itself. The German advance guard, attacking with indiscreet boldness, was pinned down by forces superior not only in numbers but in positions and fire, and a determined counter-attack might have crushed it before any help was at hand.[1]

But Bazaine had no intention of counter-attacking. The Emperor's adjurations to hurry were ringing in his head, and he was furious at this untimely battle. "I gave orders that no one should accept battle today," he stormed, "I absolutely forbid anyone to advance a yard!"[2] His adversary, Steinmetz, was equally furious when he heard of the battle: he forbade VIII Corps commander to answer any appeals for help and peremptorily ordered Zastrow and Manteuffel to break off the action.[3] But they were in no position to obey. Manteuffel was fully committed, and Zastrow had already sent up the rest of his corps to the support of von der Goltz. Moreover IX Corps of the Second Army, advancing

[1] *Guerre: Metz* I: Docs. annexes 178–90, 194–204, 215–17. *G.G.S.* I i 308–12.
[2] General Zurlinden, *La Guerre de 1870–71* (Paris 1904) 125. *Trois mois à l'Armée de Metz*, par un officier de génie 75.
[3] Cardinal von Widdern, *Kritische Tage* I i 64–5.

on Steinmetz's left towards Peltre, had taken the gunfire to indicate just that attack on the First Army which it was standing by to prevent, and moving towards Metz as fast as it could came up on the left flank of the combatants opposite Grigy. By 6 p.m. the engagement was too general to be stopped by anything short of a victory or the coming of night.

The battle was inconclusive and unsatisfactory. The Prussians could only throw in reinforcements as they came up at weak points in the line without attempt at a plan, VII Corps trying to heave itself out of the ravine on to the plateau beyond, I Corps pressing down the Vallières valley and surging up the slopes to the north of it towards the village of Mey. Between the two corps commanders there seems to have been no liaison. The French corps also fought in complete independence; but Bazaine rode about the battlefield under fire with the phlegmatic and infectious calm for which he was famous, receiving, and ignoring, a violent blow on the shoulder from a fragment of Prussian shell. The French 2nd Corps on the right wing did not fully get back into action, and here, with the Prussian advance masked by the heavy woods around Ars-Laquenexy, the position might have been dangerous; but the Prussians developed their attack against Grigy only as darkness was falling, and the great guns of Fort Queuleu helped to hold them in respect. In the centre the Westphalians of VII Corps did not show quite the careless courage that had characterised them at Spicheren; troops in action for the second time seldom do; and General Castagny's division, deployed in thick lines in the fields before Borny, easily held them in check. The fight was fiercest on the French left flank, on the heights north of the Vallières valley. Here Ladmirault's Corps returned just in time to occupy the village of Mey and the surrounding slopes, threatening Manteuffel's right flank and throwing back all Prussian attempts to debouch from the valley. Manteuffel's troops attacked with all the zest of enthusiasts fresh in action. Time after time they established themselves in the little wood east of Mey, and had to be driven back by the furious counter-attacks at which the French troops excelled and which no German troops were able to withstand, and the struggle for the possession of the wood went on well into the night.[1]

At 8 p.m. Steinmetz reached the battlefield and ordered Manteuffel and Zastrow back to the Nied. This was a serious thing to do. So long as the Prussian troops could bivouac in the positions they had so laboriously

[1] *G.G.S.* I i 317–30. *Guerre: Metz* I: Docs. annexes 223–31, 286, 289, 303. L. Patry, *La Guerre telle qu'elle est* (Paris 1907) 71–7.

gained, they could claim a victory—as, with their regimental bands playing *Heil dir im Siegerkranz* about the watch-fires in the Vallières ravine, they were already doing. To march tamely back to the Nied would be to admit complete repulse. Zastrow simply ignored the order; Manteuffel refused to receive it except from Steinmetz in person, and then did not carry it out until next day. To complete Steinmetz's discomfiture, Royal Headquarters made it clear that they approved of the action of his subordinates. The King ordered the troops to remain where they were, and next day came up in person to congratulate von der Goltz. Steinmetz might well have wondered why disobedience to his orders should receive such acclamation when his own initiative before Spicheren had been rewarded with abuse.[1]

Next morning, 15th August, it was far from clear what the battle of Borny had achieved. The Prussians had lost, in killed and wounded, nearly 5,000 officers and men; the French about 3,500—including General Decaen, the new commander of 3rd Corps, who later died of his wounds.[2] Both claimed a victory, the Prussians who had secured a number of positions and the French who had successfully defended all the most vital of them. The real outcome of the battle was far more prosaic and of greater importance than the defence or conquest of territory. Bazaine had lost twelve vital hours in making his escape from Metz.[3]

§ 2 Vionville–Mars-la-Tour

The French saw no cause for dissatisfaction in their work on the 14th August. For the first time they had fought as an army, and fought apparently with success. The bewildering retreat had ceased; the Prussians had been checked; and Bazaine had shown all the *sang-froid* and courage on the battlefield that the French looked for in their commander-in-chief. His appointment seemed to be causing that turn of the tide so universally expected. The imperial retinue welcomed him that night with enthusiasm, and Napoleon greeted him with the words, "You have broken the spell."[4] That the battle, however tactically advantageous,

[1] Cardinal von Widdern, *Kritische Tage* I i 104. Verdy du Vernois, *With the Royal Headquarters* 65. Bronsart, *Kriegstagebuch* 38.

[2] *Kriegsgeschichtliche Einzelschriften* XI 645–6.

[3] See the comments by the Russian General von Woyde, in his *Causes des Succès et des Revers dans la Guerre de 1870* (French edn. Paris 1900) I 243–5.

[4] D'Andlau, *Metz, Campagne et Négociations* 60–3. Jarras, *Souvenirs* 131.

was strategically a disaster, and that the delay it imposed virtually destroyed all hope of a successful withdrawal on the Meuse, seems to have occurred to no one. From corps commanders downwards, no officer in the French army had, or was supposed to have, any insight into the intentions of the commander-in-chief. The French tradition, that military formations were so many passive instruments in the hands of their commander, remained intact; and as the French army was to know nothing of the reasons which had set it marching and countermarching around the frontier, so it knew nothing of the purpose of the battle which had just been fought. It knew only that it had acquitted itself honourably, and further than that there was no need to look.

It was in this tradition that Bazaine had been brought up, and this does something to explain his inadequacies. The eyes of the army, of the country, and of the Emperor himself were now fixed on him in expectation of the next move; but he still could not believe that it was for him to take any decision, that he and not the Emperor was in effective command. It was agreed the same evening that the march on Verdun should continue, but Bazaine went to bed without doing anything about it. He was tired, he said later; he had been on horseback for several days, and his wound was hurting him.[1] Not until 10 a.m. on 15th August did orders go out to the army for a continuation of the retreat, and then they showed to the full Bazaine's complete incapacity for higher command.

The orders were these. Laveaucoupet's division of 2nd Corps, which had borne the brunt of the fighting at Spicheren, would remain to garrison the fortress. On the left flank 2nd and 6th Corps were to follow the Verdun road to Mars-la-Tour and Rezonville respectively; on the right flank 4th and 3rd Corps were to move on Doncourt and Verneville. The Guard was to bring up the rear at Gravelotte, and the two cavalry divisions were to cover the flanks. Thus the entire French army, over 160,000 men strong[2] with all its guns, its pontoon bridges, its horses and its four thousand supply-wagons, swollen by the vehicles of the civilians escaping from Metz, was directed in one huge, ill-policed convoy along a single route—the steep road which wound up the escarpment above the Moselle by the Rozerieulles heights to the plateau of Gravelotte.[3] Only at Gravelotte did the road divide in two. The

---

[1] *Procès Bazaine* 159–63.
[2] 178,688 men, less one division of 2nd Corps left as a garrison in Metz. *Procès Bazaine* 205.
[3] *D.T.* IV 183–4. Jarras, *Souvenirs* 95.

town of Metz itself was a grave enough obstacle to the passage of the army, as the weary French troops found when they piled up for hours in its narrow streets during the night after the battle. To impose a further delay by forcing the whole mass through so narrow a funnel was to make quite certain that the widely spread and swiftly moving Germans would reach the Meuse long before the French. Bazaine said later that it was the business of his staff to allot lines of march, as indeed it was. But he did not tell his staff anything about it. The orders went direct to the corps commanders, and Jarras, who had still hardly seen Bazaine, learned about the movement only after it had begun. Canrobert's laconic comment on all this is perhaps the most accurate as well as the most kindly. "Not everyone can command an army a hundred and forty thousand strong," he said later; "it is difficult to manage when one isn't used to it."[1]

2nd Corps, in the lead, might easily have reached Mars-la-Tour on the 15th, but through a confusion of orders it stopped at Rezonville, further delaying 6th Corps and the Guard, whose camps at Longeville had already been shelled by German horse-artillery across the Moselle. Lebœuf, who had assumed command of 3rd Corps the previous night, was able to get only his leading elements to Verneville and that by striking across country; while Ladmirault decided that the congestion of the roads and the weariness of his troops made it useless to think of moving 4th Corps at all. Could he not, he asked Bazaine, use the road which ran north-west through Woippy and Briey? Bazaine refused. Civil authorities were sending in reports of German cavalry on the Moselle between Metz and Thionville, and Bazaine's instinct was to draw his forces ever closer.[2]

But the threat from the south was considerably less hypothetical than that from the north. German cavalry was already well established on the left bank of the Moselle to the south of the French army, curling round towards the Metz–Verdun road. General Forton's cavalry division was supposed to be covering this flank, and it was gingerly feeling its way towards Mars-la-Tour, on the morning of 15th August,

[1] *Procès Bazaine* 161–3. *D.T.* IV 274. The incompetent cartographical service of the French army has also much to answer for. "Pour la Lorraine, on ne pouvait trouver que quelques exemplaires fort rares de la carte dite d'état-major, qui ne donnait pas les modifications survenues dans les configurations du pays depuis son achèvement, qui ne portait pas le tracé des routes recémment ouvertes, et qui représentait encore comme sentiers impraticables des chemins devenus carrossables." Du Barail, *Souvenirs* III 174.

[2] *Procès Bazaine* 231, 294. *Guerre: Metz* II 23–36, and Docs. annexes 42. Jarras, *Souvenirs* 92.

when shells began to fall among its squadrons from German horse batteries established on the hills to the south, round Puxieux.[1] Forton halted irresolutely near Mars-la-Tour, and other German squadrons galloped up to the sound of the guns. By 11 a.m. the German cavalry brigadier, von Redern, felt strong enough to push northward and bar the main Verdun road; but his divisional commander, General von Rhein-baben, of whose dilatory unimaginativeness the Germans had already had cause to complain, arrived in time to forbid so bold a move. So von Redern's squadrons stayed where they were, observing the French cavalry; and Forton, finding himself separated from the infantry by several uncomfortable miles, fell back on Vionville.[2] As usual the French made no attempt to pierce the enemy's cavalry screen and learn the true disposition of his forces; but it was the Germans who missed the greater opportunity on 15th August. Another and bolder commander, General Constantin von Alvensleben, was to seize it next day, and repair von Rheinbaben's faults.

Bazaine later complained that the total absence of information from civil authorities about the German advance on his left misled him as to the extent of the threat[3]; but that a threat did exist was made clear by the reports which 1st and 6th Corps headquarters sent back to him that evening. Yet these stirred him to no sort of action: his orders on the evening of the 15th merely requested his corps commanders to be ready to move next morning and to notify him of their positions so that his orders—"if I have any to give you"—should reach them with the least possible delay.[4] In reply to this order Ladmirault pointed out the virtual impossibility of moving his corps, suggesting bluntly that it would be better to await a German attack where they stood rather than attempt to advance in such hugger-mugger order; and to this Bazaine, at 5.15 a.m. on 16th August, weakly agreed. The move was postponed until that afternoon; and the men of 2nd and 6th Corps, having made all the preparations to start, found themselves inexplicably waiting for an order to move which never came[5].

This postponement, which was to lead directly to the investment of Bazaine's army in Metz, was to be explained by contemporaries and by certain historians as the first step in a subtle and treasonable plan. Those who explain Bazaine's incompetence in terms of treachery seize

[1] *G.G.S.* I i 344–6. Pelet-Narbonne, *Cavalry on Service* 306.
[2] Farinet, *L'Agonie d'une Armée* (Paris 1914) 104. *Guerre: Metz* II: Docs. annexes 74.
[3] Bazaine, *Épisodes* 81.　　　　[4] *Guerre: Metz* II: Docs. annexes 40.
[5] *D.T.* IV 274–5. Bazaine, op. cit. 80. *Guerre: Metz* II 135.

on the fact that this postponement of the army's move occurred immediately after Napoleon III at last left the army to make his way to Châlons, and therefore see in it a move on Bazaine's part to make his army independent of any command save his own. Bazaine's incapacity, his preference for postponing any sort of decision, needs no such tortuous explanation as this; but there can be no doubt that Bazaine was heartily glad to be rid of the Emperor, with his depressing fatalism, his half-hearted attempts at intervention, and the great convoy of the Imperial Household which, adding to the congestion of the single road, was earning the hatred of the troops as well as their contempt.[1] They filed past the haggard old man who sat outside the inn at Point du Jour in a silence which contrasted grimly with the enthusiasm which had greeted the Emperor on his arrival at Metz a fortnight before. At dawn on the 16th he left his army. To Bazaine, when he came to say good-bye, the Emperor urged the need to get the army as quickly as possible to Verdun, where it would find supplies. An escort of dragoons and chasseurs conducted him to Verdun, through country where Uhlan patrols were already at large; and there he took train to Châlons. Behind him the guns had already begun to fire in the battle of Vionville–Mars-la-Tour.[2]

*　　*　　*

The Germans were no more backward than the French in claiming a victory on 14th August. Next morning the French had abandoned their positions, leaving all the débris of a battlefield and of an army in retreat, and clouds of dust from the hills behind Metz showed that they were pressing their retreat yet further.[3] Moltke himself was cautious. The possibility of a strong counter-attack on the First Army was not to be ruled out, and so long as it existed he was unwilling for the main body of the Second Army, which was standing along the Moselle from Frouard to Metz and clamouring for the order to advance, to press any further to the west.[4] Only the cavalry was allowed forward to gain further information and to harass any retreat along the Verdun road. But by midday on the 15th Moltke felt happier. He removed the checks on the movement of the Second Army, and X Corps (Voigts-Rhetz) and III Corps (Constantin von Alvensleben) pressed forward over the river towards Thiaucourt and Gorze almost before orders arrived.

[1] D'Andlau, *Metz, Campagne et Négociations* 66. *Procès Bazaine* 255.
[2] *Guerre: Metz* II: Docs. annexes 19, 23, 128, 471–6, 493. Lebrun, *Souvenirs* 309.
[3] Verdy du Vernois, *With the Royal Headquarters* 69.
[4] Frederick Charles, *Denkwürdigkeiten* II 168–9.

Then, as reports came in confirming the French retreat, Moltke began to see his way more clearly, and to plan his movements once again with a view to bringing about a decisive and inescapable battle. Cheated of his hopes of a decision on the Saar, he had for a week been simply advancing his army in a formation prepared for any opportunity. Now a decision seemed again to lie in his power. At 6.30 p.m. he ordered Frederick Charles to launch a vigorous offensive towards Verdun, via Fresnes and Étain, to catch the French army on the road between Verdun and Metz. Steinmetz, leaving an army corps on the right bank of the Moselle at Courcelles to observe Metz, was to take the rest of the First Army across the river to be in a position to come to the help of his colleagues.[1] Bazaine would thus be forced to fight for his communications, or find himself pushed away from Paris. Out of the confused list of possibilities, the strategy of the campaign was at last becoming clear.

The objective which Moltke had given Frederick Charles was very vague, but knowing no more of the enemy army than that it was somewhere between Metz and Verdun, he could hardly have been more precise. Unfortunately Frederick Charles was no better informed. Redern's cavalry patrols, boldly handled as they were, could send back no exact information about enemy positions. They had found Forton's cavalry at Vionville, but whether it was there as the advance-, flank-, or rearguard of the main force no one could tell. Certainly the opinion was strongly held at Second Army headquarters that Bazaine had made good his escape from Metz and that he was approaching the Meuse, if he had not already reached it. In consequence Frederick Charles gave orders that evening, not for an offensive towards the north such as Moltke had ordered, but for a continuation of the pursuit westward towards the Meuse by all his units save those of the extreme right wing. Only III Corps, with IX Corps far in its wake, was to move northwards towards the position of the French army round Vionville: X Corps, the next unit on its left, was directed north-west on Fresnes-en-Woëvre, while XII, IV Corps and the Guard continued westward; marching away from their enemy.[2]

The mistake was natural enough.[3] By Prussian standards the French

[1] *M.M.K.* 228.

[2] Frederick Charles, *Denkwürdigkeiten* II 172. *M.M.K.* 231–2.

[3] It was some time before the German official historians admitted that it had been made. For a summary of the controversy see F. Hönig, *Darstellung der Strategie für die Schlacht von Vionville–Mars-la-Tour* (Berlin 1899), and authorities there quoted; also General Palat, *Le rôle du X Corps au 16 Août 1870* (Paris 1879) 13.

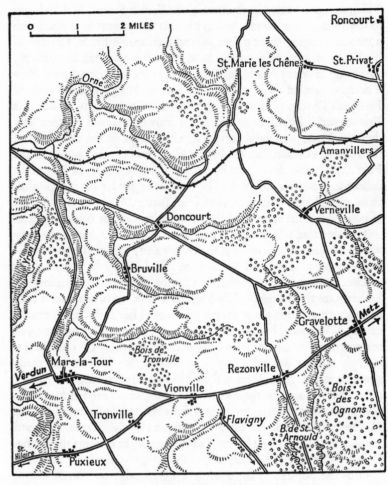

Map 7: Vionville–Mars-la-Tour

army, making full use of all available roads, should certainly have reached the Meuse by the 16th, and Frederick Charles's error in directing his army too far to the west and thus outshooting Bazaine was more pardonable than it would have been had he directed it too far to the east and missed him altogether. It remained possible, after the battle on the 16th, for the left wing of the Second Army to sweep round and complete Moltke's strategy of encirclement even more thoroughly than he had intended. None the less the error might have had grave consequences. On the 16th, the two right-flank corps, III and X, had to sustain an unsupported battle with the entire French army. Had Bazaine been more enterprising, the isolated German units might have been crushed before help could reach them, and the French, having gained one victory to set against their defeat at Spicheren, could have turned either on Steinmetz or on the remains of the Second Army and destroyed them also in detail. Such an achievement did not lie within the capacity of Bazaine; but not even Bazaine could fail, on 16th August, to gain a second tactical defensive victory to set beside that at Borny. The road to his ultimate disaster was cruelly paved with apparent success.

This then was the situation on 16th August, when Napoleon left his army for Châlons. Forton's cavalry division lay in camp at Vionville. A few miles further to the east were 2nd and 6th Corps at Rezonville, in camps which lay respectively to the north and the south of the main Verdun road. The Guard was in the rear at Gravelotte; Lebœuf had assembled most of 3rd Corps further north at Verneville, with two cavalry divisions watching out west and north; while Ladmirault, still in Metz, was trying to move up 4th Corps by every available road. Of the German troops, the First Army, and with it IX Corps, still lay east of the Moselle; half the Second Army lay south of Pont-à-Mousson; and in the immediate neighbourhood of the French there was only Rheinbaben's cavalry division at Puxieux threatening their advance, about half of Voigts-Rhetz's X Corps to the south-west at Thiaucourt, and Alvensleben's III Corps which, having crossed the Moselle at Corny, was now pressing into the valleys which led through the steep, vine-clad hills above the river and up through the village of Gorze to the broad plateau between Vionville and Gravelotte, on which the French army still lay encamped.

Bazaine's postponement of the march led to a general relaxation in the French camps. The infantry re-erected their tents. The cavalry unsaddled and watered their horses. The few desultory patrols which went out reported only isolated enemy horsemen in the neighbourhood. The officers of Forton's division did become aware of considerable troop-movements to their west at about 8 a.m.; but somebody suggested that this was 4th Corps coming up, and this fantastic explanation was generally accepted. Nearly an hour passed before the dark masses on the horizon came near enough to be identified as Germans, and then, before anything could be done, shells were already beginning to burst round Vionville. The surprise was complete.[1]

[1] *Guerre: Metz* II: Docs. annexes 142, 156, 171–2.

The Germans in question were Rheinbaben's 5th Cavalry Division, and it had taken all Voigts-Rhetz's authority to persuade him to move at all. There is at least this to be said for Rheinbaben, that he realised he had to deal, not with a rearguard, but with the entire French army.[1] Voigts-Rhetz thought otherwise, but his chief of staff, Colonel Caprivi, shared the opinion that the bulk of the French army had not yet passed Mars-la-Tour. There seemed therefore all the more reason to attack the French camp at Vionville; and it was orders for such an attack that Caprivi carried in person to Rheinbaben during the night of the 15th.

Rheinbaben remonstrated. A *coup de force* of this kind was not at all in his line, and only when news came that III Corps was moving up on his right flank would he consent to move. To the impatient eye of the able and ambitious Caprivi, who was one day to succeed Bismarck as Chancellor of the Reich, the attack was mounted with maddening slowness and carried out without determination. The cannonade did little more than alert the French, and no attempt was made to press the attack home. The attack which Voigts-Rhetz had ordered on the French camp thus never took place; and when, at about 9 a.m. the cavalry advance guard of Alvensleben appeared on the heights south of Rezonville, they found the whole camp alerted and were driven off by heavy fire.[2]

Constantin von Alvensleben, the most forceful of all Frederick Charles's corps commanders, had no doubt that the French were well on their way to Verdun, and that the best III Corps could do was to cut off its rearguard.[3] 6th Cavalry Division, which was sweeping the path before his infantry, reported as it advanced northward from Gorze that the French still lay in considerable strength before him, and the fire which drove back their advanced posts confirmed it. So much the better: the greater the number of Frenchmen that could be cut off from the main body, the more successful the action would be. Alvensleben therefore cheerfully committed his corps to action against the forces in front of him with no further investigation of their strength. While his 5th Division attacked the enemy frontally from the south, 6th Division was to sweep round to the west, cut the Verdun road at Mars-la-Tour, and prevent the French from falling back to the Étain road at Doncourt.[4]

[1] *Kriegsgeschichtliche Einzelschriften* XVIII 547.
[2] Hönig, *Darstellung* 75–82. G. Cardinal von Widdern, *Kritische Tage* II i. *Die Krisis von Vionville* (Berlin 1897) 39–41.
[3] *Kriegsgesch. Einzelschr.* XVIII 544.
[4] Cardinal von Widdern, op. cit. 40–1.

The movement would have been a bold one even if the French forces had been as inconsiderable as he believed. In view of the real strength of the French army, it was almost suicidal; and thanks to Rheinbaben's ineffectual cannonade all chance of surprise had now been lost. By the time Alvensleben's infantry emerged from the steep valleys round Gorze and began to deploy on the rolling plateau beyond, the French 2nd Corps stood ready to repel them. Bataille's division held the village of Vionville and the hamlet of Flavigny half a mile to its south-east, and Vergé's division spread across the fields south-east of Rezonville, its left flank resting on the deep ravine which separated the Rezonville plateau from the Bois des Ognons to the east. 6th Corps was deployed on their right north of the Verdun road, and 3rd Corps and the Guard provided yet further echelons of support to the north and the west.[1]

Against such dispositions III Corps could make no impression. Alvensleben first attempted to deploy his guns on the long bare heights south of Flavigny, and a determined French infantry attack taught him that this was over-bold. His infantry when it arrived did little better. In the undergrowth of the Bois de St Arnauld the German right wing could make no progress; while on the open slopes further west the troops of von Stuelpnagel's 5th Division, emerging from the Gorze ravine and committed piecemeal to the attack, suffered heavy losses from French counter-attack and French fire. It took all the authority of the German officers to hold their men steady in the face of these masses, whose advance was so confident and whose fire so intense. A determined French attack would have driven them back into the Gorze ravine. But Frossard, his corps extended in a single line, had no reserves for such a move, and Bazaine gave him neither orders nor resources to carry one out. His counter-attacks were therefore local and purely defensive. Thus it was that, although Stuelpnagel's men were repulsed, they achieved by their attacks one vital result. By 11 a.m. the heights south and south-east of Flavigny, which dominated the French positions as in a huge amphitheatre, were crowned with fifteen batteries of German guns.[2]

Meanwhile Alvensleben had acquired some idea of the gigantic task which he had so lightly assumed. He had met Rheinbaben, who gloomily assured him that they were at grips, not with the rearguard but with

---

[1] *Guerre: Metz* II: Docs. annexes 142. Frossard, *Rapport sur les Opérations du 2ᵉ Corps* 85.

[2] *Guerre: Metz* II 187–90, and Docs. annexes 231.

the entire French army. If that were so, the only way of avoiding disaster was to give the French the impression that they were at grips with the entire German army; and that could only be done by an attack which would make up in boldness what it lacked in material strength. Few decisions on the battlefield can have been harder to take, more rapidly taken, and so completely justified. The march of 6th Division northward to Mars-la-Tour was halted at Tronville, and Alvensleben directed it instead eastward in a frontal attack on the French positions at Vionville and Flavigny.[1] The conditions for the attack were good: the forces were very evenly matched in numbers; and the advantage the French had from their *chassepots* was more than outweighed by the shells which the German gunners from their commanding positions were now able to pour into their closely massed and unprotected ranks. Vionville itself was held only by a regiment of Chasseurs—the point of junction between Frossard and Canrobert, each considered the other primarily responsible for its defence—and the village fell with little struggle. But the French at once turned so heavy a weight of artillery upon it that it could not be held. The Germans had to push on if they were to defend it at all; and advancing along the road to Rezonville they found themselves opposed, not only by Bataille's division of 2nd Corps, but by Canrobert's uncommitted 6th Corps standing to the north. The blazing farmhouses of Flavigny were taken, but beyond that the attackers could make no headway. The advance of III Corps had been brought to a halt.[2]

It was now about 11.30 a.m., and an observer might have considered the German position desperate. III Corps was fully committed and had suffered heavy casualties, and only X Corps, urgently summoned by Caprivi, was near enough to come to its aid. In the French army, the intact lines of 2nd and 6th Corps were being thickened by the approach of 3rd Corps from Verneville and the Guard from Gravelotte; while further north Ladmirault was bringing 4th Corps up to the sound of the guns, and would soon be able to fall on Alvensleben's exposed left flank. The French only needed a commander who would see the situation and give the few simple orders which would lead to victory. Such a *coup d'œil*, on so vast a battlefield, was perhaps too much to ask of any

[1] *Kriegsgesch. Einzelschr.* XVIII 546–8. Alvensleben later wrote "Ich musste das aufgedrungene Schlachtterrain wohl oder übel nehmen und '*make the most of it*'. Dieses Letztere erforderte, das *physische Missverhältnis der Kräfte durch die moralische Kraft des Angriffs auszugleichen*." Ibid. 548. *G.G.S.* I i 369.

[2] *G.G.S.* I i 373. *Guerre: Metz* II 242–57. Lehautcourt, *Guerre de 1870* V 156–9.

commander except the great Napoleon himself. To manœuvre five corps, totalling 160,000 men, in an encounter-battle covering some thirty square miles, against an enemy of evident initiative and indeterminate strength, would have tested the resources of a far abler general than Bazaine. As it was, Bazaine gave evidence once more only of his valiant physical courage and his incompetence as a general. His bravery itself, confessed one of his corps commanders, was a disadvantage, because nobody ever knew where to find him on the battlefield.[1] He never for a moment thought of *defeating* the Germans. He made no attempt even to clear the Verdun road, which Alvensleben's capture of Vionville had closed. Instead, he was obsessed with the danger to his left flank—with a possible thrust which would cut him off from his base at Metz. With the fortress at his back he could not come to great harm; but to leave it and advance, even victoriously advance, was to abandon safety and place in hazard the army which, Bazaine must by now have fully realised, he was quite unfitted to lead. So on the 16th Bazaine devoted his entire energies to safeguarding his communications with Metz; ignoring the right flank, where victory might have been cheaply won, he concentrated on banishing the faintest shadow of defeat from the left; piling up round Rezonville a huge concentration of troops—the Guard, 2nd Corps, the left wing of 6th Corps and even a brigade of 3rd Corps—to repel the "enemy masses" which he hourly expected to see emerging from the ravines to the south.[2]

Nor was the basic excellence of the French situation apparent to Frossard, whose corps had supported the brunt of the attack all morning and whose right flank, pressed back from Vionville, seemed to be holding very precariously indeed. Bataille had been wounded, and his division seemed on the point of collapse. Oddly enough Frossard asked Bazaine, not for infantry reinforcements from 6th Corps, which were ready to hand, but for cavalry—an arm used, under such circumstances, only as the very last resort. Bazaine did not demur, and ordered a regiment of the Cuirassiers of the Guard to support the regiment of Lancers which Frossard already had under his command.[3] The Guards colonel, according to one account, objected strongly to charging unbroken infantry; to which Bazaine replied, with that unfortunate French talent for the unsuitably dramatic, "It is vitally necessary to stop them: we

---

[1] Bourbaki, in *Procès Bazaine* 233.
[2] *Guerre: Metz* II 275–9, 379–81, and Docs. annexes 123, 227, 416. Frossard, *2ᵉ Corps* 87, 94.
[3] *Procès Bazaine* 235. Frossard, *Rapport sur les Opérations du 2ᵉ Corps* 89.

must sacrifice a regiment!"[1] So first the Lancers and then the Cuirassiers charged, with sabres raised and howls of *Vive l'Empereur!*, over broken agricultural land which sadly disturbed their perfect alignment, down on to the German infantry before Flavigny, who stood perfectly ready to receive them. A few volleys reduced each splendid unit in turn to a line of kicking, bloodstained heaps, while the survivors galloped wildly over the battlefield until rounded up and hunted back to their own lines by the German hussars and dragoons of von Redern's brigade galloping up to counterattack. Bazaine, who had watched the defeat of his own cavalry unmoved, was supervising the placing of a battery to repel this counterattack when he was suddenly surrounded, first by German horsemen, then by French cavalry dashing to his rescue, and became the centre of a confused mêlée of sabres and horses. Then the Germans in their turn withdrew. On both sides the cavalry forays had been spectacular, invigorating and entirely ineffective.[2]

Bazaine might be unaware of the vulnerability of the German left flank north of Vionville, but for Alvensleben it was a nightmare. Caprivi had assured him that X Corps was on its way,[3] and it was here that it would make its presence felt; but it was past noon already, and the clouds of dust to the north showed that at least one more French corps was coming into action and would fall on a flank where he had no protection but cavalry. He had fed his last battalions into the Tronville wood, north-west of Vionville, and on emerging on the further side they had been checked by the fire of 6th Corps. Indeed Canrobert's artillery, deployed along the slopes north of the Vionville–Rezonville road, was pounding to pieces the German left wing; and to stave off collapse Alvensleben, his infantry reserves exhausted, called in the cavalry.[4] Both German cavalry divisions had been massed behind the left flank, at the point of greatest crisis, and the troopers most readily available were those of von Bredow's brigade. To charge guns firmly established among infantry supports was no normal duty to ask a cavalry commander. Bredow made no complaint, but he took his time about executing his mission. The brigade had to be organised; a flank-guard had to be assigned; not until 2 p.m. was he ready to go into action.

---

[1] *Guerre Metz* II 294–6. The relevant Docs. annexes however (p. 478) make no mention of this protest.   [2] Ibid 298–314.   [3] Hönig, *Darstellung* 118.

[4] *Kriegsgesch. Einzelschr.* XVIII 555, 562–3. Alvensleben had decided that if X Corps did not come up in time he would make a fighting retreat along the road to Verdun. "Bazaine konnte mich schlagen", he is reputed to have said, "aber los geworden wäre er mich noch lange nicht." T. Krieg, *Constantin v. Alvensleben* (Berlin 1903) 109.

"Von Bredow's Death Ride" was perhaps the last successful cavalry charge in Western European warfare. Its success won it a renown during the next forty years at the hands of military historians, who were to cite it to prove that cavalry was not an anachronism in battle, that the catastrophes at Morsbrunn and Sedan and to the French Guard at Rezonville were exceptions, and that von Bredow's achievement was the norm. His success was certainly remarkable. His six squadrons, partially concealed by a depression north of Vionville, were able to approach to within a few hundred yards of the French batteries; then, bursting out of the smoke, he came down on the batteries in a charge as effective as any in the Napoleonic wars. The French infantry, severely punished already by German shellfire, had in places already fallen back from the batteries, and those that remained had no time to return any organised fire. The German horsemen overran the gun-line and charged on over the slope, until checked by an accumulated mass as great as their own—two brigades of Forton's cavalry division, which fell on their flank. The survivors cut their way out of the mêlée, and returned to their own lines through heavy infantry fire. Of the 800 men who had started out, only 420 returned. But the object was achieved: the gun-line of 6th Corps was thrown into a confusion from which it was not to recover, and the threat to the German positions before Vionville was for the moment banished.[1]

Hardly was this mêlée over when Alvensleben found his left flank far more seriously threatened. Ladmirault was at last bringing up 4th Corps on the French right wing, and his men were pressing the Prussian infantry before them out of the Tronville copse, over the Verdun road, back on to Tronville itself. The cavalry covering the German flank also fell back and General Du Barail's cavalry division, covering the French right flank, advanced without opposition to Mars-la-Tour. The German line was outflanked. Ladmirault pushed his leading troops on to the road towards Tronville. Tronville was his for the taking but General Grenier, his leading divisional commander, was hesitant. It might be better to wait for more support: the Prussians had collected every available man, and might offer a stubborn defence. Ladmirault agreed. It was unwise to commit his troops piecemeal, and his second division would be on hand within half an hour. That short delay was fatal to

[1] *Kriegsgesch. Einzelschr* XVIII 562–8. *Guerre: Metz* II 342–74, and Docs. annexes 380. *G.G.S.* I i 386–8. Farinet, *Agonie d'une Armée* 134 ff. See also F. E. Whitton, *The Death Ride* (von Bredow's charge at Rezonville) in *Blackwoods Magazine* May 1933.

the French chances of victory. Before the second division of 4th Corps arrived the columns of enemy troops around Tronville began to thicken, and Ladmirault, uncertain what this might portend, pulled back his men to await events. X Corps was appearing on the battlefield at last.[1]

Voigts-Rhetz himself had been on hand for some hours. While his army corps marched on to St Hilaire, he had followed in the tracks of Colonel Caprivi, more impressed by his chief of staff's contention that the French still lay to the north-west than he would admit. As he neared the battlefield the sound of gunfire showed Caprivi to be right, and Voigts-Rhetz summoned his troops to march to the guns. 20th Division, which had just reached Thiaucourt from Pont-à-Mousson, came up at once, reaching the battlefield at about 3.30 p.m. after a twelve-mile march, to be fed in as it arrived to reinforce the Prussian troops who were still hanging on to a corner of the Tronville copse. The second division of X Corps, 19th under General von Schwarzkoppen, marching up from St Hilaire, was directed to fall on Ladmirault's flank.[2]

The order was nearly disastrous. Schwarzkoppen's men, in close formation, with no advance-guard, marched uneventfully through Mars-la-Tour, but half a mile beyond to the north they suddenly saw before them, three hundred yards away across a green valley about fifty feet deep, thick blue lines of French infantry. So far from taking Ladmirault in flank, they had blundered straight into his front. The French troops were those of Grenier's division, resting after their successful fight in the Tronville copse, and the second division under Cissey was rapidly coming up to their support. There was no time for a preliminary cannonade; the German infantry in its thick columns was launched straight into the assault across the valley. Not a man reached the further side; the French *chassepots* brought them to a dead halt. The troops who reached the bottom of the valley crouched there, too exhausted and terrified to move. For perhaps ten minutes the French fired into this inert mass; then roused by their officers and their drummers, they hurled themselves shouting into the valley and pursued the fleeing Prussians up the corpse-strewn slopes beyond.[3]

For a moment it seemed that the whole German wing might collapse.

---

[1] *G.G.S.* I i 390–2. *Guerre: Metz* II 394–422, 437, 449–63.

[2] Hönig, *Darstellung* 116, 127, 132 ff. *G.G.S.* I i 393–9. Cardinal von Widdern, *Kritische Tage* II i 64.

[3] *Guerre: Metz* II 486–507. Schwarzkoppen's leading brigade, 38th lost 60% of its strength, 45% killed. *G.G.S.* I i 412. Cardinal von Widdern, *Kritische Tage* II i 79.

Fugitives poured back over the road, horses bolted, and in Tronville Caprivi ordered all X Corps documents to be burnt.[1] Now, if ever, was the moment for the French cavalry to charge. Now was certainly the moment for Ladmirault to attack. But Ladmirault again hesitated. He was still short of one division, and his victory had already been magnificent. To advance further might be to hazard it altogether. And once more Voigts-Rhetz took a prompt decision which showed up the feebleness of his adversary. He refused to sanction any retreat. Instead, like Alvensleben three hours earlier, he sent for the cavalry. Three squadrons of Dragoon Guards and two of Cuirassiers cantered northward into the smoke, through the fugitives from Schwarzkoppen's division, and came on the French infantry just as they were emerging from the valley in pursuit. Cissey's men stood their ground and fired; but they were halted, and the impetus of the pursuit was lost. Ladmirault sent after them to return across the valley, and the last hope of clearing the road to Verdun disappeared.[2]

Ladmirault indeed had cause to worry about his own flank, which rested on the road which ran northward from Mars-la-Tour. Beyond this road a grassy sward stretched away westward towards the valley of the Yron, a standing invitation to a cavalry attack; and for such an attack Rheinbaben was already preparing. Ladmirault had, to parry it, his own cavalry division, that of 3rd Corps, and also, protecting the flank of the entire army, Du Barail's; and at the sight of Rheinbaben's advancing columns he ordered his own division to charge. The command was given a little to soon: the French cavalry had some eight hundred yards to cover, and came on the German columns disordered and slightly exhausted; but the shock was tremendous, and this was only the first wave of the French attack. More and more squadrons, French and German, charged into the gigantic mêlée until over forty were involved, Chasseurs, Uhlans, Dragoons, Hussars, in a confusion of dust wherein it became difficult to tell friend from foe. Once battle was joined all possibility of control, and thus of victory to either side, disappeared. The Germans claimed that they pressed the French back towards Bruville; the French claimed that, hearing a bugle somewhere sounding the rear rally, they deliberately disengaged.[3] In any case no pursuit was possible. Gradually the huge mass shredded itself out and

[1] Hönig, *Darstellung* 114, 126.
[2] Cardinal von Widdern, op. cit. 84–6. *Guerre: Metz* II 512.
[3] But the *Journal de Marche* of Clérembault's division, which came up too late to help, speaks of the French cavalry as a "masse confuse fuyant éperdue". *Guerre: Metz* II: Docs. annexes 256.

the German squadrons fell back in their turn, well pleased, on Mars-la-Tour.[1]

It was now 7 p.m., and daylight was beginning to wane. The battle had run the full length of the line, beginning on the slopes south of Rezonville where Stuelpnagel's 5th Division had been that morning checked, to Vionville and Flavigny which 6th Division had seized and held; from the slopes north of the Verdun road where von Bredow had charged Canrobert's guns, through the Tronville copse, along the valley north of Mars-la-Tour thick with Westphalian dead, to end in the vast cavalry mêlée on the field above the Yron. As the flame of battle passed, it left the line comparatively quiet. Infantry warily sniped at one another and gunners kept up a fire whose intensity was determined by their waning ammunition supply. In this fire-fight the German gunners, once their arc of batteries was established, undoubtedly had the upper hand. Their supply of ammunition was a constant source of worry and their shells often failed to explode in the soggy ground, but no French battery could maintain its position for long under their fire, and it was all the French infantry officers could do to hold their ranks steady.[2] The positions won by the German infantry that morning were maintained by their artillery for the remainder of the day. But the French maintained their positions equally intact, and when during the afternoon reinforcements from X Corps came up on the German right wing to 5th Division and tried again to seize the crest south of Rezonville, they also failed before the steady *chassepot* fire.[3]

As the battle died down at the west end of the front, it flared up again south of Rezonville, where it had begun. Some of Bazaine's fear for his left wing proved justified. Beyond the Moselle Steinmetz, hearing the noise of battle, had been pushing his VIII Corps across the narrow bridge at Corny as fast as he could, and its leading unit, followed by those of IX Corps, began to come up through the Gorze ravine at about 5 p.m. The forces which Bazaine had accumulated round Rezonville were ample to keep the new arrivals in check, but the fighting went on until darkness was complete.[4]

Finally the German attack in this quarter received yet another impetus. At about 4 p.m. Frederick Charles appeared on the battlefield, having remained unconscious until midday that Alvensleben had

[1] *Guerre: Metz* II 517–32. *G.G.S.* I i 409–11. Du Barail, *Souvenirs* 187–8.
[2] *Guerre: Metz* II 231–3, and Docs. annexes 455–6. E. Hoffbauer, *The German Artillery in the Battles near Metz* (London 1874) 135–46.
[3] *Guerre: Metz* II 390. *G.G.S.* I i 405.
[4] *Guerre: Metz* II 550–74. *G.G.S.* I i 415–18.

the entire French army on his hands. On arrival he gave orders for an attack on the left flank which Voigts-Rhetz, fighting to hold Tronville against Ladmirault's advance, was in no position to carry out.[1] The Army Commander, like the Crown Prince at Froeschwiller, was helpless to affect the course of the battle; but on the appearance of VIII and IX Corps he ordered, at about 7 p.m., a final attack on Rezonville, to try to force a decision before night.[2] The attack was mounted in some confusion—the infantry on the right wing was engaged already and Alvensleben's artillery commander had just ordered his guns to withdraw—but it was remarkably effective. The French on the Vionville road were taken by surprise. Two brigades of Prussian cavalry broke through their ranks, sending a flood of panic-stricken men tumbling back into the crowded streets of Rezonville. But it was now completely dark—too dark for either exploitation or counter-attack; and along the whole of the line, from Rezonville to Mars-la-Tour, the battle at last died down.

On both sides the losses had been heavy. The German Official History confessed to 15,780, the French to 13,761 officers and men;[3] but again both sides felt that the victory was theirs. The Germans, with two corps, had at heavy cost held in check the entire French army. Of this disparity in numbers the French as yet knew nothing. They had stood their ground, defended their positions successfully, and covered the fields with swathes of enemy dead. Once again they had met the Germans and smashed them; once again Bazaine had conducted himself on the battlefield with the utmost courage; there seemed no reason to suppose that next day they would not advance, destroy the remnants of the enemy army, and carry on their movement to Verdun.

Bazaine meanwhile, making his way through the immense crowds of wounded and unwounded which were streaming along the road from Rezonville to Gravelotte, returned to the inn where Napoleon had passed the previous night, and considered the situation. He at least was under no illusion about the result of the battle. The Germans had cut the road to Verdun through Mars-la-Tour; there was left only that to the north,

---

[1] *Kriegsgesch. Einzelschr.* XVIII 579–80.

[2] Frederick Charles, *Denkwürdigkeiten* 199, 204 ff. *G.G.S.* I. i 419. *Guerre: Metz* II: Docs. annexes 390, 400, 518.

[3] The German General Staff, after investigating French figures, put them rather higher, at 744 officers and 10,743 men killed and wounded, 93 and 5,379 missing. *Kriegsgesch. Einzelschr.* XI 664–5. The high number of missing can be accounted for only by the French withdrawal the following day, which left many of their wounded to the Germans. See p. 163 below.

through Étain, and there was little hope that he would be able to march along that undisturbed. Moreover, although his army had only just left Metz, its supply-organisation had broken down completely. The long, undisciplined convoy of waggons—nearly five thousand of them—had disintegrated in confusion at the sound of the enemy guns. Some civilian drivers had turned back to Metz, cutting the traces of their horses and leaving their abandoned waggons to block the single road. Elsewhere waggons were unloaded to facilitate their flight, or to make room for the wounded; and their contents were either distributed at random or dumped by the roadside, later to be abandoned or burnt. Frossard's and Canrobert's corps had received no issue of supplies at all that day, and the stocks and camping equipment of at least one division had fallen into enemy hands. Then there was the problem of ammunition, especially artillery ammunition. General Soleille, commanding the army's artillery, was worried about the expenditure during the battle, and wanted to restock from the arsenals at Metz. Finally the army had fallen into a confusion which it would take at least a day to sort out. Ladmirault had taken 4th Corps on to its original destination at Doncourt, but in the centre the units of 3rd and 6th Corps were thoroughly mixed, and in the two-mile stretch between Gravelotte and Rezonville were piled some nine infantry divisions, three cavalry divisions, and a huge quantity of artillery. There seemed no hope of getting this mass sorted out and into a position to move forward by morning. Bazaine made his decision, and at 11 p.m. wrote to Napoleon. Shortage of supplies and ammunition, he explained, made it necessary to fall back to a line running north and south from St Privat to Rozerieulles, where he could restock and reorganise before he set out again, probably by the Étain road. An hour later the orders went out to the corps commanders. The army was to fall back and the movement would begin in four hours' time.[1]

On the morning of 17th August the French army, to its bewilderment and fury, found itself marching back over the field towards Metz. Jarras had had no time to work out routes and march-tables for the columns, so the confusion was if possible even greater than that of the previous week. There were at most three or four miles to cover, but the army took the best part of eight hours to do it. Many units reached their new positions only late that night, after a day of false directions and

[1] *Procès Bazaine* 16, 18, 279, 295, 298. *Guerre: Metz* II 583 ff. and Docs. annexes 139, 166, 241. *Guerre: Metz* III: Docs. annexes 21–2. Farinet, *Agonie d'une Armée* 161. D'Andlau, *Metz* 83.

delays. The hungry and exasperated troops, marching back across their own supply lines, seized all the food they could carry from convoys and dumps which *Intendants* tried in vain to defend. Bonfires of abandoned stores marked the path of their retreat; and in Rezonville not only stores but the wounded and their attendant doctors had to be left behind for lack of transport.[1] The corps commanders in their reports to Bazaine complained of pillage, of indiscipline, of lack of ammunition and food. Canrobert in particular, much of whose artillery had been left at Châlons, spoke of desperate shortages, and objected to the position allotted to him round Verneville, where he lay somewhat forward of the line occupied by the rest of the army along the crest from Amanvillers to Point du Jour. To defend such a position, flat and shut in by woods, seemed almost impossible. Could he not, he asked Bazaine, pull his corps back to the village of St Privat which stood on the crest north of Amanvillers and commanded an excellent field of fire? Bazaine was not the man to contradict the veteran hero, and he allowed Canrobert to have his own way.[2] The French positions therefore, which originally had a certain depth, were now to consist of a single line. Their field of fire to the front was excellent, over long bare slopes typical of this part of Lorraine. The left flank rested on the steep, wooded ravines which cut into the plateau from the valley of the Moselle. But the right flank at St Privat lay completely in the air. It was held by the weakest, most incomplete unit of the Army of the Rhine; and that unit only arrived long after dark, sleepless and hungry, far too late to dig serious defensive positions even if it had had the tools to dig them; which it had not.[3]

Bazaine, still obsessed with the need to safeguard his left flank,[4] established his headquarters behind his left wing at Plappeville. The distribution of supplies to his disorganised forces gave him a few days' grace before he need think again of undertaking active operations, and this was the burden of the messages which he sent to Châlons on 17th August, both by messenger and by wire, in reply to the anxious enquiries of Napoleon. He hoped to leave for Verdun, he said, in two days' time, "if he could do so without compromising the army". But, he admitted, the operation might now present serious difficulties.[5] Did he really hope

---

[1] *Guerre: Metz* III; Docs. annexes 21–2, 32, 53, 59, 98. *Trois mois à l'Armée de Metz* par un officier de génie 86.

[2] "Maréchal Canrobert avait dix années de grade plus que moi; j'avais toujours servi sous ses ordres; il me semblait convenable d'accéder à ce qu'il me demandait." *Procès Bazaine* 166.

[3] Bapst, *Canrobert* VI 77–83.

[4] Bazaine, *Épisodes* 101.   [5] *Guerre: Metz* III 54.

to get through to Verdun? On this his own evidence is conflicting. To the Commission of Enquiry into the Acts of the Government of National Defence he later declared that he had. "It seemed to me that by fighting one or perhaps two defensive battles, in positions which I considered impregnable, I would wear down the strength of my adversary, forcing him to sustain heavy losses, which, repeated several times, would weaken him enough to oblige him to let me pass without being able to offer serious opposition."[1] But to his judges at this trial he declared that he "believed, and the Emperor believed as well, that by giving time to the army of Châlons to form, it would reach a considerable size which would allow it to come and relieve us."[2] It is hard to believe that either of these statements was more than wisdom after the event, or that Bazaine on 17th August had any plans at all. He was living from day to day, confining himself to the routine details of administration which he understood, and trusting to his good luck to pull him through.[3]

Moltke had first heard of the battle of Vionville when he arrived at Pont-à-Mousson on the afternoon of the 16th. The messages from Second Army Headquarters still played down its importance: so far it was a matter of locating "strong enemy forces" with which the army's right wing was quite competent to deal, and Stiehle suggested that the rest of his forces should press on, as previously arranged, to the Meuse. But Moltke saw the possibilities of the situation more clearly. The Meuse was unimportant: the vital thing now was to push the French forces northwards away from Paris, and the greater the force opposing Alvensleben the better. "The more enemy opposing III Corps, the greater the success will be tomorrow", he wrote, "when we can deploy against it X, III, IV, VIII, VII Corps and eventually XII." In his orders that evening he unfolded even more ambitious objectives. The French were to be pursued "up to the Luxemburg frontier, and eventually on to the territory of that country". The strategy of encirclement was taking shape.[4]

---

[1] *D.T.* IV 187.

[2] *Procès Bazaine* 168.

[3] This was the view of Jarras. "N'ayant pas su arrêter un plan de conduite, il n'avait pas un but net et précis, il tâtonnait et voulait ne rien compromettre en attendant que les événements lui ouvrissent des horizons nouveaux dont il espérait, au moyen d'expédients plus ou moins équivoques, parvenir à dégager sinon son armée, au moins sa personnalité et ses intérêts. La fortune ne l'avait-elle pas favorisé jusqu'alors au delà de ses espérances? Faute de mieux, il s'est abandonné au hasard, dernière ressource de ceux que ne comptent plus sur eux-mêmes." *Souvenirs* 132-3.

[4] *M.M.K.* 231-2.

On 17th August therefore Steinmetz pushed his forces across the Moselle, and Frederick Charles wheeled his entire army northward towards the battlefield of the previous day. There the weary battalions of Alvensleben and Voigts-Rhetz, waiting apprehensively for the French to renew the attack, were surprised and delighted when, instead of doing so, the enemy melted away towards the north-east.[1] Where were they going? Back to Metz, north to Thionville, or by Étain to Verdun? The Germans made curiously little effort to find out. On the right flank, east of Rezonville, the two armies remained in close contact, and Steinmetz, coming up with his forward units over the Moselle, could see clearly the lines of the French positions on the slopes round Point du Jour, protected by the deep depression of the Mance ravine.[2] But elsewhere contact was completely lost, and the German cavalry was too shattered by its exertions of the previous day to think of regaining it. Moltke moreover was anxious to avoid drifting into a premature engagement before he had concentrated all his forces, and Steinmetz was told so in terms which even that headstrong old man could not misinterpret. Perhaps in order to render him quite incapable of mischief, Moltke removed VIII Corps from his command altogether, leaving him, in spite of his expostulations, with only one corps in contact with the French. The First Army astride the Moselle south of Metz was to act simply as a pivot, round which the Second Army was to come up from the south in a wide wheel.[3]

From the heights south of Flavigny Moltke could see the dust-clouds made by the French army as it marched confusedly northwards and eastwards across the plain. It had no hope of getting very far, and the orders which Moltke and Frederick Charles sent out for the next day arranged for the corps of the Second Army to move north like beaters, slightly echeloned from the left, from the line Rezonville–Mars-la-Tour, and be prepared to give battle facing either north or east.[4] It was a very sensible arrangement; but a little reconnaissance would have shown Moltke that the French were settling down along a line which ran exactly at right angles to his own line of advance, in positions from which they might, under an enterprising leader, have struck at the German flank next day with considerable effect. It was

[1] Frederick Charles, *Denkwürdigkeiten II* 220.

[2] Gross Generalstab, Kriegsgesch. Abteilung I: *Studien zur Kriegsgeschichte u. Taktik, V: Der 18 August 1870* 28–9.

[3] Ibid. 33–5, 55. Bronsart, *Kriegstagebuch* 43. F. Hönig, *24 Hours of Moltke's Strategy . . . Gravelotte and St Privat* (English edn. London 1895) 5.

[4] *M.M.K.* 232.

Moltke's good fortune now and throughout the campaign that he did not have to deal with an adversary capable of profiting by his mistakes.

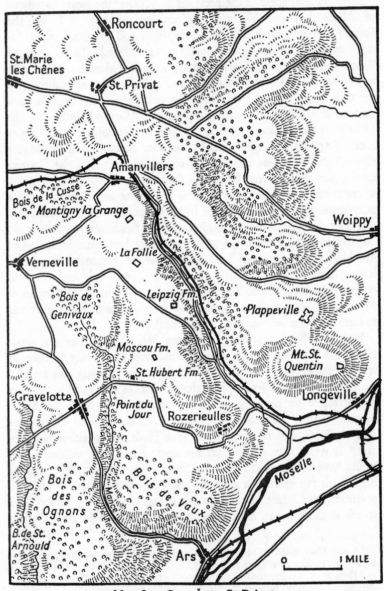

Map 8:   *Gravelotte–St Privat*

§3 Gravelotte–St Privat

The battle fought between Gravelotte and St Privat on 18th August differed from the previous engagements of the war, in kind as well as in scale. Not only was the bulk of both armed forces involved for the first time—the Germans engaged 188,332 men and 732 guns against 112,800 Frenchmen and 520 guns[1]—but the battle was deliberate and expected. The fighting at Spicheren, Froeschwiller, Colombey and Vionville had come as a surprise to the High Command on both sides, an interruption and distraction to totally different plans. The fighting at Gravelotte was deliberately willed by the Germans: Frederick Charles's orders for his army on 17th August were for it to "set out tomorrow morning towards the north to find the enemy and fight him"[2]; and it was awaited, if not immediately expected, by the French in positions which did credit to Bazaine's topographical skill and which he had some reason to consider impregnable.[3]

The left flank was particularly strong. Half a mile east of the village of Gravelotte the main road from Verdun to Metz crossed at right angles the deep ravine through which the Mance stream ran south between steep and thickly wooded slopes to join the Moselle at Ars. The gradient of these slopes and the bushes thickly covering them provided a formidable barrier to any army moving in close formation, while the road, as it rose eastward out of the ravine between a line of poplars which military artists were soon to make famous throughout the world, ran through deep cuttings and was commanded throughout most of its length by the walled farm of St Hubert, towards which it climbed in a dead straight line. Along the crest to the east of the ravine there lay three other farms —Leipzig, Moscou, Point du Jour: strongpoints commanding the fields above the Mance ravine, loopholed and barricaded by the French and connected by lines of trenches and gun-emplacements from which the French infantry and artillery commanded the long slopes before them. Frossard's 2nd Corps held the southern half of this front, based on Point du Jour, with Lapasset's brigade of 5th Corps guarding the

---

[1] *Kriegs. Einzelschr.* XI 675.
[2] Frederick Charles, *Denkwürdigkeiten* II 225.
[3] In 1944 a few German training units were to use the same positions to hold up General Patton's Third American Army as it advanced through Lorraine. See H. M. Cole, "The Lorraine Campaign", *United States Army in World War II: European Theater of Operations* (Washington D.C. 1950) 151 ff.

extreme left flank towards Ars, while the northern half, from St Hubert to Leipzig, was in the conscientious hands of Lebœuf. Beyond Lebœuf's positions the character of the country changed. The Mance ravine levelled out, the woods on its slopes spreading into the thick Bois des Genivaux, whose copses lapped up to the right flank of 3rd Corps's positions at the farm of La Folie. Beyond the Bois des Genivaux to the north there stretched wide open fields, virtually without cover, rising very gently eastwards towards the positions held by 4th and 6th Corps which were based respectively on the villages of Amanvillers and St Privat. For the *chassepot* and the *mitrailleuse* nothing could have been better; perhaps indeed it was the protection afforded by these long fields of fire that made Ladmirault and Canrobert feel excused from digging themselves in as elaborately as Lebœuf and Frossard were doing on their left.[1]

The weakness of the army's position, as we have seen, was on the right flank at St Privat; for, although the village commanded the surrounding slopes, there was nothing to prevent it from being outflanked from the north. It was not the position which Bazaine had chosen himself for his right flank, and during the course of 18th August he sent Canrobert orders to retire on a better one in rear which had been reconnoitred that morning by one of his staff. Perhaps the fact that he had already ordered such a withdrawal partly masked from Bazaine, at the end of the day, the full extent of Canrobert's collapse. But the position of his own headquarters, two miles behind the left wing at Plappeville and some four miles away from St Privat, with the Guard in reserve under his hand, was to add to the fatal weakness of his right wing.

The Germans knew all about the French positions south of Point du Jour, where Lapasset's brigade had been skirmishing with the emasculated First Army in the Bois de Vaux throughout the 17th and the ensuing night; but about the rest they remained totally ignorant. On 18th August Frederick Charles ordered his army, massed between Mars-la-Tour and Rezonville, to march northwards in the closest possible formation—straight across the front of the French positions—and then see what happened. "Whether it will be eventually necessary to make a wheeling movement to the right or the left cannot be decided at present . . . it is now only a question of a short march of a few miles."[2] IX Corps,

---

[1] Hönig, *24 Hours of Moltke's Strategy* 65–7. *Guerre: Metz* III 166, 170. Canrobert was later to complain of the frustration he felt at not having a single *mitrailleuse* on ground so well adapted to their use. *Procès Bazaine* 224.

[2] Frederick Charles, *Denkwürdigkeiten* II 228–9.

the Hessian, was on the right; XII Corps (the Saxons) and the Guard, their columns tangling and overlapping, were on the left[1]; while the battle-scarred remnants of III and X Corps followed in close reserve. So dense a mass of men could hardly move unobserved. Lebœuf saw the dust-clouds rising into the cloudless sky at about 9 a.m., and informed Bazaine. Bazaine was uninterested. He was not going to be lured from his excellent positions into the unknown hazards of battle. Lebœuf was told to sit tight and await events; and the dense, vulnerable mass of Frederick Charles's army was left to march northwards undisturbed.

By 10 a.m. the Germans saw their way more clearly. The white tents of the French lines along the crest to the east could be seen stretching as far as Montigny-la-Grange, south of Amanvillers; beyond that visibility was too difficult and nothing could as yet be observed. Frederick Charles did not think that there was anything more to see: retaining his belief that most of the French army had already escaped, he presumed—as had Alvensleben two days earlier—that he was faced with a rearguard, whose flank he had now found.[2] At 10.15 a.m. therefore he turned his army inwards. IX Corps was to make for Verneville and, with the Guard in support, attack the French positions which could be seen on the slopes beyond.[3] But a quarter of an hour later, at 10.30 a.m., Moltke issued an order for an attack by both armies. Steinmetz was to attack the forces opposite him at Gravelotte, and IX Corps was to give battle as already ordered at Verneville; but the rest of the Second Army should sweep round in an enveloping movement from the north on the supposed French flank at Amanvillers.[4] Frederick Charles may or may not have been prepared to change his plans to accord with this directive, but almost simultaneously with Moltke's order came news which certainly made some change necessary. The French camp had been sighted at St Privat; it was evident that Frederick Charles had not yet got anywhere near the enemy flank. Aides-de-camp chased after IX Corps with orders to wait until the Guard and the Saxons had time to come up on their left to join the attack; but matters had already gone too far. Shortly before midday the Hessian artillery took post in the fields beyond Verneville and fired, into the French lines

---

[1] Frederick Charles altered the order of march of his army, at great inconvenience to his troops, to get the Guard in the centre of his battle-line, instead of the Saxons, whose reliability he distrusted. See Prince Kraft zu Hohenlohe-Ingelfingen, *Aus meinem Leben* (Berlin 1915) 267.

[2] Frederick Charles, *Denkwürdigkeiten* II 232.

[3] Ibid. 237.   [4] *M.M.K.* 234.

a thousand yards ahead of them, the first shells of the battle of Gravelotte.[1]

The French guns responded at once.

> Everywhere [wrote a German officer], along the whole range, guns sent out flashes and belched forth dense volumes of smoke. A hail of shell and shrapnel, the latter traceable by the little white clouds, looking like balloons, which remained suspended in the air for some time after their bursting, answered the war-like greeting from our side. The grating noise of the *mitrailleuses* was heard above the tumult, drowning the whole roar of battle.[2]

Ladmirault's divisions rushed into position north and south of Amanvillers, abandoning in their hurry tents and haversacks which they were never to see again, and poured fire into the Hessian gun-line. Manstein pushed infantry forward to protect his gunners, but they were checked by *chassepot* fire to which their rifles could make no adequate response. The French were able to lunge forward and seize the four leading guns of the German line, while the rest hurriedly took post further back; and then the fighting between Ladmirault's and Manstein's men dwindled, for the afternoon, into an artillery duel in which the French infantry stoically endured the shellfire which, in spite of its noise and accuracy, did surprisingly little damage to their ranks, while the Hessians extended their gun-line and awaited the arrival of the Guard on their left and III Corps in their rear to enable them to renew the attack.[3]

At the first sound of IX Corps's artillery Moltke, back on the heights south of Flavigny, realised that his trap was being sprung prematurely, and sent Steinmetz a hurried message to prevent him from making it any worse. All that was happening, he said, was a minor action at Verneville, and there was no need for Steinmetz to act. When he did, he need not deploy much infantry: artillery was what was needed, to prepare the attack.[4] But the troops at Gravelotte were not, strictly speaking, Steinmetz's at all, although Steinmetz continued to behave as if they were: they were those of von Goeben's VIII Corps, which Moltke had removed from Steinmetz's direct control. On hearing the

---

[1] *Der 18 August 1870* 90–1. *Guerre: Metz* III 189, 194.

[2] Verdy du Vernois, *With the Royal Headquarters* 81.

[3] *Der 18 August 1870* 148–56. *Guerre: Metz* III 194–217, and Docs. annexes 244–75. The German Official History [*G.G.S.* I ii 37–41] claims that the Hessian infantry beat off repeated counter-attacks, but the French documents make no mention of these. A counter-attack is described by L. Patry, *La Guerre telle qu'elle est* 107–10, but this appears to have been launched later in the afternoon.

[4] *M.M.K.* 235.

guns from Verneville, VIII Corps had at once engaged.[1] Goeben pushed his leading brigade through Gravelotte and down into the Mance ravine, to attack the French lines so clearly visible at Moscou and Point du Jour. His artillery line was deployed north of Gravelotte, and soon VII Corps artillery came up to prolong it to the south. Within three hours he had well over a hundred and fifty guns, which, from noon until nightfall, never ceased pounding the French lines on the opposite slopes. Next day the Germans were able to inspect their handiwork.

In the large heaps of ruins [wrote one of them], which without an interval extended from Point du Jour to Moscou, the defenders, especially in Moscou, lay all around, fearfully torn and mutilated by the German shell; limbs and bodies were blown from thirty to fifty paces apart, and the stones and sand were here and there covered with pools of blood. In Moscou and Point du Jour some French were found burnt in their defensive positions, and a large number of the wounded showed marks of the flames, which had destroyed both uniforms and limbs. All around there lay rifles and swords, knapsacks and cartridges, the remains of limbers which had been blown up, broken gun-carriages and wheels, and a large number of hideously torn and mangled horses.[2]

Yet all this availed the Germans nothing. The French remained in their main positions opposite Gravelotte until next day, and neither German shells nor German infantry could shake them. Every attempt to assault the French positions before Moscou and Point du Jour was easily repulsed. Only at St Hubert did the Germans score any success; and that outpost lay below the crest of the ridge out of sight of the main French lines, and was held by a single battalion. It fell to a concerted rush of some fourteen German companies shortly before 3 p.m. That was the high-water mark of the First Army's success. Further attempts to advance were checked by fire from Moscou and Point du Jour; on either side lay slopes too steep and too thickly wooded for manœuvre; so Goeben's men and those sent to reinforce them could only crowd precariously in the shallow haven of safety and create on the road behind them a congestion whose consequences were nearly catastrophic.

Steinmetz had for some hours been convinced that the French troops facing him across the Mance ravine were only a rearguard covering

[1] According to his biographer Goeben "setzte diesen Angriff in etwas hinhaltender Weise ins Werk, wie sie ihm der neuen Lage der Dinge zu entsprechen schien. Hierdurch kam es, daß General v. Steinmetz den Befehl zum Vorgehen des VIII. Armeekorps wiederholt und in ganz bestimmter Form zu ertheilen sich veranlaßt sah." Zernin, *Leben des Generals v. Goeben* II 56.

[2] F. Hönig, *24 Hours of Moltke's Strategy* 63. *Guerre: Metz III*: Docs. annexes 188–94.

a general retreat; now the fall of St Hubert seemed to indicate the beginnings of that disintegration of the enemy which every commander must unhesitatingly exploit.[1] Fired with the determination not to miss his chance, he gave orders whose rashness even now seems barely credible. The French position was still intact. It could be approached only along one narrow road, from which it was almost impossible to diverge, and which was already choked with the exhausted débris of VIII Corps. Along this Steinmetz now ordered forward the available infantry of Zastrow's VII Corps; all VII Corps artillery; and, a final wild touch, the First Cavalry Division, which was ordered to pursue the defeated enemy to the glacis of Metz.[2]

Of the artillery, four batteries reached St Hubert, where three deployed only to be knocked out one by one. Of the cavalry, only one regiment could make its way to St Hubert, and that rapidly disintegrated under French fire; the remainder were halted by the unimaginable shambles in the ravine.

> Picture to yourself [wrote an observer] a continuous wall of smoke, out of which the flames of Point du Jour and Moscou rose up to heaven, a hundred and forty-four guns in action in rear of the valley ... while in front were masses of infantry, cavalry, and artillery crowding into the ravine, some of them pressing on to the front, others falling back under pressure of the enemy's fire as the range got shorter, wounded and unwounded men, infantry in order and in disorder streaming in opposite directions and jumbled together, the echo of the shells as they burst in the wood or above the trees, the whistling of the bullets from either side as they rushed overhead, and over the whole a column of dust which darkened the sun.[3]

The cavalry wheeled to extricate itself from this mass. Riderless horses bolted, and there was a general surge back towards Gravelotte. By 5 p.m. it was clear that the First Army's attack had been a total failure. The whole German position on this front was at the mercy of a strong, well-timed French counter-attack.

Such a counter-attack did not for a moment enter Bazaine's mind. At Plappeville, by a freak of acoustics, it was extraordinarily difficult to hear the noise of battle, and in consequence he did not realise how violent a conflict was raging.[4] In any case, having chosen good positions for his forces, he felt his work to be over and that it was now up to his corps commanders to defend them.[5] These were the excuses which he

[1] *Der 18 August 1870* 272.   [2] Hönig, op. cit. 110.
[3] Hönig, op. cit. 113. *Der 18 August 1870* 273 ff.
[4] *Procès Bazaine* 258. C. Fay, *Journal d'un officier de l'Armée du Rhin* 107.
[5] D'Andlau, *Metz, Campagne et Négociations* 88. Bazaine, *Épisodes* 105.

put forward in the apologias which he published after the war, and which did little to re-establish his reputation with the French army and nation. Nor was his statement to his judges any more convincing, that he was suffering a good deal from his wound, could not sit a horse, and "since 1st August had not had eight hours rest a day".[1] The latter disadvantage, after all, was one shared not only by his subordinates but by most of his enemies as well. But there can be little doubt that he was morally if not physically exhausted; that the weight of responsibility had paralysed him, annihilating all power of action and independence of will. Throughout the day he avoided the battlefield. When Lebœuf reported the advance of the enemy Bazaine told him to remain in his good positions and defend himself. When Jarras appeared and asked for orders, Bazaine sent him back with a petty administrative assignment. When Canrobert reported a threat to the right flank Bazaine only arranged for some artillery to be sent to help, and informed Canrobert that he intended the right flank to fall back in the near future.[2] When during the afternoon Bazaine finally left Plappeville, it was to go, not to the plateau which his army was defending, but in the opposite direction, to Mont St Quentin, to make sure that the batteries there were adequately sited to deal with the threat to his left flank which he obstinately continued to expect.[3] It is possible, though not easy, to find excuses for his behaviour: the French Official History does not try. His conduct, it says, "can best be compared with that of a simple soldier who abandons his post in face of the enemy."[4]

There was thus no directing intelligence on the French side to observe the disorder into which the German attack had fallen and to turn it to advantage. The rashness of the Germans was to go unpunished. But this by itself need not have led to a French defeat. On the left flank Frossard and Lebœuf were to maintain their positions unshaken until nightfall. It was on the right that the absence of an active commander was to prove fatal to the French hopes. Manstein's attack, as we have seen, had been been checked on the slopes beyond Verneville; but during the afternoon, while his infantrymen lay waiting their chance and his gunners pounded the French batteries, the rest of the Second Army was swinging round to come up on his left. Once they had passed Verneville and the copses of the Bois de la Cusse which had masked all observation to the north, the staff of the Second Army could see how

[1] *Procès Bazaine* 167.   [2] Ibid. 224, 226, 277.
[3] Bazaine, *Épisodes* 105. *Guerre: Metz* III: Docs. annexes 105.
[4] *Guerre: Metz* III 692.

entirely erroneous their conception of the extent of the French positions had been. The white tents along the heights as far as St Privat showed that IX Corps had attacked, not the flank of the French army, but almost its precise centre; and that not merely the Guard but also the Royal Saxon Corps must be deployed if the enemy was to be out-flanked. So Frederick Charles enforced caution not merely on IX Corps but on the Guard as well. Not even the French outposts in St Marie-les-Chênes, at the foot of the St Privat glacis, were to be attacked until the Saxons arrived. So the Guard, like the Hessians, took up fire-positions, deployed artillery, sniped at the French and waited for the Saxons to arrive.[1]

The Saxons came into the attack at about 3 p.m. and, assisted by the Guard and with plentiful use of artillery, took only about half an hour to drive the French defenders out of St Marie. Then the Guard's gun-line deployed south of St Marie, the Saxon to the north, the artillery of III Corps came to reinforce that of IX; and by 5 p.m. the French artillery, virtually driven from the battlefield, could do no more to protect the thick lines of infantry round St Privat from the concentrated fire of 180 German guns. As for St Privat itself, "the noise of explosions, combined with the horrible cracking of collapsing roofs and crumbling walls, the cries of the wounded mixed with the shrill whistle of bullets and the dull and impetuous shock of the shells and bombs turned the streets of the village into a splendid and horrible hell."[2] And the Saxon Corps, wisely avoiding the open slopes below the village, pushed north-wards, towards the village of Roncourt, and thence round to the east, their cavalry to fan out into the lower Moselle valley and their infantry to fall on the unprotected flank of the defence.[3]

So far the attack of the Second Army, with the wise restraint of its infantry and its reliance on artillery fire while it manœuvred to find the enemy flank, might have been contrasted with Steinmetz's bloody and fruitless impetuosity as a model of how an attack should be conducted against a well-armed enemy in positions well adapted for defence. But at about 6 p.m. the commander of the Guard Corps, Prince Augustus of Württemberg, took a decision which was to make the name of St Privat even more tragic in German military annals than that of Grave-lotte. His reasons are obscure. According to some accounts the sudden silence of the French guns led him to believe that Canrobert was

[1] *Der 18 August 1870* 166. Frederick Charles, *Denkwürdigkeiten* II 246.
[2] *Guerre: Metz* III: Docs annexes 357.
[3] *G.G.S.* I ii 64–5. *Guerre: Metz* III 457–63.

transferring his forces to Amanvillers to attack IX Corps. Others suggest that he mistakenly believed the Saxons to be in position and ready to attack; while the belief was widespread after the battle that simple partisan jealousy prompted him to pluck the laurels for the Prussian Guard before the Saxons could appropriate them.[1] Whatever the reason, he gave the order to advance without even ordering his artillery to give covering fire, and Frederick Charles, impatient at the Saxon delay, approved it. General von Pape, commander of the First Guards Division, who from his headquarters could see both that the Saxons were not yet remotely ready to launch their attack and that the French positions at St Privat bore no sign of damage by German artillery fire, protested strongly, but the prince cut him short and ordered him forward.[2] So the skirmishing lines of the Guard, with thick columns behind them, extended themselves over the bare fields below St Privat and began to make their way up the slopes in face of the French fire.

The result was a massacre. The field officers on their horses were the first casualties. The men on foot struggled forward against the *chassepot* fire as if into a hailstorm, shoulders hunched, heads bowed, directed only by the shouts of their leaders and the discordant noise of their regimental bugles and drums. All formation disintegrated: the men broke up their columns into a single thick and ragged skirmishing line and inched their way forward up the bare glacis of the fields until they were within some six hundred yards of St Privat. There they stopped. No more urging could get the survivors forward. They could only crouch in firing positions and wait for the attack of the Saxons, which they had so disastrously anticipated, to develop on their left flank. The casualty returns were to reveal over 8,000 officers and men killed and wounded, mostly within twenty minutes; more than a quarter of the entire corps strength. If anything was needed to vindicate the French faith in the *chassepot*, it was the aristocratic corpses which so thickly strewed the fields between St Privat and St Marie-les-Chênes.[3]

By 6 p.m. then, the French had met the German attack along the length of their front and had everywhere held firm. Their pre-war theorists had not been at fault when they had foreseen the unprecedented strength which modern weapons would lend the defence. If there was any weakening, it was the result of German artillery fire—

[1] Frederick Charles, *Denkwürdigkeiten* II 252–3. Moritz Busch, *Bismarck: Some Secret Pages of his History* I 97, 195.

[2] *Der 18 August 1870* 378–9.

[3] *Ibid.* 408–65. Hohenlohe-Ingelfingen, *Aus meinem Leben* 284, and *Letters on Infantry* (London 1889) 51–2. *G.G.S.* I ii 127–35.

especially that of the Guard whose guns, cleverly directed by their commander Prince Kraft zu Hohenlohe-Ingelfingen, broke up all French attempts to counter-attack between Amanvillers and St Privat;[1] and there can be little doubt that the tremendous pressure of the Guard's attack, heavy though the cost was to the atttackers, weakened Canrobert's troops and made easier the task of the Saxons. But it was not until the Saxon outflanking movement made itself felt that the French position began to crumble. North of St Privat Canrobert could spare only a handful of men to protect his right flank, and between 6 and 7 p.m. these troops could do no more than delay the Saxons' advance through Montois and Roncourt. By 7 p.m., as twilight was falling, they had been pressed back on St Privat; the Saxons were in Roncourt, and their guns were deployed, fourteen batteries strong, in a line almost at right angles to those of the Guard, which they joined in a concentrated bombardment of the blazing and crowded village.[2]

Canrobert, his artillery crushed and his infantry caught between two fires, had already decided that he must fall back. He warned Ladmirault on his left, sent a message asking Bourbaki to cover his retreat and asked Du Barail to put in a cavalry charge, to win a little time. The last manœuvre was hopeless: German fire broke up the charge before it had covered fifty yards; and there was little to check the Prussian Guard and the Saxons when, at 7.30 p.m. they charged cheering on to the disintegrating French position, fifty thousand strong, drums and bugles sounding and colours waving in the setting sun. There were about nine French battalions in the village, and some fifteen Prussian and Saxon battalions attacking. Some French units were retreating in good order, others had collapsed, a few remained firing in the burning houses. Not for an hour could any kind of order be established. Then the Germans found themselves in possession of the village, and the French were in full retreat down the Woippy road in a long straggling column, covered only by a few devoted battalions. The Germans were themselves too disorganised to pursue.[3]

Meanwhile Bourbaki had come up with the Imperial Guard—that élite reserve so carefully preserved by the French command that it had barely fired a shot since the beginning of the war. From the beginning of the battle Bourbaki had held his men in readiness behind the centre of the French front, waiting for an order from his listless commander-

---

[1] Hohenlohe-Ingelfingen, *Aus meinem Leben* 278–9. Patry, *La Guerre telle qu'elle est* 109   [2] *G.G.S.* I ii 138–46. *Guerre: Metz* III 508–76.
[3] *Guerre: Metz* III 519–24, and Docs. annexes 356–72. *G.G.S.* I ii 148–51.

in-chief. When earlier in the day Bazaine ordered him to send off a brigade to support Frossard, Bourbaki complied, but pointed out that it was unwise both to commit the reserve so soon and to commit it piecemeal. Bazaine's answer was typical: "You may either recall it or leave it there, as suits you best"; and no further message came from him for the rest of the day. For this abdication of the principal function of an army commander, the employment of his reserve, Bazaine later gave the curious explanation that Bourbaki, as commander of the reserve, had full powers to act as he thought best[1]—a statement on which comment is unnecessary. Bourbaki remained, anxious and inactive, behind the battlefront, without orders or information, until at about 6.15 p.m. two officers arrived from Ladmirault at Amanvillers to ask for help. Ladmirault had been counter-attacking to relieve the pressure on Canrobert and in so doing had suffered severely from German fire; but he suspected that the enemy opposite him was equally exhausted: the arrival of fresh troops might tip the scale. Bourbaki hesitated to answer this appeal. A suspiciously large number of stragglers seemed to be wandering back from 6th Corps front; he could see through his telescope signs of a battle raging round St Privat; and if the right flank was in danger, he was the only person who could retrieve it. But Ladmirault's messengers were urgent and convincing. Bourbaki yielded, and set off with one division along the road towards Amanvillers.[2]

The progress of the battle was masked from Bourbaki, as he advanced, by thick woods from which he emerged on to the plateau at about 6.45 p.m. Then he could see that his fears were realised. From St Privat a thick crowd of fugitives was pouring down the road, blocking the path of the guardsmen and shaking even their imperturbable discipline. Bourbaki turned on his guide and cursed him furiously in words drearily typical of the French generals of the time. "You promised me a victory," he stormed, "now you've got me involved in a rout. You had no right to do that! There was no need to make me leave my magnificent positions for this!" Boiling with rage, he turned his column about and began to canter away from the battlefield.[3] The result of such prima donna behaviour was disastrous. The sight of the Guard apparently in confusion and retreat not only confirmed the fears of the fugitives from 6th Corps, but panicked a section of 4th Corps as

[1] *Procès Bazaine* 167.
[2] Ibid. 282.
[3] Ibid. 233, 282. *Guerre: Metz* III 496–8 and Docs. annexes 452–3.

well. By the time Bourbaki had collected himself, the Guard was out of control and nothing would halt them. They dissolved into retreat just as the last resistance of 6th Corps collapsed, and Bourbaki could only deploy his artillery to discourage the German pursuit.[1]

Thus Ladmirault, so far from receiving support, found his right flank laid bare. There was nothing he could do but withdraw 4th Corps as well, in such order as he could manage, with the Germans pressing on his heels. Darkness made it possible for him to get away, but equally made it impossible for him to check the retreat from developing, like that of 6th Corps, into a disorderly flood of men, waggons and horses down the narrow road to Woippy and Metz.[2]

The French retreat from St Privat, however, was a precise and disciplined withdrawal in comparison with the collapse of the Germans which simultaneously occurred the other end of the front, before Gravelotte. There nothing could be done to retrieve Steinmetz's mistakes. By 5 p.m. forty-three Prussian companies were massed around St Hubert, drawn from seven separate regiments, entirely unable to advance.[3] Troops sent up to support the attack lost all cohesion as they passed through the chaos of the ravine, and their arrival merely swelled the confusion. Steinmetz's own reserves were almost exhausted; but General von Fransecky's II Corps, which had only just caught up with the advancing army, was beginning to appear in huge compact columns of fresh troops, and Steinmetz appealed to Royal Headquarters for permission to use them as well.[4] The King was at Gravelotte. He had come forward from Flavigny on receiving a totally erroneous message from Steinmetz that the heights had been carried. Now, at 7 p.m., he sanctioned a renewal of the attack on the grounds "that now, as the heights had once been carried, and then lost, everything must be done to get possession of them again". Moltke expressed disagreement only by chilly silence: he knew better than to contradict two choleric septuagenarians at the height of a battle; and as II Corps came up to the battlefield Steinmetz ordered the protesting Goeben to attack with his last reserves.[5]

[1] *Guerre: Metz* III: Docs. annexes 462–7.
[2] Ibid. 545–8 and Docs. annexes 430, 398. D'Andlau, *Metz, Campagne et Négociations* 96.
[3] Hönig, *24 Hours of Moltke's Strategy* 127.
[4] A. von Schell, *Operations of the First Army* (English edn. London 1873) 131. Hönig, op. cit. 133–7.
[5] Verdy du Vernois, *With the Royal Headquarters* 84–5. *Der 18 August 1870* 302. Zernin, *Leben des Generals v. Goeben* II 63. Moltke himself was to admit in his digest of the Official History: "It would have been better if the Chief of

The French at Point du Jour had seen the helmets of II Corps gleaming in the evening sun as they advanced over the Gravelotte plain, and knew what to expect. As the Prussians attacked, the whole firing-line sprang into life, and Steinmetz's last onslaught was met by fire at point-blank range.[1] The German infantry reeled back; in the ravine some of the horses crammed on the narrow road began to bolt; and suddenly the tension which had sustained the Germans snapped altogether. Squadrons of cavalry, teams of gun-horses went careering back through Gravelotte, and the infantry, too long patient under the French shells, ran shrieking with them in a ragged howling mass out of the ravine, through the flame-lit village streets under the astounded eyes of their Supreme War Lord, shouting "We are lost!" Staff officers, the King himself, weighed in cursing with the flat of their swords, but the flood of men swept on to Rezonville before it halted. The panic swept round the German rear; a line of retreat was reconnoitred for the King.[2] Now if the French had attacked, if they had had cavalry on hand, they might have thrown the First Army into disorder, and isolated the Second. But no attack was made. On the French side only one brigade seems to have known of the German repulse, and Jolivet, its commander, wrote in his report: "I did not think I should pursue them, having been ordered to remain on the defensive." Such an army does not deserve victory.[3]

The horrors of the Mance ravine had still not been exhausted. Against the tide of panic II Corps was beginning to advance into action. No deployment was possible in the ravine and both divisions of the Corps advanced *en bloc*. Beyond the ravine deployment was easier, and a few units brought their fire to bear on the dark masses of what they took to be the French ahead. But they were not the French: they were the remainder of VII and VIII Corps still holding firm round St Hubert, and at this sudden volley out of the darkness their precarious

Staff, who was personally on the field at the time, had not allowed this movement at so late an hour. A body of troops, still completely intact, might have been of great value the next day; it was not likely this evening to affect the issue." Moltke, *The Franco-German War* (London 1891) I 78.

[1] Nearly all German sources speak of a French counter-attack, but there is no evidence of this in the French documents. At most a few units made limited lunges at the Germans immediately before them. See, e.g. *Guerre: Metz* III: Docs. annexes 96, 101.

[2] *Kriegsgesch. Einzelschr.* XIX. *König Wilhelm auf seinem Kriegszuge in Frankreich* 43–4. *Der 18 August 1870* 307. Hönig, op. cit. 140–43. Verdy du Vernois, op. cit. 88. F. von Rauch, *Briefe aus dem grossen Hauptquartier* (Berlin 1911) 54.

[3] *Guerre: Metz* III: Docs. annexes 103.

control also collapsed. Of the confusion that followed no coherent account is possible: they "fell to pieces like a house of cards and poured to the rear in a wild panic, rushing, shouting, and quite out of their senses, to an extent indeed which has seldom happened in the history of war." II Corps could do no more than take over the positions they abandoned and sound the cease-fire, to stop any further mutual slaughter. At 9.30 p.m. the battle on this part of the front also came to an inglorious end.[1]

The King and his staff rode slowly back to Rezonville. There, while orderly officers tried to find them lodgings in the tiny houses already overflowing with wounded and administrative troops, they stood round a bonfire discussing what to do next. There was little cause for satisfaction with the day's work. The First Army had clearly suffered crippling losses, and its morale was severely shaken. From the Second Army nothing had been heard for several hours. The French line was apparently intact. In the royal entourage the view was frankly expressed, that the German armies had reached the end of their tether; and it was only on Moltke's insistence that the King gave the order to renew the attack next day. Not until after midnight did Moltke learn from Frederick Charles that the French right wing had collapsed and that the day was won.[2]

Next morning, even when the French were found to have slipped away, there was little feeling of victory. The slaughter had been too great, and it was clear that the Germans had suffered most. The King was overwhelmed by the reckless squandering of his Guard, and when Bismarck declared that "people are fed up with Steinmetz's butchery" he was voicing an opinion being generally expressed in still more forcible terms. "I have given up asking after friends", commented Verdy, "as I get to each question no other answer than 'dead' or 'wounded'." Roon, who had to find the replacements, was particularly appalled. "We have too few officers even in peacetime!" he lamented.[3]

---

[1] Kunz, *Kriegsgeschichtliche Beispiele aus dem deutsch-französischen Kriege von 1870–71* I. *Das Nachtgefecht vom 18 August 1870*, (Berlin 1897) 83–94. Hönig, op. cit. 127, 156. Zernin, *Leben des Generals v. Goeben* II 265. Bronsart and Verdy both believed II Corps attack to have succeeded, and Bronsart, according to his own account, rode back to Royal Headquarters shouting: "Die Schlacht ist gewonnen, das II Armeekorps hat die Höhe 'tambour battant' gestürmt und den Feind nach Metz hinuntergeworfen!" Bronsart, *Kriegstagebuch* 45.

[2] Verdy du Vernois, *With the Royal Headquarters* 91–2.

[3] Frederick III, *War Diary* 65. Bamberger, *Bismarcks Grosses Spiel* 173. Verdy du Vernois, op. cit. 94. Roon, *Denkwürdigkeiten* III 193. F. von Rauch, *Briefe aus dem Grossen Hauptquartier* 56, 61–2.

The First Army alone had lost 4,219 men, while the casualties of the French units opposing it—2nd Corps, and 3rd and 4th Divisions of 3rd Corps—totalled only about 2,155.[1] The Guard as we have seen lost over 8,000. The official German figure of losses is 20,163 officers and men; Bazaine's return, incomplete and approximate, totalled 12,273.[2] Only Moltke seemed unmoved as he viewed the carnage, and as he drove back to Pont-à-Mousson next day he made only one singularly inappropriate comment. "I have learned once more", he murmured, "that one cannot be too strong on the field of battle."[3]

On 19th August Bazaine took stock of his position.

> The troops are tired with these endless battles [he wrote plaintively to Napoleon], which do not allow them to recover (*ne leur permettent pas les soins matériels*); they must be allowed to rest for two or three days. . . . I still reckon to move northwards and fight my way out via Montmédy on the Ste Ménéhould–Châlons road, if it is not too strongly occupied; if it is, I shall go on through Sedan and Mézières to reach Châlons.[4]

That the Germans might interfere with these plans does not seem to have entered into his calculations. If the French troops needed rest and reorganisation, rest and reorganisation they must have. So on 19th August the Army of the Rhine, weary but by no means defeated, fell back into positions under the fortress of Metz. Its active part in the war was over.

It is tempting to rank the double battle of Rezonville-Gravelotte among the decisive engagements of the Western world; not because of what occurred during its course but because of what failed to occur. The strategic and tactical errors committed by the German commanders were so considerable that at the hands of a reasonably competent adversary they might have suffered, both on 16th August and on 18th August, an absolute defeat. Such a defeat might not have changed the ultimate outcome of the struggle, but the effect on belligerent morale and neutral opinion could have been sufficiently profound to alter the whole character of the war and of the peace which followed it. For these errors Moltke was only in part to blame: the main responsibility for misjudging the position of the French army both on 16th August

---

[1] *G.G.S.* I ii. App. XXIV. I take these figures in preference to the slightly lower ones in *Kriegsgesch. Einzelschr.* XI, which omit certain subsidiary skirmishes. *Guerre: Metz* III: Docs. annexes 94.

[2] *G.G.S.* I ii. App. XXIV. *Guerre: Metz* III: Docs. annexes 79.

[3] Verdy du Vernois, op. cit. 101.

[4] Bazaine, *Épisodes* 107–8. See p. 189 below.

and on 18th August, and thus exposing first III Corps to annihilation and then the Second Army to a flanking attack, must lie with Frederick Charles. Even when the French failed, through the strict passivity of their defence, to exploit either of these opportunities, they were given one more chance by Steinmetz, who flung away his army in the Mance ravine and left the most vulnerable flank of the German forces open to counter-attack; while at lower levels of command the recklessness with which the Prussian infantry was squandered in frontal attacks in close order against an enemy entrenched in strong positions and armed with a far superior rifle, on the orders of commanders in no position to appreciate what they were asking their men to do, foreshadowed with horrible accuracy the worst of the fighting in the First World War. The fault of the French lay in failing to follow their successful defensive with a resolute attack. The indictment against Bazaine is not that he lost the battles of Rezonville and Gravelotte: it is that he failed to win them when victory lay within his grasp.

CHAPTER V

The Army of Châlons

§1 Beaumont

NAPOLEON, in a third-class railway carriage, reached Châlons on the evening of 16th August, and there, as he expected, he found his second army in course of formation. Palikao had laboured heroically. The three right-wing corps of the old Army of the Rhine, 1st, 5th and 7th, were coming in by train from Chaumont and Belfort, and their depleted ranks were being filled up with recruits from the class of 1869. The new 12th Corps was there, under Trochu; one of its divisions formed of good regular troops from the Spanish frontier, one of Marines who could no longer be used for landing in Germany, and one of newly joined, untrained men. Armaments were also arriving in more than adequate quantity. By 21st August, when it set out on its brief and disastrous campaign, the Army of Châlons, under the command of MacMahon, totalled 130,000 men, with 423 guns; a remarkable testimony to the traditional powers of improvisation of which the French army was justly so proud.[1]

In spite of all this activity, Napoleon cannot have found the sight encouraging. The regular troops, broken by battle or wearied by their long retreat, sprawled about in haggard exhaustion, deaf to the commands of their officers. "It was an inert crowd," wrote one observer, "vegetating rather than living, scarcely moving even if you kicked them, grumbling at being disturbed in their weary sleep."[2] The new blood infused into this sluggish body consisted of raw recruits or depôt troops, hardly able to march in step and quite unable to load or fire their weapons. During the few days spent at Châlons it was impossible even to begin turning them into soldiers, and in the halts on their subsequent marches every available moment had to be devoted to training.[3] Finally there were the eighteen battalions of the *Garde Mobile* of the

---

[1] *Guerre: Armée de Châlons* I 4–17.
[2] D'Hérisson, *Journal of a Staff Officer* 18.
[3] *Guerre: Armée de Châlons* I: Docs. annexes 104–5.

Seine, who had brought with them all the turbulent iconoclasm which had for so long been their birthright as citizens of Paris. To the cry of *Vive l'Empereur!* they responded, with military precision, "*Un! Deux! Trois! Merde!*"[1] They did not share the provincial conscript's disinclination to fight at all; they only manifested a marked unwillingness to fight outside their own doorstep. They had greeted Canrobert with yells of "*à Paris!*" "My children," he replied politely, "I am probably rather deaf. Don't you mean *à Berlin?*" They did not; and the marshal, as we have already seen, urgently advised Palikao to distribute them among the fortresses of the north.[2]

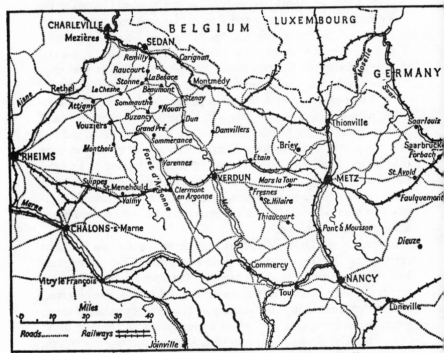

Map 9: *The Marne, the Meuse and the Moselle*

Men and arms were adequate, but supplies and services were not. The men of 1st Corps and Conseil's Division of 7th Corps had left their packs on the battlefield of Froeschwiller, and these could be replaced only on the basis of one between two men. The artillery of 7th Corps,

[1] D'Hérisson, *Journal of a Staff Officer* 21.
[2] *D.T.* IV 272.

held up by the congestion on the railways, did not reach the army until the eve of the battle of Sedan; in several divisions medical services were almost totally absent; and, it need hardly be said, there was a chronic shortage of maps.[1] Given time and an able commander, these difficulties could have been overcome, as Chanzy, Aurelle, and Faidherbe were to overcome far worse a few months later. Compared with the Armies of National Defence, the Army of Châlons, with its trained commanders, its excellent artillery and cavalry and its nucleus of regular infantry, was a respectable instrument of war—one which in the hands of the first Napoleon might have inflicted mortal damage on the enemy, and even now, under a competent leader following a cautious and correct strategy, might yet have held the Germans in play for long enough for Bazaine to take the offensive and for new forces to assemble under the walls of Paris. Distressing as were the inadequacies of the army assembling under MacMahon, they do not by themselves explain the disaster of Sedan.

On 17th August, the day after his arrival, Napoleon summoned a conference to discuss future plans. It was attended by MacMahon, by Trochu, commander of the newly formed 12th Corps and Schmitz his chief of staff, by Berthaut the commander of the *Garde Mobile*, and by Prince Napoleon, who had reached the camp several days before. The Emperor, as had been usual with him for months, was listless and silent, allowing the arguments to flow over his head. There was as yet no question of collaboration between the two armies or of help for Bazaine: reports from local officials about the battle which had been fought the day before spoke on the whole of a French victory.[2] The political issue seemed more urgent than the military: the position of the Emperor and the régime itself, and what could be done to maintain them. The lead was taken by the Emperor's cousin: he was, as Trochu later remarked, the only Napoleon who now counted. The Emperor himself murmured sadly in a moment of self-critical reflection, "I seem to have abdicated", and the Prince sharply took him up. "You abdicated the government at Paris; at Metz you have now abdicated the command of the army."[3] If the régime was to be saved he must reassert himself, both as Emperor and as commander-in-chief. He should set himself at the head of the army and return with it to Paris. There revolution was already threatening, and only one act, maintained the Prince, could stop it: the appointment of Trochu, liberal, prescient,

[1] *Guerre: Armée de Châlons* I 4-15.   [2] Ibid. I: Docs. 29.
[3] *D.T.* II 278.

and popular, whose Cassandra-like words of warning had passed unheeded, as Governor of the city. Nobody opposed the project, and when the Emperor, only half-convinced, suggested that the Empress should be consulted, his cousin broke in brutally, "Aren't you the sovereign? This has got to be done at once." Trochu supported the argument with sound military reasoning: around the inviolable fortress of Paris the army, under MacMahon's command, could manœuvre at will, and recruit its strength. So it was agreed: Trochu was to hand over the command of 12th Corps to General Lebrun, and return to Paris that evening, taking the *Mobiles* with him. The idea that they should be distributed among the fortresses of the north was opposed by the Emperor and Trochu with doctrinaire obstinacy. "They must defend their homes, that is their duty." The army of Châlons was to follow them in a few days.[1]

But that afternoon the situation was transformed. A message arrived from Bazaine—the telegram he had despatched late the previous night after the battle of Vionville.[2] The wording was confident enough: the enemy has been repulsed, the French were passing the night on their "conquered positions", and they would fall back on Metz to revictual and start out again in two days. The substance of the message, however, was disquieting: why should the army need to fall back? Napoleon responded "Tell me the truth about your position so that I can act accordingly." Later that night a telegram arrived from Palikao, begging Napoleon to reconsider his plans. To fall back on Paris, he said, would look like deserting the Army of Metz, "Could you not make a powerful diversion against the Prussian Corps, already worn out by several engagements?" Napoleon began to vacillate once more.[3]

Meanwhile Trochu's appearance in Paris filled the Government with consternation. Palikao and the Emperor had sent him to Châlons largely to get rid of him, as they had sent the *Mobiles*, and their simultaneous return seemed a most sinister political move. Palikao, finding all his plans reversed with no attempt at consultation, threatened to resign. The Empress bluntly declared to Trochu that there could be no question of Napoleon returning to Paris; only his enemies, she added, meaningly, could advise him to do so. Palikao also pointed out that if the army returned to Paris the whole system of supplies and reinforcements would have to be reorganised—a point which the Châlons conference had

[1] Trochu, *Œuvres posthumes* I 114–30. *D.T.* I 28–9. MacMahon's Memoirs in *Guerre: Armée de Châlons* I: Docs. annexes 14–16. Lebrun, *Bazeilles-Sedan* (Paris 1884) 3.
[2] See p. 162 above.   [3] *Guerre: Armée de Châlons* I: Docs. annexes 16–17.

apparently overlooked. So Napoleon reversed his decision. The attempt of the Prince Napoleon to combat the influence of the Empress had failed. All that remained of his plan was the presence in Paris of the suspect Trochu and his mutinous *Mobiles*.[1]

Thus Trochu's brief excursion into the sphere of higher strategy for the moment ended; and a few days later the despatch of Prince Napoleon to Florence in a last attempt to secure Italian intervention removed the only other figure capable of inspiring the Emperor to independent action.[2] The disposal of the Army of Châlons now lay in the hands of MacMahon. An appeal to Bazaine, his nominal superior, for instructions, remained totally without result: "I presume that the minister will have given you orders," the latter replied unhelpfully on 18th August, "your operations being at the moment entirely outside my zone of action."[3] MacMahon knew that his army was in no condition to take the field. No move was administratively possible until 21st August; but then a decision could still be delayed by a movement on Rheims, whence he could either advance to join Bazaine or fall back to cover Paris.[4] All depended on Bazaine's own plans; and the difficulty of ascertaining them was not only increased by the growing difficulty of communication, but made absolute by the fact that they did not exist. MacMahon waited on Bazaine and Bazaine waited on Providence.

On 18th August Bazaine's aide-de-camp reached Châlons, bringing details of the battle of Vionville and confirming his commander's intention of setting out for Châlons, after two days of reorganisation, by a detour to the north.[5] Then the telegraph-line was cut between Metz and Châlons; thereafter communication depended on individual messengers slipping through increasingly well-guarded German lines. The interruption of communications made it seem improbable to MacMahon that Bazaine would be able to move as easily as he claimed, and on 19th August he expressed his fears in a frank message to Metz: "If, as I believe, you are forced to retreat in the near future, I cannot see, at this distance, how I can come to your aid without uncovering Paris. If you see the matter differently, let me know."[6] Another twenty-four

---

[1] *D.T.* I 150, 219, 264. *D.T.* II 280. Trochu, *Œuvres posthumes* I 142–50.

[2] Lehautcourt, *Guerre de 1870* VI 130 suggests that Napoleon was deliberately getting rid of an embarrassing witness. One suspects the hand of the Empress, but there is no documentary evidence to suggest it. See A. Darimon, *Notes pour servir à l'histoire de la Guerre de 1870* (Paris 1888) 194 ff. for the course and outcome of this mission.   [3] *Guerre: Armée de Châlons* I: Docs. annexes 39.

[4] *Guerre: Armée de Châlons* I: Docs. annexes 45, 67.

[5] Ibid. 44.   [6] Ibid. 62–8.

hours of silence made him still more uncertain. Bazaine seemed lost.
A sheaf of telegrams was sent out from Châlons to the garrison commanders and the civil officials in the neighbourhood, asking for news. Had
he broken out to the south?[1] MacMahon was unwilling to move at all
until he had more certain information. But a commander in the field
who hesitates long enough can always rely on the enemy making up his
mind for him: and so it was now. On the afternoon of 20th August
enemy cavalry was reported within twenty-five miles of Châlons itself.
MacMahon's hand was forced; and on 21st August, leaving behind a
cavalry division to collect stragglers and destroy the stores that remained
in the camp, the Army of Châlons, still uncertain of its rôle and its
ultimate destination, set out for Rheims. With it, a passive and useless
passenger, went the Emperor, and all the cumbersome apparatus of his
suite.

In Paris, meanwhile, the Council of Ministers had decided that if
Bazaine was in danger of being blockaded in Metz, he must be rescued
at almost any cost. It was not a military matter only: if the government
abandoned Bazaine to his fate, it could not hope to survive the explosion
of Parisian wrath that would inevitably follow. It was, in the words of
one of its members, "an imperative duty for us to avoid any act which
might bring about a revolutionary movement".[2] Rational deliberation
and sound strategy under such a pressure are rarely possible, and for
the civilian ministers the decision to rescue Bazaine was a counsel of
despair. But Palikao considered the rescue operation perfectly feasible.
In 1792 Dumouriez had carried out a flanking operation in the Argonne
against the invading Prussians with spectacular success. Why should
not MacMahon, over the same ground and against the same enemy,
repeat the triumph of Valmy? To make it easier he devised a stratagem
to divide the German armies. A false despatch ordering MacMahon to
retire on Paris was to fall into the hands of the Crown Prince, whose
army would then continue to march on the capital in supposed pursuit
of their foe. Meanwhile the Army of Châlons, a hundred and thirty
thousand strong, could fall on the remaining German forces with a
nearly twofold superiority. The siege of Metz would be raised, Bazaine
would attack, and the German armies would be caught between two
fires.[3]

---

[1] *Guerre: Armée de Châlons* I: Docs. annexes 90–1.
[2] Brame, in *D.T.* I 192. Palikao expressed the same view in a letter to Napoleon
on 22nd August. *Les Papiers secrets du Second Empire No. 3* (Brussels 1871) 64.
[3] Palikao, *Un Ministère de la Guerre de 24 jours* (Paris 1871) 96–102.

On the afternoon of 21st August Rouher, President of the Senate and the most influential of all imperial politicians, went to Rheims to convey the Council's new decisions to MacMahon. MacMahon, however, after seeing his army on the march for a day, had now made up his mind that any such action was out of the question. "It is impossible to rescue Bazaine", he confessed to Rouher. "He has no munitions, no supplies, he will be forced to capitulate and we shall arrive too late."[1] The only hope lay in marching the Army of Châlons back to Paris, and reorganising under the protection of the guns of the fortress. Rouher, confronted with the military realities at first hand, accepted Mac-Mahon's judgment. He drafted an imperial proclamation appointing MacMahon Commander-in-Chief of the Army of Châlons and of all the troops in and around Paris; he drafted a proclamation by MacMahon outlining his intention of making of his army the core of a new Nation in Arms to match the Prussians; and he returned to Paris to face the Empress's wrath.[2]

Within a few hours this decision also was reversed, and once again Bazaine provided the cause. His message of 19th August[3] reached Rheims, with its confident assertion that he intended to break out from Metz, either via Ste Ménéhould or via Sedan. This put matters in a different perspective. Bazaine was not after all going to let himself be shut up in Metz: he was, possibly at this very moment marching to join MacMahon. It was no longer a question of marching to his relief, but of joining him to give battle in the open field. MacMahon at once reversed his decision. The orders for the retreat on Paris were cancelled: instead MacMahon informed both Bazaine and Palikao that he would set out for Montmédy, and in two days would be on the Aisne. On 23rd August the Army of Châlons set out on the second stage of its journey.[4]

*   *   *

[1] *D.T.* I. 238–9.
[2] His drafts are reprinted in *Les Papiers secrets du Second Empire No. 5* (Brussels 1871) 13–16.   [3] See p. 181 above.
[4] *D.T.* 32, 240. *Guerre: Armée de Châlons*: Docs. annexes 135, 140. Later that evening another message reached MacMahon's headquarters from Bazaine, despatched on 20th August. This virtually duplicated that of the 19th, but added " L'ennemi grossit toujours autour de nous et je suivrai très probablement pour vous rejoindre, la ligne des places du Nord, et vous préviendrai de ma marche, si toutefois je puis l'entreprendre sans compromettre l'armée."
About this message an extraordinary controversy was to rage. MacMahon claimed that he never saw it, and that if he had he would have realised how hesitant Bazaine was about marching and would in consequence have fallen back on Paris. Baron Stoffel, who was now attached to MacMahon's staff as

The Germans no less than the French needed a pause for rest and reorganisation after their exertions round Metz. In his orders of 19th August Moltke provided for it, but without letting the initiative slide from his hands. Two tasks now confronted him—the containment of Bazaine's intact army, and the pursuit and destruction of the new forces assembling at Châlons. The Crown Prince, whose cavalry was already advancing west from Nancy towards the Marne, would not be strong enough to deal with MacMahon on his own; but if one of the armies at Metz was detached to help him, the other would be inadequate to hold Bazaine. The problem could be solved only by abandoning the tripartite organisation of the German armies and dividing them into two approximately equal groups. The Second Army was therefore split into two. The Guard, IV and XII Corps, together with the two cavalry divisions, were pared off and constituted into a separate army called, provisionally, the Army of the Meuse, under the Crown Prince of Saxony, the commander of XII Corps.[1] The appointment was not only politically tactful but militarily sound, as the Prince's highly competent handling of his troops before St Privat had clearly shown. This army, as its name suggests, was to advance to the Meuse in pursuit of MacMahon. The remaining four corps of the Second Army would stay at Metz with the First Army, and Frederick Charles assumed command of the whole investing force.

The advantages of such an arrangement were not only strategic. It provided, in addition, an excellent opportunity to get rid of Steinmetz. Nobody expected that he would acquiesce in his subordination to Frederick Charles, and Moltke gave the Prince *carte blanche* to dismiss him at the first sign of trouble.[2] Frederick Charles had less than three weeks to wait. On 7th September he complained that Steinmetz was deliberately withholding from him the customary civilities due to a superior officer. The King was furious at an action presented to him as an insult to a Prince of the Royal House; and on 15th September Steinmetz was transferred to honourable retirement as Governor of

chief of intelligence and on whom the blame fell for failing to forward the message, claimed that it had gone up to the Marshal who had simply failed to attach any importance to it. Stoffel's explanation seems convincing: it would only be in the light of later events that Bazaine's qualifications became significant. Stoffel was later accused, by the *rapporteur* at Bazaine's trial, of suppressing the telegram on the orders of Napoleon. A natural but indiscreet explosion of wrath led to his being sentenced to three months' penal detention. Stoffel, *La Dépêche du 20 août* (Paris 1874). *Guerre: Armée de Châlons* I 89–91, and Docs. annexes 219–20. Lehautcourt, *Guerre de 1870* VI 183 n. 3.

[1] *M.M.K.* 235.   [2] Bronsart, *Kriegstagebuch* 70–2.

Posen.[1] With his disappearance Moltke's supremacy in the German armies emerged unchallenged at last.

His reorganisation complete, Moltke gave orders on 21st August for the advance to begin two days later.[2] At that moment the French army was beginning its march from Châlons to Rheims. The Third Army already stood along the Meuse south of Commercy, and its cavalry patrols had reached the Marne, and the railway which ran beside it, between Vitry and Joinville, hard on the heels of the last train-loads of French troops bound for Châlons. Moltke's left wing was thus already echeloned forward, and this formation he proposed to retain on the march in the hope that it would have the effect of scooping the French army away from Paris wherever it was encountered. Once again Moltke was preparing his strategy so as to be in an advantageous position for any possible battle; and though he could not foresee the change of direction which would be forced on him during the next few days, this preliminary formation gave him, as it turned out, a very considerable advantage.

On 23rd August therefore, while Frederick Charles completed the investment of Bazaine in Metz, the rest of the German armies began again to move west, the right wing towards Ste Ménéhould, the left wing on Vitry-le-François, the cavalry—especially that of the Third Army—scouting far ahead. Two great fortresses still barred the way, Toul and Verdun, and both, after attempts to bombard them into surrender with field-guns had failed, had to be expensively masked until siege artillery could be brought up to reduce them. But the delay imposed by such fortresses was in inverse ratio to the size of the invading army. From the numbers which Moltke was deploying, investing forces could be easily spared and labour could be drawn to build by-pass roads or even, as at Metz, railways.

Moltke's principal difficulty in planning his advance lay in his ignorance of the position of the enemy army. On 23rd August, the day that his march began, the French were reported to have left Châlons. Cavalry patrols reached the deserted camp on 24th August, and confirmed the news which was reaching Moltke from other quarters—that MacMahon had fallen back to Rheims. But the purpose of this move was still obscure. Royal Headquarters assumed that it was all part of the scheme to cover Paris. Blumenthal considered it to be the

[1] Bronsart, *Kriegstagebuch* 70–2, 79. H. von Kretschman, *Kriegsbriefe* (Stuttgart 1904) 99–100. H. von Krosigk, *General-Feldmarschall von Steinmetz* (Berlin 1900) 285.
[2] *M.M.K.* 239.

orthodox manœuvre of taking up a position on the flank of an enemy line of advance. The possibility that political necessity might compel MacMahon to discard military prudence and march to the relief of Bazaine was mooted, but Moltke did not yet take it seriously enough to modify his course of action. The orders which were drafted for 25th August, although prescribing considerable reconnaissance to the north and visualising the possibility of a detachment towards Rheims, did not provide for any change in the general direction of the German advance.[1] It was not till the night of 24th August that more definite news arrived. It took the form of a dispatch from London, based on reports in the Paris press, which spoke of MacMahon "endeavouring to form a junction" with Bazaine. Yet to Moltke the movement still seemed improbable. More information than this would be needed if the German armies and their supply columns were to be halted, given a new direction and sent lumbering northwards through the forest-lanes of the Argonne. The orders which Moltke issued for 25th and 26th August played for time. The armies were to change direction slightly to the right, making for Rheims rather than for Châlons; the cavalry of the right wing was to reconnoitre north-west, as far as Vouziers and Buzancy; and on the 27th, if no further orders were received, the advance was to pause along the line Vitry-le-François–Ste Ménéhould.[2]

Thus prepared for any eventuality Moltke spent the 25th waiting for more definite news and working out one of those complex march-tables at which constant practice had made his staff so adept, and which would enable him to intercept MacMahon, he reckoned, near Damvillers by 29th August. In the evening the news for which he was waiting at last arrived—a bundle of Paris newspapers which not only canvassed the project of a march to rescue Bazaine but in at least one instance— *Le Temps* of 23rd August—unequivocally declared that MacMahon had already marched north-east from Rheims to do so.[3] The picture was becoming clear.

Yet the evidence was still indirect. It might be deliberate deception. No reports had been received from the cavalry of the Army of the Meuse to substantiate it. Moltke was faced with one of those decisions which arise only once or twice in the course of a campaign, which can be

[1] *M.M.K.* 246. *G.G.S.* I ii 199. Blumenthal, *Journals* 102. Bronsart, *Kriegstagebuch* 49.

[2] *M.M.K.* 248.

[3] In a Havas agency dispatch. "En ce moment même, l'armée de MacMahon se dirige vers le nord pour aller donner vers l'est la main à Bazaine." A. Darimon, *Notes* 223.

taken only by the supreme commander and in which no amount of skill or training can help—only that most necessary quality of all soldiers, lovers, and gamblers: luck. Moltke decided to take the risk and believe the reports. The orders which he sent to the Crown Prince of Saxony contained an escape clause, if cavalry reconnaissance to the north-west belied this evidence.[1] If the French were moving north, he said, the Army of the Meuse must concentrate on its right, between Verdun and Varennes, and the two Bavarian Corps, on the right wing of the Third Army, would swing round to the north as well; "but we cannot decide to undertake this without reports which His Royal Highness will have received and whose arrival here we cannot afford to wait for." The Crown Prince of Saxony was thus empowered to decide on his own, but to help him Moltke sent Verdy through the night to the Meuse Army Headquarters with much the same mission that he had been given, three weeks earlier, to the Crown Prince of Prussia—to ensure that the Army Commander acted in accordance with Moltke's ruling will.[2]

The Prince did not hesitate. He decided to start the movement without waiting for his cavalry reports, and at once the orders went out for his four infantry corps to wheel round to the north. Next day Moltke confirmed them. The Army of the Meuse was to advance north into the Argonne, carrying three days' provisions and leaving behind all baggage not absolutely necessary. The Third Army also was to swing round in its entirety, for Blumenthal refused to co-operate in a plan which deprived him of half his forces and all part in the victory.[3] Finally a message went to Frederick Charles at Metz, asking for two of his corps to be sent off so as to reach the neighbourhood of Damvillers—where Moltke still expected the clash to take place—by the 28th. If necessary he was to raise the investment on the right bank of the Moselle, for MacMahon could be crushed before Bazaine could fight his way out to the east and march round to join him. Even if the two corps on the Third Army's left wing could not come up in time, Moltke would thus still have seven corps against the French four. Then Moltke himself and his headquarters rode north towards Clermont-en-Argonne, while his staff calculated how best to steer the 150,000 men under their control, with all their guns and supply-waggons, over the few poor roads which led north through the Argonne forest—roads which the

---

[1] *M.M.K.* 250.
[2] Verdy du Vernois, *With the Royal Headquarters* 113.
[3] *M.M.K.* 251. Blumenthal, *Journals* 104.

ceaseless tramp of German columns and the no less ceaseless downpour
of rain were rapidly rendering almost impassable. Confusion was probably reduced to a minimum, but it could not be eliminated. Marches
were prolonged, routes overlapped, supply-columns went astray, and
many German units were tried almost beyond their strength. Moreover
with the sudden change in the weather the sickness-rate shot up
alarmingly. But all was to be worth while. That very afternoon, as

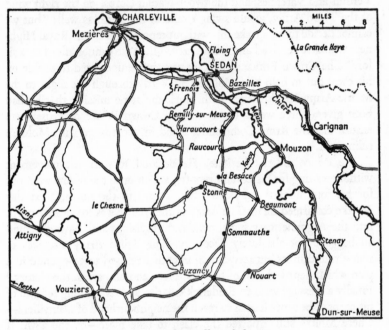

Map 10:   The Valley of the Meuse

Moltke was approaching Clermont, the Saxon cavalry, scouting
northwards towards Vouziers and Grand Pré, found MacMahon's army
at last.

*   *   *

Once MacMahon decided to march to the help of Bazaine with his
demoralised and unprepared army, his destruction was virtually certain.
His only chance, not so much of success as of avoiding catastrophe,
lay in speed; and of speed his huge, ill-trained and ill-supplied columns
were incapable. The difficulties which the *Intendance* found in supplying
so large a force marching through unprepared country were increased,

first by the inability of the French staff to plan that controlled dispersion on the march which enabled the Germans to move their far greater numbers so swiftly and flexibly, and secondly by the growing indiscipline of the columns themselves. There were plenty of supplies piled in Rheims station—though they were being rapidly reduced by pillage—and MacMahon ordered his corps to draw four days' rations before leaving the town. But the officers of the *Intendance* had neither time, staff, nor transport to organise distribution, and the fatigue-parties sent to draw rations were sent empty away.[1] During the first day's march from Rheims to the Suippe therefore the troops broke ranks and remorselessly pillaged the surrounding countryside.[2] MacMahon shrugged it off with the old campaigner's answer, that if the administration had collapsed the troops must live off the country, but even he realised that such *débrouillage* would not really suffice. The country over which the army was to advance was not richly cultivated. There were few towns, and no railways. Before going further the army had to replenish its supplies and this it could do only by returning to the railway at Rethel eighteen miles further north, at right angles to his line of march. On 24th August therefore the Army of Châlons veered sharply away from Metz towards the north—tactically a lunatic change of direction which does much to explain the failure of the German cavalry to locate the French for another two days. It was not until 26th August that Mac-Mahon could resume his interrupted march to the east.[3]

By now MacMahon's doubts were growing. Nothing more had been heard from Bazaine; MacMahon sent him a worried message confessing that "I do not think I can move much further east without having news of you and knowing your plans, for if the Crown Prince's army marches on Rethel I shall have to fall back"[4]; and on the 26th the cavalry of 7th Corps, on the right flank of the army, found itself involved with the Saxon cavalry patrols near Grand Pré. Douay, fearing to find himself at grips with the whole Prussian army, halted and deployed his entire corps. MacMahon sent up 1st Corps towards Vouziers in support and the whole French army lumbered to a halt. Once again the boldness of the German cavalry had paid good dividends.[5]

[1] *D.T.* I 32. Lebrun, *Bazeilles-Sedan* 44. *Guerre: Armée de Châlons* I 97. Lehautcourt, *Guerre de 1870* VI 200.

[2] *Guerre: Armée de Châlons* I: Docs. annexes 167–77. Sarazin, *Récits sur la dernierè guerre* 85.

[3] *Guerre: Armée de Châlons* I: Docs. annexes 189. Lebrun, op. cit. 42–4.

[4] *Guerre: Armée de Châlons* I: Docs. annexes 251.

[5] Ibid. 257. Bibesco, *Belfort, Reims, Sedan* 54–7.

Morning revealed to the French how exaggerated had been their fears. 1st Corps retraced its steps, and the army wearily continued pivoting on 7th Corps, which remained paralysed near Vouziers watching the Saxon cavalry patrols. This eastward advance brought the French yet more directly into the path of the German army pressing north-ward through the Argonne. The advance-guard of the Saxon cavalry division encountered 5th Corps at Buzancy, and after a brisk cavalry skirmish both sides fell back.[1] The main body of both German armies were still entangled far back in the muddy passages of the Argonne; but on their right flank the Saxons had reached the crossings of the Meuse at Dun and Stenay, and with their arrival MacMahon's last hope of reaching Montmédy without a fight vanished. By the evening of 27th August indeed, with German infantry reported before him on the Meuse, German forces occupying Châlons and Rheims in his rear, and German cavalry debouching from the Argonne to harass his right flank, Mac-Mahon at Le Chesne realised the full hopelessness of his position, and decided to give up the whole operation. Orders went out to the army to abandon its eastward march and instead turn north, and messages were sent to Bazaine warning him that if no news arrived of his march within the next few hours the Army of Châlons would be forced to withdraw on Mézières. Finally, MacMahon reported to Palikao what he was doing and why. There was no news from Bazaine, he pointed out, and if he advanced any further he would be attacked by the First and Second German Armies in front, while the Crown Prince came up from the south to cut off his retreat. Withdrawal to the north offered the only hope of escape.[2]

It was this message that sealed MacMahon's doom. Palikao's response was prompt and disastrous.

If you abandon Bazaine [he replied, in a message which reached MacMahon at 1 a.m. on 28th August], revolution will break out in Paris, and you will yourself be attacked by the entire enemy forces. . . . You have at least thirty-six hours' march over [the Crown Prince], perhaps forty-eight; you have nothing in front of you but a feeble part of the forces which are blockading Metz. . . . Everyone here has felt the necessity of releasing Bazaine, and the anxiety with which we follow your movements is intense.[3]

[1] *Guerre: Armée de Châlons* I: Docs. annexes 285–8, 298. *G.G.S.* I ii 215.
[2] *Guerre: Armée de Châlons* I: Docs. annexes 277–8.
[3] Ibid. 278–9. *D.T.* I 32.

It was this very anxiety, both over the political situation and for the success of the plan he had fostered which blinded Palikao to the realities of the military situation. For some days past he had been bombarding MacMahon with optimistic reports about the low morale of the German army, the mutinous attitude of the German reservists, the political dissatisfaction of the non-Prussian units, the ravages of dysentery and typhus in the German ranks and the likelihood of Austrian intervention: reports which he was no doubt quite ready to believe himself. But he was making, in addition to these egregious errors, one very natural mistake. He did not know of the existence of the Army of the Meuse. MacMahon, so far as he knew, had to deal only with the Crown Prince of Prussia; and the Crown Prince of Prussia was still bringing up his army south of Ste Ménéhould, the outer files in Moltke's huge right-wheel. It was thus impossible for Palikao to understand what MacMahon had to fear, and he was able to persuade the Council of Ministers that these fears were groundless. A few hours later he reinforced his personal message with a direct order carrying all the weight of ministerial authority. "In the name of the Council of Ministers and the Privy Council, I require you to aid Bazaine, taking advantage of the thirty-six hours' march which you have over the Crown Prince of Prussia."[1] In view of the cavalry already nibbling at the French flank, this last sentence made no sense at all. But MacMahon was a soldier and this was an order. He was not a man either to seize the initiative or to threaten resignation. From the Emperor's quarters came a gentle and wise whimper of protest; but Napoleon even more than MacMahon had surrendered all right to command. Obediently MacMahon counter-manded his orders and enquired about crossings of the Meuse below Stenay.[2] The last hope of escape had gone.

Some sense of this communicated itself to the troops on 28th August, as they marched on apprehensively in the rain, openly watched by German horsemen from the hills to the south.[3] The progress of 5th and 7th Corps, which were following one another between Vouziers and Buzancy, was watched throughout its entire length by German cavalry, which entered Vouziers as soon as 7th Corps had left it and had to be cleared from Buzancy before 5th Corps could enter. Even the two northernmost French corps, marching from Le Chesne towards La

[1] *Guerre: Armée de Châlons* I: Docs. annexes 279.
[2] M. Defourny, *L'Armée de MacMahon et la bataille de Beaumont* (Bruxelles 2nd edn. 1872) 78.
[3] Bibesco, *Belfort, Reims, Sedan* 80.

Besace, had their convoys panicked by Uhlan patrols. MacMahon was still hoping to cross the Meuse at Stenay, but during the day his cavalry found the bridges firmly held; so for 29th August he ordered his army to incline to the north again and make for the crossings at Remilly and Mouzon.[1]

For the two northern corps that was simple enough. Lebrun reached Mouzon with 12th Corps without much difficulty, and 1st Corps Raucourt six miles farther west. But for the two corps farther south it was not so easy to disengage themselves. 7th Corps, harassed by German cavalry, could cover barely half its prescribed journey to La Besace; while to Failly's 5th Corps near Buzancy, the most exposed of all the French units, the order to change direction northwards never penetrated at all. The staff-officer carrying it fell into German hands, and in consequence Failly went on eastwards towards Stenay. Thus it happened that a squadron of 5th Corps cavalry scouting a few hundred yards ahead of the main body, breasted a rise near Nouart and were received with a salvo of rifle-fire from infantry at point-blank range. They turned and slid wildly back down the hill on to their startled infantry; but not before they had seen on the slopes round Nouart, the whole of the Royal Saxon XII Army Corps deployed and ready for action.[2]

Hitherto only the German cavalry, spread out in a long screen from the Meuse towards Rethel, had been in contact with the French; now the infantry also was within striking distance. By 29th August the confusions consequent on the change of direction were over, and the pattern of Moltke's armies was once more clear. The Army of the Meuse had reached a line between Buzancy and Dun-sur-Meuse, the Guard on the left, the Saxons on the right and Gustav von Alvensleben's IVth Corps lying in reserve between them. Echeloned back on the left, the Third Army was coming up between Monthois and Sommerance, its cavalry scouting out westwards towards Attigny and Rethel.[3] Saxon advance-guards held the Meuse bridges at Stenay, barring the road to Montmédy, and Moltke had therefore been able to send back to Metz the two corps summoned from Frederick Charles. There were still sceptics among the German high command. Blumenthal grumbled about the constant change of orders on the basis of inadequate information; Gustav von Alvensleben declared that the whole change of direction was a terrible

[1] *Guerre: Armée de Châlons* I: Docs. annexes 323, 325, 327, 338.
[2] *Guerre: Armée de Châlons* II: Docs. annexes 6–9, 36–43, 58–68. Bibesco, op. cit. 82–4. *G.G.S.* I ii 228.
[3] *G.G.S.* I ii 236–8.

mistake[1]; but Moltke himself and his staff, once they realised that MacMahon had abandoned all idea of falling back to the north, measured the distance to the Belgian frontier and began to see the possibilities which lay within their grasp.[2] Moltke's orders on the evening of 28th August provided for a concentration of the Meuse Army, in preparation for a possible French attack on 30th August. The Meuse Army was to act as an anvil for the hammer of the Crown Prince sweeping round from the west. But the information which came back next day made him decide to make it take the offensive itself. The Meuse Army was ordered to advance on Beaumont with XII and IV Corps, and the Guard in reserve, while the Third Army, coming up on the left, was to push two Corps towards Buzancy and the rest round by Le Chesne. With any luck MacMahon could be pinned against the Meuse by both armies and hammered to pieces.[3]

The first contact occurred between French and German infantry on 29th August when, as we have seen, Failly blundered head-on to the left wing of the Saxon corps. The two sides blazed away at each other across the little valley of the Wiseppe all afternoon, and suffered about 600 casualties between them. The French withdrew as soon as darkness fell through the woods towards Beaumont. It was a pitch-dark night, and the troops stumbling along the forest-tracks took more than six hours to traverse the seven miles to their destination. When they emerged from the woods at Beaumont they threw themselves down at random and slept as best they could. The rearguard came up at 5 a.m. next morning, as dawn was breaking; and then, on the camp pitched haphazard on the slopes south of the village, there fell the silence of exhaustion.[4]

It was an unwise moment to rest. On 30th August, in accordance with Moltke's orders, the two Bavarian corps began to move on Sommauthe, and von Kirchbach's V Corps on Stonne; and on the right XII and IV Corps advanced through the thick woods that led to Beaumont.[5] The leading troops of IV Corps and of the I Bavarian Corps on 30th August came almost simultaneously in sight of Beaumont as they emerged from the woods; and at the sight of Failly's camp, lying

---

[1] Blumenthal, *Journals* 107. Bronsart, *Kriegstagebuch* 86. H. von Grolman: *E. E. von Krause: ein deutsches Soldatenleben* (Berlin 1901) 91.

[2] Verdy du Vernois, *With the Royal Headquarters* 117. The orders which Moltke issued at 7 p.m. on August 28th had been based on the assumption that MacMahon had abandoned his march on Montmédy and was falling back on Mézières. The reports of 5th Corps' advance on Buzancy led to these being modified. *M.M.K.* 259.

[3] *M.M.K.* 263.   [4] *Guerre: Armée de Châlons* II: Docs. annexes 11–26.

[5] *G.G.S.* I ii 286.

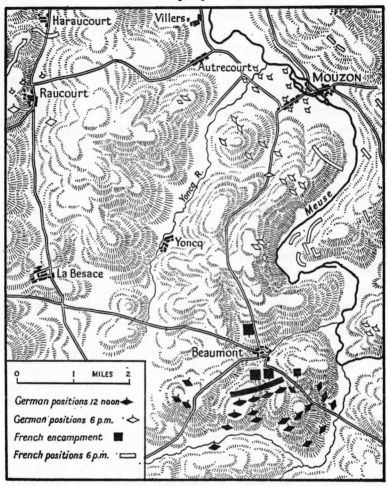

Map 11: The Battle of Beaumont

apparently at their mercy without sentries posted, without horses
saddled, without batteries in place, they could hardly believe their
eyes. It seemed almost unfair, the Germans said afterwards, to open
fire on such a target.[1] For a moment they considered whether it would
not be better to wait until all the advancing columns had drawn level,
and then launch a pulverising attack; but as the leading division of IV
Corps watched, they saw the beginnings of apprehensive movement;
and without further delay their artillery opened fire.

[1] Defourny, *La bataille de Beaumont* 108.

The French reacted with remarkable rapidity. "Like a startled swarm of bees" the infantrymen hurried forward from the camp and opened a violent fire.[1] A few regiments were already under arms, and advanced with beating drums to drive the Germans back into the woods. Elsewhere officers collected the first men who lay to hand into improvised battle-groups; but within the camp and the village, crowded with men and vehicles, there was total confusion. Staff-officers tumbled out of their billets, drivers tried to harness their plunging horses, guns, limbers, and waggons jammed the streets, masses of civilians and troops fled northward to Mouzon and eastward to the Meuse.[2] Within half an hour the rest of the corps followed in scarcely better order. The Saxons were appearing in the valley to the east of the village, the Bavarians on the heights to the west. The French had to fall back; and during their retreat the *élan* which had at first sustained them was hard to maintain. Only in a few units were the officers able to retain control during this most difficult of all military operations, and organise an orderly retreat by bounds; yet these regiments, and some hurriedly harnessed guns, did succeed in imposing respect on the cautious and methodical Germans. An adequate gun-line was formed on the slopes north of the village, which the Prussian IV Corps did not enter until 2 p.m. The Bavarians, emerging from the woods, were also checked by *chassepot* fire from the farms on the slopes above the Yoncq. There was no German cavalry on hand to harass the retreating French. When, at about 3.30 p.m., IV Corps and the Guard began to advance from Beaumont, they found that Failly had established himself in a good position a mile or so further north, against which it was necessary to mount a formal attack.[3]

Failly's colleagues could do little to help him. Douay, six miles to the west at Stonne, heard the gunfire; but he was obsessed with the problem of getting his cumbrous convoys across the Meuse, and it was easy to find excuses for doing nothing.[4] Lebrun was better placed, and did his best. 12th Corps was safely across the Meuse at Mouzon. Its left wing had taken up a position some kilometres upstream on the right bank, and was able to harass the Germans with artillery fire. One division started to

[1] *G.G.S.* I ii 247.
[2] *Guerre: Armée de Châlons* II: Docs. annexes 103–5, 117, 126, 176–95. Defourny, op. cit. 98–100.
[3] *G.G.S.* I ii 246–64. Helvig, *Operations of 1st Bavarian Army Corps* 58–60. *Guerre: Armée de Châlons* II: Docs. annexes 199–128, 173–4. See also H. von Hopffgarten-Heidler, *Die Schlacht bei Beaumont* (Berlin 1897) 24–88.
[4] Bibesco, op. cit. 104.

return across the river at Mouzon to bring Failly more immediate aid, but MacMahon forbade it. He was probably right. His task was to get across the river: Failly must fend for himself. If the army was sucked into a battle with its back to the Meuse, it would almost certainly be destroyed. Lebrun's aid was limited to the provision of a single brigade to protect the crossing of the convoys of 5th and 7th Corps, but even this help arrived too late to be effective. The Germans had already secured a foothold on the slopes overlooking Mouzon, and their fire broke up the advancing regiments and drove them back on the river.[1]

Failly's new positions quickly crumbled under determined attack. The country was close and wooded, with few effective fields of fire; the French had not recovered from their disorder; and the Germans, pressing closely, were able to drive them from position to position among the close copses and steep knolls without giving them time to draw breath. By 6 p.m. nothing lay between the Germans and the river but a plain covered with abandoned vehicles and crowds of troops streaming towards the bridges at Villers and Mouzon, in a retreat which German gunfire quickly turned into a rout. Lebrun tried to push some troops forward over the Meuse to form bridgeheads through which 5th Corps could retreat, but the disorder was too great. His men, beating against the tide of fugitives, could barely force their way as far as the bridges. Failly had recourse to the usual desperate expedient of hard-pressed commanders: he launched a cavalry attack at the advancing Germans to try to disengage his infantry. As was to be expected the cavalry, charging uphill and over broken ground, achieved glory but nothing more. Their remnants were caught up with the débris of 5th Corps crowding across the Mouzon bridges, or, despairing of making their way through the press, flung themselves into the Meuse. Some batteries of guns were doing the same, and in a horrible confusion in the middle of the river guns, horses and riders were lost. Only the fire of Lebrun's troops from beyond the river, and that of a gallant group of infantry and gunners on the left bank, kept the Germans at a distance long enough for the remains of Failly's Corps to cross to safety. Not till 7 p.m., as the light was fading, were the Germans able to close up to the river, and gather in their harvest of supplies, horses and vehicles, guns and prisoners.[2]

---

[1] *Guerre: Armée de Châlons* II: Docs. annexes 232–4. *G.G.S.* I ii 265–69.
[2] *Guerre: Armée de Châlons* II: Docs. annexes 105, 109, 152, 160–1, 200, 256–7. *G.G.S.* II ii 264–80, 285, 297. Hopffgarten-Heidler, *Die Schlacht bei Beaumont* 103–86.

In the disaster the French had lost nearly 7,500 men, mainly from 5th Corps. The German casualties were not light—3,500, mainly sustained by IV Corps during its rapid but gruelling advance from Beaumont to the Meuse.[1] It was General Gustav von Alvensleben's first major engagement, and his men could hardly have acquitted themselves better. As for the Bavarians, bundling the French back through Raucourt, they had frankly enjoyed themselves. "The beauty of the scenery," wrote their official historian, "the mildness of the weather, the ludicrous manner in which the enemy had been surprised ... the certainty of victory, everything in fact combined to produce a lively and joyful advance."[2] Royal Headquarters, scrambling up in the wake of its army, had been able only to catch glimpses of the battle, and failed at first to understand Alvensleben's full achievement. But that night the watch-fires of the army shone on the hills in a vast crescent, whose horns lay only ten miles from the Belgian frontier, and in Mouzon MacMahon was ordering his corps commanders to fall back on the fortress of Sedan.[3]

§2 Sedan

The French government had already decided to replace Failly. The fury in Paris was so great at his apparent betrayal of MacMahon at Froeschwiller that the Empress urged her husband to take a "necessary decision, however painful". There was a highly competent successor, suggested Palikao, in General de Wimpffen, the governor of Oran, who like all French officers left in Africa had been pestering the Ministry for a command ever since the war began, and whom indeed he had considered as the commander of a possible diversion on the Rhine.[4] Napoleon confirmed the appointment and Wimpffen reached Paris on 28th August. There he lunched with Palikao, listened to his

[1] *Guerre: Armée de Châlons* II: Docs. annexes 271. *G.G.S.* I ii 287.
[2] Helvig, *Operations of 1st Bavarian Army Corps* 65.
[3] Lebrun, *Bazeilles, Sedan* 74.
[4] *Guerre: Armée de Châlons* I: Docs. annexes 218. Palikao, in *Un Ministère de la Guerre de 24 Jours* 120, writes that he summoned Wimpffen to succeed Trochu in command of 12th Corps; but as Lebrun succeeded Trochu on August 17th [*Bazeilles-Sedan* 3] this appears to be an error. Palikao however denies [op. cit. 122] Wimpffen's statement that he offered him the command of 14th Corps in Paris as a counterweight to the suspect Trochu [*Sedan* 122].

lamentations about the fatal influence which the presence of the Emperor was having on the Army of Châlons, and probably discussed other matters as well; for next morning, when he mounted the train to Rethel, a last-minute message arrived from the Ministry of War, the contents of which were too important to have been entirely unexpected. "In the event of any mishap befalling Marshal MacMahon", it ran, "you will take command of the troops now under his orders." Armed with these fatal instructions he made his way to the army by way of Rethel and found it on the road between Sedan and Carignan, streaming to meet him in disorderly retreat.[1]

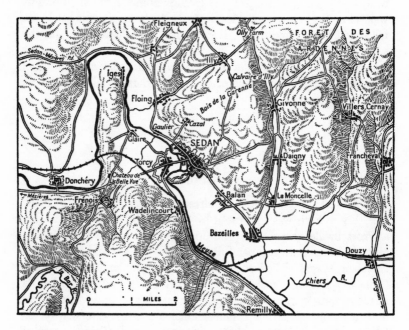

Map 12: Sedan

MacMahon's sole object in falling back on Sedan was to gain time— a day or so to reorganise and re-equip his scattered, demoralised forces and consider his next move. There was indeed little else that he could do, but if he thought his position desperate he kept the thought to himself. His first intention was probably to make a stand.[2] The fatigue and

---

[1] De Wimpffen, *Sedan* (Paris 1871) 124, 137–9.
[2] *D.T.* I 37–40. *Guerre: Armée de Châlons* II 235.

confusion of his troops could only be increased by further retreat. He still greatly under-estimated the forces of the enemy, and the hills round Sedan seemed to offer another *position magnifique*. Sedan itself was a tiny de-classed fortress with seventeenth-century fortifications, of which the principal historic interest for the French lay in its being the centre of the rebellious Bouillon family and the childhood home of Turenne. The valley of the Meuse, broad and marshy, protected it from the south and west. To the north lay an irregular triangle of high ground, sloping upwards away from the town. Sedan lay in the middle of the base of this triangle; its corners were marked by the villages of Floing to the west and Bazeilles to the east, and the sides were clearly marked to the east by the Givonne valley and to the west by a deep combe running south-west to join the Meuse valley at Floing. In the centre of the triangle a large wood, the Bois de la Garenne, sprawled across the crest of the hills, and at its apex, giving access to the high ground further north, was a col known as the Calvaire d'Illy. To the north the hills merged into the Ardennes, tumbling in receding wooded ridges towards the Belgian frontier, seven miles away.

As the French troops came up on 31st August they were disposed in positions round this triangle. Douay marched 7th Corps up to the north-west side—to the long open crest which ran from the Calvaire down towards Floing. Ducrot's men of 1st Corps were placed facing east, on the slopes dominating the Givonne valley. On their right was Lebrun's 12th Corps, which continued the line to and garrisoned Bazeilles; while the débris of 5th Corps, which Wimpffen took over during the course of the day from the aggrieved Failly, was placed in reserve in the centre, except for some units which MacMahon sent up at Douay's urgent request to hold the Calvaire and cover 7th Corps's right flank.[1] Douay's further protests about the inadequacy of his positions and the need to dig trenches were dismissed by MacMahon with a shrug. They would not be there for long enough, he said. He had no intention of sheltering under a fortress like Bazaine, but proposed rather "to manœuvre in front of the enemy". But the enemy was hard on his heels. The guns of I Bavarian Corps were already shelling 12th Corps from beyond the Meuse, and clouds of dust were rising in a menacing semicircle beyond the wooded hills to the south. "M. le Maréchal," replied Douay gloomily, "tomorrow the enemy will not give you time."[2]

[1] Ibid. 8–20. Wimpffen, *Sedan* 217.
[2] Bibesco, *Belfort, Reims, Sedan* 124.

If it had been MacMahon's intention to stand and fight at Sedan, he did not adhere to it for long. The stocks of ammunition in the station would not suffice for a battle which might be prolonged for days.[1] At Mézières, fifteen miles to the west, lay General Vinoy with his newly formed 13th Corps, and MacMahon told Vinoy's liaison officer that he intended to march his army back to Mézières by a road to the north of the Meuse, too newly completed to be on the German maps. But there were arguments against such a course. The Empress was still urging him on to Metz, and during the afternoon of the 31st German columns were reported at Frénois, even at Donchéry, threatening the French retreat.[2] MacMahon began to wonder whether it would be best to move east towards Carignan after all; but his deliberations gave no impression of urgency. Even if the Germans did cut off his retreat, he reasoned, they would be too tired and in insufficient strength to oppose a serious attempt to break through[3]; and in any case, before taking any decision he must have more information. He decided therefore to send out reconnaissances east and west next day, 1st September, to test the strength of the enemy resistance, and meanwhile the army was to rest and refit. Orders to this effect went out to all units. In the turmoil of events which followed at least one corps never opened these orders at all, and it was not until the following evening, among the débris of the greatest disaster that French arms had ever suffered, that an orderly officer found the neglected paper and read it. It began: "*Repos aujour-d'hui pour toute l'armée.*"[4]

MacMahon's insouciance was in remarkable contrast with Moltke's clear appreciation of the position. The tremendous possibilities which lay before him had first become evident when on 27th August the occupation of Stenay had virtually barred the French road to the west. From that moment the importance of the Belgian frontier had begun to loom large. On the evening of the 30th Bismarck warned the Belgian government that unless the French army was disarmed the moment it crossed the frontier, the Prussian forces reserved the right to pursue it[5]; and Moltke issued his orders for the sealing of the French armies against this barrier. The Meuse Army was to advance down the right bank of

[1] *Guerre: Armée de Châlons* II: Docs. annexes 279.

[2] *Guerre: Armée de Châlons* II: Docs. annexes 276, 280, 314. Wimpffen, *Sedan* 145.

[3] *D.T.* I 37. General Vinoy, *Siège de Paris* (Paris 1872) 35.

[4] *La Campagne de 1870 jusqu'au Ier Septembre. Par un Officier de l'Armée du Rhin* (Brussels 1870) 108.

[5] Bismarck—Prussian Minister in Brussels, von Balan, in *Gesamm. Werke* VI b No. 1771 p. 464.

the river with its right flank on the Belgian frontier; the Third Army was to move north towards the river on a broad front and seal off the French with its left wing. "Should the enemy enter Belgium and not be disarmed at once," went on the order, "he is to be followed thither without delay"—an instruction to which the Crown Prince of Prussia added the prudent qualification "Otherwise any violation of the Belgian frontier is to be studiously avoided."[1]

The two army commanders implemented their orders with enthusiasm. On 31st August the Saxons advanced beyond the Meuse up to the Chiers without incident, and the Guard coming up on their right established a line of outposts up to the frontier at La Grande Haye. The Crown Prince pushed his forces forward on a broad front till they emerged above the Meuse and began shelling the railway from Remilly through Sedan as far as Donchéry, where the advance-guard of XI Corps found a bridge over the Meuse intact and crossed it to destroy the railway line.[2] At Bazeilles the Bavarians also found the bridge undamaged, but here they could see the French already laying charges. Von der Tann mounted an attack at once. A battalion rushed the bridge, drove off the French, threw the powder-barrels into the river and maintained a precarious toehold in Bazeilles against the counter-attacks of Lebrun's Marines until they were withdrawn across the river late in the afternoon. The shellfire of the engagement set fire to the village, and all that night a huge column of flame-tinted smoke poured up into the sky. MacMahon, learning what had happened, ordered the bridge to be blown at once; but through another tragic and typical muddle this was not done. In any case it did not matter, for by nightfall the Bavarian engineers—apparently undisturbed by French artillery—had thrown two pontoon bridges across the river.[3]

Moltke, visiting the Third Army with the King, inspected the maps and rubbed his hands. "Now", he said, "we have them in a mouse-trap",[4] and later that evening he ordered Blumenthal to close the mouth of the trap by pushing XI Corps, weary as it was, across the river to seal off all French retreat to the west and attack at dawn. Nothing

---

[1] *G.G.S.* I ii 291, 297–8.
[2] Ibid. 299–300. MacMahon had sent a detachment to destroy the bridge, but as soon as the personnel had dismounted from the railway train in which they travelled the engine driver roared on at full speed to the safety of Mézierès, taking all their tools and explosives with him. A second detachment found the bridge already occupied. *Guerre: Armée de Châlons* II: Docs. annexes 277.
[3] Ibid. 117, 322, 328. Helvig, *Operations of the 1st Bavarian Army Corps* 71–4. Lebrun, *Bazeilles-Sedan* 87–9. [4] Blumenthal, *Journals* 110.

more remained to be done.[1] The French generals, observing the positions of the German watch-fires, began to realise what lay in store for them; and Ducrot, marking up his maps, summed up the situation in a single deathless sentence: "*Nous sommes dans un pot de chambre, et nous y serons emmerdés.*" Sleep was out of the question; he wrapped his cloak around him, sat by the bivouac fire of one of his Zouave regiments and waited stoically for the morning.[2]

*   *   *

Once again it was the impulsiveness of a subordinate commander that began the battle early on the morning of 1st September. It seems probable that Moltke would have preferred to wait until the two German wings had folded more closely round the French before he launched any general attack, for von der Tann was ordered to keep I Bavarian Corps in position near Remilly and join in the battle only when the Army of the Meuse had closed in from the east. But, claimed the Bavarian general's apologists, a verbal order authorised him to attack earlier if he wished[3]; and, fearful that the French might be slipping away under cover of darkness, he began at 4 a.m. to push his men across the Meuse towards Bazeilles. It was not yet light, and a cold mist lay heavily over the Meuse valley. The French pickets on the river-bank had withdrawn, and the Bavarians, swarming across the railway and the pontoon bridges, were able to penetrate deep into the village before any alarm was given. Then in the darkness fighting began. Bazeilles was skilfully barricaded, and its defenders, the Marines of Lebrun's corps, were the finest troops in the Army of Châlons. Ensconced in the solid stone houses, enthusiastically if unwisely abetted by the inhabitants, they fought with bitter determination. The village was blazing: to the fires started by shellfire were added those deliberately lit by both sides to smoke out their enemies; and the attempts of the villagers to help the defence brought down on them the fury of the enraged Bavarians. All civilians found with arms in their hands were shot at once, and it is unlikely that the troops were nice in their distinctions. It was thus a significant as well as a ferocious engagement. Had Moltke realised it, there was emerging, out of the funeral pyre of the Imperial French Army, a far more formidable enemy which was to try his talents even more highly: the French People in Arms.[4]

[1] *M.M.K.* 268. Verdy du Vernois, *With the Royal Headquarters* 126.
[2] Sarazin, *Récits sur la dernière guerre* 114–15.
[3] Helvig, op. cit. 77.
[4] *G.G.S.* I ii 312–15. *Guerre: Armée de Châlons* III 25, 29. Helvig, op. cit. 80–1. For the alleged Bavarian atrocities in Bazeilles see *The Times*, 15th

Between 5.30 and 6 a.m., as the light grew stronger and the fighting in Bazeilles slowed to deadlock, General Lebrun from his position on the hillside above the village could see the heads of further columns approaching from the east, beyond the Givonne, and batteries deploying on the slopes above the valley, far out of range of the French guns.[1] It was the Saxon Corps, the first arrivals of the Army of the Meuse. Gradually the German attack spread up the valley of the Givonne. Sixteen batteries deployed on the slopes above La Moncelle; one Saxon column took the village and linked up with the Bavarians on their left, another on the right threatened Daigny. But here Ducrot, as soon as it was light, had pushed a division across the river, to protect the Daigny bridge, and the Saxons advancing across the slopes towards the valley found themselves briskly counter-attacked by enthusiastic Zouaves. It was about three hours before the Saxons could bring up enough men and guns to force back this sizeable covering party, and Daigny did not fall until shortly before 10 a.m. Then the French withdrew in some disorder. They lost several guns, and, as they scrambled up the steep slopes west of the Givonne to regain their main positions, German fire brought down both the divisional commander, General Lartigue, and his chief of staff.[2]

The German gunners could already claim an even more distinguished victim. MacMahon had ridden out towards Bazeilles as soon as he heard of the Bavarian attack, in order, as he explained later, "to be able to give orders for a movement either towards the west or towards the east". Almost at once a shell-fragment pierced his leg, and he had to be carried back to Sedan. Knowing nothing of Wimpffen's appointment, he designated as his successor General Ducrot, the most competent and experienced if not the most senior of his corps commanders. Ducrot had not even seen MacMahon for days, let alone discussed plans with him. He did not know the position of the other corps, nor of the Germans, nor what supplies were available. But unlike MacMahon he realised that if the French army stood and fought it would be destroyed. It was not, he thought, too late to get away. He at once issued orders for an immediate retreat to the west.[3] Having only reached his positions late the previous evening, he had not heard of

September 1870, and for von der Tann's comments, Helvig, op. cit. 95. See also Lebrun, *Bazeilles-Sedan* 297, and Busch, *Bismarck: Some Secret Pages of his History* I 198–202.

[1] Lebrun, *Bazeilles-Sedan* 92–4.
[2] G.G.S. I ii 329. *Guerre: Armée de Châlons* III: Docs. annexes 78–91.
[3] Ibid. 4, 14. Sarazin, *Récits sur la dernière guerre* 120–1.

the German advance on Donchéry. As yet the German attack was limited to Bazeilles and the Givonne valley, but as a veteran of Froeschwiller he knew that it was only a matter of time before they carried out an enveloping movement of the greatest extent which their forces would allow. The only hope lay in falling back as quickly as possible. When his staff-officers objected that the attack was being held, that all was going well, and that he should at least wait, he imperiously overruled them. "Wait? What for?" he demanded. "Wait till we are completely surrounded? There isn't a moment to lose!"[1]

But Lebrun also objected, and an officer of his seniority could not be so brusquely overruled. 12th Corps, he pointed out, were putting up a spirited and successful defence; a disengagement in the heat of action would be difficult, if not impossible; and to get the corps and all its trains across the broken and wooded country that lay between Bazeilles and Illy would take hours. "The enemy is simply playing with us here while he gets round our flanks", retorted Ducrot. "The real battle will be fought behind us, at Illy." But he did not press the matter. Only after half an hour, during which the volume of German gunfire increased and the fighting crept towards the north—as at Froeschwiller it had crept towards the south—he could stand it no longer, and at 8 a.m. he gave Lebrun a direct order to retreat. Lebrun ceased arguing and began to withdraw his men from Bazeilles.[2]

Hardly had Lebrun given out his orders when, at about 8.30 a.m., Wimpffen appeared: a furious and unfamiliar figure, his whole mien expressing the old ardour, the *furia francese* which had been drained out of the rest of the army by the misery, muddle and apprehension of the last week. *He*, he announced, was in command, and there was no question of a withdrawal. If the army retreated at all it would be to the east, not to the west; Lebrun was to stay where he was; reinforcements would be sent up from 7th Corps and later they would swing over to the offensive. The hapless Lebrun agreed to stay and do his best and countermanded his orders for the retreat.[3] To Ducrot, Wimpffen sent a note announcing his appointment and asking him to "use all your energy and skill to secure a victory". Ducrot, aghast,

---

[1] Sarazin, op. cit. 121. A. Ducrot, *Journée de Sedan* (Paris 1871) 22–3. *Guerre: Armée de Châlons* III: Docs. annexes 14–15.

[2] Ibid. 306. Ducrot, op. cit. 27. Lebrun, *Bazeilles-Sedan* 101–4.

[3] Wimpffen was later to allege [*Sedan* 162] that the retreat already carried out by 12th Corps caused the loss of vital positions in Bazeilles and the Givonne valley. The war diaries of the units concerned however do not suggest that the order for retreat ever reached them at all.

sought out Wimpffen and tried to convince him of the need for an immediate retreat; but Wimpffen was immovable. "We need a victory," was all that he replied to these arguments, and Ducrot abandoned the attempt. "You will be very lucky, *mon général*," he answered, "if this evening you even have a retreat!" He was right. The retirement on Mézières might conceivably have saved some fragment of the French army, though even this is unlikely; Wimpffen's effort to redeem the disasters of the past month was to ensure its total destruction.[1]

On one point Wimpffen was certainly better informed than Ducrot. Unlike Ducrot, he knew of the German advance on Donchéry, and so had cause to feel less hopeful about the chances of a break-out to the west. We have seen how on Moltke's orders that advance had been hastened. The leading units of V and XI Corps had in fact begun to cross the Meuse at Donchéry at 4 a.m., almost simultaneously with the Bavarian attack on Bazeilles. By 7.30 a.m., without encountering even a French cavalry patrol, the German columns had reached the Sedan–Mézières road and turned east to march to the sound of the guns. With two corps moving on a single road there was confusion and delay, and not until 9 a.m. did the first troops of XI Corps reach the outskirts of Floing, while V Corps struck off into the hills to the left towards Fléigneux to complete the circle round the trapped army.[2] Gradually the batteries of both corps took post on the slopes opposite the long crest south of the Floing–Illy ravine where Douay's men were standing to arms. The infantry followed, and as they advanced over the slopes to the Floing–Illy road a strong detachment of French cavalry galloped across the valley to check their progress. The charge broke against the volleys of the infantry; the horsemen wheeled right and left in confusion, to be still further broken up by the shells which crashed among them from the German gunners on either side. Some regained their own lines; but many, lost or out of control, plunged away to the north past Fléigneux into the Ardennes before this last gap was closed. Other cavalry units also found their way out by this narrowing gap, hardly knowing, in the growing tumult, what they were doing or where they were going. Many of these fell victim to the guns of V Corps; others wandered, with thousands of stragglers on foot, over the frontier; only a lucky minority found their way

[1] Lebrun, op. cit. 111–12. Wimpffen, op. cit. 162. Sarazin, op. cit. 123.
[2] *G.G.S.* I ii 353–5. Frederick III, *War Diary* 84.

through the forest safely to Mézières and remained at liberty to fight again.[1]

The gap did not remain open for long, for the Guard Corps, on the right flank of the Meuse Army, was already marching up from the east to link up with the left flank of the Third Army. Their infantry came up on the right of the Saxons to carry the fight into the valley of the Givonne, and Hohenlohe deployed his batteries on the slopes above the valley to begin a sustained cannonade on the helpless masses of Ducrot's 1st Corps in front of the Bois de la Garenne. The Guard Cavalry Division swept round to the north towards Fléigneux, and shortly before midday its leading detachment found the leading troops of V Corps in the farm of Olly at the head of the Givonne valley. The circle was complete.[2]

It was now a superb day, and Moltke's staff had found for the King a vantage-point from which a view of the battle could be obtained such as no commander of an army in Western Europe was ever to see again. In a clearing on the wooded hills above Frénois, south of the Meuse, there gathered a glittering concourse of uniformed notabilities more suitable to an opera-house or a race-course than to a climactic battle which was to decide the destinies of Europe and perhaps of the world. There was the King himself; there was Moltke, Roon and their staff officers watching the crown to their labours, while Bismarck, Hatzfeldt and the Foreign Office officials watched the beginnings of theirs. There was Colonel Walker from the British army and General Kutusow from the Russian; there was General Sheridan from the United States, Mr W. H. Russell of *The Times*, and a whole crowd of German princelings; Leopold of Bavaria and William of Württemberg, Duke Frederick of Schleswig-Holstein and the Duke of Saxe-Coburg, the Grand Duke of Saxe-Weimar and the Grand Duke of Mecklenburg-Strelitz and half a dozen others, watching the remains of their independence dwindling hour by hour as the Prussian, Saxon, and Bavarian guns decimated the French army round Sedan.[3]

At first the morning mist and the smoke from the guns and fires at Bazeilles had hidden the battlefield, but as the sun mounted and the mist cleared the whole scene was unveiled: Sedan itself lying behind a

[1] *La Vie militaire du Général Ducrot* II 411. *Guerre: Armée de Châlons* III 112–17, and Docs. annexes 103, 116 ff.

[2] *G.G.S.* I ii 339–45. 362. Hohenlohe-Ingelfingen, *Aus meinem Leben* 309 ff.

[3] Frederick III, *War Diary* 92. Busch, *Bismarck: Some Secret Pages of his History* I 143. *Personal Memoirs of P. H. Sheridan* (London 1888) II 403. W. H. Russell, *My Diary during the Last Great War* (London 1874) 186 ff.

glittering sheet of flood-water, so near that with a good glass one could look into its agitated streets; the slopes behind it thickly crowded with the bivouacs which the red trousers of the French troops made so conspicuous; the long line of the Bois de la Garenne, outlining the summit of the crest; behind again, the open slopes above Illy and Givonne, which the two wings of the German army were beginning to crown with their batteries; and the dark crests of the Ardennes forming a backcloth to the whole scene. In the fields below the spectators, between Frénois and Wadelincourt, II Bavarian Corps had deployed a long gun-line, and IV Corps had done the same towards Remilly on the right: for it was the task of these two corps to provide a firm base along the south bank of the Meuse while the wings closed in from either side. At Bazeilles the Bavarians had by midday fought their way through the village and established their guns on the slopes beyond; and from their right flank there stretched an almost continuous circle of batteries—the Saxons above Daigny and the Guard above Givonne, the Silesians of V Corps before Fléigneux, the Hessians of XI Corps north of Floing—which smashed all the attempts of the French gunners to retaliate, and rained shells on the massed lines of infantry which waited with no trace of cover on the open slopes to repel an attack that never came.[1] There was to be no repetition of the carnage at St Privat; this time the German commanders left the decision to their guns.

In the French lines disorganisation was mounting. It is impossible to say which corps was suffering the most heavily—Lebrun's from the Bavarian and Saxon fire, Ducrot's from the Guard, or Douay's from the guns of V and XI Corps; but it was about the Bazeilles front, where he intended to make his break-out and where the Bavarians were advancing, that Wimpffen felt most anxious, and he rode up to 7th Corps to see whether Douay could send help. Douay was optimistic. He assured his commander that he would hold his position so long as the Calvaire dominating his right flank was firmly held, and for this Wimpffen promised him troops from 1st Corps. "In a moment we'll have more men on the plateau than we need," he assured him. "Come on, cheer up, we must have a victory!"[2] Thus encouraged, Douay sent off the best part of a division to the Bois de la Garenne towards the south. There Wimpffen tried to collect a force for his break-out towards Carignan. His first intention had been to attempt it at once; then he decided to wait until after dark; but by midday even he was

[1] *Guerre: Armée de Châlons* III. Docs. annexes 104, 215.
[2] Wimpffen, *Sedan* 218. Bibesco, *Belfort, Reims, Sedan* 146.

beginning to understand his desperate situation. No time must be lost. He certainly had plenty of troops: not only Lebrun's reinforced 12th Corps, but the right wing of Ducrot's and an entire division of 5th Corps as yet uncommitted; while 7th Corps and the left wing of 1st Corps could fight off the Germans in rear. After a last wrangle with Ducrot Wimpffen gave his orders at about 1 p.m., and he sent to Sedan for Napoleon to come and place himself at the head of his troops.[1]

Napoleon would not come. As on so many other occasions he took a more realistic view than his generals, and he knew that the venture was useless. Moreover, not only did no Emperor appear, but very few troops. Wimpffen had made no allowance for the Clausewitzian element of friction in war. The units could not be found. Messengers lost their way. Commanders, without maps, mistook the direction. Some units were unable to move under the shellfire, others found the roads blocked by burning waggons, rearing horses, or bodies of troops moving in the contrary direction. Only at Balan, between Sedan and Bazeilles, did Wimpffen succeed in mounting a sustained attack which forced II Bavarian Corps to send up reinforcements. Elsewhere the orders went astray, or the movements which they initiated withered away under German fire. Wimpffen, angry and determined, was still trying to rally his troops when there swept down behind him from the Bois de la Garenne a tidal wave of men, horses, guns, and waggons, leaderless, panic-stricken, making for the useless shelter of Sedan. 7th Corps's front had broken.[2]

Douay later explained the collapse of his troops by the capture of the Calvaire d'Illy, "the key position"; but the war diaries of his regiments indicate rather a gradual disintegration under the weight of the German shells. The despatch of his troops to help Lebrun had coincided with an advance by the German infantry, who succeeded at about 1 p.m. not only in establishing themselves in Illy, opposite his sensitive right flank, but in creeping up the hill from Floing and threatening to out-flank his left. Anxiously he rode towards the Calvaire to make sure that all was well there. It was not. There were no French troops to be seen. If Wimpffen had sent any they had not yet arrived, or if they had arrived they had fled into the Bois de la Garenne—which Ducrot,

[1] Lebrun, *Bazeilles-Sedan* 119–20. *Guerre: Armée de Châlons* III 194–5. Memoirs of Général de Castelnau in *Revue de Paris* vol. 154 (Sept-Oct 1929) p. 853.
[2] Wimpffen, *Sedan* 172, 271. Lebrun, *Bazeilles-Sedan* 122. *Guerre: Armée de Châlons* III 228–31.

coming up himself to inspect the Calvaire, found full of stragglers from 7th Corps. Ducrot also saw that his worst fears were realised. The Calvaire was defenceless; if the Germans occupied it they could press a wedge into the French positions which would split them in two. By 2 p.m. the German infantry were appearing on the Calvaire and could now fire straight into the Bois de la Garenne. Ducrot and Douay began to scrape up troops from any unit, from any part of the shrinking front, and flung them into the gap where they stood and fought blindly, fragments of regiments mixed pell-mell, under the hammering of the ninety guns which XI Corps had deployed south of Fléigneux. By 3 p.m., in spite of Ducrot's efforts to rally them, even the bravest of the French troops were falling back into the precarious safety of the woods.[1]

The threat to Douay's left flank above Floing was no less grave. Here he had dug in his troops on the spur in two lines of trenches, two hundred yards apart, and all morning they had, with rifle and artillery fire, been able to check all attempts by the Germans to debouch from the village. But by 1 p.m. their artillery was crushed and the German 22nd Division began to find its way round the French flank in the dead ground at the foot of the spur. Successive French infantry counter-attacks down the hill could not halt this advance; two squadrons of Lancers launched a charge which checked—though at terrible cost—the Germans who appeared over the edge of the plateau; and with his artillery shattered and his infantry nearly overwhelmed Ducrot could only turn to the last, most splendid, most useless weapon of all: the cavalry of General Margueritte.[2]

The plan which Ducrot outlined to Margueritte was desperate. The cavalry was not only to repulse the advancing Germans; it was to act as a battering-ram to force a passage for the French infantry, which would make one last attempt to break out towards the west. While the squadrons collected in a hollow above Cazal, sorting themselves out under shellfire into two massive lines, Margueritte rode out to reconnoitre the slopes towards Floing and the Meuse down which the charge was to be made. He was hit: a bullet passed through his face, mangling his jaw and tongue, and his appalled squadrons saw the figure of their general returning over the crest, supported by his two aides, with

[1] *Guerre: Armée de Châlons* III 153, 158, and Docs. annexes 264, 267. Bibesco, op. cit. 123. *G.G.S.* I ii 369.

[2] *G.G.S.* I ii 369–72. *Guerre: Armée de Châlons* III 168, and Docs. annexes 237–52.

enough strength only to raise one arm to point towards the enemy before he collapsed. An angry murmur came from the ranks—" *Vengez-le !*" and the whole mass of horsemen moved up over the crest, past the disorganised lines of their infantry, to increase speed slowly from trot to canter to gallop until they were thundering down the slope in an avalanche which it seemed that no human power could arrest. But as at Morsbach, as at Vionville, it was shown that when faced with resolute men armed with breech-loading rifles all the anachronistic splendour and courage of French chivalry was impotent. The German skirmishing-lines were overrun, but the supporting formations stood immovable and poured their volleys into the advancing mass. At no point was the German line broken. The cavalry torrent divided and swept by it to either side, northwards towards Illy to return to their own ranks, southward to crash into the quarries of Gaulier or to be rounded up in the valley towards Glaire, leaving the carcasses of horses and the bodies of their riders lying thick in front of the German lines.[1]

As the survivors of the charge rallied, Ducrot sought out their commander, General de Gallifet, and asked him whether they could try again. "As often as you like, *mon général*," replied Gallifet cheerfully, "so long as there's one of us left." So the scattered squadrons were rallied and once more the watchers above Frénois saw them plunging down the hill to certain destruction. King William was stirred to exclaim at their courage in words still carved on their memorial above Floing: "*Ah! Les braves gens!*" but it was not for him to lament that it was courage tragically wasted. Even now the cavalry were not exhausted. At 3 p.m. Ducrot, his front everywhere crumbling, threw them in yet again, while he and his staff rode along the ranks of the infantry trying in vain to rouse them to advance in the wake of the horse. This last attack, its cohesion gone, was repulsed as decisively as the rest, and with the greatest bloodshed of all. A pleasing legend speaks of Gallifet and his last followers passing exhausted within a few feet of the German infantry regiment. The Germans ceased fire; their officers saluted; and the Frenchmen were allowed to ride slowly away, honoured and unharmed.[2]

Now Douay's corps began to disintegrate. The German infantry

---

[1] Ducrot, *Sedan* 410–19. *Guerre: Armée de Châlons* III: Docs. annexes 364 ff. W. H. Russell, *My Diary during the Last Great War* 200–3. Rozat de Mandres. *Les Régiments de la Division Margueritte et les charges à Sedan*. (Paris 1908).

[2] *Vie militaire du Gén. Ducrot* II 418–19. This speaks of the unit concerned as 81st Prussian Regiment, but no such unit appears to have been present on the battlefield. Possibly the 82nd or 83rd was meant, both of which were present on this front.

closed in on every side, from Fléigneux on the Bois de la Garenne, across the Floing brook in a frontal attack on the French positions on the ridge, and from Floing eastwards towards Cazal to cut off all retreat on Sedan. From left to right the French line collapsed. The officers fighting opposite the Calvaire, leading their men forward sword in hand, found they had no longer any men to lead. The army had dissolved into a mass of fugitives, seeking shelter in the Bois de la Garenne or pressing back down the hill into Sedan. The gates of the fortress were locked against them, but they swarmed into the moat and over the walls, their panic growing minute by minute under the German shells.[1]

The flood came from the north-east of the battlefield as well as the north-west; for as 7th Corps had been broken by the guns of the Germans between Fléigneux and Floing, so 1st Corps had collapsed under the hammering of the artillery of the Saxons and the Guard. The Saxons crossed the Givonne valley and established not only their infantry on the heights west of Daigny, but the whole of their gun line as well. Further north Hohenlohe kept the Guard artillery back to bombard systematically the whole of the Bois de la Garenne. With each of his ten batteries taking a different section of the wood and each gun in the battery firing at a different elevation there was no corner of this last shelter of the French army which was not saturated by the German guns. If any unit appeared on the edge of the wood trying to escape, the full force of the corps's artillery was turned on it to drive it back.[2] Never before had gunfire been used in war with such precision. When at 2.30 p.m. the guns after one final salvo fell silent and the infantry of the Guard advanced into the wood, they found only masses of demoralised infantry, incapable of organised resistance. Whole battalions piled their arms and waved handkerchiefs in token of surrender. Some units, still intact, trying to fight their way back from the Calvaire, found their way blocked not only by the enemy but by French troops who would not hear of any prolongation of the fighting and intervened *en masse* to stop it.[3] The Third Army closed in on the wood to the north and west, the Saxons from the south. By 5 p.m. the clamour of the guns had died away; the wood and its thousands of occupants were in German hands.

Meanwhile Lebrun, Douay, and Ducrot had independently made their way back to Sedan to find the Emperor. Napoleon had spent the

[1] *G.G.S.* I ii 376–9. Ducrot, *Journée de Sedan* 137–40. *Guerre: Armée de Châlons* III 179, 188–90, 197, 201.

[2] Hohenlohe, *Letters on Artillery*, 94–5, *Letters on Infantry* 45–7, *Aus meinem Leben* 315–17.   [3] *Guerre: Armée de Châlons* III: Docs. annexes 191.

morning riding to and fro on the battlefield, seeking a death which obstinately evaded him. Now, determined to end the carnage, he had hoisted a white flag in Sedan. When Lebrun appeared the Emperor demanded that a *parlementaire* be sent to the enemy with a formal request for an armistice. But who was to sign it? Favre, MacMahon's Chief of Staff, refused. Ducrot pointed out that he himself no longer commanded the army; it could only be Wimpffen. So a letter was written optimistically requesting an armistice for the discussion of terms "equally acceptable to both armies", and Lebrun set off, an N.C.O. with a white pennant accompanying him, to find the commander-in-chief.[1]

Wimpffen was still on the road to Balan. Seeing the white pennant, he at once began to protest. There could be no question of surrender. They still held good positions and could go on fighting; and Lebrun must come back to Sedan with him to collect troops for yet another attack. Lebrun again acquiesced; it did not really matter, at this stage, what they did. So they returned to the crowds of demoralised men who lay sprawled outside the fortifications of Sedan, persuaded some thousand by urging and entreaties to follow them, found two or three guns, and set off in one last hopeless charge down the road to Balan. Their numbers increased as they went and the momentum and ferocity of their assault, coming without warning on a part of the front where all had been quiet for an hour or more, secured an immediate success. The troops of II Bavarian Corps were driven out of the village, and the alarmed German commanders alerted their batteries and their reserves on both sides of the Meuse to check any attempt to exploit the attack. But no such attempt was made. The brief flame which Wimpffen had kindled died as quickly as it had risen, and when he and Lebrun tried to press forward beyond Balan not a man followed them. Even Wimpffen had to admit defeat. With Lebrun by his side, surrounded by the last of his fighting troops, he rode silently back to the fortress. The gunfire had stopped. The evening was golden and peaceful; and the Bavarians, pressing up to the town on the heels of the retreating French, saw for the first time that the white flag was flying above the fortress walls.[2]

Moltke had seen the white flag. He despatched Bronsart von Schellendorf to ascertain its significance and Napoleon sent him back with an officer of the Imperial Suite, General Reille, who bore the famous letter which was not the least of the title-deeds of the Second German Reich.

---

[1] Lebrun, *Bazeilles-Sedan* 132. Ducrot, *Journée de Sédan* 130.

[2] Wimpffen, *Sedan* 173–5. Lebrun, op. cit. 135–40. *Guerre: Armée de Châlons* III: Docs. annexes 229–30, 256. *G.G.S.* I ii 397–400.

Monsieur mon frère [it ran],
    N'ayant pas pu mourir au milieu de mes troupes, il ne me reste qu'à remettre mon épée entre les mains de Votre Majesté. Je suis de votre Majesté le bon frère.   Napoleon.[1]

On the hillside above Frénois there reigned a certain feeling of awe. At the news that a French emissary was on the way a cheer was started, but nobody echoed it: emotions were too profound for such easy expression.[2] Reille, coming bare-headed up the hill, found the King standing ready to receive him, with the Princes pressing in an eager semi-circle behind. The King and Bismarck studied the letter and Bismarck dictated an answer. Reille returned to his master with the reply:

Monsieur mon frère,
    En regrettant les circonstances dans lesquelles nous nous rencontrons, j'accepte l'épée de Votre Majesté, et je la prie de vouloir bien nommer un de vos officiers muni de vos pleins pouvoirs pour traiter de la capitulation de l'armée, qui s'est si bravement battue sous vos ordres. De mon côté, j'ai désigné le Général de Moltke à cet effet.[3]

When Reille rode back down the hill to Sedan the group at Headquarters broke up to seek lodging for the night. The magnitude of the victory dazed them: they could barely realise how it had come about, much less what it meant for Germany and for Europe that the pattern of power had been so completely changed. Even celebration seemed out of place; it was a moment only for thanksgiving; and as darkness fell there rose into the night from the bivouac fires of the German armies one resonant chant: *Nun danket alle Gott.* . . . Only the words and music of the old Lutheran chorale could fit such a victory as this.[4]

Wimpffen protested as violently as had his colleagues at being charged with the conduct of negotiations for the capitulation of his army, but for him there was no escape. As Ducrot mercilessly told him, "You assumed the command when you thought there was some honour and profit in exercising it. . . . Now you cannot refuse."[5] So that evening, accompanied by General de Castelnau of the Imperial Suite as the

---

[1] *G.G.S.* I ii 402.
[2] Bronsart, *Kriegstagebuch* 61. Frederick III, *War Diary* 90–3. Busch, *Bismarck: Some Secret Pages of his History* I 143–7, 322.
[3] *G.G.S.* I ii 403.
[4] Verdy du Vernois, *With the Royal Headquarters* 135. Frederick III, *War Diary* 93.
[5] Ducrot, *Journée de Sedan* 51–3.

Emperor's personal representative, he made his way to the house at Donchéry selected for the meeting of plenipotentiaries where Bismarck and Moltke awaited him. It was a thankless task to deal simultaneously with the greatest political and the greatest military genius of the age, but Wimpffen did his best.[1] To the Prussian demand for the surrender of the entire French force as prisoners of war he opposed a demand for "honourable capitulation": the army to march out with arms and baggage and full military honours and take an engagement not to take up arms against Prussia and her allies for the duration of the war. But such a civilised custom, appropriate as it might be to the garrison of a beleaguered fortress, was hardly applicable to a national army. Bismarck pointed out that it was Prussia's concern to end the war as quickly as possible, and the quickest way of doing so was to deprive France of her army altogether; and when Wimpffen threatened to defend Sedan to the last, Moltke intervened to point out that the French army, reduced to 80,000 strong, with food for only forty-eight hours and very little ammunition, was in no state to continue to fight against a besieging force now 250,000 strong, armed with five hundred guns.

Wimpffen then tried another approach, and one which took him to the heart of the problem, both of the long-term relations between France and Germany and of the nature of the French State. Generosity, he argued, was the only possible basis for a lasting peace. Draconian methods would awake all the evil instincts lulled asleep by the progress of civilisation, and endless war between France and Prussia would be set on foot. Bismarck's reply to this sane observation is interesting. France, he argued, was not—as Austria had been in 1866—a stable Power with whom war could be conducted on a limited, eighteenth-century basis. French political restlessness had menaced the stability of Europe for eighty years, her military ambition had troubled Germany for two hundred. As Moltke had summed up the position of the French army, Bismarck now analysed for Wimpffen the problem of the French nation—and indeed of all nations where democracy is pushed to its logical extreme. "One should not, in general, rely on gratitude," said Bismarck, "and especially not on that of a people." If France had solid

---

[1] The account of negotiations which follows is based on Castlenau, *Revue de Paris* 154 pp. 857 ff, Wimpffen, *Sedan* 239 ff, and the narrative of Capt. Orcet preserved in the Archives de Guerre and reprinted in *Guerre: Armée de Châlons* III 248 ff. The German sources, Verdy du Vernois, *With the Royal Headquarters* 136 ff., Bismarck in Busch, *Bismarck: Some Secret Pages of his History*, and Graf Nostitz in *Deutsche Revue 1898* III 1–13, do not conflict on any essential point.

institutions, if, like the Prussians, she had reverence and respect for her institutions, if she had a sovereign established on a throne in a stable fashion, "we might be able to trust in the gratitude of the Emperor and his son and set a price on that gratitude." But French governments were kaleidoscopic: "One can rely on nothing in your country." Moreover—and here a note of atavistic emotion began to creep into Bismarck's reasoned statesmanship—the French were a nation "irritable, envious, jealous and proud to excess. It seems to you that victory is a property reserved for you alone, that the glory of arms is your monopoly." The Germans had been a peaceful, inoffensive people, but during the past two hundred years the French had declared war on them thirty times. It was too much. Now this must end, and they must have security—a glacis between themselves and France. "We must have land, fortresses and frontiers which will shelter us for good from the enemy attack."

Wimpffen's reply was that such a view of the French character was anachronistic. What may have been true of the France of Louis XIV and Napoleon was no longer true of the France of Louis-Philippe and Napoleon III. The French were a nation no longer military but bourgeois. "Thanks to the prosperity of the Empire all minds have turned to speculation, business, the arts; everyone is seeking to increase the sum of his well-being and his pleasures and thinks much more of his private interests than of glory." Bismarck was not impressed: the last six weeks, he said, had belied Wimpffen's arguments. The delight with which the press and population of Paris had greeted Gramont's declaration of war showed that France had not changed, and it was this population, these journalists, whom Bismarck was determined to punish. The German army must therefore march on to Paris. Thus he concluded with his first argument: "The fortune of battle has delivered to us the best soldiers, the best officers of the French army; to voluntarily set them free to risk seeing them march against us again would be madness."

It was now that General de Castelnau for the first time entered the discussion. The Emperor, he said, had surrendered only in the hope that the King's heart would be touched, and would grant the army the honourable terms which it had earned by its courage. This raised a very profound issue and Bismarck pounced on it. The sword which the Emperor had surrendered, he asked, was it his own, or that of France? For if it was that of France then the whole situation was different; it would not be the French army alone which was surrendering but the

French State. There was a sudden tension in the air; and when Castelnau replied that the Emperor's surrender was purely personal, Moltke at once intervened, and declared his conditions unchanged. The moment quickly passed; but in retrospect it can be seen that the first passes had been exchanged in a duel between Moltke and Bismarck which, in significance and intensity, was to come almost to rival the war itself.

There was nothing more to be said. Wimpffen made one last attempt at bluff, but when Moltke showed him on a map the ring of batteries which surrounded the doomed army, he weakened in the face of facts so obstinately and insistently presented. He asked for time to consult his colleagues, and the truce was prolonged till 9 a.m. next day. With this Wimpffen and Castelnau rode back to Sedan.

Napoleon, in a last effort to save the army from the consequences of its own inefficiency, decided to appeal to the King of Prussia behind the back of his advisers, and early on the morning of 2nd September drove out towards Donchéry. Bismarck met him on the road, impassively heard his request and politely wrecked Napoleon's attempt to by-pass him. On the excuse that the King was too far away to be fetched at once he himself took the Emperor to a nearby cottage and explored his intentions. Once he discovered that Napoleon considered himself a prisoner, incompetent to conduct any political negotiations, Bismarck lost interest. When Moltke appeared, the Emperor suggested the possibility of transferring the whole of the French army to Belgian soil; but Moltke was inflexible. It became clear to Napoleon that he had no hope of seeing King William until the capitulation was signed.[1]

Meanwhile in Sedan Wimpffen had consulted his generals, who accepted the inevitable; and at 11 a.m., in the Château de Bellevue on the river near Frénois, he signed the terms which Moltke presented to him. They were brief. The army was to surrender as prisoners-of-war, with all its arms and material, and with the fortress of Sedan. The only concession granted was that officers who gave their parole "not to take up arms against Germany nor to act in any way prejudicial to her interests until the close of the present war" were to be allowed to go free. Of this permission 550 officers took advantage.[2]

The Germans had taken 21,000 prisoners during the battle, and to these 83,000 were now added. In addition they captured over 1,000 waggons, 6,000 horses, and 419 guns. Their own losses during the

[1] Castelnau, *Revue de Paris* 154, p. 864.
[2] *Guerre: Armée de Châlons* III 260–3. *G.G.S.* I ii 406, and Appendix XLVIII. Bismarck, *Gesamm. Werke* VI b Nos. 1773–4, pp. 466–70.

battle came to 9,000 officers and men—only 850 more than those suffered by the Guard in the attack on St Privat.[1] France's first-line army was still trapped in Metz; the second-line army had ceased to exist.

With the business of the day safely over, Bismarck considered it safe to send for the King of Prussia. The interview between the sovereigns was brief and embarrassed. There was little for Napoleon to say, except to compliment William on his army—above all on his artillery—and lament the inadequacy of his own.[2] He asked only one favour—that he might go into captivity, not by the same road as his army, but through Belgium, which would avoid an embarrassing passage through the French countryside. Bismarck approved. Napoleon might still be useful "and it would not even do any harm if he took another direction . . . if he failed to keep his word it would not injure us".[3] Peace would eventually have to be made, and it could hardly be negotiated with a captured sovereign. Napoleon free in London—or even on French soil—would be no less inclined to end the disastrous war. His word would carry more weight with his countrymen, and a weak empire would be as good a régime for France in Bismarckian Europe as any other.[4] And if Napoleon was no longer the legal sovereign of France, who was?

So on 3rd September Napoleon with his suite, his powdered postilions, and the train of waggons which had so encumbered the movements of his army, drove into captivity, bound for the palace of Wilhelmshöhe above Cassel. His troops, marching through pouring rain to the make-shift internment camp which the Germans had improvised for them in the loop of the Meuse round Iges—*le camp de la misère* as they called it after a week of starvation under pelting rain—watched his departure with indifference punctuated by abuse. Both Moltke and Bismarck watched the carriage drive away. Moltke wondered, a little tortuously, whether Napoleon might not have devised the whole operation to secure his untroubled retreat from his responsibilities. Bismarck merely remarked reflectively, "There is a dynasty on its way out."[5] Then both returned to the gigantic problems which their victory had set them to solve.

[1] *G.G.S.* I ii 408.

[2] L. Schneider, *Aus dem Leben Kaiser Wilhelms*, II 219.

[3] Busch, op. cit. 159.

[4] While Napoleon and King William were talking Bismarck was assuring Castelnau that Prussia had no grudge against the Empire as such. "C'est donc encore l'Empire qui nous va le mieux, et loin de faire quoi que ce soit contre cette forme de gouvernement, nous désirons vivement qu'elle résiste à la crise qu'elle traverse en ce moment." Castelnau, *Revue de Paris* 154 p. 866.

[5] Bronsart, *Kriegstagebuch* 65.

CHAPTER VI

The Government of National Defence

§1 Ferrières

THE NEWS of Sedan stunned Paris. Palikao was too immersed in the detailed work of raising fresh armies, of putting Paris in a state of defence, and of planning a possible diversion on the Rhine to have weighed in cold blood MacMahon's chances of survival. He took it for granted that the march would succeed; the news of the disaster was incredible. For several days rumours of improbable victories had filled the city and when on the morning of 3rd September a Havas telegram from Brussels announced the capitulation of the French army, this seemed a far more improbable defeat. The messages reaching the Ministry of the Interior from local officials reporting the arrival of fugitives from the battlefield gave the Government some idea of what to expect; and it was to the Ministry of the Interior, at 4.30 p.m. on 3rd September, that the Director of Posts and Telegraphs brought the telegram in which Napoleon announced to the Empress his own captivity and that of the entire army. Such was the atmosphere in Paris that the immediate reaction in political circles was to speculate, not about the strategic implications of this disaster—for nowhere was it equated with national defeat—but about its effect on the Imperial régime.[1]

By 4th September the Ministers had recovered their wits and drafted a scheme for power to pass into the hands of a "Council of Regency and National Defence" to be nominated by the Corps Législatif, with Palikao as Lieutenant-General. Jules Favre and the deputies of the Left on the other hand demanded the overthrow of the Empire and the appointment of a parliamentary commission to organise the National Defence; while Thiers proposed a subtle compromise which would leave it uncertain whether the Empire had been overthrown or not. When the Assembly met at midday to consider these rival proposals, a

[1] Palikao, *Un Ministère de la Guerre de 24 Jours* 69–75, 126. *D.T.* I. 154, 266

huge crowd, inquisitive rather than hostile but very conscious of its revolutionary traditions, penetrated into the palace, flooded the tribune, and brought business to a standstill. As so often before, the people of Paris had paralysed the government of France; and the deputies of the Left, breathing again the heady air of 1848, knew their cue. They broke up proceedings in the Chamber of Deputies and forced their way through the crowds to the Hôtel de Ville, to proclaim yet another republic, and like their predecessors of 1848 they found at the Hôtel de Ville their sinister cousins of the Paris Clubs, Rochefort, Félix Pyat, Delescluze, in the process of forming a rival government. As in 1848, a *modus vivendi* had to be found between the extremists and the *ralliés*; but the deputies of 1870 were more skilful than their predecessors in excluding their rivals. It was agreed that a new Government of National Defence should be formed out of the deputies elected by the Department of the Seine—a decision which had the advantage, not only of asserting the primordial Parisian right of governing France, but of placing power firmly in the hands of the moderate Left. The old Ministers, also well learned in revolutionary traditions, melted away. The Empress was smuggled out of a side door of the Tuileries and set out on the road to England which French sovereigns now knew so well. There had been no violence, nothing which could be described as a riot: the Second Empire dissolved, as the monarchies of Charles X and Louis-Philippe had dissolved before it, leaving a vacuum of power to be filled by the first comers.[1]

The principal offices were quickly allotted: Jules Favre took the portfolio of Foreign Affairs, Léon Gambetta the Interior, Ernest Picard Finance, Isaac Crémieux Justice. The veteran Thiers would not accept office, but set out on a tour of Europe to enlist the sympathy and, if possible, the aid of the neutral Powers for the new régime. But a military colleague, if not a military leader, was needed, one whose name would carry weight with the army as well as with the people of Paris; and the obvious candidate was General Trochu. Trochu was not unwilling. He regarded the revolution as a natural cataclysm against which resistance was absurd. Favre, Gambetta, and their colleagues, he knew, were as firmly pledged as any of their countrymen to the defence of France against her enemies; and on being assured that they were prepared also to uphold those three pillars of orderly society—religion, property and the family—he agreed to join the Government as President of the

[1] *D.T.* I 15–16, 223, 232, 331, 380–3, 647. Trochu, *Œuvres posthumes* I 203. Jules Favre, *Gouvernement de la Défense Nationale* (Paris 1873) I 62, 77.

Council and to take charge, in the middle of the disasters which he had so long foreseen, of the military destinies of France.[1]

It was natural enough under the circumstances that military problems should at first take second place in the minds of the new ministers. "*Nous ne sommes pas au pouvoir mais au combat,*" declared the Government in its proclamation to the army on 5th September[2]; but government *is* a question of power, and the new Ministers had to make sure that they possessed it. They had seized control of an administration staffed by Imperialist officials, and conservative public opinion in the provinces had already, in 1848–1851, stifled one Paris revolution. The immediate danger to the Government of National Defence seemed to lie on the Right, and the extremists of the clubs were at first regarded as loyal if unruly allies. Crémieux, the new Minister of Justice, was notoriously sympathetic to the Left; and Étienne Arago, the new Mayor of Paris, appointed as mayors of the *arrondissements* men who in political extremism were outshone only by the committees which rapidly formed to supervise them.[3] The Ministry of the Interior, with its vital control over provincial administration, was seized by Léon Gambetta from under the nose of the more moderate Ernest Picard; and Gambetta made up for what he lacked in extremism by his energy, his youth—he was thirty-two—and immense personal dominance. He was a born leader, one who consciously trod in the footsteps of Danton. "There was authority even in his laugh", wrote an observer. "Before him the will bowed even if the intelligence was not conquered; and it seemed as natural for others to obey as for him to command."[4] Within a few weeks he was to emerge as a war leader of outstanding renown; but his immediate task was to make the new government's writ run through France, bending to obedience not only the Imperial bureaucracy but the republicans who had independently seized power at Lyons, at Marseilles, and at other provincial centres, with programmes which seemed to threaten not merely the social structure but the very political unity of France.

The first need was to appoint new Prefects, and within ten days this had been done in eighty-five departments.[5] In addition the more conservative members of the new Government felt strongly that their

---

[1] Trochu, op. cit. 198. Favre, op. cit. 80. *D.T.* I 198, 279.

[2] Joseph Reinach, *Dépêches, Circulaires . . . et Discours de Léon Gambetta* (Paris 1886) Hereafter referred to as Reinach, I 6.

[3] J. P. T. Bury, *Gambetta and the National Defence* 82. Jacques Desmarest, *La Défense Nationale* (Paris 1949) 76–83.

[4] Qu. Desmarest, op. cit. 64.

[5] *D.T.* II 13.

authority needed a stronger moral basis than the suffrage of the Parisians if they were to make peace, carry on the war, or gain the recognition of the Powers. In consequence they demanded that elections should be held as soon as possible. The doctrinaire Republicans all strongly objected. 1848 had shown that the peasants and petty bourgeoisie who made up the mass of the French population voted, whenever they had the chance, solidly against the republics foisted on them by the politicians and agitators of Paris. Elections would sweep this Government of National Defence into the limbo of the First and Second Republics and leave the nation defenceless against the Germans.[1] But so long as there seemed a chance of gaining reasonable peace-terms from the enemy, the arguments of the moderates were unanswerable, that only a Government fully authorised by public support and international recognition could sign a treaty of peace. During the first weeks of September such a settlement seemed possible. It had been the Emperor's war; the Emperor and his ministers had been swept away; now the French people could liquidate the war and return to the natural condition of peace. Elections therefore were fixed for 16th October; and then, to facilitate peace-making, in spite of the anguished protests of the Republicans, they were pushed forward to 2nd October.[2]

The peace which the new Government was prepared to consider was one which would not require France to yield, in the words of the circular letter which Jules Favre despatched on 6th September to the chancelleries of Europe, "an inch of her soil or a stone of her fortresses"[3]; but such a peace, as General Wimpffen already knew, Bismarck had no intention of granting. The war had not arisen out of a simple conflict of claims or interests which could be settled by the French accepting defeat. Its roots lay in historic national animosities which war could not appease but could only intensify. Such feelings might be rationalised by Bismarck into a claim to a frontier which would protect Germany for ever against her aggressive neighbour[4]; but even this hardly satisfied the emotion which military success was awakening in the German press and the minds of her soldiers and people. France

[1] Ducrot, *Défense de Paris* (Paris 1875-8) III 353. Bury, op. cit. 103-9.

[2] Reinach I 13. A. Dréo, *Gouvernement de la Défense Nationale: Procès Verbaux des Séances du Conseil* (Paris 1906) 128. *D.T.* I 385. Favre, *Défense Nationale* I 225-6 and 406-8.

[3] Reinach I 9-12.

[4] See e.g. Bismarck to Prussian Ambassador in St Petersburg, 16th September 1870, in *Gesamm. Werke* VI b No. 1806 p. 499. "Wir fordern Elsass und Lothringen nicht als Vindikation alten Besitzes ... nur Deckung gegen den nächsten Angriff wollen wir."

must be thoroughly and permanently humiliated: such is the view that we find in diary after diary kept by German officers as they advanced westward. "They must be made to feel what it means to challenge a peaceable neighbour to a struggle for life or death," wrote Verdy; "the whole French nation must be made sick of fighting, no matter whether a Napoleon reigns, or an Orleans or a Bourbon or anything else." A negotiated peace he thought unlikely: "the demands that we shall have to make on France are so heavy that the French people will not give up the game so easily, no matter what Government may be at the helm."[1] Roon wrote to the same effect. "We can, for the sake of our people and our security, conclude no peace that does not dismember France, and the French Government, whatever it may be, can for its peoples' sake make no peace that does not preserve France's inheritance intact. Therefrom necessarily follows the continuation of the war till the exhaustion of our forces."[2] Blumenthal believed that they "should treat the French as a conquered army and demoralise them to the utmost of our ability. We ought to crush them so that they will not be able to breathe for a hundred years."[3] Sentiments of this kind and their open expression in the German press were already beginning to lose for the German cause the sympathy which it had enjoyed among the neutral powers when the war began. But it was not only the extremists in the German army and nation who considered that the acquisition of Alsace, Protestant, German-speaking and a part of the original German Reich, should be the minimum reward for the expenditure of so much German blood and treasure. For the Liberals, who desired the German flag to wave wherever the German tongue was spoken, the possession of Alsace was Germany's manifest destiny; while all who concerned themselves with military affairs saw in the province, and its neighbour Lorraine, a glacis to protect Baden and the Palatinate against any renewal of the French attack which had threatened in July and which, but for the inefficiency of the French army, would certainly have been launched.[4] With Alsace and Lorraine went the two great fortresses round which the whole system of defences on the French north-east frontier had been built and which were now under siege, Strasbourg

---

[1] Verdy du Vernois: *With the Royal Headquarters* 61, 108.

[2] Roon, *Denkwürdigkeiten* III 214.

[3] Blumenthal, *Journals* 119, 123-4. See also *Feldbriefe von Heinrich Rindfleisch* (Göttingen 1905) 28, 73.

[4] For British evidence of German opinion on this point see Sir Robert Morier, *Memoirs and Letters 1826-1876* (London 1911) II 171, and Sir Frederick Ponsonby, *Letters of the Empress Frederick* 110.

and Metz. Jules Favre's hope that the victorious Germans would abate their claim to these spoils of war in the slightest degree was optimistic.

The German position, however, was not so assured as it seemed. It was hard to believe that a victory so overwhelming would not be followed at once by a suitably victorious peace; yet the more Moltke and Bismarck examined the difficulties which confronted them, the more intractable these appeared to be.

In the first place military operations were by no means over. Within half an hour of signing the capitulation of Sedan on 2nd September, Moltke had issued his orders for the advance on Paris. Bismarck had his doubts about the wisdom of this step: "My wish", he confided in a letter to his son, "would be to let these people stew in their own juice, and to install ourselves comfortably in the conquered provinces before advancing further. If we advance too soon, that would prevent them falling out among themselves."[1] Yet he did not make an issue of this as he had under very similar circumstances when, after the Battle of Sadowa, he had overruled Moltke's proposal for a similar advance on Vienna. Perhaps the desire to "punish" the people of Paris, which he had expressed to Wimpffen, overruled his discretion and made him acquiesce in the arguments of the soldiers, that only the possession of Paris would root out all possibility of future resistance. Whatever the reason, he raised no open objection when, on 7th September, the advance on Paris began.

The advance itself presented few problems. The German armies, spread thinly over the countryside, were able to subsist very largely on requisitions, which the humbled local authorities made little attempt to refuse. Attempts at resistance were unco-ordinated and ineffective, and such road-blocks and demolitions as the invaders encountered had been carried out so hurriedly and with so little skill that the delays they imposed were negligible. In some villages indeed the prudent inhabitants forcibly intervened to prevent the demolitions which their authorities planned.[2] By 15th September Royal Headquarters had reached Château-Thierry, and there Moltke gave out his orders for the investment of Paris. The Army of the Meuse was to occupy the right bank of the Marne and Seine, the Third Army the left bank, with their cavalry divisions making contact beyond the city.[3] There was no question of an assault

---

[1] Bismarck to Herbert Bismarck, 7 Sept., qu. Wilhelm Busch, *Das Deutsche Grosse Hauptquartier und die Bekämpfung von Paris im Feldzuge 1870–1* (Stuttgart and Berlin 1905) 10.

[2] *Guerre: Investissement de Paris* II Docs. annexes 16.

[3] *M.M.K.* 297–8.

on the fortifications: Moltke planned a siege *en règle*, and with 150,000 men at his disposal in the two armies he considered this perfectly feasible. On 20th September his two armies duly joined hands at St Germain en Laye, and Paris was cut off from the outside world.[1]

It was here that the difficulties began. These forces would have to remain in position either until an adequate park of siege-guns had been accumulated or until hunger forced the surrender of the city, and during this time they would have to be supplied. Only two direct railway lines linked Germany to Paris.[2] The northernmost, through Rheims, Sedan and Metz, was still blocked by a number of fortresses—Soissons, Mézières, Montmédy, Thionville, Metz—which would have to be by-passed or reduced. The other, through Châlons-sur-Marne, Bar-le-Duc, Nancy and Lunéville, was blocked until 23rd September by the fortress of Toul. Not only the fortresses but demolished bridges and destroyed tunnels made the repair of these and other ancillary lines a tedious process even for the excellent railway corps which Moltke had far-sightedly organised; and their defence against sabotage was to be an unending source of worry. Moreover on either flank of the lines of communication other French fortresses remained intact; Péronne, La Fère, and Lille, among others, to the north and west, Langres, Belfort, and Strasbourg to the south and east; and unless these were neutralised or destroyed they provided troublesome bases for sorties, and cover behind which new armies could assemble. Finally, Moltke knew that the Government of National Defence was already building up another army behind the Loire. The military resources of Prussia and her allies were considerable; already the troops held in North Germany to repel a French landing had been formed into a XIII Corps under the Grand Duke of Mecklenburg-Schwerin, and brought up to protect the lengthening lines of communication, and further levies of the Landwehr could always be raised; yet neither the civil nor the military authorities welcomed the prospect which such a prolonged effort held in store for them, and the holiday mood which followed the victory of Sedan very rapidly waned.

The political problems were even more baffling than the military. With whom, in the first place, was peace to be made? Bismarck was understandably dubious about the capacity of the Government of National Defence to negotiate on behalf of France. Napoleon was a prisoner and his Empress was in exile, but there had been no formal abdication. The only considerable military force left in France, the

---

[1] See further pp. 323–5 below   [2] See map at end of this volume.

Army of the Rhine, was still bound by its oath of allegiance to the Emperor. As Bismarck himself expressed it, in an announcement which he caused to appear in the Rheims newspapers on 11th September,

> The German Government could enter into relations with the Emperor Napoleon, whose Government is the only one recognised hitherto, or with the Regency he appointed; they would also be able to treat with Marshal Bazaine, who has his command from the Emperor. But it is impossible to say what justification the German Government would have in treating with a power which up till now represents only a part of the Left Wing of the former Legislative Assembly.

When Bismarck learned that Jules Favre was seeking an interview, he showed no alacrity to see him; whereas the self-accredited Imperial envoy Edouard Regnier, whose only authorisation was a picture of the front at Hastings signed by the Prince Imperial, gained access to him without difficulty. Only slowly and with reluctance did Bismarck come to realise that the Empire was irrevocably a thing of the past.[1]

The adventures of M. Regnier we shall consider in due course. Favre gained access to the Chancellor, thanks to the good offices of the British Embassy,[2] on 18th September, as Royal Headquarters was establishing itself in the huge Rothschild palace at Ferrières. He had set out from Paris without the knowledge of his colleagues, who were less ready than he to believe that, since the war had arisen solely from the ambitions of the overthrown régime, the Prussians might be persuaded by an appeal from the genuine representatives of the French people to accept a just and lasting peace without annexations. Favre hoped at least to secure an armistice, so that a National Assembly might be summoned to elect a properly authorised Government; but even in this hope he was to be disappointed. To his pained surprise he found himself regarded by Bismarck not as the spokesman of a temporarily misled people, but as the representative of a nation with a record of constant aggression which it could not be trusted not to renew at the first opportunity. Bismarck was quite prepared to recognise Favre's peace-loving protestations as genuine; but he would not accept him as being in any way typical of the French people. Therefore Prussia, he insisted, would accept no peace which did not leave her with a frontier so secure as to guarantee her absolutely against the revenge which the French would now constantly meditate. This must involve the city of Strasbourg—"the key to

[1] See Joachim Kühn, "Bismarck und der Bonapartismus im Winter 1870/1," in *Preuss. Jahrbücher* CLXIII (1916) 51.

[2] Lord Newton, *Lord Lyons: A Record of British Diplomacy* (London 1913) I 321.

our house"[1]—the province of Alsace and part of the province of Lorraine, including Metz and Château-Salins.

A more experienced diplomat might have treated this as an extreme demand put forward for bargaining purposes and started to haggle: Favre only burst into tears, and cried, "You want to destroy France!". As for an armistice to enable a National Assembly to be elected, Bismarck would consider it only on terms that would give no military advantage to France. Toul and Strasbourg must be surrendered, and if supplies were to be permitted to enter Paris, one of its protective forts must be surrendered in recompense. On hearing these terms Favre collapsed. "I made a mistake in coming here," he confessed; "it is to be an endless struggle between two peoples who ought to stretch out their hands to each other. I had hoped for another solution," and he returned to Paris in despair.[2]

Favre was indeed wrong to go to Ferrières if he could do no better than that; for he did have, had he only realised it, a few court-cards in his hand. Bismarck's aim was the establishment of a peace which would guarantee Germany against any further trouble on her western frontiers; and such a peace could best be secured by agreement with a friendly and reliable Government on terms genuinely acceptable to the nation. It was only failing such a settlement that Bismarck turned to the second and far inferior alternative—the establishment of a military barrier so strong that, although it might constantly provoke irredentism, it would be proof against any attempt to overthrow it. But where was the friendly and reliable Government to be found? Could a restored Emperor reassert his authority in France? Could a régime apparently thrown up by a Paris street-brawl be trusted? Would a National Assembly produce a ministry prepared both to negotiate and to abide by their agreement? So long as Bismarck was uncertain on these issues, he would be unable to oppose valid arguments against the nationalists who demanded Alsace and the military specialists who insisted on the fortresses of Belfort and Metz. A Talleyrand might have discerned this weakness in his position; would perhaps have accepted short-term military humiliation to secure the election of a National Assembly; and

---

[1] Favre appears to have coined this phrase. "Strassburg, welches Herrn Favre mich als den Schlüssel des Hauses bezeichnen lässt ... wurde von mir ausdrücklich als der Schlüssel *unseres* Hauses bezeichnet, dessen Besitz wir deshalb nicht in fremden Händen zu lassen wünschten." Bismarck, Circular to Diplomatic Missions of 27 September 1870, in *Gesamm. Werke* VI b No. 1835, p. 519.

[2] Jules Favre, *Gouvernement de la Défense Nationale* I 156–87. Bismarck, *Gesamm. Werke* VI b loc. cit.

would have worked to incline this Assembly to moderation, while Bismarck struggled with his own chauvinists, as he had struggled with them after the Battle of Sadowa.

Yet perhaps by 1870 it was already too late. The Austro-Prussian War had been a struggle for power uncomplicated by national animosities. Bismarck may have viewed the war with France in the same light, but his countrymen did not. For them it was a chance to pay off two centuries of old scores, besides redressing an uneasy feeling of inferiority whose roots were buried in a thousand years of history.[1] As for the French, Bismarck was correct in discerning how impossible it was to expect one government to bind its successors. However pacific the French peasant might be, his indifference to events in Paris—save when his property was threatened—had left the machinery of state too long at the disposal of the first comer; while the traditions of the Left and of the Right were too deeply impregnated with memories of military glories for the leaders of either wing to accept tamely and for ever a settlement which, however moderate its terms, would relegate France to an inferior position in Europe. The defeat of the Imperial Army— the numerically insignificant defenders of a doubtfully popular régime— could not be accepted as the defeat of France, so long as there was still the man-power and the resources to fight on. If the Germans were unappeased by victory, the French were still unconvinced of defeat. Favre was right. After Ferrières the struggle was no longer to be an affair of professional armies fighting in the interest of a balance of power: it was to be a savage war of peoples; and it is to this aspect of the struggle that our attention must now be turned.

§ 2 The Nation in Arms

France has not always been willing to follow unhesitatingly the lead given by the people and the politicians of Paris. In 1830 she accepted the July Revolution tranquilly enough; but in 1848 the French peasants

---

[1] See for example Moritz von Blanckenburg to Roon, 28th July 1870: "Was man seine ganze Jugend hindurch gehofft hat: eine gründliche Herstellung des Übergewichts der deutschen Nation und Revanche für die Unthaten der Gallo-Franken seit 200 Jahren—das musste man noch erleben." Roon, *Denkwürdigkeiten* III 169.

showed by their votes and, in the June of that year, by their arms, that the ideals of the *faubourgs* were not those of France; and the dictatorship of the third Napoleon, like that of the first, had rested largely on the acquiescence of peasant landowners in a régime which guaranteed them against clerical reaction and socialist revolution. Yet the news of the September Revolution was received in the provinces at worst with calm and at best with riotous delight. At Lyons and Marseilles the Republicans did not wait for the news from Paris before seizing power, and at Nîmes, Nice, Mâcon, St Étienne, and Bordeaux insurrections broke out as soon as the news from Paris arrived. The more stolid provinces of the centre and north accepted the change *faute de mieux*, and the Prefects either acknowledged the new régime or handed power over to local republican committees.[1] The capture of the Emperor and the flight of the Empress deprived the Bonapartists of any rallying-point, while Legitimism and Orleanism were still political sentiments rather than parties organised for action. The reports both of the Imperial Prefects and of the Republicans whom Gambetta at once sent to replace them speak almost unanimously of *calme et ordre partout* and, only a shade less unanimously, of the general determination to continue the war and defend the national soil. The Government's wisdom in stressing its rôle as the non-partisan leader of *La Défense Nationale* had the success it deserved. Even in Brittany, the stronghold of Legitimism, where the proclamation of the Republic was greeted with universal dismay, the determination to resist the foreign enemy overcame issues of domestic politics and there was a general cry for arms to carry on a guerrilla campaign in the *Chouan* tradition.[2] Even when enthusiasm was luke-warm, it was aroused when Favre published the terms on which Bismarck, at Ferrières, had declared himself ready to make peace. "There can be no answer to such insolent demands," declared the Government communiqué, "but *guerre à outrance*"; and throughout France, from the cities to the small mountain-towns, mass demonstrations pledged the nation to see the struggle through.[3]

The new Prefects, many of them men of small political experience,

[1] F. F. Steenackers and F. le Goff, *Histoire du Gouvernement de la Défense Nationale en Province* (Paris 1884) I 70–80.

[2] *Enquête parlementaire sur les actes du Gouvernement de la Défense Nationale: Dépêches télégraphiques officielles* (Versailles 1875) Hereafter referred to as D.O., I 400. The Prefect of Finistère however reported "Tout le monde prêt à la lutte contre étranger, mais après la paix complications très-probables." *D.O.* I 277.

[3] See, e.g. Prefects' reports from Chambéry, Mende, Quimper, Périgueux, Tulle for Sept. 24–30, in *D.O.* I.

were a little dazzled by the torchlight processions, the deputations and the demonstrations which filled the streets. When the first excitement subsided it became clear that enthusiasm for the war and support for the new Government were less than they had at first supposed.[1] The Prefects in Burgundy, the Jura, the Cévennes, and the Pyrenees had to confess that the peasants of the countryside seemed indifferent to the great national struggle. From Nantes the Prefect complained that the peasants would do better as Prussians than as French soldiers and urged the Government on 22nd September, "Make peace if you can—a plebiscite would ratify it."[2] From Mende the Prefect complained, "The torpor of the Lozère country is really impossible to shake"; the peasant was "completely brutalised by the all-powerful clergy of the country". Similar reports came from the Sarthe.[3] Marc Dufraisse noted, on travelling from Switzerland to Paris early in September, "the despondency of the population, their torpor, a kind of sad and distracted resignation".[4] Gambetta himself, when he arrived at Tours, reported to Paris that "the country districts are inert, the bourgeoisie in the small towns are cowardly, and the military administration either passive, or desperately slow."[5] For many of the Republican officials, lawyers or journalists by profession, this was their first contact with that self-absorbed indifference of the peasantry on which two Napoleonic dictatorships had rested and which differed so profoundly from their idealised conception of the French People. As they found their measures and their appeals frustrated by official timidity, legal restrictions, and public apathy, they began to demand more sweeping powers to suppress critical newspapers, or to replace officials of the old régime, to whose deliberate and politically motivated opposition alone, they believed, the difficulties of the administration could be attributed. The central Government thus came under growing pressure from its own representatives to denounce the political truce on which its power rested. It seemed intolerable, for example, that they should have to collaborate with Imperial magistrates, at whose hands the Republicans had suffered imprisonment and exile, or with the municipal councils which were full of Imperial nominees. "In keeping the Imperial officials," complained one official, "we are losing France . . . France can be saved by the

---

[1] *D.O.* I 220, 251, 305, 428, 549.
[2] *D.O.* I 404. This report however was made before the Ferrières meeting.
[3] *D.O.* I 428. "Hostilité passive et défiance . . . Impressions de 1848 encore vivaces" ran notes on reactions in the Sarthe area which the Germans later found in Tours. Helvig, *Operations of 1st Bavarian Army Corps* 238.
[4] *D.T.* IV 417.   [5] Reinach I 70.

Republic if the Republicans alone have the leadership. If you do not act thus, the Republicans will rise and we shall have civil war."[1]

The Government indeed was to suffer at least as much from the enthusiasm of its supporters as from the indifference of the masses. At Nice, at Marseilles and at Lyons it had to deal with disorders which the operations of such anarchist conspirators as Cluseret and Bakunin kept trembling on the verge of outright revolution; while all over France enthusiasts were pressing for measures born rather of the romantic myths of 1792 than of any precise calculations of what was possible in 1870. Local committees of defence, impatient of the delays of the central Government, got into touch with one another and began to form regional associations. These—the *Ligue du Midi*, the *Ligue du Sud-Ouest*, the *Ligue de l'Ouest*, the *Ligue du Plateau Central*—well-intentioned as they were, held the possibility that these areas might escape from the military and indeed the political control of Paris altogether.[2] There was a general clamour for weapons to arm both the population for local defence and the bodies of volunteers which formed everywhere and demanded to be led against the enemy. "The population and the local defence committee want arms and I have got to have them", wrote the Prefect from Bordeaux; and his colleague at Tarbes declared, "My situation is untenable if I cannot distribute at least the 3,000 rifles so long promised."[3]

Arms seemed to exist in plenty in the military and naval arsenals, and the first demand of the republican agitators—and one not always perhaps inspired by considerations of local defence alone—was that these should be distributed to the people. This led to direct conflicts with the local military commanders. They were for the most part dug-out generals of second-rate quality, who were anyhow mistrusted as the potential instruments of a reactionary *coup d'état*.[4] These suspicions apart, there was plenty of material for friction between the determination of the Prefects to mobilise every local resource in arms and man-power for local defence, and the refusal of the local military commanders to depart from *règle* without the authorisation of a Minister

[1] *D.O.* I 382. See also Gambetta to Favre, 31 October 1870, in Reinach I 104–8.

[2] Gambetta however shrewdly described the situation as "de l'anarchie et cela n'avait pas le caractère de sécession". *D.T.* I 555. See the evidence also of Challemel-Lacour, *D.T.* II 465; Laurier, Ibid. 15, 28; Rouvier, Ibid. 485; Esquiros, Ibid. 504–5; Gatien-Arnoult, ibid. 548.

[3] *D.O.* I 313, 547.

[4] See Crémieux's views in *D.T.* I 583 ff. and Steenackers and Le Goff, *Gouvernement de la Défense Nationale* 60.

of War who was, until Gambetta assumed that office, as punctilious as themselves. The Prefect of Haute Marne, a department directly threatened by invasion, complained that his military colleague was "the greatest obstacle to any initiative in defence that I have met", while from Lille the Prefect alleged, "There is a positive conspiracy here of all the generals, who wish to do absolutely nothing . . . at Amiens and Arras it is the same thing; it is a deliberate plot."[1] In the cities of the south the Prefects, caught between on the one hand mobs clamouring for arms and for justice against treacherous reactionaries and, on the other, military commanders who understood nothing of the political difficulties which faced them and would obey the orders only of their hierarchical superiors, were in an impossible position. At Lyons after three weeks of intermittent rioting these conflicts reached their most dramatic climax. There the able Prefect Challemel-Lacour demanded, and received from the Government, full civil and military powers to resolve these difficulties; and when the military commander General Mazure refused to recognise them for lack of notification by the Minister of War the Prefect had the General arrested and had to keep him in prison for two weeks before popular feeling abated sufficiently for him to be smuggled out to take up another command.[2]

It was with this situation in the provinces, as well as with the immediate problem of the Prussian invasion and the defence of Paris, that the Government of National Defence had to deal. But the situation developed only gradually. The telegrams which came in during the first few days after 4th September were on the whole reassuring. Trochu and his colleagues can be forgiven for failing to anticipate the magnitude and the complexity of the problems, political as well as administrative, which the organisation of the National Defence would involve. They certainly did not foresee that Moltke would be able to render Paris useless as the capital of France. At most they considered that the city might be isolated for a week.[3] But the Diplomatic Corps was less sanguine, and the disinclination of the representatives of the leading European Powers to remain within the beleaguered city led the Government on 12th September to send a small delegation under their most elderly member, Isaac Crémieux, to represent them at Tours, with a senior official to carry on the work of each ministry.[4] A few days later the reports

---

[1] *D.O.* I 459, 492.   [2] *D.O.* II 11 ff. *D.T.* II 408–25, 456–73.
[3] See e.g. Garnier-Pagès in *D.T.* I 444.
[4] This was voted on the 11th. Certain governmental services had been sent on the 7th. See A. Dréo, *Procès-Verbaux des Séances du Conseil* 85, 108. *D.T.* V ii 188. *Guerre: Investissement de Paris* I 22–3. Only the American Minister, the

of revolutionary activity in Lyons made them send two of his colleagues, Glais-Bizoin and Admiral Fourichon, the Minister of Marine, to strengthen his hand.

This Delegation was regarded as a channel of communication between the Government and the provinces, with no initiatory powers of its own. "Such was the habit of centralisation in France" wrote one of its officials, "that instinctively no one could admit any superior authority except that of Paris, and in spite of the full powers accorded to the Delegation, the Government of the capital went on sending out its orders until the last moment."[1] The members of the Delegation were not chosen for administrative ability. Crémieux and Glais-Bizoin were elderly, inexperienced, and talkative. Fourichon, who looked after not only his own office but the Ministry of War, was stolid and inelastic, and with good reason mistrusted the ability of his colleagues. Conferences were long, disorderly, and unfruitful.[2] The provincial struggle between the civil and military powers was reflected in incessant conflicts between Fourichon and his colleagues, and when Crémieux and Glais-Bizoin upheld the actions of Challemel-Lacour in Lyons, Fourichon finally on 3rd October resigned the Ministry of War, and Crémieux in title assumed it. The Delegation could give no lead to the country, and the able assistants who served it—Colonels Lefort and Thoumas at the Ministry of War, M. Laurier who deputised for Gambetta at the Interior, M. Steenackers the Director of Posts and Telegraphs—could only create machinery which their leaders did not know how to turn to effect. Steenackers voiced in a letter to Picard the general dissatisfaction with the Delegation. "Around me there is only inertia and hesitation . . . anarchy; no consistent or energetic direction, no strategic plan"; and another official summed it up: "The provinces need to be roused, and nobody is doing it."[3]

The Government in Paris was not at first worried by the inefficiency of its representatives. The course of the war would, in its view, be settled by a great battle under the walls of Paris, and within a few days it would resume direct control of France. But by 15th September the reports from the provinces were beginning to cause it serious alarm,[4]

Papal Nuncio, and the representatives of certain minor powers remained in the city. See E. B. Washburne, *Recollections of a Minister to France* (London 1887) I 127.

[1] General Thoumas, *Paris, Tours, Bordeaux* (Paris 1893) 79.

[2] Ibid. 51. *D.T.* III 212, IV 420. C. Chevalier, *Tours capitale. La délégation gouvernementale et l'occupation prussienne* (Tours 1896) 36.

[3] *D.O.* II 261, 255.   [4] Dréo, *Procès-Verbaux* 121–2.

and when the Delegation passed from inertia to positive disobedience it was compelled to take action. The Government's decision to hold national elections on 2nd October stirred the Prefects to almost unanimous protest. "You know our peasants," wrote one; "you will have Bonapartist municipalities and a Bonapartist Constituent Assembly." The Prefect at Nantes wrote with more foresight that an election "would deliver France up to an Orleano-Legitimist coalition."[1] When Gambetta ignored their complaints, many of the Prefects, anxious for national rather than local power, sent in their resignations and offered themselves as candidates for the National Assembly. Then came the interview at Ferrières. This made it clear that peace was out of the question; and the Republicans with their reluctance to appeal to a hostile populace were joined by the soldiers who were unwilling to divert national energies from the task of defence. "We could not have elections without an armistice," Gambetta put it later; "and the effect of an armistice would be to relax the efforts of the defence."[2] So on 24th September the Government decreed that both local and national elections should be indefinitely postponed.[3]

The decision created consternation at Tours. Crémieux needed an Assembly to which he could abdicate the authority which he knew he and his colleagues could not sustain. Foreign Office officials lamented the effect abroad; Laurier, in charge of the Ministry of the Interior, thought it would intensify secessionist feeling in the south; while the ardent Republicans feared that any delay would only give their opponents the chance to organise, and so be fatal to their cause.[4] It was generally felt that Paris, whose last land-link with the outside world was cut when the Prussians dredged up her submarine cable from the bed of the Seine on 27th September, was no longer in a position to lay down the law for France. On 29th September the Delegation assumed responsibility itself, and announced that elections would after all be held.[5]

It was to reverse the effects of this decree that the Government despatched Gambetta on his famous balloon voyage on 7th October.[6] As Minister of the Interior he could best deal with the question of elections; the Prefects were his nominees, many of them his personal friends; while his youth, energy, and superb oratorical powers would

---

[1] *D.O.* I 378, 403. [2] *D.T.* I 552. [3] Dréo, op. cit. 154–5.
[4] *D.T.* II 15; IV 421–2. Steenackers and Le Goff, *Gouvernement de la Défense Nationale* I 381.
[5] *D.T.* V ii 203. [6] Reinach I 32–8.

enable him to give that impulse to the organisation of the National Defence which the Delegation so patently lacked.[1] War indeed was a less alien element to him than to his more elderly colleagues. He had never shared their optimistic and irenical beliefs: for him the traditions of the Republic were always those of 1792, and he had once lamented "to see how our republican traditions are being weakened and effaced by the influence of humanitarian doctrines".[2] Almost alone among the statesmen of the Left he had understood the implications of Sadowa, and had discerned the coming of the inevitable clash with the growing forces of Prussia. His record and his abilities both marked him out as the man of the hour.

The impact of Gambetta on the disordered provinces was immediate. "One immediately had confidence", said one of his avowed enemies, "in a man who spoke so well."[3] From Tours he issued a heartening proclamation which made victory seem not only desirable but a perfectly reasonable aim.

> We must set all our resources to work—and they are immense. We must shake the countryside from its torpor, guard against stupid panic, increase partisan warfare and, against an enemy so skilled in ambush and surprise, ourselves employ ruses, harass his flanks, surprise his rear—in short inaugurate a national war . . . Tied down and contained by the capital, the Prussians, far from home, anxious, harassed, hunted down by our reawakened people, will be gradually decimated by our arms, by hunger, by natural causes.[4]

For such inspiring vigour and confidence men were prepared to overlook the strain of partisan Republicanism which could also be traced in his proclamations. Victory was an object in pursuit of which all parties could combine, and it seemed as if Gambetta might attain it.

Gambetta's first act, once he had brought the Delegation to heel over the question of elections, was to take over the Ministry of War. There was everything to be said for the Ministry of the Interior, responsible as it was for mobilising and equipping the *Garde Nationale* of which the French forces were now largely to consist, and the Ministry of War, responsible for deploying them in action, being combined under one hand. Fourichon himself voted for it; and since Gambetta

---

[1] Trochu, *Œuvres posthumes* I 304–5. Jules Favre, *Gouvernement de la Défense Nationale* I 260.

[2] J. P. T. Bury, *Gambetta and the National Defence* 36.

[3] Desmarest, op. cit. 179. "Enfin nous avons *une direction*" wrote the Prefect at Perpignan, "il était temps", *D.O.* I 555.

[4] Reinach I 41–5.

had thoughtfully provided himself with a casting vote before leaving Paris, he and Fourichon between them were able to overcome the opposition of their two colleagues to this concentration of power. The next step was to break the opposition within the Ministry of War itself to the ruthless and unorthodox measures on which Gambetta insisted. "I have determined", proclaimed Gambetta, "to quit the usual paths. I wish to give you young and active chiefs capable by their intelligence and their energy of renewing the prodigies of 1792. Therefore I have no hesitation in breaking with the old administrative conditions."[1] It was not an attitude to endear him to the regular officers who staffed the ministry, and Colonel Lefort, who had headed it with considerable ability since its departure from Paris, soon resigned. Gambetta, he complained later, "complained of delays. I told him that we would go no faster without departing from routine. I added that we might do things faster, but that disorder would result."[2] Disorder *did* result, and Gambetta's boldness led him to make gigantic mistakes; but one may wonder whether routine could in the time available have achieved anything at all. Another official of the Ministry, more flexible in his attitude, admitted that

> perhaps in these circumstances we needed men who were not used to service routine but were able on the contrary to shake off all restraint. These men could do nothing by themselves, but with experienced assistants able to translate into action intentions or desires expressed in general terms with no concern for the difficulties to be overcome, their initiative may have good results.[3]

The administrative machine could only bear a certain strain without collapse, but it could bear more than its peace-time guardians realised. Certainly it needed the force of a driving will behind it to achieve any results at all.

Such a will was soon to be provided. Charles de Freycinet was not a soldier but a professional engineer, a civilian with the precise mind and immense powers of industry of an outstanding administrator. Like many other professional men in Tours he had realised that the organisation of a modern nation for war, the mobilisation of its industrial potential and its man-power, was not basically a military matter; that it demanded a far wider range of skills and more plenary authority than any soldier could command. His conclusion he published in a memorandum which appeared in Tours a few days before Gambetta's

---

[1] J. T. P. Bury, *Gambetta and the National Defence* 136.
[2] *D.T.* III 79–80.   [3] Thoumas, *Paris, Tours, Bordeaux* 97.

arrival. In it he urged that the Minister of War should be a civilian, that a Military Council of War should assist him in conducting operations, and that all questions of administration and organisation should be handled by a "Delegate" who should also be a civilian. These plans coincided nearly enough with Gambetta's own ideas; within a few hours of his arrival he appointed Freycinet to the post of Delegate which he had himself devised. But there was one important difference between Freycinet's project and Gambetta's implementation of it. The Military Council of War was never created. Freycinet became Gambetta's plenipotentiary in matters operational as well as administrative— Gambetta confessed himself to be no more than "a will supplying an impetus"[1]—and his achievements in the latter field were to be overshadowed, and rightly, by his catastrophic failures in the former. Moreover he was to make himself almost universally and unnecessarily unpopular with the Army which he directed. "He was to offend it daily," wrote General d'Aurelle de Paladines, "by his harshness, his demeanour, his haughty words, and his complete ignorance of hierarchical principles which he had anyhow determined to tread under foot."[2] No doubt Aurelle spoke only for himself and the small group of regular officers who commanded the higher formations; but the feelings of these men at such a moment, were not unimportant.

Gambetta's arrival and assumption of office at least resolved the conflict between the civil and the military powers. The senior officers, offended as they were by the revolutionary tone of his proclamations and sceptical about the strategic combinations of Freycinet and his civilian friends, were to obey him, even in carrying out orders which they knew to be absurd. In return Gambetta urged obedience on the raw troops who were always liable to confuse republican liberty with indiscipline and licence. "You have at your head", he told them, "energetic and devoted chiefs, as wise as they are bold. They must be blindly obeyed. They preoccupy themselves ceaselessly with you. In return they have the right to demand order, discipline, courage: republican virtues of which they set you the example every day."[3] The professional soldiers were none the less able to argue convincingly after the war that they had no responsibility for the disasters which overtook the Armies of National Defence. The failure of the amateurs in the second half of the war did much to atone for the failure of the professionals in the first.

[1] Bury, op. cit. 132.
[2] General d'Aurelle de Paladines, *La Première Armée de la Loire* (2nd edn. Paris 1872) 36.
[3] Proclamation of 24th November, *D.T.* V ii 245.

Freycinet and Gambetta did however understand one aspect of modern war better than did the professional soldiers, whether French or German. The summoning of a nation to arms involved not only the conversion of civilians into soldiers but the conscription of such civilians as scientists, engineers, railway executives, telegraph operators, business men, doctors, and architects, to employ their own professional skills in a common enterprise in which the movement of armies was only the final result. Freycinet's comprehension of this gave to the organisation of the National Defence an amplitude which far surpassed anything on the German side, and which was not to be seen again until the First World War was far advanced on its course.[1] For example, all state engineers, architects, and public-works contractors were put under requisition, and a civil engineering corps took the place of the military engineers. All qualified civilians, suitable accommodation and stores were requisitioned for the medical services, and the entire *Intendance* services—pay, transport, supply—were put under civilian control. The civil administrative services and communications-network were put at the disposal of a *Bureau des Reconnaissances*, which dealt not only with the collection and dissemination of intelligence, but with the destruction of communications in front of and behind the enemy lines; with the evacuation of supplies from invaded areas, and where possible with the enforcement of conscription in the occupied provinces. A *Bureau Supérieur d'Études Topographiques*, calling on the service of local photographers, provided the necessary quantity of military maps; a *Commission d'Armement* was set up consisting largely of businessmen and presided over by Jules Lecesne, one of France's leading men of affairs, to supervise the allocation of war contracts at home and abroad; while the nation's scientific and technological resources were surveyed and exploited by two overlapping organisations, the *Commission Scientifique de la Défense Nationale* and the *Commission d'Études des Moyens de Défense*. Appointments to these bodies and their staffs had to be hurriedly, and could not always be wisely, made. They had no precedents to steer them, they worked under intense pressure and made many mistakes; and their achievements were to be largely forgotten in the general failure which overtook French arms. But if their work had received a hundredth part of the study which was lavished on the operations of the armies in the field, the great industrial nations of the world

---

[1] See Freycinet's own interesting if not totally reliable account in his *Souvenirs* (Paris 1912) I 139–56.

would have had a surer guide in planning the conduct of their twentieth-century wars.[1]

★   ★   ★

There was plenty of raw material for the creation of the new French armies. The very rapidity of the German victory had made impossible anything like a complete mobilisation of military resources by the Imperial Government; and although most of the trained man-power of France was shut up with the Army of the Rhine in Metz or on the way to imprisonment with the Army of Châlons, a huge quantity of partly trained or untrained material still remained. The paper strength of the French armed forces on 1st July 1870 had been 984,748 officers and men. To this had been added the classes of 1869 and 1870, and by the law of 10th August, all unmarried men between the ages of twenty-five and thirty-five, whether they had previously served or not; which, with voluntary enlistments, brought the total figure, including the *Garde Mobile*, up to 1,814,320. If we subtract the 500,000 casualties and prisoners of the Armies of Châlons and the Rhine, and the 260,000 troops defending Paris, there still remained well over 1,000,000 men, serving, training, or liable to military service.[2] On 2nd November, in a measure recalling the *réquisition permanente* of 1793, the Delegation issued a decree which mobilised the entire male population between the ages of twenty-one and forty, with exceptions granted only for infirmity. By the end of the war only the first group in this class, the unmarried men, had been called up, but these alone totalled 578,900. Moreover, in addition to these forces of the army, there were those of the *Garde Nationale mobilisée*, in recruiting for which the age-limit was more flexible. This was mobilised in the provinces by decree of 12th October. Every canton was to find a battalion, every *arrondissement* a legion, and every department a brigade; which, raised and equipped by the civil power, then passed for purposes of discipline and training under the authority of the Ministry of War.[3]

In a country still in the early stages of industrialisation the provision of man-power for the Army in itself presented little difficulty. It was the

[1] *Guerre: La Défense Nationale en Province* I i 29–62. Freycinet, *La Guerre en Province* 18–25, 36–8.

[2] Official statistics of the *Ministère de Guerre*, qu. Martin des Pallières, *Orléans* (Paris 1872) 12–14.

[3] Reinach II 39, 49. *D.T.* V ii 216. *Guerre: Défense Nationale* I i 110–13. It is not always easy to distinguish between the Army and the *Garde Nationale*, since registered conscripts awaiting their call to the former would serve, and if necessary fight, with the latter.

very size of these forces which raised the greatest problems for Freycinet. How, first of all, were they to be officered? On 16th September we find the commander of the military sub-division at Blois writing that he had 940 men at present under his command, was expecting 1,500 more, and had altogether six officers and nineteen N.C.O.'s to deal with them.[1] Freycinet's first step was to double the size of the infantry companies, thus halving the number of officers required: an expedient borrowed from the practice of the Federal Army in the American Civil War. The effect, as in the United States, was deplorable. It made more difficult the maintenance of discipline, and manœuvre on the battle-field became almost impossible. The Armies of National Defence were to consist of huge concentrations of men capable only of executing the simplest movements, and those with ponderous slowness. Their number could avail little against the small, disciplined and articulated forces of the Prussians: it made them only a more vulnerable target for the rifles of the enemy when they attacked and for his artillery when they stood on the defence. Certainly the officer-problem was eased, but it was far from being solved. The Law of 10th August, which recalled to the army all men up to the age of thirty-five who had previously served, produced a number of ex-officers and also of ex-N.C.O.'s who were made eligible for commissions. Gambetta's resolute departure from routine did much to ease matters still further. By decree of 13th October all restrictions on promotion were abolished, and it became possible to give General's rank to such energetic young officers as Colonels Billot, Cremer, and de Sonis.[2] The following day a decree grouped together all troops not belonging to the regular army, the *mobiles*, the *mobilisées*, the *francs-tireurs*, in an Auxiliary Army—another American expedient—in which anyone, regardless of back-ground or experience, could be appointed to hold any rank.[3] Thus it became possible to give army commissions to foreigners such as Giuseppe Garibaldi, or naval officers like Admirals Jaurès and Jauréguiberry. Yet however wide the net was spread, there was still not enough good material available. In the units formed towards the end of the war complaints were constant of the idleness, cowardice and indifference of the regimental officers, which was reflected in the gradual deterioration of discipline, and of the inefficiency of the staff.[4] Inaccurate calculation of march-tables, faulty railway administration, failure in the supply

[1] *Guerre: La 1re Armée de la Loire I*: Docs. annexes 99–100.
[2] Reinach II 9.   [3] Ibid. II 10.
[4] See Gambetta's circular of 25th January 1871, *D.T.* V ii 304.

services, all were to increase the miseries and reduce the fighting effectiveness of the Armies of National Defence.[1]

In the *Garde Nationale* the officer-problem was not only administrative but political. The regimental officers of the *Garde Nationale sédentaire*, intended as it was primarily for local defence, were by tradition elected, and in the decrees of mobilisation of 10th August and 12th October this tradition was confirmed.[2] The officers of the *Garde Mobile*, a force intended for service in the field, were appointed by the Ministry of War, usually with the advice of the local Prefects, whose main concern was with their political reliability; and the presence of royalist or Imperialist officers who had no sympathy with the events of 4th September awoke agitation in the more excitable provinces, to say nothing of Paris itself.[3] Under pressure of the Parisian agitation the Government, on 7th September, extended election of officers to the *Garde Mobile* as well. To the immediate protests of civil and military authorities in the provinces Gambetta replied soothingly that "in most cases the *Mobiles* will confirm the existing choice and the officers will have new authority". But he was too optimistic. Complaints poured in from officers who had lost their place and who were too old or had been commissioned for too long to serve in the ranks, and who objected, correctly, that they could not be deprived of their commissions without the authority of a Council of War. The Delegation left it to the discretion of Prefects whether elections should be held or not. In most departments they were not; and in Paris, after three months of torment at the hands of the uncontrollable *Mobiles*, the Government at last had the courage, on 18th December, to revoke the electoral principle altogether.[4]

Then there was the problem of arming these masses. Since *chassepots* could not be manufactured in sufficient quantity, older models of rifle were taken and adapted to breech-loading, while French agents scoured the markets of the world for arms and ammunition. French naval supremacy gave unrestricted access to the arsenals of Great Britain and the United States, where manufacturers gratefully seized the opportunity to unload stocks of obsolescent rifles and to experiment with new models. In spite of official protests from Berlin and mounting rage in Germany, armaments and military equipment were

[1] Freycinet, *Guerre en Province* 335–42. *Guerre: La Défense Nationale en Province* I ii 66–90: Docs. annexes 55–67.   [2] *D.T.* V ii 216.

[3] Reports in *Guerre: Investissement de Paris* I ii: Docs. annexes 22–5.

[4] *Guerre: Investissement de Paris* I i 39 and I ii Docs. annexes 28–35. *Guerre: Défense Nationale* I i 92. *D.O.* II 248.

freely imported across the Channel and the Atlantic. Yet this very profusion was embarrassing. Enfields, Springfields, Spencers, Sniders, Winchesters, Scharps, Remingtons, came pouring into the country in every sort of condition—eighteen different types in all, each needing a different calibre of ammunition. The French agents were not always skilful nor the foreign agents scrupulous, and the *Garde Nationale*, rightly mistrusting the substitutes with which they were supplied, continued vainly to demand *chassepots*.[1]

Artillery presented fewer problems. At Bourges, Toulouse, Rennes, Nantes, Lyons, Besançon, and Douai the foundries and arsenals which had grown up during the industrial boom of the Second Empire were available to turn out guns virtually in whatever quantity the Government required. Of the total of 1,500 demanded, 1,270 had been provided from French sources by the armistice, while imports from Britain and America easily made up the balance. When the war ended the armies had some two hundred batteries in action with a further twenty-two available at the depôts: a proportion of something over two guns to every thousand men. The real shortage was not of guns but of gunners. Even less than infantrymen could artillerymen be improvised, and for lack of them even the guns available could not be put to full effect.[2]

The task of arming the forces was shared between the Central Government and the departmental authorities. Each department was ordered to provide a complete battery for every 100,000 of its population. Prefects were encouraged to use their own initiative in arming the *Garde Nationale*, and repayment of two-thirds of the departmental expenditure was guaranteed by the State.[3] But this division of labour had unfortunate results. In Britain, America, and Belgium local and central government agents unwittingly bid against each other, and the price of armaments soared. Moreover they competed not only for arms: uniforms, saddlery, shoes, every sort of equipment, all were urgently needed. Normally these were turned out by factories in and around Paris, and huge stocks still lay uselessly in the besieged capital. Now they had to be hurriedly secured in a sellers' market, at home and abroad, by inexperienced or venal negotiators, whose mistakes or dishonesty clothed thousands of men in shoddy cloth or shoes which fell to pieces as they marched.[4] As one of the Delegation's leading officials

[1] Thoumas, *Paris, Tours, Bordeaux* 143–4. D.T. III 299, 511.
[2] Reinach II 17. *Guerre: Défense Nationale en Province* I i 249, 300–1.
[3] Ibid. 274, 284.
[4] D.T. I 50, 526. Thoumas, op. cit. 71. Gen. L. Faidherbe, *Campagne de l'Armée du Nord* (Paris 1871) 75–80. *Guerre: Défense Nationale en Province* I i 366.

later put it, "Naturally when one does things in a hurry one does not do them well; but we had to do things by halves or not do them at all"[1]; and before the Delegation could learn from its own mistakes the war was over.

The standard of equipment of the armies and of the *Garde Nationale* thus varied from department to department according to the skill, the energy or simply the good fortune of the responsible officials. The standard of training and discipline varied with the date of embodiment of the units. The first two army corps raised, 15th and 16th, contained all that was left of the regular army, and most of the old soldiers recalled to service; and this accounts, quite as much as does the ability of Generals Aurelle, Martin des Pallières and Chanzy, for the success with which they fought around Orléans. But the corps created thereafter deteriorated with pathetic rapidity, and "the last units sent to the theatre of operations", in the grim words of the French General Staff analysis, "were made up of men who knew how to get killed, but not of soldiers".[2]

The attempts of the Delegation to train its new armies failed; partly from lack of cadres, largely through lack of time. Training of all fighting units was the responsibility of the Ministry of War, which set up training camps all over the country to which troops from the departments were sent before being drafted to the armies in the field. But the camps were hurriedly constructed on ill-chosen sites, were seldom ready in time to house the floods of men sent to them, accommodated them at best in miserable discomfort, and were only able, for lack of instructors, arms and equipment, to provide the barest vestiges of training when they were able to provide any at all.[3] An English journalist visited one training area at Boulogne, and reported:

> The scene was simply ludicrous. The officers, with one or two exceptions, kept aloof, talking with their friends. . . . Many of the men were engaged in position drill. Then they formed in battalion, and performed sundry evolutions in so clumsy a manner that the officers gave it up in despair, split the battalion into squads of six and ten men, and ordered skirmishing again. . . . 'It is difficult to teach what one is ignorant of oneself,' remarked one officer to another. Of discipline there was none. The men never saluted their officers, and spoke to

---

[1] Testelin, in *D.T.* III 559.

[2] *Guerre: Défense Nationale en Province* I i 128.

[3] Ibid. : Docs. annexes 701–6. *D.O.* II 89, 163–5. 192–4. The camp at Cherbourg, reported the local Prefect on 22nd December, "n'est que tracé, pas construit, et déjà plus de 20,000 hommes y ont été dirigés," *D.O.* I 452.

them with easy and in some cases impudent familiarity. . . . Everything about them was dirty. [1]

Sometimes operational urgency was so great that units, in spite of protests from their local authorities, were sent straight to the front without even a day's training. At the height of Bourbaki's campaign in the East, for example, we find one colonel refusing point-blank to take his untrained troops into action and being arrested in consequence.[2] Local demonstrations against the departure of conscripts multiplied, and they deserted *en masse* on the way to the camps and from the camps themselves, having to be rounded up by civil and military authorities with flying columns and forced back to their units.[3] It was the votes of these men and their families that were, after five months of struggle, to sweep Gambetta from power, and instal an Assembly empowered, at whatever cost in humiliation, to give the wretched Frenchmen the peace for which they yearned.

§ 3 The Francs-Tireurs

Was it really necessary for the Delegation to raise these huge and miserable armies and encounter the Prussians in the open field at all? The original ideas of the Delegation seemed to be cast on very different lines. On 21st September Fourichon advised his commanders to use their *Mobiles* as partisans "whose rôle is less to fight than to harass the enemy. . . . To obstruct him in his requisitions. . . . Above all to carry out *coups de main* and *pointes*, to capture convoys, cut roads and railways, destroy bridges. . . . These troops must wage real partisan war, and for that they will need vigour, dash, intelligence and above all a great deal of cunning." Gambetta's advice was the same. "Harass the enemy's detachments without pause or relaxation," he advised the Delegation from Paris on 26th September, "prevent him from deploying, restrict the area of his requisitions, make him thin out before Paris, disturb him day and night, always and everywhere—that is the object for you to attain." Only in second place "from this war of *chicanes*, of *chouannerie*, you will pass gradually, as our forces increase, to more serious operations, susceptible of being more directly linked to the

---

[1] *War Correspondence of the Daily News* (London 1871) II 162–3.
[2] *D.O.* II 89. *D.T.* III 518.
[3] *D.O.* I 303, 310, 335, 548. II 192.

defence of Paris".[1] The proclamation he issued three weeks later on arriving at Tours shows that his thoughts were still running in the same channels. Many voices were raised in the Republican ranks to advocate the inauguration of ruthless guerrilla war. "We will make France into one great guerrilla," wrote one, "Paris into a Saragossa!"[2] At Tours Steenackers suggested the formation of small groups "which will cut off convoys, harass the enemy and hang from trees all the enemies they can take well and truly by the neck, after having mutilated them". In addition he suggested recruiting 20,000–30,000 Kabyle tribesmen "and throwing them into Germany with leave to burn, pillage and rape all they find on the way. . . . In short I suggest the type of war which the Spaniards waged against us under the First Empire and the Mexicans under the Second."[3]

Had the Delegation devoted its resources to organising such resistance on a large scale the war would have plumbed even greater depths of horror than it did; but though the outcome is unlikely to have been changed, this might have been a more effective way of organising the man-power available than the attempt to form it into armies which never stood a chance against the Prussians in the open field. Only Gambetta's determination to relieve Paris at all costs can account for his abandonment of these early ideas of guerrilla warfare in favour of the creation of large armies to conduct a regular campaign. Large-scale guerrilla activities might harass and decimate the Germans until they abandoned the occupation in despair, but Paris would long since have fallen, and the relief of Paris had to be the first object of the Delegation's strategy. Thus guerrilla operations could only be subsidiary to the main French military preoccupation: the formation and operations of the Army of the Loire.

There was at first plenty of enthusiasm in France for a war of guerrillas. In Alsace and Lorraine bodies of volunteers had been organised and training ever since the Luxemburg crisis of 1868, and from the beginning of the campaign a substantial element of the population had shown itself unwilling to leave the conduct of the war in the hands of the professional soldiers. The Germans were embarrassed by guerrilla activity even before they reached the Meuse. German cavalry crossing the Moselle on 15th August reported that they were "constantly fired at" by the inhabitants of the villages, and they hanged the culprits— or the suspected culprits—whenever they caught them. A fortnight later, on the eve of Sedan, the Crown Prince spoke of this *franc-*

[1] *D.O.* II 258.　　　[2] *D.T.* I 380.　　　[3] *D.O.* II 256.

tireur activity as being now general. "Single shots are fired, generally in a cunning, cowardly fashion, on patrols, so that nothing is left for us to do but to adopt retaliatory measures by burning down the house from which the shots came or else by the help of the lash and forced contributions."[1] When the antiquated and under-gunned fortress of Laon surrendered to German cavalry on 9th September the custodian of the magazine set off his stock of gunpowder in an immense explosion which killed or wounded a hundred enemy troopers and three hundred Frenchmen.[2] Sharpshooters haunted the roads between Sedan and Paris. "We are hunting them down pitilessly", Bismarck told Jules Favre. "They are not soldiers: we are treating them as murderers." And when Favre pointed out that the German people had done the same in the Wars of Liberation, he replied unanswerably, "That is quite true; but our trees still bear the marks where your generals hanged our people on them."[3]

Along the main German lines of communication such sporadic resistance quickly died down. The occupation forces established a reputation for prompt and sometimes indiscriminate retaliation, and the local authorities collaborated in the repression of what they could only regard as acts of useless terrorism. The population sank into acquiescent apathy.[4] When at Soissons on 27th October a German official was attacked, the municipal council issued a formal condemnation of the act "in the name of its feelings of loyalty".[5] But on the fringes of the occupation area, in districts visited only by occasional patrols or swept by cavalry, *franc-tireur* units operated with increasing boldness. Among the woods and mountains of the Vosges they were so effective that considerable forces had to be detached, from the troops besieging Strasbourg, in a sustained campaign to clear Alsace.[6] It was not until the German occupation had extended south into Franche-Comté that *franc-tireur* activity in the Vosges died down and the German territories beyond the Rhine felt themselves safe from raids. South and west of Paris German cavalry penetrating down the Oise and the Seine

[1] Pelet-Narbonne, *Cavalry on Service* 322. Bronsart, *Kriegstagebuch* 42. Frederick III, *War Diary* 75. On 30th August the sub-prefect at Rheims reported to the Ministry of the Interior that he had distributed 6,000 rifles and that the population, "hesitant at first, seems disposed to defend itself energetically". *Guerre: Armée de Châlons* II: Docs. annexes 90.

[2] *M.M.K.* 291. *Guerre, Investissement de Paris* II 120–33. Lehautcourt, *La Campagne du Nord en 1870–1* (Paris 1897) 7–11.

[3] Jules Favre, *Gouvernement de la Défense Nationale* I 163.

[4] *G.G.S.* II iii 137. Lehautcourt, *Campagne du Nord* 217.

[5] Ibid. 34.   [6] *G.G.S.* II i 82–6.

encountered local resistance so stiff that they were forced either to abandon the area or occupy it *en règle*. At Ablis, near Epernon, a detachment of German cavalry billeted in the village was surrounded and attacked by *francs-tireurs* and only just got away—an escapade for which the French paid by seeing the village burned to the ground. The town of Châteaudun, when attacked on 18th October, put up a resistance which has passed into legend. By the end of October it was clear to the Germans that the war had entered a stage in which terror and counter-terror were to play a formidable part.

The *franc-tireur* companies were raised by local or individual enterprise, and at first the Government did no more than encourage their formation and vote funds for their pay.[1] They multiplied quickly. An official calculation puts the total number of units at three hundred, totalling 57,600 members.[2] There were plenty of Frenchmen willing to die for their country but unwilling to undergo the boredom and discomfort of military life, and their ranks were swelled by foreign sympathisers of every kind: Spanish Republicans, Polish exiles, Americans of French descent, adventurous young men from England and Ireland, above all Italians with the great Giuseppe Garibaldi himself at their head. The French companies reflected every hue of the complex political spectrum, from the violently radical *francs-tireurs* of the Seine to Colonel de Cathelineau's legitimists from Vendée, from the wealthy bourgeois *tirailleurs volontaires* from the Gironde to the companies of papal Zouaves which Colonel de Charette brought back to France after the Italian occupation of Rome. Even the grooms of the Imperial Household, to the embarrassment of the local authorities, raised a regiment of cavalry. All crowded the streets of Tours, armed and uniformed according to their own fancy. One company was dressed in the romantic if impractical style of Alexandre Dumas's Musketeers, with plumed hats, huge cloaks, boots, sabres, and daggers. The *francs-tireurs* of Nice wore grey Tyrolean jackets and hats, the *francs-tireurs* of the Pyrenees berets, the *Partisans du Gers* carried black banners ornamented with crossbones; a mounted company from South America appeared with lassos; and companies from North Africa wore the burnous.[3] Their military performance was unequal: not all could match the performance of Ricciotti Garibaldi at Châtillon, or of Lipowski's *francs-tireurs* at

[1] Decrees of 7th and 29th September. See Martin des Pallières, *Orléans* 343, 349.

[2] *Guerre: Défense Nationale en Province* I i 552.

[3] Thoumas, *Paris, Tours, Bordeaux* 119. Chevalier, *Tours Capitale* 61, 149. Steenackers and Le Goff, *Gouvt. de Défense Nationale* I 151-3.

Châteaudun, or the sustained, disciplined courage shown by the Bretons under de Cathelineau; while the general impression they left on the countryside in which they operated was one of a rapacious indiscipline even more terrible than the methodical exactions of the Germans. They were, according to one observer, "the terror and the ruin of the country-side which they should have protected".[1] Successive measures had to be enacted to bring them under military discipline. On 29th September they were placed on the same disciplinary footing as the *Gardes Mobiles*, and on 4th November Gambetta placed them under the authority of the regular military commander within whose area they were operating, demanding at the same time that the commander of each unit should submit a regular report on the strength and achievement of his men. Any unit deemed not to have acquitted itself with honour in the face of the enemy was made liable to dissolution; and in January violent measures were decreed against *soi-disant* members of free corps who "wandered far from the armies in the towns and villages, and scandalised the population by their vagabondage, their idleness, and often their misbehaviour".[2]

Among the most controversial of the *franc-tireur* units were those commanded by the veteran hero, Giuseppe Garibaldi. His offers of help were greeted by the Government with some embarrassment. Gouty and unwell, he was past his military prime, and as the foremost revolutionary of the age he was a doubtful political asset. Garibaldi saw the war purely in Mazzinian terms, as the struggle of the French section of the Universal Republic against the forces of reactionary monarchy and clericalism, an aspect of the sacred and titanic conflict which had driven Austria and the Papacy from Italy and would end with the liberation of mankind from the chains of feudalism and bigotry. Even Gambetta was uneasy. The co-operation of Garibaldi would appal the conservatives and the Catholics[3]; it would raise grave diffi-culties for Thiers in Rome; and there was a distinct danger that Gari-baldi might demand as his price the liberation of those Imperial ac-quisitions which the Republicans had no intention of relinquishing, his

---

[1] Chevalier, op. cit. 63. Complaints by local authorities in *D.O.* I 413, II 92, 175.
[2] Freycinet, *Guerre en Province* 388. *D.T.* IV. 25, V ii 291. *Guerre: Défense Nationale en Province* I ii 557.
[3] The Archbishop of Tours lamented: "Je croyais que la divine Providence avait comblé la mesure des humiliations qu'elle imposait à notre pays; je m'étais trompé: il nous était reservé de subir une suprême humiliation, celle de voir Garibaldi arriver ici, en se donnant la mission de sauver la France." C. Chevalier, *Tours Capitale* 101.

native provinces of Nice and Savoy.[1] His chief French disciple, a naval surgeon by name Dr Bordone, had a criminal record.[2] But help from so distinguished a source could not be rejected. Garibaldi was coolly received at Tours,[3] but given a general command over the *francs-tireurs* in the east of France. He raised his standard at Lyons, with Bordone as his chief of staff; and there flocked to him a collection of revolutionaries of both sexes, survivors of 1848 and precursors of the nihilists and anarchists of the '80s and '90s, of whose behaviour the authorities at Lyons vigorously complained.[4] Once embodied, the force moved to the Côte d'Or and established its headquarters at Autun, where its military effectiveness was to prove considerable. But the contempt and violence with which the Garibaldians treated the establishments of the Church earned them an unenviable reputation which not all their intermittent success in battle could expunge. If the French came near to reviving the heroic days of 1792-3, they were forced to remember that those were years, not only of resistance to the invader, but of bitter civil war.[5]

With the growth of *franc-tireur* units the line between soldier and civilian became blurred. The measures which the Delegation decreed for local defence destroyed it altogether.

The Imperial Government had left its local authorities to work out for themselves how to deal with the invaders, and their actions varied from commune to commune. Some mayors ordered the inhabitants to receive the Germans well; others, with memories of 1814-15, organised local guards to cut off enemy patrols, and carried out with enthusiasm Palikao's instructions to arm the local *Garde Nationale*. The mood of the inhabitants of North-West France seems to have been one of resistance, but one which needed a focus and a lead[6]; and this was provided by Gambetta within two days of his taking over the Ministry of the

[1] *D.T.* IV (Marc Dufraisse) 430. Gambetta to Trochu, 10th October 1870 in Reinach I 78.

[2] It is printed in *D.O.* II 157.

[3] The Delegation sent him enthusiastic messages of welcome when he landed at Marseilles on 7th October, but did their best to have him stopped at Valence. *D.O.* II 268-9.

[4] *D.O.* II 31-3. For a fuller description see J. Theyras, *Garibaldi en France 1870-1* (Paris 1891) 32-110 and Bordone's own work *Garibaldi et l'Armée des Vosges* (Paris 1871).

[5] See, e.g., Chevalier, *Tours Capitale* 107. *D.T.* IV 27, 77-101. Cardinal Archbishop of Besançon to Gambetta, 11th November: "Garibaldi arrête, menace fusiller curés, Doubs, Jura, Haute Saône. Effroi général, défense compromise. Réprimez - Éloignez." *D.O.* I 256. Compare however n. 1, p. 409 below.

[6] Wimpffen, *Sedan* 131.

Interior. On 6th-7th September he sent out orders to the Prefects of all departments threatened with invasion to organise the defence of their territory using *Gardes Nationales, sapeurs-pompiers,* forest officials, and "all the men of goodwill they can arm". They were to arouse all local energies, had complete powers of requisition, and were to create to assist them local committees of defence.[1] Some Prefects showed all the enthusiasm Gambetta could desire. Spuller, in Haute-Marne, replied on 14th September, "I am forming an army of 40,000 *Gardes Nationales Sédentaires,* at the head of which I shall place 4,000 *francs-tireurs . . .* this force, on the enemy flank, will strike blows which will echo throughout France."[2] Others showed less initiative. West and south of Paris organisation lagged; the Prefect at Auxerre complained that "nearly all the mayors and magistrates are hindering the defence, not openly but by inertia". By the middle of October the progress of the Germans south of Paris and of Strasbourg had made it clear that no form of local defence had been developed which could deal with anything stronger than scattered patrols. The local authorities of Dreux and Mont-didier handed over their towns with a complaisance which roused particular fury.[3] By a decree of 14th October Gambetta took the matter in hand. All departments within a hundred kilometres of the enemy were declared to be in a "state of war", and military committees were empowered to organise their defence and erect road-blocks, field-works, and demolitions. Subsequent orders provided for a "scorched earth" programme. Areas threatened by invasion were to be stripped of livestock and crops, which were whenever possible to be evacuated to safer areas; where it was not they were to be destroyed, and the owners would be indemnified by the State. All the population not capable of fighting was also to be evacuated, and the remainder would take their place at the barricades. The mayor, the curé, the schoolmaster, and other local notables were to be responsible for carrying out these orders, and anyone contravening them was to be dealt with by a military court.[4]

The instructions of the Delegation and the detailed preparations in the departments constituted an impressive blueprint for national resistence, but in execution they met the fate of all plans which depend upon *l'homme moyen sensuel* behaving in a consistently heroic fashion without being first conditioned and armoured by military discipline. Whenever German troops appeared in any quantity local defence

---

[1] *D.O.* II 216, 227.   [2] *D.O.* I 459.
[3] Steenackers and Le Goff, *Défense Nationale en Province* II 112–14.
[4] Reinach II 11–14.

measures crumbled away. Colonel de Cathelineau, who had to co-operate with the local *Garde Nationale* in defending the Forest of Orléans, agreed that on paper their organisation was perfect; "but when the enemy appeared, nobody was there. On every road, behind every bush, there were men armed with rifles, and not one came to join the line when he heard the firing."[1] When at the beginning of the new year Frederick Charles's army penetrated westward towards the Sarthe, the indifference of the population drove the authorities to despair. "I warn you", wrote the Prefect of the Orne to the Mayor of Beaumont-sur-Sarthe on 13th January, "that if, when you get this despatch, you have not blown the two bridges at Beaumont . . . you will be immediately arrested, brought before a court martial and shot on the spot." Four days later he ordered the Sub-Prefect at Argentan to destroy all communications between Argentan and Alençon. "Use every means, requisition tools, conscript man-power . . . if the people won't work, force them to, revolver in hand."[2] But the bridges were not blown; the roads were not destroyed; the boldness of Gambetta and the heroism of his most ardent followers were more than could be long sustained by the nation as a whole. The Prefect of Calvados showed more realism when, on being informed that all the troops in his area were being withdrawn into the Cherbourg peninsula, he replied, "Very well then, I agree. But . . . you must not set up the defence of the soil foot by foot as an inviolable principle . . . After indicating anyone who does not resist to the end as an object of scorn for men of honour, to remove from us, as you do today, all means of resistance, is quite simply to organise our disgrace." The French peasants continued to harvest their crops, to tread their grapes, to tend their beasts and to look after their children; submitting where necessary to the exactions of the invader, obeying whichever administration had the means to enforce obedience, growing steadily more hostile to the fanatical idealism of their leaders, and longing only, at whatever price, for the coming of peace.

[1] Pallières, *Orléans* 376.   [2] *D.O.* I 520–2.   [3] *D.O.* I 169.

CHAPTER VII

Metz and Strasbourg[1]

IN ORGANISING his new forces after 4th September Gambetta acted as if the Imperial army, like the Empire itself, had ceased to exist. It was a natural assumption; yet by far the greater part of the professional army on which Napoleon had at the beginning of the war relied for the defence of France was still on French soil lying organised, armed and disciplined, in complete inactivity around the fortress of Metz. It comprised five army corps, the finest of which had hardly been in action at all: 154,481 men strong, fully armed, complete with cavalry and artillery and abundant ammunition.[2] Gambetta and Bazaine made little attempt to communicate with one another, and did not take the existence of the other's forces into serious consideration in formulating their own plans.[3] An astounded and outraged nation could afterwards find no explanation for the inactivity of the army of the Rhine except in the rank treachery of Bazaine, and once the war was over it relieved its feelings by trying him for his life and setting him in the pillory for all posterity. Yet the evidence which emerged, both in his trial and in the inquiry which the Third Republic conducted into the actions of the Government of National Defence, does not support a charge of treachery, or even of simple self-seeking. The picture it gives is one of incompetence and paralysis in face of a situation with which only a commander of outstanding military and political ability could have dealt. The real accusation lies not against Bazaine himself, but against the military system which bred him and allowed him to rise to the command of the French army. Nations get the generals, as well as the governments, they deserve. But some account must be given of the events in Metz

---

[1] See for this chapter the map on p. 138.

[2] Palat, *La Capitulation de Metz* (Paris 1908) 15 and n. The strength of the investing force on 19th August was slightly higher: 154,000 infantry, 14,435 cavalry, 642 guns.

[3] For an analysis of Bazaine's outgoing messages, and evidence of the attempts of the Delegation to get in touch with him, see ibid. 304–5.

between 19th August and 27th October, when the fortress and the army eventually capitulated, if we are to estimate where the responsibility really lay. We shall consider first the military events, which are relatively easy to disentangle, and then the political, which are not.

Neither the German nor the French commanders fully realised on 19th August that they were beginning a siege. Moltke's orders were for six corps of the First and Second Armies to line the left bank of the Moselle to prevent the French breaking through to the west. An easterly break-out would encounter only I Corps and a Landwehr Division, who were instructed to oppose no serious resistance. All that mattered was to keep Bazaine and MacMahon apart. To Frederick Charles, who showed no enthusiasm for this unglamorous assignment, Moltke promised that the business would not last very long. Either the French would attempt a break-out, and could be pursued, or they would capitulate for want of food, and then, he wrote soothingly, "your Royal Highness will reap, on the occasion of the capitulation, one of the greatest successes which military history has to record".[1]

Quickly however a line of fortifications was woven around Metz, twenty-five miles in perimeter, which Prussian thoroughness and diligence made virtually impregnable on the right bank of the Moselle as well as on the left. Every road was barricaded; each village was turned into a small fortress and linked by communication-trenches to its neighbours; every wood was blocked by *abattis* or cleared to give a field of fire. Everywhere fire-trenches and support-trenches were dug, and battery positions were created for field-guns on carefully chosen sites. Roads were diverted, built, resurfaced; additional bridges were thrown across the Moselle; a telegraph network was woven between all major headquarters; observation posts and light-signalling towers were built at intervals round the perimeter, and the main railway-line from Paris to the Rhine was so diverted as to run well outside these lines. For the troops crowded into inadequate billets in the villages behind their trench system, life was tedious and uncomfortable. At first the villages were so full of the wounded of both armies that the Prussians had to construct makeshift huts out of brushwood which were hardly adequate as protection against the autumn cold and rain. Rations were short until the *Intendantur* had the railway in proper working order; while the inevitable marauding among the vineyards and orchards of the Moselle brought its melancholy result in an outbreak of dysentery and diarrhoea. The health of their troops altogether gave the Prussian authorities

[1] *M.M.K.* 242–3.

considerable concern. Many of their bivouacs lay in the fields around Gravelotte and Amanvillers where thousands of corpses lay decomposing under a light covering of soil, which the heavy rain of the next few weeks was repeatedly to wash off, with deplorable effect on German health and morale. The Prussians set their men to work therefore with all the more diligence at digging, constructing and revetting. Week followed rainy week and the army in its cramped billets grew steadily more bored and discontented; but as the wounded were sent back to Germany and more buildings became available for billets, as rations became more plentiful and the flow of post from home increased, the living conditions of Frederick Charles's men improved as markedly as those of Bazaine's army within the fortress were deteriorating.[1]

The French army which fell back into Metz on 19th August, though dazed and urgently in need of rest and re-equipment, did not feel itself defeated.[2] Only 6th Corps and the right wing of 4th Corps had suffered serious damage at Gravelotte, and Bazaine's plans gave some colour to the explanation that their rout was really a planned withdrawal. The rest of the army, conscious of having fought bravely and, for all it knew, successfully, fell back in resentful bewilderment and looked forward to the chance of fighting again. Shortages of equipment and ammunition were quickly made up from the stocks piled in disorder round the station at Metz.[3] On 21st August the corps commanders sent in unanimously cheerful reports on the condition of their units. Their only general complaint was of a shortage of officers, which in Frossard's corps was having bad effects on morale; while Lebœuf frankly stated that in his corps the officers were "naturally a little inclined to be critical".[4] But in general the troops had no conception of their situation. Bazaine, they believed, had thrashed the Germans at Colombey and Vionville and had fallen back on Metz only in order to play some master-stroke.

Quite what this stroke would be nobody could tell. Bazaine, withdrawn into the solitude of his headquarters in the well-to-do suburb of Ban-St Martin, discussed the situation with nobody, not even with his corps commanders; and they, disciplined in the Napoleonic tradition,

[1] *G.G.S.* I ii 173–5, 474–8, Appendices XXVII, LV. H. von Kretschman, *Kriegsbriefe* (Stuttgart 1904) 71, 136.

[2] See, e.g. Montaudun, *Souvenirs militaires* II 106.

[3] On 22nd August General Soleille reported the Army to be completely re-equipped with ammunition. *Procès Bazaine* 176.

[4] Bazaine, *Épisodes* 153–5.

did not expect that he would. It is difficult even today to discover how Bazaine's mind was moving; the apologias he wrote many years later afford no real clue; but there is nothing to suggest that he did not at first intend to attempt a break-out if the occasion offered. The Prussians barred the way to the west, but two other courses lay open to him: to march northwards as he had originally intended and link up with MacMahon via Montmédy and Sedan; or to break out to the south, cutting destructively across the German lines of communication and establishing himself on the plateau of Langres, whence he could draw supplies from south and west. The last plan was the boldest and promised the most success[1]; it was the one which Moltke thought the most likely[2]; but it would have demanded a degree of boldness in conception and skill in execution which Bazaine did not possess. His orders from the Emperor were to link up with the Army of Châlons, which could be done only by the north; and on 23rd August he smuggled out to Napoleon, through the still loosely guarded lines on the lower Moselle, a message announcing his intention of "undertaking the march which I spoke about before, through the northern fortresses, in order not to run any risk (*afin de ne rien compromettre*)".[3]

The break-out was planned for 26th August, and was to take place towards the north-east, down the right bank of the Moselle. The staff work was as slovenly as ever. Jarras was again ignored; orders went out only at the last moment; no attempt was made to co-ordinate movement over the Moselle bridges; and—most amazing omission of all—no bridging equipment was taken to enable the army to negotiate the rivers on its way.[4] These preparations, in certain quarters, were viewed with considerable alarm. On the evening of 25th August two senior officers visited Bazaine, the commander of the fortress of Metz, General Coffinières de Nordeck, and the commander of the army artillery, General Soleille; and they put the case against the proposed break-out in the strongest possible terms. Coffinières pointed out that if the army left Metz, the fortress would fall to the Germans in a fortnight—an eventuality, Bazaine might have replied, which, fatal as it might be to the General's own career, would not necessarily be so to the destinies of France. Soleille argued with more force that the ammunition stocks of the army, although adequate for one great battle, would hardly suffice

---

[1] It was widely discussed by Bazaine's staff. Jarras, *Souvenirs* 171.

[2] Moltke to Frederick Charles, 22nd August 1870, in *M.M.K.* 242.

[3] *D.T.* IV 232.

[4] Bazaine later explained, rather lamely, that he had given no orders that it should *not* be taken. *Procès Bazaine* 179.

for the series of engagements to be foreseen before a junction was made with MacMahon. And where, he asked, *was* MacMahon? Rather than launch into the unknown, with the risk of being overwhelmed in open country, would it not be better to wait until some definite news arrived from the Army of Châlons?[1]

Bazaine did not at first cancel the operation, and next day the army began to move at 4 a.m. But he countermanded the orders for his own headquarters, and he summoned his corps commanders to hear Soleille present to them the arguments which he and Coffinières had urged the previous evening. The unfortunate generals, consulted for the first time on the conduct of a campaign about whose strategy they knew nothing, did not take long to make up their minds. Frossard considered that morale would not survive another unsuccessful battle. Canrobert admitted that for the army to make its way across the country with all its baggage was nearly impossible. Ladmirault and Bourbaki agreed, very much against their will, that if ammunition was as short as Soleille maintained there was nothing to be done. Lebœuf, perhaps the only man present who had enough knowledge of the general situation to formulate a correct judgment, burst out into a long and unhelpful apologia, declaring that "to that day he had sustained the burden of accusations launched against his administration, but nobody had ever listened to him or asked his advice".[2] Moreover Soleille not only expounded the dangers of the proposed manœuvre; he pointed out the positive advantages of remaining where they were. They would be able to paralyse the German army by raiding their communications; and —and here for the first time the voice of defeatism was heard, and heard unrebuked—if France had to sue for terms, the possession of Metz would be a powerful bargaining counter which might well ensure the possession of Lorraine.[3] Outside, the rain which had been threatening all day was now seething down on to the columns of troops jamming the roads. Bazaine had said little during the Council; now, with the general acquiescence of his subordinates, he ordered the operation to be broken off. The heads of the columns were halted and, turning about, tried to force their way back through the crowded roads behind. Guns and limbers stuck in the mud, blocking the roads still further. The troops inched their way back through the downpour as slowly as they had set out;

[1] Bazaine, *Épisodes* 158. *D.T.* IV 276.
[2] Minutes of the meeting kept by General Boyer, reprinted in Bazaine, *Épisodes* 164–7.
[3] Loc. cit. *D.T.* I 56.

and not until 6 a.m. next morning, after twenty-six hours on the road, did the last of the troops settle into their quarters.[1]

The effect of this fiasco was unsettling, not least on Bazaine. Perhaps he clutched at Soleille's comforting suggestion, that even by remaining in Metz the army could serve a useful purpose, as a sheet-anchor in a situation he felt to be beyond his control. But within a few days he had again to nerve himself for action. On 30th August a message from Mac-Mahon was smuggled in from Thionville.[2] This had been despatched, it will be remembered, on 22nd August when MacMahon had received Bazaine's note of 19th August; and it announced the Army of Châlons was on its way to the relief of Metz. "I will be on the Aisne the day after tomorrow," it concluded, "whence I shall act as circumstances allow to come to your help."[3] Bazaine's phlegmatic reception of this infuriated his more excitable staff officers. "The day after tomorrow" was the 25th; a further five days' march should have brought MacMahon to the neighbourhood of Montmédy; Soleille's argument, that to break out would be to launch wildly into the blue, no longer had any relevance.[4] But Bazaine's calm was deceptive. Plans for a sortie had been under review ever since the 26th, and it was now possible to draw up and issue orders for battle the following day.

Once again the attempt was made on the weakly guarded right bank. With five army corps Bazaine should have had no difficulty in breaking through a front held by one army corps alone, which could be reinforced at best, during the course of the day, by only two more; and his failure to do so, combined with his curious conduct during the battle, certainly raises doubts whether the explanation is entirely to be sought in his military incapacity. One hostile observer could only draw the conclusion that he was playing a very deep game. MacMahon was to be deliberately left to himself. If he was beaten peace would certainly follow, the Empire might fall, and Bazaine, the commander of an intact and unbeaten army,

[1] D'Andlau, *Metz, Campagne et Négociations* 134–7. Bazaine was later to claim (*D.T.* IV 190) that he had ordered the movement "de faire supposer à l'ennemi que l'on voulait tenter un effort sur la route de Thionville, et de l'obliger ainsi à montrer de ce côté les forces qu'il avait en position".

[2] Much of the odium later cast on Bazaine came from the testimony of two of his staff officers, Baron d'Andlau and Colonel Lewal, that this message arrived on 23rd August, which made the failure to persevere on the 26th unforgivable. Bazaine's assertion that he heard nothing till the 30th was vindicated by the evidence at his trial. Palat suggests [*Capitulation de Metz* 62] that Bazaine received a purely unofficial message on the 23rd, announcing the departure of the Army of Châlons.

[3] *Procès Bazaine* 177.

[4] D'Andlau, *Metz, Campagne et Négociations* 121.

would be the man of the hour. If MacMahon was victorious, Bazaine would secure a comparatively easy triumph over the forces opposing him.[1] Such a thesis can neither be conclusively proved nor rejected out of hand, but it is not necessary to look so far for an explanation of Bazaine's hesitant and ambiguous leadership on 31st August and 1st September. If a break-out was achieved, he would then have the responsibility of conducting his army across perhaps 60 miles of country to effect a problematic junction with MacMahon, pursued by a swifter, stronger and more skilful enemy, at whose hands he could hardly hope to avoid defeat. By failing to break out and preserving his army intact, he not merely avoided disaster; he could still make a contribution of definite military value; and possibly the luck which had brought him thus far without disaster would produce some twist of events, some stroke of fortune which would enable him to extricate himself intact and even with credit. This cautious but hopeful fatalism seems a more probable guide to Bazaine's actions than the cold-blooded political calculations attributed to him by his accusers. Whichever view one takes, it is hard to avoid the conclusion that Bazaine, after issuing orders on 31st August for attack next day, had second thoughts about the desirability of breaking out at all; and that on 31st August and 1st September he was less than wholehearted in his desire for success.[2]

Once again Jarras was ignored in the drafting of orders. But the lessons of 26th August could not be totally forgotten, and on this occasion Bazaine's staff took rather greater trouble to move the army from the left bank to the right in a rapid and orderly manner. Their pains availed them little. The delays within the corps themselves combined with the wilfulness of their commanders to produce a disorder little better than that of six days earlier. Thus although 3rd Corps, which was already in position opposite the Germans on the old battlefield between Grigy and Noisseville, opened fire as instructed at 8 a.m. on 31st August and drove the German outposts from Colombey, nothing further occurred for eight hours. Manteuffel's outposts had reported the concentration of French troops in the fields round Borny; they noted

[1] D'Andlau, op. cit. 172–3. Du Barail (*Souvenirs* III 202) suggested that there was a bitter personal feud between the two Marshals, dating back to their service in Africa when MacMahon, then Bazaine's superior officer, refused him permission to marry.

[2] The following account of the battle of Noisseville is based on *G.G.S.* I ii 498–531, C. Fay, *Journal d'un officier de l'Armée du Rhin* 144–55, D'Andlau, *Metz, Campagne et Négociations* 162–71, L. Patry, *La Guerre telle qu'elle est* 131–55.

with surprise that no attack followed; and finally they saw with amazement that this menacing host of the enemy had piled its arms and was
placidly beginning to cook a midday meal. Meanwhile long columns of
dust crossing the Moselle valley north and south of the town showed
that Frederick Charles was rushing across reinforcements to the right
bank in time to deal with the French troops which were slowly edging
their way through the suburbs of Metz. These dust-clouds were pointed
out to Bazaine, who seemed quite unconcerned. "That's good," he
remarked calmly, "those are the troops coming over from the left
bank." By midday the whole of the French Imperial Guard was still
on the left bank; and at 6 p.m. the army artillery, which should have
been in the very forefront of the army to blast a way through the German
positions, had still not crossed the river. Bazaine held a leisurely conference with his corps commanders at which he gave out their orders for
the battle; he informed them that the attack was not to begin until he
gave the signal, by a gun fired from the Fort St Julien; but he did not
give the signal until three heavy guns had been laboriously dismantled
from St Julien and sited under his supervision so that they could bombard the German positions. The signal gun was eventually fired at 4 p.m.
and the French at last advanced.

The French object was to clear the Prussians from the slopes round the
village of St Barbe, which would open the road which led through
Bettlainville to the Lower Moselle. 3rd Corps and 4th Corps were to
advance along either side of the Vallières valley, the former to seize
Noisseville and the latter Servigny, while 6th Corps guarded the left
flank, 2nd Corps the right, and the Guard, as usual, was kept in reserve.
Against them they had only von Manteuffel's I Corps whose outposts
were some five battalions strong. Manteuffel knew that help was on the
way: the 3rd Landwehr Division was in close reserve, and divisions of
VII and IX Corps were hurrying over from the other bank; but
even when they came the French would still enjoy a considerable
superiority, and there was little hope of their arrival before nightfall. To
resist the attack of the entire French army Manteuffel was thus thrown
on his own resources. He decided to conduct the battle in his outpost
positions and throw everything into the fight for Servigny and Noisseville rather than fall back on St Barbe; so before Servigny he deployed a
formidable gun-line, sixty guns firing unresisted on to the French infantry while the French artillery were still negotiating the crowded
bridges of the Moselle. This successfully slowed down Ladmirault's
advance; but by contrast that of Lebœuf was all the more spectacular.

3rd Corps stormed back across their old battlefield. Pushing across the Vallières ravine they drove a deep salient into the German positions which enabled them to help 4th Corps by attacking Servigny from the south across the valley of Noisseville. The German gun-lines fell back, and the infantry fought for the possession of Servigny far into the night. To the north of Servigny 6th Corps was established in the outskirts of Failly; and when at about 11 p.m. the fighting at last died down, the French had bitten deeply into the German positions after an exhilarating and successful advance which did much to compensate for the frustrations and the miseries of the previous week.[1]

Meanwhile Bazaine, without waiting to hear the latest news from the battlefield, had gone to bed; and the orders which he gave out next morning were, for the commander of an army successfully advancing against inferior forces, very strange indeed.

> If the dispositions which the enemy may have been able to make opposite you permit [he told his corps commanders], we should carry on the operation undertaken yesterday which should (1) lead to the occupation of St Barbe, (2) facilitate our march on Bettlainville. In the contrary case, we must hold on to our positions, consolidate them, and this evening we shall then retire under St Julien and Queuleu.

As soon as these uninspiring orders had been sent off, he wrote two messages to Napoleon. The first, to be sent off in case of success, announced that he was on the march to Thionville; the second, longer and more circumstantial, declared that he had been repulsed and was again in Metz "with little reserve of field-artillery ammunition, meat or biscuit, and finally in sanitary conditions which are far from ideal, as the fortress is full of wounded".[2] This prudent measure was hardly the action of a man confident of victory. On the other hand Manteuffel, although his forces still numbered only half those of the French, had received enough reinforcements during the night to feel justified in attacking all along the line. Before the mists of an early autumn morning had dispersed, the French troops at Flanville, at Noisseville and before Failly found themselves under heavy fire. It was at Noisseville that the fight was fiercest. This was the most dangerous of the French gains; it threatened the flank of the position at Servigny which the Germans so precariously occupied; and if Servigny fell the whole French line could surge forward to engulf St Barbe. Manteuffel therefore called up the

---

[1] *Trois mois à l'Armée de Metz,* par un Officier de génie 127. L. Patry, *La guerre telle qu'elle est* 140–6.
[2] Jarras, *Souvenirs* 183. D'Andlau, *Metz* 160–1.

Landwehr Division and launched it across the valley from the north-east. The village was held by Bastoul's division of 2nd Corps, which had been put under Lebœuf's command, and they defended it stubbornly. But the fire of 114 massed German guns made the position even less tenable and no French artillery came forward to combat them. Indeed, while Bastoul and Manteuffel contended for this vital position, the rest of the French army stood idly by. Ladmirault had his hands full before Servigny and Lebœuf had three divisions engaged on either side of Noisseville. But both 2nd and 3rd Corps had a division uncommitted; 2nd Corps artillery lay idle; Canrobert had two divisions doing nothing; and the Guard, the army artillery, and the great, elegant, useless mass of the French cavalry were not called upon at all. Bazaine made no more attempt to fight the battle of Noisseville than he had those of Vionville and Gravelotte; and when at about 11 a.m. Bastoul had finally to fall back from Noisseville to avoid being encircled, Bazaine took this as a proof that the break-through was impossible and ordered his corps to abandon their attacks. Throughout the afternoon the armies faced one another in expectant silence, and in the evening the French trooped back again into Metz. Each army had lost something over 3,000 men.

The break-out had failed; and within a few days Bazaine learned that there was no chance of relief from outside. On 3rd September dust-clouds on the northern horizon had awoken in the garrison a buzz of excited rumours, and three days later Frederick Charles ensured that Bazaine should learn the melancholy truth by exchanging for a group of Prussian prisoners a number of Frenchmen who had surrendered at Sedan.[1] There were no French forces left in the field; Bazaine was on his own; and when the news from Paris, furnished by German outposts, showed that politically as well as militarily the Empire had been swept away, the army of Metz became as inert and grotesque as an amputated limb. Neither Napoleon nor Eugénie had sent Bazaine any instructions before their disappearance, and the new Government in Paris apparently ignored him. The army at Metz remained an island of Imperial authority doubly isolated, militarily by the German forces in occupation of north-eastern France, and politically in a Republic which seemed to have forgotten its very existence.

Armies are very self-sufficient communities. The entire *raison d'être* of the army in Metz may have collapsed, but life within its ranks could go on much as usual; for in this, as in all other human organisations, the object of its existence could be easily forgotten in the time-filling

---

[1] *G.G.S.* II i 177. Jarras, *Souvenirs* 202–6, 252.

routine of merely existing. Rations still had to be issued, returns made, kit checked and replaced; drills and exercises had to continue as usual, and discipline be maintained. It seemed to some observers that Bazaine now deliberately emphasised questions of routine and administration so as to divert the minds of his subordinates from more dangerous speculations. There was work to be done on the incomplete fortifications, and the veterans of Sebastopol, with all the resources of the arsenal of Metz behind them, were able so to strengthen the defences that they could boast them impregnable to any force Frederick Charles might bring against them. Sorties were undertaken into no-man's-land to collect food-stocks from abandoned villages and farm-houses, which were successful until the Germans started to clear the stocks themselves and burn the farms. But by the end of September it was obvious even to Bazaine that unless the army undertook a major action it would sink into inglorious capitulation without firing a shot.[1]

On 6th October therefore Bazaine summoned his corps commanders, and with the diffidence which he habitually showed in dealing with his distinguished subordinates he suggested a plan for a break-out down the Moselle towards Thionville. There was little consideration of what should happen if it succeeded—where the army should go and what it should do: it was action simply to avoid complete idleness. The generals raised no major objections; preliminary orders were given about baggage, about the garrisoning of the fortress and disposal of the sick and wounded; and on 2nd October the necessary jumping-off positions were successfully seized. Then Coffinières intervened again. He had 25,000 sick on his hands; a further 15,000 wounded might be expected as a result of this action; and the fortress, thus encumbered with sick and wounded, with no doctors and inadequate supplies, could hardly be expected to hold out by itself. He must be left a garrison of at least 20,000 men. "God grant", he wrote piously, "that 150,000 inhabitants and garrison, as well as your own army, may not be the victims of the decisions you are going to take."[2] His arguments were reinforced by the news, gleaned from newspapers captured in German outposts, of the Ferrières negotiations: if peace was really a possibility it would be unforgivable to squander the lives of French troops to no purpose. The project of a break-out was therefore abandoned, and instead, on 7th October, the army was launched on a large-scale raid to seize the harvest

[1] *G.G.S.* II 180–5. D'Andlau, *Metz* 185–6, 218–19.
[2] The figure of 150,000 was absurdly exaggerated. A Prost, *Blocus de Metz* (Nogent-le-Rotrou 1898) gives the population, native and refugee, as 70,000.

stored in the farms immediately behind the German outposts on the lower Moselle. The expedition was not very successful. The farms themselves were seized, but the attempt to silence the batteries on either side of the valley failed and the Germans could bring to bear an artillery fire so heavy that the French had to abandon all attempts to load their waggons, and withdraw empty handed with a loss of more than a thousand officers and men.[1]

Within army and city confidence in Bazaine was waning fast. On 24th September a civilian deputation had petitioned that the army should take some action. "We believe", it said forcefully, "that the army assembled beneath our walls is capable of great things, but we also think it is time that it did them."[2] It might be expected that his corps commanders would have urged some action, but his relations with them were uneasy, marked by the lack of self-confidence which distinguished all his actions. He gave none of the clear orders which they had been bred to expect; rather he gave them indications and made suggestions which it would have needed the training and enterprise of a Prussian commander to bring to fruition. At a meeting on 12th September, for example, he had suggested a policy of raids to keep the Germans on the alert, and left it to the corps commanders to work out the details "I can't be everywhere", he pointed out. This was an intelligent technique of command so far as it went; but he did nothing to follow up his original suggestions, and if his generals pointed out the difficulties of a proposed operation he meekly abandoned it and complained in private that his subordinates would neither co-operate nor obey. He completely failed to provide that driving will and moral force for which troops look in a commander. When he gave orders, Jarras noted, they were couched in vague and often ambiguous terms, as if to cover himself if things turned out badly.[3] The corps commanders, receiving no impulse from above, ignorant of the general situation, and concerned to preserve their men, were not prepared to provide the impetus which Bazaine lacked. Rather they immersed themselves, as did their commander, in the comforting anaesthetic of professional routine.

Combined with this military deadlock there was a political situation of a complexity far beyond Bazaine's power to resolve. He was not merely the commander of an army which still carried on all its functions

---

[1] Bazaine, *Épisodes* 190–1. Fay, *Journal d'un Officier* 209, 214–20. Jarras, *Souvenirs* 233–8, D'Andlau, *Metz* 278–82. *D.T.* I 62.

[2] Prost, *Blocus de Metz* 17 ff. 236.

[3] D'Andlau, *Metz* 140. Jarras, *Souvenirs* 189, 200. Fay, *Journal d'un Officier* 246.

in the Emperor's name; he was also the sole representative of Imperial authority on French soil, and thus in Bismarck's eyes a possible intermediary through whom peace might be concluded.[1] Like most of his colleagues Bazaine looked with disfavour on the Government of National Defence, in which such unspeakable politicians of the Left as Gambetta and Rochefort had joined forces with the odious Trochu[2]; and, as he told Jarras, he could not give it his allegiance until the Emperor had released him from his oath of loyalty. But it was the *de facto* Government of the country, and was recognised as such by the civil authorities in Metz; and Bazaine, in an Order of the Day of 16th September announcing the formation of that Government, declared, with masterly equivocation, "Our military obligations towards the country remain the same. Let us then continue to serve her with devotion and the same energy, defending her land against the foreigner, the social order against evil passions."[3] Was this a declaration of obedience or of independence? Perhaps Bazaine did not know himself. The last six words may have been added to reassure his officers; but they contain a marked suggestion that the army might have a political rôle to play—and not necessarily one favourable to the Government of National Defence.[4]

It was exactly a week later, on 23rd September, that the mysterious M. Edmond Regnier arrived in Metz.[5] For a decade the French were to consider him a sinister figure, almost certainly an agent of Bismarck. They would have been more justified in thinking him a buffoon. Yet there is something which commands respect about this man who had the energy, the pertinacity and the self-confidence to gate-crash into the field of high diplomacy, like some member of the audience wandering on to the stage during a grand opera and boldly taking a hand. He was a businessman with a chequered past and an English wife, whose only qualification, apart from his misplaced courage, was a passionate devotion to the Empire. He was convinced, with some reason, that Bismarck

[1] See p. 231 above.

[2] *D.T.* IV (Canrobert) 277–9. Garnier-Pagès maintained (*D.T.* I 443) that Trochu's presidency in the Government explained Bazaine's failure to make contact with it.

[3] Bazaine, *Épisodes* 178.

[4] It is perhaps significant that on the same day Bazaine secretly sent General Boyer, his A.D.C. and factotum, with a letter to Frederick Charles requesting information about the condition of France. The Germans themselves saw in this an attempt to open negotiations. See Annaliese Klein-Wuttig, *Politik und Krieg-Führung in den deutschen Einigungskriegen* (Berlin 1934) 102.

[5] For the whole of the Regnier episode, see his own account, *Quel est votre nom?* (Brussels 1870) which has won general acceptance as being in substance accurate.

would prefer to negotiate with the Imperial régime rather than with the Government of National Defence, and he had therefore written out of the blue to the Empress in her exile at Hastings, urging her to denounce the revolutionary Government, put herself under the protection of the fleet, and summon the loyal section of the army and nation to rally round her person. The Empress did not reply to a proposal so irresponsible in its provenance and its implications, and refused to receive its author. Regnier decided therefore to take his proposal to the Emperor; and as an aid to securing access to him he scraped acquaintance with the young Prince Imperial and persuaded the boy to write a few words of greeting to his father on the back of a picture of the Hastings sea-front. Equipped with this remarkable document Regnier made his way to German headquarters at Ferrières, which he reached on 20th September, to obtain from Bismarck leave to proceed to Wilhelmshöhe. The Chancellor was already in negotiation with Jules Favre, but in Regnier he saw a possible second string to his bow. There was, after all, as much to be said for doing business with the doubtfully accredited emissary of the legitimate Empire as with the accredited representative of a doubtfully legitimate Republic.[1] He therefore greeted Regnier with remarkable warmth, and explained his perplexities with equally remarkable frankness. In the course of their conversation Regnier elaborated his plan. He would go to Metz and Strasbourg, where the remains of the Imperial armies still held out, and persuade their commanders, when they capitulated, to do so in the name of the Emperor. Then the Empress would summon—presumably under the protection of this army—the members of the Senate, Legislative Body and Council of State, declare the Government of National Defence overthrown, resume the reins of government, and negotiate for peace. The plan did not seem totally impossible. It held out hopes of providing that Government *de jure* and *de facto* which was indispensable to the conclusion of peace. So Bismarck equipped Regnier with a more formal *laissez-passer*, and sent him off to Frederick Charles's headquarters with instructions that he was to be given every facility to enter the fortress. Thus at twilight on 23rd September, in his capacity as an official of the Red Cross, still clutching his picture of Hastings, Regnier presented himself before the French outposts at Metz.

Bazaine found Regnier's credentials no more impressive than had Bismarck; but he was even readier than Bismarck to clutch at any straw.[2]

---

[1] Busch, *Bismarck: Some Secret Pages of his History* I 197.
[2] Bazaine, *Épisodes* 179, D.T. IV 199.

Nor can Regnier's project have been entirely disagreeable to him. He felt no loyalty to the Government in Paris, and Regnier offered a means of escaping the inglorious capitulation which was already hanging over his head. But he made it clear to Regnier that if his army did leave Metz it must be as a free agent, with all arms and baggage, and that there could be no question of yielding up the fortress itself.[1] The immediate suggestion which Regnier had to make was that Bazaine should send a representative to propose his scheme to the Empress, preferably one of the two officers with whom she was on most friendly terms, Bourbaki or Canrobert. Bazaine was agreeable, but Canrobert, to whom the rejection of embarrassing appointments was now second nature, flatly refused to go. Bourbaki, however, yielded when Bazaine gave him one of his rare direct orders; and on 25th September, furtive and embarrassed in a borrowed civilian suit and a Red Cross uniform cap, he left the fortress *en route* for England. As soon as he reached Brussels he began to suspect that he was on a fool's errand, and on arriving in England his suspicions were confirmed. Eugénie disowned all knowledge of the affair, and gallantly refused to lend her name to anything which might hamper the activities of the Government of National Defence. With her refusal to endorse Regnier's scheme the whole web of his intrigues collapsed.[2]

This incident however had the effect of further embittering the conflict which was fast developing between Bismarck and Moltke, and the feelings of the latter were shared at Second Army headquarters. The fate of Bazaine's army was there considered a purely military affair, and both Moltke and Frederick Charles watched with apprehension lest, thanks to Bismarck's meddling, this magnificent prize should slip through their fingers. "Under no circumstances ought the sacrifices and endeavours of the army before Metz to lead to an entirely negative military outcome", wrote Moltke sympathetically to Frederick Charles's Chief of Staff, General von Stiehle; and he complained to Manteuffel that in view of the King's wilful support of Bismarck his hands were completely tied and Regnier and Bourbaki must be allowed to pass.[3]

---

[1] Bazaine, *Armée du Rhin* (Paris 1872) 125–6. *D.T.* IV 242.

[2] *D.T.* III (Bourbaki) 345–6. Bismarck, *Gesamm. Werke* VI b No. 1839 p. 526, No. 1848 p. 532. Regnier, after a few more ventures into high politics, died as manager of a laundry at Ramsgate, "a field" as Philip Guedalla happily put it, "in which his genius for confusion could be exercised without international consequences." *The Two Marshals* (London 1943) 211.

[3] *M.M.K.* 309. Frederick Charles, *Denkwürdigkeiten* II 286. Stadelmann, *Moltke und der Staat* 225–30.

But Frederick Charles was able to score one rather cheap point. Bourbaki's pass had been misdated in error, and in consequence the authorities of the Second Army, when he returned from England and attempted to re-enter the fortress, informed him that it was no longer in order and that his permission to re-enter the fortress had lapsed. It was a foolish attitude to adopt, as Moltke had the sense to realise. Bourbaki was less dangerous to Prussia inside Metz than outside, and the information about the condition of France which he would take into the fortress was not likely to stiffen Bazaine's will to resist. But Moltke's orders to let him through did not arrive until 9th October and by then it was too late: Bourbaki had given up the attempt to return and had placed himself at the disposal of the Government of National Defence.[1]

Bourbaki's letter announcing the failure of his mission was handed over by the German outposts to Metz on 29th September. With it was a courteous note to Bazaine from Frederick Charles informing him that Strasbourg had capitulated.

*   *   *

For nearly two centuries Strasbourg had ranked with Metz as a major bastion of north-eastern France, and one of the greatest fortresses in Europe. In fact the two places were not comparable. Metz at least was equipped with outlying forts which protected the fortress from effective bombardment by anything except the heaviest siege artillery and made investment of the place impossible except for a sizeable army; but little had been done to improve the defences of Strasbourg since the days of Vauban. Vauban had fortified the town with the complex and mutually supporting fortifications of masonry and of water which characterised his later period. The *enceinte* wall was furnished with its due number of bastions, and beyond the fosse outworks proliferated; *lunettes*, hornworks, *raviolins*, designed to keep seventeenth-century artillery beyond range of the main defences. The inner Citadel was fortified as a fortress in its own right; and the flat countryside surrounding the town could be easily inundated. Until the mid-nineteenth century Strasbourg deserved its reputation as a great fortress; but times had changed. The increased range of artillery dwarfed Vauban's outworks. The town could now be shelled without difficulty from German soil, and nothing could have kept the German guns out of range except weapons of equal calibre within the fortress itself. Secondly, Strasbourg had since 1815 grown a peaceable *embonpoint* of industrial and resi-

[1] *M.M.K.* 323–4. *Procès Bazaine* 187. Bronsart, *Kriegstagebuch* 116.

dential suburbs which sprawled beyond the fortifications, impeding their field of fire, and which the municipal authorities had refused to destroy until the last possible moment. Thirdly, little had been done to provide the town with the underground shelters for garrison, inhabitants, stores and especially ammunition, which would be essential if it were to withstand a bombardment by modern artillery.[1] In general the French military authorities, paralysed by shortage of funds and obstinately visualising the campaign in terms of a French invasion of South Germany, had done little to equip Strasbourg for a siege. There were food stocks for sixty days, and bread could be supplied for three times as long; but there were in the fortress only some 250 guns of fifteen different types, many of them smooth-bore, which were quite insufficient to arm the batteries on the ramparts. The only gunners to man them were troops from two artillery regimental depôts of Mac-Mahon's corps. No provision had been made for a regular garrison: MacMahon had left behind one regiment of the line, which after 6th August was reinforced by numerous fugitives from Froeschwiller; and *gardes mobiles, gardes nationales,* customs officials and *sapeurs pompiers* brought the total to some 17,000 men. At their head was General Uhrich, who had succeeded Ducrot as commander of 6th Military Division: a sixty-eight-year-old "dug-out" officer, honourable, courageous, and unimaginative, who was to conduct a brave but totally unenterprising defence.[2]

The assailants of Strasbourg were primarily the troops of the neighbouring Grand Duchy of Baden under General von Werder, who were detached from the Third Army by the Crown Prince after the battle of Froeschwiller to capture the city; and they were joined, by Moltke's order of 13th August, by two Prussian Landwehr Divisions released from their task of watching the North Sea coast; making a siege corps about 40,000 strong. The leading elements of this force advanced on Strasbourg immediately after the battle of Froeschwiller and on 14th August began with their field-guns a desultory bombardment of the fortifications and the town while Werder pondered how best to attack. To invest the fortress and await its fall by hunger was out of the question. It would tie down troops badly needed elsewhere, and Strasbourg was too valuable a prize, in terms of national prestige, to be left dangling

[1] See R. Wagner, *Geschichte der Belagerung von Strassburg im Jahre 1870* (Berlin 1874) I 22–60, for the attempts to modernise the fortress between 1861 and 1870, and their frustration through inertia and economy.

[2] See the comments of C. Rousset, *Histoire générale de la Guerre Franco-Allemande* (n.d. but 1894) VI 230–1.

indefinitely out of reach. Opinion was divided, at Werder's head-quarters, between undertaking a siege *en règle* in the traditional form, with an approach by parallels, bombardment of the fortifications and finally assault through a breach; or, on the other hand, hastening the surrender of the fortress by bombarding the town and thus striking at the defenders through the *morale* of the civil population. This last course, commonplace as it has become among belligerents of the twentieth century, was in 1870 a comparatively novel expedient. It was not that earlier generations of besiegers had been more humane, but their guns had seldom possessed the necessary range. Any moral doubts the Germans may have felt were set at rest by the French action, on 19th August, in bombarding the open town of Kehl on the right bank of the Rhine[1]; and although the sceptics as to the efficacy of such a course remained unconvinced, the bombardment began, after formal warning had been served on Uhrich, on the night of 23rd August.

The effect on the civil population was at first all that Werder could desire.[2] After four nights of continuous bombardment by explosive and incendiary shells whole quarters of the city had been reduced to ashes and a thick pall of smoke hid the sun. The principal public buildings had been destroyed or damaged: the picture gallery, the famous city library with its treasures, the Palais de Justice, the great Huguenot Temple Neuf, the Arsenal, all had been burned to the ground, and fire had destroyed much of the roof of the Cathedral itself. The population kept terror at bay only by frantic activity in rescue work; but the Archbishop drove to the Prussian outposts to beg for a cease-fire, and the municipality asked Uhrich to forward to Werder the suggestion that the town should pay a ransom of 100,000 francs for each day it was left in peace.[3] Neither request was granted; nor did Uhrich yield to a second summons to surrender on 26th August. It was a situation with which his straightforward soldierly nature perfectly qualified him to deal, and his firmness rallied the bulk of civilian opinion to his side. Militarily as well as morally his decision proved correct. On 26th August Werder learned that ammunition supplies would not permit the continuation of bombardment at such a rate, and he had to admit that the attempt to terrorise the population into surrender had failed.[4] On balance, as on subsequent occasions when violence was employed against

[1] See Werder's protest to Uhrich of 19th August, reprinted in Wagner, op. cit. Beilage 68.

[2] For an eyewitness account see G. Fischbach, *Le Siège et le Bombardement de Strasbourg* (Paris 1871).

[3] Rousset, op. cit. VI 233.   [4] *G.G.S.* I ii 453.

civil population for military objects, the German cause had probably been harmed rather than helped, and the example stiffened opposition in military circles to the proposed bombardment of Paris. Werder cut his losses, reduced his bombardment to a slow harassing fire, and began instead a formal siege.

Within two decades developments in gunnery and in fortification were to make the formal siege as anachronistic as the cavalry charge; but in 1870 its procedures, devised by Italian engineers in the sixteenth century and formalised by Vauban to the precise rhythm almost of a dance, were still effective. The Germans selected the point in the fortifications where they proposed to make their breach. On the night of 29th–30th August they opened their first parallel, 500 metres from the French outworks, and installed eleven batteries to bombard the selected spot at close range. Three nights later they opened their second parallel, 150 metres nearer the fortress, repulsing a sortie made by the garrison in a vain attempt to interrupt them; and on 9th September, working with a speed that amazed the French, they began work on the third parallel, a few metres from the glacis. Meanwhile, firing with nearly a hundred heavy guns and mortars, they smashed the fortifications and buildings all around and behind the point of attack. On 11th September a Swiss delegation allowed into the place to arrange for the evacuation of non-combatants found the whole quarter of the town north of the canal in ruins; and by 17th September the Germans had battered a breach in the *enceinte* wall.[1]

"A practicable breach", in the ritual of siegecraft, was the signal for honourable surrender. But the walls had to be no longer defensible and the assaulting force must be poised for attack. This situation had not yet been reached; but Werder had hit on a weapon more effective than any artillery in disposing the garrison to surrender. The Swiss representatives whom he had allowed to pass through his lines of investment brought the Strasbourgeois their first certain news of events in France. From them they learned of the annihilation of the Army of Châlons and the incarceration of the Army of the Rhine. There was no hope of relief, there seemed little point in further resistance, and the morale of the population, worn down by a month of sleepless nights, steeply declined.[2] On 19th September Uhrich refused yet another demand from the municipality that the fortress should be surrendered; but the same day the Germans captured their first outwork, and were able to bring such an intensity of fire to bear on the ramparts that no

[1] *G.G.S.* II i 87. [2] Fischbach, op. cit. 208.

defence was possible. On 27th September Uhrich, advised that the breach was practicable and indefensible and assault imminent, asked for terms, and next day the fortress capitulated, yielding its material intact as booty and its garrison as prisoners-of-war.

Uhrich had conducted the defence with resolution and with a courteous correctness matched by Werder's own. They corresponded politely, negotiations between outposts and *parlementaires* were carried on with friendliness, and on his surrender Uhrich received the chivalrous attention due to a brave but defeated foe. Such observance of protocol was little to the taste of the French. The garrison, to whom the privilege was accorded of marching out with honours of war, streamed out of the gates undisciplined, humiliated, and many of them drunk; breaking or throwing away their arms rather than yield them to the enemy. Uhrich gave his parole and left, first for Tours, then for Switzerland; and in his exile found himself the object of bitter attacks from his countrymen who declared that his courtesy towards the enemy and his "premature" surrender were alike symptomatic of treason.[1] In a Peoples' War there was no room for such courtesies, and they were seldom to be repeated. In one of its aspects the siege of Strasbourg can be seen as the last example of a mode of conducting warfare which had ruled in Europe since the Middle Ages; but in another, the deliberate bombardment of civilians, it was to be no less typical of a new military age.

*   *   *

Neither bombardment nor assault was needed to reduce Metz. By October both town and army were beginning to go hungry. For four weeks they had lived with little worry on the huge stocks piled up for the campaign, and Bazaine was reluctant to weaken, by drastic rationing, the strength of an army which might attempt to break out at any moment. In addition to the normal stocks of meat available there was a great supply of horseflesh from the horses of the train who had failed to escape from the city, and of which distribution began on 4th September. But this sickly meat was palatable only if liberally salted, and salt was the first commodity to run short. In Metz the price rocketed to eighty times its normal level, and on 20th September, after the town had been searched for stocks, the army ration was reduced by three-quarters.[2] Within a few days the medical services were reporting an alarming increase in cases of dysentery and diarrhoea.[3] The supply of horsemeat

---

[1] See Uhrich's letters in Fischbach 273 ff.
[2] Prost, *Blocus de Metz* 78. D'Andlau, *Metz* 181–2.
[3] Bazaine, *Épisodes* 193. D.T. IV 237.

continued tragically to grow as even the cavalry began to slaughter their animals for lack of fodder to feed them. Each corps sent fifty-five daily to the slaughter house from 30th September, and five days later this number had to be increased to seventy-five to keep pace with the increasing mortality. Sugar and coffee stocks began to run short; on 20th September the ration was reduced by a third and made up in the accepable but barely nourishing substitute of *eau de vie*.[1] The condition of the horses was already pathetic, and now the troops themselves, bivouacking in their camps under intermittent rain, began to be in little better case. Those who could afford it crowded into the cafés of the town, where prices of unrationed foods quickly rocketed out of their reach and out of that of many of the townsfolk. Coffinières accused the army of eating food stocks intended for the civil population; the corps commanders in return accused the civilians of hoarding supplies.[2] There were scenes between civilians and soldiers, and Bazaine had to reinforce the city gendarmerie to quell them. Bitterness grew also between the troops and the officers who alone could afford the inflated prices, and further exacerbated the political discontents of the town. The crisis came on 7th October, when Coffinières reported to Bazaine that he had flour to meet the ration for only ten more days, and that if the bread ration was reduced by two-fifths he might just prolong this to eighteen. The same day occurred the failure of the army's foray down the Moselle. The possibility could no longer be concealed, that the French army might have to capitulate without a fight.[3]

On 8th October Bazaine wrote to his corps commanders to explain the situation. "The moment is approaching", he said, "when the Army of the Rhine will find itself in perhaps the most difficult position that a French army has ever had to endure ... supplies are beginning to run short and in what can only be a very short time they will run out completely." The corps commanders were in touch with the troops, would know what to expect from them; so before coming to any decision Bazaine wanted their advice.[4] All save one—Lebœuf—replied that, with the horses of the cavalry and of the artillery so reduced, no new

---

[1] D'Andlau, *Metz* 182–3, 267.

[2] Bazaine, *Épisodes* 261–2. Jarras, *Souvenirs* 243. Rationing for civilians was not considered until 13th September. Eleven days later it was decided to introduce bread cards, but the administrative complexities of this could not be mastered before 14th October, when the ration was fixed at 400 grams. Until that date foodstuffs were rationed only by the purse. Prost, *Blocus de Metz* 15, 22, 67 ff. App. XXV.

[3] D.T. IV 233. Fay, *Journal d'un Officier* 224.

[4] Bazaine, *Épisodes* 194.

sortie was possible, and negotiations should be opened for honourable terms. Lebœuf was in favour of one more battle, and Ladmirault merely replied in a soldierly fashion that his troops were still prepared for anything.[1] Coffinières reported that supplies could last out only until 20th October; and on 10th October, when Bazaine summoned his commanders to a Council of War, he repeated this in yet more forthright terms, adding that this included all supplies for the army as well as for the town. There were, he added, 19,000 sick, and typhus and smallpox were beginning to appear.[2]

In view of all this the Council of War reached the following conclusions. The army should in any case hold on until all stocks were exhausted: it was immobilising 200,000 men whose intervention against the armies on the Loire might be decisive. But negotiations should be opened, and at once, to try to secure honourable conditions; and should those fail, a last effort might be made to break out. Bazaine's aide-de-camp General Boyer was to go to Versailles to begin negotiations.

Bazaine's request to the Germans to receive an intermediary opened once again the precariously healed rifts in the unity of Royal Headquarters. Stiehle forwarded the request to Versailles with the advice that it be refused and that the matter be left *rein militärisch*. At Moltke's headquarters opinion was the same: the whole matter should be left to Frederick Charles.[3] The King supported Bismarck and gave orders that Boyer should be allowed to pass; but these orders did not reach Metz until 12th October; and although Boyer set off immediately, this left the garrison with only eight days' food in hand.

Boyer reached Versailles on 14th October, and was affably received by Bismarck. Peace with the Republic seemed no nearer, and it might not be too late to reach some agreement along the lines suggested by Regnier. The proposals which Boyer brought from Bazaine were an elaboration of his ideas, and when Bismarck heard them he drew Boyer conspiratorially out into the garden, out of earshot of the representatives of the General Staff. "There are people next door who speak French," he said mysteriously: "Walls, as they say, have ears."[4]

Bazaine's letter was at least frank. It admitted military defeat, appealed to the European forces of order against the revolutionary

---

[1] Reports reprinted in *Épisodes* 195–205.

[2] Jarras, *Souvenirs* 243.

[3] Frederick Charles, *Denkwürdigkeiten* II 287 ff. Bronsart, *Kriegstagebuch* 120–4. Frederick III, *War Diary* 155–6.

[4] Bazaine, *Épisodes* 219–20. Boyer's account as quoted here differs in several particulars from that in *D.T.* IV 246–9.

Government of Paris, and promised a stable régime in France, supported by the Imperial Army, to guarantee the social order and an enduring peace. All this was well calculated to appeal to Bismarck who still believed that a restored Empire would offer more lasting hopes of peace than would the Government of National Defence[1]; but in such matters Bismarck was not his own master. Moltke opposed any terms short of a capitulation of the army and the surrender of the fortress with a stubbornness which the King found it difficult to resist. Even if this military opposition could be overcome, there were other questions. Would the Regency be prepared to accept the terms for which German public opinion was now clamouring? And if the Regency accepted the terms, could it enforce them on a France which was energetically girding itself to national resistance? Bazaine's troops might follow him in suppressing revolution; but would their discipline stand up to enforcing a humiliating peace? In any case nothing could be done until the Empress had been sounded to see whether she had in any way modified her attitude; and meanwhile the garrison at Metz was within a few days of starvation.

Boyer returned to Metz on 17th October, and next day the Council of War met to hear him explain the situation. The main question to be considered was whether the troops could be relied on to carry out the scheme proposed. The corps commanders believed that they could, though some feared that the army would simply melt away once it got outside the walls of Metz.[2] Certainly no other plan seemed to offer any hope of success. So Boyer set out again next day, reached London on 22nd October, and went at once to Chislehurst to explain the desperate situation. Eugénie declared herself prepared to do almost anything to help; but what peace-terms, she asked, was she being asked to accept? The Prussian Embassy, when asked to clarify the matter, was evasive. They had not, in fact, been settled; and it was evident that the Regency was being asked to sign a blank cheque.[3] This was impossible. All that Eugénie and her advisers could do was to play for time. Through Boyer she sent a message to Bismarck, requesting an immediate armistice at Metz for a fortnight to enable the army to revictual, and again asking

[1] Joachim Kühn, "Bismarck und Bonapartismus" in *Preussische Jahrbücher* CLXIII (1916) 163. On 30th September Bismarck had explicitly denied to Busch any intention of restoring Napoleon to the throne, but this denial did not exclude the possibility of a Regency; and on 17th November he said that a restoration was "not entirely impossible". Busch, *Bismarck: Some Secret Pages of his History* I 233, 311.
[2] *D.T.* IV 212, 283–5. Bazaine, *Épisodes* 217–8.   [3] *D.T.* IV 252

for the conditions of peace; and to King William she sent a personal
message, appealing to his "royal heart, his soldierly generosity. I
implore Your Majesty to be favourable to my request; its success," she
concluded, with a pathetic attempt at bluster, "is the indispensable
condition for the continuation of negotiations."[1]

It was hopeless. The Prussians quite properly wanted solid guarantees, and these were not and could not be forthcoming. The King's
reply was courteous but firm.

> I desire with all my heart [he wrote] to restore peace to our two
> nations, but to secure this it would be necessary to establish at least
> the probability that we shall succeed in making France accept the result
> of our transactions without continuing the war against the entire
> French forces. At present I regret that the uncertainty in which we
> find ourselves with regard to the political dispositions of the Army of
> Metz, as well as of the French nation, does not allow me to proceed
> further with the negotiations proposed by Your Majesty.

To Bazaine Bismarck wrote on 23rd October to the same effect.
"The proposals which have reached us from London are, in the
present situation, absolutely unacceptable, and I declare to my great
regret that I can see no further chance of reaching a result by political
negotiations." Boyer's mission had failed.[2]

Bismarck's message was considered at a Council of War in Metz on
24th October. Coffinières had, as threatened, ceased to provide food
for the army on 20th October—the civilian bread-ration was now down
to 300 grams per day—and the army's own stocks had lasted for only
two more days. The troops, unless they could pay the famine prices
of the town cafés, were reduced to a diet of horsemeat soup; and to
add to their miseries the weather, which for the first ten days of October
had been fine, cold and dry, suddenly broke. Rain pelted down on to the
camps, turning them into lakes of mud where the few remaining horses
gnawed at each other's manes and tails and the troops lay in the inadequate shelter of their bivouac tents. Some wandered round the fields
in a hungry search for potatoes which the Germans were often too
humane to interrupt; others, in an ever-swelling stream, presented
themselves at the German outposts in apathetic surrender which the
Germans refused to accept.[3] There could now be no hope of a break-out;
but Bazaine left it to his corps commanders to state this openly. He

[1] *D.T.* IV 268.
[2] *D.T.* IV 268. Bismarck, *Gesamm. Werke* VI b No. 1886 p. 558.
[3] D'Andlau, *Metz* 377. Fay, *Journal d'un Officier* 247, 260. Farinet, *Agonie
d'une Armée (Metz)* 294. Kretschman, *Kriegsbriefe* 110, 118, 144.

opened the Council on 24th October by assuming that a break-out must take place, as agreed, and inviting suggestions as to how it could best be done. Only Desvaux, who had succeeded Bourbaki as Commander of the Imperial Guard, and who in spite of his juniority rapidly won the reputation of being the most outspoken of Bazaine's lieutenants, took him seriously, and suggested an attack towards St Privat. Ladmirault, Frossard, Coffinières, and Lebœuf bluntly said that their men would never follow them in such an operation; and Soleille pointed out that even if they did the German guns would make mincemeat of them before they got anywhere near the enemy lines. Canrobert was the most optimistic: a third of the army, he thought, might get through, but it would then disintegrate for lack of supplies, and the Prussians would simply add another laurel to their victor's crown. The outcome of the Council was not in doubt. Even now nobody spoke the shameful word "capitulation". It was merely agreed that a convention should be negotiated honourable to French arms. The Prussians should treat separately with the army and the fortress, accept the army's parole not to fight again in the war, and let it go free.[1]

Such hopes were absurd. The Prussian commander knew only too well that this civilised eighteenth-century expedient had no place in the Peoples' War such as was now being waged on the Loire. He was prepared to liberate the officers on parole, as had been done at Sedan, but this the French themselves refused to accept.[2] The terms offered by the Prussians were very simple, and no discussion was permitted. The fortress was to be surrendered, the army was to become prisoner, and all material of war was to be handed over intact. On 26th October the Council of War accepted these terms. Somebody suggested that at least the guns should be spiked and the powder damped, but opinion was against it. Such a breach of the terms would not be *en règle*; it would expose the army to reprisals; and it would lead to that indiscipline and disintegration which is, in the eyes of the regular soldier, more shameful even than defeat.[3] In the extremity of misfortune the army should accept its lot with dignity and with loyalty to its plighted word.

It fell to Jarras, as Chief of Staff, to work out the details of the capitulation. The Prussians insisted again that all material should be collected and handed over, and with this they included all the colours

---

[1] Bazaine, *Épisodes* 230–2. Jarras, *Souvenirs* 282–94. D'Andlau, *Metz* 354–6. Farinet, *Agonie d'une Armée* 312, 317.
[2] *G.G.S.* II i 200. Jarras, op. cit. 309–11. Frederick Charles, *Denkwürdigkeiten* II 295.
[3] D'Andlau, *Metz* 396.

of the French army. Bazaine's alacrity in enforcing obedience to these conditions earned him perhaps more odium than any other episode in the entire campaign. In his Order of the Day on 28th October, in which he invoked the precedents of Kléber, of Masséna, and of Gouvion Saint-Cyr who had "like you, also gloriously fulfilled their duty to the extreme limit of human endurance," he expressly forbade the destruction of arms. He gave particular orders for the colours to be stacked at the Arsenal; and his later protests, that he intended them to be burned there but that the order went astray and that the Prussians strictly forbade it, do him even less credit. Certain regiments refused to surrender them at all but concealed them about the town. General Desvaux had those of the Imperial Guard burnt before his eyes.[1]

Finally Bazaine completed the shame of his army by refusing even the honours of war which the Prussians spontaneously offered. The French might have marched into captivity with one last flourish of glory, arms in hand, bands playing, officers riding at their head. As it was, the embarrassed Jarras had to tell the Prussians that Bazaine would accept honours of war only if they were not actually carried out: the weather, he explained lamely, was too bad. Bazaine's later explanations made a bad case worse. The troops were not fit enough; he would have broken his sword rather than command such a parade; and if his men were to find themselves armed in the presence of the Prussians, he could not answer for the consequences.[2] It is hard to avoid the conclusion that his real fears were for himself, the leader whom the troops had barely seen since the beginning of the siege and whose incompetence had betrayed them; for on 29th October, the day of the surrender, he slunk away on his own to the German outposts. He was not expected until the evening; so he spent the day waiting in a suburban villa while the rain poured down on the overgrown garden outside. It was the final tragedy of a man whose one redeeming feature was a physical courage outstanding even among the soldiers of France, that he should at the last crown his incapacity by an act of personal cowardice.

For the capitulation itself Bazaine cannot seriously be blamed. With an army which was now beyond question *hors de combat* no other decision was possible. Nor is it easy to see what purpose would have been served by an attempt to break out once the only army capable of bringing him relief had been annihilated at Sedan. It is on two different

[1] D'Andlau, *Metz* 401–2. Bazaine, *Épisodes* 240, *Procès Bazaine* 201–2. Jarras, *Souvenirs* 320–1, 330.
[2] D'Andlau, op. cit. 381, 386. Jarras, op. cit. 319. *D.T.* IV 220.

counts that he must be condemned. The first is his failure to persevere with his plans for a break-out in August, when his army was still intact and MacMahon, he knew, was marching to his help; and the second was his failure to decide, after Sedan, either to regard his army as a military asset in the service of the Government of National Defence, or to make up his mind to use it as an instrument for the restoration of internal order and international peace. His duty as a Frenchman pointed to the former course: so to plan his defence as to keep his army as a force in being and thus to paralyse the armies of Frederick Charles, for as long as possible. By far-sighted and ruthless rationing both of army and town from the day that the news of Sedan first reached him he might have prolonged his resistance at least into mid-November. Had he done so it is highly probable that Moltke would have been forced to divert his forces from Paris to deal with the Army of the Loire, and Trochu's sortie from Paris might then have taken place under far more favourable conditions.[1] A reversal of the final military decision was unlikely; but the French failure would have been less ignominious, their military assets less ruinously dissipated and their bargaining power at the conference-table notably increased. Alternatively, if Bazaine believed that the revolution of 4th September absolved him and his army of all loyalty to the French government, he should have acted with yet greater ruthlessness and despatch. A commander who combined the devious patriotism of a Dumouriez with the skill of a Talleyrand might have played a notable and not dishonourable part in the tragedy of the French collapse. As it was, Bazaine's half-heartedness made his intrigues as ludicrous as his military achievement was pathetic. Yet he still deserves our sympathy. Other soldiers have since been confronted by circumstances with decisions no less agonizing; and not all have emerged from the ordeal with any greater credit than did Marshal Bazaine.

[1] See p. 300, n.1, below.

Note: *Bazaine, coupable ou victime?* by Général Edmond Ruby and Général Jean Regnault (Peyronnet 1960) appeared while this book was in the press. In consequence no use could be made of the documents therein quoted from the archives of the German Foreign Ministry which reveal, among other things, the extent to which Napoleon at Wilhelmshöhe associated himself with Regnier's project. The book is an ably argued defence of Bazaine, which not only destroys completely the charge of treachery but does much to explain his apparently equivocal attitude over the burning of the colours. But it does nothing to clear him of the charge of military incompetence, and I see no reason to modify the judgments expressed in the above pages.

CHAPTER VIII

The Battles for Orléans

§1 Coulmiers

THE CAPITULATION of Metz and of the Army of the Rhine on 29th October marked the end of the campaign which the King of Prussia and his allies had undertaken in July against the Second Empire. The King and his military advisers could pride themselves on the astonishing fact that the entire military force which Napoleon had put into the field had become, except for a handful of individuals, either casualties or prisoners-of-war. The history of modern Europe showed no precedent for such a victory, and there is little cause for wonder that it should have gone to the collective German head. The Prussian government made it clear that it had no intention of ever relinquishing the fortress, which would henceforth be embodied in the western defences of Germany; and the King celebrated the occasion by creating both Frederick Charles and the Crown Prince Field-Marshals and bestowing on Moltke the title of Count.

There was however more immediate and practical reason than the lustre which it bestowed on German arms for rejoicing at the fall of Metz. If the war against the Empire was over, the war against the Republic was well under way. The armies of the Crown Princes of Prussia and Saxony were pinned down before Paris, while in their rear, in a wide arc from the Somme through Normandy and Brittany to the Loire and the Saône, the forces which Gambetta was stamping out of the ground were making growing demands on the limited resources of German manpower. For Moltke Bazaine's capitulation came not a moment too soon, and the forces it released were a godsend for him. To the First Army, now commanded by General von Manteuffel, he assigned the task of reducing the fortresses which still lay across or threatened the German communications—Verdun, Thionville, Montmédy, Mézières—and then advancing westward to the Oise to break up the French forces which were assembling in the north. As for the Second Army, his need for it was yet more urgent. Frederick Charles had received his marching orders on the

23rd, as soon as the capitulation was certain; and on 3rd November he set out to deal with the critical situation which was developing on the Loire.[1]

Once the plains and water-courses of northern France have been abandoned to an invader, the curving course of the Loire provides a natural line of defence: a moat protecting the inner citadel of Central France whence attacks can be launched northwards or eastwards, and behind which troops can be switched to meet attack from any direction. If military considerations alone dictated strategy it would always be wise for French armies, once beaten back from their frontier fortifications, to abandon Paris and the North and fall back on this strong inner defence-line, possibly preserving also a redoubt in Brittany to take the enemy in the flank.[2] Such were the plans which Napoleon had made in 1814 and 1815; and Palikao had already done much towards organising such a defence when the events of 4th September swept him from power. But military considerations are not always paramount; factors of policy and sentiment are often much more significant; and once Paris has fallen to the enemy no French government in modern times has ever yet been able to prolong a war. The war in the provinces in 1870 was not the defence of an inner line: it was always subsidiary to the siege of Paris, and the relief of Paris, rather than the attrition and defeat of the German armies, was the objective at which the Delegation aimed. "*Toute l'armée de la Loire sur Paris!*" had been Gambetta's first words to the crowd that greeted him at Tours.[3] Only if this is understood does the strategy of the Delegation become intelligible. The determination to remain as close as possible to the beleaguered city made them hang on doggedly to the indefensible bastion of the Forest of Orléans. The desperate determination to relieve the city before its supplies were exhausted dictated the series of premature, ill-planned offensives with untrained troops, who might, had the Delegation been content to bide its time, have been built up into a force as formidable as it was numerous. And finally the repeated attempts at immediate relief delayed until it was too late the adoption of a strategy far richer in possibilities—that of attacking, not the German armies round Paris, but the precarious supply-lines which linked them to their homeland. Speculation about alternative strategies is usually deceptive. The eventual collapse of the

---

[1] *Staatsanzeiger*, 30th October, qu. by Albert Sorel, *Histoire diplomatique de la Guerre Franco-Allemande* II 62.

[2] Colmar von der Goltz, *Die Operationen der II Armee* (Berlin 1873) 429 ff.

[3] C. Chevalier, *Tours Capitale*, 99.

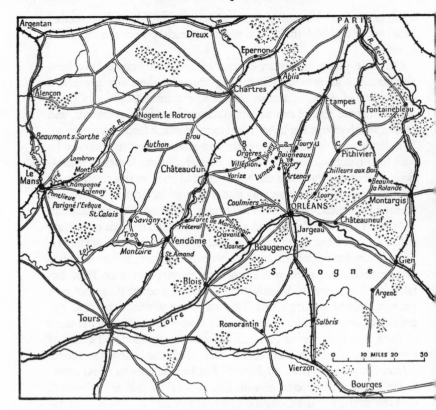

Map 13: The Campaign of the Loire

armies of the Loire before the attacks of Frederick Charles may make
one sceptical about the chances of the armies of National Defence,
however good their positions, if they had had to meet the full force of
Moltke's armies in the open field. None the less by linking the outcome
of the war to the defence of Paris, the Delegation not only shortened
the conflict, but made its length mathematically calculable; it could be
measured in terms, not of the military and moral potential of the nation
as a whole, but of the food supplies of the capital.

The fighting on the Loire began spontaneously, before any guiding
strategy had been shaped by either side. As the German armies advanced
on Paris, the cavalry on their extreme left wing, reconnoitring and requisitioning far to the south of the main body, entered the region of

the Forest of Orléans, a belt of scrub and woodland north of the Loire where the first organised troops of the provincial armies were beginning to assemble. There was a little skirmishing, during which the French troops evacuated Orléans in panic and reoccupied it again without opposition[1]; and by the beginning of October French and German outposts faced one another on a vestigial front which ran roughly eastwards from Artenay along the northern edge of the Forest of Orléans.[2]

The French forces on the Loire had by now been organised into an army corps, the 15th, under General de la Motte Rouge, and the Delegation, more mindful of a press and a public clamouring for action to relieve Paris[3] than of elementary military realities, ordered him to attack with as many troops as he could accumulate. He moved forward on 5th October, and had little difficulty in forcing the German cavalry outposts which faced him to fall back as far as Étampes.[4] Unsound and premature the French attack may have been, but Moltke had to take steps to deal with it. He could not tell what was the ultimate aim of the French, nor what forces they were prepared to commit to attain it. He had reluctantly to admit that a strong detachment was necessary, from the thinly held lines of investment about Paris, to contain this new threat, and he had to persuade an even more reluctant King to sanction it.[5] The troops most readily at hand were the I Bavarian Corps, which had as yet, apart from the struggle at Bazeilles, seen little action. Its reputation was not brilliant and von der Tann, its commander, though gallant enough in battle, was considered to be over-cautious in command.[6] But he was unlikely to have to deal with anything very formidable, and 22nd Prussian Division, under the exceptionally able Major-General von Wittich, was put under his command as a makeweight. Von der Tann wanted time to make preparations, but the messages from cavalry outposts scouting up to Artenay spoke so alarmingly of French concentrations, and the orders from Versailles were so

---

[1] For these operations see *Guerre: La 1re Armée de la Loire* I Hereafter referred to as *Guerre: Loire* I: Docs. annexes 109, 123–31, 145, 153–8, 191, 216. D.T. III (Borel) 483.

[2] *G.G.S.* II i 148.

[3] E.g. report from the Prefect at Chartres, 3rd October, in *Guerre: Loire* I: Docs. annexes 197. Also Lehautcourt, *La Campagne de la Loire* (Paris 1893) I 22.

[4] *Guerre: Loire* I: Docs. annexes 198 ff. *G.G.S.* II i 148–9. Gen. de La Motte Rouge, *Souvenirs et Campagnes* (Paris 1898) III 416–91.

[5] Frederick III, *War Diary* 148.

[6] Bronsart, *Kriegstagebuch* 129. Frederick III, op. cit. 159. Hönig, *Der Volkskrieg an der Loire im Herbst 1870* (Berlin 1893–7) III 222–4, paints a more charitable picture.

peremptory, that on 9th October, flanked by cavalry divisions, he began to move ponderously southwards from Étampes, with instructions to clear the rear of the investing armies as far south as Orléans and as far west as Chartres; and to push on, if occasion offered, to Tours itself.[1]

With 28,000 men and 160 guns he attacked the French positions on 10th October. By midnight on the 11th he had burst through the French defences and captured the city of Orléans, with all the stores accumulated there and more railway rolling-stock than the hard-pressed administration could afford to lose. Gambetta at once demanded that La Motte Rouge should be court-martialled. The officials of the Ministry of War persuaded him with difficulty that this would be undesirable, so he contented himself with depriving him immediately of his command, summoning in his place the veteran General d'Aurelle de Paladines.[2]

Aurelle had commanded a division in the Crimea, and was as fine a soldier as any in France—simple, religious, brave, with a magnificent presence which made itself felt as soon as he took over command of the shaken troops which had collected in the Sologne south of the Loire. He moved them back into safety at Salbris, thirty-three miles from the Germans at Orléans, and set about the task of restoring confidence and discipline to an army which showed no traces of either. His success was considerable. The soothing routine of a well-organised camp life, the salutary punishment of notorious malcontents,[3] the ubiquitous presence of the General who visited each regiment in turn and addressed them briefly and movingly about the traditions behind them, the tasks before them and the inexorable necessity of the hour—all this helped to transform a leaderless and demoralised rabble into a disciplined and reasonably confident army. Moreover to the efficiency of the soldier Aurelle added the zeal of a *dévot*. Chaplains were appointed in the reconstituted Army of the Loire, and were welcomed by the conscript peasants they served. Under Aurelle's hand the new army, disciplined and pious, began to acquire much of the patina of the *ancien régime*.[4]

Gambetta and Freycinet were too thankful at having an army at all

[1] *G.G.S.* II i 150. Helvig, *1st Bavarian Corps* 125.

[2] Helvig, op. cit. 141–54. Lehautcourt, *Campagne de la Loire* I 45–56. *D.T.* V (Cochéry) 102–13, III (Lefort) 76–7.

[3] A decree of the Delegation on 2nd October had authorised the setting up of summary courts-martial empowered to pronounce the death sentence for a variety of offences, including murder, desertion, straggling, theft, pillage, disobedience, indiscipline, abandonment or destruction of arms and ammunition. *Guerre: Défense Nationale en Province* I i 573–6.

[4] Martin des Pallières, *Orléans* 40 ff. Freycinet, *Guerre en Province* 71. Aurelle de Paladines, *La Première Armée de la Loire* 9–16. *D.T.* III (Aurelle) 189.

to make unnecessary trouble, but a conflict of some sort was hardly to be avoided. In Aurelle a professional mistrust of politicians went together with a good Catholic's hatred of Republicanism. Gambetta and Freycinet were young, energetic, confident and doctrinaire. Their minds were shaped by legends of '92 when, they believed, the enthusiasm and ruthlessness of young men such as themselves had triumphed over the timidity and doubtful loyalty of professional soldiers and won impossible victories. Moreover they were obsessed with the urgent necessity of relieving Paris. *De l'audace, de l'audace, toujours de l'audace* —this was the formula which had saved France once, and they reckoned would do so again. For such men the professional caution of the old general was even more infuriating than his political antagonism; and for Aurelle the attitude they adopted towards himself and the army under his command was a source of more profound irritation even than the impossible evolutions they required him to carry out. Gambetta was bad enough, with his egalitarian proclamations and speeches; but it was with Freycinet that Aurelle was in most constant contact, and for Freycinet he acquired feelings bordering on hatred. So intense indeed were the conflicts between the conservative soldier and the radical politician that the wonder is they were able, between them, to devise and execute any strategy at all.[1]

The location of the Delegation at Tours and its concentration on the immediate relief of Paris ensured that the centre of French resistance should be on the Lower Loire. From that centre, however, two irregular wings extended north and east in a crescent which partly enclosed the German armies surrounding Paris and might have provided the opportunity for a more flexible strategy. The left wing ran through the bases of Le Mans, Rouen, and Amiens, and rested on the fortresses of the northern frontier; the right extended more irregularly across the upper Loire and the Côte d'Or to the valley of the Saône and Dijon, thence to the intact fortresses of Besançon, Belfort, and Langres and the mountainous country of the Vosges.

On each wing the French could count on certain advantages. The Vosges, in particular, provided ideal cover for *francs-tireurs*—far better than did the flat and thickly populated lands of northern and central France. Forces operating there could threaten the Strasbourg–Paris railway, the jugular vein of the German armies round Paris, and also keep the inhabitants of the Grand Duchy of Baden in lively fear of raids across the Rhine. The advantages of this eastern theatre were

[1] See Aurelle, op. cit. *passim*, esp. vii, 36, and Chanzy, in *D.T.* III 217.

appreciated at the very outset by Trochu's Minister of War, the able and cantankerous General Le Flô, one of whose first acts on assuming office was to despatch a brigade of regular infantry to provide a nucleus for *franc-tireur* operations in the Vosges.[1] As commander of the area he appointed General Cambriels, an officer who had been so severely wounded in the head while fighting with the Army of Châlons that the Germans had released him from captivity after the battle of Sedan. These forces operated with such effect during September that Werder had had to make sizeable detachments from the siege corps at Strasbourg to protect his communications; and as soon as the city fell he had concentrated his forces for an expedition to clear the Vosges altogether. Simultaneously Cambriels was planning an equally concentrated blow against the Paris–Strasbourg railway-line. The forces clashed on 5th October near St Dié, and the French were forced back through the mountain passes, first to Épinal and then to Besançon, which they reached on 14th October in a state of drunken and mutinous collapse.[2]

To the Republican authorities in Besançon the failure of Cambriels to hold fast in the Vosges seemed inexplicable. "Is he mad?" they asked Gambetta, "is he incompetent, or a traitor?"[3] Gambetta paid a personal visit to Besançon and Cambriels explained to him some of the elementary facts of military life.

> To undertake with these bands a serious and considerable operation [he warned] will be to expose ourselves to a real disaster. If you are counting on this army of the East, which is at present in an embryonic condition, you must give it time to acquire a proper organisation, clothes, shoes and above all to learn some discipline. Then when the time is ripe, and I shall do my best to ensure that this is as soon as possible, I shall start moving and fall on the enemy lines of communication.

Gambetta had heard the same argument from Aurelle, but he attached to operations on the Loire an urgency which did not, in his view, apply to those in the east; so for a little Cambriels was left in peace.[4]

It was a pause which Werder was reluctant to disturb. The weather was vile, his own troops were tired, and his lengthening communications were at the mercy of *francs-tireurs*. After probing the strength of the French outposts on the Ognon he abandoned all thoughts of attack. Instead he turned south-west into the valley of the upper Saône and on

[1] *Guerre: Loire* I 10.
[2] *G.G.S.* II i 83–6, 205 ff. *M.M.K.* 313–5. L. Löhlein, *Operations of the Corps of General von Werder* (English edn. n.d.) 4 ff. Henri Genevois, *Les premières campagnes en l'Est* (Paris 1909). Grenest, *L'Armée de l'Est* (Paris n.d. but 1895).
[3] *D.O.* I 255.   [4] *D.T.* III 463.

31st October, after a day of fighting, he seized the city of Dijon—a centre vital for billets, communications and prestige.[1] It was a move which threatened to sever the communications of the French right wing, and put an end to all hope of an offensive northward from Besançon. Cambriels, rendered *hors de combat* by his wound, resigned his command, and his successor, General Michel, was an old-fashioned cavalry leader who proved even less capable of mastering either the political or the strategic difficulties of the situation. He declared that to undertake any operation with the forces under his command was quite out of the question, and instead prepared to fall back on Lyons. He lasted in command for five days before Freycinet dismissed him. His successor, the level-headed General Crouzat, evacuated Besançon on 8th November but fell back no farther than Chagny, between Beaune and Châlon-sur-Saône; a well-chosen position from which he could contest any further German advance to the south and communicate easily with the Army of the Loire.[2] Within a few days he and his army were summoned by Aurelle to join the advance on Paris, and the main burden of resisting Werder fell on the *francs-tireurs* of the Côte d'Or, commanded by Giuseppe Garibaldi. About their adventures we shall have more to say in due course.

Meanwhile the French army in the north, on the extreme left wing of the provincial armies, was also pinning down a large German force. The plains of Picardy and Artois did not lend themselves, as did the Vosges, to the operations of *francs-tireurs*; but the network of fortresses on the Belgian frontier provided an excellent base which only a major offensive could eliminate completely; the wealthy industrial area round Lille provided the economic basis for a thriving war-effort, and supplies of every kind could flow unrestricted over the Belgian frontier or through the Channel ports. There was no shortage of men, for recruits came in large numbers from the occupied provinces of the north-east,[3] and a nucleus of regular officers was provided by prisoners-of-war who escaped from Bazaine's army at Metz or from the somewhat cursory surveillance to which they were subjected in Germany.[4] The area was considered sufficiently independent, and its communications with the Loire were sufficiently tenuous, for the Delegation to appoint a General Commis-

---

[1] *G.G.S.* II i 222–4. Löhlein, op. cit. 43–4.

[2] Freycinet, *Guerre en Province* 105–7. Lehautcourt, *Campagne de l'Est* (Paris 1896) I 28–35.

[3] Faidherbe to Gambetta, 9th January 1871 in *Guerre: Campagne de l'Armée du Nord* III: Docs annexes 78.

[4] Op. cit. I: Docs. annexes 28.

sioner for the North: a Dr Testelin, a physician of Lille who was known as a staunch Republican and who rapidly showed himself a stout-hearted and competent administrator[1]; and in the middle of October command over its military forces was assumed by no less a figure than General Bourbaki himself.

Bourbaki, repulsed from the gates of Metz, had received an enthusiastic welcome from Gambetta at Tours. Whatever his political sympathies, Bourbaki was still considered to be one of the greatest soldiers in Europe. It had yet to be seen how far age and discouragement had rotted a military capacity which had perhaps always been rated higher than its deserts. Gambetta offered him command of the Army of the Loire, but Bourbaki prudently declined a post which could only, he foresaw, involve him in spectacular failure.[2] It was his own suggestion that he be given command of the Army of the North. When he left Tours for Lille on 17th October it was in the hope that he might with the troops assembling there bring some help to Bazaine in Metz.[3] A study of the resources available in the north had suggested that he might be able to raise there an army corps 12,000 strong with an artillery of thirty-six guns; but on arrival he found himself entirely deceived. In the first place units were being despatched to the Loire as quickly as they were formed, and he was able to arrest this movement only by a threat of resignation. Secondly, after a brief inspection of the forces available he came to the conclusion, like Aurelle and Cambriels, that it would take months of training to turn them into soldiers capable of taking the field against the Germans. For the present he considered them capable only of fighting defensive actions under the guns of the fortresses.[4] Such pessimism was as unwelcome and unintelligible to the Republican officers with whom he had to collaborate as were the similar views of Cambriels in Besançon. They, like Gambetta, were obsessed with the need to bring rapid help to their comrades in Paris, and into Bourbaki's hesitations they read the darkest motives. He had been a favourite of the Imperial Government; his suite was still filled with Imperial courtiers; and no satisfactory explanation had yet been given of his escape from Metz. After Bazaine's surrender his position became impossible. The widespread suspicions of his loyalty found expression in open demonstrations and lampoons. With the greatest possible reluctance Bourbaki

[1] Op. cit. I 1.

[2] Lord Newton: *Lord Lyons: a Record of British Diplomacy* I 328.

[3] *D.T.* III, (Bourbaki) 346. Gambetta to Favre, 19th October, *D.O.* II 277.

[4] Louis d'Eichthal, *Le Général Bourbaki: par un de ses anciens officiers d'ordonnance* (Paris 1885) 110–12. *Guerre: Armée du Nord* I 9–21.

agreed, on 14th November, to undertake an advance through Amiens on to the German positions at Beauvais and Clermont, but he had hardly set the movement on foot when Freycinet yielded to the demands of his critics and recalled him to Tours.[1]

The disposition of the French armies, as they developed during October, might thus have lent itself to an interesting variety of strategic combinations. The main German armies, firmly held round the fortress of Paris, were threatened from three different directions. Each of the three groups of French forces was largely self-sufficient and independent. Those in Lille and Amiens drew men and supplies from the industrial north, Britain, and Belgium, those of the Loire from the south-east and the Atlantic ports, those in the Saône and Doubs valleys from Lyons, the Midi and Marseilles. To wipe out any one of these groups and occupy its supply-area would have taken all the forces still available to Moltke apart from those besieging Paris, and would not necessarily have affected the resistance of the other two. Working independently or in unison the French armies, given a high enough standard of professional competence, might have made the German position almost untenable; and their professional chiefs were almost unanimous in advising that no operations should be undertaken until that standard had been reached. But there was no time for such a delay. Paris had to be relieved before she capitulated from starvation; and an even greater urgency was lent to Gambetta's planning by the arrival of a message from Favre, on 21st October, that Trochu was planning a break-out from Paris during the course of November, and was counting on the support of the provincial armies.[2] This demand for direct collaboration ruled out the project which Freycinet had been considering, of throwing the weight of the French armies on to the right flank in the east, and launching an attack which would not only cut German communications but relieve Metz. Such an expedition would take far too long. A movement on the left flank, with the Armies of the Loire and the North converging on Rouen and striking up the Seine valley under Bourbaki's command seemed to offer greater possibilities. But Bourbaki was discouraging. It was, he pointed out, a complex operation to ask of untrained troops (though the same might be said of any offensive by the provincial armies); it would involve a long flank march in face of a bold and enterprising enemy; and success would depend on a detailed co-operation with the Paris garrison which, given all the

[1] Ibid. 30–32. *D.T.* III (Testelin) 563–4.
[2] Freycinet, *Guerre en Province* 78. See p. 334 below.

circumstances, was out of the question. He was prepared to undertake it if ordered; but in face of this marked lack of enthusiasm Gambetta and Freycinet did not insist further.[1] Instead they turned their attention to the only remaining offensive possibility—the recapture of Orléans and a direct attack on Paris from the south.

Such a plan had obvious advantages. It was simple; it would afford the most immediate relief to the capital; it would enable the army to continue to cover the inconveniently vulnerable city of Tours, and it afforded the best prospect of avenging the loss of Orléans. Aurelle now had at his disposal about 70,000 men, divided between 15th Corps, reconstituted under his eye at Salbris, and the newly formed 16th Corps, untrained and under-equipped, which had assembled at Blois to cover Tours.[2] Such a force should be ample to deal with the 20,000 German troops under von der Tann in Orléans. By intelligent use of the railway system, the French forces could be concentrated rapidly at any point and to the advantage of numbers add that of surprise—or so at least Freycinet hoped. On 24th October he visited Salbris and explained his plan. 15th Corps, with the exception of one division, was to entrain for Tours, giving the impression that it was on its way to Le Mans to threaten Paris from the west. From Tours it was to move up the Loire to join 16th Corps at Blois, and attack Orléans from the south-west. Simultaneously its remaining division, 30,000 strong under General Martin des Pallières, would march to the upper Loire at Gien and advance down the river to take the Germans in the rear. Aurelle raised various objections. He did not consider his troops fit to conduct an active campaign, and he feared that an attack up the Loire would lay them open to a blow on their left flank. It would be far better, he suggested, for them to take up good defensive positions and await attack. But such a course, however sound militarily, was politically out of the question. Aurelle could suggest no better form of attack; General Borel, his able chief of staff, considered the plan to be feasible; and it was decided that the operation should begin on 27th October.[3] The army, it was reckoned, should be in its new positions by 29th October, and by 1st November at latest have taken Orléans.

The movement of an army by railway is not, as we have seen, any business for amateurs. The staff-officers of the Imperial army had shown themselves incompetent enough the previous summer, and it

[1] *Guerre: Armée du Nord* I 13 *D.T.* III (Bourbaki) 347. Eichthal, *Bourbaki* 113–16. [2] Aurelle, *1re Armée de la Loire* 19.
[3] Freycinet, *Guerre en Province* 79–82. Pallières, *Orléans* 64.

was not to be expected that Aurelle's hastily assembled staff and the scratch team of civilians at the Ministry of War would do any better. Freycinet expected the movement to be completed within thirty-six hours.[1] In fact it took three days, and all the mistakes were committed which had proved so disastrous the previous July. Civil traffic still ran uninterrupted. The troops spent hours at railway stations because of miscalculation of the time it would take them to entrain. Time-tables were disrupted, and there were no facilities at stations for the reception of masses of men and stores. Horses spent long days in their trucks; men became separated from their baggage, guns and ammunition; and when the whole force had at last been disgorged higgledy-piggledy at Blois, Aurelle claimed with every show of reason that it was in no condition to attack. Heavy rain, soaking the roads and clogging all movement, was an additional source of irritation and delay. Freycinet was furious, but could do nothing. "As we must give up the idea of winning with odds of two to one, when once we conquered one against two", he wrote, on 29th October, in a letter which can have done nothing to endear him to Aurelle, "let us speak of it no further, and try to make the best we can of the situation . . . when you feel yourself in condition to march on the Prussians, you will let us know."[2] With relief Aurelle delayed for a week the attack which he was convinced would anyhow fail.

This week's pause was to contribute no little to the disasters of the Army of the Loire. On 29th October Metz capitulated, and two German armies were released for action. Speed was essential if the operation to relieve Paris was to have any hope of success. Had Bazaine not by his capitulation released Frederick Charles, Moltke would have been compelled to make detachments from his already over-stretched lines of investment around Paris to deal not only with the Army of the Loire but with the forces which Bourbaki was collecting at Amiens. Certainly von der Tann by himself could not deal with the forces which Aurelle assembled against him. Since the capture of Orléans, indeed, his conduct of operations had caused considerable dissatisfaction at Versailles. It had been left to his discretion whether he advanced beyond Orléans. Moltke had suggested that he should advance to Bourges, one of the chief arsenals of the Government of National Defence[3]; but Tann felt

---

[1] *D.T.* III 29.   [2] Aurelle, 1re *Armée de la Loire* 61.

[3] Moltke to Blumenthal, 12th October, *M.M.K.* 326–7. His appreciation of the strategic importance of Bourges was very shrewd: see Thoumas, *Paris, Tours, Bordeaux* 807.

isolated enough already, and had no intention of taking further risks by advancing into the inhospitable wastes of the Sologne. The Bavarians therefore remained apprehensively on the Loire, while the task of sweeping westwards was left to the 22nd Prussian Division and a strong detachment of cavalry. These troops had to contend only with a screen of local *mobiles* and *francs-tireurs*, inadequately commanded from Le Mans by General Fiéreck[1]; but isolated units put up a stubborn resistance to which the Germans retaliated with a strictness bordering on savagery. At Châteaudun on 18th October they mounted a full-scale attack against a detachment about 1,200 strong under the *franc-tireur* leader Colonel Lipowski, and fought from house to blazing house far into the night.[2] At Chartres two days later the civil authorities intervened before fighting could begin and surrendered the town in return for the peaceful departure of the French occupying troops. By the end of October the original task of von der Tann's force was accomplished, and the rear of the German armies was cleared to Chartres and Orléans. But the Germans knew that beyond this arc patrolled by their cavalry, at Le Mans, at Tours, at Bourges, preparations were in hand for an attack on a scale which they would be quite unable to meet. Nor could they be sure where the French would strike. Freycinet's deception plan was effective; Royal Headquarters expected not so much an attack on Orléans as a movement from Le Mans on Versailles, and discounted the anxious reports of von der Tann.[3] Moltke, unwilling to spare further detachments from the siege, would make no more troops available, and merely demanded that von der Tann should show more activity in sending out fighting patrols to disrupt the French movements, as the Prussians and the cavalry were already doing to the west.[4]

Urged by the impatient Freycinet, Aurelle began his advance on 7th November. The confusion of the march along the muddy lanes of the Forest of Marchénoir, the disorganised columns piling up and halting for hours in the pouring rain, confirmed all his fears, and next day he sent back another message to Tours expressing the profoundest gloom about the outcome of the operation. But Freycinet was inexorable; so on

---

[1] Gambetta to Favre, 26 November, *D.O.* II 316.

[2] *G.G.S.* II i 165–6.

[3] Bronsart, *Kriegstagebuch* 129, 134. Frederick III, *War Diary* 185.

[4] *M.M.K.* 360. As to the King's views, there is a conflict of evidence between Waldersee, who alleged "Der König wünscht ihn (Tann) zu verstärken; Moltke und Podbielski sträuben sich dagegen" (*Denkwürdigkeiten* I 106) and the Crown Prince. Frederick III, *War Diary* 179–83.

9th November Aurelle advanced again, with a fatalistic resignation paralleled only by that of his equally pessimistic adversary in Orléans.[1]

About 100,000 Frenchmen were now closing in on the Bavarians. Aurelle had his left flank covered by Lipowski's *francs-tireurs* from Châteaudun; a detachment was advancing through the Sologne from Salbris; Pallières was on his way from Gien, in von der Tann's rear; and far in the west the French forces gathering at Le Mans made a demonstration to pin down the German right flank. On 7th November a strong German fighting patrol stumbling through the misty copses of the Forest of Marchénoir came upon 16th Corps. The Germans were partially surrounded, wholly defeated and regained their positions with a loss of 150 men.[2] This revelation of French strength, combined with reports of Pallières's advance from Gien, was enough for von der Tann. He decided not to await the closing pincers in Orléans. Instead, on the night of the 8th, he abandoned the city and marched out, in conformity with the best military principles, to deal with the strongest of the two forces threatening him while the other was still out of range. If he were victorious he could reoccupy Orléans and deal with Pallières at leisure, while if he were defeated his line of retreat to the north was still secure. It was an orthodox and correct military response which disrupted Freycinet's strategy: the battle occurred prematurely, without Pallières's participation and without the subsequent encirclement at which the French had aimed.[3]

The German forces took up their position on 8th November round the village of Coulmiers, about twelve miles north-west of Orléans along the main road to Le Mans. It was a moderately good position for defence. The village and the park of the château before it could be made into passable strong-points, the woods in rear masked the movement of reserves, and a shallow depression, hardly deserving the name of a valley, running north from the village through the hamlets of Cheminiers and Champs gave the right wing a reasonable field of fire. On the left wing however the country was closer, its copses and slopes affording better opportunities for surprise; and it was perhaps the vulnerability of this flank that made von der Tann concentrate here the bulk of his strength. With his three cavalry and four infantry brigades he mustered under 20,000 men, and he pinned most of his hopes on the proved effectiveness of his 110 guns. He did not anticipate having to contend

[1] Freycinet, *Guerre en Province* 89–91. Aurelle, *1re Armée de la Loire* 87–9. *D.T.* III (de Serres) 31.
[2] *G.G.S.* II i 269. General Chanzy, *2me Armée de la Loire* (4th edn. Paris 1872) 14–15.　　　[3] Helvig, op. cit. 179.

with 70,000 men,[1] and even more disastrous than his miscalculation of the enemy's strength was his misjudgment of their line of advance. He expected no French effort north of Coulmiers and had virtually no troops on hand to meet one. In fact Coulmiers was the objective of the French right wing, 15th Corps; the whole strength of 16th Corps, the command of which had just been assumed by the vigorous General Chanzy, was directed further to the north, towards the Châteaudun road. With better fortune, or better judgment,[2] the French might thus have achieved on the battlefield that total encirclement which von der Tann, by his premature forcing of battle, had hoped to avoid.

The morning of 9th November was cold and grey and the French troops, denied bivouac fires during the night by the nearness of the enemy, advanced shivering across the bare fields of the Beauce. But they advanced with confidence. The disaster to the German patrol on the 7th, with its revelation that the Germans were not invincible, had had a galvanic effect on the entire army, and it attacked not only with *élan* but with a totally unexpected confidence and skill. From their gunners they received support of a kind which the Imperial army had never known; for the Delegation had suppressed the time-fuses which had so hampered the efficiency of the Imperial artillery, and instead fitted their shells with percussion-fuses which exploded, like those of the Germans, on impact. The Bavarians held out all day, but by 4 p.m. von der Tann had decided that the position was untenable, and begun to withdraw towards Artenay and Toury, the onset of darkness, and with it a driving mixture of sleet and rain, concealing the full extent of his retreat. The French bivouacked in the fields over which they had fought, and not till next morning did they realise that they had won their first victory of the war. Then Aurelle and Pallières marched into Orléans, and all the bells in the city pealed a welcome. The first round in the People's War seemed to be won.[3]

---

[1] I do not here accept Lehautcourt's reduction of Aurelle's force to 40,000 by eliminating estimated "non-effectives", nor his increase of the Bavarian to 23,500 over Helvig's estimate of 14,543 infantry and 4,450 cavalry. *Campagne de la Loire* I 151–2.

[2] Aurelle might still have encircled his enemy had he taken Chanzy's advice and attacked with a strong left wing, to press the Germans back on the Loire. Lehautcourt attributes his failure to do so to "une enfantine préoccupation de régularité en plaçant à la droite de l'armée le corps le premier à marcher dans l'ordre de bataille." *Campagne de la Loire* I 115.

[3] For details of the battle see Helvig, *1st Bavarian Corps* 186–210. *G.G.S.* II i 271–9. Aurelle, *1ʳᵉ Armée de la Loire* 102–13. Chanzy, *2ᵐᵉ Armée de la Loire* 25–35. Lehautcourt, *Campagne de la Loire* I 130–52.

§ 2 Beaune-la-Rolande

At Versailles the news of von der Tann's defeat caused less surprise than might have been expected. The Prussians could not conceal their satisfaction at the inability of the Bavarians to stand on their own feet, and Blumenthal laid the blame at Moltke's door for failing to send reinforcements as he had urged. Moltke himself viewed the situation with the calm of the dedicated technician. "We are now living through a very interesting time", he observed, "when the question of which is preferable, a trained army or a militia, will be solved in action. If the French succeed in throwing us out of France, all the Powers will introduce a militia system, and if we remain the victors, then every State will imitate us with universal service in a standing army."[1] He had, in any case, no cause for alarm. The fall of Metz had put at his disposal sufficient forces to deal with the new enemy—forces depleted by sickness, their casualties of the summer replaced by inexperienced new drafts, but a happy windfall none the less.[2]

On 10th November Moltke summoned Frederick Charles's forces— III, IX and X Corps—to the neighbourhood of Fontainebleau, where they could deal with any attempt by Aurelle to advance on Paris. Four days later, when the situation seemed easier and it was clear that the French were attempting neither an immediate advance from the Loire nor, as yet, a sortie from Paris, he summarised the position as he saw it in a long letter to Stiehle.[3] The Army of the Loire, he reckoned, was not strong enough to attack towards the north, but it was unlikely to remain on the defensive at Orléans. Its most probable course of action was to move west, join forces with Bourbaki, and attack towards Versailles. Such an attack might not raise the siege, but it would come in among all the headquarters and artillery parks of the German armies, and the political consequences might be grave. His original intentions for the Second Army, a direct march on Bourges and Tours, must therefore for the moment be abandoned. Instead it was to take over the defence of the Orléans–Paris road. The forces hitherto operating south and west of Paris, I Bavarian Corps, three cavalry divisions and 22nd Prussian Division, would form an independent Detachment, together with 17th Division, under command of the Grand Duke of Mecklenburg, and would deal with the threatened attack from the west. The position was

---

[1] Hohenlohe-Ingelfingen, *Aus meinem Leben* 355.
[2] Hönig, *Volkskrieg an der Loire* I 67.   [3] *M.M.K.* 373, 376.

not an easy one; and Moltke frankly confessed that "we are very thankful for the rapid arrival of His Royal Highness Prince Frederick Charles; it has helped us to get over a kind of crisis".[1]

By 24th November the Second Army, having marched briskly through Chaumont, Troyes, and Fontainebleau, was taking up its positions along the northern edge of the Forest of Orléans and testing the strength of Aurelle's defences. The Grand Duke of Mecklenburg, who had been concentrating his forces in the region of Chartres, was now free to seek the enemy in the west, and he set out on 17th November to look for French activity on the Eure.[2] His task, as Moltke admitted, was not easy. Its difficulty lay "in being able to recognise correctly the vital point against which a drive is to be directed with assembled forces".[3] But the fact that he was opposed, not by an organised force but by a loose cordon of some 50,000 troops in every stage of training scattered over sixty miles and reinforced by local *Gardes Nationales*, made this almost impossible. Detachments of French troops would take up a defensive position, force the Germans to deploy, and then slip away to harass supply-columns in the rear. In face of an enemy so active and a population so hostile the German cavalry did not dare to act with the boldness it had shown three months earlier in Lorraine; and for nearly two weeks Mecklenburg blundered unhappily round the sad, rain-swept countryside, from Dreux to Nogent-le-Rotrou and on towards Le Mans, in search of an enemy who always eluded him.

The spirits of Mecklenburg's troops, never very high, now began to sink alarmingly. They had left the open plains of the Beauce, where enemy activity could be seen from afar and broken up by gunfire, and were now marching through close country ideal for ambush and surprise. The marches were long, often through thick mud and pouring rain. Boots and equipment rotted and could not be replaced; troops were reduced to wearing peasant sabots stuffed with straw; and the columns were daily lengthened by requisitioned waggons carrying men no longer able to march.[4] It quickly became clear that Moltke's original assessment

---

[1] Frederick Charles considered the crisis to have been even more acute. If Metz had fallen a day later, he maintained, the siege of Paris would have had to be raised. "*Das ist klar und wird allgemein anerkannt.*" *Denkwürdigkeiten* II 394. This was the general view among civilians at Versailles. See Rauch, *Briefe aus dem grossen Hauptquartier* 159, and Hermann Oncken, *Grossherzog Friedrich I von Baden und die deutsche Politik von 1854–1871* (Stuttgart 1927) II 175. [2] Hönig, *Volkskrieg* I 120–28.
[3] *M.M.K.* 385. [4] Helvig, *1st Bavarian Corps* 227–40.

of French intentions was completely at fault. The centre of French strength had not been shifted from the Loire. On 22nd November therefore Moltke ordered Mecklenburg's Detachment, which had just fought its way into Nogent-le-Rotrou, to leave a covering force to watch westward and march south towards Beaugency, to join forces with Frederick Charles.[1] In purely military terms this was a wise decision. Moltke was too far away to direct the two armies effectively, and to make Frederick Charles Commander-in-Chief of the whole theatre seemed a sound solution. But the two royal cousins disliked one another, collaborated uneasily, and when Mecklenburg's Detachment returned to the neighbourhood of Orléans the operations of the two forces were to be distinguished by a very remarkable lack of liaison.

By now the French were reacting to the German movements. To Freycinet Mecklenburg's advance seemed significant mainly as a threat to Tours, and he rapidly assembled at Châteaudun a force, dignified by the name of 17th Corps, to cover the city. To the command of this corps Aurelle appointed an energetic young regular soldier, General de Sonis; and de Sonis realised that if anybody was menaced it was Mecklenburg himself, marching westward across the French front with his communications wide open to a counter-stroke from the south. On 25th November a brief advance from Châteaudun brought de Sonis upon a Bavarian supply-column, which he pursued as far as Brou. For a glorious moment he thought of pushing on to Nogent and cutting Mecklenburg's communications altogether. The German forces now stretched between Authon and Savigny; with de Sonis at Brou in their left rear their position, in the dry words of the Bavarian official historian, "was to say the least of it very peculiar". But so was that of de Sonis, and both he and Freycinet lost their nerve. On 26th November de Sonis fell back hurriedly to the south, abandoned Châteaudun and shepherded his forces towards the Forest of Marchénoir.[2] With almost comic simultaneity Mecklenburg, summoned by a peremptory telegram from Frederick Charles, pulled back his no less exhausted men from the salient into which he had marched them, and turned back towards the east.[3]

At Royal Headquarters Mecklenburg's movements were observed with growing disapproval. By 26th November, according to Moltke's

[1] *M.M.K.* 390.

[2] Aurelle, *1re Armée de la Loire* 207–10. Helvig, *1st Bavarian Corps* 241 D.T. III 257–8.

[3] Frederick Charles, *Denkwürdigkeiten* II 338. Hönig, *Volkskrieg* I 312.

order of 22nd November, Mecklenburg should have been at Beaugency, ready to take part in the offensive against Orléans. As it was, he was still considerably nearer to Le Mans than to Beaugency, with his troops exhausted and his lines of communication straggling dangerously across the front of the French army. It was also clear that the incompetence of Mecklenburg's staff, which consisted largely of his own personal entourage, was increasing the delays of the Detachment and the trials of its troops; so on 26th November Moltke placed Mecklenburg under the direct orders of Frederick Charles, and next day despatched the head of his *Intendantur*, Lieut.-General von Stosch, to take over the duties of Chief of Staff to the Grand Duke. Thereafter the movements of Mecklenburg's Detachment showed a very marked improvement.[1]

Mecklenburg was not the only army commander whose delays were watched with impatience from Versailles. The stock of Frederick Charles was slumping as well. His immediate task had been purely defensive, and he was reluctant to pass to the attack. To do so, he realised as he inspected the thick copses of the Forest of Orléans, was more difficult than he had foreseen. He had to attack a numerically superior enemy situated among a sympathetic population and holding strong defensive positions—an enemy very different from the small, ill-organised forces which von der Tann had brushed aside so easily the previous month. Moreover reports of French troop movements indicated that Aurelle was himself going to attack.[2] Moltke, prepared as ever to over-estimate the military sagacity of his enemies, thought this improbable, but he pointed out to Stiehle that it would be most desirable if he did. "He would then have to come out into the open", he wrote, "where your superiority in artillery and cavalry would be at its most effective." So Frederick Charles confined himself for the moment to patrolling and collecting information, with Moltke's reluctant consent.[3]

There was also a deeper reason for the Second Army's delays: Frederick Charles and Moltke were in fundamental disagreement about the whole object of the campaign on the Loire. Moltke was concerned with the protection of his lines of investment, and with the frustration of Aurelle's impending attack. Frederick Charles saw his task as the destruction of the French army, and that would not be achieved by a

[1] Blumenthal, *Journals* 202. Stosch, *Denkwürdigkeiten* 206–7. Bronsart, *Kriegstagebuch* 197. Hönig, *Volkskrieg* I 172, 313, 353.

[2] *M.M.K.* 382.

[3] *M.M.K.* 401. Hönig, *Volkskrieg* I 225–6. Stiehle to Moltke, 26th November in Frederick Charles, *Denkwürdigkeiten* II 337–8.

frontal attack which would simply push Aurelle back behind the Loire. Only an enveloping movement against his communications would be effective, with the Second Army driving south-west through Châteauneuf and Gien towards Bourges and Mecklenburg's Detachment moving south-east to meet them in Aurelle's rear. Frederick Charles therefore received Moltke's demands for a frontal attack with little enthusiasm, and possibly he was right. Had operations gone as he planned, the campaign would have been over by the end of November and both French and Germans would have been spared the useless sufferings of two bitter months on the Doubs and the Sarthe.[1]

These views were not shared at Versailles. There the King was growing increasingly anxious about the situation of his armies, and for a moment his trust in Moltke faltered. He determined to obtain an independent view of the events on the Loire; so on 25th November unknown to Moltke, he sent the able young Colonel von Waldersee, the former Military Attaché in Paris and Moltke's eventual successor as Chief of Staff, to Second Army headquarters to report on the position, and to point out to Frederick Charles the grave consequences to the entire German situation if he allowed himself to be defeated.[2] The arrival of Waldersee gave Frederick Charles the chance to send the King a convincing statement of his case. It would be foolish for him, with less than 50,000 men, to plunge into the thickly held Forest of Orléans; the strong possibility that the French might attack from the upper Loire towards Fontainebleau made it necessary to keep his forces dispersed; and he confessed that he could not tell where the main French strength lay. German cavalry was even less bold in reconnaissance than it had been the previous summer. It would, he admitted, be foolish for the French to venture out; "but we have already in this campaign experienced some amazing things—I mean the order from Paris to MacMahon for the relief of Metz which led eventually to Sedan. So lawyers' orders may now decree that the Loire army shall under any circumstances undertake the advance on Paris"[3]; and about this he was, of course, perfectly right.

For if Frederick Charles was able to reassure his anxious superiors about his ability to handle the situation, Aurelle in Orléans met with

[1] Hönig, *Volkskrieg, passim*, especially I 185.

[2] Ibid. I 334–6. Waldersee did not even visit Moltke's staff officers before leaving, as it was "die Absicht des Königs, mich unbeeinflusst von Generalstabsansichten die Verhältnisse betrachten zu lassen. Er war misstrauisch, dass man ihm nicht die volle Wahrheit sage". Waldersee, *Denkwürdigkeiten* I 107.

[3] Frederick Charles, *Denkwürdigkeiten* II 341.

much less success. The conflict of opinion which had so embittered relations between Aurelle and Freycinet before Coulmiers had been renewed after the battle with an even greater intensity. For Freycinet and Gambetta Coulmiers was only the first step to Paris. They had informed Trochu of their victory by carrier-pigeon and urged him to break out to meet them; thus they believed that the need to advance on the capital was more urgent than ever if the whole operation was not to end in disaster. Aurelle, on the contrary, considered that the approach of Frederick Charles made any further advance impossible. All he could now do, he maintained, was to strengthen the defences of Orléans and await attack—the sound strategy which Moltke presumed he would pursue. The problem was discussed in a Council of War at Orléans on 12th November. At this stage it was still possible for both sides to agree, since not even Freycinet could deny the need to consolidate Orléans as a firm military base and there accumulate the greatest possible strength before undertaking any further advance.[1] Freycinet contented himself with pointing out that Orléans should be regarded as a base for operations from which strong patrols should go out to exercise the troops and harass the Germans. Gambetta issued a resounding order to the army which left no doubt about the rôle for which he intended them. "You are today on the road to Paris", he wrote. "Never forget that Paris is waiting for us and honour demands that we should wrest it from the grasp of the barbarians who are threatening it with pillage and fire." Aurelle was therefore allowed to remain at Orléans, while the Delegation assembled every available man in their new armies in preparation for the forthcoming attack.[2]

Aurelle's force consisted, on paper, of six corps, or more than 200,000 men. 15th Corps (commanded now by Pallières) and Chanzy's 16th Corps lay in the centre before Orléans, to the right and left respectively of the Paris road, their flanks and front covered by *francs-tireurs*. On the left at Châteaudun was de Sonis's 17th Corps, while General Fiéreck lay at Le Mans with his shadowy 21st Corps. On the right, at Gien, was 18th Corps, temporarily without a commander and controlled by its Chief of Staff Colonel Billot, but soon to be taken over by Bourbaki; and finally, on 15th November, Freycinet summoned General Crouzat, the commander of the forces confronting the Germans in the Saône valley, to bring the best of his troops over to the Loire by train and

---

[1] Freycinet to Aurelle, 27th October. Aurelle, *1re Armée de la Loire* 133.
[2] Freycinet, *Guerre en Province* 103, 110–11. Aurelle, *1re Armée de la Loire* 121–58. *D.T.* III 61.

come into line, as 20th Corps, between Billot and Pallières. It was an impressive total; but in practice only 15th and possibly 16th Corps constituted military formations worthy of the name. 21st Corps was incapable of moving from Le Mans; 17th Corps almost disintegrated when de Sonis hurried it from Châteaudun to the Forest of Marché-noir; while 20th Corps, officered by retired regulars promoted to ranks which they were quite unfitted to hold, was armed only with a miscellany of firearms for which it was almost impossible to provide ammunition.[1] Only courage and enthusiasm made such formations anything more than flocks of sheep herded for the slaughter-house; and these, under the circumstances, were diminishing assets.

Freycinet and Aurelle regarded these gathering forces with very different eyes. Freycinet looked at their numbers, of which he formed perhaps an exaggerated estimate. Aurelle was conscious of their imperfections, and his view of these, perhaps also exaggerated, strengthened his determination not to move from Orléans. Such men would be stubble for Frederick Charles's sword, and he was not prepared to risk them even on the limited offensive operations which Freycinet urged.[2] After Aurelle had remained apparently idle for a week Freycinet wrote on 19th November urging him to attack. He had, Freycinet pointed out, 250,000 men at his disposal. "We cannot stay at Orléans for ever," he argued; "Paris is hungry and demands our help. *Paris a faim et nous réclame.*"[3] This began an exchange of letters which revealed how profound was the misunderstanding between the civil Government and its Commander-in-Chief. Aurelle replied that Freycinet's estimate of the army's strength was wildly false. "It would be dangerous to trust to the deceptive mirage of figures on paper and take them for reality."[4] The strength of the German forces and the continuing bad weather made any offensive out of the question; and anyhow no operation could be planned except in collaboration with Trochu. Freycinet replied, reasonably enough, that such collaboration was impossible; and as for the numbers of the enemy and the badness of the weather, these conditions were not likely to improve before famine forced Paris to surrender.[5] Aurelle abandoned argument and fell back on dignified obscurity. "You recommend that I should think out a plan of operations with Paris as my ultimate objective," he wrote, on 23rd November; "the solution of this problem is not the least of my preoccupations. To resolve it, there

---

[1] Lehautcourt, *Campagne de la Loire* I 206–9.
[2] Aurelle, *Ire Armée de la Loire* 157–67.
[3] *D.T.* III 193.   [4] Aurelle, *Ire Armée de la Loire* 187–8.   [5] *D.T.* III 197.

must be co-operation and agreement between the Government and the Army represented by the leaders whom you have entrusted with your confidence."[1]

Freycinet decided to take matters into his own hands; but his decision was precipitated less by the determination to relieve Paris than by fear for the safety of Tours itself. The advance of Mecklenburg's Detachment threatened the capital, and the forces on the French left wing were in no condition to parry it. The only chance of forcing the Germans to relax their pressure seemed to lie in striking strongly at another part of their front. Freycinet had already decided that the break-out from Orléans, when it came, should be directed north-east towards Fontainebleau, in order to join forces with Trochu on the Upper Seine; so it was reasonable that this attack should be carried out by the French right flank, and that it should aim, not merely at relieving pressure on the left, but at seizing Pithiviers as a spring-board for the advance on Paris.[2] For these reasons Freycinet, on 22nd November, sent Aurelle the direct order to transmit instructions to the corps commanders of his right wing for an advance.

Aurelle's reaction was scrupulously correct. He forwarded the orders, and submitted a strong protest to Tours. The tone of Freycinet's reply showed that he had now lost patience with Aurelle altogether. "If you were to bring me a better plan than mine, or even if you were to bring me any plan at all, I could abandon my own and revoke my orders," he wrote. "But during the twelve days that you have been at Orléans you have not, in spite of the repeated requests of M. Gambetta and myself, proposed any sort of plan."[3] In his exasperation, Freycinet had, as he later admitted, constituted himself the effective commander-in-chief of the French army, and had taken matters into his own hands.[4]

On 24th November, controlled at long range from Tours, the operation began, and its very beginning was unfortunate. In the course of the first day's fighting the Germans captured letters from Gambetta and army orders which enabled Frederick Charles to anticipate the entire French move.[5] The movement of the three French corps through the forest was slow, cumbrous, and distinguished by an almost complete lack of liaison; but all went well until, on 28th November, they came up against the main German position: the village of Beaune-la-Rolande and the adjacent hamlets, held by the Hanoverian troops of General

---

[1] Aurelle, op. cit. 214–21.
[2] Freycinet, *Guerre en Province* 114–19.　　　[3] Ibid. 122.　　　[4] *D.T.* III 3.
[5] Hönig, *Volkskrieg* I 290.

Voigts-Rhetz's X Corps. On this position Freycinet ordered 18th and 20th Corps to converge, with a joint strength of some 50,000 men. The Hanoverians had only two brigades to hold the position, about 9,000 men in all,[1] and each was attacked, and surprised, by an entire French corps. But they were phlegmatic and experienced troops, well-armed and well-commanded, with first-class gunners and plenty of ammunition. They were established in stout farm-houses against which the French could only advance *en masse* across an open plain, and the garrison of Beaune-la-Rolande had the advantage of a thick and well-sited town wall, inside which they had erected firing platforms to give the maximum efficacy to their fire. Crouzat was reluctant to direct against them the full force of an artillery which, though it might break their resistance, would heavily damage the town as well. He preferred to trust to the mass of his infantry, which he launched in attack after unsuccessful attack throughout the day, waiting impatiently for 18th Corps to come up on his right and join him. 18th Corps were held up before the hamlets on the Châteauneuf road, and could join 20th Corps only in the last assault which Crouzat led in person at nightfall— an assault to which they contributed confusion rather than strength.[2] By then the Germans had been reinforced. There had been a moment, shortly before 2 p.m., when Voigts-Rhetz, despairing of holding on to his positions, had almost ordered a retreat, and he had been dissuaded (by Caprivi) with difficulty. It was not until after midday that Frederick Charles had decided that the strength of the attack warranted his sending III Corps down from Pithiviers to help.[3] Rapid marching brought up their advance-guard by 4 p.m., and their pressure on the French left flank, combined with the onset of darkness, forced Crouzat to abandon the attack. He had lost 1,300 men in killed and wounded, and 1,800 prisoners fell into German hands; while the Germans had lost something under 900 men.[4]

[1] Ibid. II 279–80.

[2] *D.T.* III (Crouzat) 264, 279–81. (Billot) 467. G. H. Rindfleisch, *Feldbriefe* 104–5.

[3] Hönig, *Volkskrieg* II 274. Frederick Charles, *Denkwürdigkeiten* II 356–8.

[4] For accounts of the battle see *G.G.S.* II i 314–21. Hönig, *Volkskrieg* II 80–267. Gen. von Voigts-Rhetz, *Briefe aus den Kriegsjahren 1866 und 1870–71* (Berlin 1906) 203 ff. Lehautcourt, *Campagne de la Loire* I 249–65. Frederick Charles remained unaware even after the battle of the scale of the fighting, reporting to the King only that X Corps had held its position with fighting "zum Teil sehr ernst" against 30,000 men. *Denkwürdigkeiten* II 360. He visited the battlefields only on 30th November, and then confessed that the corpse-covered fields were comparable only to those before St Privat, Hönig, *Volkskrieg* III 64.

For French observers able to watch the progress of the war with clear eyes and balanced judgments, the results of the battle for Beaune-la-Rolande were discouraging. The hopes founded on legends of '93 and on the victory at Coulmiers were belied; it was clear that numbers and enthusiasm were no match for the discipline and fire power of German troops in good defensive positions. But Freycinet was not cast down. Mecklenburg's abandonment of his march to the south-west was seen at Tours as the direct result of pressure on the German left flank, so the battle could be counted a strategic success[1]; but more important even than this was the impact of a message, which reached Tours on 30th November, that the garrison of Paris was attempting a break-out at last. Despatched from Paris by a balloon which had drifted to Norway, it announced that the operation would begin on the 29th. If the message was correct—as in essence it was—the attack had been in progress for twenty-four hours already, and there was not a moment to lose. Freycinet dashed up to Orléans, where he ordered Aurelle to prepare to attack as soon as more definite news arrived from Paris. 17th Corps was to stay guarding Orléans; 15th and 16th Corps were to advance on Pithiviers from the west, 18th and 20th Corps from the east; and then the victorious army, 170,000 strong, was to press on to the Forest of Fontainebleau to join hands with their comrades from Paris.[2]

Even if the French troops had been in a state to give battle, such an attack, by a thin line of units, over-extended and with no reserve, promised little success. In fact they were in no condition to undertake any sort of advance. 20th Corps was immobilised for want of uniform and camping equipment; and Crouzat pathetically asked Freycinet: "Let me have a few days' rest to refit. The morale of my men is good, but they have too many deficiencies for this cold and wet weather." Freycinet was unimpressed. "You seem to me", he wrote, "to lose confidence very easily. . . . If the attitude of this corps continues to appear so uncertain, I shall hold you personally responsible for it, and you will have to account to the Government for whatever consequences this situation may have." As a final insult Crouzat was put under the command of Billot, acting commander of 18th Corps, of whose failure to reinforce him adequately at Beaune-la-Rolande Crouzat was already bitterly complaining.[3]

Nor was all well on the left flank. De Sonis's precipitous retreat from

[1] Freycinet, *Guerre en Province* 130.
[2] Freycinet, *Guerre en Province* 133–6. Aurelle, *1re Armée de la Loire* 269–78.
[3] Aurelle, op. cit. 245–7.

Châteaudun on 26th November had laid Chanzy open to attack from the west, and only a stand by Lipowski's *francs-tireurs* at Varize on the river Conie enabled him to make dispositions to defend himself against Mecklenburg. The eastward movement on Pithiviers which was now demanded of him would involve a flank-march across Mecklenburg's front; and under the energetic direction of Stosch Mecklenburg's army was developing a concentration and an aggressiveness which it had until then notably lacked.[1] Before he could move eastward to collaborate with Pallières Chanzy had therefore to attack northwards to eliminate the immediate threat to his flank; and he advanced to do this on 1st December.

The rain had now stopped, and a light frost had set in: welcome to gunners and drivers who no longer had to manhandle their vehicles through rivers of mud, welcome also to the German troops for whom a resourceful *Intendantur* usually found billets in farm and barns, it increased the hardships of the French troops whose generals, stubbornly clinging to African precedent, kept them under the canvas of their in-adequate bivouac tents. Only Chanzy had abandoned this pointless practice and begun to find billets for his men; who were thus on 1st December able to advance on the German positions in good heart, moving rapidly across the iron-hard fields lightly powdered with snow.[2] They were confronted by the Bavarians, who were loosely spread out among the sparse villages in the plain west of Artenay, and unable to offer any immediate resistance. The French guns fired with accuracy and the infantry advanced with *élan*; the Bavarians were driven from position after position until they found in the walled farm of Villépion a strongpoint where they could rally and in rear of which Stosch could hurriedly organise an effective defence. But the French were encouraged and the Bavarians shaken; and at twilight Chanzy's leading divisional commander, Admiral Jauréguiberry, led an assault which swirled round the farm, smashed through the walls and overwhelmed its defenders. It was the second victory of the Army of the Loire, and was to be the last.[3]

That evening Chanzy sent back an ecstatic report which did nothing to belittle the achievement of his troops. For Gambetta it was the

---

[1] On 1st December Stosch urged Frederick Charles to allow him to take the offensive. Stosch to Stiehle, 1st December, Hönig *Volkskrieg* III 198.

[2] Chanzy, *2ᵉ Armée de la Loire* 62.

[3] For accounts of the battle see *G.G.S.* III 327–9. Hönig, *Volkskreig* III 236–47. Helvig, *1st Bavarian Corps* 256–65. Chanzy, op. cit. 62. Lehautcourt, *Campagne de la Loire* I 294–8.

climax to a day of excellent news. He had already received a second despatch from Paris, sent like its predecessor by balloon, which described, also without understatement, the results of the first day's fighting in the attempted break-out at Champigny. This despatch stated that the village of Épinay had been taken—Épinay-sur-Seine, that is, which had been captured in a diversionary attack northwards from St Denis. But at Tours this was taken to mean Épinay-sur-Orge, a village a dozen miles due south of Paris, far behind the German lines of investment; and its capture could only mean that Trochu had broken through.[1] On 2nd December Gambetta issued a proclamation in language as lyrical as it was politically unwise.

> The genius of France, for the moment veiled, is appearing anew! [he wrote.] The Prussians can now judge the difference between a despot who fights to satisfy his whims and a People in Arms determined not to perish. . . . France and the universe will never forget that Paris first set the example, taught this policy and thus founded its moral supremacy in remaining faithful to the heroic spirit of the revolution. Long live Paris! Long live France! Long live the one, indivisible Republic![2]

It would have been difficult to outrage more profoundly or more succinctly the feeling of the officers who still led the French armies, and the largely Catholic, largely Royalist provinces whose wealth, industry, and manhood furnished the bulk of their strength. Only victory could have rendered such sentiments acceptable; and there was to be no victory.

§ 3 Loigny

This was the climax of the People's War in France. The events of the next two days were to destroy Gambetta's plans, not only on the Seine where Trochu abandoned as hopeless the attempt to break through the German lines, but on the Loire, where the exaggerated expectations aroused by Coulmiers and Villépion were shattered. Chanzy was the first to suffer. At first light on 2nd December, after a night of intense cold, Chanzy sent his columns forward from Villépion to assault Mecklenburg's main positions which stretched from north of the village of Loigny to the château of Goury and through the villages of

[1] *D.T.* I 560. See p. 343 below.
[2] Reinach I 59–64.

Lumeau, Baigneux, and Poupry to the Chartres road. The great snow-covered fields, bare of cover and sloping slightly down from Goury, put the attackers at a disadvantage; yet at first they met with some success. The Germans, who had themselves been preparing to attack, were taken by surprise.[1] The Bavarians only just had time to occupy Goury, and on their left 17th Division had to fight its way back into Lumeau. On the French left flank the *élan* of Jauréguiberry's division forced the Bavarians back yet further, and their *chassepots* smashed every attempt to counter-attack; but the garrison of Goury held out until the Prussians of 17th and 22nd Divisions recaptured Lumeau and took the French forces assaulting the château in the flank, driving them back in disorder. At the same time the German cavalry was advancing alarmingly round Chanzy's left flank. With both flanks menaced and its impetus exhausted 16th Corps began to fall back on the village of Loigny; and gradually the superior training of the Germans began to tell. From Loigny the French with their *chassepots* should have been able to beat off the Germans as they themselves had been beaten off from Goury; but they could not. They were weary, ill-officered, demoralised; ever larger groups were sidling off to the rear, and whole regiments were streaming back towards Orléans. Determined assaults by the Germans recaptured Loigny and drove the French back to their starting-point at Villépion, where the arrival of de Sonis with reinforcements from 17th Corps enabled them to make a stand. De Sonis himself, acting like the colonel he was rather than the corps commander he should have been, attempted at the head of a few hundred Papal Zouaves to lead a last counter-attack through the twilight on Loigny; but the Germans had reserves to meet it, and before their fire the charge collapsed, de Sonis falling badly wounded with more than half his men.[2]

Chanzy did not have to fight alone. General Peytavin's division, the left wing of 15th Corps, lay only a few miles to the east of Artenay, and had loyally marched to the guns, arriving soon after midday to menace the German flank at Poupry. 22nd Prussian Division swung round to meet the threat, and in the copses north of the village a tough and even battle swayed to and fro throughout the afternoon. But at Poupry as at Loigny the French were thwarted in their attempt to break the German line. It was not surprising. To the 45,000 French troops attacking the

---

[1] See Mecklenburg's orders of 6 p.m. 1st December, in Hönig, *Volkskrieg* IV 16.

[2] Hönig, op. cit. IV 133. *D.T.* III (de Sonis) 259–61. H. de Sonis, *Le 17ᵉ Corps à Loigny* (1909).

Germans had been able to oppose 35,000 men, and an equal number of guns.[1] Altogether during the day the French suffered between six and seven thousand casualties and inflicted 4,139, leaving 2,500 prisoners in German hands.[2]

Aurelle meanwhile had spent the day at Artenay, listening to the noise of Chanzy's battle and waiting for the moment to carry on the advance to Pithiviers. According to Freycinet, most of the German strength had been withdrawn from the Loire to deal with the sortie from Paris, and he had only a thin screen of troops before him.[3] But that night the news of Chanzy's repulse made it clear that the whole advance must be abandoned. Aurelle assumed the responsibility of which his civilian superiors had for so long deprived him, and, hoping that he might still save his army, ordered a general retreat to Orléans. It was too late. Freycinet's optimistic appreciation of the German intentions and movements could hardly have been further from the truth: in fact Frederick Charles was at last preparing to attack. That very day, 2nd December, Moltke had sent him a direct order to advance on Orléans.[4] The Prince still had his doubts—doubts which, thanks to Waldersee's presence at his Headquarters, he could and did communicate to the King. He did not believe that the main body of the French lay before him on the main Orléans–Paris road south of Artenay, and he was obsessed by the fear that, if he attacked in the centre, the French would march past his flanks northwards towards Paris.[5] But Moltke was obdurate, and the Prince ordered an offensive for 3rd December. IX Corps was to capture Artenay and drive straight down the main Orléans road; III Corps was to advance from Pithiviers on Chilleurs-aux-Bois and through the forest to Loury; X Corps was to move in from the left flank and act as a reserve. To Mecklenburg he assigned the task of closing in on the Orléans road from the west, to drive the French on to Orléans.

Stosch objected. He had hoped to operate independently, driving south and west to cut off Chanzy's retreat; but the Prince refused to modify his strategy. The entire strength of the German forces was to

---

[1] Lehautcourt's figures, in *Campagne de la Loire* I 325.
[2] For accounts of the battle see *G.G.S.* II i 330–43. Helvig, *1st Bavarian Corps* 268 ff. L. von Wittich, *Aus meinem Kriegstagebuch 1870–71* (Cassel 1872) 248–68. Hönig IV *passim*. Stosch, *Denkwürdigkeiten* 212–3. Freycinet, *Guerre en Province* 144–51. Chanzy, *2ᵉ Armée de la Loire* 70–7. Aurelle, *1ʳᵉ Armée de la Loire* 306–9.
[3] Aurelle, op. cit. 321.
[4] Frederick Charles, *Denkwürdigkeiten* II 382.
[5] Frederick Charles, op. cit. 378. Hönig, *Volkskrieg* III 41, 60, 117–20.

be concentrated against the French centre; and there lay not, as Moltke believed, the bulk of the French army, but only Pallières's thinly extended 15th Corps. It is not surprising that the Germans, in spite of their numerical inferiority, were to break clean through the Forest of Orléans and cut the Army of the Loire in two. But the victory was easy at the price of being inconclusive. The Army of the Loire was to be defeated, but not destroyed.[1]

The weather was now worsening, and the next few days and nights were horrible with wind and snow. To hold the untrained, ill-clad French troops together under such conditions would have been difficult even if they had been advancing triumphantly as Freycinet had hoped; under Frederick Charles's blows they disintegrated. He attacked on the morning of 3rd December, mainly against the two villages of Artenay and Chilleurs-aux-Bois. The Germans themselves, advancing through thick woodland in two isolated columns along icy roads against an enemy in long-prepared positions and believed to be in overwhelming strength, were more conscious of the peril of their own position than of the threat they presented to the enemy[2]; but fortune was to favour III and X Corps as remarkably as it had at Vionville, and so did the improved German tactics. Daylight revealed the plains before the French positions to be covered with German troops, and at once a weight of artillery fire came down on the villages which reminded veterans of the siege of Sebastopol and to which Pallières's few batteries could make no reply. Frederick Charles was using the methods of Sedan; he did not launch his infantry to attack until his artillery had crushed all resistance.[3] For most of the day the French units remained under control, falling back by orderly bounds, and Aurelle still hoped that under the guns of Orléans he would be able to halt, reorganise, and re-establish his positions. But that night he took stock of the condition of the army and realised that any such stand was impossible. The night was bitterly cold; snow

---

[1] Frederick Charles, op. cit. 379–82. Hönig, op. cit. IV 204 ff., Stosch *Denkwürdigkeiten* 213.

[2] See Alvensleben's comments in Hönig op. cit. V 78–9.

[3] Frederick Charles wrote in his notebook at the beginning of November: "Meine Taktik soll darin bestehen, Ansammlungen von Feinden nicht zu verhindern, sondern durch Zuwarten zu unterstützen, damit man einigermassen grosse und vernichtende Schläge führen kann. . . . Resultatlose Frontalgefechte sind also zu vermeiden. Bei allen uns etwa noch bevorstehenden Kämpfen, besonders um Dörfer oder Städte, muss noch mehr als bisher die Artillerie gebraucht werden, die Nester in Brand stecken, und ganz zuletzt erst darf die Infanterie ins Gefecht und dann umfassend, um die Gesellschaft in Empfang zu nehmen." *Denkwürdigkeiten* II 315.

had fallen heavily during the evening; and the army was falling to pieces. Only in a few units were men still obeying their officers, and Aurelle saw for himself that the road back to Orléans was covered with panic-stricken regiments which, having fought bravely all day, were now openly abandoning the battlefield. This was 15th Corps, the experienced nucleus of his army; reports from the flanks showed that 17th and 20th Corps were in an even worse state. Aurelle drew the only possible conclusion, that Orléans must be abandoned and the army once again withdrawn to the safety of the Sologne.[1]

Freycinet could hardly believe the news. There would be no need for the retreat of an army of 200,000 men, he wired, "if their leaders could stiffen their courage and patriotism by their own resolute example". Why, he asked Aurelle, could he not call in Billot and Crouzat, who were lying idle on the right wing? Aurelle replied that it was too late, and the troops were too demoralised for such a manœuvre to succeed. He was on the spot and could judge: unless a general retreat was sanctioned there would be no army left.[2]

For Gambetta and Freycinet the blow was a terrible one. They had built their hopes and their reputations on the success of the attack and they could hardly bring themselves to abandon it. To spread the responsibility Gambetta consulted for the first time Crémieux and Glaise-Bizoin, who could only acquiesce in a state of affairs which was none of their making; and on the morning of 4th December he sent off formal permission for the abandonment of Orléans.[3] But then Aurelle telegraphed again; he thought he might after all be able to hold the city. Orléans was still strongly armed; retreat was concentrating the French forces; and the reliable Pallières had withdrawn at least one of his divisions in fair order. But a consultation with his commanders showed that such hopes were illusory. 15th Corps barely existed any longer as an organised formation. Officers and men were scattered through the town, in hotels and *cafés* and private houses, shaking off the slender ties of duty and obedience and seeking in sleep or drunkenness some solace for the horrors of the past twenty-four hours. Everywhere reigned the confusion and impotence which attend on armies in defeat. When at 4 p.m. Aurelle finally decided to abandon the city and leave Pallières to form the rear-guard, nobody told Pallières. When he learned

---

[1] *D.T.* III (Pallières) 238–9, (Borel) 492. Aurelle, *1re Armée de la Loire* 320–33.

[2] Freycinet, *La Guerre en Province* 164–6. Borel (*D.T.* III 486) confirmed Aurelle's judgment, that 18 and 20 Corps were now militarily useless.

[3] J. P. T. Bury, *Gambetta and the National Defence* 192.

of his rôle he could find no troops to carry it out, and the advancing Germans were held in check only by a few groups of infantry and gunners, who fell back through the suburbs step by step and were able in that close, built-up country to delay the fall of the city until night.[1]

From Chanzy there was no news. He was falling back to the south-west before the advance of Mecklenburg's Detachment, and trying in vain to rally his own shaken forces to strike at Frederick Charles's flank. Bourbaki, who had assumed command of 18th Corps during the battle, was shepherding his troops up the Loire to Gien; and Crouzat, bringing back 20th Corps through the forest from the east, found him-self cut off from Orléans by the German advance and was barely able to get his men across a partly demolished bridge at Jargeau. By late afternoon the Germans had reached the river on either side of the city. To the west trains were still running on the railway to Tours; in one of them was Gambetta, coming to see the situation for himself. A few shells from a German horse battery provided explanation enough, and his train reversed in the nick of time.

By 8 p.m. the Prussian 17th Division had driven between the French 15th and 16th Corps north-west of Orléans, and its commander, General von Tresckow, sent in a formal *parlementaire* to demand the surrender of the city on pain of bombardment. It was largely bluff: the main German forces had been ordered to halt for the night,[2] and only a spearhead—and that without any heavy guns—was available to carry out the threat. But Pallières was glad to accept; only by doing so, he believed, would he be able to get his men away.[3] Large numbers of *débandés* remained to watch with drunken indifference the Germans march into the city; and soon after midnight on 4th–5th December Orléans was, for the second time, and finally, in German hands. Aurelle's army was scattering east, west and south, having lost 18,000 prisoners, 2,000 wounded and dead[4]; and earlier the same day Ducrot's army had abandoned the battlefield of Champigny and marched half-frozen back into Paris.

[1] Pallières, *Orléans* 215 ff. Aurelle, op. cit. 344.
[2] Army Order of 6.45 p.m. Hönig, *Volkskrieg* VI 94.
[3] *D.T.* III (Pallières) 240–1. T. Krieg, *Hermann v. Tresckow* (Berlin 1911) 92–5.
[4] Lehautcourt, *Campagne de la Loire* I 378. *G.G.S.* II i 364.

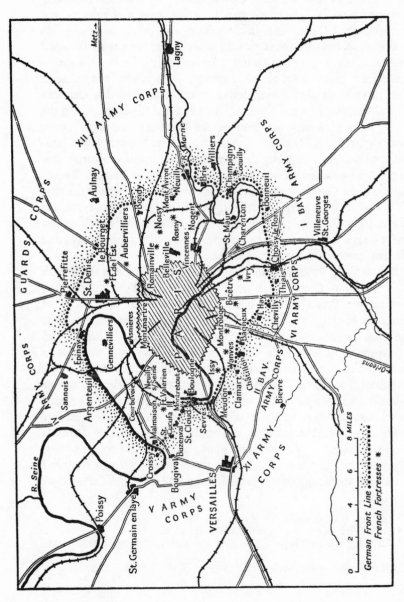

Map 14: The Siege of Paris

CHAPTER IX

The Siege of Paris

§1 The Investment

SINCE 19th September the official Government of France had been immured in Paris. For its members the conduct of the war therefore consisted of measures for the defence and relief of the capital, and this conception had been with them since they first assumed office. The defence of the city, in Trochu's words, was to be "our great and final effort. Nobody then considered", he admitted, "what the provinces might be able to do." In a proclamation of 6th September the *Journal Officiel* asserted that "power must be where the fighting is. . . . It is on Paris that the invading army is now marching: it is on Paris that the hopes of the country are concentrated." This proclamation determined the course of the remainder of the war.

It was not unreasonable to argue that Paris was the supreme objective whose capture would decide the issue of hostilities. Strategy is not a matter of geometry but of politics, and politics in their turn are a matter of tradition and sentiment. So successfully have the monarchs of France centralised power in their capital that even in the twentieth century no Government deprived of its resources of administration and prestige has been able to command the loyalty of the nation. With Paris in the hands of the Germans, resistance could be no more than sporadic guerrilla activity by groups enjoying a decreasing degree of public support. The arguments for defending Paris were overwhelming; but the argument that the Government should remain on the spot, and attempt to organise the National Defence from a beleaguered city, made no sense at all. It is misleading, however, to talk of the Government's "decision" to remain at Paris: only a handful of its members considered doing anything else[1]; and when at the last moment the Delegation was sent to the provinces, the object was largely that of sparing

[1] *D.T.* I 548.

their more elderly members the hardships of a siege.[1] In retrospect such an attitude may seem ludicrous; but one must bear in mind, not simply the egotism from which the politicians of Paris are even now not totally immune, but the difficulty of conceiving that Paris, that vast and populous *ville lumière*, the centre of civilisation and so recently, at the Exhibition of 1867, the hostess to the world, could really, in the second half of the nineteenth century, be invested, bombarded and assaulted like a fortress in the wars of Louis XIV.[2] The fortifications were there, and preparations for a siege were being made; there could be no doubt that the Germans had men enough to invest the city, though it was doubtful whether the railways could supply them. But even so a siege was inconceivable; as inconceivable, perhaps, as we find war with thermo-nuclear weapons today.

Preparations for the defence of the city had, in one form or another, been going on for fifty years. The first Napoleon had bitterly regretted that Paris was not fortified, and to this he attributed in very large measure the failure of his final campaigns. "If Paris had still been a fortress in 1814 and 1815, able to hold out for only eight days, what influence would that have not had on the events of the world?" he demanded.[3] Others had drawn similar lessons; but nothing was done until 1840, when the Near East crisis, which made European war a possibility for the first time since 1815, enabled Thiers, that enthusiastic amateur of strategy, to equip Paris with a gigantic series of fortifications at a cost of 140 million francs. Then the city was surrounded by an *enceinte* wall thirty-three feet high, provided with ninety-four bastions and covered by a moat ten feet wide. Barring all approach to the city, as the increased range of artillery now made necessary, were fifteen detached forts. The west, where the triple bend of the Seine gives good protection against assault, was covered only by the commanding height of Mont Valérien. The north was protected by the fortified village of St Denis, which was linked to Paris by two smaller forts, de l'Est and Aubervilliers. To the east a group of forts covered the heights on the right bank of the Marne—Romainville, Noisy, Rosny, and Nogent; and between the Marne and Seine lay the fort of Charenton. South of the Seine lay the five forts of Ivry, Bicêtre, Montrouge, Vanves, and Issy—barring access

---

[1] Jules Favre, who as Foreign Minister had the best claim to leave the city, insisted on remaining "là où était le combat, là où serait la souffrance." See Desmarest, *La Défense Nationale* 121.

[2] *D.T.* (Garnier-Pagès) 433, (Picard) 487, III (Ducrot) 108.

[3] Qu. in *Guerre: Investissement de Paris* I 44. From this work I have taken the details of the arming and provisioning of Paris which follow.

to the *enceinte*, it is true, but uncomfortably overlooked by the Châtillon heights to the south, where only one fortified work, the Châtillon redoubt, had been erected, and that on the extreme northern edge. The total perimeter of the fortifications was thirty-eight miles; and to encompass this the investing army would need to cover about fifty miles—a task which seemed almost unthinkable, even in 1870, and which only Moltke's huge armies could have achieved.

It can be well imagined that work on the defences of Paris received a very low priority at the outbreak of a war which was to be fought, according to popular and official expectation, in Germany; but the news of Spicheren and Froeschwiller shocked the authorities into activity. A mixed committee of civilians and soldiers was established to deal with the fortifications, of which the veteran Marshal Vaillant, a survivor of the original 1840 Commission, became the president, and equipped with a credit of twelve million francs it set to work. Additional redoubts were constructed; roads were broken up; vast obstructions were erected round the city; woods and buildings were razed to provide a field of fire, the ornamental woods at Vincennes, Meudon, St Cloud and Boulogne being saved only by their size. Mines, electrically detonated, were laid in likely lanes of approach. All quarries and excavations outside the walls were mapped and where necessary sealed. Road and rail entrances to the city were blocked, and a barricade was laid across the Seine. With the assistance of the navy, more than three thousand heavy guns were collected, of which about half were posted in the forts, a further eight hundred were mounted within the *enceinte*, and the remainder were kept in reserve, with teams of horses standing by to draw them.[1] Every arsenal and suitable workshop in the city was set to work to produce shells; workshops were improvised for the transformation of muzzle-loading rifles, and the manufacture of *mitrailleuses* and *chassepots*.[2] Finally, a small but powerful flotilla, originally intended to sail on the Rhine, was collected on the Seine to provide mobile fire power. By mid-September the city had become one of the most powerfully armed fortresses that Europe had ever seen.

By 4th September the provisioning of the city, with its garrison and its population swollen by refugees, was already far advanced. A stock of

[1] *D.T.* I 137.
[2] 400 breech-loading guns were manufactured, but only 40 were accepted by the military authorities as safe. Vinoy, *Siège de Paris* 287. No *chassepot*, in fact, was completed before the end of the siege, but their manufacture at least kept the workers busy. Armaments workers played little part in the riots during the siege. *D.T.* I (Dorian) 525–6.

flour and corn had been accumulated which was expected to last for eighty days, and forty thousand oxen and a quarter of a million sheep were set to browse in the Bois de Boulogne.[1] There was not enough room for all; many had to be killed at once and salted; and no provision was made for milch cows—an oversight from which the children of the city were to suffer terribly.[2] As for fuel, the gas companies reckoned, on 22nd August, to have coal for seventy-eight days,[3] and no one expected the siege to last into the winter. It was generally presumed that the Germans would attack. The city would be able to repel their attacks, inflicting huge casualties, for about a month; and by then a relief army would have been raised in the provinces, to fall on the rear of the enemy and complete its rout.

Troops were available in almost embarrassing quantity. In the first place there were the two new corps, 13th and 14th, which Palikao had formed in Paris. To call these "regular forces" would be misleading, for both consisted almost entirely of untrained conscripts and depôt troops who had forgotten what little of the military art they had ever known. 14th Corps, commanded by General Renault, had never left the city, and its organisation was at first so faulty that for several days the troops had nothing to eat, and swarmed in the streets begging from passers-by. General Vinoy's 13th Corps contained the only regular regiments still at liberty—the 35th and 42nd, which had formerly garrisoned Rome. This corps, despatched to join MacMahon, had been at Mézières when the Army of Châlons surrendered at Sedan. Vinoy had extricated it with some skill from under the noses of the German cavalry and brought it back to the capital, together with about 10,000 refugees from MacMahon's forces.[4] In addition there were about 3,000 Marines, who had not formed part of Lebrun's corps in the Army of Châlons, and 8,000 sailors, disciplined and reliable. These forces of the regular army and navy totalled something over 106,000 officers and men. Then there was the *Garde Mobile*; not simply the eighteen battalions brought back by Trochu from Châlons, but a further 100,000 summoned from the provinces to the defence of the capital. The ruling principle of Trochu's strategy seems indeed to have been the accumulation of the largest possible force inside Paris. Over this issue he had strongly opposed Palikao, when the Minister of War had insisted on

---

[1] *Guerre: Investissement de Paris* I: Docs. annexes 126. *D.T.* I (Ferry) 418, (Magnin) 512.
[2] *Guerre: Investissement de Paris* I: 180–5.
[3] Ibid. 187.
[4] Ibid. I 13, II 51. *D.T.* III (General Vinoy), 112–15.

sending 13th Corps to join MacMahon; now he had as colleagues only civilians whose views were even more parochial than his own. So every train from the provinces brought in further crowds of *mobiles* and of *sapeurs pompiers*; village fire-brigades from the depths of the Midi or the uplands of Auvergne who wandered round the boulevards wearing fantastic helmets and speaking unintelligible patois, until in the nick of time they were rounded up again and sent back to their native villages as suddenly and inexplicably as they had come.[1]

The fall of the Empire and their return to Paris had done nothing to mollify the ferocious indiscipline of the *Mobiles* of the Seine. Indeed renewed contact with the fountain-head of revolution at Belleville and the Faubourg St Antoine made them yet more unmanageable. They had played a considerable part in the events of 4th September: at their camp at St Maur the presence of crowds of their friends and relations made discipline impossible; and their touching faith in the innate superiority of free Frenchmen over the disciplined hordes of the Prussian tyrant excused them, in their own eyes, from practising the more tedious branches of military science. Their value both political and military was doubtful; and they faced the regular military commanders across a gulf of mutual suspicion hardly less profound than that which separated them from the Prussians themselves.

In addition to the *Garde Mobile* there was the *Garde Sédentaire* of Paris: all male citizens between the ages of twenty-five and thirty-five, about 200,000 men all told, armed with anything available. The original qualification, that membership should be confined to electors, had gone by the board. No longer was the National Guard a bourgeois counter-revolutionary militia: it was the People of Paris in arms, and the Government may well have wondered against whom these arms were to be used. Finally there was a multiplicity of private volunteer formations, armed and uniformed as the fancy took them, which a harassed Ministry of War tried to reduce to uniformity with mediocre success. There were the *Légion des Volontaires de France*, composed of Polish exiles; *Les Amis de France*, an organisation of Belgian, Italian and British residents in Paris; the *Francs-tireurs de la Presse*, a literary unit raised by the novelist Gustave Aymard; and innumerable groups of provincial, suburban and metropolitan *guerrillas, francs-tireurs*, and *carabiniers*.[2]

[1] Comte d'Hérisson, *Journal of a Staff Officer* 43. Henri Guillemin in *Cette curieuse Guerre de 70* (Paris 1956) a stimulating but partisan work, suggests plausibly that the object of summoning them was to keep the population of Paris in order.

[2] *Guerre: Investissement de Paris* I 365–87.

This heterogeneous concourse was assembled for a monster review on 14th September in the Champs Elysées, and most of Paris turned out to cheer them.

> More than a million human creatures [wrote Trochu afterwards], soldiers and sailors in uniform, National Guardsmen and armed civilians, and watching crowds filling with their intermingled and tightly squeezed ranks the great roads which stretched from the Place de la Bastille to the Arc de Triomphe, through the boulevards, the Place de la Concorde and the Champs Elysées! At every window of surrounding buildings, on the balconies and the terraces there were further ranks of moving heads, of flags, of patriotic emblems. Every voice was shouting, all arms were moving, it was a delirium!

"Never has any general", ran, with some truth, Trochu's Order of the Day, "had before his eyes such a spectacle as you have just given me"; and he went on to demand, hopefully, "order, calm and devotion".[1]

Such were the forces at Trochu's disposal. What did he propose to do with them? The passive defence of the fortifications presented few difficulties. The forts themselves were held by sailors, who were ordered to defend them as they would their ships.[2] The *enceinte* was divided into nine sections, each with its own artillery and engineer commands, and held by the *Garde Sédentaire*; the *Mobiles* provided first-line reserves, and the two regular corps were kept back as second-line reserves. But was this huge garrison simply to sit within the city walls? Was any attempt to be made to delay the German advance, to fight for the Châtillon plateau, even to occupy the additional outworks which had been constructed by Lebœuf? Should communications to the south be kept open? What should be done with the cavalry of 13th and 14th Corps? All these problems were resolved for Trochu by his belief, which the review of 14th September did nothing to shake, that the men under his command were in no condition to meet the Germans in the open field. Most of his cavalry he despatched to the Loire. The rest of the troops were to remain within the fortifications and await the German assault. Even if the Germans breached the walls, the city would be defended street by street, and in such fighting the indiscipline and lack of training of the French forces would be unimportant. And if the Germans did not attack? Then, Trochu told Picard, "the siege will become a heroic folly which we will commit to save the national honour when all else is lost".[3]

---

[1] Trochu, *Œuvres posthumes* I 218-21.
[2] *D.T.* III (Admiral Pothuau) 564. See also Baron de la Roncière, *La Marine au Siège de Paris* (Paris 1872) *passim*.   [3] Trochu, *Œuvres posthumes* I 303.

One useful ally had arrived to help Trochu in his task—the ubiquitous General Ducrot, who had succeeded in escaping from captivity in the confusion which attended the evacuation of MacMahon's army from Sedan to Germany. Trochu appointed him to the command of the two regular army corps in the city; not without bitter offence to their commanders. Vinoy was ten years senior to Ducrot, and he showed dissatisfaction on every possible occasion; and this factor additionally complicated a structure of command which was already quite complex enough.[1] Ducrot and Trochu had much in common. Both had long foreseen and prophesied the *débâcle*, and both realised the futility of the operations to which they were now pledged. But whereas Trochu, anxious to avoid useless bloodshed, wished to keep operations down to the minimum consonant with political pressure and national honour, and to allow the Germans to batter in vain against the great labyrinth of Paris, Ducrot, ardent by temperament and anxious to reap some revenge for the disasters through which he had passed, was determined to attack if it was humanly possible. In particular, to abandon without a fight the Châtillon redoubt which so decisively dominated the southern forts of Paris seemed to him military lunacy. Finally, whereas Trochu, in spite of his devout Catholicism, glumly accepted revolution as the inevitable destiny of France, and belonged to the school of soldiers who were prepared to place their swords at the service of any régime, Ducrot was an authoritarian, a man of December, whose passion for order revolted against the ideas and aspirations of the Left. As head of a Republican Government Trochu had to treat the moderate Left with the respect due to his masters; as Governor of Paris he felt bound to avert civil war by appeasing the extremists of the Left up to the limits of possibility. With such prevarication Ducrot had no patience. If Trochu wanted to postpone the military and political disasters which threatened Paris, Ducrot preferred to rush on both, sword in hand, and achieve heroic victory or heroic defeat. But neither for one minute considered submitting to the national enemy so as to deal the better with *le péril intérieur*. The political quarrels were local: Ducrot, Trochu, Rochefort, and Delescluze stood in genuine if short-lived national unity to meet the forces which swept down on Paris from the north.

* * *

Moltke had given out his orders for the investment from Château-Thierry on 15th September, and on the 17th the two German armies

[1] A. Ducrot, *La Défense de Paris* (Paris 1875-8) I 211.

began their encirclement. The Crown Prince of Saxony established his forces opposite the northern forts without opposition, the northern arm of a pair of pincers curling round the city, but for the Crown Prince of Prussia the investment of the southern half presented much greater problems. On 17th September his leading troops, moving westward towards the Seine at Villeneuve St Georges, became involved with a strong force of Vinoy's 13th Corps which had marched out in a last-minute attempt to clear a depôt of supplies, and the Germans had to force a passage by brisk artillery fire.[1] Next day, while cavalry scouted ahead to Versailles—whose governor reconciled honour and common sense by refusing to surrender the town except to a force of respectable size—the infantry was drawn into episodic but unpleasant skirmishes with the French outposts south of the city; and on the 19th it was involved in a battle of considerable proportions. Ducrot had persuaded Trochu that some attempt at least should be made to defend the Châtillon heights and established 14th Corps between Meudon and Châtillon with instructions to defend the plateau for as long as they could.[2] The line of their outposts flanked the German line of advance from the Seine towards Versailles, and to allow the enemy to defile past him undisturbed was more than Ducrot could stand. With Trochu's hesitant approval he launched his men, on the early morning of 19th September, in an offensive movement towards the Versailles road. He hoped that the limited task he had set them was not beyond their capacity; but he was wrong. The French troops were too inexperienced and under-officered to be deployed: they advanced southward through the morning mists in thick masses which offered a splendid target to the German guns. Shellfire brought them to a halt, the right wing collapsed completely and streamed down through the woods to Meudon to carry into the outskirts of the city their dismal, vicious cry "We are betrayed!" The rest of the corps disintegrated in confusion, and Ducrot was able to find only a handful of regiments and batteries to attempt a last stand behind the fortifications of the Châtillon redoubt, to strengthen which engineers had been working through the night. But even this position proved indefensible: its water came from the works at Choisy-le-Roi, and these in the confusion which attends almost all retreating armies had been destroyed the previous day to prevent their falling into German hands. During the afternoon Ducrot abandoned the position, and its garrison followed the rest of the army down the

---

[1] *G.G.S.* II i 38. Vinoy, *Siège de Paris* 136–40.
[2] *Guerre: Investissement de Paris* I 96, II 262.

slopes towards Paris, leaving a rich booty in colours, equipment, and guns. By evening German patrols occupied the entire edge of the plateau and looked down in wonder and satisfaction at the sea of houses which lay at their feet: Paris, the Queen of Europe, the modern Babylon; to all appearances at their mercy.[1]

Thus the siege of Paris began. The Germans cut the railway to Orléans on 17th September, and on the 20th the cavalry patrols of both German armies met near St Germain-en-Laye, sealing off the last road to the west. For communication with the outside world the city now depended on two unorthodox channels. The first was by river. With great secrecy a cable had been laid on the bed of the Seine, its existence known only to a few members of the Government and officials of the *Postes et Télégraphes*. It did not come into operation until 23rd September, and then it functioned properly only for twenty-four hours. Next day it was badly damaged and on 27th September the Germans dredged it up and, finding themselves unable to decipher the telegrams they intercepted, destroyed it.[2] Another ingenious project for floating messages down the river in hollow zinc globes, to be intercepted by nets, also broke down.[3] It was introduced only at the onset of winter, and the nets were almost at once carried away by ice-floes. The Parisians were thus entirely dependent on the second and even less orthodox means of communication: balloons.

Balloons were by no means new in war. During the Wars of the Revolution the Committee of Public Safety, whose ingenuity in pressing science into the service of their war machine was a worthy precedent for the Government of National Defence, had experimented with them for observation and for communication; but Napoleon had ignored them, and their use disappeared from European armies. But by 1870 the development of coal gas had made balloons a more reasonable proposition than they had been eighty years earlier, and in the early days of the war an enthusiastic inventor, M. Godard, pressed them on the attention of the Ministry of War. Lebœuf paid little attention, but Palikao, to whose brief ministry so many measures of the Government of National Defence can be traced, took the matter up. After experiments had been made with captive balloons a daring aeronaut set out from Montmartre

---

[1] For the battle of Châtillon see *G.G.S.* II i 44–51. *Guerre: Investissement de Paris* II 400–74. Ducrot, *Défense de Paris* I 18–50.

[2] *D.T.* II (Steenackers) 82. *Guerre: Investissement de Paris* I 215. Verdy du Vernois, *With the Royal Headquarters* 170. Darimon, *Notes pour servir à l'histoire* 260–66.

[3] *D.T.* II (Rampont) 75.

on 23rd September, was wafted over the investing lines at a height of ten thousand feet and three hours later came safely down sixty-five miles away near Evreux.[1] After three more experimental flights a contract was placed with Godard to provide balloons, to be used primarily for carrying mail, and carrier-pigeons to make the return journey. On 26th September a regular postal service was introduced, balloons leaving two or three times a week. Photography was brought into play to facilitate the delivery of inward messages. All messages for transmission by pigeon were centralised at Tours, typed in columns like a newspaper and reduced to microscopic size. Postal orders were treated in the same way, as was the *Moniteur Universel*, and so perfected did this system become that eventually thirty thousand messages could be sent by a single pigeon.[2] As for outward messages, a total weight of 10,675 kilograms was sent out of Paris in sixty-five balloons, as well as 164 passengers, 381 pigeons and five dogs.[3] Such a method was irregular and uncertain. Pigeons went astray and thousands of messages with them. Balloons were wafted out to sea, or fell into the hands of the Germans with a mass of valuable information about Parisian morale.[4] But on the whole the city preserved contact with the outside world to a remarkable degree; and this contact did something to make more tolerable the lives of the inhabitants which, after the first exhilaration and strangeness had died away, grew ever more depressing.

Paris was the first great urban community to experience the ordeals of wartime shortage and regimentation which were to become so drearily familiar to the cities of Europe during the twentieth century; and those ordeals were embittered by the political struggles which grew sharper as food and fuel dwindled. The Government had taken minimal measures to regulate consumption. Grain was requisitioned and the slaughter of cattle controlled; meat-rationing was introduced at the beginning of October. But bread, though its quality deteriorated, remained unrationed until the last weeks of the siege; and the prices of all foodstuffs rose so steeply that the poor of the city faced a serious prospect of starvation.[5] The flocks of oxen and sheep grazing in the

[1] C. Chevalier, *Tours Capitale* 79.   [2] *D.T.* II (Rampont) 70.
[3] Steenackers, *Les Télégraphes et les Postes pendant la guerre de 1870–1* (1883) 392, 394, 457. Georges Brunel, *Les Ballons du Siège de Paris* (Paris 1933).
[4] Frederick III, *War Diary* 190.
[5] Jules Ferry, the Minister responsible, denied the practicability of rationing. "Je le tiens, appliqué à une population civile . . . pour la plus immense chimère que l'on puisse imaginer. Nous avons eu à lutter contre cette folie. C'était un des grands griefs du parti démagogique. . . . Le rêve de ce parti était de faire un universal emmagasinage et d'appeler tout le monde à la gamelle patriotique."

Bois de Boulogne melted away like snowdrifts in summer, and the Government turned to horsemeat to honour the ration. There can be little doubt that all Parisians who possessed prudence and resources had laid in large stocks before rationing was introduced, and the restaurants of the well-to-do never ran seriously short. Rats and cats were served in wealthy houses only *"par bravade de dilettantisme"*[1]; the famous menus composed entirely from the flesh of animals from the Jardin d'Acclimatation, from which a zebra, a yak, two buffaloes, two wapiti, two camels, and two elephants were hauled off to the butchers, were the results of ingenious exhibitionism rather than stark necessity. But for much of the population normal fare was not available. Fresh vegetables and milk disappeared, cat and dog butchers multiplied in the meaner streets. The queue, that ubiquitous symbol of total war, became an intrinsic part of Parisian life. The city grew colder as fuel ran short, darker as gas was economised, and increasingly hungry. The romantic enthusiasm of the early weeks, when everyone swaggered in a home-made volunteer's uniform with a rifle and the noisy patriotism of the theatres and cafés spilled over into the boulevards, all died gradually away. Café life dwindled under increasing Government restrictions, and the population became obsessed with the problem of collecting enough food to keep alive.

For the men it was not so bad. The army rationing-system functioned separately and reasonably well. The *Garde Nationale* was provided with food and occupation, and the Government made provision for the unemployed.[2] But, as always, it was the women who suffered most, especially the women of the lower middle classes: queueing outside the food-shops, scrounging for milk for their children, working grimly to keep their families alive in a world which their husbands had so deplorably mismanaged. Cases of pillage and open robbery increased; towards the end of the year large mobs were tearing down wooden palisades, trees, hutments, anything that could be burned, and the police could do nothing to stop them.[3] The rage of the Parisians against

---

"Au lieu de ration, nous avons changé la qualité du pain. C'était, j'en conviens, du pain détestable. J'en porterai jusqu'au tombeau la responsabilité." *D.T.* I 419, 421.

[1] Desmarest, *La Défense Nationale* 335. D'Hérisson, *Journal of a Staff Officer* 224–6.

[2] "C'était les ateliers nationaux de 1848 sous une autre forme." Ducrot, *Défense de Paris* III 223 n. 1. *Cantines municipales* were also set up, where five centimes bought a meal of rice, soup, bread, vegetables, and potatoes. *D.T.* I 536, IV 414.

[3] See Police Reports for December in *D.T.* V ii 147 ff.

the invaders became tinged with a sullen anger against their own governors, and neither emotion was to be appeased by the conclusion of peace.[1]

How was a Government largely composed of doctrinaire Liberals to deal with a situation which demanded the greatest degree of government control? Their helplessness in face of demands so totally outside their experience aroused general discontent, and, on the Left, increasing fury. The press attacks were unceasing, garnished with reiterated demands for all the nostrums of '93—the Commune, the *levée en masse*, the Committee of Public Safety. The wildest rumours were circulated. The German fleet was prisoner; all the Poles in the German army were planning a mass surrender; in Berlin demonstrations were being held against the war. Military information was freely printed, and the Germans had little difficulty in keeping fully abreast of their enemy's plans. Ernest Picard, one of the more realistic members of the Government, openly demanded the suppression of all newspapers during the siege. Jules Favre strongly opposed the suggestion; but by the end of November, on Favre's own admission, the newspapers were making government almost impossible.[2] Yet the Government took no action; partly from fear of the political consequences which might follow, but largely from a genuine desire not to fall back into the evil paths of the Empire. Arago, Ferry, Simon, and their colleagues had been the leading advocates of the ideals of free speech and of the Nation in Arms. Now they had translated the ideal into reality; but they could not admit that in engaging in armed conflict they were entering an element in which the absolutes of their Liberalism could not survive.[3]

The political difficulties of the Government were not even redeemed by any ray of military hope. Trochu, as we have seen, believed that the city could be defended only if the Germans launched a headlong attack. Within a few days of the investment it was clear that Moltke was

---

[1] On 5th January 1871 the police reports noted: "il faut prendre garde, la désorganisation sociale y aidant, à ces colères des citoyens les uns contre les autres. Il se creuse ainsi dans la population des abîmes, et le danger de la guerre civile double de plus en plus celui de la guerre étrangère". *D.T.* V ii 158.

[2] Ducrot, *Défense de Paris* III 359. Favre, *Gouvernement de la Défense Nationale* I 297.

[3] Among the enormous literature on the siege of Paris, Georges D'Heylli, *Journal du Siège de Paris* (3 vols Paris 1871) provides by far the best collection of source material. Melvin Kranzberg, *The Siege of Paris 1870–1871* (Cornell 1950) gives a good, if brief, account of life in general. Among personal accounts, J. Adam, *Mes illusions et nos souffrances pendant le siège de Paris* (1906) is particularly illuminating.

proposing to do nothing of the sort. His troops were settling in around the city for a siege.[1] On the right bank of the Seine IV Corps occupied a segment from Croissy to Pierrefitte opposite the guns of St Denis. To their left the Guard held Le Bourget as a precarious outpost, the rest of their strength in reserve positions a mile or more in rear. The Royal Saxon Corps lay between Aulnay and the Marne; the Württemberg Division lined the south bank of the Marne as far as the peninsula of St Maur, and XI Corps carried the line on to the Seine at Choisy-le-Roi. Then came VI Corps, between Choisy and the Bievre; II Bavarian Corps on the Châtillon plateau; and V Corps covering Versailles, the headquarters of the Third Army and, after 5th October, of the King himself. Most of the villages in the occupied area had been abandoned by their inhabitants, who had fled to swell the population of the beleaguered city; consequently the German troops found billets with little difficulty, and with great thoroughness set about making their own positions as impregnable as the fortifications which they confronted. The fields north of the city were inundated by breaching the neighbouring canals. Villages were fortified and linked by communication-trenches. The woods and gardens which embellished the suburbs of the Seine round Bougival and Malmaison and St Cloud were devastated by Major-General von Sandrart of V Corps with a thoroughness which made the *Sandrartschen Verschönerungsverein* famous throughout the German army. Few villas escaped either outright destruction or transformation into strongpoints. The Palace of St Cloud itself, conveniently poised on a bluff above the Seine, served as an ideal observation-post until on 13th October it was destroyed by the guns of Mont Valérien. Everywhere the forward German line consisted only of lightly held outposts; behind lay a thick belt of defended localities, throughout which batteries were sited in depth; while far in rear of these, especially to the south and west, roamed the cavalry divisions, patrolling ever deeper into the centre of France to extend the requisition areas, sweep the country clean of *francs-tireurs*, and give warning of the appearance of any relieving force. Thus comfortably settled, Moltke proposed to await the capitulation with such patience as he could muster; meanwhile sending to Germany for siege-artillery in case the Parisians needed assistance in making up their minds.[2]

---

[1] *G.G.S.* II i 98–109.
[2] *M.M.K.* 324–6, 334. "Ich denke, sie sollen in ihren Barrikaden, Minen, Petroleum und Torpedos ersticken, wir wollen gar nicht hinein, sie sollen zu uns herauskommen." Moltke to Goeben, 20th October.

The French did not allow the siege works to continue undisturbed. Their heavy guns fired regularly, doing more good to French morale than damage to the enemy, and the German troops soon acquired that almost contemptuous familiarity with the guns of the other side which comes to all troops in static warfare. Friendly relations were quickly established between the outposts of the two armies. German sentries watched benevolently as Frenchwomen scoured the fields for potatoes; working arrangements were made for the alternate use of inns and bakers' shops lying between the two positions; and a direct traffic grew up between the two armies, winked at by the German General Staff, whereby the German sentries traded their rations for information, brandy, and newspapers.[1] For official parleying, or the transmission of communications by neutral powers, a post was established at Sèvres. There the bugles on either side of the river would sound a cease-fire. Then, for a mere parley, the officers concerned would clamber over the barricades at either end of the bridge and converse across the gap blown in the middle. For more extended negotiations, or for the conveyance of neutrals into or out of the city, a boat was provided by the French; a miserable affair, so constantly shot at on its journeyings by undisciplined or ill-informed troops on either side that the journey, which the cultured emissaries of both armies constantly compared to the crossing of the Styx, came rather to resemble the even more hazardous voyage of the Jumblies.[2] On this tenuous thread hung the Government's official relations with the outside world.

Among the first to entrust themselves to this Stygian passage, on 1st October, were two American officers, General Burnside of Fredericksburg fame, and Colonel Forbes. Officially they came as independent neutral observers under parole, interested only in the technicalities of the siege, and as such Trochu arranged for them to be conducted round the strongest points of the fortifications.[3] In fact they, Bismarck, and Favre himself were quite prepared to use the occasion of their visit to try to break the political deadlock; but they could make no progress beyond the stalemate reached at Ferrières. Both sides agreed that an armistice was desirable so that an assembly might be elected to make peace. But the French insisted that the armistice should last a fortnight

[1] Bronsart, *Kriegstagebuch* 183, 189. Stosch, *Denkwürdigkeiten* 208. Hohenlohe-Ingelfingen, *Aus meinem Leben* 353. H. Abeken, *Ein schlichtes Leben in bewegten Zeit* 450–1.

[2] D'Hérisson, *Journal of a Staff Officer* 154. Verdy du Vernois, *With the Royal Headquarters* 226.

[3] D'Hérisson, op. cit. 145.

and Paris be revictualled—a proposal which Moltke found entirely unacceptable.[1] All that the American visit achieved was to make the state of mind of each party a little clearer to the other. To the Germans they pointed out that the French were not yet prepared to buy peace with territory. Favre himself was reconciled to the loss of Alsace, but he could never carry Paris with him.[2] As for Trochu, they made clear their conviction that his fortifications would avail him little: Bismarck counted on civil disorder in the city to do his work for him, and he was probably right. To this Trochu could only reply that hunger would be necessary to compel capitulation, as well as riot; but neither side could remain any longer under the illusion that a siege, with all its tedium and suffering, could be either avoided, or brought to a premature end.[3]

§2 Le Plan Trochu

In face of the evident refusal of the Germans to attack, Trochu had to reconsider his plans. He had at his disposal 400,000 men, their armament daily growing with the intensive activities of the city factories, to confront a force of 236,000 thinly spread over a perimeter of fifty miles. True, more than a quarter of his force was composed of the *Garde Nationale*; but this force made up in enthusiasm what it lacked in experience, or at least so it believed. It drilled devotedly, often by gaslight, and asked nothing better than to be led to battle. This Trochu was not prepared to do; yet even without their aid he had the numbers to strike a considerable blow at the over-extended German lines. But what purpose would it serve? Trochu did not relate the defence of Paris to any general plan for the conduct of the war. It was no part of a general strategy of attrition to wear down the Germans, provoke political discontent beyond the Rhine and force them to an early and generous peace. "I had no idea", he later admitted, "of strategy and none of tactics. I had no object in view except to get the Germans involved in another Saragossa."[4] And if the Germans refused to become so involved, how could he force their hand?

[1] Jules Favre, *Gouvernement de la Défense Nationale* I 436–8.
[2] Frederick III, *War Diary* 145.
[3] Trochu, *Œuvres posthumes* I 308. Albert Sorel, *Histoire diplomatique de la Guerre Franco-Allemande* II 14–20.
[4] *Œuvres posthumes* I 273.

In default of a German attack, and spurred by the agitation of the Press and the clubs, the French commanders undertook one or two brief and limited offensive operations. Ducrot, after his experiences at Châtillon, rated the capacity of his troops even lower than did Trochu, and begged in vain to be permitted to leave Paris by balloon and organise resistance in the provinces. Vinoy was more optimistic: his army corps contained all that remained of the regular army, and he was unwilling to see them restrained indefinitely from action by the incapacity of their comrades in arms. Trochu therefore permitted him, on 30th September, to launch that most useless of military operations, an "offensive reconnaissance" up the left bank of the Seine. With 20,000 men, under the guns of forts Bicêtre and Ivry, he stormed the villages of L'Hay, Chevilly, and Thiaïs, only to see his forces decimated and driven back in disorder.[1] A fortnight later Trochu launched another limited attack which met with slightly more success. Moltke's reorganisation of the Third Army positions in order to release von der Tann's forces to march on Orléans seemed to indicate a concentration for that attack on Paris in which Trochu had not yet entirely lost faith; so on 13th October, to disturb these presumed preparations, Vinoy was launched on another offensive reconnaissance to the south—this time against the villages of Clamart, Châtillon, and Bagneux, which lay on the forward slopes of the plateau of Villacoublay and were thus vulnerable to bombardment by the guns of the southern forts. The positions were garrisoned by II Bavarian Corps, whose resistance was unlikely to be so strenuous as that of the Prussians. The French had learned certain tactical lessons. They moved with greater caution, relied more heavily on covering fire, and successfully drove the Bavarians from their outposts in Clamart, Bagneux, and all but the upper part of Châtillon. There they were out of sight of the enemy guns, and the batteries which the Bavarians brought up to the edge of the plateau to fire down on them were driven back by the heavy guns of the forts. In the afternoon the French fell back undisturbed. They had merely nibbled at the edge of the German line; an advance over the edge of the plateau had been out of the question; but the results of the enterprise—some 400 casualties on either side, but 200 prisoners borne triumphantly back to Paris—gave the French, very reasonably, the impression that they had had the better of the engagement.[2]

[1] Vinoy, *Siège de Paris* 183–98. G.G.S. II i 111–14.
[2] G.G.S. II i 118–19. Trochu, *Œuvres posthumes* I 320–34. Vinoy, op. cit. 211–19.

This success only gave added impetus to the demands of the *Garde Nationale* that it should be given something to do. The patrol activity to which it was restricted in no way corresponded to the *sortie torrentiale* which the Left-wing press was continuing insistently to demand.[1] Nor could Ducrot reconcile himself to awaiting indefinitely an attack which by now, clearly, would never come. The *Garde Nationale* might be useless, but there were some troops in Paris who could fight, and for the first time Ducrot began to consider operations in relation to the national war effort as a whole. A break-out would be useless unless it could lead to a continuation of operations in conjunction with the new forces which the Delegation was raising on the Loire; thus if a break-out was attempted, it would have to be in a direction whereby contact might be made with Gambetta's troops. The German defences on the south side of the city seemed impregnable, but to the west the situation appeared more promising. At first sight the triple bend of the Seine looked an insuperable obstacle; yet for this very reason the German defences in this area, the point of junction between the two armies, were very much weaker. It might be possible for a force of about 40,000 picked men, under the guns of Mont Valérien and the Seine flotilla, to force a crossing on to the Argenteuil peninsula, fight forward on to the Sannois plateau, and then, with their left flank protected by the Seine, make for Rouen and there, in Normandy and Brittany, create a redoubt, firmly in touch with the Loire armies by sea. The objections were obvious, but no greater than those to any course of action that might be considered. It was after all, as Trochu later put it ruefully, a plan. Trochu, Ducrot, and their immediate staffs began to work on it in great secrecy—but not so great that rumours did not seep out on to the boulevards, and references seep in to the *cafés chantants* about "*l'plan Trochu*".[2]

Before the main break-out was attempted, Ducrot decided, it was necessary to fight a limited action in the sector chosen for the attack: partly to test the German defences, partly to assure more strongly the possession of the necessary jumping-off ground, and partly to cement and reassure the morale of the French troops. It was one of those attacks against well-prepared positions, too modest in its scope either to achieve much or to come to great harm, which were to become so familiar

---

[1] Trochu stubbornly maintained that the rôle of the *Garde Nationale* was internal security. *Compagnies de Guerre* were however formed of the youngest and fittest men and put into the field on 20th–25th November. Ducrot's report on them was scathing. Trochu, op. cit. 285. *D.T.* III (Ducrot) 99.

[2] Trochu, *Œuvres posthumes* I 325–7. Ducrot, *Défense de Paris* I 301–21.

forty-five years later in the trenches of Flanders and northern France. Three columns, totalling something over 8,000 men accompanied by 120 field-guns, carried it out on 21st October, across the rolling allotments and gardens of the Gennevilliers peninsula south-west of Mont Valérien against the long ridge between St Cloud and Bougival where the Germans had established their forward line. Once again they got no further than the Prussian outposts; and as at this point the Prussian defences were at their deepest and thickest it would have been of little value if they had. The heads of their columns pushed through the park at Malmaison, seized Buzenval and worked their way through the woods to the eastern slope of the Cucufa ravine. But on the western slope and on the crest behind Buzenval the main Prussian position remained intact behind its barricades, and the Prussian guns did heavy damage to the rear of the columns halted uncertainly in the open fields. Confronted by such a defence the French superiority in numbers was useless, and the *élan* of the attack was already exhausted when Prussian reserves came up and began to push them back again. Twilight came early to cover the French as they withdrew, leaving behind 120 prisoners and losing 500 wounded and dead. They had made no impression whatever on the German defences, but Ducrot was not ill-pleased. The operation could not be written off as a failure, for it had hardly aimed at success, and his troops—even the *Mobiles*—had manœuvred creditably, fought, in places, gallantly, and remained fairly steady under fire. It was a very fair augury for the success of the Plan.[1]

The sortie was planned for the third week in November. As it turned out, Ducrot was not to feel himself ready even then; but the necessary weeks of waiting were more than the hotter tempers of Belleville could bear. The honeymoon period of the National Defence had quickly come to an end; the old suspicions, military and political, again became dominant; and at the end of October three events combined to end the uneasy truce between Republicans and revolutionaries and arouse the spirit of civil war within Paris from its uneasy sleep.

*　　*　　*

The village of St Denis was so heavily fortified as to be almost a fortress in its own right, a detached bastion covering all approaches to the city from the north. In command was General Carey de Bellemare, an able, energetic and ambitious regular soldier who resented both his subordination to Trochu and his enforced inactivity. Under his com-

[1] *G.G.S.* II i 122–6. Ducrot, op. cit. I 373–409.

mand was one of the most vociferous and active of the irregular formations of the city, the *francs-tireurs* of the Press. On the night of 27th
October this unit carried out a fighting reconnaissance across the fields
in front of their positions to the village of Le Bourget, which an outpost
of the Prussian Guard held in uncomfortable isolation. The Prussians,
taken by surprise, fell back. The *francs-tireurs* summoned up reinforcements and occupied the village; Bellemare rode into Paris to inform a
delighted population and an embarrassed Trochu about this splendid
victory—the first since the beginning of the siege, if not the beginning
of the war—for French arms. He demanded reinforcements, artillery
and—according to Trochu—immediate promotion.[1] Trochu was unco-
operative. The captured position was of no value; German artillery
fire would make it untenable; and his staff considered, with the gloomy
common sense of trench warfare, that the action would "merely increase
the death-roll for all".[2] Curiously enough the Germans were taking the
same view. The Guard themselves believed, and reported to their army
commander, that the position, dominated as it was by the French forts,
was hardly worth recovering; and when the Crown Prince of Saxony
ordered its recapture Moltke's headquarters had considerable mis-
givings.[3] The German troops, snug in their houses and hoping to be
home by Christmas, had lost their enthusiasm of the summer. The
end of the war was now only a matter of time, and they wanted to be
alive to see it.[4] None the less the Guard counter-attacked on the early
morning of 30th October, after a day of shellfire; and their attack is a
small landmark in military history in that for the first time the problems
of infantry advancing against a position defended with breech-loading
rifles had been carefully and successfully worked out. The company
columns breaking up into a skirmishing line had given way to loose lines
of widely spaced men, making all possible use of cover, offering small
targets and advancing by bounds, supporting one another by fire[5]—
tactics which the British army was to learn expensively from the Boers
thirty years later, and the German and French armies were to have
entirely forgotten before 1914. These open formations enabled the
Prussians to advance across the open fields in spite of *chassepot*-fire

[1] Trochu, *Œuvres posthumes* I 348.
[2] D'Hérisson, *Journal of a Staff Officer* 187.
[3] Bronsart, *Kriegstagebuch* 158.
[4] Moltke to Stiehle, 9th October: "Jeder fühlt mehr oder weniger, dasz
eigentlich der Feldzug zu Ende ist, und wünscht selbst kleinere Verluste zu
vermeiden." *M.M.K.* 324–5.
[5] Hohenlohe-Ingelfingen, *Letters on Infantry* (London 1889) 135–6.

from the village and shellfire from the forts, to outflank Le Bourget on either side and close in for a battle in the streets which left the village and 1,200 prisoners in their hands at a cost of 500 German dead.[1]

The exaggerated enthusiasm with which the capture of Le Bourget had been greeted in Paris increased the shock of disappointment at its loss. The blame was generally laid on Trochu, for failing to send up the reinforcements demanded, and de Bellemare did nothing to discourage this interpretation. But the fall of Le Bourget was only one factor in bringing the agitation in Paris to a head. Rumours were already circulating that Bazaine had opened negotiations for the surrender of Metz. The capitulation was reported in at least one Left-wing journal on 27th October with circumstantial details, and the Government promptly and in good faith denied the report as *infame et fausse*.[2] But on 30th October confirmation came from an unimpeachable source—Adolphe Thiers, who on that day returned to Paris by the Stygean passage at Sèvres.

Thiers's attempts to enlist the aid of the Powers of Europe had everywhere failed. He had been received with respect and listened to with courtesy, but nobody was willing to take any action. The Czar was taking advantage of the French misfortunes to denounce the Black Sea clauses of the Treaty of Paris, and had in any case little sympathy with a Republican régime. At Vienna the last traces of Beust's hopes of revenge had been swept away by the echoes of the guns at Sedan. At Florence Victor Emmanuel was turning the confusion in Europe to advantage by consolidating his kingdom with the seizure of Rome; and in England, although the unanimous delight aroused by the victory of a traditional and consanguineous ally over a traditional enemy was wavering, and fears were beginning to take shape about a new threat to the balance of power in Europe, there was neither the will nor the military ability to intervene. Lord Granville offered his good offices in mediating an armistice between the belligerents, and this offer was the only fruit which Thiers gathered during his long journey.[3] He returned to France profoundly pessimistic, and his spirits were not raised by what he saw of the Army of the Loire on his journey from Tours.[4]

---

[1] Hohenlohe-Ingelfingen, *Aus meinem Leben* 346 ff. Ducrot, *Défense de Paris* II 14–24. *G.G.S.* II i 131–2. H. Kunz, *Die Kämpfe de preussischen Garde um le Bourget während der Belagerung von Paris*. (Berlin 1891).

[2] Jules Favre, *Gouvernement de la Défense Nationale* I 312–13. D'Herisson, op. cit. 184.

[3] For a full account of Thiers's negotiations see Albert Sorel, *Histoire diplomatique* II 30–60.   [4] Favre, op. cit. 319.

By the time he reached Versailles he was convinced that peace must be made on the best terms available, and he willingly made himself an intermediary to reopen negotiations for an armistice. Bismarck allowed him into Paris to ascertain the French terms, and on 30th October he re-entered the city and consulted the Ministers of the Government of National Defence. His advice was to accept any German terms so long as elections could be held which would return a Government authorised to make peace.[1] Trochu was in principle agreeable, but insisted on two stipulations: the elections must extend to the threatened provinces of Alsace and Lorraine, and Paris must be allowed to revictual herself during the armistice. This last stipulation, as Thiers knew, made negotiations impossible, but on it the Government was obdurate; so on 31st October Thiers returned to make his report to Versailles.[2] That morning the *Journal Officiel* carried a brief hint of the opening of negotiations; an announcement of the loss of Le Bourget; and, at last, official confirmation of the fall of Metz.

The mixture was a strong one, and nearly fatal to the Government. It was a cold gloomy morning, very different from the glorious Sunday when Paris had overthrown the Empire. The delegates of twenty *arrondissements*, meeting in the Place de la Concorde, agreed to march on the Hôtel de Ville to proclaim the downfall of the Government and the inauguration of the Commune. Nor was the shame and alarm awakened by the *Journal Officiel* confined to the Left wing. The *Garde Nationale* itself was divided and uncertain, and there was a substantial bourgeois element in the crowd which shouted "*Pas d'armistice!*" and "*La guerre à outrance!*" outside the Hôtel de Ville, where the Ministry was in session.[3] The extremists took advantage of the confusion to invade the Hôtel de Ville. As a pacific gesture the Ministers agreed to grant the demand, which the mayors of the *arrondissements* had been pressing during the past few weeks, for the election of a municipal body, in spite of their forebodings that its inevitably Left-wing composition would have a disastrous effect on the provinces.[4] It was the Commune in all but name. But it was *not* the Commune

---

[1] Favre, op. cit. 317–18.

[2] Trochu, *Œuvres posthumes* I 368. In a memorandum to Bismarck, Moltke insisted that revictualling should be allowed only in return for the surrender of all Paris forts south of the Seine. *M.M.K.* 346.

[3] Jules Ferry later declared "la population parisienne nous était, de haut en bas de l'echelle, absolument hostile." *D.T.* I 395. See also Favre, *D.T.* I 337, and D'Hérisson, op. cit. 191–2.

[4] Ducrot, *Siège de Paris* III 356.

in name; and a detachment of the *Garde Nationale* burst into the room where the Ministry was in session to declare the Ministers captive and the Government overthrown. There followed hours of confusion and turgid oratory, but by the evening it was evident that the insurgents had no idea what to do next. Power lay within their grasp but at close quarters the reality seemed less attractive than the prospect. The mood of the crowd began to change, and a friendly battalion of the *Garde Nationale* smuggled Trochu and a few other Ministers out of the building.

Meanwhile Ducrot had decided that the time had come for the military to intervene. Now was the moment for the Army to show its value as the *palladium* of the social order. With a strong body of troops he set out down the Champs Elysées, prepared to break up all resistance with *mitrailleuses*, bombard the Hôtel de Ville into surrender, and execute the revolutionaries *en bloc*. "The repression would have been terrible", he said later, "and the whole thing would have been finished."[1] But at the Louvre he found Trochu, and although Trochu agreed that strong action was necessary he insisted that it should be carried out not by the army but by the moderate battalions of the *Garde Nationale*, under command of Jules Ferry, the Prefect of the Department of the Seine. A direct attack would endanger the lives of the captive Ministers; so Ferry instead began to negotiate with the rebels, who, conscious of their impotence and of the changing mood of the crowd, were now less interested in revolution than in withdrawing with dignity and safety. Thus when Trochu and Ducrot themselves reached the Hôtel de Ville at 4 a.m. on 1st November they found all was over. Partly as the result of agreement, partly because Ferry had lost patience and summoned up his forces, the insurgents had disappeared and the Ministers were free.[2]

Now if ever was the moment for the Government to assert itself. The impotence of the extreme left had been revealed; its leaders, as members of the *Garde Nationale*, had laid themselves open to trial by court-martial on a charge of mutiny; and the plebiscite held on 3rd November showed how tiny was the numerical support they enjoyed, 557,976 votes being cast in favour of the Government and only 62,638 against.[3] The results of the plebiscite—and the results of the municipal elections which followed—were an open invitation to the Ministers to crush the insurrection and assume dictatorial powers with a wide

---

[1] *D.T.* III 88.   [2] D'Hérisson, op. cit. 202–3.
[3] Dréo, *Procès Verbaux* 275.

measure of public support—powers such as Gambetta had not hesitated to assume at Tours. But it was an invitation of which no one in France was less likely to take advantage than the men who made up the Government of National Defence. It took two days for the Ministers to decide on the arrest even of the leaders of the insurrection of 31st October; and when they did so Henri Rochefort and Edmond Adam, the Prefect of Police, both resigned. The events of 31st October settled nothing. The political clubs and the Press continued to agitate, political dissension still vitiated the effectiveness of the *Garde Nationale*, and under the tightening screw of privation the rift of social fear and hatred, which divided the classes of the city and had been temporarily closed by the presence of the common enemy, opened a little wider with every day that passed.[1]

The events of 31st October confirmed the worst expectations of Adolphe Thiers. He left Paris in a state of agitation which he made little attempt to conceal from Bismarck; and Bismarck naturally took full advantage of a situation from which he could reap nothing but benefit. It is hard to believe that he was seriously perturbed by disorders on which he had counted all along, but they provided an excuse for abandoning the conciliatory attitude which he was finding it difficult to maintain in face of the hostility of Moltke and the General Staff.

On 5th November Thiers returned to Paris with the Prussian terms— an armistice for long enough to convoke a National Assembly, but no revictualling of Paris unless a fort was surrendered to compensate for the military setback which the Prussians would suffer thereby. Trochu felt that the situation in the city was not yet secure enough either for Thiers to enter Paris or for himself to leave, so he sent Ducrot to represent him, and the two met with Favre in a depressing no-man's-land, a deserted and shell-torn house at Sèvres. Thiers again urged the acceptance of the German conditions: there was nothing to hope from the provinces, and further resistance would only lead to harsher terms of peace. Favre with the shouts of the insurgents fresh in his ears, replied that Paris would never accept such conditions, and Ducrot added that she should not.[2] It was their duty, he said, to continue the struggle, to blot out the stain of Sedan and Metz. Thiers sighed. "General", he replied, "you talk like a soldier. That's all very well, but you're not talking in political terms." But Ducrot maintained that resistance would serve

---

[1] On the *émeute* of 31st October see the document printed in Georges d'Heylli, *Journal du Siège de Paris* II 593–625.

[2] Favre, *Gouvernement de la Défense Nationale* II 25, and *D.T.* I 338.

political ends as well—that the Prussians might be wearied and worn down into offering more acceptable terms. Thiers in fact had the same problem with him as Bismarck had with Moltke. Both soldiers spoke in terms of honour, and of victory through attrition. The first concept was irrelevant to a sound peace; the second was disastrous to it. But in wartime soldiers sometimes represent the mood of the nation more exactly than statesmen, and in Paris that evening the Ministers unanimously applauded Ducrot's attitude. Trochu declared that they owed it to the country, "if not to triumph, at least to succumb gloriously after having fought valiantly", and with this disastrously *chevaleresque* pronouncement the Government concurred. In face of such an attitude neither Thiers nor Bismarck could find anything more to say, and the situation returned to a purely military footing.[1]

*   *   *

Throughout these political and diplomatic disturbances Trochu and Ducrot had been pushing ahead with plans for their sortie. Much still remained to be done. Not only did batteries have to be sited, ammunition accumulated, and bridging-material prepared, but a complete reorganisation of the armed forces was necessary. The 100,000 men who were to attempt the sortie were organised into three army corps under the command of Ducrot; 70,000 men, largely *Mobiles*, constituted a second force under Vinoy with a diversionary rôle; and out of the *Garde Nationale* a third army was formed, some 130,000 strong, which was to act as the garrison of the city.[2] Naturally enough all this came to the ears of the Germans and their involuntary hosts in the towns outside Paris, and both looked forward with confidence of different kinds to a sortie in the middle of November.[3] The date anticipated by Ducrot was 15th November, but the preparations by then were still far from complete, and on 14th November two events occurred which forced Trochu to reconsider the entire plan. The first was a sudden rise in the level of the Seine, which would have forced the postponement of the operation even if it had already begun. The second was the arrival of a pigeon from Tours, "like the dove returning to the Ark", with the news of Aurelle's victory at Coulmiers.[4]

The news that the provinces had raised armies which could fight, and not only fight but win, awoke as much amazement as delight in

[1] Ducrot, *Défense de Paris* II 72–7, 362–8, III 365.
[2] Ibid. II 92.
[3] Verdy du Vernois, *With the Royal Headquarters* 212.
[4] Ducrot, op. cit. II 3. Desmarest, *Défense Nationale* 300.

Paris. Trochu for one had not believed this possible: for him the war began and ended in Paris, where the only remaining troops of the regular army were concentrated; and the armies at Tours, if they existed, could act at best in an ancillary rôle.[1] Trochu had already sent Gambetta a message suggesting that he should concentrate forces on the lower Seine, based on Rouen, drawn either from Bourbaki's troops in the north or from the Army of the Loire. In addition he gave to an official who left Paris for Tours by balloon on 11th October an outline of his plans for the sortie, to be explained to the Delegation. The message was delivered, but Gambetta was unenthusiastic. On Bourbaki's advice he had dismissed the possibility of operations on the lower Seine, and planned simply for an advance northward from Orléans.[2] He followed the message announcing the victory of Coulmiers with a second, which reached Paris on 18th November, describing the positions he held north of Orléans and suggesting that Trochu should cooperate by attacking southwards. But he also admitted the possibility that Trochu might continue with his break-out towards the west: "attempting a vigorous break-out towards Normandy which will let you get out of Paris, hitherto impregnable, 200,000 men who are not necessary to her defence and who, holding out in the open country, will act as a counter-weight to the forces which Prince Frederick Charles is bringing from Metz".[3]

There was thus nothing in Gambetta's intentions which obliged the forces in Paris to abandon their plans; but cold reason does not always play the part it should in formulating military strategy. The Press of Paris, intoxicated with the news of Coulmiers, was sending up the cry "*Ils viennent à nous: allons à eux !*" There was in the air a feeling of wild hope, that the miraculous was at last going to happen, that the *sortie torrentielle* might at last take place and, bursting through the Prussian wing, meet Aurelle's men in the Forest of Fontainebleau. Trochu, who assessed the success of Coulmiers at its true worth, did not share this view, but all the other Ministers did.[4] On 19th November

[1] Trochu, *Œuvres posthumes* I 325. According to Ducrot, when Trochu was asked on 2nd October about the prospects of the Army of the Loire, he replied that "la formation de cette armée est impossible et qu'il ne faut compter que sur la défense de Paris. Le siège est d'ailleurs bien moins inquiétant que la façon dont agit la Délégation du Gouvernement à Tours." Ducrot, op. cit. III 355.

[2] *D.O.* II 278. Freycinet later said that he understood Trochu's intentions, but "entre une intention manifestée comme celle-ci, et un plan arrêté il y a une différence". *D.T.* III 3.

[3] *D.O.* II 303.

[4] Trochu, *Œuvres posthumes* I 407–8.

the Government decided to suspend the preparations for a breakout down the Seine and instead to launch an operation towards the south, to link up with Gambetta; and next day this decision was conveyed to an astonished and indignant Ducrot.[1]

Ducrot's disappointment, as he later mildly put it, "was not less than his embarrassment". The task which he was now called upon to undertake was absurd, and it speaks volumes for the efficiency of his staff-officers and the enthusiasm of the Parisians that it was accomplished at all. Four hundred heavy guns had to be brought back through the streets of Paris; fifty-four pontoon bridges; and some 80,000 men, with all their field-artillery, transport, and supplies. These forces had to be deployed to attack the Germans in one of the strongest sectors of the entire perimeter. The only point at which Ducrot believed success possible—or rather failure not totally inevitable—was to the east, in the loop of the Marne between Champigny and Brie, where both flanks of his army might rest on the river, with the St Maur peninsula on one side and Mont Avron on the other. Thus protected, and covered by the guns of the eastern forts, it should be possible to reach the plateau of Villiers and Coeuilly, give battle under reasonably advantageous conditions, and, if the fortunes of war were favourable, to push on to join the Army of the Loire in the Forest of Fontainebleau. General Exéa's Corps on the left was to cross the river at Nogent-sur-Marne and seize Brie, while General Carey de Bellemare's division protected his flank at Neuilly. Renault's Corps, debouching from the Bois de Vincennes, was to advance on Champigny; and Vinoy's army was to make its diversion on the left bank of the Seine, attacking towards L'Hay and Choisy-le-Roi and intercepting the reserves which the Germans might bring up from the west.[2] The baggage-train, so vulnerable in breakthrough operations, was eliminated; the men carried six days' supplies, and such waggons as followed them contained only artillery ammunition. Even blankets were discarded to lighten the army for its supreme effort. Ducrot set the tone of the operation with one of those heroic and disastrous Orders of the Day in which this history abounds. "As for myself", he wrote, "I have made up my mind, and I swear before you and before the entire nation: I shall only re-enter Paris dead or victorious. You may see me fall, but you will not see me yield ground." Even Trochu, himself not given to moderation in his public declarations, considered this phrase doubtfully wise.[3] The people of

---

[1] Ducrot, *Défense de Paris* II 109.   [2] Ibid. II 135–45.
[3] Ibid. II 156–7.

Paris were not to forget it when, a few days later, Ducrot reappeared among them, defeated and alive.

The attack was to take place on 29th November. It had little chance of securing surprise: the Germans had been on the alert for ten days, and ever since 26th November the gunfire from the forts had been so intense that many thought the long-awaited German bombardment of the city had begun.[1] Nor did it require much insight to discern where the French were most likely to attempt a break-through if they wanted to link hands with the Army of the Loire. The threatened sector was held by the Württemberg Division, and the Crown Prince of Saxony had received explicit orders to reinforce it rapidly in case of need.[2] Moreover the French were denied even tactical surprise. On the night of 28th November the Marne flooded, the pontoons so laboriously accumulated were found to be too short, and the whole operation had to be postponed for twenty-four hours. By then it was too late to countermand the establishment of fresh batteries on Mont Avron, in full view of the Germans; too late to conceal the huge accumulation of men and guns under the walls of Paris; and too late to stop the attack which Vinoy directed, on the morning of the 29th, against Choisy-le-Roi and L'Hay. The troops launched on these now pointless operations could not be extricated until they had lost 300 prisoners and 1,000 men wounded or dead.[3] When the main attack at last began, at dawn on 30th November, attempts were made to mask it by further diversionary operations. A division attacked southwards between Seine and Marne, seizing the isolated hump of Mont-Mesly and the neighbouring village of Bonneuil before the Württembergers could rally enough strength to counter-attack and push it back with artillery fire to its original positions. On the opposite side of the city a detachment of Marines, debouching under heavy bombardment from St Denis, forced their way into the village of Épinay and maintained their position there throughout the day—an operation whose success was, as we have seen, to have disastrous consequences on the operations of the Army of the Loire. These attacks, and a third launched by Ducrot's left wing against Neuilly-sur-Marne, achieved a measure of success in pinning down the German reinforcements; and the main attack could go in as planned,

---

[1] Bamberger, *Bismarcks Grosses Spiel* 233. Rauch, *Briefe aus dem grossen Hauptquartier* 168, 171.

[2] *M.M.K.* 403. Bronsart, *Kriegstagebuch* 200.

[3] Vinoy, *Siège de Paris* 253–60. For general accounts of the operations between 29th November and 3rd December see *G.G.S.* II i 370–89. Ducrot, *Défense de Paris* II 152–316, III 5–67. Trochu, *Œuvres posthumes* 432–62.

with two full corps and a third in reserve, against the thinly held and as yet unreinforced lines of the Württemberg Division between Champigny and Brie.

Ducrot, after the rout at Châtillon, knew very well that numbers were a doubtful advantage when they were made up of troops so poorly trained as his. He still did not dare to deploy them in the open formations which the Prussian Guard had used with such success at Le Bourget, for fear they might go to ground and become unmanageable. They had to remain in the close order which made them so vulnerable to artillery and rifle fire; and Trochu watched their advance into action with the gloomiest apprehension. The inadequacy of their own artillery could to a large extent be compensated for by the guns of the fortress, but the range even of these was limited. The twin hearts of the Württemberg defence-system were the villages of Villiers-sur-Marne and Coeuilly, lying about a mile apart and dominating a gently undulating plateau which barred all egress from the Marne. This plateau fell steeply to the river at Champigny and Brie, riverside villages isolated by the slopes behind them and tenable only by outposts too weak to put up any effective resistance to a French river-crossing. Thus in the initial stages of the attack all went well. The German positions were neutralised by artillery fire; the pontoons were laid and the French crossed them in the cold dawn twilight without interference; the two wings established themselves after a brief fight in Champigny and Brie, and the whole French line closed up to the edge of the plateau.

Then the difficulties began. All further advance withered away in face of the fire which poured across the fields from the two fortress villages, where the Württembergers had dug themselves in so securely that no amount of artillery fire could get them out. Ducrot had foreseen that there would be difficulty at this stage, and had arranged for his third corps under General Exéa, which was crossing the river on the extreme left at Neuilly, to come round and assault Villiers from the north while his centre attacked from the south and west. But Exéa did not get his bridges across the Seine until the early afternoon; then, seeing the disastrous outcome of all attacks on Villiers, he hesitated to commit his own troops to action until it was too late to operate effectively with the rest of Ducrot's forces. His attack, when it was eventually launched, was irresolute, isolated, and as useless as its predecessors. By evening the fields before the park and village of Villiers were thick with French dead. The right wing debouching from Champigny to attack Coeuilly could do no better, and sharp counter-attacks from the south drove it back over the edge of the plateau in confusion. The constant energy of the generals, from Trochu downwards, was needed to keep the French line together at all. Ducrot showed a suicidal courage which matched the hyperbole of his proclamation,[1] and General Renault, commander of 14th Corps, received a wound from which he died a few days later, after lying in a delirium in which he raved wildly and uninterruptedly against Trochu. By nightfall the French were fighting simply to preserve the positions they had won that morning—Champigny, Brie, and a foothold on the edge of the plateau between them; and Ducrot decided, as he rode back along the ice-bound road to his headquarters, that the operation had failed. It would be futile to renew the attack next day.

As in all their previous attacks, the French had failed to penetrate even the first belt of the German defences; yet they had succeeded in throwing the German forces into an unusual state of agitation. The attack at Neuilly had delayed the arrival of the reinforcements which the Crown Prince of Saxony sent over the Marne, and the intensity of the French attack had worn down both the Württembergers and the Saxons who came to their aid. Alarming reports filtered back to Versailles. The Saxons in particular, it was reported, "did not make their stand, fight it out and take their part in the action when they were ordered".[2] Moltke, worried at the sluggishness with which the Crown Prince of Saxony seemed to be dealing with the threat, ordered Blumenthal to send up II Corps and one brigade of VI Corps to deal with the situation; and next day he removed the operations from the immediate control of the Crown Prince of Saxony by giving General von Fransecky, commander of II Corps, control of all operations between the Seine and the Marne.[3] But there was unusual confusion about the movement of these reserves: although they had stood by on the 30th to deal with the threat to Mesly, they had then marched back ten miles to their billeting areas, and Fransecky had to be roused in the small hours by orders from Versailles to return to the battlefield.[4] By then it was too late to mount any attack that day, and the Germans greeted the quiescence of the French with considerable relief.

1st December was thus a day of recuperation and ultimately of a

[1] Trochu, op. cit. 439, 459.

[2] Frederick III, *War Diary* 208. Bronsart, *Kriegstagebuch* 201.

[3] Blumenthal, *Journals* 208.

[4] Bronsart, *Kriegstagebuch* 202. Verdy du Vernois, *With the Royal Headquarters* 217–19. General von Fransecky, *Denkwürdigkeiten* (ed. Walter von Bremen, Leipzig 1901) 541.

formal truce, with burial parties from both sides working amicably together, gleaning the fields of their ghastly harvest under a leaden sky. Since Ducrot ordered no further advance, the French devoted themselves to putting their newly won and precarious positions into a state of defence. It was as well that they did, for at dawn on 2nd December the Germans counter-attacked in force. Fransecky had questioned the necessity of doing so: the main German defences were still intact, and neither Champigny nor Brie could be adequately defended even if they were retaken.[1] But the Crown Prince of Saxony was as inflexible in demanding their recapture as he had been at Le Bourget, and the attack was launched with a suddenness which carried the attackers into the middle of Champigny and nearly broke the French line on the hills above. Visibility was too bad for the French fortress-artillery to come into action, and the guns on the St Maur peninsula which might have taken the assault in flank had been withdrawn. Thus it was an infantry fight, and the *Mobiles*, after their initial panic had been checked by Trochu and Ducrot, stood their ground and fought very well. The Germans found themselves as incapable of making any headway against rifle-fire as the French had been two days earlier, and once the morning mists cleared the gunners on Mont Avron were able to open aimed fire in support of strong French counter-attacks. The fighting went on all day, neither side able to make much progress, each showing stubborn courage, and both, when darkness came, ending up exhausted. The Crown Prince of Saxony, who came up to watch operations, was appalled at the condition of his troops, and sent Moltke such a gloomy account of the situation that Moltke began to make preliminary plans to deal with the French if by any chance they did break through the following day.[2]

But Ducrot did not intend to attempt anything of the sort. His men could endure no more. The Germans at least had their blankets and extra wool-lined cloaks for guard duty, and their *Intendantur* succeeded in finding billets for nearly all their troops. The French had spent three freezing nights in the open without the cover even of blankets, and with no cooked food since the operation had begun. Ducrot found them, on the morning of 4th December, "crouched on the frozen ground, exhausted and shivering, their bodies and souls enfeebled by weariness, suffering and lack of food"; and without even

[1] Fransecky, loc. cit. Frederick III, *War Diary* 208–9.

[2] *M.M.K.* 409–11. P. Hassel, *Aus dem Leben des Königs Albert von Sachsen* (Berlin 1900) II 442–3.

finishing his inspection he decided to abandon the battlefield and re-treat into Paris.[1] Not even the arrival of a despatch from Gambetta, announcing the approach of the Army of the Loire 120,000 strong, could shake his resolve.[2] A thick mist hid his movements, making it possible for all his men to recross the Marne without loss. The French had no more fight left in them; during the past three days they had lost 12,000 officers and men, and that evening Ducrot urged Favre to treat for peace.[3]

Next day Trochu received a courteous letter from Moltke, informing him that the Army of the Loire had been defeated and Orléans re-occupied; inviting him to send an officer to make sure that the news was true. Both sortie and relief had simultaneously and finally failed.[4]

§3 Versailles

The German armies awaited the fall of Paris with growing impatience, but most of them were able to await it in comfort. Ever since the arrival of Royal Headquarters on 5th October Versailles had taken on all the appearance of a capital city. Strategically it was a nonsensical place to select as the command-post of the German armies. Not only was it so near the lines of investment that every demonstration made by Trochu in that direction set the more nervous hangers-on packing their bags, but no town on the periphery of Paris could have been worse placed for communication with Germany. But not even the vast halls of Ferrières could house Moltke's staff, the Royal retinue, Bismarck's officials and a crowd of *Schlachtenbummler* which, once the war had bogged down, swelled enormously. These included, by the end of the year, Prince Charles and Prince Adalbert of Prussia, Prince Leopold of Bavaria, the Grand Dukes of Oldenburg, Saxe-Weimar, Baden, and Mecklenburg-Schwerin, the Dukes of Holstein, Oldenburg, Saxe-Meiningen, Saxe-Altenburg, Saxe-Coburg-Gotha, and the Landgrave of Hesse; and the King ordered the Trianons to be reserved in case any even

---

[1] Ducrot, *Défense de Paris* III 63.

[2] Trochu, *Œuvres posthumes* I 462. Favre acknowledged it on 2nd December: "A 3 heures nous recevions au Gouvernement votre dépêche du 30, elle nous a comblés de joie. Le droit enfin triomphe. Vous vous approchez, nous allons à vous. Nous touchons aux termes des maux de la patrie." Ducrot, op. cit. II 426.

[3] Favre, *Gouvernement de la Défense Nationale* II 160.

[4] *M.M.K.* 424.

more exalted Royalty should care to join them; for the neurotic King of Bavaria might yet respond to Bismarck's invitations. To these more or less official residents were added a swarm of visitors who passed through the common mess at the Hôtel des Réservoirs; visiting military experts like General Burnside from America, politicians from every state in Germany negotiating over the question of unification, war correspondents, artists, diplomats, and a crowd of miscellaneous notabilities. Military security, in the modern sense, barely existed, and even common administrative efficiency was difficult to maintain. "If only the King with all the Princes and his Staff would go away" wrote Blumenthal in his diary in despair, "we could make short work of the business and soon bring peace within measurable distance."[1] It was an interesting, glittering, gossiping community, but hardly a happy one; and as the weather grew bleaker and peace came no nearer, its happiness grew still less.

Versailles combined the traditional intrigues and jealousies of a Royal Court with those, no less intense and much more familiar to our own times, of a great military headquarters. The personal rivalries and disagreements about policy which had been almost forgotten during the hectic weeks of victory were quick to reappear after Sedan; and they bred prolifically in the atmosphere of frustration and bewilderment which possessed the German forces as week followed week and there still came no prospect of peace. It was not only the delay in the ending of the war which worried the Prussian commanders, the disappearance of all prospect of getting their armies home by Christmas as they had so confidently hoped. The longer the struggle lasted the greater became the political complications, the greater the danger of that intervention of the Powers which the rapid victories of the summer had so far postponed.[2] The French Government was continuing to launch eloquent appeals to the neutral states, and although these had no effect on the policy of their Governments, they were not without influence on the opinion of their peoples.

The longer this struggle lasts [wrote the Crown Prince on New Year's Eve], the better for the enemy and the worse for us. The public opinion of Europe has not remained unaffected by the spectacle. We are no longer looked upon as the innocent sufferers of wrong, but rather as the arrogant victors, no longer content with the conquest of the foe but fain to bring about his utter ruin. No more do the French appear

[1] *Journals* 193.
[2] For Bismarck's fears on this count see Zernin, *Leben des Generals v. Goeben* II 75 n.

in the eyes of neutrals as a mendacious, contemptible nation, but as the heroic-hearted people that against overwhelming odds is defending its dearest possessions in honourable fight.[1]

Towards the end of the year therefore all the German military and civil leaders were in a state of explosive irritation. The King himself set the tone. Already at the beginning of November he was showing himself impatient and depressed at the course of events, and by the first week in January, when Bourbaki's appearance before Werder suddenly created a huge new problem for the German armies, he was in a state of hysterical despair almost beyond the capacity even of Moltke to appease.[2] He was in no state to inspire his subordinates, civil and military, with unity and confidence, and their lack of these qualities became daily more apparent.

Relations between Moltke and Roon worsened as the demands of the General Staff for men and material voraciously increased. Moltke and his staff compared the achievements of their own Ministry of War unfavourably with those of the French, whose fresh armies were beginning to confront them on all sides. The normal system of replacements sufficed to keep the field army up to strength, reported Moltke, in a letter to Roon of 8th December, but it was essential that more Landwehr forces should be brought from Germany if the lines of communication were to be properly guarded.[3] Roon released eighteen battalions, whose arrival enabled two regiments to be released from occupation duties for active service; but this Moltke did not consider nearly adequate in face of the efforts being made by the French. Could not yet new battalions be raised? Roon replied with a protest against the undertaking of operations which placed such a strain on German resources[4]; whereat Bronsart, whose diary-entries grew ever more bilious, noted, "God protect us from our friends! . . . He [Roon] appears to stand as a strategist on about the same level as Count Bismarck; but as a comedian he anyhow ranks immeasurably higher."[5]

This was the least of the enmities boiling up at Versailles. The army commanders were as jealous as prima donnas. The Crown Prince wondered, when Frederick Charles was promoted Field-Marshal after the

---

[1] Frederick III, *War Diary* 240.
[2] Ibid. 180, 251, 259, 263. Bronsart, *Kriegstagebuch* 301. Hermann Oncken, *Groszherzog Friedrich I von Baden* II 225. Schneider's statement in *Kaiser Wilhelm*, III, 56 that he had "nie die geringste Unruhe oder Gereiztheit an ihm bemerkt" seems disproved by these authorities.
[3] *M.M.K.* 430.
[4] Ibid. 445.
[5] Bronsart, op. cit. 241.

fall of Metz, "how long the possession of this rank he has laid claim to will satisfy his boundless ambition and overweening vanity ?" Manteuffel on the other hand he recorded as being hurt at not receiving the same promotion.[1] Moltke was openly critical of the competence of the Crown Prince of Saxony in handling the French attack on 30th November; and there was no love lost between the Crown Prince's Headquarters and Moltke's staff, living as they did in uncomfortable proximity. Blumenthal mistrusted the interference of the "demigods", "meaner spirits who always liked to have a finger in the pie". Bronsart and Verdy equally mistrusted the English influence which they believed to dominate the Crown Prince's entourage, inclining him to unmilitary softness and desire for an early, over-generous peace. This was a mistrust which Bismarck most emphatically shared; but it was one of the very few questions on which Bismarck and the General Staff found themselves in agreement.[2]

In their dislike of the Chancellor all the soldiers, with the exception of Roon and Stosch, made common cause. To deal with this adversary even Moltke abandoned his Olympian detachment. They resented the very presence of this civilian masquerading in his reservist uniform as an officer,[3] and they regarded as intolerable his attempts—or so they considered them—to influence the conduct of operations. They remembered, and resented, the part he played in shaping strategy in 1866, and were determined that this situation should not recur.[4] Unfortunately the spheres of civil and military authority overlapped, as they always will, and nobody could tell precisely where the line of distinction should be drawn.[5] Bazaine's surrender was a political as well as a military matter; the terms of the capitulation of Verdun, claimed Bismarck, should also have been referred to him since they included provision for the return of the captured war material after hostilities were ended; and in Moltke's letter to Trochu announcing the fall of Orléans Bismarck

[1] Frederick III, *War Diary* 182, 255. See also Stosch, *Denkwürdigkeiten* 204.

[2] Oncken, *Groszherzog Friedrich I von Baden* II 178. Blumenthal, *Journals* 149. Stosch, loc. cit.

[3] The wearing of a cuirassier's greatcoat, noted Bronsart acidly, was no aid to military understanding. *Kriegstagebuch* 281.

[4] Wilhelm Busch, *Das Deutsche Grosse Hauptquartier und die Bekämpfung von Paris im Feldzuge 1870-71* pp. 6–7.

[5] The first overt friction arose in September, over a question of responsibility for appointment of administrative officials in the occupied area. "Wenn ich mit solcher Ressort Verwirrung im Zivil haushalten sollte," wrote Bismarck to his wife, "wäre ich längst gesprungen wie eine Granate." Haeften, "Bismarck und Moltke" in *Preuss. Jahrbücher* (1919) CLXXVII 89. See also Bismarck, *Gesamm. Werke* VI 6 No. 1797, p. 490.

saw, not altogether wrongly, an attempt by the Chief of Staff to open political negotiations.[1]

In general Bismarck heartily reciprocated the soldiers' mistrust and dislike. He grew increasingly impatient at the obstacles which he felt Moltke was putting in his way in his attempts to make an acceptable peace. "For years past", he complained, "he has devoted himself to one single subject, and he has come to have no head and no interest for anything else." He complained violently and repeatedly that he was kept in complete ignorance of military plans and operations: even the newspapers, he lamented, got more information than he did.[2] These complaints were resented by the Staff as further attempts by the Chancellor to worm his way into the control of military affairs; and they remained adamant in their refusal to give him access to military information and decisions. Only the repeated intervention of the King himself could shake their determination on this vital point of principle.

Finally Bismarck, like Roon, watched with concern the enormous demands which the General Staff were making on the resources of Prussia and her allies. In October Bronsart was already complaining of the difficulty in requisitioning enough rolling-stock in Germany: "people seem generally to have forgotten in the victory celebrations that we are at war", he wrote, "and they must learn to put up with its exigencies, even if, as a result, private traffic in Germany is somewhat restricted". Count von Itzenplitz, the Minister of Commerce, continued to protest at the exigencies of military demands, and Bismarck supported him. The army anyhow, he maintained, wasted its resources: 2,600 trucks were standing idle waiting to provision Paris on its capitulation; and he strongly urged Itzenplitz to refuse to release any more.[3] In return Moltke, not surprisingly, complained of Bismarck's "arbitrary and despotic attitude. In military matters no less than in political", he complained, "the Federal Chancellor is resolved to decide everything himself, without paying the smallest heed to what the responsible experts have to say"[4]; while Bismarck lamented the days of "men like Frederick the Great, who were generals themselves and also knew something

---

[1] A. Klein-Wuttig, *Politik und Kriegführung* 136–8. Bismarck, *Gesamm. Werke* VI b No. 1950 p. 615. Bronsart, *Kriegstagebuch* 212. Bamberger, *Bismarcks Grosses Spiel* 244. See further p. 437 below.

[2] Moritz Busch, *Bismarck: Some Secret Pages of his History* I 310. Bismarck to Moltke, 22 October 1870, in *Gesamm. Werke* VI b No. 1885 p. 558, and 17th December 1870, No. 1977 p. 637. Bronsart, op. cit. 234–5, 281.

[3] Bronsart, op. cit. 120, 279–80. Busch, op. cit. 438.

[4] Frederick III, *War Diary* 253.

about administration, acting as their own ministers. . . . But here, this eternal talking and begging!" "I came to the war", he declared in lighter vein, "disposed to do everything for the military authorities, but in future I shall go over to the advocates of Parliamentary Government, and if they worry me much more, I shall have a chair placed for myself on the extreme Left."[1] He criticised, loudly and publicly, the military conduct of the war: the unnecessary advance into the centre of France,[2] the dissipation of forces piecemeal throughout the country, the languid progress of operations before Paris, and above all, the delay in beginning the bombardment of the city.[3]

It was over this last question that all the quarrels and jealousies in Versailles came to a head.[4] When he undertook the investment of Paris, Moltke had set on foot preparations for a possible bombardment of the forts and fortifications. Neither he nor Roon thought at this time that it would ever be necessary: Moltke indeed expressed the belief that Paris would capitulate as soon as the milk-supplies ran out.[5] None the less siege-guns had been ordered up from Germany, including the 15-cm. cannon and 21-cm. mortars manufactured by Krupps and never yet tested in action. A siege-park was established at Villacoublay, and siege-ammunition was added to the long list of items which competed for priority on the overworked railway-line which linked the German armies to their base.[6] On 30th October a plan was put forward for the bombardment of Forts Issy and Montrouge and the section of the *enceinte* which lay behind them, and for a subsidiary bombardment of St Denis as a feint, and on 9th October this received royal approval.[7] But Moltke and his staff showed no enthusiasm for bombarding either the fortifications or the city itself. The bombardment of Strasbourg, pointed out Bronsart, had wasted ammunition, alienated the population, and not hastened capitulation by a single day.[8] Even if the city itself

[1] Moritz Busch, op. cit. 293–4, 325.

[2] On this see in particular his *Immediatbericht* to the King of 28th December 1870, in *Gesamm. Werke* VI b No. 1990 p. 648.

[3] Oncken, *Friedrich I von Baden*, II 221. Bismarck, *Letters to his Wife from the Seat of War* 94.

[4] See, for the attitude of the General Staff on the whole question, W. von Blume, *Die Beschiessung von Paris 1870/1 und die Ursachen der Verzögerung* (Berlin 1899).

[5] Roon, *Denkwürdigkeiten* III 218 n. 1.

[6] *Kriegsgeschichtliche Einzelschriften* I Heft 4. *Die Thätigkeit der Belagerungsartillerie vor Paris* 2–9. It was reckoned that 299 guns were the minimum adequate for the bombardment. By 15th October only 235 had arrived.

[7] W. Busch, *Das Deutsche Grosse Hauptquartier* 15.

[8] *Kriegstagebuch* (3rd October) 109.

was not attacked Blumenthal estimated that no assault on the forts would be possible before December, and none on the *enceinte* before January, and on this calculation Moltke agreed that "it would never come to be a question of bombardment, as the French would be starved out long before that could arise".[1] The Crown Prince, to whose army the bombardment was entrusted, summed up the general opinion of senior German officers when he wrote on 26th October: "All persons in authority, I at the head of them, are at one in this, that we must use every endeavour to force Paris to surrender by hunger alone."[2]

For the soldiers the bombardment was a technical question, and one of such difficulty that they wanted to avoid having to undertake it if they possibly could. But it was a project which aroused the most heated emotions within Germany itself. The desire to avenge the damage wreaked by generations of French armies on German soil, and a gloating Protestant satisfaction at having the modern Babylon at their mercy—a satisfaction such as that felt by Charles V's *Lanzknechten* when they wrecked Rome in 1527—combined with deeper, even less creditable emotions to produce within Germany a public agitation that the bombardment should take place; not a bombardment as the soldiers visualised it, directed against the fortifications as part of the normal operations of siege-warfare, but a general attack on the civil population as an act of national revenge.[3]

Bismarck did not hesitate to foster this emotion by the powerful influence he exercised in the German press. Whether or not he shared it—and it was by no means alien to his temperament—he certainly believed, according to his statements after the battle of Sedan, that the journalists and agitators of Paris, the root of all the political evil in Europe, must be brought to their senses. Moreover, with one eye cocked on Thiers's progress round the courts of Europe and his finger on the languid pulse of the South German States, he was anxious for a rapid

---

[1] Blumenthal, *Journals* 165. See also *With the Royal Headquarters* 183 for Verdy's agreement with this view.

[2] Frederick III, *War Diary* 165, 169. There was one notable exception, however, in the Crown Prince of Saxony, who was a keen advocate of the bombardment. Had its preparation been entrusted to him it might well have occurred earlier. The difficulties in accumulating a siege-park were real enough, but Blumenthal showed little enthusiasm in overcoming them. Nor did Stosch, the Intendant-General, who claimed an absolute priority on rail transport for supplies. P. Hassel, *Aus dem Leben des Königs Albert von Sachsen,* II 432. Hohenlohe-Ingelfingen, *Aus meinem Leben* 374. Hönig, *Volkskrieg* III 80–1. Waldersee, *Denkwürdigkeiten* I 103.

[3] M. Busch: *Bismarck: Some Secret Pages of His History* I 107. Roon, *Denkwürdigkeiten* III 220. Frederick III, *War Diary* 175.

end to the war. If the French could prolong their resistance for long enough, not only might the Powers intervene but the whole German alliance might collapse. Only the fall of Paris could bring about the end of the war, and only bombardment, he was convinced, could hasten the fall of Paris.[1] He brushed aside the technical arguments of the soldiers. The bombardment was being delayed, he was convinced, only because of womanish scruples in the Court and the Army, fostered by the Crown Prince and through him by the Princess Victoria and her English friends.

> There hangs over this whole affair [he wrote in an outburst to his wife on 28th October] an intrigue contrived by women, archbishops and professors. . . . Meanwhile the men freeze and fall ill, the war is dragging on, the neutrals waste time discussing it with us, while the time passes and France is arming herself with hundreds of thousands of guns from England and America. . . . All this so that certain people may be praised for saving 'civilisation'.[2]

And as further weeks passed, and ammunition dribbled into the park at Villacoublay with a slowness which even Moltke's staff found disappointing, Bismarck saw even darker influences at work. Monsignor Dupanloup, the Archbishop of Orléans, was bringing pressure to bear on the Queen; the Freemasons were getting at the King. There were people, he hinted darkly, "for whom the German cause and German victories were not the main questions; but rather their anxiety to be praised in the English newspapers"; and he ordered the obedient Busch to stoke up yet higher the pressure in the newspapers at home.

By the end of November Bismarck could contain himself no longer, and on 28th November he addressed a formal démarche to the King. The danger of neutral intervention, he considered, had been alarmingly increased by the forthcoming Conference of European powers convoked at London to discuss the Russian denunciation of the Black Sea clauses of the Treaty of Paris; and the longer the war went on, the greater that danger grew. The fall of Paris was not merely a military matter. The Army might be in a position to wait until hunger forced the city to capitulate; none the less, he concluded, "political considerations make

---

[1] *Immediatbericht* to the King of 28th November, *Gesamm. Werke* VI b No. 1933 p. 602. Waldersee, *Denkwürdigkeiten* I 100, 103. Oncken, *Friedrich I von Baden* II 210-11, 216-17.

[2] *Letters to his Wife from the Seat of War* 74. M. Busch, op. cit. 333. See also Roon's suspicions of "Weiber-Intriguen" in *Denkwürdigkeiten* III 248, and Hatzfelt's of "irgendwelche geheime, starke Einflüsse". Graf Paul Hatzfeldt, *Feldzugsbriefe* (Leipzig 1907) 215.

an acceleration of this by a bombardment of the forts very desirable".[1]
The King was sympathetic. Three days earlier, on 25th November,
General von Hindersin and Lieut.-General von Kleist, the Inspectors-
General of artillery and engineers, had broken the news to him that the
bombardment, originally planned to begin on 1st December, could not
now possibly open until the New Year; and William made no difficulties
about passing Bismarck's view on to Moltke, together with a strongly
worded expression of his own dissatisfaction at the delay.[2] To this
Moltke replied at once; and his memorandum, drafted for him by Bronsart, expressed the impatience which was being widely voiced in military
circles with the "military ignoramuses behind their green tables".[3]
One historian, indeed, has suggested that he deliberately exaggerated the
technical difficulties so that "the civilian should learn that the tempo of
war was not dependent on civilian desires, that the signal to attack,
like the signal to halt, would be given exclusively by the fighting
troops".[4] "The question", stated Moltke, "when the artillery attack
on Paris should or can begin, can only be decided on the basis of military views. Political motives can only find consideration in so far as
they do not demand anything militarily inadmissible or impossible."
To begin the bombardment prematurely was inadmissible, and to speed
the collection of material was impossible. He had only the one railway
line at his disposal and that ended fifteen miles short of the siege-park.
"In this alone," he stated, "lies the sole explanation for the delay in
the artillery attack." But he made it clear that he still regarded bombardment as an expensive and inefficient weapon, to be used only if hunger
failed.[5]

This view infuriated Roon. He was one of the few senior soldiers
who agreed with Bismarck that the bombardment was desirable and
necessary.[6] He had long suspected that a little more efficiency on the
part of the Third Army would speed up the stockpiling of ammunition,
and had himself taken charge of the collection of waggons to transport
the ammunition from railhead to park.[7] Now he asked Moltke to
explain himself. Why should they go to the immense trouble of

---

[1] *Gesamm. Werke* VI b No. 1933 p. 602.
[2] *M.M.K.* 415–16. *Kriegsgesch. Einzelschr.* I Heft 4 30.
[3] Blumenthal, *Journals* 196–8. Frederick III, *War Diary* 201.
[4] R. Stadelmann, *Moltke und der Staat* 234.
[5] Moltke to William I, 30th November, *M.M.K.* 417.
[6] Roon, *Denkwürdigkeiten* III 244 ff. See also his (undated) letter to the King
in Hönig, *Volkskrieg an der Loire* III 74.
[7] M. Busch, op. cit. I 345. Oncken, *Friedrich I von Baden* II 260.

accumulating material for an operation which the High Command did not intend to carry out ?[1]

Moltke's reply made it clear that he did not consider the bombardment impossible or useless: he merely thought it difficult, and not to be carried out without elaborate preparations, during which time hunger might force a capitulation and make their task unnecessary.[2] He was, however, now prepared to consider a "purely political" bombardment—that is, an isolated act which would not commit the Germans to following it up with an assault.[3] The attacks at the end of November, both from Paris and from the Loire, had shown the French to be very much further from exhaustion than Moltke's staff had believed, and demands for action multiplied. A telegram came from Delbrück in Berlin, which Bismarck thoughtfully forwarded to Moltke, saying that he expected trouble in the Assembly if the bombardment did not begin at once.[4] Another message from Berlin reported the belief in Foreign Office circles that the French were only waiting for the bombardment to begin before entering into negotiations. The Nationalist Press was roaring with one voice for the beginning of the bombardment. Moltke's staff, knowing Bismarck's part in manufacturing the material which he now used as weapons, were not very impressed. Nevertheless it was agreed at a Council of War on 17th December—a Council from which Bismarck was excluded—that the bombardment of the southern fortifications of the city should be put in hand as soon as a ten-day supply of shells, 500 per gun, had been accumulated at Villacoublay. It was also agreed that the full bombardment should be prefaced by an experimental shelling of Mont Avron, the isolated position to the east of the city which the French had occupied before the Battle of Champigny. Finally the conduct of the bombardment was put into the hands of the formidably competent Prince von Hohenlohe, commander of the artillery in the Guard Corps, who was ordered by the King to press on with the matter as quickly as possible. The question, he was informed, should be considered not from the technical view-point of a gunner, but from that

---

[1] Roon to Moltke, 11th December, *M.M.K.* 445.
[2] Moltke to Roon, 12th December, *M.M.K.* 446.
[3] Blumenthal, *Journals* 219.
[4] Bronsart (*Kriegstagebuch* 227) quotes one jingle from the Berlin press:
> Guter Moltke, gehst so stumm
> Immer um das Ding herum.
> Bester Moltke, sei nicht dumm,
> Mach doch endlich: Bumm! Bumm! Bumm!
> Herzens-Moltke, denn warum ?
> Deutschland will das: Bumm! Bumm! Bumm!

of a strategist—a broad hint that technical problems could no longer be regarded as an excuse for delay.[1]

The bombardment of Mont Avron presented few problems. Its batteries had been hastily and inadequately constructed, and were exposed to German gunfire from north, east and south. The Germans opened a sustained fire with seventy-six guns on 27th December and fired continuously for two days. The French had only forty-five guns, poorly sheltered, and they were quickly silenced.[2] Shells exploded lethally on the iron-hard ground, gun emplacements were wrecked one by one, and on the night of 28th December Trochu abandoned the position after losing more than a hundred men. The rapidity of this success surprised the Germans themselves, and made most of the sceptics think again about the efficacy of bombardment. The Crown Prince in particular confessed himself converted, and admitted that "the bombardment may perhaps lead to important results".[3] Moltke had also made up his mind. His hesitations were dispelled by the failure of Frederick Charles to bring the war in the provinces to an end; it was now necessary, he declared at a conference on 31st December, to use any and every means to bring about the fall of Paris and release the German forces to deal with Gambetta's new armies. Hohenlohe reported himself ready; and the King ordered the bombardment to begin on 4th January.[4] As it happened thick fog that morning forced a further postponement; and it was not until 5th January that the first rounds were fired of that bombardment for which the entire army was waiting, according to Bronsart, "like the Jews for the Messiah".[5]

§4 The Bombardment

When Bismarck had taken exception to Moltke's letter to Trochu announcing the fall of Orléans, Bronsart noted scoffingly that the

---

[1] W. Busch, *Das Deutsche Grosse Hauptquartier* 70–1. Bronsart, *Kriegstagebuch* 248, 251. The King informed Hohenlohe that his objective was "den souveränen Pariser Pöbel, der in der Stadt Paris das entscheidende Wort spreche, durch die mittels eines Bombardments zu erzeugende Furcht vor Gefahr zu einer Kapitulation und einen Frieden geneigter zu machen, da die Entbehrungen, welche die Cernirung erzeugte, nicht ausreichten." Hohenlohe-Ingelfingen, *Aus meinem Leben* 367.

[2] Trochu, *Œuvres posthumes* I 515. *G.G.S.* II ii 137. Ducrot, *Défense de Paris* III 233–43.

[3] Frederick III, *War Diary* 247. Hassel, *König Albert von Sachsen*, II 454.

[4] Hohenlohe-Ingelfingen, op. cit. 376–7.

[5] *Kriegstagebuch* 271. Hönig, *Volkskrieg* III 109, corroborates this.

Chancellor was beginning to be "ripe for the madhouse". But the French Government shared Bismarck's view that this communication was more than an act of ironical courtesy. Ducrot saw in it an overture for peace from a war-weary enemy addressed to the only element among the French authorities with whom he was prepared to treat, and he urged that it should be followed up at once while Paris was still in a position to negotiate from strength.[1] So did the moderates in the Government, Favre and Picard. Their view was shared by nobody else in the Ministry, least of all by Trochu. The Governor believed, with some reason, that the Germans would never grant terms acceptable to an undefeated country, and with the approval of the Government he returned a non-committal answer to Moltke's letter and pressed on with his plans for a sortie.[2] The failure at Champigny had not reduced his determination to break out and join the provincial armies which he now knew were marching to his aid. Aurelle might have been defeated, and the German positions south of the Marne had proved impregnable; but there was another force at large and intact—the Army of the North[3]; and this force lay not in a direction to which the approach was barred by a flooded river and barricaded hills, but across a bare plain on which the Germans, if they emerged to do battle, could be dealt with by French artillery. This was a disadvantage, however, from which the French would suffer no less, and the possibility that the German infantry might remain as stubbornly under cover behind their fortifications as they had at Villiers had to be ignored. The essential thing was to get the French forces into action again before the precarious *élan* aroused in them by the Champigny attack had totally died away.

It was not until 21st December that Trochu launched his attack. By then, according to all accounts, his troops had recovered a large measure of confidence and their morale was remarkably high.[4] Their immediate objective was Le Bourget, which, since its recapture by the Prussian Guard on 30th October, made an uncomfortable salient in the French line. This could be attacked from two sides—by a force debouching from St Denis on the west and one advancing from Bondy and Noisy to the south-east; and a pincer movement of this type was

[1] *D.T.* III 96.

[2] Favre, *Gouvernement de la Défense Nationale* II 170 Trochu, *Œuvres posthumes* I 467–9. Dréo, *Procès Verbaux* 379–85.

[3] See p. 390 below.

[4] For accounts of the battle see Trochu, *Œuvres Posthumes* I 480–9. Ducrot, *Défense de Paris* III 106–93. D'Hérisson, *Journal of a Staff Officer* 266. G.G.S. II ii 130–6. Hohenlohe-Ingelfingen, *Aus meinem Leben* 359–65.

prepared, with a mingled force of regular troops, *Mobiles*, *francs-tireurs* and Marines constituting the left pincer and a force under Ducrot the right. It was for the first group to seize Le Bourget, whereon the second would press through and exploit their success. The Marines, moving through early morning mists, reached the village with their left wing, where they hung on and fought bitterly among the houses. But German gunfire broke up all attempt to reinforce them; and when Ducrot, having waited vainly for the success signal from Le Bourget church tower, launched his troops into the attack, they also were checked and thrown into confusion by the accuracy and intensity of the German shell-fire which slammed into their densely packed ranks. The French gunners could make no reply: there was nothing for them to shoot at. The cold, bleak plain stretched empty before them: no enemy infantry was in sight, and his artillery betrayed its presence only by distant clouds of smoke.

Trochu watched all this with a sinking heart, and when the early winter twilight began to fall he ordered his troops to return to their own lines. He was still not prepared to confess final defeat; such an admission, he knew, would be politically intolerable and would re-awaken all the disorders in the streets of Paris which had been so recently and with such difficulty repressed. He gave orders therefore for an advance on Le Bourget by digging parallels, as if for a formal siege. Such orders were unrealistic. Nobody could dig in that icy, rock-like ground; and the morale of his men, badly shaken by the German shells during the day, was shattered by the agonies of cold which they had to endure during the night and the following day. There was no fuel for fires; the ground was too hard for the erection of tents; the men lay in the open, ill-clad and unprotected against the cutting north wind. Nearly a thousand collapsed with frostbite. It was plain to everyone who saw the army that the last flicker of fight had died in it, and could never be revived again.

Trochu was quite right in prophesying political trouble if the attack on Le Bourget failed. The clubs were still maintaining what Trochu called "*le dada des Parisiens militants*", and attributing to the generalship of Trochu the failure at Champigny and Le Bourget. "We shall sally forth without Trochu's generals," declared one; "we have no need of generals. Once we reach the battlefield the generals will emerge on their own."[1] But now the Government also was losing confidence in the military command. A capitulation, with Paris in its present mood, seemed unthinkable: the military operations *must* succeed. But

[1] Ducrot, *Défense de Paris* III 198.

if they did not, even the unthinkable must be thought about; and after Champigny some of the more moderate members of the Government began to brace themselves for unpleasant decisions. Civilian bread-supplies, it was reckoned on 15th December, would last until 10th January, army supplies for a fortnight beyond that. Favre went down to Vincennes, where Trochu had established his headquarters away from the turmoil of Paris, to warn the Governor that the Government of National Defence would not accept the responsibility for exposing the city to famine.[1] Trochu's air of confidence, his assurances that the Germans were also at the end of their strength, were unconvincing; and there was some talk of putting him under the direction of a Commission of Generals, even if he resigned in protest.[2] At the time nothing further had been done; but the shambles before Le Bourget compelled the Government to take action. Favre drove out to Trochu's headquarters after the battle, saw for himself the miserable state of the troops, and on his return firmly declared that the Government must take back the control of military operations into its own hands.[3]

Yet this would not eliminate the need for a soldier to advise the Government and put its orders into effect, and where was such a soldier to be found? Trochu was quite prepared to resign. But Ducrot could not succeed him: he was now openly defeatist, and his hostility to the Liberals made his appointment unthinkable. Vinoy was still the most optimistic of the senior commanders, obstinately believing that with massed forces operating against a decisive point (where? asked Ducrot tartly) something might be achieved; but he had an Imperialist background which made him as unacceptable as Ducrot. The Left-wing members of the Government would trust nobody but Trochu: Arago indeed stated bluntly that "his first care would be to demand of any candidate for the command a profession of Republican faith". All they could do was to urge Trochu to attempt "extraordinary efforts, beyond all orthodox military principles"; and Trochu could only reply that the troops were as yet too exhausted for any further efforts, but that he would certainly deliver battle as soon as he could,[4] and then he would do so in style.

[1] Dréo, *Procès Verbaux* 399–406.
[2] Ibid. 437.
[3] Favre, *Gouvernement de Défense Nationale* II 198. Dréo, *Procès Verbaux* 440–4.
[4] D'Hérisson was perhaps reflecting Trochu's own views when he reported a feeling at his headquarters that "in order to cure Paris of her fever and reduce her excitement, some pints of blood must be taken from her." *Journal of a Staff Officer* 270.

There would be no more capitulations: "when the last hour comes, the Governor of Paris will propose to you a supreme enterprise which may perhaps turn into a disaster, but which might also produce unexpected results." Favre remained unconvinced; and on New Year's Eve, when a meeting of the mayors of *arrondissements* demanded the appointment of a Council of War with a civilian element to supervise Trochu and an immediate attack, he found himself in unexpected alliance with them against his own colleagues.[1]

Such was the French state of mind when, on 5th January, the German bombardment began. At first the fire was aimed at the forts to the east and the south; but during the evening one gun began to shell the city itself.[2] For this attack on the civilian population, as for that at Strasbourg, there was no military reason. Its only excuse, and it was to be one increasingly used by belligerents of all lands with equally little justification, was that by directly attacking their morale it would incline the stubborn Parisians the earlier to peace.[3] The hands of all nations are now so stained with civilian blood spilled under this and analogous pretexts that to pronounce a moral judgment would be hypocritical; about the practical inefficiency of this action, however, there can be no question. Like several commanders since, the Germans both underestimated the morale of the civilian population and over-estimated the destructive effect of explosive in a built-up area. The range of the new siege-guns certainly astonished both sides: to throw a shell from the Châtillon heights to the Île St Louis—although this range demanded extra-heavy charges which wore out the guns[4]—was an achievement hitherto unimaginable. Between three and four hundred shells fell daily in the city, but they did astonishingly little damage. Most of them exploded harmlessly in open spaces, and even when buildings were hit—and the public buildings which suffered included the Sorbonne, the Panthéon, the Salpêtrière and the Convent of the Sacred Heart—the damage was often superficial. Parisians at first flocked curiously to the Left Bank, which bore the brunt of the bombardment, and were disappointed to find how little could be seen.[5] Small boys were doing a thriving trade in shell-fragments, and the effect if anything was to strengthen the hand of the Government. Trochu, more enthusiastic than

---

[1] Dréo, *Procès Verbaux* 444–53. Trochu, *Œuvres posthumes* I 491–5, 515–16. Ducrot, *Défense de Paris* III 203–11, 254–75.
[2] *Kriegsgesch. Einzelschr.* I Heft 4 86.
[3] See e.g. Bronsart, *Kriegstagebuch* 278, and William I, in n. 1 p. 357 above.
[4] *G.G.S.* II ii 369. Verdy du Vernois, *With the Royal Headquarters* 240.
[5] Desmarest, *La Défense Nationale* 397.

discreet, penned a proclamation giving honour to St Geneviève, protectress of Paris, who "has providentially inspired in the enemy the thought of the bombardment which is dishonouring German arms, which dishonours civilisation"; but the radical printers at the Imprimerie protested and the Governor's colleagues persuaded him not to go ahead with his publication. Even the Parisian sense of humour had its limits.[1] Trochu was on surer ground when he protested to Moltke about the bombardment of hospitals in Paris; and Moltke's grimly jesting reply, that he hoped soon to get his batteries near enough to pick out the Red Cross flags more clearly, did much to sway the public opinion of Europe which had been steadily veering round to the support of the French ever since the siege began.[2]

Moltke's expectation of moving his batteries closer to Paris was not idle. The shells which had been falling on the city were a tiny proportion of those which were landing daily on the outer forts, especially on Issy, Vanves, and Montrouge. The sailors who garrisoned the forts responded nobly to their instructions to man and fight them as if they were ships, and their shells did considerable damage to the unmasked German batteries[3]; but it was an uneven fight, in both calibre and number of guns involved. The French worked at night to repair the havoc wrought during the day, but gradually, during the first fortnight in January, their defences fell into ruins and their retaliatory fire became even more spasmodic.[4] After three days the German batteries were able to close in. As they came nearer, so the area of bombardment was extended. From the east the fire crept round the north, and on 21st January St Denis was taken under fire. From there also came a vigorous reply, but there also the defence began to crumble under the concentrated weight of German shells; and the inhabitants of the town had to flee into the city itself.

The effect of the bombardment on the people of Paris was thus not that expected by Bismarck, and Blumenthal, unbending in his opposition to the whole operation, lost no opportunity of rubbing this in. But some effect it did have, and one by no means unfavourable to the German cause. It strengthened the clamour in Paris that something

[1] Trochu, *Œuvres posthumes* I 507–9.
[2] Trochu, op. cit. 511. *M.M.K.* 517. D. N. Raymond, *British Policy and Opinion* 287.
[3] *G.G.S.* II ii 366–9. Frederick III, *War Diary* 249. Ducrot, *Défense de Paris* IV 6–9.
[4] Rauch, *Briefe aus dem grossen Hauptquartier* 250. There is a good description of the damage done to the forts in Vinoy, *Siège de Paris* 382 ff.

positive should be done. The city was now bitterly cold and for the most part very hungry, with the death-rate increasing every week; but so long as nothing was happening the bulk of its population was sinking into a drab, grumbling apathy.[1] The Germans shells stirred them from this like the sting of a wasp, and provoked a violent desire for retaliation and vengeance. "There are 400,000 of you," was the cry of the Paris women, "and you let them shell us!"[2] The demands of the clubs for a *sortie torrentielle* had never abated, and various schemes were now put forward by members of the Government. Could not the entire population paralyse the Germans, suggested one, by breaking out at every point on the perimeter? Another, perhaps with dim recollections of classical antiquity, proposed that the members of the Government, together with the clergy, the magistracy, the religious corporations and choirs of virgins, should lead a procession marching straight on the German lines.[3] Among the soldiers, Ducrot could suggest only breakouts by small groups of picked men, to swell resistance in the provinces. Ducrot was in any case longing to resign, and was kept at his post only by the pleas of Trochu.[4] Trochu himself was determined to keep his sortie as an absolutely last resort, and he was not stirred from this determination even by the arrival on 9th January of despatches from Gambetta which roused the rest of the Government to a frenzy of excitement.

These despatches, dated 22nd December, announced a movement by Bourbaki against the German lines of communication which might yield "immense results", and, more imaginatively, a renewed march by the Armies of the Loire and the North on Paris. "The Prussians," they stated, not untruly, "without having experienced anything like a defeat, seem however to be demoralised."[5] In view of this development Trochu's inactivity seemed all the more intolerable, and the scepticism which he showed as to the probable effectiveness of these provincial plans only made matters worse. It was strongly rumoured that he was in contact with the Germans: indeed, so widespread did these rumours become that he felt it necessary to issue a reassuring proclamation. It was not one of his happier efforts. "Nothing will ever make us relinquish our arms," it declared, "... the Governor of Paris will not capitulate!"[6]

[1] See police report for 5th January, *D.T.* V ii 159.
[2] Dréo, *Procès Verbaux* 526.
[3] Ducrot, *Défense de Paris* III 310–12.
[4] Trochu, *Œuvres posthumes* I 522.
[5] Favre, *Gouvernement de la Défense Nationale* II 215.
[6] Trochu, *Œuvres posthumes* I 520.

Meanwhile on 12th January Trochu told his colleagues that Paris could barely hold out until the effects of Bourbaki's movement began to be felt by the Germans, and draconian measures must be taken to discover hidden food stocks and suppress public discontent. If the food situation was desperate, he pointed out unhelpfully, it was the fault of the Government for failing to take strong measures in time; to which Favre riposted that it was also the fault of the Governor for failing to secure any military success. In any case, maintained Picard, the measures which Trochu advocated would be feasible only "if the voice of the guns drowns the mutterings of the people"; and to this his colleagues unanimously agreed.[1]

Trochu and Ducrot had shot their bolt with regard to any further military operations,[2] but there were junior generals who were prepared to submit plans. When Gambetta's despatch arrived the Government already had before it the project drafted by General Berthaut and supported by Trochu's Chief of Staff, General Schmitz, for an attack from Mont Valérien to crash through the defences on the neck of the Gennevilliers peninsula to Versailles. It was an attack on the German works at their strongest point, and Trochu and Ducrot knew that with the troops under their command it did not stand a chance of success.[3] But the Government, like the clubs, had now had enough of military calculations.[4] The attack was to be launched, if only in a last frenzy of despair, and if only to convince the enthusiasts in the only way they could understand of the hopelessness of their position. On 16th January the Council of Ministers ordered the operation to be put in hand, and in spite of Trochu's objections that the preliminary planning would not possibly be completed before 20th January they ordered it to be launched two days later, on the night of 18th–19th January.

It would be easy to quote this as an example of political leaders demanding the militarily impossible, and liken it to Gambetta's instructions to Aurelle; but it is doubtful whether such a view would be altogether correct. Trochu's staff regarded the operation as a necessary blood-letting to cure the fever of the clubs; and it is possible that the enthusiasm which certain members of the Government showed for the attack was due less to any belief that it would succeed than to a desire to show the Parisians that success was now out of the question and to

[1] Ducrot, op. cit. III 290.
[2] *D.T.* III 101–2.
[3] "Cela ne réussira pas," admitted Trochu, "mais il faut que Paris tombe debout." *D.T.* II 316.
[4] See Em. Arago's testimony in *D.T.* I 459.

prepare for a now inevitable capitulation. If that were so, the sooner the ordeal was over the better, and the degree of failure was unimportant. At their meeting on 15th January the Ministers for the first time discussed capitulation seriously, and Favre admitted that he had been associating the mayors of the *arrondissements* with the Government's decisions during the past week so as to implicate them in any responsibility. That capitulation would involve violent disorders was generally agreed; but the disorders might be less after the *sortie torrentielle* so hotly demanded had definitively and bloodily failed.[1]

The battle of Buzenval, as it was to be called, settled the fate of Paris. More, it destroyed once for all the belief that a People in Arms could overwhelm a trained enemy by sheer numbers and burning zeal. It was the action for which the clubs had for so long yearned—the *sortie en masse*. Nearly 90,000 men were involved, of whom about half came from the *Garde Nationale*, and at dawn on 19th January they debouched from Mont Valérien, and advanced against the German defences between Bougival and St Cloud along a four-mile front. Ducrot had attacked here three months earlier and been repelled; since then Sandrart had done nothing to weaken his renowned defences. Their forward lines still ran along the Montretout-Buzenval ridge, commanding the low ground in front of Valérien across which the French had to attack. The flanks still rested on the Seine; and the works were continued in depth, a tangle of trenches, redoubts, *abattis*, and obstructions, reaching as far as Versailles. The French plan involved a simultaneous attack by three columns, the left under Vinoy against the Montretout Heights above St Cloud, the centre under Bellemare against Buzenval Park and the ridge of La Bergerie, and the right under Ducrot, who had resolutely refused all part in planning the operation,[2] over the old battlefield of Malmaison. The attacks were to begin simultaneously, on a signal-gun to be fired from Mont Valérien, on Trochu's orders at 6 a.m.

From the beginning everything went wrong.[3] It had been foreseen that the passage of 90,000 men over the two bridges available—the road bridge at Neuilly and the railway-bridge at Asnières—would take all night. But nobody remembered that the roads approaching these bridges were blocked by barricades which admitted the passage only of

[1] Dréo, *Procès Verbaux* 530–38. Ducrot, *Défense de Paris* III 294 ff.
[2] *D.T.* III 101–2.
[3] For accounts of the battle see *G.G.S.* II ii 375–85. Trochu, *Œuvres posthumes* I 528–33. Ducrot, *Défense de Paris* IV 72–164. Vinoy, *Siège de Paris* 396–419. *D.T.* III 123.

one vehicle and a few men at a time. Nothing was done to prevent a huge convoy of private vehicles accompanying the army as voluntary ambulances. Nobody foresaw the delay imposed by the heavy rain which had recently so soaked the fields and roads that both rapidly turned under foot and wheel into cloying mud. By 6 a.m., after a night of total darkness and pouring rain, not one of the columns had reached its starting positions, and Trochu himself, struggling to make his way through the confusion, was nowhere near Mont Valérien. An hour later there was still no sign of Trochu, and Ducrot's column, which had the longest distance to cover, was still far from its start line. But it was growing light; the left-wing column was in position in front of Valérien and dangerously visible to enemy guns; so the commandant of the fortress took the responsibility on himself and fired the signal gun.

The columns of the left and centre, launched close-packed into battle, secured some initial surprise as they loomed up through the frosty mists in front of the German outposts. On the left they outflanked the foremost German positions before Montretout and fought their way into St Cloud itself. In the centre they swept up the steep ridge and through Buzenval Park until they were checked before the German stronghold of La Bergerie and the tough defences in the wood between Buzenval Château and the Cucufa ravine. But once the first *élan* was lost, nothing could take its place. The German infantry, driven from their forward defences, renewed their fire from positions further back. The French commanders summoned up artillery; but the guns had been delayed for hours on the approach march, and when they arrived they could not negotiate the slippery slopes of the Buzenval ridge. Engineers went forward to dynamite the German obstructions; but the dynamite was frozen and would not explode. The attack dwindled into a stationary fire-fight in which the thick French columns could only huddle passively on the slopes under the Germans shells, their morale ebbing towards panic. On the left Ducrot's column, coming up into the positions some four hours late, could make even less impression. The Germans in Malmaison and at Longboyau were ready for them and did not yield a yard. Everywhere the French advance was checked, and the precarious discipline of the *Garde Nationale* began to disintegrate.

Trochu, watching the battle from Mont Valérien, could do no more. He had no reserves of artillery or infantry, and there was no hope of getting round the flanks. It was a check which he had foreseen as certain, and which he accepted as final. He himself showed personal courage of the highest order, riding up with his staff to check an incipient collapse before Montretout and drive the wavering National Guardsmen back to face the enemy; but the insouciance with which he risked his own life did not infect his conduct of the battle. After an afternoon spent watching his troops defend themselves—and defend themselves successfully—against counter-attacks, he glumly at nightfall gave the order to retreat.

The disengagement itself was carried out with some skill. To one isolated detachment fighting in the middle of St Cloud the order failed to get through, and it had to surrender the following day; but otherwise the French were able to withdraw from the battle without the Germans being aware of it. This was just as well; for once the French troops began to approach their own lines they fell into a truly monstrous confusion. During the long hours which the forward columns had spent vainly battering at the German defences there had accumulated behind them a host of vehicles: ambulances, supply-waggons, ammunition-trains, guns and limbers, jamming the roads in expectation of an advance. Now this collection, trying vainly to turn and withdraw in the narrow, muddy lanes, piled up into one huge and impassable barrier against which the fighting columns found themselves jammed. The advance from Paris the previous night had been a miracle of order in comparison with the situation which now developed. The winter night was mercifully long and the moon was bright, but not until 6 a.m. were the last rearguards able to fall back, and when the mist lifted five hours later the Germans could see huge columns still covering the roads to the bottle-neck at Courbevoie; leaving the plain littered, not only with dead and wounded but with abandoned ambulances, waggons and guns.

The French losses were not very heavy—a total of some 4,000 killed and wounded, which, taken with the derisory German losses of just over 700, are sufficient evidence of the lack of enthusiasm with which the attack was pressed.[1] But the disorder into which his forces had been thrown by the battle inspired Trochu to demand an armistice of two or three days to clear the battlefield. "We shall need for that, time, effort, very well harnessed carriages, and plenty of stretcher-bearers", he informed Favre.[2] For Favre this was the last straw. He had on 19th January received a long and bitter despatch from Gambetta accusing Paris of doing nothing while the provincial armies were bleeding to

[1] Ducrot, *Défense de Paris* IV 188.
[2] Ibid. IV 159.

death. The Prussians had detached 200,000 men to deal with Chanzy, maintained Gambetta, 100,000 to deal with Bourbaki: why did the Parisians still wait?[1] Small wonder that Favre found the accusation intolerable. When he found Trochu openly convinced that capitulation was now inevitable he demanded that Trochu should be dismissed and the attack renewed at once. But within a few hours another despatch arrived, and from a more reliable source than the sanguine Gambetta—Chaudordy, the *Chargé d'Affaires* of the Foreign Ministry at Bordeaux. This frankly admitted that the Delegation's forces had been crushingly defeated at Le Mans, with the loss of 10,000 prisoners, and that his entire army had collapsed. There was no longer any force capable of marching to the relief of Paris. Jules Favre at last resigned himself to the inevitability of capitulation; and the word was now spoken openly in the Paris streets.

Favre found little sympathy among his colleagues. Picard supported him, but the rest spoke of trying one more attack, of holding out, if need be on horsemeat, after the bread reserves were exhausted. The press and the clubs were unabated in their ardour, fixing responsibility for the failure at Buzenval firmly and solely on the shoulders of Trochu. This view was also held by the mayors, whom Favre and Trochu met on the afternoon of 20th January. They were subdued neither by views which Favre gave them of the defeat at Le Mans nor by Trochu's harangue on the military situation. After so much hardship and hope they could not accept the prospect of capitulation. Rather than capitulate, they said, they would die of starvation, or be buried beneath the ruins of the city: better to die of hunger than of shame. They demanded yet another *sortie torrentielle*: Buzenval did not count. The *Garde Nationale* wanting nothing better, they said, than to be led against the enemy: this time their victory would be certain.[2]

Only one of their points made any sort of sense—the demand that Trochu should resign. Trochu refused. Such a course, he considered, would in a soldier be dishonourable. He placed on the shoulders of the Government the responsibility of his dismissal, and rode out on 21st January to seek among the German shells at St Denis a death which there evaded him as obstinately as it had evaded Napoleon III at Sedan. To this problem at least the Government was equal. It suppressed the Governorship of Paris altogether; it persuaded Trochu to remain as President of the Council; and that evening it offered the com-

---

[1] Ducrot, op. cit. IV 192–203. Favre, *Gouvernement de la Défense Nationale* II 334–9. [2] *D.T.* IV 389. Favre, loc. cit. 340–2.

mand of the armies, which Ducrot refused, to Vinoy.[1] It may seem surprising that the Republicans should have overcome their scruples against the former Imperial senator, and even more surprising that Vinoy should *in extremis* have accepted such a command. But the appointment was neither made nor accepted with a view to carrying on the war. Vinoy's task was to deal with the explosion within Paris which could not in anyone's view be averted any longer. Vinoy was to be the new Cavaignac, and it was a rôle he was quite happy to play.[2]

The rising, such as it was, came on 22nd January, and did not at all fulfil the apprehensions it had inspired. Only the clubs of the extreme Left took part: the mayors of the *arrondissements* had perhaps been more impressed by Trochu and Favre than they were willing to confess, and any lingering doubts were dispelled when they consulted a number of junior officers and found them as determined as their seniors on the futility of further resistance.[3] The demonstrations on 22nd January were thus fomented by a minority as small as it was violent. The imprisoned revolutionary leaders had been liberated the previous night, and during the morning crowds swarmed round the Hôtel de Ville. Jules Ferry received delegates who demanded that the conduct of operations should be taken over by the municipality, and one of whom simply asked that he should be given supreme command. "There is in me the stuff of Kléber, of a Marceau", he explained. Eventually a detachment of *Garde Nationale* appeared before the Hôtel de Ville, and suddenly opened fire on the group standing outside the doors. From the windows there came a furious answering volley, and the square cleared. Fusillades echoed round the streets all afternoon, while the Government, in session at the Hôtel de Ville learned that the flour-supply would barely last the city for two more days. "Civil war was a few yards away," wrote Favre later; "famine, a few hours."[4]

---

[1] *D.T.* III 100. Favre, op. cit. II 351–2. Trochu's acquiescence was unenthusiastic. "I am the Jesus Christ of the situation" he told his staff. D'Hérisson, *Journal of a Staff Officer* 280.

[2] Dréo, *Procès Verbaux* 558–61. Ducrot, *Défense de Paris* IV 211–20. *D.T.* III 118. Favre, op. cit. II 353.

[3] *D.T.* III 100. IV 406. V *Pièces Diverses* 54–5.

[4] *Gouvernement de la Défense Nationale* II 360. The report was exaggerated. Ferry later reported that on 27th January, the last day of the siege, 35,000 quintals of flour remained in stock. Since 18th January daily consumption had been 5,300 quintals, which gave seven more days. Three or four more days' supplies were available at the retailers, so Paris might if necessary have held out for ten more days—until the end of the first week in February. See Ferry, *D.T.* I 417, and Magnin, *D.T.* I 515. A full report of the session is in Dréo, *Procès Verbaux* 562–70.

This sudden, mad little fusillade of the insurgents was like the bursting of a long-festering boil. The long-delayed appearance of force enabled the Government itself to use force, and in the show-down which occurred on 22nd January it became clear how little support the extremists really enjoyed. Vinoy's whiff of grape-shot restored the Government's freedom of action and emboldened it to do what all its members now knew to be unavoidable: to ask the Germans for terms. Paris had reached the end of her resources.

So also had the rest of France. Now we must retrace our steps, and consider the course which the war in the provinces had taken since, at the beginning of December, Gambetta's armies had been driven from Orléans.

CHAPTER X

Guerre à Outrance

§1 The Deepening Conflict

B Y ALL the normal customs of warfare observed by the regular armies
and the traditional statesmen of Europe, the defeats suffered by the
French armies between 30th November and 5th December should have
made the Government of National Defence sue for peace; and it was
assumed by the Germans and by Europe that they would do so.
Opinion in the provinces, as members of the Delegation privately confessed, was now strongly in favour of ending the war. The generals
who led the French armies, excepting only a tiny minority, either
threw in their hands in disgust or continued to fulfil from a dogged
sense of duty a task which they knew to be hopeless. In military logic
there now seemed no prospect of defeating the Germans, nor was there
any reason to suppose that a prolongation of the war would secure a
more favourable peace. The struggle was kept alive only by the will and
the energy of a few men at the centre of power, who inflexibly refused to
admit defeat.

As the war progressed the political truce on which the authority
of the Delegation rested had become ever harder to maintain, and the
Delegation indeed showed ever less interest in maintaining it. For
Gambetta and his followers the victory of France was inseparable from
the establishment of the Republic, and it was only a short step from
that belief to the conviction that all who opposed the Republic were
actual or potential traitors. Gambetta had restrained and even disowned
the extreme Republicans of the South; but he had announced the
surrender of Metz in terms designed to create an outburst not merely of
national but of Republican fervour. "There is one thing that cannot
and must not capitulate," he proclaimed, "and that is the French Republic . . . so long as an inch of sacred soil remains beneath our feet, we
shall hold firm the glorious flag of the French Revolution!"[1] The

[1] Reinach, I 48.

outburst had come, in riots and demonstrations throughout the land, and Gambetta seized on these as evidence that "the party of *la guerre à outrance* has decidedly gained the upper hand."[1] "The combination of the military and the political situation of the country", he concluded, "demands that the system of toleration . . . should give place to a more energetic programme, of a type to upset the supporters of the fallen régime." Nerved by this belief, the Delegation took more and more violent measures. Local councils were dissolved; the magistracy and teaching profession were purged, and a Government newspaper was circulated to "spread into every commune the news of official decrees and to help in the political education of the people". Not only was this to be publicly displayed, but compulsory readings from it were to be given every week by the local schoolmaster, who was to emphasise particularly those articles whose object was "to make clear this essential truth, that the Republic alone, by its institutions, can assure the liberty, the greatness of the future of France".[2]

Such notions on the part of an unpopular minority Government would have been barely tolerable even if it had been leading the nation to victory. When, after the fall of Orléans, it became clear that Gambetta, for all his energy and his brave professions, could not avoid eventual defeat, opposition to the Delegation hardened. Press attacks multiplied, local officials became more stubborn, conscripts more unwilling and desertions more numerous. Gambetta could not believe that France did not share his hopes and his creed, and that the obstacles which he encountered sprang from anything more than the malignancy of a small political clique.[3] At the beginning of the New Year he unburdened himself in a long letter to Jules Favre.

The whole country understands and wants a war to the end, without mercy, even after the fall of Paris, if that horrible misfortune, must befall us. The simplest clearly understand that since the war has become a war of extermination covertly prepared by Prussia for thirty years past, we must, for the honour of France and for our security in the future, finish for good with this odious power. . . . It is because the enemies of the Republic are afraid of seeing her assure the deliverance of our country that they are taking advantage of the extreme liberty which they enjoy to hamper, cry down or misrepresent the military measures taken by the Government. . . .

[1] Gambetta to Favre, 31st October, *D.O.* II 287.
[2] Reinach II 53-4.
[3] For opposition to Gambetta and open expression of public opinion see e.g. *War Correspondence of the Daily News* II 49-50, 310-11.

At bottom France is growing more and more attached to the Republican régime. The mass of the people, even in the countryside, understand, under the pressure of unfolding events, that it is the Republicans ... who are the true patriots, the true defenders of the nation and of the rights of man and of the citizen. ... We shall prolong the struggle to extermination, we shall ensure that there cannot be found in France a man or an Assembly to adhere to the victory of force, and we shall thus strike with impotence conquest and occupation.[1]

Success would have justified Gambetta, as it justified the inflexibility of George Washington, of Danton, of Trotsky, or, to choose a closer analogy, of Charles de Gaulle. Failure places him in the same category as Hitler or Napoleon or Charles XII of Sweden, sacrificing the lives of his people and embittering posterity in the pursuit of an impossible ideal which most of his fellows did not share. At what point does nobility become inexcusable pride? Should it not be the duty of the statesman to represent the immediate desires of his people for security to till their land and bring up their families rather than to force them to endure sacrifices whose benefit, if any, will be felt only by generations long after theirs? It is impossible to frame an answer to these questions which would be valid for both Washington and Jefferson Davis, for both Churchill and Hitler, for both Gambetta and de Gaulle. The quality of a historical action cannot be judged in isolation; even a decision correct in terms of isolated individual morality may be disastrous for a nation. Politics, in war as in peace, is the art of the possible, and the great statesman, like the great soldier, discerns or creates possibilities unseen to the general eye, and can detect with abnormal acuteness the weakness of the enemy and his own nation's latent sources of strength. He is not an irrational hero who, guided by absolutes alone, challenges fortune without weighing the odds and drags down a whole people in his own dramatic ruin.

Yet *was* Gambetta's task impossible? The Germans were certainly less conscious of the hopelessness of the French fight than of the enormous strain which it was imposing on their own already overtaxed resources; and if Metz had held out for a few weeks longer it is difficult to see how this strain could have been met. The release of the First and Second Armies rescued Moltke from a serious dilemma, and even these forces were hardly adequate for the multiple tasks which the growth of French resistance compelled them to undertake. The full strength of the Second Army was needed to deal with the Army of the

[1] Reinach I 197–212.

Loire. This left only the three corps of Manteuffel's First Army to undertake the reduction of the fortresses which still lay across the German lines of communication, the protection of the vulnerable gap between Frederick Charles on the Loire and Werder in the Upper Saône valley, and the destruction of the troops assembling in the north and north-west threatening the rear of the Army of the Meuse. Apart from these active operational requirements there was still the passive need to guard the armies' lengthening communications against the intensifying attacks of the *francs-tireurs*, and this could be done only by drawing more Landwehr units from Germany. About the tension which this caused among the authorities at Versailles something has already been said.

To deal with the organised forces which Bourbaki had raised in the north, Moltke at the beginning of November despatched Manteuffel with two of his corps, I and VIII, and a cavalry division; something over 40,000 men, with 180 guns. Marching westward through Rheims and Compiègne, this force should have had little difficulty in scattering the small Army of the North, 17,000 strong, which barred its way; but on 24th November at Villers-Bretonneux, on the long spur which runs just east of Amiens, the troops trained by Bourbaki fought with a stubbornness which took the Germans by surprise, and inflicted as many casualties—about 1,300—as they received.[1] But the day's fighting was enough to destroy all French hopes of an advance on Beauvais and to send them, disorganised and defeated, to shelter in the fortresses of Arras and Lille, whither Manteuffel did not attempt to follow. Another centre of equally troublesome resistance seemed to be growing up at Rouen, and Moltke had ordered him to deal with that as soon as Amiens had been taken. Rouen was occupied without resistance on 5th December, and the French troops assembling there fell back on Le Havre. Moltke advised a *coup de main* against this last stronghold in the west, but Manteuffel could not spare the men.[2] The forces at Arras lay too menacingly on his flank, and by mid-December their activities compelled him to recall VIII Corps to the neighbourhood of Amiens, leaving I Corps alone to pacify the unceasingly hostile citizens of Rouen and the *francs-tireurs* who infested the close country of the lower Seine.

By December the German forces extended south to Dijon, south-west

[1] H. von Wartensleben, *Operations of the First Army from the capitulation of Metz to the fall of Peronne* (English edn. 1873) 50–70. *Guerre: Campagne de l'Armée du Nord* I 80–119. Lehautcourt, *Campagne du Nord* (Paris 1897) 55–75.
[2] M.M.K. 429.

to Orléans and west to the English Channel at Dieppe; and they were dependent upon a railway system still mutilated by demolitions, shackled by intact fortresses and harassed by *franc-tireur* attacks. The very backwardness of French railway communications now proved to be a positive advantage, much as the primitive nature of the Russian road-system was to hamper the German invaders in 1941.[1] Only three lines crossed the Franco-German frontier, at Saarbrücken, Wissembourg, and Strasbourg. The southern line ran to Paris through Mulhouse, Vesoul and Chaumont, but the fortresses of Belfort and Langres denied it to the Germans throughout the war. The northern line reached Paris through Metz, Mézières and Rheims; but this was blocked by the fortresses of Thionville, Montmédy and Mézières, and not until 2nd January did the fall of Mézières render it available. All German rail transport had therefore to pass over a single stretch of railway between the Moselle valley at Frouard and the Marne valley at Blesme. Even this line was not freed until Toul fell on 25th September, and even then demolition of bridges and tunnels in the Marne valley made it impossible to bring the railhead forward beyond Château-Thierry for another two months. Traffic on the last stretch of this line was relieved by the fall of Soissons on 15th October, which made it possible to supply the Army of the Meuse and later the First Army through Rheims; and the fall of La Fère on 27th November opened up another branch to feed Manteuffel's army in its advance to the west. The supply of the Second Army on the Loire was very much more difficult. Until 9th December the railhead was at Chaumont, demolitions in the valleys of the Seine and Yonne rendering the lines to Montereau and Montargis impassable. Then it was moved forward to Troyes, whence supplies had to go forward by road through Sens and Nemours. The whole line passed within easy striking distance of *francs-tireurs* operating from the plateau of Langres and the mountains of the Côte d'Or, and on 28th November the remaining army corps of the First Army, Zastrow's VIIth, was detached to protect it, establishing its headquarters at Châtillon-sur-Seine.[2]

[1] For German rail communications and *Etappen* organisation in general see E. Schäffer, *Der Kriegs-Train des deutschen Heeres* (Berlin 1883). E. A. Pratt, *The Rise of Rail Power in War and Conquest* 128–32. *M.M.K.* 318, 323, 327, 391, 393, 398. W. Blume, *Operations of the German Armies in France from Sedan* (English edn. 1872) 28 ff. *G.G.S.* I ii 457–68, II i 135–6, 260, II iii 103–38.

[2] For the operations of VII Corps in this area see Hans Fabricius, *Auxerre-Châtillon: Die Kriegsereignisse und Operationen in der Lücke zwischen der II Deutschen Armee und dem XIV Armee-Korps bis zum 20 Januar 1871* (Berlin 1900).

The reduction of the French fortresses was only a matter of time and concentration. All, with the exception of Belfort where extensive improvements had at least been begun, suffered from the weaknesses that we have noted in the story of Strasbourg. Their fortifications were old-fashioned, their guns were outranged by the German, they lacked bomb-proof shelters and they were mostly garrisoned by undisciplined *gardes mobiles*. In few instances were the civil population able to stand up to intensive bombardment or the military governors capable of resisting the pressure of the civil authorities to surrender once the bombardment began. In this alone Strasbourg had been exceptional. Once the Germans had sited their siege-batteries and opened fire, twenty-four hours was usually enough to bring about capitulation.[1] But since there were not enough siege-guns to go round, the fortresses could only be attacked one by one, and until they *were* attacked troops had to be found to observe them. Thus the nuisance-value even of an out-of-date fortress was found to be still considerable. The lesson was not lost on Europe, and after the war military experts returned to the art of fortification with newly-whetted zeal.[2]

Even when a railway-line was cleared of fortresses, grave difficulties still lay in the way of its smooth operation. Demolitions were often skilful and extensive. The destruction of the viaduct at Xertigny severed all rail communication between Dijon and Lunéville. At Nanteuil-sur-Marne the explosion of six mines had filled the railway tunnel with 4,000 cubic yards of sand, and repeated landslides ruined all attempts at repair. Eventually it was necessary to build a loop-line, which was not completed until 22nd November; so for two months the Third Army before Paris—which was responsible for the accumulation of siege-material—had to fetch all its supplies by road from Château-Thierry, fifty miles away. Then as railway-lines became increasingly available men and rolling-stock had to be found to work them. As French railwaymen could not be found in sufficient numbers, some

[1] The policy of deliberately bombarding the civilian quarters of the towns instead of the fortifications, which aroused horror both in France and in England, was justified by the Germans on the grounds that it shortened the siege and thus reduced total suffering; and General Faidherbe, writing of the bombardment of Péronne, admitted "Le système leur a si bien réussi en France qu'ils seraient autorisés à dire que l'humanité même y a trouvé son compte." *Campagne de l'Armée du Nord* (Paris 1871) 56-7.

[2] For surveys of the fortress-warfare in 1870-1, see *Studien zur Kriegsgeschichte und Taktik* IV: *Die Festung in den Kriegen Napoleons und der Neuzeit* (Berlin 1905), and H. von Müller, *Der Thätigkeit der deutschen Festungsartillerie bei den Belagerungen . . . im deutschen-französischen Krieg* (4 vols. Berlin 1898–1904).

3,500 Germans had to be imported. Only fifty French locomotives had been captured, so 280 had to be brought from Germany, causing considerable shortage and dislocation at home. And finally the network had to be protected against the attacks of the *francs-tireurs*.

These attacks were not so numerous or so successful as might have been expected; partly because of the weaknesses of the *francs-tireurs* themselves which we have discussed elsewhere,[1] and partly because of the effectiveness of German counter-measures. Yet their occasional successes and the continual threat forced Moltke to great and growing efforts to keep them at bay. *Francs-tireurs* in the Vosges harassed the line from Wissembourg to Nancy until in September Werder mounted his sustained operation to clear Alsace. The wooded country between Seine and Marne south of Épernay was never cleared of *francs-tireurs*; and attacks on the roads and railways in the upper Seine, Armançon and Yonne valleys died down only with the arrival of VII Corps at Châtillon at the end of November, and even then well-planned and damaging raids continued until the end of the war. The most successful coup of all occurred on the night of 22nd January 1871, when a small group made their way sixty miles across country from Langres and blew up the viaduct at Fontenoy-sur-Moselle, on the vital stretch between Frouard and Blesme over which all German traffic had to pass. Tragically for the French, their heroism was useless. The fall of Mézières had already put the northern lines at the disposal of the Germans, and these had come into operation a few days before. If this attack had been made three months earlier as part of a planned interdiction programme, it is hard to see how the German supply system could have been saved from total, if temporary, collapse.[2]

Responsibility for the defence of communications lay partly with the *Etappen* commands in the various armies and partly with the Governments-General which Moltke set up to administer the occupied areas. One was established for Alsace, one for Lorraine, one, based on Rheims, for the departments between Paris and Lorraine, and one, based on Versailles, for the departments north, south and west of the capital. From these authorities came repeated requests for more troops which neither Moltke nor Roon were conceivably able to fulfil. As it was, the total number of men engaged on *Etappen* and general occupation duties by the end of the war was, according to a reliable estimate,

---

[1] See p. 253 above.
[2] See *Kriegsgeschichtliche Einzelschriften* 2. *Der Überfall bei Fontenoy 22 Jan. 1871*, and H. Genevois, *Les Coups de Main pendant la Guerre* (Paris 1896) 111 ff.

over 110,000, found almost entirely from the Landwehr.[1] Partly by intensive guarding of the lines, partly by taking prominent Frenchmen on the trains as hostages, partly by holding localities responsible for acts of sabotage committed within their boundaries—the inhabitants of Fontenoy were punished with a fine of ten million francs—the Germans were able to keep their services running with reasonable regularity; but they were never able to maintain more than the slenderest margin of supplies for their forces in the field.

As for the *francs-tireurs*, Moltke laid it down at the beginning of the campaign that whereas the *Garde Nationale* were to be treated as *bona-fide* belligerents, the *franc-tireur* had no belligerent rights and was liable to be summarily shot.[2] Later he amplified these instructions. Where individuals could not be brought to book the entire community was to be held responsible. "Experience has established", he informed the Second Army, "that the most effective way of dealing with this situation is to destroy the premises concerned—or, where participation has been more general, the entire village"[3]; and to Werder in Burgundy he wrote: "The very severest treatment of the guilty as regards life and property can alone be recommended to your Excellency, whole parishes being held responsible for the deeds of their individual members when these cannot be discovered."[4]

The German forces carried out these instructions with a thoroughness which did nothing to endear them to the inhabitants, and which left memories that poisoned relations between the two nations for generations to come. The severity of the sentences passed by the court set up in Nancy to try offences against German troops awoke protests even in Berlin.[5] Nor can all their actions come under the heading of "reprisals". The German armies which invaded France, according to the overwhelming evidence of not only neutral but of French observers, were as disciplined, moderate and sober as any Europe had seen. Frenchmen sadly noted the contrast which the orderliness and efficiency of the German marches and the punctiliousness and the moderation of their requisition arrangements showed with the marauding drunkenness of their own troops.[6] It was a contrast, not simply between the

---

[1] Général Derrécagaix, *La Guerre Moderne* (Paris 1890) I 321-2.
[2] *M.M.K.* 239, 241.   [3] Ibid. 368.   [4] *G.G.S.* II ii. App. CXII.
[5] Frederick III, *War Diary* 202.
[6] E.g. Du Barail, *Souvenirs* III 221. Lehautcourt, *Campagne du Nord* 31. On 8th August a Royal Order of the Day had declared "It is the duty of every honour-loving soldier to protect private property and not to suffer the good name of our army to be tarnished, even by isolated instances of indiscipline." Frederick

Teuton and the Latin or—as was more generally believed on the German side—between disciplined Lutheran piety and the degenerate looseliving of the revolutionary free-thinkers, but between two different ages in the conduct of war. French troops straggled, looted and drank as European armies had for four hundred years past. Neither Turenne nor Marlborough nor Saxe nor Napoleon nor Wellington would have seen anything strange in it. But with a staff and supply service organised as was Moltke's such behaviour was unnecessary and could for the first time be eliminated. Marches worked out with scientific precision and efficiently policed eliminated stragglers. Regular and abundant supplies made plunder unnecessary. The German troops were not *dépaysés* by long service but reservists fresh from civil life who on the whole still respected the life, property and women of their enemies. But no army on enemy territory behaves with total restraint, and in every army there are exceptions. The progress of the German troops across France—like that of the French troops—was accompanied by irresponsible looting; and it was scarred with occasional horrors which remained in the mind of the world long after the disciplined restraint to which they were exceptions had been forgotten.[1]

Moreover as the war dragged on into the winter and *franc-tireur* activity grew, the Germans learned an ever-deeper hatred of the nation which was in their eyes prolonging the struggle so uselessly, and by such underhand means. "The war", wrote a German officer campaigning on the Loire in November, "is gradually acquiring a hideous character. Murder and burning is now the order of the day on both sides, and one cannot sufficiently beg Almighty God finally to make an end to it."[2] "We are learning to hate them more every day", wrote another, a sane and civilised man who watched with horror the deterioration which bitterness and brutality were working among his troops. "I can assure you that it is also in the interests of the civilisation of our own

Charles reminded his troops that the French people were not responsible for the atrocities of Napoleon's armies and exhorted them to show them "dasz in unserem Jahrhundert zwei Kulturvölker die Gebote der Menschlichkeit nicht vergessen." *G.G.S.* I i 278. Frederick Charles, *Denkwürdigkeiten* II 148.

[1] At Remilly in August Bamberger found scenes of sacking and brutality for which he blamed the Hessians. *Bismarcks Grosses Spiel* 160–3. On 29th August a battalion of *Gardes Mobiles* which fell into German hands was massacred by its guards at Passavant, and on 29th August a cavalry patrol had, apparently wantonly, burned the village of Voncq. Anon. *Massacre des Mobiles à Passavant, 25 août 1870* (Bar le Duc 1887). *Guerre: Armée de Châlons* I: 128, II: Docs. annexes 8.

[2] F. von Rauch, *Briefe aus dem grossen Hauptquartier* 162. Also Stosch, *Denkwürdigkeiten* 210, and Hatzfeld, *Briefe* 227.

people that such a racial struggle should be brought to an end. Atrocious
attacks are avenged by atrocities which remind one of the Thirty Years
War." The discipline which during the summer had forced the German
troops to respect civilian property was gradually relaxed.

> At first we were forbidden, with the severest penalties, to burn
> vine-posts in bivouacs, and woe to him who used unthreshed corn
> for his palliasse! Child-like innocence! Now no one asks whether you
> are using garden fences or the doors of houses or waggons for fuel,
> and only scrupulous idealists like ourselves care whether a hurriedly
> abandoned fire will catch the straw nearby and then one's host's roof;
> no Frenchman can any longer lay claim to property or means of
> livelihood.[1]

Thus throughout the autumn and winter of 1870 the terrorism of the
francs-tireurs and the reprisals of the Germans spiralled down to new
depths of savagery. If the French refused to admit military defeat,
then other means must be found to break their will. The same problem
had confronted the United States in dealing with the Confederacy six
years earlier, and Sherman had solved it by his relentless march through
the South. Moltke had believed war to consist in the movement of
armies; but General Sheridan, who was observing the war from German
headquarters, pointed out that this was only the first requirement of
victory.

> The proper strategy [he declared after Sedan] consists in inflicting
> as telling blows as possible on the enemy's army, and then in causing
> the inhabitants so much suffering that they must long for peace, and
> force the government to demand it. The people must be left nothing but
> their eyes to weep with over the war.[2]

Bismarck took this advice more seriously than did Moltke. The more
Frenchmen who suffered from the war, he pointed out, the greater
would be the number who would long for peace at any price. "It will
come to this, that we will shoot down every male inhabitant." Every
village, he demanded, in which an act of treachery had been committed, should be burned to the ground and all male inhabitants
hanged. To show mercy was "culpable laziness in killing".[3] Bismarck's

---

[1] Rindfleisch, *Feldbriefe*, 101, 108, 133, and *passim*.
[2] Busch: *Bismarck: Some Secret Pages of his History* I 273. Waldersee
(*Denkwürdigkeiten* I 100) gives a slightly different account. "Sie verstehen es
einen Feind zu schlagen, wie keine andere Armee, aber ihn zu vernichten, das
haben Sie noch nicht weg. Man muss mehr Rauch von brennenden Dörfern
sehen, sonst werden Sie mit den Franzosen nicht fertig."
[3] Busch, op. cit. I 224, 254.

letters and conversations at Versailles were loaded with such sentiments. "Decidedly brutality fits in with his instincts," wrote Bamberger, "as I noticed in 1866. *Il préfère les procédés violents.*"[1] But there are two things to notice about Bismarck's anger. First, it was a matter of words alone and in no way affected his actions. The French negotiators at Versailles in January 1871 were to find him as cool-headed and courteous as he had been at Ferrières in September, and when incidents of wanton and impolitic German brutality were reported to him he condemned them with the violence with which he attacked the *francs-tireurs*.[2] Secondly, his expressions were no worse than those which were becoming common among German civilians as a whole. Even Bismarck protested at his wife's suggestion that all the French should be "shot and stabbed to death, down to the little babies",[3] and the German Press abounded in similar ideas. Nor did the French lag behind in urging suitable torments for the invaders. Each nation came to believe that it alone was upholding civilisation against a race of barbarians which could only be bullied into submission by brute force. Forty-four years later that belief was to be even more disastrously revived.

§ 2 Chanzy[4]

It was not, admittedly, for Gambetta to sue for peace after the fall of Orléans. The Government was in Paris, and its actions were dictated neither by reason nor by military necessity but by the pressure of the extreme Left-wing "clubs". Yet Gambetta regarded the fall of Orléans and the scattering of his armies as no more than an unpleasant episode. The French armies were defeated, but not annihilated; the Delegation's position at Tours was plainly no longer tenable and on 10th December the centre of government was shifted to Bordeaux; but there was no question but that the war should go on and that the offensive should be renewed with the briefest possible delay. Aurelle, who had retired with 15th Corps on Salbris, was made the scapegoat for the loss of Orléans

---

[1] Bamberger, *Bismarcks Grosses Spiel* 152–3.

[2] E.g. his attitude towards the exactions of the German Prefect in Beauvais, General von Schwarzkoppen. Busch, op. cit. I 561.

[3] Busch, op. cit. I 273. Paul Déroulède later suggested in *Avant la Bataille* (Paris 1886) 7, that these words should be engraved on the walls of all French schools.

[4] See map on p. 286.

and the command-in-chief was abolished. The Army was to remain in the two fragments into which it had fallen under the pressure of Frederick Charles's attack. Chanzy was to retain command of 16th and 17th Corps, retreating along the northern banks of the Loire; while 15th, 18th, and 20th Corps, whose flight was carrying them towards the south, were combined into a second army of which Bourbaki assumed command.

It was not until 6th December that Gambetta learned of Ducrot's defeat, and so long as he believed that the armies of Paris were marching south to meet the armies of the Loire nothing, not even the loss of Orléans, could make him abandon his determination to attack. On 5th December Bourbaki and Pallières, shepherding their fleeing troops across the Loire, were ordered to concentrate at Gien and attack northward towards Fontainebleau, while 16th and 17th Corps recaptured Orléans. The generals were stupefied by these orders. Their troops, they pointed out, were frozen and exhausted, and such a movement was out of the question. For once their protest was accepted.[1] Gambetta, visiting Salbris, saw enough of the state of 15th Corps to realise that they spoke no more than the truth, and in any case the news of Ducrot's repulse removed the urgent need to attack. On 7th December therefore he authorised Bourbaki to withdraw to Bourges where he was to take command of 15th and 20th as well as 18th Corps, and rest and refit; but "once you have them all collected under your hand", he added, "I reckon that you will be really ready for a decisive action."[2] Pallières, as soon as he had got his men back to safety at Bourges, resigned his command. Nothing, he said, would induce him to remain any longer "at the disposal of the military fantasies of the telegraph from Tours".[3]

While Bourbaki fell back on Bourges, Chanzy was reforming his army on the Loire before Beaugency. There were several reasons why his force should have been in better shape than Bourbaki's. It had not suffered the full impact of the German attack as had 15th Corps, and it had not, like 18th and 20th Corps, been disorganised by a long retreat. But all other reasons are insignificant beside the competence and personality of Chanzy himself. Like most of his colleagues in the Loire armies, he had arrived too late from Africa to find employment in the Imperial forces before they were engulfed at Metz and Sedan; but unlike his colleagues he was not discouraged by the material he now had to command. He neither tried to fit his untrained citizen-soldiers into the mould of the regular army nor gave them up in despair. He

---

[1] *D.T.* III 349, 380, 469. Eichthal, *Bourbaki* 139.
[2] *D.T.* III 405.   [3] Pallières, *Orléans* 262, 284. *D.T.* III 243-5.

knew what could be expected from them, and how to extract it: where other commanders overstrained their forces till they collapsed into an unmilitary rabble, Chanzy kept his in hand and knew when he could stand and fight. Alone perhaps among the generals, he never allowed himself to doubt the possibility of ultimate success. Until the very end of the war he was fertile in devising plans and enthusiastic in urging them. He had already shown himself an inspiring leader in the attack, but his full genius was to show itself in the patience, resolution, and fighting capacity with which he led his armies in unbroken retreat, in the dead of winter, for seven terrible weeks. Chanzy deserves better of his country than many of the names which glitter on the roll of Marshals of France; but it is habitual for nations to give exaggerated glory to generals who lead them to victory, and forget those whose talents merely stave off or mitigate defeat.

Chanzy's new position was well chosen, his right wing resting on the river and his left on the Forest of Marchénoir, but he halted, he later confessed, mainly because to retreat further would mean the total disintegration of his forces. It was a courageous decision, and its correctness can be judged by comparing the condition of his forces with that of Bourbaki's men when they reached Bourges. A fight in good positions might restore their shaken morale; a continuation of the retreat could only destroy them. A large proportion of 16th Corps had already streamed back to Blois out of reach, but enough remained for Chanzy to take up a position along the Binas–Beaugency road, with 21st Corps, which had come up to join his command, posted in the forest on his left; while in rear of these positions he prudently posted a cordon of cavalry, to deal with fugitives.[1]

Chanzy did not have long to wait. Moltke was urging Frederick Charles to a rapid pursuit, advising him to press on to Bourges and Nevers while Mecklenburg, whose independent command was restored, advanced down the river to Tours. It was necessary to make up as quickly as possible for the failure to annihilate the French at Orléans and to ensure that, when it came to peace negotiations, the French should not still have as a bargaining-counter an army 100,000 strong in the field.[2] But Frederick Charles could not rid himself of the fear that Bourbaki might resume the offensive against his left flank, and not until 7th December did he advance from Orléans.[3] Then the Second

[1] Chanzy, 2me *Armée de la Loire* 122.
[2] *M.M.K.* 425. Bronsart, *Kriegstagebuch* 211. Frederick Charles, *Denkwürdigkeiten* II 408.　[3] Stosch, *Denkwürdigkeiten* 214.

Army fanned out from the city, III Corps marching upstream towards Gien and IX Corps and a cavalry division crossing south into the Sologne. Mecklenburg's Detachment was already feeling its way down the river towards Beaugency and Blois. On 6th December his cavalry had run into Chanzy's outposts beyond Meung, and on the 7th he advanced to attack. He did so unskilfully, his forces widely dispersed, expecting little resistance after the rout of Orléans, and the French had little difficulty in holding his surprised troops in the vineyards before Beaugency. His cavalry could not deploy among the vines, his artillery was ineffective against the tough French farm-buildings, and the *chassepot* came once more into its own. The day ended in a humiliating check.[1]

On the 8th therefore Mecklenburg deployed his full forces for battle, 17th Division on his left wing opposite Beaugency, the Bavarian Corps in the centre and 22nd Division on the right. North-west of the Loire the country was open and rolling, only villages and farms providing cover among the bare snow-covered fields; and the fighting was to consist of a succession of battles for these vital *points d'appui* which dominated the landscape in every direction. Chanzy did not await attack in his positions. The advancing German troops were met by thick columns of infantry, covered by an artillery fire whose speed and precision astonished them. For the village of Cravant in the centre of the French position a vigorous battle raged all day, while between there and Le Mée the Bavarians were subjected to an attack by 17th Corps under which they very nearly broke. Only nightfall and artillery fire prevented their complete collapse, and they left scores of men on the battlefield too exhausted even to retreat. These extraordinarily vigorous attacks checked the German advance everywhere except at Beaugency where, unknown to Chanzy, Freycinet, alarmed by the German advance on the south bank of the Loire, had ordered the garrison to withdraw from this potential salient to more defensible positions behind the town. This decision, correct enough in terms of military manœuvre, was disastrous in terms of men and morale. The troops in the town had fought effectively so long as they were in good static positions. Once they were withdrawn they began to panic and most of them streamed back to Blois. The Germans were thus able to make their way into Beaugency that evening and use it as a base for further advance next day.

[1] For accounts of the battle of Beaugency see *G.G.S.* II ii 47–61. Helvig, *1st Bavarian Corps* 299–353. Chanzy, *2me Armée de la Loire* 104–51.

That night Chanzy reported his troops "at the end of their strength and incapable of making a serious effort next day". Nevertheless he attacked again at dawn on the 9th, attempting in vain to reoccupy Beaugency and making such strong demonstrations in the centre that the Germans gathered their strength to meet a renewed attack. Curiously enough the German historians speak of attacks on their right flank as well, where in fact Chanzy was far too prudent to allow the untrained men of 21st Corps to debouch from the Forest of Marchénoir; and it was to relieve this purely imaginary pressure that Mecklenburg ordered his 17th Division to attack from Beaugency against the French right flank. There they met with no resistance and penetrated deep into the French rear—a success which enabled 22nd Division to drive hard against the French centre until they were within a few hundred yards of Chanzy's headquarters at Josnes. Darkness halted them. Had they ignored it they might have secured one of the most significant successes of the war; for not only Chanzy but Gambetta was at Josnes, almost within their grasp.

Gambetta had come up to assess the chances of further resistance, and they seemed slight. Chanzy admitted that his men were exhausted. He was prepared to hold on if he must, but he urged a withdrawal while it was still possible. Since the Government was abandoning Tours and the protection of that city was no longer essential, the best direction for such a withdrawal was westward, to the base of Le Mans where the army could rest and refit. Between them they decided to hold off the German attack for one more day, and then to retreat westward towards Vendôme and the valley of the Loir.

It proved unnecessary to hold the Germans on the 10th. Moltke had now realised that Mecklenburg had been set a task far above his strength. With 24,000 men he had no hope of shaking a concentrated force of 100,000. At one moment Mecklenburg began to talk despondently about retreat, and Stosch had to exert all his energy to banish his discouragement. Frederick Charles was still hypnotised by the presence of Bourbaki in Bourges and reluctant to offer him an open flank by going to Mecklenburg's help. He attributed the check suffered by Mecklenburg's forces purely to the incapacity of their commander. "The Grand Duke is a very brave gentleman but no commander," he told Waldersee. "Believe me there's nothing in front of him. He simply has not the energy to attack." Personal animosity obviously affected his judgment, but it was reasonable to rate the threat offered by 16th and 17th Corps under an unknown commander lower than that of the larger force commanded by a general of world renown. Stosch, despairing of his voluntary help, had to telegraph directly to Moltke, who at once sized up the situation. The German plan of fanning for a pursuit must be abandoned; they must instead concentrate for a fight.[1] On 9th December therefore Frederick Charles, on orders from Versailles, resumed command of Mecklenburg's forces, sent X Corps down to support them from Orléans and ordered III Corps, which was marching up river towards Gien, to turn about and advance by forced marches on Blois. Mecklenburg was to stay where he was for the 10th December, and await relief.[2]

Thus on the 10th Chanzy found everything much easier than he had expected, and indeed began to wonder whether he need retreat at all. The only immediate threat now came from the German advance south of the Loire, where at twilight on the previous evening Hessian infantry had wrested the castle of Chambord from the *mobiles* defending it, and on the 10th Hessian cavalry had appeared opposite Blois; but this advance was highly vulnerable to a counter-attack by Bourbaki from Bourges.

Ever since his arrival at Bourges Bourbaki had been bombarded by messages from Tours urging action, but to all such demands he responded that his men were unfit to fight. "The men", he reported, "are in a state of misery and demoralisation of which you cannot form any conception."[3] His force was composed of the least experienced troops in the army, and not even defeat in battle is so demoralising as prolonged and hurried retreat. Gambetta, who went straight to Bourges from Josnes, was forced to admit that Bourbaki did not exaggerate. His forces, he wired to Freycinet, were in "veritable dissolution: it is the saddest sight I have ever seen."[4] On 12th December Bourbaki did attempt a limited advance which had the effect of forcing a German cavalry outpost to abandon Vierzon and checked the uninterrupted march of the Hessian Corps on Tours[5]; but then he lost his nerve completely. The bulk of the German forces, he wired Gambetta, was concentrating against him and not against Chanzy. For a moment it was doubtful whether he could be persuaded to remain in Bourges at all.[6] With no hope of support from

[1] Waldersee, *Denkwürdigkeiten* I 110–12. Stosch, *Denkwürdigkeiten* 215.
[2] *M.M.K.* 438.
[3] *D.T.* III 368–9.
[4] Lehautcourt, *Campagne de l'Est 1870–1* (Paris 1896) I 119. Reinach I 267.
[5] *G.G.S.* II ii 67.
[6] *D.T.* III 369, 372. For further correspondence between Bourbaki and the Delegation, see Eichthal, *Bourbaki* 150–71.

Bourbaki, Chanzy had no alternative except to retire, and on 11th December he disengaged his troops.

Chanzy's fears about the effect of further retreat on his troops proved correct. A thaw had set in, turning the snow on the ground to slush and soaking the troops with rain.[1] Even the cold had been better than this soggy misery and Chanzy's troops began in thousands to throw away their weapons and abandon their ranks. The Germans found the Forest of Marchénoir full of stragglers, wet, hungry and shaking with fever. The local peasants did nothing to mitigate the sufferings of their compatriots. They displayed the harshest indifference towards the struggle which was being uselessly prolonged by a Government they disliked, and of the two armies they preferred the Germans who could pay for what they took.[2] Only the caution of the German cavalry saved the whole army from disaster as it floundered across the muddy plain and enabled it to reach its new positions on the Loir, on either side of Vendôme by 13th December. 16th Corps provided a bastion in front of Vendôme, while on the right flank General Barry and the troops which had been holding Blois had fallen back to St Armand.[3] Strategically the French were well placed. They threatened the flank of any German advance on Tours, covered the line of retreat to Le Mans, and menaced the direct communications between the German forces and Paris; so Chanzy decided that rather than prolong the horrors of the retreat he would remain there and await events.[4]

But Chanzy did not anticipate the size of the force that Frederick Charles was now able to deploy against him. Mecklenburg's troops, almost as exhausted as the French, were held on the river at Fréteval, but III and X Corps came up on their left and began on 15th December to exert a pressure which their adversaries could not possibly resist. Chanzy still struggled against the decision to fall back again; but on top of the fighting of the 15th there came a night of such terrible suffering for his men, camped fireless in the mud under a new onslaught of sleet and snow, that the corps commanders next morning reported any serious resistance to be impossible. Chanzy therefore gave the order to

[1] For a heart-rending account of this retreat see C. Chevalier, *Tours Capitale* 164–5.
[2] Voigts-Rhetz, *Kriegsbriefe* 240–1.
[3] Chanzy, *2ᵐᵉ Armée de la Loire* 158–77.
[4] Blois had been abandoned on the 12th. Only Gambetta's personal intervention had prevented the civil authorities from surrendering it on the 10th, when the Hessians summoned it to capitulate on pain of bombardment—a threat which the Prince of Hesse did not carry out. (Report of Gen. Barry, in Chanzy, *2ᵐᵉ Armée de la Loire* 505.)

retreat on Le Mans, abandoning all hope both of co-operating with Bourbaki and of covering Tours; and behind river-mists his forces were able to get away undisturbed. As he had feared the remaining forty-five miles to Le Mans completed the destruction of his army. The country it had to traverse was close and hilly, the fields small, the hedges high and impenetrable, the lanes twisting and sunk deep between high banks. The infantry had to flounder across fields or tear their way through vine trellises, while guns and waggons choked the lanes, breaking their surfaces into muddy morasses in which entire convoys stuck fast. Chanzy's army eventually reached Le Mans in a state of miserable exhaustion little better than that in which Bourbaki's had arrived in Bourges.[1]

Had Frederick Charles pressed his pursuit it is doubtful whether Chanzy would have reached Le Mans at all. But the German troops were quite as weary as the French. A large proportion now consisted of young recruits, hastily trained and of low physical stamina; they were weakened by sickness and fatigue, their boots dropping to pieces on their feet.[2] Moreover the further he moved from Orléans, the more uneasy the Prince became. He was conscious of his lengthening communications, and had never rid himself of his obsession with the threat which Bourbaki still offered to his left flank. Finally, as the Second Army was massing on 15th December to attack Vendôme there came alarming though baseless reports of an attack on Gien far in its rear. Frederick Charles therefore pursued no further and sent only cavalry to harass Chanzy's retreat, and two days later Moltke formally confirmed that there should be no further pursuit.[3]

§ 3 Faidherbe

Meanwhile at Versailles Moltke considered the situation which faced him. The armies of Republican France had been defeated as decisively as those of the Empire. Ducrot, Aurelle, Chanzy, Bourbaki, every general who had attempted to meet the German armies in the open

---

[1] Chanzy, op. cit. 196–207. Rindfleisch, *Kriegsbriefe* 109.
[2] Frederick Charles, *Denkwürdigkeiten* II 423–5. Rindfleisch, *Kriegsbriefe* 115 ff. Kretschman, *Kriegsbriefe* 216–7. Rauch, *Briefe aus dem grossen Hauptquartier* 190.
[3] *M.M.K.* 462.

field had failed. But still there was no sign of peace. Not one of the French armies had been destroyed. Ducrot had fallen back into the fortress of Paris, which the Germans were as yet in no position to assault; the provincial armies had withdrawn out of reach; and within the area occupied by the German armies unceasing vigilance was necessary to prevent communications and administration from being disrupted by *francs-tireurs*. The prestige of Sedan was dribbling away, and with it all hope of securing a peace as cheap and successful as that which had followed Sadowa. The dilemma seemed insoluble: rapid victory was vital to prevent the neutral powers of Europe enforcing a humiliating arbitration, but rapid victory could be secured only by an expenditure of manpower which might not only strain the loyalty of the German allies, but reopen the scarcely healed army-crisis in Prussia. Bismarck's recipe was to keep war-fever stoked up in the German Press, and to demand the immediate bombardment of Paris, in the hope that this would bring about the capitulation of the capital and the end of the war. Moltke, as we know, had no belief in bombardment as a short cut; but he accepted the thesis that the operations in the provinces were subsidiary to the siege of Paris, and that the fall of the capital was needed to end the war. The main effort of the German armies had therefore still to be directed against Paris, and operations in the provinces must be confined to the minimum necessary to protect the lines of investment.

The means of implementing this strategy Moltke outlined in despatches to the commanders of the First and Second Armies on 15th and 17th December.[1] The enemy, he explained, could be pursued only so far as was necessary to rout their main forces and make their reassembly impossible for a long time. He could not be followed to his bases at Lille, Le Havre or Bourges, and distant provinces such as Normandy or the Vendée could not be permanently occupied. The German armies should if necessary withdraw from untenable positions, and concentrate their forces in a few strong points from which mobile columns could operate against *francs-tireurs*. The First Army should thus be based on Beauvais, with strong detachments in St Quentin, Amiens, and Rouen. Mecklenburg, based on Chartres and Dreux, should resume responsibility for the west; and the Second Army at Orléans was to abandon the left bank of the Loire and occupy only Gien and Blois. Zastrow's VII Corps at Châtillon and Werder's troops in the Saône valley completed these lines of circumvallation. Beyond them the French armies could be left for the time being to lick their wounds in peace.

[1] *M.M.K.* 462.

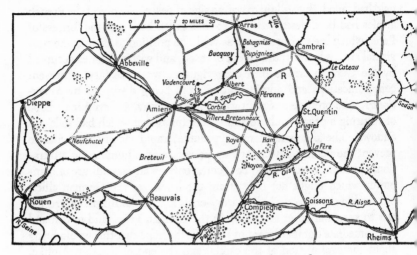

Map 15: The Campaign in the North

Gambetta and Freycinet did not hesitate to take advantage of this lull. Their resources were still on paper enormous: nearly a million men serving or available for military service, backed by an industry which was now beginning to produce war-material in quantity, and by ports through which armaments from America and Great Britain could freely flow. If all this was borne in mind there was no need to despair of renewing the attack, and Gambetta did not despair. Bourbaki at Bourges was refashioning an army three corps strong, capable of once more taking the offensive. Chanzy had been barely a week in Le Mans before he was pushing out columns to harass the Germans on the Loir and urging Gambetta to renew that attack. And finally General Faidherbe had taken charge of the Army of the North.

The fall of Rouen had almost isolated the northern departments of France from the provinces of the centre and south where the heart of the resistance lay. Thereafter Lille became virtually a capital city, linked to Bordeaux only by semaphore, or by telegraph-lines running through England and Le Havre. With its limited resources the area could never be more than a nuisance to the Germans; but if those resources were properly used the nuisance could be considerable. There was the industrial potential of Lille and the surrounding districts; there was a strong Republican spirit, as Bourbaki had found to his cost; there was an intricate barrier of fortresses, into which the Germans hesitated to venture, while a flow of escaped prisoners-of-war from Germany provided the army with a cadre of professional troops.[1] These forces were already being marshalled with great ability by Colonel Farre, Bourbaki's Chief of Staff, and had fought bravely at Villers-Bretonneux, when, at the beginning of December, General Faidherbe came to take command.

Faidherbe,[2] like Chanzy, had been in Algeria during the first stage of the war. Previously he had been Governor of Senegal, where his intelligent administration had enriched the colony and gained him an honourable place among the galaxy of soldier-administrators which France bred during the nineteenth century with such prolific ease. A lifetime in Africa had ruined his health, and a winter of campaigning in Picardy was an unceasing martyrdom. Wracked by fever and constantly exhausted, he had to go to bed at five o'clock every evening, rising again at midnight to dictate his orders.[3] If he lacked something of Chanzy's amazing resilience, he shared his cool insight into the strength and weakness of the citizen armies he commanded, and added a luminous intellectual courage of his own. Unlike Chanzy, he saw no hope of victory: he did his work as a soldier, and fought on until the Government told him to stop.[4] But like Chanzy he won the confidence of the Republican officials and collaborated with them cheerfully and without friction. The qualities required in a disciplined army, he pointed out, were exactly those which Gambetta had demanded in the nation as a whole: contempt for death, discipline and *austérité des mœurs*; and these he announced his intention of enforcing. From those who found *austérité des mœurs* beyond their strength—and many evidently did—he demanded "at least dignity, and in particular temperance". The slightest acts of violence, rapine, and looting, he proclaimed, would be punished with the utmost severity. Unlike the Armies of the Loire, whose discipline collapsed under the strain of constant fighting and campaigning, the Army of the North, safe within its fortresses and carrying out only limited operations with a specific end, was at the mercy of its police, its N.C.O.s, and all the officials whose ungrateful task it is not to assist in a battle but to create, in the rear areas, those habits of obedience and that military mien without which no army can exist. But for all this

[1] Altogether some 5,000 escaped prisoners joined the Army of the North. *Guerre: Armée du Nord*: Docs. annexes I 28.
[2] See J. M. Brunel, *Le général Faidherbe* (Paris 1890).
[3] General de Villenoisy, in *Guerre: Armée du Nord* I 138.
[4] *D.T.* III 542.

time is vital, and Faidherbe never had enough. Faidherbe knew the deficiencies of his forces: "My army is 35,000 strong," he told Gambetta on 5th January, "of whom half fight seriously. They decrease at each encounter. The remainder are only useful for making a show on the battlefield."[1] He had not enough arms and equipment: neither the contracts placed in Britain nor those in Belgium, he complained, were producing enough. "We are making great efforts," he assured Gambetta, "but be assured that a flock of men without arms, without leaders and without training is a source of weakness and useless expense. The improvised officers, ignorant, good-for-nothing, are a menace and disorganise everything."[2] One of his divisional commanders indeed, General Robin, a former captain of Marines, who was notorious for his corruption, his loose living and his incompetence, on one occasion established his headquarters in the hospitable premises of a local brothel. Faidherbe could defend him only on the grounds that he was energetic, that he was good with his troops, and that at least he was better than his chief of staff who could not even mount a horse.[3]

Like Bourbaki at Bourges, Faidherbe wanted time to knock his forces into shape; but unlike Bourbaki he realised that time was under the circumstances a luxury he could not afford. On 7th December Gambetta ordered him specifically to "direct his army corps with a view to a possible junction with General Ducrot's army, which would break out via St Denis and march north-east"; Manteuffel was just then in Rouen, and the opportunities seemed favourable. Such a movement might at least halt the German threat to Le Havre, the last link between north and south; and Faidherbe replied at once that within three days he would have three divisions on the Somme ready to march.[4] He was as good as his word and even better, for he sent a column which on 9th December, in darkness and a snowstorm, fell on the town of Ham, successfully surprised the German garrison, and recaptured the fortress for the Government of National Defence.

This brilliant *coup de main*, which severed the rail-communications between Rheims and Amiens, was followed next day by the appearance of Faidherbe with his entire army, and caused the Germans considerable alarm. From Ham Faidherbe might strike at Amiens, at Paris, or even at the important supply-centre of Rheims.[5] Manteuffel at Rouen

---

[1] *Guerre: Armée du Nord* III: Docs. annexes 63.

[2] 9th January 1871. *Guerre: Armée du Nord* III 5, and Docs. annexes 78.

[3] *D.T.* III 539.

[4] *Guerre: Armée du Nord* II 32.

[5] Bronsart, *Kriegstagebuch* 220.

repeatedly ordered Graf von der Groeben, who had been left in charge at Amiens, to retake Ham at once, but this Groeben decided he could not do. Worse, he decided that Faidherbe's appearance on the Somme made Amiens untenable and on 16th December he withdrew from the city, leaving only a garrison in the citadel. The furious Manteuffel then turned to General von Kummer, who was in command at Breteuil, ordered him to recapture Amiens and to take over from Groeben until General von Goeben could arrive with VIII Corps from Dieppe to restore the situation.[1] Meanwhile Moltke was sufficiently alarmed by this new threat, and by the incompetence with which it was being met, to take a hand himself.[2] On 13th December he ordered Manteuffel to concentrate his whole force in the region of Beauvais, whence he could meet an attack on Paris from any direction. It was a wise move. The concentration of his army gave Manteuffel time to see that Faidherbe was aiming, not at Paris, but at Amiens; and once this became clear he was able to reach the danger-spot rapidly in sufficient strength.

Faidherbe's first movement from Ham had been eastward towards the Oise valley, where he might find easier pickings on the German line of communications. But he found his path barred by the fortress of La Fère, which could not be rushed and which he was unwilling to bombard. So he turned back and marched down the Somme towards Amiens. These marches were very different from the depressed shambling of the Armies of the Loire. The weather was cold but fine, the chalk hills firm under foot, and the troops slept in billets every night. "It is a pleasure to feel oneself in a solid army, well-organised and well-commanded," wrote one *mobile* under Faidherbe's command; "we are convinced that at the first encounter General Faidherbe will win a great victory."[3] Certainly Faidherbe did not intend to risk a great defeat. The recapture of the town of Amiens was made more difficult by the action of the German commander of the citadel, who had prudently taken the leading French citizens and officials into the citadel to discourage French bombardment and who threatened on Faidherbe's approach to turn his guns on the town[4]; and the approach of Manteuffel with all available troops of the First Army made the reoccupation out of the

[1] Wartensleben, *Operations of the First Army* 126–37.
[2] *M.M.K.* 451.
[3] L. Gensoul, *Un bataillon de mobiles pendant la Guerre de 1870–1. Souvenirs de l'Armée du Nord* (1914).
[4] Wartensleben, *Operations of the First Army* 123. *Guerre: Armée du Nord* II 56.

question until he had been met and defeated in battle. Faidherbe had little hope of defeating him; but he realised, like Chanzy, that a defensive battle fought under favourable conditions would do his army more good than ignominious retreat. He decided to stand and fight.[1]

The position he chose was about five miles north-east of Amiens along the Albert road, and he could hardly have found a better. His front and right flank were covered by the course of the Hallue, a stream flowing south into the Somme, and his left flank was covered by the Somme itself below Corbie. His outposts lay in the villages of the Hallue valley from Vadencourt to Daours, but his main positions were on the hills behind them—bare chalk slopes, then covered with a light fall of snow, which provided as excellent fields of fire for the *chassepot* and *mitrailleuse* as they did for German machine-guns when, forty-five years later, 60,000 British soldiers were mown down in a single day trying to assault just such slopes a few miles up the valley. To defend his five-mile front Faidherbe had about 40,000 men and eighty guns, organised into two corps, 22nd and 23rd. One division of the latter consisted of untrained *Gardes Nationales* under the incompetent Robin, and Faidherbe kept it well back in reserve behind his right wing. The other divisions he deployed in two lines, with the regular troops in first line and the *Mobiles* behind. On 22nd December he rehearsed his men in taking up these positions before returning them to their customary billets; and on 23rd December he marched them up to fight.[2]

To assault this position Manteuffel had at his disposal VIII Corps and a brigade of I Corps. Another brigade was on its way from Rouen, and Moltke had ordered up the 3rd Landwehr Division from Mézières; but rather than wait for these reinforcements Manteuffel decided to attack at once with the 25,000 men and 108 guns at his disposal. Reconnaissance revealed the French positions on the hills between Daours and the Albert road, but, like Moltke at Gravelotte, Manteuffel could not tell how far these positions extended to the north. Like Moltke he directed part of his force—the 15th Division—against the visible enemy positions, and sent the rest in a sweep to the north to find the French right flank. Like Moltke's his attack failed. The 15th Division, attacking on the morning of 23rd December, had no difficulty in clearing

[1] Faidherbe, *Campagne de l'Armée du Nord* 33.
[2] For general accounts of the battle of the Hallue see *G.G.S.* II ii 110–17. Zernin, *Leben des Generals v. Goeben* II 87–90. Wartensleben, *Campaign of the First Army* 152 ff. *Guerre: Armée du Nord* II 72–121 and Docs. annexes. Faidherbe, *Campagne de l'Armée du Nord* 36–41. Lehautcourt, *Campagne du Nord en 1870/1* (edn. of 1897) 124–39.

the outposts in the valley villages before the centre of the position, but then exhausted itself in fruitless attempts to assault up the bullet-swept slopes beyond; while on the extreme left flank French marines held on to the village of Daours, which sealed the Somme valley. The 16th Division after a circuitous march arrived at about 3 p.m. in the villages of Montigny and Béhencourt, further up the Hallue, to discover that they had not found the French flank at all, but were involved in a tough frontal attack. All along the valley the Prussian attack was held. Not even their superior gun-power could help them, for the French gunners, equipped with percussion-fuses, were able to make a vigorous and effective reply. By 4 p.m., as the short winter day was ending, Faidherbe judged that the impetus of the attack was exhausted and the moment was right for counter-attack. All along the line the French rose and charged cheering down the slopes into the misty valley beneath. The movement was ill-judged. A concentrated attack against a single point might have had some effect on the Prussians; as it was the counter-attack spent itself in confused and desultory house-to-house fighting in the burning villages, until Faidherbe, once darkness was absolute, summoned his troops back to the slopes above.

That night the French did not withdraw to billets. Faidherbe made them sleep on the battlefield, the only certain criterion of victory, and he himself slept among them. Next morning Manteuffel, judging his forces too tired to renew the attack, saw the French still encamped on the hills above him and resigned himself to a defensive battle for Amiens. But no attack came. Faidherbe had attained his objective of giving successful battle; he knew that German reinforcements were on the way; and his army could not stand another night on those freezing hills. During the night of Christmas Eve he retired with his forces along the Albert road to the safety of Arras. Each side had lost about a thousand men and Faidherbe had lost a thousand more in prisoners or deserters who fell to the Germans during the retreat. Manteuffel did not pursue him far; Moltke's orders of the 15th had been explicit on this point. Besides, his departure from Rouen had been a signal for the revival of intensive *franc-tireur* activity in that area, and I Corps was urgently demanding reinforcements. Manteuffel therefore returned to Rouen and left to General von Goeben, commander of VIII Corps, the protection of Amiens and the Somme.

By Christmas the Germans had thus established relatively stable fronts on the Somme, on the Loir and on the Loire, and wanted only to be left in peace. Gambetta and Freycinet had abandoned their schemes for concentric advances on Paris, and were staking everything on the ambitious campaign of Bourbaki in the east. The west and the north therefore became comparatively quiescent; but Chanzy and Faidherbe could be relied upon to ensure that this quiescence was neither prolonged nor absolute. Goeben in particular was kept in a state of apprehension. The fortress of Péronne, invested by a Landwehr Division, was still in French hands, and threatened German communications between Amiens and Rheims. Goeben took up a position at Bapaume to cover it against any attempt by Faidherbe at relief, but he acknowledged that if Faidherbe advanced on Péronne he would not have the strength to stop him.[1] Faidherbe knew that his armies were in no state to move; but if no relief was attempted Péronne would certainly fall, and both military and political considerations demanded that this should be prevented at almost any cost.[2] So on 2nd January he advanced to the attack.[3]

Faidherbe's forces were two corps strong, and the Germans barring his way at Bapaume had only one division and a little cavalry; and that was deployed to meet an attack from Cambrai rather than from Arras. But Faidherbe also had misjudged the enemy positions. He expected to find the bulk of them west of Bapaume at Bucquoy, and he directed his best corps, indeed his only passable corps, the 22nd, against that point. Only his 23rd Corps advanced straight on Bapaume, and half of that, Robin's division, was useless. It was not good country for the attack: the snow-clad plain of Picardy was naked under a lowering sky and the Germans in the sparse villages possessed the only available cover. Thus a weak German brigade ensconced in the villages of Sapignies and Béhaignies was able to check one French division on the main Arras-Bapaume road,[4] while further east Robin allowed his division to be halted almost at once by a handful of cavalry. Not until 3rd January was Faidherbe able to bring 22nd Corps to bear against Bapaume; by then the Germans, concentrated and reinforced, seemed ready to contest the town house by house. Rather than subject its citizens to the horrors of a direct assault Faidherbe decided to use his superior numbers to outflank and surround the garrison. Throughout 3rd January 22nd Corps pushed its way round through the villages west of Bapaume,

---

[1] Zernin, *Leben des Generals v. Goeben* II 447, 449.

[2] *Guerre: Armée du Nord* II 136.

[3] For the Battle of Bapaume see authorities quoted in n. 2 p. 394 above, and A. von Schell, *Operations of the First Army* (English edn. 1873) 24–41.

[4] For Goeben's own part in this action see Zernin, *Leben des Generals v. Goeben* II 93–5.

till by nightfall it was well across the Albert road. But Robin's division of 23rd Corps, which should have provided the left-hand arm of the pincer, advanced in line without any reconnaissance and was halted by a few mounted batteries, under whose shells the French left wing broke and ran.

Faidherbe, himself exhausted, felt that he could ask no more of such troops. Later he explained that German reinforcements were on the way and that he believed he had achieved his purpose and lifted the siege of Péronne. Such a course was in accordance with his policy of shaping his operations to the abilities of his troops[1]; but his order to withdraw was received with amazement by the victorious 22nd Corps and was in fact tragically unnecessary. The Germans were outnumbered, weary, and short of ammunition. 15th Division had been uninterruptedly engaged since it left Metz, and its endurance was almost at an end; and while Faidherbe was giving orders for the abandonment of the attack on Bapaume, Goeben was arranging for the evacuation of the town and the lifting of the siege of Péronne.[2] Had Faidherbe persevered Bapaume might have fallen to him on 4th January and another victory would have been achieved to rank with Coulmiers in softening the bitterness of final defeat. As it was, the French and Germans withdrew north and south like exhausted boxers to their corners at the end of an inconclusive round; and five days later, after a week of continuous bombardment, Péronne capitulated at last.

§ 4 The End in the West

Chanzy meanwhile had been growing bolder in harassing the Germans before him; perhaps too bold. Manteuffel, with the troops at his disposal and his commitments on the Lower Seine, could not pursue Faidherbe into his fortress-belt and crush him: thus Faidherbe possessed those two essentials for successful operations, an enemy he could meet on approximately equal terms and a secure base. Chanzy had neither. Frederick Charles and Mecklenburg had adequate forces to deal with him; and the security of his base at Le Mans depended not on geographical or artificial defences of its own but solely on the difficulty which the Germans found in supplying troops fighting so far to the west —difficulties which their staff found means to overcome. Chanzy was

[1] See Faidherbe's "Note supplémentaire" in *D.T.* V, *Réclamations* 139.
[2] Schell, *Operations of the First Army* 15.

thus dependent for his survival on German forbearance; and he would have done well, being so placed, to have exercised something of Faidherbe's caution, even if Faidherbe could have afforded something of Chanzy's zeal. As it was Chanzy grudged even the minimum time for the restoration of order to his armies. Within a few days of reaching Le Mans he was submitting plans to Bourbaki for new concentric attacks on Paris, which Gambetta and Freycinet, now immersed in Bourbaki's eastern expedition, persuaded him with some difficulty to postpone.[1] Even they could see that with the forces at his disposal he stood no chance of success; but if he waited until the second week in January, pointed out Gambetta, his army would be strengthened by two new army corps now being raised at Cherbourg and at Vierzon, and Bourbaki's expedition against the German lines of communication would have taken effect.[2] It was a new experience for Freycinet to have to restrain the ardour of one of his military commanders.

Meanwhile to cover his concentration at Le Mans Chanzy sent out two strong columns to keep the Germans at bay, harass them in their positions and dominate the considerable no-man's-land between the valleys of the Huisne and the Loir. One of these advanced up the Huisne valley to Nogent-le-Rotrou to oppose any advance from Chartres, where Mecklenburg lay with 22nd and 17th Divisions (now reconstituted as XIII Corps); while the other, a division strong under General Jouffroy, was sent against the Second Army's positions in the Loir valley. Jouffroy was given a very free hand, and on 27th December he ambushed two German battalions at Troo below Montoire. The Germans stolidly shot their way out again, but Jouffroy was encouraged and pressed on to Vendôme, sending back to Chanzy an excited demand for support. On New Year's Eve he mounted a very respectable attack on the town and on 5th January he prepared to attack again. This time he failed disastrously, and no wonder; for he ran head on into a full scale German offensive.

It had not taken Moltke long to tire of the strict defensive which he had imposed on his armies in the provinces. It was not in his nature to leave the initiative to his enemies for any longer than was absolutely necessary—least of all to an enemy of such proved energy and ingenuity as Gambetta. He knew well with what zeal the two armies of the Loire were being overhauled at Le Mans and at Bourges, and rightly suspected

---

[1] Freycinet, *La Guerre en Province* 277. Chanzy, *La 2me Armée de la Loire* 234.

[2] Chanzy, op. cit. 237–54.

that the urgent needs of Paris would soon force them to renew the
attack. If Frederick Charles remained passive he might find himself
overwhelmed. Safety lay only in taking the initiative, so on 1 January
1871 Moltke ordered the Second Army, with Mecklenburg's forces
again under command, to advance westward to crush Chanzy for good,
before any such joint attack could develop.[1] Frederick Charles arranged
his forces in a loose arc for a concentric advance on Le Mans, with
XIII Corps on the right with its right flank advancing down the Huisne,
X Corps on the left advancing down the Loir and clearing resistance
further south, and in the centre III and IX Corps following one another
along the main road through St Calais to Le Mans. This advance
began on 6th January, and Jouffroy ran into it just outside Vendôme.
He resisted for twenty-four hours, then the Germans began to close
in on Le Mans.[2]

There followed six days of campaigning which remained like a nightmare in the memories of all the participants, French and German
alike.[3] The midwinter retreat through the narrow twisting lanes and
steep valleys of this district had already broken Chanzy's new army,
and now the horror had to be repeated by French detachments with
Germans hard on their heels. The Germans suffered little less from the
difficulties of the advance. They could not move off the roads; even on
the roads, icy and muddy by turns, the movement of guns and waggons
was a major problem; while the shortness of the days set its own limit
to the speed of operations. A well-sited *mitrailleuse* manned by a
resolute crew might check a division for an entire day while infantry
sought openings for a flanking attack and unemployable guns and cavalry
blocked the lanes behind. Under these circumstances the speed of the
German advance, fifty miles in six days, was remarkable. Chanzy
considered it inexcusable. On 8th January he sent out Admiral Jauréguiberry, his most trusted lieutenant, to take charge of all the columns
except that on the left flank and to impose some order on their retreat,
and for a day the German left wing was held. But in the centre III Corps
was forging steadily up the St Calais road, and Chanzy had on 9th
January to send out a division which checked it ten miles short of
Le Mans at Ardenay, and held out until dark in heavy snow. But such
isolated stands could achieve little: only a general counter-attack could
check the Germans, and this Chanzy, to gain time to complete his

---

[1] *M.M.K.* 493–4.   [2] *G.G.S.* II ii 145–84. Chanzy, op. cit, 271–307.
[3] E.g. Kretschman, *Kriegsbriefe* 252–57, Rindfleisch, *Feldbriefe* 155–61
C. von der Goltz, *Die sieben Tage von Le Mans* (Berlin 1873) passim.

defences before Le Mans, ordered for 10th January. "I really don't know what I am going to do to make them march this evening", said one corps commander. "If it is possible we'll do it. Everyone says that it can't be done, but we'll see."[1] In this glum mood Chanzy's generals led their troops through the snow to encounter the German forces whose foremost troops were now within five miles of Le Mans. In the Huisne valley, round Champagné, they held firm; but further south they were driven from position after position, and at Parigné l'Evêque they streamed from the battlefield in total collapse.

Chanzy himself was sick and exhausted,[2] but his resolution never faltered, and now he summoned up his last resources of energy and ransacked Le Mans for every available man. He had his three corps and their reinforcements, and he had in addition twenty-two battalions of Breton *Gardes Nationales* from the training camp at Conlie, fifteen miles north of Le Mans, whom he had summoned in spite of the protests of their commander that they were neither trained nor armed. A large proportion of them arrived equipped only with American muzzle-loaders left over from the Civil War. Their ammunition was soaked by rain and snow; it was of the wrong calibre; and the troops did not know how to load. Even had they been able to do so the defective mechanism of the rifles would have made them impossible to fire. No cleaning equipment was provided, but it is doubtful whether anything would have made any impression on the thick coating of rust which had accumulated in the six years since the Civil War had ended. These wretched men, armed only with these execrable weapons, had to take their place in the line.[3] Trenches had been dug before Le Mans, roads barricaded, guns provided with stocks of ammunition; and on the evening of 10th January Chanzy issued orders through which he tried to inspire his broken troops with his own resolve. His strict instructions, he complained, had been disobeyed. The offensive which he had demanded had not been launched, and he publicly reprimanded the generals responsible. Now he called on his men to defend Le Mans as they had defended their positions above Beaugency. Cavalry posted behind them would make sure that they did. Fugitives would be shot, and if need be the bridges would be blown up in the army's rear, to leave it no alternative except to fight to the last.[4]

[1] Chanzy, 2me *Armée de la Loire* 570.
[2] See Lehautcourt, *Campagne de la Loire* II 246.
[3] *D.T.* III (Jauréguiberry) 299, V (Genl. de la Lande) 16. Lehautcourt, op. cit. II 279–84.
[4] Chanzy, op. cit. 307.

If anything could have saved Le Mans it would have been orders such as these, and the sort of cheering encouragement which Chanzy gave his men as he rode down their lines in front of the town on the morning of 11th January. They were cleverly posted. 21st Corps north of the Huisne guarded the left flank against Mecklenburg's encircling advance. Two divisions of 17th Corps held the long plateau between Yvré and Champagné, their flanks on the Huisne and their front covered by raking fire from the guns on the hills west of Yvré; while the French right wing lay before Pontlieue, its flanks resting on the Sarthe and the Huisne and its front along the Chemin aux Bœufs which ran in a straight line north-east between the two rivers. It was here that the unfortunate Bretons were posted, together with the detachments which were still falling back into position under the super-vision of Jauréguiberry. X Corps, pursuing them, did not arrive before the French right wing until late in the afternoon, after III Corps had already become heavily and not altogether successfully involved on the left. With heavy fire the French had been driven from the hills above Champagné, but the fugitives found themselves checked by the sabres of their own cavalry, the guns of their implacable commander and the icy waters of the Huisne. The advancing Germans were shelled by the guns beyond the river, and a French counter-attack recaptured part at least of the abandoned crest. On the extreme left 21st Corps stood firm; and on the right, when at 7 p.m. Voigts-Rhetz arrived with a weary X Corps before the Chemin aux Bœufs, he found himself confronted by a line of earthworks and trenches which it seemed hopeless to ask his troops to attack. Nevertheless with the least possible delay he did attack, and after driving in the French outposts he launched a battalion in close columns straight up the main road. Most of the troops even of Chanzy's army could probably have held such an attack and repulsed it, but by ill-luck Voigts-Rhetz had chosen to assault the point held only by the almost defenceless Breton *Mobiles*.[1] They collapsed completely, and with them the entire French right wing. Jauréguiberry spent the whole night trying to rake troops together to counter-attack, and failed. The columns he assembled disintegrated on the march and men slipped away or collapsed from fatigue. Gradually his whole front dissolved like melting ice, the troops wandering back to La Mans with a quiet deliberation which was far more final than any panic.

Next morning the admiral reported to his commander than an immedi-ate retreat was essential. Throughout the night Chanzy had been hearing,

[1] Voigts-Rhetz, *Kriegsbriefe* 280–5. Rindfleisch, *Feldbriefe* 157.

and dismissing, identical reports from his other commanders, but Jauré-guiberry was a man whom he knew he must believe.[1] He at once drafted orders for a retreat up the Sarthe to Alençon. Typically the opening paragraph stated that the army had "to reconstitute itself as quickly as possible and under the best possible conditions, so that it may erase the sad events of today and resume its rôle". The French left wing was still intact and the Germans as yet had no conception of the extent of the collapse on the right, so by a great effort some quantity of the stores accumulated in the town could be removed before the Germans followed Jauréguiberry's retreating columns. On the left wing counter-attacks kept III Corps at bay long enough for the last French troops to be withdrawn safely across the Huisne; then the entire French army began its pilgrimage again through thick snow, north and west, in a miserable search for safety.

The Germans had no strength left to follow. They were themselves near exhaustion and thankful to rest, and Frederick Charles sent forward only the minimum necessary force to keep contact with the re-treating French.[2] Chanzy had lost more than 25,000 men in casualties and prisoners, and twice that number had deserted; but he did not allow this to affect his plans. He moved to Alençon, not to retreat, but to be in a position to advance again on Paris, and it was only on Gambetta's urgent instructions that he agreed to change the direction of his march and on 13th January to fall back westward towards Laval. There he again began tirelessly to plan an advance with the ex-hausted, hungry, mutinous horde which hardly any longer deserved the name of an army. He was still so planning when the armistice was signed.

* * *

The collapse at Le Mans no more discouraged Gambetta than had the collapse of Orléans. He believed that Paris could hold out until the end of the month, that Bourbaki's strategy would soon make its effect

[1] Chanzy, 2me *Armée de la Loire* 327.

[2] On 12th January both Alvensleben and Voigts-Rhetz had reported their men incapable of further effort; and the Bavarians had long been withdrawn from active operations as no longer battle-worthy. Frederick Charles noted in his diary: "Wenn man sieht, dass nach solchen Niederlagen und nach solchem wüsten Marsch durch Le Mans der Feind eine Meile von hier bei Chaufour die erste Nacht blieb und jetzt immer hartnäckigeren Widerstand leistet, statt auseinanderzulaufen, so drängen sich doch eigentümliche Betrachtungen auf, z.B. dasz ein Verlust von 30,000 Mann für ihn nichts ist, da er 50,000 aus Rennes sofort zur Disposition hat, die Lücken zu ergänzen, während unser Verlust von 3,000 Mann zunächst nicht zu ersetzen ist. Soll man unter solchen Umständen überhaupt verfolgen oder bloss schlagen?" *Denkwürdigkeiten* II 424.

felt, and that the armies of the provinces must now gird themselves, as Chanzy had consistently urged, for one last concentric attack. On 17th January he met and harangued Chanzy's officers at Laval, and from there went on by sea to the north. In Lille he spoke superbly.

If each of you had the same conviction, the same profound passion as myself, it would not take weeks and months to annihilate the invading armies: the ruin of Prussia would be immediate; for what could 800,000 men do, whatever the power of their organisation, against thirty-eight million resolute Frenchmen who had sworn to conquer or die?[1]

But it was too late for such appeals. Neutral observers saw that his speeches no longer awoke any responses, and Testelin, the Republican Commissioner in the north, told him with brutal frankness that "the mass of the nation is going to hold the Republic and yourself responsible for our material disasters, and will prostrate itself at the feet of the first-comer who will give it peace".[2]

Testelin spoke perhaps with the more feeling since Faidherbe's army had just fought its greatest battle and suffered its most decisive defeat. After the German recoil from Bapaume Faidherbe had held his forces in readiness between Bapaume and Albert, while Goeben, who on 8th January had succeeded Manteuffel in command of the First Army, remained south of the Somme. Faidherbe had been stirred again to action by a demand from Freycinet that he should make a diversion to help the Paris garrison on their last attempt to break out. His task was thus not necessarily to fight the Germans but to cause them the greatest possible anxiety. An advance on Amiens or southwards on Paris itself would only bring on a fatal collision with the bulk of the German forces; but by a stroke eastwards towards St Quentin and the valley of the Oise he might evade Goeben, create havoc among German communications, and return to his fortresses without engaging the First Army at all.[3]

It was an intelligent plan but one difficult to execute. The few good roads which ran south-eastward from Bapaume and Albert passed through Péronne; and the fall of Péronne left Faidherbe only a few indifferent lanes for moving his troops. The northward bulge of the Somme between Amiens and Ham gave the Germans good interior lines, and enforced on the French a long march across their front which would have been dangerous with the best of troops and the best of roads. Finally Faidherbe now had a more formidable opponent than Manteuffel to deal with. Goeben was a masterly commander, as

[1] Reinach I 71–6.   [2] *D.O.* I 505.
[3] *D.T.* III (Faidherbe) 538. *Guerre: Armée du Nord* IV 12.

cool and clear-headed as Moltke himself. He concentrated his forces behind the Somme to be ready for movement in any direction, and he used his cavalry boldly in reconnaissance.[1] On 15th January he realised from the intensity of French reconnaissance that something was brewing, and warned Moltke; on the 16th a French column descended from Cambrai to seize the weakly guarded town of St Quentin; and at dawn on the 17th the discovery by a cavalry patrol that Albert was deserted showed that this was not just a feint: Faidherbe was really moving east. So Goeben also moved east to intercept him, concentrating his forces between Péronne and Ham.[2] He had at his disposal four divisions of infantry and one of cavalry. In addition Moltke sent him a Saxon brigade from the lines of investment at Paris, and by arranging for XIII Corps to take over the defence of Rouen he enabled Goeben to withdraw most of his forces from there as well. Assured of the approach of these reinforcements Goeben felt well justified in offering battle to an army only 43,000 strong.[3]

Thus everything went wrong with Faidherbe's plans. His army, floundering along narrow lanes ankle-deep in muddy slush, could not keep to the time-table he had prescribed. Supply-arrangements collapsed. German cavalry watched quite openly the snail-like progress of his troops. Goeben's infantry raced east to forestall him on the Oise, and on 18th January the wings of the two armies became entangled in an encounter-battle between Péronne and St Quentin which halted half Faidherbe's army and disorganised his entire movement. It was clear to Faidherbe that the Germans had been too quick for him. There was nothing he could do but fall back on St Quentin and if necessary offer battle there.[4]

The result of the battle of St Quentin was not a foregone conclusion.[5] In infantry Goeben had only about half his opponent's strength, and

[1] Schell, *Operations of the First Army* 86, 89.

[2] Ibid. 94–5. Zernin, *Leben des Generals v. Goeben* II 103 ff. A detailed analysis of this movement is to be found in *Kriegsgeschichtliche Einzelschriften* XIV. *Der Rechtabmarsch der I Armee unter General von Goeben auf St Quentin im Januar 1871* (Berlin 1895).

[3] *G.G.S.* II ii 259, 263. *Guerre: Armée du Nord* IV 47. For the Battle of St Quentin itself Lehautcourt gives 40,000 Frenchmen and 99 guns against 36,000 Germans and 161 guns. *Campagne du Nord* 246.

[4] *Guerre: Armée du Nord* IV 26–9, 69: Docs. annexes 35, 47–60, 91, 95–6. Schell, op. cit. 107–17.

[5] For general accounts of the battle see *G.G.S.* II ii 264–76. *Guerre: Armée du Nord* IV 70–146. Schell, op. cit. 128–67. Lehautcourt, *Campagne du Nord* 251–79. Zernin, *Leben des Generals v. Goeben* II 106–11. *Kriegsgesch. Einzelschr.* XIV 142–8.

the open hills round the town made any attack doubly difficult. The circumstances of the battle were no less favourable to the French than they had been in the battle of the Hallue. But Faidherbe's army, though numerically stronger, was far weaker in morale than it had been a month before. Wearied and dispirited by its marches in the rain, disordered by the fighting of the previous day, it looked forward with reluctance to battle. The gendarmes had to search the town for deserters and drive them forcibly out to fight. Positions were taken up hurriedly, without adequate reconnaissance, and at least one set of vital orders went astray. Faidherbe had intended that 22nd Corps, which contained his most reliable troops, should guard the Somme valley in positions reaching from the Ham to the La Fère road, while 23rd Corps and the reserve lay behind its right flank to cover his line of communications to Cambrai. But the orders never reached 22nd Corps, which took up positions before the villages in which it had spent the night, Castres, Grugies, and Gauchy, on the left bank of the Somme. Thus each corps fought a separate battle on either side of the Somme valley, 22nd Corps defending the hills to the south-east against the attacks of the 16th and 3rd Landwehr Divisions, and 23rd Corps, north-west of the river, meeting the attacks of 15th and von Groeben's divisions between the Ham and the Cambrai roads.

The morning of 19th January was foggy and dark, with a chill rain churning the clay fields into mud. The Germans advanced on St Quentin up both banks of the Somme and found the French barely ready to receive them. But 22nd Corps, in spite of its lack of orders, found excellent positions on the hills round Grugies, firing from behind piles of sugar-beet and manure, and when the Germans began to attack at 10.30 a.m., they could make no impression. Beyond the Somme 23rd Corps with inferior troops fighting in closer country crumbled more easily before the assaults of the German left wing. It is curious, under the circumstances, that Goeben, when the first impetus of his attack had been exhausted, should have chosen to reinforce his right flank, which had made little progress, rather than his left, which was doing well; especially since a break-through by his left wing would have cut the Cambrai road which was Faidherbe's main line of retreat. As it was, hearing the noise of battle loudest to the south of the Somme, he sent the regiment and the thirty guns which he had been keeping in reserve to that part of the front; and with the help of these reinforcements and an encircling movement up the La Fère road the German right wing was able to dislodge 22nd Corps from its hill-tops and force it back towards the single bridge over which retreat to St Quentin was alone possible. By 4 p.m. resistance south of the Somme was broken. So was resistance to the north. 23rd Corps, never very steady, shredded gradually away under the German fire, and by 4.30 p.m. was falling back uncontrollably towards the Faubourg St Martin; and when Faidherbe galloped back through St Quentin to seek reinforcements, he found that 22nd Corps had also collapsed and was flooding back across the Somme.

Faidherbe had made no plans for retreat; he knew as well as Chanzy that retreat could only destroy an army such as his. His first reaction on finding that his defences were collapsing was to fight on in St Quentin to the last. "The papers make fun of us and say that we are always falling back", he grimly told a staff officer. "Very well. This time we won't fall back."[1] But nothing he could do could now halt his troops. Belatedly recognising a *fait accompli*, he ordered a retreat—an order, which in the darkness and confusion of the streets of St Quentin, did not reach the commander of 23rd Corps until he was almost surrounded in the outskirts of the town. Fortunately the Germans were in a state of confusion as great as the French and in no condition to pursue the defeated army as it trailed through the night, shedding stragglers at every farm-house, along the slippery *pavé* roads to Le Cateau and Cambrai; and by morning most of Faidherbe's men had made their way back to safety. They had lost over 3,000 casualties, and more than 11,000 were missing—for the most part falling unwounded to the Germans as prisoners. Faidherbe had lost more than a third of his army and he did not pretend, to himself or to anyone else, that he could do anything with the débris that remained. He distributed them among the fortresses of the north and Goeben was content to leave him in a peace which remained unbroken until, on 28th January, they learned that an armistice had at last been signed.[2]

---

[1] *Guerre: Armée du Nord* IV 145, quoting de Courson, *Opérations de l'armée française du Nord*. See also Faidherbe's "Note supplémentaire" in *D.T.* V. *Réclamations* 142.

[2] Goeben and Faidherbe, both scholarly men, continued to fight their battles over again. Faidherbe's work, *Campagne de l'Armée du Nord*, which appeared in 1871, was at once criticised for its inaccuracies and misjudgments by Goeben in the *Allgemeine Militär. Zeitung* 36–47 (1872). Faidherbe replied with a *Réponse à la relation du général von Goeben* (Paris 1873) and Goeben riposted in the *Allgemeine Militär. Zeitung* 17–19 (1873). The writer has been unable to trace any further published reply by Faidherbe, though Goeben's biographer states that he received "ein sehr artiges Schreiben" from him after Goeben's death. Zernin, *Leben des Generals v. Goeben* II 116.

§ 5 Bourbaki

The campaigns of Chanzy and of Faidherbe, strenuous as was the effort they involved, were subordinate to military events elsewhere in France. Their object was not to defeat the forces opposed to them but to pin down the greatest possible number of German troops and by their attacks to facilitate the relief of Paris. Gambetta clung to the hope of a direct march on the capital long after Orléans fell. Bourbaki's forces in Bourges were still intended for an attack on Paris through Gien and Montargis. Not until the middle of December, when Frederick Charles temporarily abandoned the pursuit of Chanzy and returned to Orléans, did Gambetta begin seriously to consider another possibility—that of forcing the Germans to raise the siege by cutting their communications in eastern France with an advance northwards into Lorraine from the valley of the Saône.

A substantial proportion of the forces in eastern France, it will be remembered, had been transferred to the Loire to participate in Aurelle's offensive in November, and now constituted 20th Corps in Bourbaki's army. There were left three bodies of troops, in addition to those who still held out at Langres, Besançon, and Belfort. At Lyons General Bressolles was forming an army corps out of the *Gardes Nationales* of the Midi and had about 15,000 men under arms. Garibaldi's *francs-tireurs* were based on Autun and dominated the Côte d'Or; and in the Saône valley below Dijon lay a force of 18,000 *Gardes Nationales* whose command was shared, and bitterly contested, between Generals Bressolles, Crevisier, Crémer, and Pelissier; four commanders whose suspicion of one another was surpassed only by their loathing for Garibaldi.[1] They were watched, not without anxiety, by von Werder at Dijon, whose forces had now been reorganised under the label of XIV Corps. Until VII Corps came to his help at the end of November Werder was solely responsible for the protection of the main German communications against attacks from the south. It was not an easy task, and the Prussians at Versailles did not consider that Werder and his Baden troops did it particularly well.[2] But nobody at Versailles could understand how a rabble of badly armed conscripts and undisciplined *francs-tireurs*, who were scattered wherever they were brought to battle, could possibly

[1] For the confusion in the command of these forces see *D.O.* II 34–5, *D.T.* III 505, 533, *D.T.* V 70–2. Ultimately Crémer emerged as the effective commander.

[2] E.g. Bronsart, *Kriegstagebuch* 214.

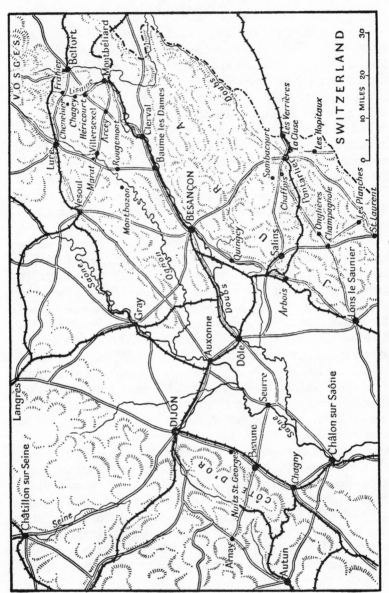

Map 16: The Campaign in the East

cause so much trouble. Only this persistent under-estimation can explain why Moltke should have left a scratch formation, and one largely composed of non-Prussian troops, to take care of an area so strategically vulnerable and so difficult to pacify.

Regular soldiers are inclined to underestimate, as amateurs to over-estimate, the value of irregular forces in the conduct of war. At best they consider them erratic, uncertain, and expensive, and dismiss their spectacular achievements either as otiose, or as accidental, or as achieved at far too great a cost. Certainly if the operations of Garibaldi are considered as a whole they furnish a tragic list of efforts wasted and opportunities missed; yet it cannot be denied that during the last fortnight of November and the first fortnight of December, he operated against Werder to considerable effect. Conditions were favourable. Werder, his corps isolated and his communications uncertain, had commitments far beyond his effective strength to fulfil. His resources were overstretched and the population actively hostile. The Garibaldians could bring pressure on his corps, not simply by overt military operations, but

> by restricting the zone of its free operations, and, what was still more important, the area from which its supplies were drawn; . . . nothing decisive [said Werder's official historian] could be done to destroy this nuisance; the enemy force consisted mostly of flying columns, which, marching only at night, appeared each day at some different point in the line of outposts, attempting surprises of patrols, and attacks of small parties.[1]

The most spectacularly successful of these operations occurred on 14th November, when a small force under Ricciotti Garibaldi suddenly descended on Châtillon and surprised a draft of five hundred men on their way to the Second Army. But Garibaldi's forces were less effective when they offered pitched battle, and this Ricciotti's success unfortunately encouraged them to do. On 26th November they attacked Dijon from the north-west, and once they appeared in the open the discipline and fire power of the Germans inevitably told. They fell back disorganised on their base at Autun and Werder sent a task force to pursue them and finish off the nuisance for good. Autun was under shellfire and Garibaldi was planning its evacuation when, on 2nd December,

---

[1] Löhlein, *Operations of the Corps of General von Werder* 56–7. A British war correspondent at Mâcon "found a population so enthusiastic in its praise of the Garibaldians that I and a captain of the general's staff . . . could hardly appear in the street without attracting a considerable crowd, which followed us about wherever we went, shouting "Vivent les Garibaldians! Vive Garibaldi!" *War Correspondence of the Daily News* II 80.

Werder urgently summoned his troops back to Dijon. New French forces had appeared in the Saône valley and a German detachment had been roughly handled at Nuits St Georges. The Germans returned to Dijon, having to fight through a well-contrived ambush on the way, and Garibaldi was able to breathe again.[1]

The forces whose appearance caused Werder so great alarm consisted merely of the *Gardes Nationales* round Chagny whose commanders were stirred to action by the threat to Autun; and their success in driving the Germans back on Dijon led them also to contemplate more ambitious operations. On 12th December they agreed to attempt a co-ordinated movement on Dijon with all their forces from the Côte d'Or and the valley of the Saône.[2] But they were not the only Frenchmen with plans for the theatre. On 13th December Freycinet sent a brusque telegram to Bressolles at Lyons demanding an immediate march to relieve Belfort, making the alarming suggestion that Garibaldi, the only man who had yet achieved anything positive in the East, should be given overall command.[3] On 16th December Bordone, who was consulting Gambetta in Bordeaux, sent Garibaldi news of yet a third plan, whereby his force was to march north towards the Vosges while Bressolles and Crémer pinned down the Germans in the Saône valley. But their plans came to nothing: Werder struck first. The arrival of VII Corps at Châtillon relieved him of responsibility for guarding the communications of the Second Army and enabled him to act against the movements threatening from the south with unexpected force. On 18th December he sent General von Glümer and the Baden Division towards Beaune to carry out a reconnaissance in force. Simultaneously Crémer was advancing northward from Beaune towards Dijon with a slightly smaller force, and the two bodies met in the vineyards around Nuits St Georges. They fought all day and then fell back in mutual exhaustion. Each side had suffered about a thousand casualties—the French losing a further thousand prisoners and deserters—and neither wished for a further encounter. In Lyons indeed the news of Cremer's repulse provoked riots of such violence that nothing but a visit from Gambetta could pacify the city. It was evident that considerable reinforcements would be needed if the French forces in the eastern theatre were to take the offensive with any hope of success.[4]

---

[1] Löhlein, op. cit. 69–74. *D.T.* IV (Bordone) 3–4. Theyras, *Garibaldi en France* 172–247.

[2] *D.T.* III 506, V 77.

[3] Freycinet to Rolland, qu. Lehautcourt, *Campagne de l'Est* I 68.

[4] On the Battle of Nuits St Georges see Löhlein, *Campaign of the Corps of*

At Bourges meanwhile Bourbaki's army was undergoing a thorough reorganisation. Two corps commanders, Pallières and Crouzat, had resigned in exasperation; their places at the head of 15th and 20th Corps were taken by Generals Martineau des Chesnez and Clinchant, and 18th Corps was again in the hands of Billot. Of the two operations which Gambetta had originally envisaged for Bourbaki, a diversion to save Chanzy and an advance through Gien and Montargis to the relief of Paris, the first was rendered unnecessary by Chanzy's successful withdrawal to the west and the second impossible by the return of Frederick Charles to Orléans. The latter plan was still under consideration at Bourges by Gambetta and Bourbaki as late as 17th December[1]; but Freycinet, informed by telegram at Bordeaux, argued against the suggestion very forcefully indeed. Such a movement, he pointed out, stood no chance of success. With only 50,000 men, Bourbaki would have neither hope of co-operation from Ducrot if he succeeded in advancing nor the use of Orléans as a base if he were forced to retreat. In the eastern theatre, however, his army might be used with decisive effect, and Freycinet despatched to Bourges the ablest of his assistants, a young civil engineer named de Serres, to explain what he had in mind.[2]

Freycinet's plan was impressive. Bourbaki, leaving 15th Corps to cover Bourges, was to transfer 18th and 20th Corps by railway to the Saône valley. At the same time Bressolles was to bring his troops, now constituted as 24th Corps, north from Lyons. The two forces combined with Cremer's, Garibaldi's, and the garrison of Besançon, would amount to 110,000 men—an army strong enough to recapture Dijon, raise the siege of Belfort and Langres and press northward to sever German communications and even combine in an operation with Faidherbe. The prospect was dazzling and the arguments, for those who equated numbers with military strength, unanswerable. Gambetta and Bourbaki agreed at once. Gambetta had already contemplated the idea himself; as for Bourbaki, there may well have been something in Gambetta's subsequent view, that he welcomed any scheme which postponed an encounter with the German forces, of whose outcome he despaired. No murmur of doubt seems to have been voiced by any of the senior

---

General von Werder 80–90. *G.G.S.* II ii 102–3. Lehautcourt, *Campagne de l'Est* I 71–81. *D.T.* III 535, V 77. For the Lyons riots see *D.O.* II 41, *D.T.* II (Challemel-Lacour) 475–7.

[1] Eichthal, *Bourbaki* 169–70.

[2] Freycinet, *Guerre en Province* 222. Lehautcourt, *Campagne de l'Est* I 146.

officers whom they consulted; and on 19th December de Serres sent back a triumphant telegram: "*affaire réglée*".[1]

If the conduct of armies consisted only of the geometrical movement of forces in space, no scheme could have been better. Had it been worked out and executed by experienced staff-officers, disciplined troops, and a resolute and resourceful commander, it might have achieved far-reaching results. The bulk of the German armies were pinned down before Paris; the remainder were contained by the growing forces of Chanzy and Faidherbe; there were barely enough troops in the rear areas to deal with *franc-tireur* activities; and the very existence of the huge German organisation was dependent on the functioning of a railway-line, duplicated over barely half its length. Moltke was in the classical position of military weakness: he had over-extended his forces by an offensive pressed to extremes, laying himself open to a counter-attack at his weakest point; and his weakest point lay in the east of France on the flank guarded so precariously and so apprehensively by Werder. The first Napoleon would not have hesitated long.

Gambetta however did not hesitate for nearly long enough. He and Bourbaki accepted the plan without any examination of the logistical problems involved. They took it for granted that two army corps could be moved over the available railways, which could then be used to supply a force 110,000 strong in the middle of winter. This might have been possible, but only if the Ministry of War devoted to the planning an amount of time and a degree of skill which it did not have at its disposal. There was, in the first place, some confusion about the precise objective of the operation. Freycinet later stated that he intended Bourbaki to take Dijon and march northward, while Bressolles from Lyons moved on Besançon and relieved Belfort. But the plan which de Serres explained to Bourbaki was for the entire force to move eastward to relieve Belfort before moving north—a scheme which not only gave the Germans time to devise counter-measures to protect their communications, but involved a flank-march across Werder's front. Bourbaki thought only of drawing the German troops away from Paris, and he relied on Garibaldi to guard his left flank while this march was being carried out. But Garibaldi was neither put under his command nor given any orders by the Ministry of War. He was, according to Freycinet, to "be requested to be so good as to accept the proposals of

---

[1] *Guerre: Campagne du Général Bourbaki en l'Est* I 47–58. D.T. I 559–60, III 497. For Gambetta's ideas of a movement to the East see Gambetta to Freycinet, 12th December. Reinach I 267.

General Bourbaki"; but Bourbaki was not told to make any such proposals. The most complicated question of liaison and command was thus ignored.[1]

Finally failure was virtually guaranteed by the retention of Bourbaki himself in control of the operation. The shrewdness of Faidherbe or the energy of Chanzy might have achieved some results; the pessimistic and unimaginative Bourbaki could only head for disaster. Freycinet had urged his replacement, by Billot, even before the eastern campaign was devised. "How can you still base any hopes on Bourbaki", he asked Gambetta, "after all that has happened in this campaign and earlier in the north? It is this making a fetish of our old military glories that has ruined us."[2] Gambetta, though lamenting Bourbaki's pessimism, was not convinced; but he did agree that de Serres should accompany Bourbaki as the Minister's personal representative; and through him Freycinet hoped to conduct the campaign himself. "I want it to be well understood", he told de Serres, "that no decision must be taken before being submitted to me. It is only in case of urgency commanded by military necessity that action is permissible without my orders." De Serres even carried, for use at his discretion, an order for Bourbaki's dismissal.[3] It was an absurd and pathetic arrangement, the more so as everyone in Bourbaki's headquarters knew why de Serres was there; but it is doubtful whether it really made any worse the disasters of the campaign.[4] In fact Bourbaki and Borel both found de Serres a courteous and agreeable colleague who did not unduly interfere with operations, who provided useful liaison with Garibaldi, and who was helpful over problems of rail-transport and supply.[5] De Serres himself became progressively more humble as he gradually discovered how very much more complex were the problems of conducting such a campaign than he had ever realised.

The worst disasters occurred within de Serres's own particular sphere of rail transport, as a specialist in which he had first been employed

---

[1] *D.T.* III 351, 384. *Guerre: Campagne en l'Est* I 55–62. Eichthal, *Bourbaki* 358.

[2] Lehautcourt, op. cit. I 119.

[3] "Je n'ai qu'une crainte: c'est d'avoir à faire bien rapidement usage des pièces que vous m'avez confiées. Plus je vais, plus je renforce ma conviction sur l'insuffisance du personnage." De Serres to Gambetta, 24th December. *Guerre: Campagne en l'Est* I 88, 253.

[4] Lehautcourt I 164.

[5] *D.T.* III 356, 497. See also Thoumas's friendly comments in *Paris, Tours, Bordeaux* 132

by Freycinet in the Ministry of War.[1] It is doubtful whether anything could have been gained by using the railways for the movement of troops. Rolling-stock was short, much of it was immobilised on supply-duties, and the interruption of civil traffic provided a pointer for the Germans, had they cared to take any notice of it, as to what was being prepared. In any case the troops could have reached their destinations quite as quickly by marching. De Serres had reckoned that it would take two days to move Bourbaki's two corps, 18th and 20th, to the Saône from the Loire and he arranged for the movement to begin on 22nd December. But on 22nd December no trains appeared. The troops, who had already spent three freezing nights in bivouacs,[2] waited for hours on the platforms of Nevers and La Charité. When at length trains arrived they were too few for the task, and the entraining dragged out into days. Once the men were in their carriages—cattle-trucks with rough planks for benches—they stayed in them for as much as a week before reaching their destinations at Chagny and Châlon-sur-Saône. The lines had not been cleared of stationary trucks; one recently completed stretch was still considered unsafe by the railway authorities[3]; there were minor break-downs on the line; all contributed to immobilise the troop-trains for days, while their occupants sickened with cold and hunger. Several died. Rations were consumed voraciously and no more appeared; then, unless food could be requisitioned locally, the troops starved. The men cursed their officers, the officers cursed the Minister, Freycinet and his staff cursed the inexperienced and over-worked railway officials, all of whom, said the *intendant-en-chef*, should be shot. General Palat magisterially declared that the responsibility for this disaster

> rests as much on the Minister who gave impossible orders as on the generals and their staffs, who all too often lacked foresight, on the corps who daily gave evidence of indiscipline, on the intendants and the artillery, who daily sacrificed the general interest to that of their own service, and finally on the railway officials who often lacked good-will and above all initiative.[4]

It is a sweeping condemnation, but it would be difficult to draw up one more precise.

To this indictment may be added the failure of the authorities to provide any clear chain of command. Gambetta went to Lyons to assist

---

[1] *D.T.* III 28.

[2] On 24th December Martineau reported that in 15th Corps "depuis plusieurs nuits les hommes meurent au bivouac de froid et d'épuisement; le suicide même commence." *Guerre: Campagne en l'Est* I 209.

[3] *D.T.* III 37. [4] Lehautcourt II 13.

Bressolles in organising 24th Corps; de Serres was at Bourbaki's headquarters; Freycinet remained at Bordeaux; and these three key-figures quickly lost touch with one another's actions and intentions. Gambetta, who before his departure had given de Serres full powers to organise the expedition, by 23rd December felt entirely out of touch with events. "I cannot administer from here", he wired from Lyons "but I wish to be kept informed."[1] Freycinet, for example, had arranged for Bressolles to de-train at Besançon. De Serres suddenly switched him to Dôle: why?[2] Anyhow, he reported, Bressolles's troops were in a state of such disorder that 24th Corps could not move for a week and would be of little use when it did.[3] Freycinet, for his part, found that de Serres's energy and initiative had its drawbacks, and on 2nd January wired to reprimand him. "I know that your intervention is inspired by the patriotic wish to come to the help of the radical inadequacy of the commanding general," he wrote, "but that is an impossible task, and you will only increase the difficulties by trying to sort them yourself."[4] But without de Serres it is doubtful whether anything would have been done at all. The only hope of rescuing a campaign so fecklessly begun was a continuing genius for improvisation and unwearying energy, and this de Serres showed. He bull-dozed his way through obstructive railway officials, requisitioned labour to clear and mend the railway-tracks, wheedled Garibaldi and charmed the generals. His task was impossible; but his efforts to perform it were Herculean.

Not until 30th December was Bourbaki in any condition to advance. By then 24th Corps had come up from Lyons and constituted his right wing at Besançon; 20th Corps was further down the Doubs at Dôle, 18th Corps was approaching the Upper Saône at Auxonne, and Crémer's troops had entered Dijon on the heels of the German garrison which Werder, in alarm at the rumours which reached him, had pulled hurriedly back. It was now up to Bourbaki to begin operations. He took his immediate objective to be the relief of Belfort, and to isolate the investing force he proposed first to move on Vesoul.[5] But now Freycinet and de Serres took fright. German movements north-west of Dijon (in fact the most cautious of protective reconnaissances by VII Corps) gave Freycinet cause to fear that the delay on the railways had been fatal and that the Germans were now massing to crush Bourbaki between two fires. To de Serres and Bourbaki he sent, on 30th and 31st

[1] *Guerre: Campagne en l'Est* I 165–9.   [2] *D.O.* III 395.
[3] *D.O.* III 383–5.   [4] *Guerre: Campagne en l'Est* I 47.
[5] Bourbaki to Freycinet, 30th December. *Guerre: Armée de l'Est* I 351.

December, anxious messages urging them to hurry. If they did not get to Vesoul quickly, he warned them in wild exaggeration, they would have 150,000 men on their hands, to say nothing of reinforcements coming from Germany. He urged Bourbaki, in a message as disagreeable as it was inaccurate, to get out of his army "a little of the mobility which the Prussian army is showing us at this very moment". And he decided to send over 15th Corps from the Loire.[1]

The decision to send 15th Corps was another error, and Freycinet made it worse by taking complete charge of its movement. The subsequent confusion was the greatest that France had yet seen. Freycinet not only made all the usual mistakes: he decided to de-train the corps, not at Besançon, where there was adequate platform-space, but further up the Doubs at Clerval, where there was not. The resulting delays brought all troop-trains to a halt which not only reduced their occupants to a state of hunger, exhaustion and cold worse even than that of their predecessors but blocked the entire railway system and prevented adequate supplies from reaching the rest of the army.[2] 15th Corps added to Bourbaki's numerical strength but its arrival not merely decreased his speed: it brought him to a dead halt.

Meanwhile the Germans during the past fortnight had been thoroughly bewildered, and Moltke lost something of his sureness of touch. He confidently expected that Bourbaki would strike on the upper Loire, possibly in conjunction with an offensive from Vendôme by Chanzy, and he ordered VII Corps to advance from Châtillon to Auxerre to meet him. But as early as 21st December rumours were reaching Werder of extensive troop-movements on his fronts, and on the 24th came the news that the railway between Lyons and Besançon had been closed to all civilian traffic.[3] On Christmas Day Werder forwarded to Moltke a report from Switzerland that a massive relief of Belfort was being prepared, and Moltke wired back a report that Bourbaki's army had left the Loire and was on its way to the east.[4] Werder assembled his troops at Vesoul, evacuating both Dijon and Gray, and prepared to block the approaches to Belfort. Moltke sent him reinforcements from

---

[1] *Guerre: Campagne en l'Est* I 377–9, II 49–51.
[2] *Guerre: Campagne en l'Est* I 399–400, II 5, 104, 278. *D.T.* III 19. F. Jacqmin, *Les Chemins de Fer pendant la Guerre* 184–5.
[3] On 20th December Bronsart noted a rumour from Vienna that Bourbaki might move East, but he discounted it, believing that Bourbaki must move straight on Paris, where the decision lay. *Kriegstagebuch* 243. But by 27th December Moltke recognised that Gambetta's presence in Lyons was significant. Moltke to Zastrow, *M.M.K.* 487–9.   [4] *M.M.K.* 485.

Lorraine and ordered VII Corps to fall back again from Auxerre to Châtillon, whence it could rapidly reinforce Werder if the need arose.[1] But as soon as Moltke removed his shield from the upper Loire he began to have doubts. There were reports that Bourbaki was still in Bourges after all. Moltke halted VII Corps and sent it back to Auxerre. Werder's reports of movements on his front were discounted, and Moltke unsympathetically ordered him to clarify the situation by taking the offensive himself.[2] Versailles settled down to dismiss the whole episode as another example of Werder's cold feet, and when Werder reported on 5th January that large French forces were attacking his outposts south of Vesoul, Moltke replied that these could only be Bressolles's troops from Lyons—"according to our information Bourbaki is still at Bourges" —and urged him again to attack. It was only when, later the same evening, a report from the Prussian Legation in Berne confirmed Bourbaki's arrival in the east that Moltke at last decided that the threat was real.[3]

Until now the Germans had shown little signs of that mobility which Freycinet had cited to put Bourbaki to shame; but once the situation was clear Moltke showed formidable dispatch. Within twenty-four hours he organised a new army, the Army of the South, out of XIV, VII, and II Corps.[4] He ordered Werder to cover Belfort at all costs, and to engage Bourbaki closely until II and VII Corps could arrive and take the French in rear. The troops in Lorraine were alerted to protect the lines of communication; and the War Minister of Baden was warned to prepare for a French crossing of the Rhine if Bourbaki did succeed in breaking through to Alsace.[5]

To command the Army of the South Manteuffel was summoned from Rouen. No commander on the spot was suitable. Werder was too junior, Frederick Charles too cautious, Zastrow was too old; whereas Manteuffel's energy in dealing with Faidherbe had been noted at Versailles with approval. He rose very well to the occasion, reaching Versailles on 9th January and Châtillon three days later, where he at once gave out his orders. II and VII Corps were neither to concentrate nor to rest; they were to begin marching on 14th January across the Langres plateau to reach Werder with the least possible delay. The risks were considerable; Manteuffel had to move his troops through a gap

---

[1] *M.M.K.* 474–5. Löhlein, *Operations of the Corps of General von Werder* 94 ff. [2] *M.M.K.* 491, 492.

[3] Ibid. 503. Bronsart, *Kriegstagebuch* 274. Fabricius, *Auxerre-Châtillon* 260–2.

[4] II Corps, since its intervention in the battle of Champigny, had been posted at Montargis in anticipation of a possible attack from the Loire.

[5] *M.M.K.* 508–11.

barely forty miles wide, flanked on one side by the fortress of Langres and on the other by Garibaldi's forces round Dijon. The area was mountainous, lending itself to ambush, and communication between the marching columns would be almost impossible. "I herewith ratify in advance all measures for which my sanction is necessary," stated Manteuffel in his orders, "so that the hands of the commanding generals may not be tied by any regulations"[1]; the commanders were given their objectives, the most general of instructions, and left to themselves. No greater contrast with the meticulous French practice could be imagined. The system worked. The roads were good, though slippery with ice; a few harassing attacks from the flanks were easily beaten off; and on 17th January, after a four-day march, the two corps were out of the mountains and across the main highway from Dijon to Langres. Next day II Corps reached the Saône at Gray, and there learned that Werder had already engaged Bourbaki in a three-day battle and beaten him back. The entire French army was in retreat.[2]

* * *

Moltke's orders had not reached Werder until 10th January, five days after he first found himself at grips with the French. By then they were hardly necessary. On 5th January the French advance-guards had clashed with his outposts south of Vesoul, and the prisoners taken during the encounter revealed the size of Bourbaki's forces. Werder realised that he was considerably outnumbered; he could only concentrate his forces and hope for the best. But no attack came on 6th January, and on the 7th, when Werder moved tentatively southward, he found no sign of the French. In spite of his huge superiority, Bourbaki had decided not to attack. The official reason which he gave to his protesting subordinates was that he could force Werder to abandon Vesoul by manœuvring. He would take a strong position, he said, between Vesoul and Belfort and force Werder to attack himself. "I have taken Dijon without fighting, Gray without fighting, I will take Vesoul without fighting, the same with Lure, Héricourt, and we shall thus reach Belfort which will fall in the same way."[3] It was an unconvincing argument and he did not use it in his private communications with Freycinet and de Serres. To Freycinet he explained that a defeat before Vesoul would compromise the whole operation, and to de Serres he repeatedly

---

[1] H. von Wartensleben, *Operations of the South Army in January and February 1871* (English edn. London 1872) 16.

[2] *G.G.S.* II iii 1–9. Fabricius, *Auxerre-Châtillon* 63–127.

[3] *Guerre: Campagne en l'Est* II 156.

urged the impracticability of frontal attacks with the troops at his disposal. In short, he lost his nerve. It was absurd to hope to relieve Belfort, let alone cut the German communications, without a battle, and at Vesoul he had Werder at his mercy. Instead, he lamely explained that he preferred to turn the Prussian flank, as the Prussians had so often turned the French.[1]

It was true that the Prussians, often in spite of themselves, had found that outflanking was the best way to overcome an enemy armed with modern weapons. But outflanking is effective only under two conditions. The enemy must be pinned down by some measure of frontal attack; and the movement must be too rapid for him to transfer forces to meet it. Bourbaki fulfilled neither of these requirements. He halted his forces short of Vesoul, not even sending a screen to watch Werder's movements, and thus completely lost touch with the enemy; and he moved with extraordinary slowness. This was not entirely his fault. His under-officered army could not be subdivided to move across country, and had in consequence to crawl along the few main roads; and the chaos on the railways behind him caused a stoppage in the delivery of supplies. Only gradually could his units be deployed. The frozen, hungry and mutinous battalions of 15th Corps[2] had to be slowly unloaded at Clerval and deployed on the left bank of the Doubs. Bressolles's 24th Corps lay on the right bank, with Clinchant's 20th Corps round Rougemont and Billot's 18th Corps beyond the Ognon at Montbazon. Only by the evening of 8th January all were, after a fashion, ready to move.

Bourbaki had written to Chanzy on 7th January[3] to say he expected to encounter the Germans at Villersexel, where the southernmost of the two main roads from Vesoul to Belfort crosses the Ognon. His estimate was correct. Werder, after a day of hesitation, had decided to make for Belfort.[4] His main line of advance was the northernmost of the

---

[1] *D.T.* III 43.

[2] The journey of one typical battalion was as follows. At 9.30 a.m. on 7th January it reached its entraining-point at Bourges. At 9 p.m. it was ordered to entrain. At 10 p.m. the order was cancelled. At 4 a.m. on 8th January entraining began and the first train left at 11 a.m. During the night of 8th-9th and the day of 9th January, the day of 10th January, the night of 11th-12th and the day of 12th January the trains were stationary, and the regiment detrained at Baume, after a a journey of 230 miles, on 15th January. For the journey it carried rations for two days. This was not the worst. A trainload of cavalry was unloaded after it had been immobilised for three consecutive days and nights, and several horses were found dead. Lehautcourt, *Campagne de l'Est.* II 7–9.

[3] *Guerre: Campagne en l'Est.* II 250.

[4] Both Löhlein and the German General Staff History state that Werder

two roads but his right wing used the Villersexel road, and its advance-guard reached the town on the morning of 9th January to find it in French hands. Standing high on the left bank of the Ognon, which there divided into a wide sprawl of channels, the town effectively barred the passage of the river. The château of the Marquis de Grammont lay immediately west of the town in wooded grounds sloping sharply down to the river-bank. It commanded the main bridge over the Ognon and the only other means of crossing then was a precarious affair of ropes and a lock at the extreme western end of the park which could also be commanded from the wooded heights above. The Marquis showed the French troops the best positions in his park, and the townsfolk co-operated in barricading the bridge. The position should have been excellent for a defensive battle.

Unfortunately there were at first very few French troops available to fight it. Bourbaki's orders for 9th January did not reflect his avowed expectations of a clash on the Ognon: they provided only for a forward movement of four kilometres by each of the four corps along approximately parallel lines of advance, and, like most French orders, they furnished neither information about the enemy position or the purpose of the advance, nor instructions for co-operation in the event of attack.[1] Villersexel lay on the route of only one corps, 20th. 18th Corps followed a course beyond the Ognon which would also bring it in contact with the Baden Division, but 24th Corps's course lay north-east away from the battle, and 15th Corps beyond the Doubs was far out of reach. On the morning of 9th January only 200 troops of 20th Corps's advance-guard had reached the village, and in spite of the advantages the position gave the defenders the German infantry, after its first check, was able to get across the lock and the rope-bridge and take the defenders of the main bridge in rear. By noon, when the main body of 20th Corps appeared on the scene, the Germans were masters of the château and the town.[2]

18th Corps's advance-guard meanwhile had already encountered the Germans north of the Ognon, round the village of Marat. The usual bad staff work had tangled up the main body in long delays, and it never

intended to fall on Bourbaki's flank, but his route hardly bears this out. It is more probable that he was making for Belfort to join hands with the investing force before Bourbaki could get between them. So far from him falling on Bourbaki's flank, Bourbaki fell on his.

[1] *D.T.* III 413. *Guerre: Campagne en l'Est* II 299–300.
[2] For accounts of the battle of Villersexel see ibid. II 345 ff. Löhlein, op. cit. 109–13. *G.G.S.* II ii 313–18.

untangled itself sufficiently to mount a proper attack on the small force that blocked its path. 20th Corps was thus as unsupported on its left flank as it was on the right, where Bressolles, in spite of reiterated messages from Bourbaki, was marching 24th Corps further and further away from the battle. Bourbaki himself came up to 20th Corps Headquarters before Villersexel during the afternoon. In the familiar atmosphere of the battlefield he forgot the melancholy caution which had beset him since the beginning of the war. "You only have fifteen thousand men before you," he told the divisional commander (a wild exaggeration); "take the position for me. You should have done it already. At your age I would have marched on them cane in hand." The old fire galvanised the officers and for the first time a flicker of something like martial ardour passed through the ranks of that wretched army. The regiments advanced cheering through the twilight across the snow-covered fields and stormed into the village; and Bourbaki returned to his headquarters to send back to Gambetta the despatch: "All the positions indicated by the movement-order have been reached. Villersexel, key of the position, has been taken with cries of *Vive la France!*"[1]

Bourbaki's satisfaction was premature. Werder, anxious to avoid battle until he had joined forces with the troops investing Belfort, had hurried up to Villersexel at noon to order the troops engaged there to occupy the town with as small a garrison as possible and to press on with the advance. The troops in Villersexel began to withdraw, and it was during their withdrawal that 20th Corps had attacked. The French thus penetrated into the town and the château with comparatively little difficulty; but their success threatened to throw the German movement into such confusion that the divisional commander resolved to ignore Werder's order and hang on to the town. The French thus found that the fighting was by no means over. The Germans came crowding back, and spasmodic fighting went on in the snow-covered streets far into the night. A party of Germans forced their way back into the château on the ground floor while the French were still holding out on the first floor, and for hours a macabre fight went on in the dark corridors and halls until the flames kindled by the combatants took control and brought the roof crashing down to consume French and Germans alike in a huge funeral pyre.[2] Not until midnight did the situation become quiet enough for the Germans to withdraw again and continue their march.

[1] *Guerre: Campagne en l'Est* II 515. *D.T.* III 141.
[2] Lehautcourt, *Campagne de l'Est* I 225.

The casualties sustained were not such as to cripple either army, and both sides with equally little reason claimed the encounter as a victory.[1] The French pointed out that they had been left in possession of the battlefield; but their possession of Villersexel in no way impeded Werder in his vital objective of racing Bourbaki to Belfort. The German claim was more disingenuous. "The object of the day had been fully attained," wrote their principal historian of the campaign; "Bourbaki could not now reach Belfort before the XIV Army Corps."[2] This was nonsense, and Löhlein must have known it. In the first place Werder had had no "object" except to disengage his forces from an unexpected encounter as rapidly and as cheaply as possible. In the second place, the battle imposed no check on Bourbaki's snail-like progress: all his corps, as he proudly informed Gambetta, had reached the destinations for which they had set out on the morning of the 9th. Finally, on the morning of 10th January Bourbaki was still in a position to reach Belfort with his right wing before Werder, if he had cared to push 24th and 15th Corps rapidly up the banks of the Doubs. But he did not. "All the tactical and strategical advantages gained by the French command, in spite of its faults, and thanks to those of its adversary," wrote the French Official History truly, "were going to be lost in a few hours of timidity and indecision."[3] Bourbaki's brief blaze of offensive ardour had burnt out: once again he thought only of dispositions to resist the attack which the enemy was bound to make. Thus during three days, from 10th to 13th January, the French army advanced altogether five miles, while Werder prepared at his leisure a strong position on the Lisaine to block the road to Belfort; and while Manteuffel away to the north-west gathered his forces for the dash over the plateau of Langres.

One can detect in Bourbaki's actions during these days a listless, almost masochistic fatalism reminiscent of Bazaine's attitude in the battles around Metz; the acquiescence of a man who knows himself impotent to control events, able only to watch their unfolding in hypnotised passivity. He showed little interest in the reports of Manteuffel's movements which began to reach him on 12th January. "If we are to believe the information received from various sources", he commented, "the greater part of Prince Frederick Charles's army [sic] is moving against us"—a movement, he pointed out, which ought to free Chanzy

[1] The French lost 1,390 men, the Germans 579. *Guerre: Campagne en l'Est* II 500. *G.G.S.* II ii 318.   [2] Löhlein, op. cit. 115.
[3] *Guerre: Campagne en l'Est* III 4.

to march on Paris.[1] Also like Bazaine, he proved incapable of handling the huge bodies of men under his command. The Prussian tactics of dispersing to move, concentrating to fight, were far beyond him and his makeshift staff. He could only concentrate, calling Crémer from the north-west and Martineau from the south-east to swell the three corps already moving with glacier-like slowness towards Belfort. Five German battalions round the village of Arcey seemed to threaten the security of the railhead at Clerval, and on 13th January Bourbaki ponderously deployed five divisions of his right wing to force them back. That exhausted his ideas. He wrote back to Freycinet that evening that he was pushing on to Héricourt and Belfort, but added pathetically, "Please let me know what you think would be best for me to do. This depends completely on the march of Frederick Charles's forces [sic], which I must meet under good conditions. Do not be sparing either of advice or of information."[2] He then began to prepare to attack the German positions on the Lisaine.

The Lisaine is a small stream which rises in the Vosges a few miles north-west of Belfort and flows into the Doubs at Montbéliard through a broadening valley flanked on either side by thick woods. The stream is itself a slight obstacle, and at that season was covered with thick ice; but the valley north of Héricourt is flanked with steep, wooded slopes, narrowing in places to ravines; round Héricourt the heights to the east, though lower, more open, and rising more gently, still dominate the valley; between Héricourt and Montbéliard the valley again narrows, running between shallower, regular hills which close in to dominate the steep streets of Montbéliard. Werder occupied the eastern slopes of the valley from Montbéliard to the Lure road at Frahier, a distance of twelve miles. His troops worked hard and effectively to strengthen the position. They brought up siege-guns, dug trenches and mined the bridges; they cut paths through the thick woods behind their lines, laid a complex of telegraph-wires, covered icy roads with sand and manure, lit fires to melt the worst patches of ice, and broke up the ice along the Lisaine.

Everything that ingenuity could devise and industry achieve the Germans accomplished. Even so they were only 40,000 men against 110,000; and Werder made matters worse by a radical miscalculation

[1] *D.T.* III 414–15. *Guerre: Campagne en l'Est* III 67. Bourbaki's ignorance of the formation of the South Army is an interesting parallel to Palikao's ignorance five months earlier of the formation of the Army of the Meuse.

[2] Lehautcourt, *Campagne de l'Est* II 49.

of Bourbaki's intentions. The French dependence upon the railway, he reckoned, would force them to attack in the southern part of the valley; in consequence he disposed the bulk of his forces between Héricourt and Montbéliard. He had eight battalions to guard the eight miles of difficult country between the Doubs and the Swiss frontier, but the vital Lure road, running through open country on his right flank, he guarded with three battalions only. Bourbaki, while preparing to attack the Germans along the whole length of the Lisaine, had the forces available to outflank them to the north as well. 20th, 24th and 15th Corps were to engage the Germans from Héricourt to Montbéliard, but this was to be only a holding attack. The decisive blow was to be launched in the north by 18th Corps against Chagey, and by Crémer's division against Chenebier and Frahier, where Bourbaki, believing that Werder's positions stretched no further north than Héricourt, hoped for a bloodless success.[1]

The initial French movements on 14th January made Werder realise that the forces opposite him were greater even than he had expected, and for a moment his spirits quailed. He wired to Moltke, "Whether Belfort is to be held against these enveloping movements I request may be urgently considered. I believe Alsace can be held, but not at the same time Belfort, unless the existence of the Corps is to be imperilled. By holding on to Belfort I am deprived of all freedom of movement. The rivers are passable in the frost."[2] The message created some uneasiness at Versailles, but Moltke promptly replied: "Attack is to be awaited and battle is to be accepted in the strong position covering Belfort ... the advance of General Manteuffel will make itself felt within a few days."[3] These orders reached Werder on the evening of 15th January; by then he was already engaged and had no opportunity of disobeying them.

The battle of the Lisaine lasted for three days,[4] and brought both armies to the limits of human endurance. The cold was intense: constantly below freezing-point, the thermometer on the night of 15th January touched eighteen degrees of frost. Werder got his men back into billets whenever possible, but for the French it was not possible at

[1] Werder's expectations were fulfilled, however, in that Bourbaki concentrated nine divisions against the main German positions and had only four to attack on the left. As events were to show, even these four could hardly make their way through the forest tracks north-west of Héricourt.

[2] *G.G.S.* II ii. App. CXL.

[3] Stosch, *Denkwürdigkeiten* 224. Löhlein, op. cit. 131.

[4] For general accounts of the battle see *G.G.S.* II ii 332–58. Löhlein, op. cit. 134–50. *Guerre: Campagne en l'Est* III 208–96.

all. The nearness of the enemy made commanders prohibit the lighting of camp-fires, but they were lit none the less, out of smouldering green wood, and everyone, from General to private, huddled round them to gain enough warmth simply to keep alive.[1] The forest-roads were choked with snowdrifts, but whereas the Germans had cleared them in advance the French had not; and this made no small contribution to the failure of their attack. It was over the worst of these tracks that Billot's 18th Corps and Crémer's Division had to move. They constituted the striking force of the French army. Bourbaki had given strict orders that the corps of his centre and right were to act simply as a pivot, and "lean on" the enemy until these units had developed their attack against the un-guarded enemy right wing. But the progress of Billot and Crémer on the morning of 15th January was made slower by a confusion of orders.[2] Their columns met in the forest, crossed, caused hour-long delays. Thus the French troops which closed up to the Lisaine between Héricourt and Montbéliard during the morning with a three-fold superiority did not press their attack across the river. 18th Corps was able to attack Chagey only during the afternoon, and then in such a piecemeal fashion that it was easily repulsed; and Crémer arrived before Chenebier as darkness was falling, far too late to attack at all.

Bourbaki's plan had gone wrong, but there was still time to save it from total failure. On 16th January the French again attacked all along the valley. They were cold, tired and hungry, and made little attempt to press forward once they were checked by the German fire. But at least they forced Werder to commit all his reserves; and when Crémer, reinforced with a division from 18th Corps, marched to attack the sprawl-ing village of Chenebier, they fell back down the road to Belfort. Pursuit might have turned their retreat to a rout; the whole of the over-strained German position might have collapsed and the road to Belfort would then have been open. But Crémer did not pursue. His forces were disorganised, his casualties considerable; he had no orders to pene-trate beyond Chenebier[3]; and Bourbaki had anyhow decided not to press this outflanking attack. "I would be obliged to abandon the Besançon-Montbéliard railway", he told Billot, "and if we were cut off there, how should we eat?"[4] So Crémer dug himself in at Chenebier, and remained firmly on the defensive throughout the day.

Elsewhere the French again attacked, but with even less enthusiasm than they had shown on the 16th; and Bourbaki, riding along his

---

[1] Freycinet, *Guerre en Province* 243.   [2] *D.T.* V (Col. Poullet) 85–7.
[3] Loc. cit. 88.   [4] *D.T.* III (Billot) 476.

positions under an icy rain, saw that the game was up. He could ask no more of his troops, and all his corps commanders except Billot advised him to fall back. A young officer suggested a night attack, but Bourbaki shook his head. "I'm twenty years too old", he said. "Generals should be your age."[1] He gave the order to withdraw. The orders, and his report to Freycinet, still kept up appearances: he was merely retiring, he said, a few kilometres to better positions where supply would not be such a problem, and where, with any luck, the Germans would try to attack him. But the fiction did not last long: twenty-four hours later, learning that Manteuffel was nearing the Saône, he began to fall back on Besançon. In the fields and forest beyond the Lisaine the advancing Germans were to find 4,500 French wounded and 1,500 dead.[2]

Bourbaki's lack of spirit; the terrible weather; the clumsiness of his staff-work and supply-organisation; the inexperience of his troops: all this, together with the cool competence with which Werder and his forces had held their positions fully explain his repulse. The approach of Manteuffel turned the repulse into a retreat which was to end in one of the greatest disasters that has ever overtaken a European army. Why was Manteuffel able to march unhampered? The forces in and around Dijon numbered nearly 50,000 men, half of them Garibaldi's. Skilfully handled, they might at least have embarrassed the Army of the South. As it was they achieved nothing. Admittedly no precise plans had been made for them. De Serres had visited Autun on 23rd December and obtained vague but enthusiastic assurances of co-operation; but from the beginning of the operation little co-operation was forthcoming.[3] Garibaldi would not move from Autun to Dijon unless rail transport was made available, and although his concern for his men at such a season was reasonable it was hardly a moment to ask Freycinet for rolling-stock. Crémer's division had therefore been delayed guarding Dijon until Garibaldi arrived on 8th January. At the critical moment, when Manteuffel was descending from the plateau of Langres on the Upper Saône, Garibaldi fell ill and Bordone in reply to Freycinet's polite urgings ("How can it happen that the enemy dares to show himself in the neighbourhood of your brave army?") declared that he could not leave Dijon until he had put it in a state of defence,

---

[1] Bourbaki was fifty-four: hardly an excessive age for a general of his seniority.
[2] *D.T.* III (Pallu) 441. Löhlein, op. cit. 150.
[3] *Guerre: Campagne en l'Est* II 61, 92. Freycinet, *Guerre en Province* 228. *D.T.* IV 47.

and that the danger was greatly exaggerated.[1] The fall of Gray belied him, and on 19th January Freycinet's patience collapsed. "You have given Bourbaki's army no support, and your presence at Dijon has had no effect on the enemy march from west to east. In short, fewer explanations and more action, that's what we want from you."[2]

Two days later Freycinet changed his tone. Manteuffel's flank-guard, a force of 4,000 men and twelve guns under General von Kettler, launched on 21st January a vigorous attack against Dijon with the object of keeping the garrison employed while the main German force marched east of the city to the Saône and the Doubs.[3] Garibaldi's forces together with the local French *Gardes Nationales* numbered about 50,000, but few of them were actually armed or able to fight, and Garibaldi, agonised by gout, had to command them from a carriage. But his men proved remarkably steady in battle. Kettler's attack was repulsed; when he tried again two days later it was with equal lack of success; and from under a pile of German corpses the Garibaldians unearthed an enemy colour which they sent back in triumph to Bordeaux. "At last", wired Freycinet on the 19th, "I discern again the brave army of Garibaldi and his clever chief-of-staff."[4]

The loss of one colour and 700 men was a price which Manteuffel did not grudge. On 21st January he reached the Doubs below Besançon at Dôle, and Bourbaki's doom seemed sealed. Manteuffel ordered Werder to pin down the French army until II and VII Corps could sweep up the Doubs to take them in rear. Werder would not co-operate: his troops were far too tired to pursue and engage Bourbaki without some rest. But Manteuffel's movement was still effective. The two armies were not to act as a vice squeezing Bourbaki between them, but as a net sweeping behind him to cut his communications with France and pin him against the Swiss frontier as MacMahon had been pinned against the Belgian. At Dôle Manteuffel had cut the main road and railway which ran south-west from Besançon to Châlons and Chagny; this left only the road and railway to Lons-le-Saunier and Lyons, and once they were gone Bourbaki would be thrown back on a few mountain-routes through the snow-blocked uplands of the Jura; and these could easily be sealed.[5]

[1] Bordone to Freycinet, 14th January. *D.T.* IV 43. See also *D.O.* I 224–5. "Ne pourrions laisser Dijon entre les mains d'autorités civiles et militaires incapables et mal intentionnées."

[2] Lehautcourt, *Campagne de l'Est* II 127–8.   [3] *G.G.S.* II iii 15–24.

[4] *D.T.* IV 39. Theyras, *Garibaldi en France* 564–77.

[5] Wartensleben, *Operations of the South Army* 41.

The capture of Dôle astonished Freycinet and Bourbaki. Freycinet had already devised another grandiose plan by which Bourbaki was to return to the Loire, collect reinforcements and drive north again through Auxerre and Troyes to join forces with Faidherbe. Bourbaki was confident of holding out along the Doubs, manœuvring around Besançon which, he presumed, contained ample supplies,[1] and on 22nd January he told Freycinet that he hoped to break through at Dôle. Thus his despatches to Bordeaux still had a confident ring: even Manteuffel's movement towards the Lons-le-Saunier road does not appear to have alarmed him, and he sent over a division of 15th Corps to Quingey to check it. But when he reached Besançon his tone changed. The *Intendant* of the army had told him that he had had no instructions to stock up Besançon, and he had food for the army for barely a week.[2] For the first time Bourbaki realised the hopelessness of his position. One by one his escape-routes were cut. On 23rd January Crémer's division was repulsed as it moved down the Doubs towards Dôle; the division sent to Quingey panicked at the sight of VII Corps's advance-guards and the Lons road was lost; and Werder's appearance was enough to make 24th Corps abandon the rear-guard positions they were holding round Baume-les-Dames. On 24th January Bourbaki consulted his corps commanders, and it was agreed that the only hope lay in plunging into the Jura and finding a way out through Pontarlier.[3]

Freycinet, when the news reached him, was incredulous. His tone too had changed since the battle of the Lisaine. Chastened perhaps by Garibaldi's failure to stop Manteuffel, he had applauded Bourbaki's recoil on Besançon; but when Garibaldi showed fight at Dijon and Bourbaki announced himself cut off from Lyons, the familiar acid note crept back into his despatches. He laid the blame on Bourbaki for his slowness. "In my opinion," he wired on 23rd January, "there is now only one course for you to take, which is to reconquer at once without losing a minute the lines of communication which you have regrettably lost, and to prevent the fall of Dijon that the renewed attempts of the enemy may bring about, in spite of Garibaldi's heroism." When he learned that the decision to fall back on Pontarlier had been taken he was

---

[1] *D.T.* III 396.

[2] Later investigation revealed that the stocks in the town and piled up round the railway station could have fed Bourbaki's forces for six weeks. *D.T.* III 524–6. Lehautcourt, *Campagne de l'Est* II 175–6, 185.

[3] Only Billot disagreed and suggested that they should fight their way out to the north-west; but he refused to take over the command which Bourbaki at once offered him. *D.T.* III 399, 478.

flabbergasted. "Haven't you made a mistake about the name?" he wired. "Do you really mean Pontarlier? Pontarlier, near Switzerland? If that is really your objective, have you envisaged the consequences? What will you live on? You will certainly die of hunger. You will be forced to capitulate or to cross into Switzerland . . . at all costs you must break out. Otherwise you are lost."[1]

Freycinet was right. But what Bourbaki knew, and he did not, was that nothing would make the French troops stand and fight the Germans, much less fight their way through them. The retreat from the Lisaine had completed the army's demoralisation: it fell, as one general put it, into "a kind of instantaneous decomposition".[2] Units were held together only by the need for food. Convoys and trains were pillaged by bands of hungry men, who then threw away half they took. Boots had been replaced by bundles of rags, and Werder found his way paved with a litter of abandoned arms and equipment. When units were brought up to face the Germans a few shells sent them streaming in flight. Hence the decision to move on to Pontarlier: "It is the only direction that the moral and physical condition of the troops allows them to take", Bourbaki wired on the 24th January. "If this plan does not suit you I really would not know what to do; believe me, it is a martyrdom to exercise the command at this moment . . . if you think that one of my corps commanders could do better than I, do not hesitate to replace me . . . the task is beyond my strength."[3] For two more days he tried to hold off the Germans closing in from north and south while the baggage trains lumbered eastward into the Jura. Then on the evening of the 26th he gave orders for the army to follow next day, and while they were being drafted he retired to his room and shot himself through the head.[4]

Poor Bourbaki! Even this escape was denied him. The bullet only grazed his skull, and he was out of danger within a week. But Freycinet had already decided to take him at his word, and instructions for Clinchant to take over command of the army were already on their way. Clinchant could only continue the march to Pontarlier, through the ravines and jagged crests to the broad plateaus where movement was easier. Yet he could not outdistance the Germans. On 26th January II Corps had forced the gorge at Salins, and two days later it was across the Lons–Pontarlier road at Onglières. Clinchant, waiting at Pontarlier

[1] *D.T.* III 355, 377, 433. Freycinet, *Guerre en Province* 263–6.
[2] Pallu de la Barrière, *D.T.* III 442.
[3] *D.T.* III 375.
[4] For the details of Bourbaki's suicidal attempt see Eichthal, *Bourbaki* 345–54.

while his columns dragged their way over the mountain roads, sent forward an advance-guard under Crémer to hold open the last good road along the frontier at St Laurent and Les Planches, and Crémer's cavalry reached these vital junctions on 29th January to find them still free. But the infantry following them could not keep up over the snow-bound roads, and a few hours later the German advance-guards appeared and with a little brisk artillery fire swept away the slender French outposts. There was left now only a narrow mountain-track blocked by snow over which it was impossible for the whole French army to pass. Further north VII Corps advancing from Salins had joined battle with the main French forces a few miles west of Pontarlier. 3,000 men surrendered to a single battalion in the village of Sombacourt, but at Chaffois the Germans ran into stiffer resistance. Night fell, but brisk firing continued on each side; until suddenly an officer arrived from Clinchant with orders for the cease-fire. An armistice had been signed at Versailles.[1]

It seems in retrospect as though fate had decided that there should be no humiliation which the French army should be spared. An armistice had indeed been signed, and Manteuffel at Arbois knew of it almost as soon as Clinchant at Pontarlier. But for reasons which we shall consider later the fighting in the departments of Doubs, Jura, and Côte d'Or was exempted from its provisions, and by an incredible error Jules Favre had omitted to inform Bordeaux of this exception. Manteuffel knew therefore that the armistice did not apply to him, and on 30th January went on with the movements which barred to the French every avenue of escape. To Clinchant's furious emissaries he pointed out with the greatest courtesy that he would be delighted to receive "such proper proposals as are in conformity with the military situation prevailing here at this moment."[2] But Clinchant was not going to deliver up yet a third army to German prison-camps. Already tentative conversations had been opened with the Swiss about the safe conduct of wounded across the frontier, and when on 31st January Clinchant learned officially from Bordeaux that his hopes of armistice were delusory he concluded a convention with the Swiss authorities at the frontier-post of Verrières.[3]

On 1st February therefore the French troops, lost to all semblance of order, crowded the roads from Pontarlier to the frontier, leaving a

---

[1] Lehautcourt, *Campagne en l'Est* II 222–5. For the controversy over the question whether the roads could have been kept open or not, see, e.g. *D.T.* IV (Bressolles) 324–5, *D.T.* V 96–8 (Rivière).

[2] Wartensleben, *Operations of the South Army* 80. *D.T.* III 331.

[3] *D.T.* III 340.

wake of abandoned guns and equipment, exhausted horses and men which alone checked the German pursuit. A last stand was made at the gorge of La Cluse four miles beyond Pontarlier by a handful of men from the army reserve. Here, supported by a battery firing from the lofty castle of La Cluse, they held out all day while the Germans vainly looked for a way round and the rest of the French army filed over the frontier at Les Verrières and Les Hopitaux. Then they too slipped away and filed into Switzerland with the rest, throwing their arms on the huge piles by the roadside.[1] A few units filtered through the mountains to the south, dodging the German outposts, and at length reached Lyons. Crémer got most of his cavalry away, and other generals escaped individually, including Billot, whose 18th Corps had alone preserved some appearance of order until the end. Others attempting to escape missed their way, sometimes deliberately misled by peasants anxious to see the last of them. Altogether Clinchant led 80,000 men into Switzerland. Freycinet's gamble had come to its ignominious end.[2]

---

[1] *D.T.* III 342–3, 444–8. For the final skirmishes in the campaign see H. Genevois, *Les dernières Cartouches* (Paris 1893) 175 ff.

[2] On the details of the entry of the troops into Switzerland and the arrangements for their reception, see E. Davall, *Les Troupes françaises internées en Suisse* (Berne 1873): the official report based on Swiss government documents.

CHAPTER XI

The Peace

BY THE middle of January 1871 the armies of the National Defence, both in Paris and in the Provinces, had been routed and to a large extent destroyed. The civil population of France, except only for a handful of iron-willed commanders and unreasoning enthusiasts, were ready for any sort of peace. But in war the scales of fortune do not tip evenly. The growing misery of the French was not counter-balanced by any lightening of the burden which weighed on the German armies and their leaders. The troops in the field and in occupation-areas were war-weary, indifferently housed, and harassed, in many areas, by *francs-tireurs*. The task of the *Intendantur*, of supplying an army 800,000 strong over a railway-system still strangled by intact fortresses and demolitions and liable at any moment to interruption, grew no easier. And in Germany itself open complaints were now being made about the continuing demands on national resources of rolling-stock and man-power. The victories at Le Mans, St Quentin, Buzenval, and the Lisaine were loudly and properly applauded in the German press; but they seemed to bring peace no nearer.

At Versailles therefore, the centre of Prussian civil and military government, the tensions remained as great as ever. It was clear that the question of the bombardment of Paris had been an occasion for conflict rather than a cause, for the opening of fire on 5th January had led to no *détente*. It was indeed not until a fortnight later that the quarrels at Versailles were to reach their climax. The French request for an armistice was to come at an almost providential moment. Had the war been prolonged for a few more weeks, it is difficult to see how either Bismarck or Moltke could have remained in posts which each felt the other was making untenable.

The burden upon Bismarck would have been heavy enough without the additional difficulties which he considered that the military were creating for him. For four months he had been engaged in delicate and often acrimonious negotiations with Prussian party-leaders and with the princes and parliamentarians of South Germany about the form and nature of the new German Empire. Behind the magnificent ceremony which took place on 18th January in the Galerie des Glaces at Versailles, when the King of Prussia was acclaimed Emperor by the assembled Princes of Germany, there lay a succession of political crises and conflicts during which Bismarck had constantly found himself at odds both with the King, who suspected and disliked the whole Imperial idea, and with the Crown Prince, who was its most enthusiastic and often its most impolitic partisan; and the cooling in personal relationships which was the natural consequence did not make any easier Bismarck's other task, that of distilling a satisfactory peace out of the prolonged and seemingly endless war. In spite of the failure of Thiers's missions, Bismarck's fears that the Powers of Europe might decide at last to intervene remained unabated; and ironically enough his own activities had now provided a new opportunity.

On 29th October Russia, not entirely unexpectedly, had denounced the clauses of the Treaty of Paris of 1856 which declared the Black Sea to be neutralised in perpetuity and limited the number and type of naval forces which the Czar might maintain on its waters. Of the two powers responsible for imposing this restriction on Russia, France was impotent and Great Britain in a state of isolation which it had not yet occurred to any of her statesmen to describe as "splendid". It was significant of the new position which Bismarck occupied on the European scene that Lord Granville, before taking any further action, should have sent an envoy extraordinary to Versailles, Odo Russell, to invoke his aid in persuading Russia to withdraw her denunciation; failing which, Russell told the Chancellor, Britain would be compelled, with or without allies, to go to war.[1] Such a broadening of the Franco-German conflict was in the highest degree unwelcome to Bismarck. Instead he proposed a conference of the Powers to consider the matter; a conference at which he agreed to accept the presence of a French plenipotentiary.[2] Granville accepted the solution, and urged the Government of National Defence to accept as well.[3]

The French reaction was ambiguous. On the one hand both Chaudordy, the delegate for Foreign Affairs at Tours, and Favre, kept tenuously informed in Paris, determined to make the Conference an instrument for securing an armistice on their own terms. Since no conference could reach valid decisions without the presence of a French

[1] Fitzmaurice, *Life of Lord Granville* II 73.
[2] Sorel, *Histoire diplomatique de la Guerre Franco-Allemande* II 103.
[3] Granville to Lyons, 28th November. Lord Newton, *Life of Lord Lyons* I 340.

representative, they argued, the Powers would be compelled in their own interests to bring pressure on Prussia to accede to the French terms.[1] On the other hand, by insisting that the French representative at the conference should be Favre himself, and not one of the ministers or officials of the Delegation, they gave Bismarck the opportunity of thwarting the whole plan. Favre could leave Paris only by consent of the Prussians; and though that consent might be forthcoming in principle, a succession of practical difficulties could be and were raised which made it impossible for him to leave at all.

The Conference was summoned for 3rd January 1871; but Bismarck, by suspending all communication between the Prussian outposts and those of the besieged city on the excuse that the French had fired on accredited *parlementaires*, prevented the invitation from reaching Favre. The Conference was adjourned until 10th January; and Bismarck arranged for the invitation to reach Favre only on that very day. The Conference again adjourned for a week; Bismarck raised new difficulties about the precise form in which the safe-conduct should be arranged, and played on Favre's own reluctance to leave the capital at a moment of such critical danger, to debate, far from the battle, so abstract and legalistic a point of power politics. "I would permit myself to enquire", he wrote with heavy irony on 16th January, "whether it would be a good idea for Your Excellency to leave Paris now to attend a discussion on the subject of the Black Sea. . . . I can hardly believe that Your Excellency, in the critical situation to which you have so effectively contributed, would wish to deprive yourself of the opportunity of collaborating in a solution for which you must bear a share of the responsibility."[2] But such finessing could not go on for ever; and if Favre were to reach London and appeal to the conscience of Europe, Bismarck foresaw that a new and far more difficult phase might open for the relationship between the new German Empire and the neutral powers.[3]

Bismarck was thus determined that the peace settlement, when it came, should be one between Germany and France alone. Yet at the beginning of 1871 it seemed more difficult than ever to find a government in France prepared to make peace on any terms at all. Since the beginning of December there had been no word from Paris, and the Delegation seemed to grow more fanatically irreconcilable with

[1] *D.T.* (Chaudordy) II 5. Dréo, *Procès Verbaux* 412–16.
[2] Bismarck, *Gesamm. Werke* No. 2006 p. 669.
[3] Oncken, *Friedrich I von Baden* II 353.

each successive defeat. Only the Imperialist emigrés seemed to offer any kind of hope; but apart from the improbability of any Imperial restoration being practicable in France save as the most naked and impermanent form of military dictatorship, Napoleon's supporters in London, Brussels and Wilhelmshöhe had fallen, as emigrés will, into such quarrelsome factions that any agreed solution from this quarter seemed almost impossible. In Brussels Persigny and Palikao still advocated the Regnier proposals, of summoning the Corps Législatif to deliberate under the protection of the old Imperial army, which was to be released from capitivity for the purpose. In London the Empress proposed, in her capacity as Regent, to sign a peace ceding to Germany an area equivalent to the territories of Nice and Savoy which France had acquired from Piedmont ten years earlier. Finally, Prince Napoleon, irrepressibly ambitious, invited himself to Versailles to sign a peace with Germany in his own right.[1]

To all these conflicting suggestions Bismarck lent a sceptical ear. The only one which promised a remote chance of success was that of the Empress, who by the beginning of 1871 had resolved to grant to Bismarck the terms which he was in fact later to obtain from Thiers: a cession of territory, a pecuniary indemnity, and German occupation of France until the indemnity was paid. The offer was to be made officially as soon as the fall of Paris made clear to the French people the futility of any further resistance. Clément Duvernois left London in the middle of January to gain the approval of the Emperor at Wilhelmshöhe and the emigrés in Brussels to these plans, and by 19th January he was expected to arrive in Versailles.

Bismarck therefore had some reason to consider that the renewal of peace negotiations immediately after the fall of Paris would stand a good chance of success. Even if an Imperial restoration was impossible—and the growing violence of Gambetta's republicanism might make it the lessser of two evils for Germany[2]—the Imperial overtures could be used as a diplomatic lever to compel Favre to put forward proposals of his own; and nothing, he believed, should be done to make any more difficult the task of any French statesman, of whatever régime, who was willing and able to negotiate for peace. These were the views which he

---

[1] On these negotiations see Joachim Kühn, "Bismarck und der Bonapartismus im Winter 1870/1" in *Preuss. Jahrbücher* CLXIII (1916). Also Bismarck, *Gesamm. Werke* VI b No. 1952 p. 618, No. 1976 p. 637, No. 1989 p. 647, No. 1995 p. 654, No. 2001 p. 661, No. 2002 p. 662.

[2] Bismarck's Memorandum to the King of 14th January 1871, *Gesamm. Werke* VI b No. 2005 p. 665, gives a powerful statement of this argument.

had held with respect to Austria after the victory of Sadowa; and they were now, as then, to bring him into harsh conflict with Moltke and the General Staff.

Moltke during this period was under no less of a strain than Bismarck. His resources were stretched to the limit, his communications were precarious, and the victories of his forces in the field still seemed to make no impression on the hydra-headed resistance of the National Defence. The confirmation, on 5th January, of Bourbaki's movement to the East showed that he had made a serious miscalculation of his enemy's resources and intentions, and for two weeks it seemed probable that Werder might suffer a serious reverse before Manteuffel could come to his aid. The staunchest resolution was needed, at the War Council of 15th January, to forbid Werder to raise the siege of Belfort and to order him to accept battle on the Lisaine; and it was not until 18th January that Moltke could be sure that his counter-measures had been successful. Throughout these weeks of strain he maintained an icy composure which belied his real feelings. These came out only in private intercourse with his intimates; and his disciples on his Staff, Podbielski, Verdy, Bronsart and their subordinates, indignant at the sufferings to which their beloved master was subject, allowed themselves outlets in letters and conversations which Moltke denied to himself. Bismarck's open criticisms of the conduct of the campaign, his demands for access to military information, his desire for a negotiated peace, all added up, in their view, to a formidable indictment. "I have never yet known such bitterness against any man", noted the relatively neutral Stosch, on 26th January, "as prevails against Bismarck at this moment."[1]

For Moltke the fall of Paris would be an opportunity, not for making peace, but for prosecuting the war in the provinces with greater vehemence. The city was to be occupied by German troops, its garrison was to be imprisoned in Germany and its stores and weapons requisitioned, a heavy contribution was to be extorted and the administration be taken over by a German military government.[2] Meanwhile the liberated armies of investment should drive southward, Moltke told the Crown Prince at dinner on 8th January, so as to capture the enemy military resources. "We must fight this nation of liars to the very end!" he exclaimed. "Then we can dictate whatever peace we like." When the Crown Prince interposed a question about the political implications of all this, Moltke replied briefly that he knew nothing about that: "I am concerned only with military matters." When a few days later,

---

[1] Stosch, *Denkwürdigkeiten* 227. [2] Stadelmann, *Moltke und der Staat* 246.

on 13th January, the Crown Prince attempted to resolve the differences between Bismarck and Moltke by inviting both to dinner, he failed miserably. Not only did their views about the conduct of operations after the fall of Paris prove irreconcilable, but Bismarck launched an attack on Moltke's entire conduct of operations since the battle of Sedan which infuriated the Chief of Staff. It is hardly surprising that Moltke should have resented the accusation that he was overstepping the limit of his military sphere when Bismarck showed so little hesitation about invading it.[1]

If Moltke's views prevailed all hope of negotiating peace, with the Bonapartists or anybody else, would disappear; and Bismarck resolved to establish his unquestioned authority as the King's principal adviser. On 14th January, the day following the Crown Prince's dinner-party, Moltke gave him his chance. By accepting, and replying to, Trochu's letter complaining of the damage done to civilian life and property by the German bombardment, Moltke laid himself open, as he had by his earlier exchange of letters with the Governor of Paris, to a charge of entering into separate negotiations with a section of the enemy Government. In the embittered and Byzantine atmosphere of Versailles such a course of action appeared quite possible; in any case, Bismarck put on the incident the worst interpretation it could bear, and on 18th January he raised the whole question with the King—or, to give him the new title which he unwillingly assumed that very day, the Kaiser. Bismarck had already reiterated his complaint that, in spite of the Kaiser's express commands, the General Staff was still failing to provide him with the information about the progress of military affairs which would make it possible for him to carry on his diplomatic work. Now he renewed his demand that Moltke should be explicitly forbidden to enter into any independent negotiations with the enemy.[2]

The Kaiser was old and unwell. The crises with which Bismarck and Moltke were dealing separately—the creation of the German Empire and the repulse of Bourbaki—demanded decisions which ultimately he alone could make, and which imposed a heavy strain on his nerves and temper. In the conflict between his two great advisers his sympathies were openly with Moltke[3]; but Bismarck's demands were reasonable,

[1] Frederick III, *War Diary* 253, 257. Oncken, *Friedrich I von Baden* II 294–311. See also Haeften, "Bismarck und Moltke" in *Preuss. Jahrbücher* CLXXVII (1919), and Gerhard Ritter, *Staatskunst und Kriegshandwerk* I 283–6.

[2] Bismarck, *Gesamm. Werke* VI b. No. 1999 p. 658, No. 2009 p. 673.

[3] Oncken, *Friedrich I von Baden* II 306.

and to refuse them would be to provoke the resignation of the Chancellor at a moment when, for the guidance of the new Empire and the conclusion of a lasting peace, his services were more necessary than perhaps they had ever been. He yielded. On 25th January he issued two strongly worded Cabinet Orders. The first reiterated the command that Bismarck was to be kept informed of the course of military operations, and directed Moltke to take such effective steps to do so that Bismarck would have no further cause for complaint; while the second expressly ordered that in any correspondence with members of the French Government or Delegation which might have any political significance, and in the drafting of any replies, the Ministry of Foreign Affairs was always to be consulted.[1] The royal decision was unequivocal and settled the matter.

The reply which Moltke at first projected was virtually a letter of resignation. The royal order, he said, was *"ungnädig"*, un-Gracious. His communications with Trochu, he maintained, had been strictly military. All he had withheld from Bismarck was information and plans which would be of value to the Chancellor only if he as well as Moltke were advising the King about operations; and rather than have the war conducted by such a dual authority Moltke declared himself ready "to leave the relevant operations and the responsibility for them to the Federal Chancellor alone. I await", he concluded grimly, "Your Imperial Majesty's most gracious decision on the matter."[2] The letter which he actually sent, however, was considerably milder. In it he merely defended his conduct with dignity, complained at Bismarck's repeated and unjustified accusations, asked for a clear ruling about his relationship with the Chancellor, and requested the Emperor's protection against any further attacks. The Imperial secretaries drafted an anodyne reply, but it was not sent. There was no need. On 28th January an armistice was signed with the Government of National Defence. For the preservation of peaceful relations within Royal Headquarters it had come not a moment too soon.[3]

* * *

Bismarck's *démarche* of 18th January took effect almost immediately. Two days later, on the evening of 20th January, Trochu sent his request for an armistice to bury the dead after Buzenval. The Kaiser at once referred the request, not to Moltke, but to Bismarck; and Bismarck grimly

[1] Haeften, loc. cit. 98.

[2] For the successive drafts of Moltke's letters, see Stadelmann, *Moltke und der Staat* 503–6, App. 8.

[3] Bronsart, *Kriegstagebuch* 336.

refused it. The brusqueness of the refusal, the failure to take advantage of what was generally sensed in Versailles to be the beginning of the end,[1] seems so out of keeping with Bismarck's desire to renew peace negotiations that the explanation must surely be sought in Bismarck's attitude to the earlier exchanges between Moltke and Trochu. In this new overture he may have seen another move in the negotiations which he believed the soldiers to be conducting behind his back, and it is not surprising that he should have taken advantage of his new established dominance to end them. In any case he was convinced that after the failure of the Buzenval sortie capitulation could not be long delayed,[2] and then the peace-proposals of the Imperial party could be seriously considered. Clément Duvernois was expected at any moment. But Duvernois did not come: the stubbornness of the emigré group in Brussels threw his whole time-table out of joint, and before he was ready to talk to Bismarck Jules Favre had reached Versailles.[3]

Favre arrived at German Headquarters late in the evening of 23rd January. His journey followed a day of stormy debate while the Government in Paris discussed whether he should negotiate for an armistice for the fortress of Paris only or for the whole of France. The question was left open: he was instructed only to discover what terms were available, without betraying the desperate state of the city's supplies.[4] Favre himself hoped to secure, as a minimum, that there should be facilities given for the free election of a National Assembly to decide the question of war or peace; that there should be no entry of Prussian troops into Paris and no imprisonment in Germany of the garrison, and that civil war should not be provoked by an attempt to disarm the *Garde Nationale*. Failing these conditions, he was prepared to threaten a renewal of the fighting and ultimately a total surrender which would compel the Germans to accept complete responsibility for the civil administration of Paris.[5]

---

[1] Stosch, *Denkwürdigkeiten* 225. Hohenlohe, *Aus meinem Leben* 390.

[2] Busch, *Bismarck: Some Secret Pages of his History* I 485.

[3] Duvernois's delay convinced Bismarck that "dieselbe Unentschlossenheit wie seit Monaten noch jetzt herrscht. . . . Die Anerkennung des Kaisers hat für uns so viel Schwierigkeit gegenüber England, Russland und in Deutschland, dasz sie nur dann sich rechtfertigt, wenn sie der kürzeste Weg zum Frieden ist. Finden wir bei Gelegenheit der Kapitulation von Paris einen kürzern, so werden wir ohne Rücksicht auf dynastische und monarchische Fragen unsere Entschlüsse nur nach eigenem Interesse fassen." Bismarck to Count Bernstorff, 20th January 1871, *Gesamm. Werke* No. 2010 p. 673. For Duvernois's visit to Wilhelmshöhe see Graf Monts, *Napoleon III auf Wilhelmshöhe 1870–71* (Berlin 1909) pp. 128–33. [4] Dréo, *Procès Verbaux* 571–9.

[5] Favre, *Gouvernement de la Défense Nationale* II 377.

Bismarck was able to bluff much more effectively than Favre. As at Ferrières, he was able to state truthfully that he was in negotiation with the Empress, who alone represented lawful authority, for the summoning of the only legal representative body in France, the Corps Législatif. Favre's project of a freely elected Assembly he declared to be no longer realisable: under the dictatorial republicanism of Gambetta elections would not be free. He was prepared however to talk in general terms about conditions for Paris. He agreed that the garrison should not be sent as prisoners to Germany, where their presence would only be an embarrassment; he considered that although opinion in the Army and in Germany would insist on a triumphal entry into the city, the scope of this might be strictly limited; and while refusing to waive the disarmament of the *Garde Nationale*, he suggested that the most politically reliable battalions alone should be allowed to keep their arms. The contrast between these terms and the draconian conditions demanded by Moltke speaks for itself. By the end of the first evening's discussion it was evident that the chances of agreement were good. Bismarck said nothing to the curious bystanders as he left the room in which he had been closeted alone with Favre, but he whistled a hunting call of unmistakable meaning: the chase was over.[1]

Next day, 24th January, both negotiators came into the open. Clément Duvernois had still not arrived, and Bismarck consented to abandon his negotiations with the Empress if he could reach agreement with the Government of National Defence. In return Favre agreed to sign an armistice covering the whole of France, and to ensure that no resistance by the Delegation would be allowed to stand in the way of its implementation. Only the question of the armament of the *Garde Nationale* remained unsettled, and on this Bismarck, faced by Favre's convincing assurance that it would be physically impossible to disarm them without a civil war, was eventually to yield.[2] For the rest, the Government in Paris with some reason accepted Bismarck's terms as "*inespérées*".[3] Thanks to the Chancellor's diplomatic moderation, the honour of the city and the troops who had defended it would remain intact. On 25th January Favre was therefore authorised to sign an armistice for three weeks, to enable a National Assembly to meet at Bordeaux and finally resolve the question of war or peace.

[1] Favre, op. cit. II 382–6. *D.T.* I 343. Busch, op. cit. I 487. Frederick III, *War Diary* 282.
[2] *D.T.* I 343.
[3] Dréo, *Procès Verbaux* 587, 589.

So far Bismarck had carried on the negotiations single-handed. Now the military had unavoidably to be called in to settle the details of the armistice. It was unfortunate that this stage in the negotiations coincided exactly with the crisis of the quarrel between the civil and military authorities; and Bismarck rubbed salt into the wounds of his defeated rivals by insisting that the agreement with the French should take the form, not of a Capitulation, which would signify surrender, but of a Convention, which indicated only a negotiated settlement between equals. Moltke began attending conferences on 26th January, the day after his rebuff by the Emperor. The French negotiators noted, without fully appreciating the cause, the unpleasant contrast between his grim, unsmiling dourness and the easy affability of Bismarck, and Bismarck openly stigmatised Moltke's attitude as mean, pettifogging and unrealistic.[1] But the French had trouble enough with their own military representatives. Trochu's oath never to capitulate made it impossible for him to undertake the responsibility of negotiating surrender, and Ducrot had never been forgiven by the German Emperor for his apparent breach of parole after Sedan. Favre therefore found to accompany him a certain General Beaufort d'Hautpoul, who proved quite incapable of carrying on negotiations. The French attributed his peculiar condition to honourable mortification; the Germans, less charitably, said he was drunk.[2] He was succeeded after one embarrassing day by General de Valdan, Vinoy's Chief of Staff, by whom, on 28th January, the armistice was signed.

The armistice was to take effect in Paris immediately—indeed on Bismarck's suggestion the bombardment and counter-bombardment had ceased two days earlier—and was to come into action elsewhere in France in three days' time. It was to last until 19th February, during which time full facilities would be given for an Assembly to be freely elected and to meet at Bordeaux, where it would debate whether the war should continue and on what terms peace should be made. Meanwhile Paris was to pay a war-indemnity of two hundred million francs. It was to yield up its perimeter forts and dismount the guns from its walls, but the ground between the forts and the city would be considered neutral, and no German troops would enter Paris. The Germans would provide full facilities for the rapid re-provisioning of the city. 12,000 men of the Paris garrison would retain their arms, an essential minimum

[1] Busch, op. cit. 517. *D.T.* III 164, 171–2.
[2] D'Hérisson, *Journal of a Staff Officer* 305. Busch, op. cit. 507. Frederick III, *War Diary* 285.

to preserve order, as Favre insisted. The rest were to surrender their arms and remain in Paris until the end of the armistice; when, if peace had not yet been made, they were to be taken over by the Germans as prisoners-of-war.

The terms for the rest of the country were less satisfactory to the French. It was agreed that a military demarcation line should be drawn, from which both armies should withdraw ten kilometres; but Favre and his military advisers depended entirely on the Germans for information about the position of the existing front line, and Moltke was in no mood to interpret doubtful cases to his opponents' advantage. The agreed line was to involve at several points the withdrawal of French troops from positions which they had quite securely held.[1] Moreover about the operations still in progress in the Jura both Favre and Bismarck were equally ill-informed. Favre knew only that the fortress of Belfort was still intact and that Bourbaki's relieving force still held the field. To enforce an armistice in this area might be to spoil the chance of a military victory which would considerably strengthen the French hand when it came to negotiating the final peace. Moltke, though he had received little news from the swiftly moving Manteuffel, was sufficiently confident of the outcome to allow Favre to nurse his illusions; so by common agreement military operations were allowed to continue in the departments of Jura, Côte d'Or, and Doubs.[2] When Favre telegraphed the news of the armistice to Gambetta on the evening of 28th January he made the astonishing and notorious mistake of failing to inform him of this omission. How this error contributed to the final agonies of the Army of the East we have already seen.

Moltke admitted the validity of the political considerations which had led Bismarck to conclude the Convention with the Government of National Defence, but he made no secret of his dissatisfaction with the moderation of its terms.[3] In this he spoke for the Army, but not for the Army alone. His views were widely echoed throughout Germany.

---

[1] Freycinet, *Guerre en Province* 320. Bismarck to Favre, 1 February 1871 in *Gesamm. Werke* VI b No. 2021 p. 683.

[2] That there was no question of German "trickery" over this Favre makes quite clear in *Gouvernement de la Défense Nationale* II 402–3.

[3] See his message to the Crown Prince of Saxony in H. von Grollman, *E. E. von Krause* 140. "Die provisorische Regierung in Paris würde sich die extremsten Bedingungen des Siegers zwar haben gefallen lassen müssen, und Jules Favre habe dies selbst anerkannt. Wolle diese Regierung aber sich aufrecht erhalten, so könne sie nicht weiter gehen. . . . Dieselbe habe die aufrichtige Absicht, den Frieden herbeizuführen, und folglich wir ein eminentes Interesse, sie in der Gewalt zu erhalten."

On the French side it was the civilians, Gambetta and the politicians of the Paris Clubs, who wished to prolong the war long after all but a tiny minority of their military advisers had urged the conclusion of peace. The relaxing of the tension which was brought about by even a temporary suspension of hostilities undermined the strength of the extremists on both sides. The parties of *guerre à outrance* dwindled to impotent if vociferous cliques at Bordeaux and Versailles, able to embarrass the peace-makers but not to thwart them. That this was so in the French ranks was due to the openly expressed determination of the French people, through their elected representatives, to have peace at any cost. But Bismarck, in dealing with his own military party, did not enjoy a comparable advantage. Instead public opinion in Germany as overwhelmingly supported a peace of extermination as did that in the Allied nations in 1918. If the opposition to Bismarck at Versailles which had been at its height on the eve of the armistice abated rapidly once the armistice was signed, it was not because the military party was accepting defeat with a good grace. Rather it was because the final conditions of settlement presented to the French left in their view little to be desired. It had been Bismarck's armistice; but it was to be Moltke's peace.

* * *

Bismarck remained sceptical of Favre's capacity to bring the Delegation to acquiesce in his peace negotiations, and with reason. When rumours of the negotiations at Versailles reached Bordeaux, the Delegation, on 27th January, issued a public denial of their existence— "We cannot believe that negotiations of this kind could have been undertaken without the Delegation being previously notified"—and Gambetta warned Favre in a despatch of the same date that the Delegation would not consider any agreement negotiated by the Government in Paris to be binding on itself.[1] This message reached Versailles only on 2nd February. Had it arrived before the signature of the armistice of 28th January it is unlikely to have affected Favre's decision, but it might easily have shaken Bismarck's none too firm confidence in the capacity of the Government of National Defence to enforce its own agreements. As it was, Gambetta obeyed the instruction in the Government's telegram, to spread the news of the armistice and to organise elections for February 8th; but he determined that the armistice should be no more than a pause before renewing the battle yet more bitterly, and that

[1] *D.T.* V ii 305. Bury, *Gambetta and the National Defence* 248.

the Assembly should be one purged of reactionaries and pledged to the continuation of *la guerre à outrance*. When on 31st January Jules Simon, the representative despatched by the Government to inform the Delegation more fully of its intentions, reached Bordeaux, he found the streets placarded with two new decrees: one excluding from the new Assembly anyone who had held public office under the Empire, and one setting forth Gambetta's own interpretation of the Armistice.

> Let us make use of the Armistice [it ran] as a school for instruction for our young troops.... In place of the reactionary and cowardly Assembly of which the enemy dreams, let us install an Assembly that is truly national and republican, desiring peace, if peace assures our honour . . . but capable of willing war also, ready for anything rather than lend a hand in the murder of France.[1]

Behind Gambetta stood his colleagues of the Delegation, and behind them a body of opinion, at Bordeaux, Lyons, and Marseilles, which showed no hesitation, not only in continuing the foreign, but in provoking a civil war. An unwise telegram in which Bismarck angrily rebuked Gambetta for flouting the armistice-terms played into the hands of the extremists, and when Jules Simon demanded the retraction of the offending decree the Delegation flatly refused to obey. A moderate and subtle man, Simon did not avail himself of the plenary powers with which he was equipped. Instead he sent for reinforcements from the Government in Paris to out-vote the members of the Delegation. They reached Bordeaux on 6th February, but before they met their colleagues Gambetta decided to resign. He still had no doubt that the war could and should be carried on,[2] but he was a man of sense as well as honour, and his resolution was not carried to the point of irrational fanaticism. France already owed him much for his leadership during the past four months: now by his peaceful abdication of that leadership he rendered his country the greatest service that lay within his power.[3]

Gambetta's resignation did much to strengthen Bismarck's position at Versailles against the military party which considered a continuation of the war to be not only desirable but necessary.[4] Until the Assembly met, however, a renewal of hostilities could not be ruled out by either side. The Germans allowed Chanzy and Faidherbe to travel to Paris to discuss the matter with the Ministers on 7th February. Faidherbe

---

[1] Reinach, I 55–8, II 124–5.
[2] *D.T.* I 555.
[3] Favre, *Gouvernement de la Défense Nationale* III 14–32. Bury, op. cit. 261–3.
[4] Oncken, *Friedrich I von Baden* II 361–2.

was justifiably pessimistic about the chances of prolonging the campaign in the North, even if his army took refuge in the fortresses. Instead he proposed that the best of his men should be transferred to strengthen the forces in Brittany and the south; and in accordance with this plan, the cream of his army, 16,000 troops and sixty guns, were embarked at Dunkirk between 17th and 25th February.[1] Chanzy himself did not doubt for a moment that the campaign could be continued. He recommended that his own army, leaving detachments to cover Brittany and Normandy, should be transferred to the south bank of the Loire; then, aided by the local population, they should put up a foot by foot defence of French territory which would compel the Germans to maintain an army 500,000 strong in France until through sheer exhaustion she offered peace on acceptable terms.[2]

Chanzy's assumption that such a campaign would incline the Germans to greater moderation showed a depressing *naïveté*. The extreme elements among the German generals demanded nothing better,[3] and Moltke was already planning to deal with the situation. The collapse of Paris enabled him to detach troops from the armies of investment to strengthen his forces in the field, and at a Council of War of 8th February his proposals were accepted by a somewhat reluctant Kaiser.[4] IV Corps, from the Army of the Meuse, was to move to Chartres to cover Paris from the west, and V Corps, from the Third Army, was to stand on guard on the Loire between Orléans and Blois. Frederick Charles would then drive south from the Loire with the whole of his forces while Manteuffel advanced south-west with his three corps from the Saône, in a campaign to surround and annihilate whatever French forces were still left in the field.[5] Roon, who had to find the men for this, was not enthusiastic. On a demand by Moltke for twelve more Landwehr battalions he minuted his belief that it would make better sense to start sending the Landwehr home after the fall of Paris than to send any more to France. "An operation", he wrote, "which takes us to the foot of the Pyrenees is, without overstretching our resources, a task for years."[6] But in general Moltke's entourage, like Chanzy, looked forward to a renewal of hostilities with confidence and hope.

[1] *Guerre: Armée du Nord* IV 160–2.
[2] Chanzy, 2me *Armée de la Loire* 418.
[3] See e.g. Blumenthal, *Journals* 315.
[4] Frederick III, *War Diary* 298. Oncken, *Friedrich I von Baden* II 363–4. Bronsart, *Kriegstagebuch* 339.
[5] *M.M.K.* 573.
[6] Ibid. 581.

The French electors were to confound them. By their choice of an Assembly they decisively rejected the Republicans who had led them for the last five months, and with them all idea of continuing the war. Left to themselves, without pressure from a central Government, or propaganda by organised parties, the provinces turned to the leaders of local society, the gentry and aristocracy who had turned their backs on national politics since the fall of the monarchy and whose local pre-eminence had been re-asserted by the notable part they had played in the National Defence.[1] Paris and the great cities stubbornly continued to return men of the Left: Gambetta, Garibaldi, Victor Hugo, Henri Rochefort, Félix Pyat and Delescluze all found seats. But the Republicans of all shades numbered only 200, while against them was ranged an Orléano–Legitimist bloc 400 strong. Only some thirty supporters of the Empire were returned. Thiers, who since October had been publicly urging the conclusion of peace on any terms, was elected by twenty-six constituencies, and was the obvious choice as head of the new Government. Once in power, he dealt sharply with the unthinking emotionalism which had already done such irreparable harm. On 7th February, when the Assembly gave a warm welcome to a demand from the representatives of Alsace and Lorraine that France should never consent to any cession of their territory, Thiers bluntly recalled it to realities. "Have the courage of your opinions", he told them. "Either war or peace. This is serious. There's no room for childishness when it's a matter either of the fate of two very important provinces or the fate of the country as a whole." Chastened, the Assembly agreed to leave the question to the wisdom of the negotiators; and on 21st February Thiers, with Favre as his Foreign Minister, left for Versailles to see what terms were to be obtained.[2]

Thiers had few illusions. Before the fall of Metz, he told Favre, Bismarck might have been content with Alsace and an indemnity of three milliard francs. Now he reckoned that he would demand Lorraine as well, including Metz, and five milliard francs. It was a very accurate estimate. In fact the figure which Bismarck first named was six milliard —he wrote it down on a piece of paper and at the sight of it Thiers jumped "as if he had been bitten by a mad dog"—but it was generally realised that this was a bargaining ruse, and that five milliard would be

[1] F. H. Brabant, *The Beginning of the Third Republic in France* (London 1940) 62–7.
[2] Favre, *Gouvernement de la Défense Nationale* III 74–79. Sorel, *Histoire Diplomatique* II 219.

accepted.[1] Alsace was demanded, but only that northern area of Lorraine, including Metz, which had already been organised by the German administration as "the new department of the Moselle". The south of the province, round Nancy would remain French. Finally, a triumphal entry of the German army into Paris was to take place. Against all these demands Thiers protested with vigorous eloquence, but he could shake neither Bismarck nor the Kaiser himself. To all his pleas for moderation Bismarck was able to point, not without reason, to the inflexible demands of his own military party, who were already accusing him of spoiling all the victories they had won. And when Thiers threatened to appeal against his demands to the Powers of Europe, Bismarck replied, "If you speak to me of Europe I speak to you of Napoleon."[2] He had himself little faith left in the practicability of a Bonapartist restoration, but the General Staff were beginning to take up the idea with an enthusiasm which was in ironic contrast to their opposition to it the previous autumn. It was, at any rate, another weapon to use in negotiations. Against it Thiers might for his part have threatened Bismarck with Gambetta; but from this extremity even he shrank.

In fact Bismarck put forward the demand for Metz with considerable reluctance. During the campaign of the previous summer he had been enthusiastic in his demands for its annexation as part of Germany's new protective belt against French attack; but during the autumn his ardour cooled as he realised the problems which this purely French enclave would raise in an Empire whose political structure would be complicated enough without it.[3] When Thiers came to Versailles at the end of October Bismarck told him in confidence that he regarded Metz as expendable. By February the Chancellor was making no secret of his unwillingness to demand so indigestible a morsel.[4] Various alternative proposals were being canvassed at Versailles. One was that Germany should, with French approval, acquire Luxemburg as a substitute; another, that the war-indemnity should be increased; a third, that France should cede one of her overseas possessions, perhaps Saigon, instead.[5] But the Kaiser would not consider relinquishing a prize won at the cost

[1] Stosch, *Denkwürdigkeiten* 235–7. Waldersee, *Denkwürdigkeiten* I 162.
[2] Busch, *Bismarck: Some Secret Pages of his History* I 557.
[3] E.g. Busch, *Bismarck: Some Secret Pages of his History* I 99–101, 166, Bismarck, *Gesamm. Werke* VI b No. 1808 p. 500. Oncken, *Friedrich I von Baden* II 393.
[4] Newton, *Life of Lord Lyons* I 358. Bronsart, *Kriegstagebuch* 359, 369. Waldersee, *Denkwürdigkeiten* I 163.
[5] Oncken, op. cit. II 392–3.

of so much Prussian blood; Moltke was equally determined to retain a fortress which, for the defence of the new German Empire's western frontier, he assessed as the equivalent of an army 120,000 strong[1]; and the claim to Metz had been too openly and too frequently made in the German press for it to be abandoned now without a furore which Bismarck was unwilling to brave. On the question of Metz, as on the question of the entry into Paris, Bismarck yielded to the demands of the Army, and Thiers found him immovable.[2]

On one point alone did Thiers get his way. The garrison of Belfort under Colonel Denfert-Rochereau had held out, an island of conflict in a becalmed sea, until 15th February, when, with the consent of the French Government and on the recommendation of Bismarck, it had marched freely away with full honours of war.[3] If Metz was sentimentally precious to the Emperor of Germany, Belfort was equally so to the people of France, and Thiers fought energetically for its retention. If Bismarck would yield over this, he promised, peace could be made at once. If he did not, then Thiers would resign and leave Bismarck to govern France himself. It was the only card which Thiers could play, and Bismarck judged that he was not bluffing. It was not difficult for Bismarck to yield. Moltke set no great store by Belfort. In any future campaign, he reckoned, the decision would be reached either on the Main or on the plains of Lorraine, and in an invasion of France or of Germany Belfort would be of secondary value.[4] The Kaiser was agreeable: Thiers was merely offered the choice between retaining Belfort or having the Germans abandon their entry into Paris. He had no difficulty in making up his mind.

On 26th February Thiers, Favre, Bismarck, and the representatives of the South German States signed the preliminaries of Peace. The new frontier was defined and the indemnity was fixed at five milliard francs; one milliard to be paid during the course of 1871 and the rest within three years of the ratification of the preliminaries. As soon as the treaty was ratified the Germans would withdraw from the interior of Paris and the forts on the left bank of the Seine and would evacuate all departments south of the Seine. The remainder of the occupied area would be evacuated as the indemnity was paid. French civil administration would be restored in the occupied areas, and the maintenance of

---

[1] Stadelmann, *Moltke und der Staat* 223.
[2] A. Klein-Wuttig, *Politik und Kriegführung* 158–60.
[3] Favre, *Gouvernement de la Défense Nationale* III 42.
[4] Stadelmann, *Moltke und der Staat* 507.

the occupying forces would be the responsibility of the French Government. The French forces, except for a garrison in Paris 40,000 strong, were to retire behind the Loire until the definitive peace treaty was signed. Exchange of prisoners was to begin at once, and negotiations for a definitive treaty would begin in Brussels as soon as the preliminaries had been ratified by the Emperor and the French National Assembly. By an additional Convention, it was agreed that the German forces occupying Paris should not exceed 30,000 men and that they should be restricted to the area bounded by the Seine, the Avenue des Ternes and the Rue du Faubourg Saint-Honoré: a district elegant enough to satisfy German pride and far away from the working-class quarters where trouble might be expected.[1] Either party might still denounce the armistice any time after 3rd March, and reopen hostilities three days after that.[2]

The terms were harsh. The figure for the indemnity appeared astronomical, and the cession of Alsace-Lorraine was a sacrifice to which France was never to reconcile herself. A century earlier the transfer of such provinces to the sovereignty of a victorious prince had been commonplace. A century later it would have been completed by the brutal surgery of transfer of populations. To the nineteenth century, with its growing belief in national self-determination and plebiscitary voting, the process, carried out in defiance of the wishes of the populations, seemed an open flouting of that public law on whose development Europe was beginning to pride itself. Yet the treaty was not so harsh as that which the French had imposed on Prussia in 1807. There was no attempt to interfere with the internal affairs of the country. No limit was imposed on the size of the armed forces which France might keep up; no cession or destruction of naval vessels was demanded; and in spite of agitation among the mercantile interests of Hamburg and Bremen, Bismarck left French overseas possessions intact.[3] Whatever her losses and her humiliation, France remained a Great Power: too great, indeed, for German peace of mind during the coming forty years.

The National Assembly ratified the preliminaries with remarkable speed. Although a few voices were raised to demand a *levée en masse*, the ratification was voted on 1st March by 546 votes to 107. Chanzy,

---

[1] "Eine Beschränkung auf die besseren Stadtviertel liegt im Interesse aller Teile." Bronsart, *Kreigstagebuch* 347.

[2] The text of the preliminaries is reprinted in Favre, *Gouvernement de la Défense Nationale* III 517.

[3] Oncken, *Friedrich I von Baden* II 358–60. Frederick III, *War Diary* 297.

after making an eloquent protest from the tribune, voted with the minority, together with Generals Billot and Mazure; but most of his military colleagues cast their votes for peace, including Aurelle, Le Flô, Jauréguiberry, Pallières, and Ducrot.[1]

This prompt ratification gained the French one slight but gratifying advantage. The Germans, presuming that ratification would come only after a prolonged debate, had as we have seen undertaken to evacuate the interior of Paris as soon as it occurred. They had lost no time in organising their entry into the city. The limitation of the occupying force to 30,000 men had led them to arrange for their troops to enter in three relays, on successive days, beginning on 1st March. On that day, after parading before the Kaiser on the racecourse of Longchamps, a contingent from the Third Army had duly marched down the Champs Élysées under the gaze of a curious and intermittently jeering crowd. The Kaiser, who did not conceal his dissatisfaction with a triumph which fell so far short of the remembered splendours of 1814,[2] looked forward to leading in his Guard on the third day; but on 2nd March Jules Favre appeared at Versailles with news of the ratification and a demand for its immediate implementation by the withdrawal of the German troops. Bismarck did not conceal his vexation, nor Favre his pleasure; but Roon and Moltke insisted punctiliously on honouring their agreement. The Kaiser had to content himself, on 3rd March, with reviewing his troops at Longchamps as they marched out of the city. It was a disappointment, according to Waldersee, which he was never entirely to forgive or forget.[3]

This very limited triumph, if it failed to assuage the appetite of the Kaiser and his Army, failed also to arouse the passions of the Parisians. There was some cat-calling and a little stone-throwing during the parade, but afterwards, when the troops settled down in their temporary quarters along the Seine and in the Trocadéro, they mixed with their late enemies on easy and even amicable terms.[4] Crowds listened to their military bands, even joining in singing the tunes. "At the sound of the Retreat on Thursday", Bismarck wrote to his wife, "thousands of Parisians followed, arm in arm with our soldiers, and at 'Helmets off for prayer' took off their hats and said '*Voilà ce que nous manque*', and that was no doubt correct."[5]

---

[1] Welschinger, *Guerre de 1870: Causes et Responsabilités* II 178.
[2] Waldersee, *Denkwürdigkeiten* I 127.
[3] Ibid. I 163. L. Schneider, *Aus dem Leben Kaiser Wilhelms*, III 200.
[4] Frederick III, *War Diary* 322. Oncken, op. cit. II 406.
[5] *Letters to his Wife from the Seat of War* 117.

Such views probably commanded considerable support in the wealthier quarters in which the Germans found themselves; but with the end of the fighting the precarious unity of the city disappeared. Even as the German troops marched out, on 3rd March, the riots were beginning. Two weeks later the revolution which Trochu and Favre had struggled so hard to contain broke out in full force, and the revolutionary Commune seized power.

*   *   *   *   *

The events of the French civil war during the spring of 1871 are no part of this story, except in so far as they affected the negotiations between the German Empire and the French Provisional Government for the conclusion of a definitive peace. The Germans watched with sympathy the attempts by Thiers to reduce the Commune to order; offering indeed military help which was naturally refused. But military forces were certainly needed, and if they were to be French it would be necessary to revise the provision in the peace preliminaries which restricted the number of French troops north of the Loire to the 40,000 of the Paris garrison. Bismarck therefore agreed that the number should be raised to 80,000, and that the return of prisoners from Germany should be speeded up so that an army could be formed under the command of MacMahon to suppress the revolt. In addition, the Germans obligingly evacuated Versailles a week earlier than had originally been agreed, to enable the French Government and Assembly to transfer their seat from Bordeaux. But Bismarck made these concessions with an ill grace. The situation was an annoying one for the German Government. The formation of a new French army, as well as the emergence of a revolutionary force which, however localised, was very competently armed, made it necessary in common prudence for the German army to delay its withdrawal from French territory until some measure of order had been restored; but this meant a further delay in demobilisation, with all that this involved in social dislocation and financial expense. Bismarck exploited the situation with a bullying acerbity which contrasted curiously with the moderation he had shown during the armistice negotiations. Perhaps the attacks to which he had been subjected as a result of that moderation had affected his attitude; certainly he felt that his decision to rely on the capacity of Thiers and Favre to make the peace acceptable throughout France had proved to be mistaken. The result was that the rôles of Bismarck and the General Staff were now to be reversed. It was Bismarck, and his representative at Brussels, Count Harry von Arnim, who bullied and threatened. The generals were anxious only to get their troops home. Their professional assessment of French military strength gave them no cause for alarm; and in the Provisional Government they saw the best guarantee, both for the restoration of order inside France, and for the payment of the indemnity which any revolutionary administration would almost certainly denounce.[1] When in March the Kaiser and his headquarters returned to Germany and Manteuffel, the most politically active of all the Prussian generals, assumed command of the German troops in France, a period opened of genial co-operation between German soldiers and French statesmen which, paradoxically, infuriated Bismarck quite as much as had the intransigence of Moltke and his demigods during the course of the war.

While Bismarck harassed the French Government with complaints at their slowness in suppressing the Commune and by threats to take over the work himself, his representatives at Brussels haggled mercilessly over the timing and the nature of payment of the indemnity. They demanded that the full sum should be paid in specie. In addition they now put forward claims to the confiscation of the property of the *Compagnie des Chemins de Fer de l'Est* in Alsace-Lorraine, against derisory compensation; to a guarantee of the commercial *status quo ante bellum* between France and the German Zollverein; and to an indemnity for all the citizens of German States who were expelled from France during the course of the war.[2] Moreover Bismarck pointed out that, as the circumstances in which the original figure of the indemnity had been fixed had now changed, that figure could no longer be regarded as sacrosanct. On 2nd May his representative in France, General von Fabrice, a courteous Saxon nobleman who did all he could to soften the impact of the brusque communications which he was compelled to deliver, informed Favre: "Germany, so long as she has no guarantee of a solid state of affairs, cannot think of disarming. From this arises considerable new expenditure, whose extent cannot be estimated until after the conclusion of the unforeseen period which has given rise to it."[3] This hint of new and unspecified demands compelled Favre once more to seek out Bismarck in person. The ill-tempered negotiations at Brussels were suspended, and on 6th May the two statesmen met at Frankfurt-am-Main.

[1] Stosch, *Denkwürdigkeiten* 260–1.
[2] Sorel, *Histoire diplomatique* II 273. See also Hans Goldschmidt, *Bismarck und die Friedsunterhändler, 1871* (Berlin 1929) *passim*.
[3] Sorel, op. cit. II 290.

For once Favre's hope, so cruelly belied at Ferrières the previous September, that by personal negotiation he could remove misunderstandings, proved justified. Over the past five months Bismarck had acquired for him personally a considerable degree of affection and a certain measure of respect; while MacMahon's victories over the Communards during the past month had shown the Provisional Government to be not only willing but able to restore order within France. Nevertheless Bismarck now insisted that the total evacuation of French territory by the German army was impossible. 50,000 troops must remain, occupying six departments, until the German Government considered the French régime sufficiently stable to carry out its obligations. If this demand was not accepted, he declared, he would revoke all the concessions he had made since 26th February and insist on the withdrawal of the French army to the south of the Loire. To this Favre agreed; obtaining only the concession that the remaining departments should be evacuated as soon as 1,500 million francs had been paid, irrespective of the political situation within France. It was a modification of the original terms more of form than of substance. Bismarck made no secret of the clamour among both the German public and the German army for the troops to be brought home, and a prolonged occupation was equally unwelcome to both parties. On the other outstanding points agreement was quickly reached. Payment of the indemnity might be in agreed bonds as well as in specie. Commercial relations were to be restored on most-favoured-nation terms. The inhabitants of Alsace-Lorraine would have the chance to emigrate with all their possessions. No compensation would be demanded for Germans expelled from France; and in return for a slight extension of the German frontier between Luxemburg and Metz the area retained around Belfort by the French was increased from the traditional cannon-shot radius—reckoned in modern military parlance at seven kilometres—to a more defensible military zone. On 10th May Favre and Bismarck signed the Treaty of Frankfurt, and on 21st May they exchanged the ratifications authorized by their respective sovereign powers.[1] The Franco-Prussian War was over.

* * *

The German Empire had bought her victory at a cost of 88,488 young men wounded and 28,208 dead, and it had taken her five months of fighting to do it. Such speed and decisiveness were not new in warfare.

[1] Sorel, op. cit. II 309.

The military theorists of the eighteenth century, condemned to sterile campaigns and inconclusive peace, had aimed to achieve just these characteristics in their operations, and Napoleon had succeeded. If the successive Napoleonic victories had not led to the establishment of a lasting peace based on a new balance of forces, the explanation was two-fold. First there was Napoleon's own fundamental unwillingness to establish and acquiesce in such a balance, and his determination instead to create a personal hegemony resting on military conquest—a hegemony unlimited in its ambitions and far beyond the resources of France to sustain. The second was the survival, and invincibility, of an inaccessible and vindictive Great Britain, whose incessant encouragement of his domestic and subsidy of his foreign adversaries made it impossible for him to consolidate his conquests in peace. From these drawbacks Germany was not to suffer. Whatever the sympathies of the British people—and as the war progressed these veered more and more strongly to the side of France—the immediate interests of the British nation were too marginally affected by the continental struggle for its Government to consider intervention even if it had commanded the necessary military capacity; which it was shamefully obvious that it did not.[1] This neutrality Bismarck, by his careful restriction of German naval and overseas expansion, was to work assiduously to preserve; and so long as he remained in office the British were to acquiesce in a German hegemony of Europe which bore no resemblance to the pattern which they were traditionally supposed to cherish, of a European Balance of Power. Moreover Bismarck worked, as Napoleon had not, to create out of the German victory a new state-system in Europe which should rest, not on German military domination, but on general consent. Such consent, thanks to the seizure of Alsace and Lorraine, could hardly be secured from France; but so long as France was kept isolated from continental allies and encouraged to develop colonial enterprises which brought her into conflict with Italy and Britain, her irredentist ambitions could be considered a minor, if never a negligible menace, and one which was likely to decrease with time. It was thanks entirely to Bismarck's statesmanship that Moltke's victories were not to remain as sterile as Napoleon's, but were to lead, as military victories must if they are to be anything more than spectacular butcheries, to a more lasting peace.

[1] See *The Fight at Dame Europa's School: or how the German Boy thrashed the French Boy and the English Boy looked on,* and the pamphlet controversy which it set off in London, 1870-¹.

Yet there was something in the very nature of this war which was to render that peace precarious. Unlike the victories of Napoleon, Moltke's successes were not due to any brilliant generalship, either on his own part or that of his commanders. There had been little in the way of manœuvre; tactics, as often as not, were murderously clumsy; and strategic direction had been largely a matter of dour common sense. Nor had there been any significant technical superiority on the German side: the *chassepot* and Krupp's steel breech-loaders might easily have cancelled one another out. The German victories, as was universally recognised, had been won by superior organisation, superior military education, and, in the initial stages of the war at least, superior manpower; and it was these qualities which would bring victory in any future wars. The small, introvert professional army, more conscious of its social than its professional status, was no longer an effective form of military organisation; and any continental power which wished to escape annihilation as swift and overwhelming as that which overtook the Second Empire had to imitate the German pattern and create a Nation in Arms—a nation whose entire man-power was not only trained as soldiers, but could be mobilised, armed, and concentrated on the frontiers within a very few days. The military revolution which ensued in Europe had repercussions in spheres far transcending the military. Its importance has perhaps never been fully appreciated or been subjected to adequate historical analysis; but it must be left for treatment elsewhere.

It was this inherent military insecurity, rather than the single factor of Alsace-Lorraine, which was to make the peace which followed the Treaty of Frankfurt so uncertain, in spite of Bismarck's attempts to maintain it. The Powers of Europe were to grow at once increasingly militarised and increasingly anxious, and none more so than the newly constituted and victorious German Empire. It was too easy for a generation which had seen its nation founded by military strength, after centuries of division and impotence, to believe that military strength must be the chief factor in its preservation, and the military class, in consequence, the chief element in its society.[1] It was too easy

---

[1] On 27th January 1871 Sir Robert Morier wrote from Berlin to Baron Stockmar: "... such unparalleled successes as those which have attended the German arms, and the consequent absolute power which the German nation has acquired over Europe, will tend especially to modify the German character, and that not necessarily for the better. Arrogance and overbearingness are the qualities likely to be developed in a Teutonic race under such conditions, not boasting or vaingloriousness. I was painfully struck in my visit to the Camp at

to ignore the mistakes and the problems which had attended the German victories, the good fortune which had made them possible and the politic moderation which had made them fruitful. And it was too easy to believe that only by a preservation and extension of military power could the new German Empire, with the magnificent cultural tradition which it enshrined and all it made possible in the way of scientific, commercial and industrial development, be guarded against the rivals and enemies who surrounded it. For this generation the War of 1870 was a heroic epoch; the deeds of those times were to be treasured, admired and, when necessity arose, repeated. In this fashion the popular military histories were written, in spite of the scholarly and self-critical monographs which the soldiers themselves began to produce a decade after the struggle ended, in which the best traditions of German scholarship reasserted themselves among the general *Schwärmerei* of militaristic distortion and suppression. It has been left to a German historian of our own generation, writing nearly a century later, to see the full significance of the struggle: how during its course there emerged for the first time "that sinister problem of modern national War, from which the great catastrophes of our epoch have developed, and on which we have foundered twice in succession".[1] It is this which makes the Franco-Prussian War an event of importance far transcending the specialist field of the military historian, or even the historian of nineteenth-century Europe. Germany's magnificent and well-deserved victory was, in a profound and unforeseeable sense, a disaster: for herself, and for the entire world.

Metz in October by the extraordinary difference I witnessed in this respect between the language and *tenue* of the officers I met with there and those I had observed in the days which preceded the invasion of France. Is it love of exaggeration to fear that under such circumstances the German Empire based on universal suffrage, *i.e.* on the suffrages of the 800,000 men who have been fighting in France ... may have some of the faults of militarism attaching to it?" *Memoirs and Letters of Sir Robert Morier* II 243.

[1] Gerhard Ritter, *Staatskunst und Kriegshandwerk* I 329.

Note on Sources

APART from a little documentary material in the *Archives de l'Armée* at Vincennes bearing upon French diplomatic and military preparation for the war, this book is based entirely upon printed sources. The destruction and 'diaspora' (if one may use the term in this context) of the German *Heeresarchiv* at Potsdam during the Second World War was a tragic loss to military scholarship; but their contents bearing upon the war of 1870 had been so extensively used and reproduced by such independent scholars as Hönig, Kunz and Cardinal von Widdern, as well as by the anonymous authors of the publications of the *Kriegsgeschichtliche Abteilung* of the General Staff, that it may be doubted whether they would have shed very much more light on the major problems of the war as considered in this book. On the French side the relevant Army documents, from headquarters' correspondence to regimental war diaries, are reproduced in the forty-odd volumes of text and documents published by the *Revue d'Histoire* for the *Section Historique de l'Etat-Major* between 1901 and 1913. Further material both on the civil and on the military conduct of the war is to be found in the volumes of documents and evidence published by the *Commission d'Enquête Parlementaire sur les Actes du Gouvernement de la Défense Nationale*, and, for the second part of the war, in J. Reinach's *Dépêches, Circulaires, Décrets, Proclamations et Discours de Léon Gambetta*; in A. Dréo's *Procès-verbaux des séances du Conseil du Gouvernement de la Défense Nationale*, and in Georges d'Heylli's three volumes of documents on *Le Siège de Paris*. The principal protagonists on the French side in their memoirs tend to be prolific, if selective, in quotation from documents at their disposal—particularly Aurelle de Paladines, Bazaine, Chanzy, Ducrot, Jules Favre, and Freycinet.

I am conscious of a number of memoirs and biographies, especially of members of the Government of National Defence, which I have not used and which might have provided fresh material or prevented errors of fact or judgment. I have also made little use of regimental histories outside those quoted in the official French documents and German studies, or of the files of European military periodicals between 1870 and 1914, the sifting of whose contents would in itself keep a scholar busy for many months. There can be no doubt that much important information would thereby have become available, and that this book is the poorer because my spirit quailed before the task.

The list of works which follows contains only those works which have been consulted or quoted in the course of writing this book, and hardly scratches the surface of the available material. General Palat's *Bibliographie générale de la Guerre de 1870–71* (Paris 1896) must be the starting point for any serious student of the subject. An up-to-date bibliography has yet to be compiled.

Select Bibliography

ABEKEN, HEINRICH, *Ein schlichtes Leben in bewegter Zeit, aus Briefen zusammengestellt,* Berlin, 1898.

ADAM, J., *Mes illusions et nos souffrances pendant le siège de Paris,* Paris, 1906.

ALBERS, JOHANN HEINRICH, *Die Belagerung von Metz ... vom 19 August bis 28 Oktober 1870, nach französischen Quellen und mündlichen Mitteilung,* Metz, 1896.

ALVENSLEBEN, CONSTANTIN VON, see KRIEG, THILO.

AMBERT, JOACHIM, BARON, *Gaulois et Germains. Récits militaires ... L'Invasion 1870,* 4 vols, Paris, 1883–1885.

    Histoire de la Guerre de 1870–1871, Paris, 1873.

ANDLAU, BARON D', *Metz: Campagne et Négociations: par un Officier Supérieur de l'Armée du Rhin,* Paris, 1871.

ANÉ, MARC PIERRE ÉMILE, *Les Armées de province en 1870/1871,* Toulouse, 1904.

AURELLE DE PALADINES, CLAUDE MICHEL D', *Campagne de 1870–1871. La première Armée de la Loire,* 2nd edition, Paris, 1872.

BAMBERGER, LUDWIG, *Bismarcks Grosses Spiel. Die geheime Tagebücher Ludwig Bambergers,* ed. Ernst Feder, Frankfurt a/M, 1932.

BAPST, CONSTANT GERMAIN, *Le Maréchal Canrobert. Souvenirs d'un siècle,* 6 vols, Paris, 1898–1913.

BAPST, EDMOND, *Le Siège de Metz en 1870. D'après les notes manuscrites laissées par Germain Bapst,* Paris, 1926.

BARAIL, DU, see DU BARAIL.

BARATIER, ANATOLE, *L'Intendance Militaire pendant la Guerre de 1870–1871. Justification. Réorganisation,* Paris, 1871.

BASTARD, GEORGES, *Armée de Châlons. Un jour de bataille,* 2nd edition, 2 vols, Paris, 1872.

BAZAINE, FRANÇOIS ACHILLE, *L'Armée du Rhin depuis le 12 août jusqu'au 29 octobre 1870,* Paris, 1872.

    Épisodes de la guerre de 1870 et le blocus de Metz, Madrid, 1883.

    Procès Bazaine. (Capitulation de Metz). Compte rendu sténographique in extenso des séances du premier Conseil de Guerre de la première division militaire séant à Versailles, Paris, 1873.

BELL, HARRY, *St Privat. German Sources,* Fort Leavenworth, 1914.

BENEDETTI, VINCENT, COMTE, *Ma Mission en Prusse,* Paris, 1871.

BENJAMIN, HAZEL, "Official Propaganda and the French Press during the Franco-Prussian War," *Journal of Modern History,* IV (1932).

BERTIN, LEO, *Les Prussiens dans l'Eure. Vernon et ses environs pendant la guerre de 1870–1871,* Vernon, 1898.

BETHCKE, ERNST, *Politische Generale! Kreise und Krisen um Bismarck*, Berlin, 1930.

BIBESCO, GEORGE, PRINCE, *Campagne de 1870. Belfort, Reims, Sédan. Le 7e Corps de l'Armée du Rhin*, Paris, 1872.

BIERGANS, LUDWIG, *Das grosse Hauptquartier und die deutschen Operationen im zweiten Teil des Krieges, 1870/71. Abmarsch von Sedan bis zum Friedenschluss*, Munich, 1913.

BIGGE, WILHELM, *Feldmarschall Graf Moltke. Ein militärisches Lebensbild*, 2 vols, Munich, 1901.

BILLOT, PIERRE, *1870. Notes de guerre du capitaine Billot . . . publiées par M. Billot de Göldlin*, Paris, 1913.

BISMARCK-SCHOENHAUSEN, OTTO EDUARD VON, PRINCE, *Bismarck, die gesammelten Werke*, 15 vols, Berlin, 1924–32.

    Bismarck the Man and the Statesman: being the reflections and reminiscences of Otto Prince von Bismarck, written and dictated by himself after his retirement from office, 2 vols, London, 1898.

    Bismarck's Letters to his Wife from the Seat of War, 1870–1871, London, 1915.

BIZOT, VICTOR, *Souvenirs de la guerre franco-allemande en 1870–1871*, Lyons, 1914.

BLEIBTREU, CARL, *Die Wahrheit über Mars-la-Tour*, Berlin, 1905.

BLUME, CARL WILHELM VON, *Die Beschiessung von Paris 1870/71 und die Ursachen ihrer Verzögerung*, Berlin, 1899.

    Feldzug 1870–71, Die Operationen der deutschen Heere von der Schlacht bei Sedan bis zum Ende des Krieges, Berlin, 1872. (*The Operations of the German Armies in France from Sedan*, London, 1872.)

BLUMENTHAL, CARL CONSTANTIN ALBRECHT VON, GRAF, *Tagebücher des Generalfeldmarschalls Graf von Blumenthal aus den Jahren 1866 und 1870/71. Edited by Albrecht Graf von Blumenthal*, Stuttgart & Berlin, 1902. (*Journals of Field-Marshal Count von Blumenthal for 1866 & 1870/71*, London, 1903.)

BONNAL, GUILLAUME AUGUSTE, *Froeschwiller: récit commenté des événements . . . du 15 juillet au 12 août 1870*, Paris, 1899.

    L'esprit de la guerre moderne: La Manœuvre de Saint-Privat, 18 juillet–18 août 1870, 3 vols, Paris, 1904–12.

    Le Haut Commandement français au début de chacune des guerres de 1859 et 1870, Paris, 1905.

BONNIN, GEORGES (ed.), *Bismarck and the Hohenzollern Candidature for the Spanish Throne*, London, 1957.

BORDONE, J. P. T. *Garibaldi et l'Armée des Vosges. Récit officiel de la campagne*, Paris, 1871.

    L'Armée des Vosges et la Commission d'enquête sur les actes de Gouvernement de la défense nationale, Paris, 1875.

BOURGIN, GEORGES, *La Guerre de 1870–1871 et la Commune*, Paris, 1939.

BRABANT, FRANK HERBERT, *The Beginning of the Third Republic in France*, London, 1940.

BRENET, AMÉDÉE, *La campagne de 1870/1 étudiée au point de vue du droit des gens*, Paris, 1902.

BRONSART VON SCHELLENDORFF, PAUL, *Geheimes Kriegstagebuch, 1870–1871*, edited by Peter Rassow, Bonn, 1954.
  The Duties of the General Staff, London, 1905.

BRUNEL, GEORGES, *Les Ballons au siège de Paris 1870–1871*, Paris, 1933.

BRUNEL, MATHIEU ISMAEL, *Le Général Faidherbe*, Paris, 1890.

BRUNET-MORET, JEAN, *Le Général Trochu (1815–1896)*, Paris, 1955.

BURY, J. P. T., *Gambetta and the National Defence: a republican dictatorship in France*, London, 1936.

BUSCH, MORITZ, *Graf Bismarck und seine Leute während des Krieges mit Frankreich*, Leipzig, 1878.
  Tagebuchblätter, Leipzig, 1899 (*Bismarck: some secret pages of his history*, 3 vols, London, 1898).
  Mit Bismarck vor Paris. Erlebnisse und Gespräche mit dem grossen Kanzler während des Deutsch-Französischen Krieges 1870/1, edited by H. Sündermann, Munich, 1940.

BUSCH, WILHELM, *Das deutsche Grosse Hauptquartier und die Bekämpfung von Paris im Feldzuge 1870–71*, Stuttgart & Berlin, 1905.

CANROBERT, see BAPST, CONSTANT GERMAIN.

CARDINAL VON WIDDERN, GEORG, *Deutsch-französischer Krieg 1870–71. Der Krieg an den rückwärtigen Verbindungen der deutschen Heere und der Etappendienst*, 5 pts, Berlin, 1893–99.
  Kritische Tage, 5 vols, Berlin, 1897–1900.

CARTIER, VITAL, *Un Méconnu. Le Général Trochu*, Paris, 1914.

CASE, LYNN MARSHALL, *French Opinion on War and Diplomacy under the Second Empire*, Philadelphia, 1954.

CASTELNAU, HENRI PIERRE, "Sedan et Wilhelmshöhe (Souvenirs)," *Revue de Paris*, Sep. & Nov., 1929.

CHALLENER, RICHARD DELO, *The French Theory of the Nation in Arms, 1866–1939*, New York, 1955.

CHALMIN, PIERRE, *L'Officier français 1815–1870*, Paris, 1958.

CHANZY, ANTOINE EUGENE, *Campagne de 1870–1871. La deuxième Armée de la Loire*, 4th edition, Paris, 1872.
  See CHUQUET, ARTHUR.
  See FELIX, GABRIELLE.

CHESNEY, CHARLES C., and REEVE, HENRY, *The Military Resources of Prussia and France, and Recent Changes in the Art of War. Four essays, reprinted from 'The Edinburgh Review'*, London, 1870.
  and STOTHERD, R., *Reports written during a Continental Tour in 1871*, London, 1872.

CHEVALIER, CASIMIR, *Tours capitale. La Délégation gouvernementale et l'occupation prussienne, 1870–1871*, Tours, 1896.

CHEVALIER, EDOUARD, *La Marine française et la marine allemande pendant la Guerre de 1870–1871. Considérations sur le rôle actuel des flottes dans une guerre continentale*, Paris, 1873.

CHUQUET, ARTHUR, *Le Général Chanzy, 1823–1883*, Paris, 1884.
  La Guerre 1870–1871, Paris, 1895.

COCHENHAUSEN, FRIEDRICH VON, *Von Scharnhorst zu Schlieffen, 1806–1906. Hundert Jahre preussisch-deutscher Generalstab*, Berlin, 1933.

COFFINIÈRES DE NORDECK, GRÉGOIRE, *Capitulation de Metz. Réponse du général Coffinières de Nordeck à ses détracteurs*, Brussels, 1871.

CRAIG, GORDON, *The Politics of the Prussian Army, 1640–1945*, Princeton, 1955.

DAILY NEWS, *War Correspondence of the Daily News 1870–71 . . . forming a continuous narrative of the War*, 2 vols, London, 1871.

DANIELS, EMIL, *see* DELBRÜCK, HANS.

DARIMON, A., *Notes pour servir à l'Histoire de la Guerre de 1870 . . .*, Paris, 1888.

DAVALL, E., *Les troupes françaises internées en Suisse à la fin de la guerre franco-allemande en 1871. Rapport rédigé . . . sur les documents officiels*, Berne, 1873.

DECANTE, E., *Souvenirs de la campagne, 1870–1871, et du siège de Paris*, Mélun, 1914.

DEFOURNY, PIERRE GUILLAUME, *L'Armée de MacMahon et la Bataille de Beaumont, en Argonne*, Brussels, 1872.

DELBRÜCK, HANS, *Geschichte der Kriegskunst im Rahmen der politischen Geschichte. Fortgesetzt von Emil Daniels. Sechster Teil: Neuzeit (Fortsetzung). Die Politik verdirbt die Strategie. (Der deutsch-französische Krieg 1870–1871)*, Berlin, 1929.

DEMETER, KARL, *Das Deutsche Offizierkorps in seinen historisch-soziologischen Grundlagen*, Berlin, 1930.

DERRÉCAGAIX, VICTOR, *La Guerre Moderne*, 2 vols, Paris, 1885.

DESCHAUMES, E., *La Retraite infernale, armée de la Loire, 1870/1871*, Paris, 1889.

DESMAREST, JACQUES, *La Défense Nationale*, Paris, 1949.

Documents sur les Origines Diplomatiques de la Guerre de 1870, 29 vols, Paris, 1910–1932.

DORMOY, P. A., *L'Armée des Vosges: 1870/71. Souvenirs d'avant-garde*, 2 vols, Paris, 1887.

DRÉO, AMAURY PROSPER. *Gouvernement de la Défense Nationale. Procès verbaux des séances du Conseil*, Paris, 1906.

DU BARAIL, FRANÇOIS CHARLES, *Mes Souvenirs, 1820–1879*, 3 vols, Paris, 1894–6.

DUCROT, AUGUSTE ALEXANDRE, *La Journée de Sédan*, Paris, 1871.
  La Défense de Paris, 1870–1871, 4 vols, Paris, 1875–78.
  La Vie Militaire du Général Ducrot, d'après sa correspondence, 1839–71, Publiée par ses enfants, 2 vols, Paris, 1895.

DUTRAIT-CROZON, HENRI, *Gambetta et la défense nationale, 1870/1871*, Paris, 1914.

DUVEAU, GEORGES, *Le Siège de Paris, septembre 1870–janvier 1871*, Paris, 1939.

EARLE, EDWARD MEADE (ed.), *Makers of Modern Strategy*, Princeton, 1943.

EICHTHAL, LOUIS D', *Le général Bourbaki, par un de ses anciens Officiers d'Ordonnance*, Paris, 1885.

ENGELS, FRIEDRICH, *Kriegsgeschichtliche Schriften: Der Deutsch-französische Krieg, 1870/1*, edited by R. Haus, Vienna & Berlin, 1931.

ERARD, D., *Souvenirs d'un Mobile de la Sarthe*, Le Mans, 1909.

ERNOUF, ALFRED, BARON, *Histoire des Chemins de Fer français pendant la Guerre Franco-Prussienne*, Paris, 1874.

FABRICIUS, HANS. *Auxerre-Châtillon: Die Kriegsereignisse und Operationen in der Lücke zwischen der II Deutschen Armee und dem XIV Armee-Korps bis zum 20 Januar 1871*, Berlin, 1900.

    Besançon-Pontarlier. Die Operationen des Generals von Manteuffel gegen den Rückzug des französischen Ostheers vom 21 Januar 1871, 2 vols, Berlin, 1912/13.

FAIDHERBE, LOUIS LÉON, *Campagne de L'Armée du Nord en 1870–1871*, Paris, 1871.

    See BRUNEL, MATHIEU ISMAEL.

FAILLY, PIERRE LOUIS DE, *Campagne de 1870. Opérations et marches du 5e Corps jusqu'au 31 août*, Brussels, 1871.

FARINET, ALEXANDRE, *L'Agonie d'une Armée—Metz 1870. Journal de guerre d'un porte-étendard de l'armée du Rhin*, Paris, 1914.

FAVRE, JULES, *Gouvernement de la Défense Nationale du 30 juin 1870*, 3 vols, Paris, 1871–75.

FAY, CHARLES, *Journal d'un officier de l'Armée du Rhin*, Paris, 1871.

FELIX, GABRIELLE, *Le Général Chanzy*, Tours, 1895.

FISCHBACH, GUSTAVE, *Le Siège et le Bombardement de Strasbourg*, Paris, 1871.

FISCHER, GEORG, *König Wilhelm und die Beschiessung von Paris*, Leipzig, 1902.

FITZMAURICE, EDWARD PETTY, BARON, *Life of Granville George Leveson Gower, second Earl Granville, K.G., 1815–1891*, 2 vols, London, 1905.

FOERSTER, WOLFGANG, *Prinz Friedrich Karl von Preussen. Denkwürdigkeiten aus seinem Leben*, 2 vols, Stuttgart & Leipzig, 1910.

FORBES, ARCHIBALD, *My Experiences of the War between France and Germany*, 2 vols, London, 1871.

    Memories and Studies of War and Peace, London, 1895.

FRANCE, ASSEMBLÉE NATIONALE, *Enquête Parlementaire sur les Actes du Gouvernement de la Défense Nationale*, 18 vols, Versailles, 1873–75.

FRANCE, ARMY, ÉTAT MAJOR, SECTION HISTORIQUE, *La Guerre de 1870/1, publiée par la Revue d'Histoire, rédigée à la Section historique de l'État-Major de l'Armée*, Paris, 1901-1913, Includes:

    La Guerre de 1870, (i) *Juillet 1866–juillet 1870;* (ii–x) *28 juillet–23 août 1870.*

    Les opérations autour de Metz, 3 vols.

L'Armée de Châlons, 3 vols.
Mesures d'organisation depuis la commencement de la guerre.
L'Investissement de Metz.
Opérations dans l'Est (Rhin et Vosges).
La Défense Nationale en Province.
La Ière Armée de la Loire: Toury, Épernon.
Campagne de l'Armée du Nord, 4 vols.
Campagne du Général Bourbaki dans l'Est, 4 vols.
L'Investissement de Paris, 2 vols.
> All with maps and *documents annexes.*

FRANSECKY, EDOUARD FRIEDRICH VON, *Denkwürdigkeiten des preussischen Generals der Infanterie Edouard von Fransecky.* Edited by Walter von Bremen, Berlin, 1913.

FRAUENHOLZ, EUGEN VON, *Entwicklungsgeschichte des Deutschen Heerwesens,* 5 vols, Munich, 1935–41.

FREDERICK I, GRAND DUKE OF BADEN, *see* ONCKEN, HERMANN.

FREDERICK III, EMPEROR OF GERMANY, *Das Kriegstagebuch von 1870–1.* Edited by H. O. Meissner, Berlin 1926. (*The War Diary of the Emperor Frederick III, 1870–1871,* London, 1927.)

FREDERICK, EMPRESS, *See* PONSONBY, SIR FREDERICK.

FREDERICK CHARLES, PRINCE OF PRUSSIA, *Eine militarische Denkschrift von P.F.C.,* Berlin, 1862.
> *Ueber die Kampfweise der Franzosen,* Frankfurt 1860.
> *See* FOERSTER, WOLFGANG.

FREYCINET, CHARLES DE, *La Guerre en Province pendant le siège de Paris, 1870–71,* Paris, 1871.
> *Souvenirs, 1848–1893,* 2 vols, Paris, 1912.

FRIEDERICH, EDOUARD, *Das grosse Hauptquartier und die deutschen Operationen im Feldzuge 1870 bis zur Schlacht von Sedan,* Berlin, 1898.

FROBENIUS, HERMAN, *Kriegsgeschichtliche Beispiele des Festungskrieges aus dem deutsche-französischen Kriege von 1870/71,* 2 vols, Berlin, 1899–1906.

FROSSARD, CHARLES AUGUSTE, *Rapport sur les Opérations du deuxième corps de l'armée du Rhin dans la campagne de 1870,* Paris, 1871.

GAMBETTA, LÉON, *see* REINACH, JOSEPH.

GENEVOIS, HENRI, *Les dernières cartouches . . . Héricourt, Pontarlier, Villersexel,* Paris, 1893.
> *Les coups de main pendant la Guerre,* Paris, 1896.
> *Les Premières campagnes en l'Est,* Paris, 1909.

GENSOUL, N., *Un bataillon de mobiles pendant la guerre de 1870–1. Souvenirs de l'Armée du Nord,* Paris, 1914.

GERMANY: ARMY, *Sammlung der officiellen Kriegs Depeschen von 1870/1,* Leipzig, 1896.
> GENERALSTAB, KRIEGSGESCHICHTLICHE ABTEILUNG:
> *Der deutsch-französische Krieg, 1870–1,* 5 vols, Berlin, 1872–81. (*The Franco-German War 1870–1871.* Translated from the German Official Account by Capt. F. C. H. Clarke, 5 vols, London, 1874–1884.)

Kriegsgeschichtliche Einzelschriften:

Heft 2. *Der Uberfall bei Fontenoy-sur-Moselle am 22 Januar 1871*, Berlin, 1883.

Heft 4. *Die Thätigkeit der Belagerungsartillerie vor Paris im Kriege 1870/71*, Berlin, 1884.

Hefte 9, 11, 12. *Die Stärkeverhältnisse im Deutsch-Französischen Kriege 1870/71 bis zum Sturze des Kaiserreiches*, Berlin, 1889.

Heft 14. *Der Rechtabmarsch der I Armee unter General von Goeben auf St Quentin im Januar 1871*, Berlin, 1895.

Heft 15. *Die Festung Langres während des Krieges 1870/71*, Berlin, 1895.

Heft 17. *Truppenfahrzeuge, Kolonnen und Trains der I und der II Deutschen Armee bis zu den Schlachten westlich Metz*, Berlin, 1895.

Heft 18. *Das Generalkommando des III Armee Korps bei Spicheren und Vionville*, Berlin, 1895.

Heft 19. *König Wilhelm auf seinem Kriegszuge in Frankreich 1870. Von Mainz bis Sedan*, Berlin, 1897.

Heft 25. *Der Kampf der 38 Infanterie Brigade und des linken Deutschen Flügels in der Schlacht bei Vionville – Mars-la-Tour am 16 August 1870*, Berlin, 1900.

Heft 36. *Moltke in der Vorbereitung und Durchführung der Operationen*, Berlin, 1905.

Studien zur Kriegsgeschichte und Taktik:

I. *Heeresbewegungen im Kriege 1870/1*, Berlin, 1901.

II. *Das Abbrechen von Gefechten*, Berlin, 1903.

III. *Der Schlachterfolg*, Berlin, 1903.

IV. *Die Festung in den Kriegen Napoleons und der Neuzeit*, Berlin, 1905.

V. *Der 18 August 1870*, Berlin, 1906.

VI. *Heeresverpflegung*, Berlin, 1913.

GIRARD, JACQUES, *1870 . . . Récits d'un Combattant. L'Armée du Rhin—Le Siège de Metz—La Captivité*, Brive, 1909.

GIRARDET, RAOUL, *La Société militaire dans la France contemporaine 1815–1939*, Paris, 1953.

GOEBEN, AUGUST VON, See ZERNIN, GEBHARD.

GOLDSCHMIDT, HANS, *Bismarck und die Friedensunterhändler, 1871*, Berlin & Leipzig, 1929.

GOLTZ, WILHELM COLMAR VON DER, BARON, *Die sieben Tage von Le Mans*, Berlin, 1873.

Feldzug 1870–71. Die Operationen der II Armee. Vom Beginne des Krieges bis zur Capitulation von Metz, Berlin, 1873.

Feldzug 1870–71. Die Operationen der II Armee an der Loire, Berlin, 1875.

Leon Gambetta und seine Armeen, Berlin, 1877.

GRAMONT, ALFRED DUC DE, *La France et la Prusse avant la Guerre*, Paris, 1872.

GRANVILLE, EARL, see FITZMAURICE.

466 *Select Bibliography*

GRENEST, *L'Armée de l'Est*, Paris, 1895.

GROLMAN, HEDWIG VON, *Ernst Edouard von Krause. Ein deutsches Soldatenleben*, Berlin, 1901.

GROUARD, AUGUSTE ANTOINE, *Critique stratégique de la Guerre franco-allemande: Les Armées en presence*, Paris, 1906.
  Woerth et Forbach, Paris, 1905.
  Fallait-il quitter Metz en 1870 ?, Paris, 1893.
  L'Armée de Châlons, Metz, 1885.
  Blocus de Paris, 3 vols, Paris, 1889–94.

GUEDALLA, PHILIP, *The Two Marshals. Bazaine. Pétain*, London, 1943.

GUILLEMIN, HENRI, *Cette curieuse Guerre de '70*, Paris, 1956.
  L'héroïque Défense de Paris, Paris, 1959.

HAEFTEN, OBERST VON, "Bismarck und Moltke", *Preussische Jahrbücher* CLXXVII (1919).

HÄHNKE, W. VON, *Feldzug 1870–1871. Die Operationen der III Armee*, Berlin, 1873.

HALE, LONSDALE AUGUSTUS, *The "People's War" in France 1870–71*, London, 1904.

HARTMANN, JULIUS VON, *Briefe aus dem Deutsch-Französischen Kriege, 1870–1*, Kassel, 1893.

HASSEL, JOHANN PAUL, *Aus dem Leben des Königs Albert von Sachsen*, 2 vols, Berlin, 1898–1900.

HATZFELD, MELCHIOR PAUL, GRAF, *Hatzfelds Briefe. Briefe des Grafen Paul Hatzfeld an seine Frau. Geschrieben vom Hauptquartier König Wilhelms 1870–71*, Leipzig, 1907.

HELVIG, HUGO VON, *Das I bayerische Armee-Corps von der Tann im Kriege 1870/71*, Munich, 1872. (*The Operations of the I Bavarian Army Corps under General von der Tann*, London, 1874.)

HENDERSON, G. F. R., *The Battle of Spicheren, August 6th 1870, and the events which preceded it*, London, 1891.
  The Battle of Wörth, London, 1899.

HÉRISSON, MAURICE D'IRISSON D', COMTE, *Journal d'un Officier d'Ordonnance, juillet 1870–fevrier 1871*, Paris, 1885. (*Journal of a Staff Officer during the Siege of Paris during the events of 1870*, London, 1885.)

HEYLLI, GEORGES D', *Journal du Siège de Paris*, 3 vols, Paris, 1871–74.

HILTL, GEORG, *Der Französische Krieg von 1870 und 1871*, Leipzig, 1895.

HOFFBAUER, CARL EDOUARD VON, *Die deutsche Artillerie in den Schlachten und Treffen des deutsch-französischen Krieges, 1870–71 . . .*, 3 vols, Berlin, 1873–78.

HOHENLOHE-INGELFINGEN, KRAFT CARL ZU, PRINCE,
  Letters on Strategy, 2 vols, edited by W. H. James, London, 1897.
  Letters on Artillery, translated by N. L. Walford, London, 1888.
  Letters on Infantry, translated by N. L. Walford, London, 1889.

Letters on Cavalry, translated by N. L. Walford, London, 1889.

Aus meinem Leben: Aufzeichnungen aus den Jahren 1848–1871, Berlin, 1907.

HÖNIG, FRITZ. *Gefechtsbilder aus dem Kriege, 1870–1871*, 3 vols, Berlin, 1891–94.

   Das Grosses Hauptquartier und die Oberkommandos am 17 und 18 August 1870, Berlin, 1892.

   24 Stunden Moltkes cher Strategie entwickelt und erläutert an den Schlachten von Gravelotte und St Privat, Berlin, 1891 (*24 Hours of Moltke's Strategy* . . . , Woolwich, 1895).

   Der Volkskrieg an der Loire im Herbst 1870, 6 vols in 5, Berlin, 1893–97.

   Die Wahrheit über die Schlacht von Vionville – Mars-la-Tour auf dem linken Flügel, Berlin, 1899.

   Dokumentarisch-kritische Darstellung der Strategie für die Schlacht von Vionville—Mars-la-Tour, Berlin, 1899.

HOPFFGARTEN-HEIDLER, H. VON, *Die Schlacht bei Beaumont*, Berlin, 1897.

JACQMIN, F., *Les Chemins de Fer pendant la guerre de 1870–1871*, Paris, 1872.

JANY, CURT, *Geschichte der Königlich Preussischen Armee*, 4 vols, Berlin, 1928–37.

JARRAS, L., *Souvenirs du General Jarras, Publiées par Mme. Jarras*, Paris, 1892.

KEIM, AUGUST ALEXANDER, *Die Schlacht von Wörth. Eine taktische Studie*, Berlin, 1891.

KESSEL, E., *Moltke*, Stuttgart, 1957.

KEUDELL, ROBERT VON, *Fürst und Fürstin Bismarck, Erinnerungen aus den Jahren 1846 bis 1872*, Berlin, 1902.

KLEIN, CARL, *Fröschwiller-Chronik. Kriegs und Friedensbilder aus dem Jahr 1870*, Nördlingen, 1878 (*La Chronique de Froeschwiller*, Paris, 1911).

KLEIN-WUTTIG, ANNELIESE, *Politik und Kriegführung in den deutschen Einigungskriegen, 1864, 1866 und 1870/71*, Berlin, 1934.

KRANZBERG, MELVIN, *The Siege of Paris, 1870–71. A Political and Social History*, Cornell, 1950.

KRAUSE, ERNST, see GROLMAN.

KRETSCHMAN, HANS VON, *Kriegsbriefe aus den Jahren 1870–71*. Edited by Lily Braun, Stuttgart, 1904.

KRIEG, THILO, *Constantin von Alvensleben, General der Infanterie. Ein militärisches Lebensbild*, Berlin, 1903.

   Hermann von Tresckow, General der Infanterie und Generaladjutant Kaiser Wilhelms I. Ein Lebensbild, Berlin, 1911.

KROSIGK, HANS VON, *General Feldmarschall von Steinmetz. Aus den Familienpapieren dargestellt*, Berlin, 1900.

KÜHN, JOACHIM, "Bismarck und der Bonapartismus im Winter 1870", *Preussische Jahrbücher* CLXIII (1916).

KUNZ, HERMANN, *Kriegsgeschichtliche Beispiele aus dem deutsch-französischen Kriege von 1870/1*, 6 vols, Berlin, 1897–1904.

    Die Thätigkeit der deutschen Reiterei vom 19 August bis zum 1 September 1870, Berlin, 1892.

    Die Kämpfe der preussischen Garde um Le Bourget während der Belagerung von Paris, Berlin, 1891.

    Die Schlacht von Loigny-Poupry am 2 Dezember 1870, Berlin, 1893.

    Die Schlacht von Orléans am 3 und 4 Dezember 1870, Berlin, 1894.

    Die Schlacht vor dem Mont Valérien am 19 Januar 1871, Berlin, 1891.

    Die Entscheidungskämpfe des Generals von Werder, Berlin, 1895.

LACRETELLE, CHARLES-NICOLAS, *Souvenirs*, Paris, 1907.

LA GORCE, PIERRE DE, *Histoire du Second Empire*, 8 vols, Paris, 1902–3.

LA MOTTE ROUGE, JOSEPH DE, *Souvenirs et Campagnes, 1804–1883*, 3 vols, Nantes, 1888.

LAPASSET, FERDINAND AUGUSTE, *Le Général Lapasset. Par un ancien officier de l'Armée du Rhin*, 2 vols, Paris, 1897.

LA RONCIÈRE LE NOURY, ÉMILE DE, COMTE, *La Marine au Siège de Paris*, Paris, 1872.

LEBRUN, BARTHÉLEMI LOUIS JOSEPH, *Souvenirs Militaires, 1866–70. Préliminaires de la Guerre. Missions en Belgique et à Vienne*, Paris, 1895. *Guerre de 1870. Bazeilles-Sedan*, Paris, 1884.

LECLERC, ÉMILE, *La Guerre de 1870: l'Esprit Parisien*, Paris, 1871.

LECOMTE, FERDINAND, *Relation historique et critique de la Guerre Franco-Allemande en 1870–1871*, 4 vols, Paris, 1872–74.

LEHAUTCOURT, PIERRE (pseud. PALAT, BARTHÉLEMY EDMOND, *q.v.*), *La Défense Nationale*, 8 vols, Paris, 1893–98.

    Histoire de la Guerre de 1870–71, 7 vols, Paris, 1901–1908.

    Guerre de 1870–1871. Aperçu et commentaires, Paris, 1910.

    Les Origines de la Guerre de 1870: la candidature Hohenzollern, Paris, 1912.

LEHMANN, GUSTAV, *Die Mobilmachung von 1870/71*, Berlin, 1905.

LÖHLEIN, LUDWIG, *Feldzug 1870–71. Die Operationen des Korps des Generals von Werder*, Berlin, 1894 (*Operations of the Corps of General von Werder*, Chatham, 1876).

LONLAY, DICK DE, *Français et Allemands, histoire anecdotique de la guerre de 1870–71*, 6 vols, Paris, 1888–89.

LORD, ROBERT H., *The Origins of the War of 1870. New documents from the German Archives*, Cambridge Mass., 1924.

LYONS, LORD, *see* NEWTON.

MAISTRE, PAUL ANDRÉ, *Spicheren (6 Août 1870). Préface de M. le général Langlois*, Paris, 1908.

MARTIN DES PALLIÈRES, CHARLES, *Campagne de 1870–1871*, Orléans, Paris, 1872.

MARTINIEN, ARISTIDE, *Guerre de 1870–1871, La mobilisation de l'armée, Mouvements de dépots (armée active) du 15 juillet 1870 au 1er mars 1871*, Paris, 1911.

MECKEL, KLEMENS WILHELM, *Ein Sommernachtstraum. Erzählt von einem älteren Infanteristen*, Berlin, 1888.

MEYER, ARNOLD OSCAR, *Bismarck und Moltke vor dem Fall von Paris und beim Friedenschluss*, Berlin, 1943.

MOLTKE, HELMUTH CARL BERNHARD VON, GRAF, *Militärische Korrespondenz. Aus den Dienstschriften des Krieges 1870–71*, Berlin, 1897.

> *Moltkes Taktisch-strategische Aufsätze aus den Jahren 1857 bis 1871*, Berlin, 1900.

> *Geschichte des deutsch-französischen Krieges von 1870–1871.* [*Gesammelte Schriften und Denkwürdigkeiten des General-feldmarschalls Grafen Helmuth von Moltke.*] Berlin, 1891 (*The Franco-German War of 1870–71*, translated and revised by Archibald Forbes, London, 1893).

> *See* BIGGE, WILHELM.

> *See* KESSEL, E.

> *See* STADELMANN, RUDOLF.

> *See* WHITTON, FREDERICK E.

MONTAUDON, JEAN BAPTISTE, *Souvenirs militaires*, 2 vols, Paris, 1898–1900.

MONTEILHET, JOSEPH, *Les Institutions militaires de la France, 1814–1924. De l'armée permanente à la nation armée*, Paris, 1932.

MONTS, FRIEDRICH WILHELM VON, GRAF. *Napoleon III auf Wilhelmshöhe, 1870/71, nach Aufzeichnungen des Generals d. Infanterie Grafen Monts*, Berlin, 1909.

MORIER, SIR ROBERT, *Memoirs and Letters of the Right Hon. Sir Robert Morier, G.C.B., from 1826 to 1876.* By his daughter Mrs Rosslyn Wemyss, London, 1911.

MOTTE ROUGE, *see* LA MOTTE ROUGE.

MÜLLER, HERMANN VON, *Die Thätigkeit de Deutschen Festungsartillerie bei den Belagerungen, Beschiessungen und Einschliessungen im deutsch-französischen Kriege, 1870–71*, 4 vols, Berlin, 1898–1904.

NAPOLEON, III, *Œuvres posthumes et autographes inédits de Napoléon III en exil. Recueillis et co-ordonnés par le comte de la Chapelle*, Paris, 1873.

> *Note sur l'organisation militaire de la Confédération d'Allemagne du Nord*, Wilhelmshöhe, 1871.

> *Les forces militaires de la France en 1870*, Paris, 1872.

> *Les papiers secrets du Second Empire*, Brussels, 1870–71.

> and FAVÉ, J. *Études sur le passé et l'avenir de l'Artillerie*, 6 vols, Paris, 1846–71.

NEWDIGATE, EDWARD, *The Army of the North German Confederation. A brief Description by a Prussian General*, translated by Colonel E. Newdigate, London, 1872.

NEWTON, THOMAS WODEHOUSE LEIGH, BARON, *Lord Lyons. A record of British Diplomacy*, 2 vols, London, 1913.

(Officier de génie) *Trois mois à l'Armée de Metz. Par un Officier de génie*, Brussels, 1871.

(Officier de l'Armée du Rhin) *La Campagne de 1870 jusqu'au 1er septembre. Par un Officier de l'armée du Rhin*, Brussels, 1870.

OLLIVIER, ÉMILE, *L'Empire libéral. Études, récits, souvenirs*, 16 vols, Paris, 1895–1912.
 Philosophie d'une guerre, Paris, 1910.

ONCKEN, HERMANN, *Die Rheinpolitik Kaiser Napoleons III von 1863 bis 1870 und der Ursprung des Krieges von 1870–71*, 3 vols, Stuttgart, 1926.
 Grossherzog Friedrich I von Baden und die deutsche Politik von 1854–1871, 2 vols, Stuttgart, 1927.

ONCKEN, WILHELM, *Unser Helden Kaiser. Festschrift zum hundert-jährigen Geburtstage Kaiser Wilhelms des Grossen*, Berl'n, 1897.

OSTEN-SACKEN UND VOM RHEIN, JULIUS VON DER, *Preussens Heer von seinen Anfängen bis zur Gegenwart*, 3 vols, Berlin, 1911–14.

PALAT, BARTHÉLEMY EDMOND (see also LEHAUTCOURT), *Bibliographie générale de la Guerre de 1870–1871*, Paris, 1896.
 La Stratégie de Moltke en 1870, Paris, 1907.
 Une grande question d'histoire et de psychologie, Bazaine et nos désastres en 1870, 2 vols, Paris, 1913.

PALIKAO, CHARLES COUSIN DE MONTAUBAN, COMTE DE, *Un Ministère de la guerre de vingt-quatre jours, du 10 août au 4 septembre 1870*, Paris, 1871.

PALLIÈRES, MARTIN DES, *See* MARTIN DES PALLIÈRES.

PATRY, LÉONCE, *La Guerre telle qu'elle est (1870–71): Metz–Armée du Nord–Commune*, Paris, 1907.

PELET-NARBONNE, GERHARD VON, *Die Reiterei der ersten und zweiten deutschen Armee in den Tagen vom 7 zum 15 August 1870*, Berlin, 1899 (*Cavalry on Service, illustrated by the advance of the German cavalry across the Mosel in 1870*, London, 1906).

PFLUGK-HARTUNG, JULIUS VON, (ed.) *Krieg und Sieg 1870–1. Ein Gedenkbuch*, 2 vols, Berlin, 1895–96. (*The Franco-German War, 1870–71. By Generals and other officers who took part in the campaign.* Translated and edited by Major-General J. F. Maurice, London, 1900.)

PICARD, JEAN JULES ERNEST, *1870*, 5 vols, Paris, 1907–1912.

PONSONBY, SIR FREDERICK, *Letters of the Empress Frederick*, London, 1928.

PRATT, EDWIN A., *The Rise of Rail-Power in War and Conquest, 1833–1914*, London, 1915.

PROST, GABRIEL AUGUSTE, *Le Blocus de Metz en 1870*, Nogent le Rotrou, 1898.

"The Railroad concentrations for the Franco-Prussian War." *The Military Historian*, April–July 1918.

RANDON, JACQUES LOUIS, COMTE, MARSHAL OF FRANCE, *Mémoires du Maréchal Randon*, 2 vols, Paris, 1875–7".

RAUCH, FEDOR VON, *Briefe aus dem grossen Hauptquartier der Feldzüge 1866 und 1870/71, an die Gattin*, Berlin, 1911.

RAYMOND, DORA NEILL, *British Policy and Opinion during the Franco-Prussian War*, New York, 1921.

REGNAULT, J., "Les Campagnes d'Algérie et leur influence de 1830 à 1870, *Revue historique de l'Armée*, December 1953.

REGNIER, EDMOND, [*Quel est votre Nom?*] *What is your Name? N. or M. "A strange story"* revealed, London, 1872.

REINACH, JOSEPH, *Dépêches, Circulaires, Décrets, Proclamations et Discours de Léon Gambetta*, 2 vols, Paris, 1886.

REYBAUD, MARIE ROCHE LOUIS, *La Fer et la Houille; suivis du canon Krupp et du Familistère de Guise*, Paris, 1874.

RINDFLEISCH, GEORG HEINRICH, *Feldbriefe 1870–71*, Göttingen, 1905.

RITTER, GERHARD, *Staatskunst und Kriegshandwerk; das Problem des Militarismus in Deutschland*, vol. I, Munich, 1954.

ROON, ALBRECHT THEODOR EMIL VON, GRAF, *Denkwürdigkeiten aus dem Leben des General-Feldmarschalls Kriegsministers Grafen von Roon*, 3 vols, Breslau, 1897.

ROUSSET, LÉONCE, *La seconde campagne de France. Histoire générale de la Guerre Franco-Allemande, 1870–71*, 6 vols, 1895–99.

  Le 4e corps de l'armée de Metz, 19 juillet–27 octobre 1870, Paris, 1899.

  Le haut commandement des armées allemandes en 1870, Paris, 1908.

ROZAT DE MANDRES, CHARLES, *Les Régiments de la Division Margueritte et les charges à Sedan*, Paris, 1908.

RUBY, EDMOND, and REGNAULT, JEAN, *Bazaine, coupable ou victime?*, Paris, 1960.

RUSSELL, WILLIAM HOWARD, *My Diary during the last great War*, London, 1874.

RÜSTOW, FRIEDRICH WILHELM, *Der Krieg um die Rheingrenze 1870 politisch und militärisch dargestellt*, 3 vols, Zürich, 1870.

  Die Feldherrnkunst des neunzehnten Jahrhunderts, Zürich, 1857 (*L'Art militaire au dix-neuvième siècle*, Paris, 1869.)

SARAZIN, C. *Récits sur la dernière guerre franco-allemande*, Paris, 1887.

SAXONY, ALBERT, CROWN PRINCE OF, see HASSEL.

SCHÄFFER, E., *Der Kriegs-Train des deutschen Heeres*, Berlin, 1883.

SCHELL, CARL EMIL VON, *Feldzug 1870–71. Die Operationen der l'Armee unter General von Steinmetz*, Berlin, 1872 (*The Operations of the First Army under General von Steinmetz*, London, 1873).

  Die Operationen der l'Armee unter General von Goeben, Berlin, 1873 (*The Operations of the First Army under General von Goeben*, London, 1874).

SCHERFF, WILHELM VON, *Kriegslehren in kriegsgeschichtlichen Beispiele der Neuzeit, 1870–71*, 3 vols, Berlin, 1894–97.

SCHMIDT, ERNST, *General der Infanterie Graf von Werder. Ein Lebens und Charakterbild*, Oldenbourg, 1912.

SCHNEIDER, LOUIS, *Aus dem Leben Kaiser Wilhelms, 1849–1873,* 3 vols, Berlin, 1888.

SHERIDAN, PHILIP HENRY, *Personal Memoirs of Philip Henry Sheridan,* 2 vols, London, 1888.

SONIS, HENRI DE, *Le 17e corps à Loigny. D'àpres des documents inédits et les récits des combattants,* Paris, 1909.

SOREL, ALBERT, *Histoire diplomatique de la Guerre Franco-Allemande,* 2 vols, Paris, 1875.

STADELMANN, RUDOLF, *Moltke und der Staat,* Krefeld, 1950.

STAEHLIN, CARL, *Der deutsch-französische Krieg 1870–71,* Heidelberg, 1912.

STEENACKERS, FRANÇOIS F., *Les Télégraphes et les Postes pendant la guerre de 1870–1871. Fragments de mémoires historiques,* Paris, 1883. and LE GOFF, FRANÇOIS, *Histoire de Gouvernement de la Défense nationale en province, 4 septembre 1870–8 février 1871,* 2 vols, Paris, 1884.

STEINMETZ, CARL FRIEDRICH VON, see KROSIGK, HANS VON.

STOFFEL, EUGÈNE GEORGES, BARON, *Rapports militaires écrits de Berlin, 1866–70,* Paris, 1871.

    La Depêche du 20 août 1870 du Maréchal Bazaine au Maréchal Macmahon, Paris, 1874.

STOSCH, ALBRECHT VON, *Denkwürdigkeiten des Generals und Admirals Albrecht von Stosch . . . Briefe und Tagebuchblätter,* Stuttgart, 1904.

TANERA, CARL, *Ernste und heitere Erinnerungen eines Ordonnanz-offiziers im Feldzug 1870/1,* Munich, 1896.

THEYRAS, G., *Garibaldi en France—Dôle, Autun, Dijon,* Autun, 1888.

THIERS, LOUIS ADOLPHE, *Notes et Souvenirs de M. Thiers, 1870–73,* Paris, 1904.

THIRIAUX, L., *La Garde nationale mobile de 1870,* Brussels, 1909.

THOUMAS, CHARLES ANTOINE, *Les Transformations de l'armée française. Essais d'histoire et de critique sur l'état militaire de la France,* 2 vols, Paris, 1887.

    Paris, Tours, Bordeaux: souvenirs de la guerre de 1870–71, Paris, 1893.

TRESCKOW, HERMANN VON, see KRIEG, THILO.

TROCHU, LOUIS JULES, *L'Armée française en 1867,* Paris, 1867. *Œuvres posthumes,* 2 vols, Tours, 1896.

    See BRUNET-MORET, JEAN.

    See CARTIER, VITAL.

VERDY DU VERNOIS, JULIUS VON, *Studien über den Krieg. Auf Grundlage des deutsch-französischen Krieges 1870/71,* 3 vols, Berlin, 1891–1909.

    Im Grossen Hauptquartier, 1870, 71. Persönliche Erinnerungen, Berlin, 1896 (*With the Royal Headquarters in 1870–71,* London, 1897).

VICTORIA, QUEEN OF GREAT BRITAIN AND IRELAND, *The Letters of Queen Victoria 1862–78*, edited by G. E. Buckle, 3 vols, London, 1926.

VINOY, JOSEPH, *Campagne de 1870–1871. Siège de Paris, Operations du 13e Corps et de la Troisième Armée*. Paris, 1872.

VOIGTS-RHETZ, CONSTANTIN VON, *Briefe des Generals der Infanterie von Voigs-Rhetz aus den Kriegsjahren 1866 und 1870–71*, Berlin, 1906.

WAGNER, REINHOLD, *Geschichte der Belagerung von Strasburg im Jahre 1870*, 3 parts, Berlin, 1874–78.

WALDERSEE, ALFRED VON, GRAF, *Denkwürdigkeiten*. Edited by H. O. Meissner, 3 vols, Stuttgart, 1922–25.

WALKER, SIR CHARLES BEAUCHAMP, *Days of a Soldier's Life. Being letters written . . . during active service in the . . . Franco-German War*, London, 1894.

WARTENSLEBEN, HERMANN LUDWIG VON, GRAF, *Feldzug 1870–71. Die Operationen der I Armee unter General von Manteuffel*, Berlin, 1872 (*Operations of the First Army under General von Manteuffel*, London, 1873).

    Die Operationen der Süd-Armee im Januar und Februar 1871, Berlin, 1871 (*Operations of the South Army in January and February 1871*, London, 1872).

WASHBURNE, ELIHU BENJAMIN, *Recollections of a Minister to France, 1869–1877*, 2 vols, London, 1877.

WELSCHINGER, HENRI, *La Guerre de 1870: causes et responsabilités*, 2 vols, Paris, 1910.

WERDER, CARL WILHELM, GRAF, *see* SCHMIDT, ERNST.

WHITTON, FREDERICK E., *Moltke*, London, 1921.

WILLIAM I, Emperor of Germany, *Kaiser Wilhelms des Grossen Briefe, Reden und Schriften*, edited by E. Berner, 2 vols, Berlin, 1905–06.

    See ONCKEN, WILHELM.

    See SCHNEIDER, LOUIS.

WIMPFFEN, EMMANUEL FELIX DE, *Sédan*, 3rd edition, Paris, 1871.

WITTICH, L. VON, *Aus meinem Tagebuche, 1870–71*, Kassel, 1872.

WOYDE, CHARLES DE, *Causes des succès et des revers dans la guerre de 1870*, 2 vols, Paris, 1900.

WRIGHT, GORDON, "Public Opinion and Conscription in France", *Journal of Modern History* XIV (1942).

ZERNIN, GEBHARD, *Das Leben des Generals August von Goeben*, 2 vols, Berlin, 1895–97.

    August von Goeben, Königlich preussischer General der Infanterie. Eine Auswahl seiner Briefe, mit einem einleitenden Lebensbilde, Berlin, 1901.

ZURLINDEN, ÉMILE AUGUSTE, *La Guerre de 1870–1871. Réflexions et souvenirs*, Paris, 1904.

Index

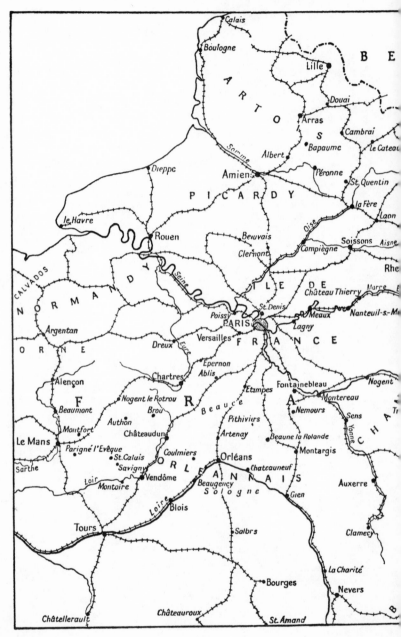

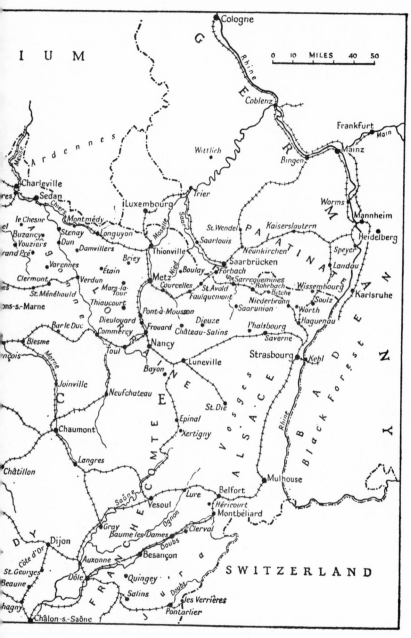